The Constitutional Convention of 1787

The Constitutional Convention of 1787

A COMPREHENSIVE ENCYCLOPEDIA OF AMERICA'S FOUNDING

Volume Two: N–Z

John R. Vile

Foreword by Jack N. Rakove

A B C · C L I O

SANTA BARBARA, CALIFORNIA   DENVER, COLORADO   OXFORD, ENGLAND

Cataloging-in-Publication data is available from the Library of Congress.

ISBN 1-85109-669-8 (hardback : alk. paper)
ISBN 1-85109-674-4 (e-book)

Design by Jane Raese
Text set in Berthold Garamond

05   06   07   08   10   9   8   7   6   5   4   3   2   1

This book is also available on the World Wide Web as an eBook.
Visit abc-clio.com for details.

ABC-CLIO, Inc.
130 Cremona Drive, P.O. Box 1911
Santa Barbara, California 93116-1911
This book is printed on acid-free paper.

Manufactured in the United States of America

Dedicated to

The delegates, and the families of the delegates, to the Constitutional Convention, who sacrificed the summer of 1787 in Philadelphia in the belief that it was possible to construct a government that would better secure liberty under law.

May the heirs of the Framers honor their predecessors by continuing to share their thirst for liberty, their love for truth, and their sacrificial spirit on behalf of justice and the common good.

Contents

List of Entries, A to Z   ix

List of Sidebars   xvii

Topical Table of Contents   xix

Entries, A to Z

Appendix A:
Materials Prior to the Constitutional Convention   855

The Mayflower Compact   855

Albany Plan of Union   856

Virginia Declaration of Rights   857

The Declaration of Independence   859

Constitution of Massachusetts, 1780   860

Articles of Confederation   874

Resolution from Annapolis Convention: September 14, 1786   878

Report of Proceedings in Congress: February 21, 1787   880

Appendix B:
Materials from the Convention Debates and after the Convention   883

James Madison's Preface to Debates in the Convention   883

The Debates in the Federal Convention of 1787 Reported by James Madison,
May 29: The Virginia Plan   889

The New Jersey Plan: June 15, 1787   891

Speech and Proposal of Alexander Hamilton at Federal Convention: June 18, 1787　894

Speech of Benjamin Franklin Delivered to Constitutional Convention: September 17, 1787　898

Resolution of Federal Convention to Continental Congress　899

Letter of the President of the Federal Convention, Dated September 17, 1787,
to the President of Congress, Transmitting the Constitution　900

The Constitution of the United States　900

The Bill of Rights　907

Amendments XI–XXVII to the Constitution　908

Federalist No. 10　912

Federalist No. 51　915

Appendix C: Charts　919

Committee Diagram　920

Signers of the U.S. Constitution　921

How Well Do You Know the U.S. Constitution?　923

Selected Bibliography　925

Selected List of Cases　953

Selected Bibliography for Schoolteachers and Students　955

Websites on the Constitutional Convention　957

Index　959

About the Author　1009

List of Entries, A to Z

⨍ Volume One ⨍

Achaean League, 1

Adams, John (1735–1826), 1

African Americans, 4

Ages of Delegates, 11

Albany Plan of Union, 11

Amending Process, 12

Amphictyonic League, 18

Annapolis Convention, 19

Antifederalists, 21

Appointments and Confirmations, 23

Aristocracy, 27

Armies, Standing, 29

Armies and Navies, Raising and Supporting, 30

Articles of Confederation, 33

Artistic Depictions of the U.S. Constitutional Convention, 37

Attainder, Bills of, 38

Attendance, 39

Authorship of the Constitution, 41

Baldwin, Abraham (1754–1807), 43

Banking, 45

Bankruptcies, 47

Bassett, Richard (1745–1815), 47

Beard, Charles (1874–1948), 48

Beckley, John (1757–1807), 50

Bedford, Gunning, Jr. (1747–1812), 51

Biblical and Religious References at the Constitutional Convention, 54

Bill of Rights, 58

Blair, John, Jr. (1732–1800), 62

Blount, William (1749–1800), 63

Borrowing Power, 64

Brearly, David (1754–1790), 65

Broom, Jacob (1752–1810), 67

Bureaucracy, 69

Butler, Pierce (1744–1822), 70

Calendar, 77

Canada, 77

Carroll, Daniel (1730–1796), 79

Census, 82

Checks and Balances, 83

Chief Justice of the United States, 84

Citizenship, 85

Classes, 86

Classical Allusions and Influences, 90

Clymer, George (1739–1813), 93

Coalitions, 95

Colonial Precedents, 97

Commemorations of the Constitutional
Convention, 98

Commerce Power, 100

Committee of Compromise on Representation
in Congress (July 2), 104

Committee of Detail (July 24), 105

Committee of Style and Arrangement
(September 8), 108

Committee of the Whole (May 30–June 19), 109

Committee on Commercial Discrimination
(August 25), 111

Committee on Interstate Comity and Bankruptcy
(August 29), 112

Committee on Original Apportionment of
Congress (July 6), 112

Committee on Postponed Matters (August 31), 113

Committee on Rules (May 25), 114

Committee on Slave Trade and Navigation
(August 22), 115

Committee on State Debts and Militia
(August 18), 115

Committee on Sumptuary Legislation
(September 13), 116

Committee to Reconsider Representation in
the House (July 9), 116

Committees at the Constitutional Convention, 117

Common Law, 120

Compromise, 123

Confederal Government, 124

Congress, Bicameralism, 125

Congress, Collective Powers, 126

Congress, Compensation of Members, 130

Congress, Continuation of under Articles, 133

Congress, Expulsion of Members, 134

Congress, House of Representatives,
Qualifications of Members, 134

Congress, House of Representatives,
Qualifications of Voters for, 139

Congress, House of Representatives,
Representation in, 140

Congress, House of Representatives,
Selection of, 142

Congress, House of Representatives, Size, 143

Congress, House of Representatives, Terms, 145

Congress, House of Representatives,
Vacancies, 146

Congress, Leaders Designated by
Constitution, 147

Congress, Limits on, 148

Congress, Members' Ineligibility for Other
Offices, 148

Congress, Militia Powers, 151

Congress, Origination of Money Bills, 154

Congress, Power of the Purse, 157

Congress, Privileges of Members, 159

Congress, Publication of Appropriations, 159

Congress, Quorums, 160

Congress, Recall, 161

Congress, Senate, Qualifications, 162

Congress, Senate, Representation in, 164

Congress, Senate, Selection, 170

Congress, Senate, Size, 172

Congress, Senate, Terms, 173

Congress, Time and Frequency of Meetings, 175

Congress, Times, Places, and Manners of Election, 176

Congressional Call for Constitutional Convention, 176

Connecticut, 178

Connecticut Compromise, 180

Constitutional Convention Mechanism, 181

Constitutional Moments, 183

Constitutionalism, 184

Continental Congresses, 188

Contracts Clause, 189

Copyrights and Patents, 191

Corporations, 192

Corruption, 193

Council of Revision, 195

Court and Country Parties, 197

Critical Period, 199

Daily Schedule of the Constitutional Convention, 201

Davie, William Richardson (1756–1820), 202

Dayton, Jonathan (1760–1834), 204

Debts, 206

Declaration of Independence, 208

Delaware, 212

Delegates, Collective Assessments, 213

Delegates, Collective Profile, 215

Delegates, Individual Rankings, 219

Delegates Who Did Not Attend the Constitutional Convention, 223

Democracy, 223

Dickinson, John (1732–1808), 225

Dickinson Plan, 232

District of Columbia, 234

Dominion of New England, 237

Dunlap and Claypoole, 238

Education of Convention Delegates, 239

Ellsworth, Oliver (1745–1807), 242

Entrepreneurs, Constitutional, 251

Equality, 251

European Influences on Delegates to the Convention, 253

Ex Post Facto Laws, 254

Expenses of Delegates, 255

Export Taxes, 256

Extradition, 259

Fame, 261

Farrand, Max (1869–1945), 262

Father of the Constitution, 263

Federalism, 264

Federalist and Democratic-Republican Parties, 268

Federalist, The, 269

Federalists, 274

Few, William (1748–1828), 276

Fitzsimons, Thomas (1741–1811), 277

Foreign Affairs and the Convention, 279

Forms of Government, 281

Founding, 286

Framers, 288

France, 289

Franklin, Benjamin (1706–1790), 290

Fry, Joseph, 298

Fugitive Slave Clause, 299

Full Faith and Credit Clause, 300

Galloway Plan, 301

General Welfare Clause, 302

Geography, 303

Georgia, 308

Germany, 311

Gerry, Elbridge (1744–1814), 312

Gilman, Nicholas (1755–1814), 322

Gorham, Nathaniel (1738–1796), 323

Governors, State, 329

Great Britain, 331

Guarantee Clause, 335

Habeas Corpus, 339

Hamilton, Alexander (1755–1804), 340

Hamilton Plan, 347

Henry, Patrick (1736–1799), 350

Holland, 351

Houston, William (1757–1812), 352

Houston, William Churchill (1746–1788), 354

Human Nature, 354

Hume, David (1711–1776), 356

Impeachment Clause, 359

Indentured Servants, 362

Indians, 363

Ingersoll, Jared (1749–1822), 365

Iroquois, 368

Jackson, William (1759–1828), 371

Jay, John (1745–1829), 373

Jay-Gardoqui Negotiations, 374

Jefferson, Thomas (1743–1826), 375

Jenifer, Daniel, of St. Thomas (1723–1790), 378

Johnson, William Samuel (1727–1819), 379

Judicial Jurisdiction, 382

Judicial Organization and Protections, 386

Judicial Review, 388

Jury, Trial by, 393

Justice, 394

Kentucky, 397

King, Rufus (1755–1827), 398

Knowledge of the Constitutional Convention, 405

Land Disputes, 407

Langdon, John (1741–1819), 408

Lansing, John (1754–1829), 410

Legality of the Convention, 413

Letter of Transmittal, 414

Liberalism, 415

Liberty, 417

Liberty Bell, 419

Library Privileges, 420

Livingston, William (1723–1790), 421

Locke, John (1632–1704), 423

Lodging of the Delegates, 424

Madison, James, Jr. (1751–1836), 427

Madison's Notes of the Convention, 438

Magna Carta, 440

Maine, 441

Marshall, John (1755–1835), 442

Martin, Alexander (1740–1807), 443

Martin, Luther (1744–1826), 445

Maryland, 450

Mason, George (1725–1792), 452

Masons, 462

Massachusetts, 463

Massachusetts Body of Liberties, 466

Massachusetts Constitution of 1780, 467

Mayflower Compact, 468

McClurg, James (1746–1823), 469

McHenry, James (1753–1816), 471

Meeting Times, 474

Mercer, John (1759–1821), 474

Mifflin, Thomas (1744–1800), 478

Military, Congressional Governance of, 479

Militia, Congressional Power to Call, 480

Militia, Congressional Power to Organize and Govern, 482

Mississippi River, 484

Mixed Government, 488

Monarchy, 488

Money, Congressional Coining, 491

Money, State Coining and Emissions of, 492

Monroe, James (1758–1831), 493

Montesquieu, Charles Louis de Secondat de (1686–1755), 495

Morris, Gouverneur (1752–1816), 496

Morris, Robert (1734–1806), 505

Motives of the Founding Fathers, 506

Mount Vernon Conference, 509

Music, 511

❦ *Volume Two* ❧

National Archives, 513

National Constitution Center, 515

National University, 516

Natural Rights, 517

Naturalization, 520

Negative on State Laws, 521

Nem. Con., 524

New England Confederation, 524

New Hampshire, 525

New Jersey, 527

New Jersey Plan, 529

New York, 532

North Carolina, 535

Northwest Ordinance of 1787, 536

Oaths of Office, 539

Occupations of the Delegates, 541

Oratory and Rhetoric, 542

Original Intent, 545

Paine, Thomas (1737–1809), 549

Paris, Treaty of, 550

Parties, Factions, and Interests, 551

Paterson, William (1745–1806), 553

Pennsylvania, 557

Pennsylvania Packet and Daily Advertiser, 559

Pennsylvania State House (Independence Hall), 559

Philadelphia, 563

Pierce, William (1740–1789), 565

Pinckney, Charles (1757–1824), 566

Pinckney, Charles Cotesworth (1746–1825), 575

Pinckney Plan, 580

Piracies, Punishing, 581

Plans of Government Introduced at the Convention, 582

Poland, 583

Polybius (ca. 198–117 B.C.), 585

Population of the United States, 586

Post Offices and Post Roads, 586

Posterity and Perpetuity, 587

Power, 588

Powers, Implied, 591

Prayer at the Convention, 592

Preamble, 594

President, Commander in Chief, 596

President, Compensation, 597

President, Council, 598

President, Disability, 601

President, Executive Power, 601

President, Number of, 603

President, Oath of Office, 605

President, Qualifications, 605

President, Selection, 607

President, Term, Length, and Re-eligibility, 614

President, Title, 615

President of the Convention, 616

Presidential Veto, 617

Press Coverage, 621

Price, Richard (1723–1791), 622

Priestly, Joseph (1733–1804), 623

Privileges and Immunities Clause, 624

Progress, 625

Property Rights, 627

Protestantism, 629

Public Opinion, 633

Puritanism, 637

Quorum, 639

Randolph, Edmund (1753–1813), 641

Ratification, Convention Debates, and Constitutional Provision, 649

Ratification in the States, 655

Read, George (1733–1798), 659

Reason and Experience, 662

Records of the Constitutional Convention, 665

Religious Affiliations of the Delegates, 667

Religious Tests, Prohibition, 669

Republic, 670

Republicanism, 672

Resolution Accompanying the Constitution, 674

Revolutionary War, 675

Rhode Island, 677

Rising Sun, 681

Rising Sun Chair, 681

Rules of the Constitutional Convention, 682

Rutledge, John (1739–1800), 685

Scottish Enlightenment, 691

Secrecy, 692

Secretary of the Convention, 696

Sectionalism, 696

Sentries, 700

Separation of Powers, 700

September 17, 1787, 704

Shallus, Jacob (1750–1796), 704

Shays's Rebellion, 705

Sherman, Roger (1721–1793), 709

Signing of the Constitution, 717

Size of the Convention, 722

Slave Importation, 723

Slavery, 726

Social Contract, 728

Society of the Cincinnati, 730

South Carolina, 733

Sovereignty, 735

Spaight, Richard Dobbs (1758–1802), 736

Spain, 739

Speeches, Number of, 740

Stability, 741

State Appointment of Delegates to the Constitutional Convention, 743

State Constitutions, 746

State Delegations to the Convention, 749

States, Admission and Creation, 750

States, Legislatures, 755

States, Limits on, 759

States, Police Powers, 760

Statesmanship, 761

Strong, Caleb (1746–1815), 763

Suffrage, 764

Sumptuary Legislation, 769

Supermajorities, 771

Supremacy Clause, 772

Supreme Court, 775

Swiss Cantons, 777

Syng Inkstand, 778

Taxes on Imports and Exports, 779

Temperatures in the Summer of 1787, 782

Tennessee, 783

Territory of the United States, 783

Three-fifths Clause, 784

Timing, 788

Titles of Nobility, 789

Treason, 790

Treasury, Secretary of the, 793

Treaty-Making and Ratification, 794

Unitary Government, 799

United Colonies of New England, 800

United States, Name, 801

U.S. Constitution, 801

Vermont, 807

Vice Presidency, 808

Vices of the Political System of the United States, 809

Virginia, 811

Virginia Declaration of Rights, 814

Virginia Plan, 815

Virtue, 820

Voting at the Convention, 823

War Powers of Congress, 825

Washington, George (1732–1799), 827

"We the People," 832

Weaver, Nicholas, 833

Whig Ideology, 833

Williamson, Hugh (1735–1819), 834

Wilson, James (1742–1798), 840

Women, 849

Wythe, George (1726–1806), 851

Yates, Robert (1738–1801), 853

List of Sidebars

A Petition against the Slave Trade, 9

Jefferson and Madison on Constitutional Durability, 16

Zip Codes, 99

Lighthouse Tax, 103

Number of Words in Original Constitution, 107

Residency Requirements for Members of Congress, Learning from Experience, 138

A Constitution for Prisoners, 185

"Founding Fathers": A Term with an Unlikely Origin, 211

Wives of the Delegates, 217

An Ambulatory Capital? 235

John Witherspoon (1723?–1794), 241

E Pluribus Unum, 267

Publius, 271

The Forefathers' Forefathers, 287

Benjamin Franklin and the Two-Headed Snake, 297

Gerry the Lightweight, 321

William Temple Franklin, 372

The Eleventh Amendment and Judicial Jurisdiction, 383

James Madison the Campaigner, 437

U.S.S. *Constitution,* 479

Potential Kings? Prince Henry of Prussia and the Bishop of Osnaburg, 490

Physical Dimensions of the U.S. Constitution, 514

Abraham Clark (1726–1794), 529

A Smoke-Filled Room? 562

Contemporary Philadelphia: A Ban on Plays, 564

Charles Pinckney and the Contradictions of Slavery, 574

Elizabeth Lucas Pinckney, a Founding Mother (1722–1793), 576

Contemporary Death of a "Witch," 632

The First American Novel, 655

Dates and Votes by Which States Ratified the U.S. Constitution, 658

Rogue's Island, 678

Riots as Expressions of Popular Sovereignty, 707

Dueling: Chapter and Verse, 746

Women Voters in New Jersey, 765

Child of Fortune, 806

John Adams on George Washington, 811

Agenda-Setting, 820

Civilian Control of the Military, 828

"Remember the Ladies," 850

Topical Table of Contents

Artifacts

Liberty Bell, 419

Rising Sun Chair, 681

Syng Inkstand, 778

Committees

Committee of Compromise on Representation in Congress (July 2), 104

Committee of Detail (July 24), 105

Committee of Style and Arrangement (September 8), 108

Committee of the Whole (May 30–June 19), 109

Committee on Commercial Discrimination (August 25), 111

Committee on Interstate Comity and Bankruptcy (August 29), 112

Committee on Original Apportionment of Congress (July 6), 112

Committee on Postponed Matters (August 31), 113

Committee on Rules (May 25), 114

Committee on Slave Trade and Navigation (August 22), 115

Committee on State Debts and Militia (August 18), 115

Committee on Sumptuary Legislation (September 13), 116

Committee to Reconsider Representation in the House (July 9), 116

Committees at the Constitutional Convention, 117

Compromises

Connecticut Compromise, 180

President, Selection, 607

Slave Importation, 723

Slavery, 726

Three-fifths Clause, 784

Congress

Congress, Bicameralism, 125

Congress, Collective Powers, 126

Congress, Compensation of Members, 130

Congress, Continuation of under Articles, 133

Congress, Expulsion of Members, 134

Congress, House of Representatives, Qualifications of Members, 134

Congress, House of Representatives, Qualifications of Voters for, 139

Congress, House of Representatives, Representation in, 140

Congress, House of Representatives, Selection of, 142

Congress, House of Representatives, Size, 143

Congress, House of Representatives, Terms, 145

Congress, House of Representatives, Vacancies, 146

Congress, Leaders Designated by Constitution, 147

Congress, Limits on, 148

Congress, Members' Ineligibility for Other Offices, 148

Congress, Militia Powers, 151

Congress, Origination of Money Bills, 154

Congress, Power of the Purse, 157

Congress, Privileges of Members, 159

Congress, Publication of Appropriations, 159

Congress, Quorums, 160

Congress, Recall, 161

Congress, Senate, Qualifications, 162

Congress, Senate, Representation in, 164

Congress, Senate, Selection, 170

Congress, Senate, Size, 172

Congress, Senate, Terms, 173

Congress, Time and Frequency of Meetings, 175

Congress, Times, Places, and Manners of Election, 176

Constitution

Authorship of the Constitution, 41

Bill of Rights, 58

Commemorations of the Constitutional Convention, 98

Constitutional Moments, 183

Constitutionalism, 184

Dunlap and Claypoole, 238

Entrepreneurs, Constitutional, 251

Father of the Constitution, 263

Founding, 286

Pennsylvania Packet and Daily Advertiser, 559

Preamble, 594

Signing of the Constitution, 717

U.S. Constitution, 801

"We the People," 832

Constitutional Principles

See Ideas, Terms, and Principles Used at the Convention heading, below

Constitutional Provisions and Considered Provisions

Amending Process, 12

Appointments and Confirmations, 23

Armies, Standing, 29

Armies and Navies, Raising and Supporting, 30

Attainder, Bills of, 39

Banking, 45

Bankruptcies, 47

Bill of Rights, 58

Borrowing Power, 64

Census, 82

Chief Justice of the United States, 84

Citizenship, 85

Commerce Power, 100

Congress (*see* Congress heading, above)

Contracts Clause, 189

Corporations, 192

Council of Revision, 195

Debts, 206

District of Columbia, 234

Ex Post Facto Laws, 254

Export Taxes, 255

Extradition, 259

Fugitive Slave Clause, 299

Full Faith and Credit Clause, 300

Guarantee Clause, 335

Habeas Corpus, 339

Impeachment Clause, 359

Indentured Servants, 362

Judiciary (*see* Judiciary heading, below)

Jury, Trial by, 393

Land Disputes, 407

Military, Congressional Governance of, 479

Militia, Congressional Power to Call, 480

Militia, Congressional Power to Organize and Govern, 482

Money, Congressional Coining, 491

Money, State Coining and Emissions of, 492

National University, 516

Naturalization, 517

Negative on State Laws, 521

Oaths of Office, 539

Piracies, Punishing, 581

Post Offices and Post Roads, 588

Powers, Implied, 591

Preamble, 594

President (*see* President heading, below)

Privileges and Immunities Clause, 624

Property Rights, 627

Religious Tests, Prohibition, 669

Slave Importation, 723

Slavery, 726

States (*see* States heading, below)

Suffrage, 764

Sumptuary Legislation, 769

Supremacy Clause, 772

Supreme Court, 775

Taxes on Imports and Exports, 779

Territory of the United States, 783

Three-fifths Clause, 784

Titles of Nobility, 789

Treason, 790

Treasury, Secretary of the, 793

Treaty-Making and Ratification, 794

Vice Presidency, 808

War Powers of Congress, 825

Convention, Miscellaneous

Calendar, 77

Classes, 86

Coalitions, 95

Knowledge of the Constitutional Convention, 405

Meeting Times, 474

Prayer at the Convention, 592

President of the Convention, 620

Press Coverage, 621

Quorum, 639

Records of the Constitutional Convention, 665

Rules of the Constitutional Convention, 682

Secrecy, 692

Secretary of the Convention, 696

Signing of the Constitution, 717

Speeches, Number of, 740

State Appointment of Delegates to the Constitutional Convention, 743

Timing, 788

Voting at the Convention, 823

Culture

Artistic Depictions of the U.S. Constitutional Convention, 37

Commemorations of the Constitutional Convention, 98

Music, 511

See also Artifacts heading

Delegates

Ages of Delegates, 11

Attendance, 39

Biblical and Religious References at the Constitutional Convention, 54

Classical Allusions and Influences, 90

Compromise, 123

Delegates, Collective Assessments, 213

Delegates, Collective Profile, 215

Delegates, Individual Rankings, 219

Delegates Who Did Not Attend the Constitutional Convention, 223

Education of Convention Delegates, 239

Expenses of Delegates, 254

Fame, 261

Library Privileges, 420

Lodging of the Delegates, 424

Motives of the Founding Fathers, 506

Occupations of the Delegates, 541

Oratory and Rhetoric, 542

Original Intent, 545

Religious Affiliations of the Delegates, 667

Speeches, Number of, 740

State Appointment of Delegates to the Constitutional Convention, 743

Statesmanship, 761

See also People heading

Documents

Albany Plan of Union, 11

Articles of Confederation, 33

Bill of Rights, 58

Congressional Call for Constitutional Convention, 176

Declaration of Independence, 208

Dominion of New England, 237

Federalist, The, 269

Galloway Plan, 301

Letter of Transmittal, 414

Madison's Notes of the Convention, 438

Magna Carta, 440

Massachusetts Body of Liberties, 466

Massachusetts Constitution of 1780, 467

Mayflower Compact, 468

New England Confederation, 524

Northwest Ordinance of 1787, 536

Paris, Treaty of, 550

Resolution Accompanying the Constitution, 674

State Constitutions, 746

United Colonies of New England, 800

U.S. Constitution, 801

Vices of the Political System of the United States, 809

Virginia Declaration of Rights, 814

Events

Annapolis Convention, 19

Jay-Gardoqui Negotiations, 374

Mount Vernon Conference, 509

Revolutionary War, 675

Shays's Rebellion, 705

Forms of Government

Aristocracy, 27

Confederal Government, 124

Democracy, 223

Federalism, 264

Forms of Government, 281

Mixed Government, 488

Monarchy, 488

Republic, 670

Unitary Government, 799

Groups Connected to, or Affected by, the Convention

African Americans, 4

Antifederalists, 21

Classes, 86

Coalitions, 95

Federalist and Democratic-Republican Parties, 268

Federalists, 274

Indians, 363

Iroquois, 368

Masons, 462

Parties, Factions, and Interests, 551

Society of the Cincinnati, 730

Women, 849

Historical and Philosophical Influences

Classical Allusions and Influences, 90

Common Law, 120

Court and Country Parties, 197

European Influences on Delegates to the Convention, 253

Progress, 625

Protestantism, 629

Puritanism, 637

Reason and Experience, 662

Republicanism, 672

Scottish Enlightenment, 691

Social Contract, 728

Whig Ideology, 833

Ideas, Terms, and Principles Used at the Convention

Checks and Balances, 83

Corruption, 193

Founding, 286

Human Nature, 354

Judicial Review, 388

Justice, 394

Liberty, 417

Mixed Government, 488

Natural Rights, 518

Parties, Factions, and Interests, 551

Powers, Implied, 591

Public Opinion, 633

Reason and Experience, 662

Separation of Powers, 700

Sovereignty, 735

Stability, 741

Virtue, 820

Judiciary

Chief Justice of the United States, 84

Judicial Jurisdiction, 382

Judicial Organization and Protections, 386

Judicial Review, 388

Jury, Trial by, 393

Miscellaneous

Critical Period, 199

Foreign Affairs and the Convention, 279

Geography, 303

Legality of the Convention, 413

Mississippi River, 484

Pennsylvania Packet and Daily Advertiser, 559

Population of the United States, 586

Posterity and Perpetuity, 586

Rising Sun, 681

Sentries, 700

September 17, 1787, 704

Sumptuary Legislation, 769

Temperatures in the Summer of 1787, 782

United States, Name, 801

"We the People," 832

Nations and Leagues Cited at Convention

Achaean League, 1

Amphictyonic League, 18

Canada, 77

France, 289

Germany, 311

Great Britain, 331

Holland, 351

Poland, 583

Spain, 739

Swiss Cantons, 777

People

Delegates Who Attended

Baldwin, Abraham (1754–1807), 43

Bassett, Richard (1745–1815), 47

Bedford, Gunning, Jr. (1747–1812), 51

Blair, John, Jr. (1732–1800), 62

Blount, William (1749–1800), 63

Brearly, David (1754–1790), 65

Broom, Jacob (1752–1810), 67

Butler, Pierce (1744–1822), 70

Carroll, Daniel (1730–1796), 79

Clymer, George (1739–1813), 93

Davie, William Richardson (1756–1820), 202

Dayton, Jonathan (1760–1834), 204

Dickinson, John (1732–1808), 225

Ellsworth, Oliver (1745–1807), 242

Few, William (1748–1828), 276

Fitzsimons, Thomas (1741–1811), 277

Franklin, Benjamin (1706–1790), 290

Gerry, Elbridge (1744–1814), 312

Gilman, Nicholas (1755–1814), 322

Gorham, Nathaniel (1738–1796), 323

Hamilton, Alexander (1755–1804), 340

Houston, William (1757–1812), 352

Houston, William Churchill (1746–1788), 353

Ingersoll, Jared (1749–1822), 365

Jenifer, Daniel, of St. Thomas (1723–1790), 378

Johnson, William Samuel (1727–1819), 379

King, Rufus (1755–1827), 398

Langdon, John (1741–1819), 408

Lansing, John (1754–1829), 410

Livingston, William (1723–1790), 421

Madison, James, Jr. (1751–1836), 427

Martin, Alexander (1740–1807), 443

Martin, Luther (1744–1826), 445

Mason, George (1725–1792), 452

McClurg, James (1746–1823), 469

McHenry, James (1753–1816), 471

Mercer, John (1759–1821), 474

Mifflin, Thomas (1744–1800), 478

Morris, Gouverneur (1752–1816), 496

Morris, Robert (1734–1806), 505

Paterson, William (1745–1806), 553

Pierce, William (1740–1789), 565

Pinckney, Charles (1757–1824), 566

Pinckney, Charles Cotesworth (1746–1825), 575

Randolph, Edmund (1753–1813), 641

Read, George (1733–1798), 654

Rutledge, John (1739–1800), 685

Sherman, Roger (1721–1793), 709

Spaight, Richard Dobbs (1758–1802), 736

Strong, Caleb (1746–1815), 763

Washington, George (1732–1799), 827

Williamson, Hugh (1735–1819), 834

Wilson, James (1742–1798), 840

Wythe, George (1726–1806), 851

Yates, Robert (1738–1801), 853

Interpreters of the Constitution

Beard, Charles (1874–1948), 48

Farrand, Max (1869–1945), 262

Non-Americans Who Were Influential

Hume, David (1711–1776), 356

Locke, John (1632–1704), 423

Montesquieu, Charles Louis de Secondat de (1686–1755), 495

Polybius (ca. 198–117 B.C.), 585

Price, Richard (1723–1791), 622

Priestley, Joseph (1733–1804), 623

Other Americans Who Did Not Attend but Were Influential

Adams, John (1735–1826), 1

Henry, Patrick (1736–1799), 350

Jay, John (1745–1829), 373

Jefferson, Thomas (1743–1826), 375

Marshall, John (1755–1835), 442

Monroe, James (1758–1831), 493

Paine, Thomas (1737–1809), 549

People Who Served, or Aspired to Serve, at the Convention

Beckley, John (1757–1807), 50

Fry, Joseph, 298

Jackson, William (1759–1828), 371

Shallus, Jacob (1750–1796), 704

Weaver, Nicholas, 832

Places Other Than States and Nations

National Archives, 513

National Constitution Center, 515

Pennsylvania State House (Independence Hall), 559

Philadelphia, 563

Plans of Government at Convention

Dickinson Plan, 232

Hamilton Plan, 347

New Jersey Plan, 529

Pinckney Plan, 580

Plans of Government Introduced at the Convention, 582

Virginia Plan, 815

President

President, Commander in Chief, 596

President, Compensation, 597

President, Council, 598

President, Disability, 601

President, Executive Power, 601

President, Number of, 603

President, Oath of Office, 605

President, Qualifications, 605

President, Selection, 607

President, Term, Length, and Re-eligibility, 614

President, Title, 615

Presidential Veto, 616

Ratification of the Constitution

Antifederalists, 21

Bill of Rights, 58

Federalist, The, 269

Federalists, 274

Ratification, Convention Debates, and Constitutional Provision, 649

Ratification in the States, 655

Rules and Procedures

Committee on Rules (May 25), 114

Nem. Con., 524

Quorum, 639

Rules of the Constitutional Convention, 682

Secrecy, 692

Secretary of the Convention, 696

States, Provisions Related to

Contracts Clause, 189

Ex Post Facto Laws, 257

Fugitive Slave Clause, 299

Full Faith and Credit Clause, 300

Governors, State, 329

Guarantee Clause, 335

Slave Importation, 723

States, Admission and Creation, 750

States, Legislatures, 755

States, Limits on, 759

States, Police Powers, 760

States and States in the Making

Connecticut, 178

Delaware, 212

Georgia, 308

Kentucky, 397

Maine, 441

Maryland, 450

Massachusetts, 463

New Hampshire, 525

New Jersey, 527

New York, 532

North Carolina, 535

Pennsylvania, 557

Rhode Island, 677

South Carolina, 733

Tennessee, 783

Vermont, 807

Virginia, 811

$\mathcal{N}$

NATIONAL ARCHIVES

Although the Constitution was written in Philadelphia and signed in the State House (today's Independence Hall), the original embossed copy of the document is on display at the National Archives in Washington, D.C. (the new National Constitution Center in Philadelphia has one of the first printed copies of the document). The Archives also contain the original embossed copies of the Declaration of Independence and the Bill of Rights, each of which has been carefully preserved and each of which is elaborately guarded and secured in the event of an attack against the nation. These "Charters of Freedom" are displayed in the Rotunda of the Archives (murals by Barry Faulkner

President George W. Bush praises the work of America's founders as the Rotunda of the National Archives reopens after a two-year renovation, in Washington, September 17, 2003. The Declaration of Independence, left, the Constitution, center, and the Bill of Rights are preserved in new cases built from gold-plated titanium and filled with argon to slow decay. (AP/Wide World Photos)

Physical Dimensions of the U.S. Constitution

The original engrossed copy of the U.S. Constitution was prepared by Jacob Shallus and is now housed at the National Archives in Washington, DC. It consisted of four sheets. They measured about 28 ¾ by 23 ⅝ inches each. This paper was slightly smaller than that used for the Declaration of Independence, which measured 29 ⅞ by 24 ⁷⁄₁₆ inches.

FOR FURTHER READING

"Constitution of the United States: Questions and Answers." http://www.archives.gov/national_archives-experience/constitution_q_and_a.html.

---

celebrating the Constitution and the Declaration adorn the walls), which Harry S Truman opened on December 15, 1952, with an address. These documents can be viewed on the website of the National Archives at http://www.archives.gov/.

The Constitution has not always been on public display. The original document was initially carried by the Convention secretary William Jackson to the president of the Confederation Congress in New York City. He stored it in congressional archives from where it was later transferred to George Washington who turned it over to the State Department. The Constitution moved with changes in the nation's capital from New York, to Philadelphia, to the District of Columbia.

President James Madison's secretary of state, James Monroe, transferred the Constitution and the Declaration of Independence from the State Department to Leesburg, Virginia to protect them during the War of 1812. They were returned to the State Department where they remained until being transferred to the Library of Congress on September 19, 1921. Exhibited there with the Declaration of Independence until December 23, 1941, they were transferred to Fort Knox for safekeeping during much of World War II before being brought back to Washington, D.C. As noted above, the documents were transferred to the National Archives, where they are now displayed, on December 15, 1952.

The value of the documents is demonstrated by the fact that, before they were displayed in the National Archives, they were surrounded by helium and preserved within sealed bronze and glass containers against abrasion, drying out, molding, and ultraviolet light using state-of-the art technology. In the event of an emergency, they can be lowered in a steel and concrete vault designed to withstand even a nuclear attack (Plotnik 1987, 80–83).

After the discovery that microscopic droplets were forming within the protective casings, they were reopened in 1998. At this time scientists cleaned the document, flattened the manuscript, and reattached loose particles of ink. The document was redisplayed in the fall of 2003 (Nicholson and Ritzenhaler 2002).

See Also Bill of Rights; Declaration of Independence; National Constitution Center

FOR FURTHER READING

Lieberman, Jethro K. 1987. *The Enduring Constitution: A Bicentennial Perspective.* Saint Paul, MN: West Publishing Company. (See especially 153, "Constitutional Peregrinations.")

Mearns, David C., and Verner W. Clapp, comps. 1952. *The Constitution of the United States Together with an Account of Its Travels since September 17, 1787.* Washington, DC: Library of Congress.

Nicholson, Catherine, and Mary Lynn Ritzenhaler. 2002. "Tales from the Vault." *Common-Place* 2, no. 4 (July). http://www.common-place.org.

Plotnik, Arthur. 1987. *The Man behind the Quill: Jacob Shallus, Calligrapher of the United States Constitution.* Washington, DC: National Archives and Records Administration.

Visitors enter the new National Constitution Center on Independence Mall in Philadelphia during its grand opening Friday, July 4, 2003. (AP/Wide World Photos)

Twiss-Garrity, Beth A. 2002. "Object Lessons: Relics, Reverence, and Relevance." *Common-Place* 2, no. 4 (July). http://www.common-place.org.

NATIONAL CONSTITUTION CENTER

There are many places that serve as reminders of the Constitutional Convention and its work. Among the most famous are the Pennsylvania State House (Independence Hall), the nearby Liberty Bell, the seats of the three branches of government (all in Washington, D.C.), homes of the Framers and early presidents, the National Archives in the nation's capital (where the original engrossed, or handwritten, copies of the Declaration of Independence, the U.S. Constitution, and the Bill of Rights are located), and the like.

An additional site was added on July 4, 2003, with the opening of the National Constitution Center at 525 Arch Street on Independence Mall in Philadelphia. Constructed from federal, state and local government, and private contributions of about $185 million (governments provided $100 million and private contributions $85 million), the idea for the site dates to the 1980s when celebrations were being planned for the bicentennial of the U.S. Constitution. The building has a modern glass and marble exterior. The words of the Preamble of the U.S. Constitution are inscribed on the top right outside of the building as visitors enter; the words face toward Independence Hall.

Visitors get a pass to the museum ($6.00 each in 2003) that entitles them to view a 17-minute multimedia presentation entitled "Freedom Rising." Visitors then go to a circular display of events from American constitutional history beginning in the 1760s and continuing to the present. Many displays are interactive. Thus visitors may take the presidential oath of office, wear robes like those of U.S. Supreme Court justices, vote for their favorite president, and even leave posted notes concerning their views of contemporary constitutional questions, like gun control and the posting of the Ten Commandments in public buildings. A highlight of the display is "Signers' Hall," with life-size bronze statues of each of the signers with which visitors may mingle. The museum also has a copy of the first public printing of the U.S. Constitution on display.

The Constitution Center contains a gift shop, a lunchroom, and various auditoriums and meeting rooms for educational activities related to the U.S. Constitution. It is the site of discussions of contemporary books on the Constitution and the Founding period that are sometimes broadcast on public television.

See Also Commemorations of the Constitutional Convention; Pennsylvania State House; Philadelphia

FOR FURTHER READING

"National Constitution Center: Visitor's Guide and Map." 2003. http://www.constitutioncenter.org.

NATIONAL GOVERNMENT

See FEDERALISM; UNITARY GOVERNMENT

NATIONAL UNIVERSITY

Relatively late in the Convention proceedings (September 14), Virginia's James Madison and South Carolina's Charles Pinckney proposed to vest Congress with the power "to establish an University, in which no preferences or distinctions should be allowed on account of religion"

(Farrand 1937, II, 616). Unfortunately, there was almost no discussion. Pennsylvania's James Wilson was recorded as supporting the motion whereas Gouverneur Morris, of the same state, argued that such a power would not be necessary since "The exclusive power at the Seat of Government, will reach the object" (II, 616). The Convention then voted against the proposal by a vote of 4-6-1, and the matter was dropped.

The exasperating feature of the debate is the difficulty of ascertaining whether delegates rejected the idea because they did not want to vest such power in Congress or because they agreed with Gouverneur Morris in believing that such a power was already encompassed within the congressional power over the nation's capital. Unfortunately, early congressional debates do not settle the matter.

Pennsylvania's Dr. Benjamin Rush, who had also favored a uniform American system of elementary education (Messerli 1967, 419), appears to have been the first individual to suggest a national university. He broached this proposal in an article in the January 1787 issue of the *American Museum* (Castel 1964, 280), and members of the Convention may well have read his essay. President George Washington subsequently reiterated support for a national university in his first annual message to Congress. Scholars have traced the desire for such a university to the following factors: a strong devotion to learning, the thought that higher education was essential to republican government, the relatively sad state of existing institutions of higher learning within the nation, the desire to keep Americans within their home country for further study, and the hope that a national university would be a force for national unity (Castel, 281). Despite such reasons, Washington's proposal was no more successful than proposals that Presidents Thomas Jefferson, James Madison, James Monroe (who, like Jefferson, however, thought that such an act would require a constitutional amendment), John Quincy Adams, Ulysses S. Grant, and Woodrow Wilson later advanced (Castel, 292–297).

A scholar who has examined this issue has observed that although much of the opposition to a national university stemmed from fairly parochial concerns, the ultimate decision to reject the idea may have been sound. He observes that the elitism implicit in such an idea may have been contrary to American democracy, that it is doubtful that the idea would have promoted national unity (he observes that Robert E. Lee and Jefferson Davis both went to West Point), that a single institution could only have served a limited number of persons, and that it would have been difficult to keep such an institution from being wrecked by sectional divisions (Castel, 298).

The Constitution's failure to mention a national university is part of a larger omission, that of education in general. The adoption of provisions for education in the Northwest Ordinance of 1787 appear to indicate that delegates expected such power to be subsumed, as under the Articles of Confederation, in the provision granting Congress to make rules and regulations for the territories (Denenberg 1979, 229). They likely regarded education within individual states primarily as a matter for states themselves to take care of.

See Also Education of Convention Delegates

FOR FURTHER READING

Castel, Albert. 1964. "The Founding Fathers and the Vision of a National University." *History of Education Quarterly* 4 (December): 280–302.
Denenberg, Dennis. 1979. "The Missing Link: New England's Influence on Early National Educational Policies." *New England Quarterly,* 52 (June): 219–233.
Farrand, Max, ed. 1937. *The Records of the Federal Convention.* 4 vols. New Haven, CT: Yale University Press.
Messerli, Jonathan. 1967. "The Columbian Complex: The Impulse to National Consolidation." *History of Education Quarterly* 7 (Winter): 417–431.

NATIVE AMERICANS

See INDIANS

NATURAL RIGHTS

The concept of natural rights embraces the idea that human beings are unique and that they are entitled to certain rights as to how they are treated simply as a result of their common humanity. Natural rights theorists, most notably Britain's John Locke, had hypothesized that men began, or could best be understood to have begun, in a "state of nature" when their rights were insecure and that they had joined in society and formed governments largely to protect such rights. This doctrine stemmed in part from earlier notions of natural law dating back to the Greek philosopher Aristotle, and to Roman Stoic philosophers like Cicero. This concept was based on the conviction that existing laws and institutions had to be measured against that which was right by nature. This conviction, in turn, served as a basis for resisting laws that were thought to violate such rights—a

Greek philosopher Aristotle (Ridpath, John Clark, Ridpath's History of the World, 1901)

doctrine to which Dr. Martin Luther King, Jr. later appealed in the civil rights protests of the 1950s and 1960s. The idea of natural rights is often connected to the idea of self-evidence. Alexander Hamilton thus observed in 1775 that "the sacred rights of mankind are not to be rummaged for, among old parchments, or musty records. They are written, as with a sun beam, in the whole volume of human nature, by the hand of the divinity itself; and can never be erased or obscured by mortal power" (quoted in Jordan 1988, 500).

The colonists often associated natural rights with the customary rights that they believed they shared as Englishmen. They identified such rights by reference to ancient English documents (like the Magna Carta), colonial compacts and charters, and their newly written state constitutions. Larry Kramer has thus observed that the texts of these new state constitutions "were situated within an established constitutional tradition, and they took their place alongside existing practices and understandings, many of which remained viable" (2004, 40).

The best-known articulation of natural rights in America remains the Declaration of Independence. In that document, Thomas Jefferson proclaimed the colonists' conviction ("self-evident" truths) that all men were created equal and that they were thus all equally entitled to the rights of "life, liberty, and the pursuit of happiness." This entitlement served as a basis for questioning and seeking to overthrow a government (that of Great Britain) that was governing arbitrarily and not adequately securing the people's happiness. Like writers before him, Jefferson associated natural rights with the customary rights of Englishmen and colonists (Kramer, 36–37).

Articulation of the Idea Prior to the Convention

Believing that governments were designed chiefly to secure individual liberties, during the revolutionary period, a number of states prefaced their constitutions with declarations of rights. Virginia's Declaration of Rights, largely written by George Mason, was the most prominent of these.

Although many of these early statements were largely declaratory in nature, over time these provisions became enforceable in court. They were thus translated from natural rights into what are called positive, or legal, rights. Ideally, a constitution will secure through positive law protection for all the important natural rights.

The idea of natural rights, which the colonists had used to justify their struggle with Great Britain, was widely accepted in America at the time of the writing of the Constitution. Such a doctrine would therefore have united the delegates more than it would have divided them (see Wright 1962, 123–148). At the Convention, however, delegates were not generally concerned with abstract natural rights but with concrete governmental institutions.

Discussions at the Constitutional Convention

Virginia's James Madison was among the delegates who thought that one of the weaknesses of the Articles of Confederation was that it did not adequately provide for protecting the rights of the people. Thus on June 6, he pointed to the need "of providing more effectually for the security of private rights, and the steady dispensation of Justice" (Farrand 1937, I, 134). He focused largely on the idea, later reiterated in *Federalist* No. 10, of creating a large republic in which factions would be multiplied and the chance that anyone would dominate would be mitigated. Virginia's George Mason announced on July 26 that "his primary object, . . . the pole star of his political conduct," was "the preservation of the rights of the people" (II, 119). He subsequently opposed ratification of the Constitution partly on the basis that, without a bill of rights, it did not adequately protect liberty. At the Convention, Pennsylvania's Gouverneur Morris later cited the fact that government was "instituted for protection of the rights of mankind" as a basis for his emotional condemnation of slavery (II, 222).

At times it was difficult at the Convention for delegates to separate the idea of the rights of men from the doctrine, embodied in the notion of state sovereignty under the Articles of Confederation, of the rights of states. In the controversy over representation for the small states and the large ones, Maryland's Luther Martin portrayed the states—as social contract theorists like Thomas Hobbes and John Locke had portrayed individuals prior to society—as "in a state of nature towards each other" (I, 324). He added that "they entered into the confederation on the footing of equality; that they met now to amend it on the same footing, and that he could never accede to a plan that would introduce an inequality and lay 10 States at the mercy of Va. Massts. and Penna." (I, 324). By contrast, Pennsylvania's James Wilson said that he "could not admit the doctrine that when the Colonies became independent of G. Britain, they became independent also of each other" (I, 324). Gouverneur Morris of Pennsylvania later charged that delegates from the smaller states who were demanding equal representation in Congress were demanding "greater rights as men, than their fellow Citizens of the large States" (I, 552). Notes that Virginia's Edmund Randolph composed during his work on the Committee of Detail contained some observations about a preamble for the Constitution. The initial paragraphs of the Declaration of Independence and of many state constitutions had articulated the doctrine of natural rights. Randolph thought that the goal of the national Constitution should be different:

> A preamble seems proper not for the purpose of designating the ends of government and human polities—This business, if not fitter for the schools, is at least sufficiently executed display of theory, howsoever proper in the first formulation of state governments, is unfit here; since we are not working on the natural rights of men not yet gathered into society, but upon those rights, modified by society and interwoven with what we call the right of states. [some crossed out materials omitted] (II, 137)

Ratification Debates

Debates over natural rights seemed to heighten during the ratification debates. Both Federalists and Antifederalists supported the idea. Federalists, who conceived of the entire structure of the new government as a kind of bill of rights, initially argued that a bill of rights was unnecessary to protect such rights. Indeed, they argued that such a bill could even prove dangerous in the event that rights not specified might be in jeopardy. Antifederalists and some friends of the Constitution, like Thomas Jefferson, asserted that such a bill was required both as a means of educating the public and providing for redress in the courts.

Although not all Federalists appear to have been convinced of the necessity of such a bill to protect rights, enough were persuaded of the need to promise the addition of such a bill to get the Constitution ratified, that such a bill of rights was initially adopted. By incorporating such provisions into the fundamental law, early Americans hoped to provide legal enforcement for rights that the national government might not otherwise heed. The provisions in the Bill of Rights initially bound only the national government. James Madison's desire for provisions limiting state governments did not become a reality until after the adoption of the Fourteenth Amendment in 1868. The U.S. Supreme Court later used this amendment to apply most of the provisions in the Bill of Rights, which once limited only the national government, to the states as well.

One of the reasons that has been cited for the widespread adulation of the U.S. Constitution has been its association in the popular mind with the idea of natural, or higher law (Corwin 1981, 79–139). The idea of the Constitution as higher law has served as one of the pillars of the power of courts to exercise judicial review, the power to strike down acts of legislation that they judge to be unconstitutional.

See Also Bill of Rights; Declaration of Independence; Jefferson, Thomas; Judicial Review; Liberalism; Locke, John; Mason, George; Natural Rights; Ratification in the States; Virginia Declaration of Rights

FOR FURTHER READING

Barrett, Randy E. 2004. *Restoring the Lost Constitution: The Presumption of Liberty.* Princeton, NJ: Princeton University Press.

Corwin, Edward S. 1981. *Corwin on the Constitution.* Vol. 1: *The Foundations of American Constitutional and Political Thought, the Powers of Congress, and the President's Power of Removal.* Ed. Richard Loss. Ithaca, NY: Cornell University Press.

Cranston, Maurice. 1973. *What Are Human Rights?* New York: Taplinger Publishing Co.

Farrand, Max, ed. 1937. *The Records of the Federal Convention.* 4 vols. New Haven, CT: Yale University Press.

Hamburger, Philip A. 1993. "Natural Rights, Natural Law, and American Constitutions." *Yale Law Journal* 102 (January): 907–960.

Jordan, Cynthia S. 1988. "'Old Words' in 'New Circumstances': Language and Leadership in Post-Revolutionary America." *American Quarterly* 40 (December): 491–513.

Kramer, Larry D. 2004. *The People Themselves: Constitutionalism and Judicial Review.* New York: Oxford University Press.

Lyons, David. 1979. *Rights.* Belmont, CA: Wadsworth Publishing.

Sherry, Suzanna. 1987. "The Founders' Unwritten Constitution." *University of Chicago Law Review* 54 (Fall): 1127–1177.

Wright, Benjamin Fletcher. 1962. *American Interpretations of Natural Law: A Study in the History of Political Thought.* New York: Russell and Russell.

NATURALIZATION

Article I, Section 8 empowers Congress "to establish an uniform Rule of Naturalization . . . throughout the United States," a power that it pairs with the power to establish uniform laws related to bankruptcies. The provision relative to naturalization engendered little debate at the Constitutional Convention. It appears to have originated in a provision in the New Jersey Plan, which William Paterson presented to the Convention on June 15. It provided that "the rule for naturalization ought to be the same in every State" (Farrand 1937, I, 245). The report of the Committee of Detail to the Convention on August 6 established the current language of the provision (II, 167). There is no recorded debate at the Convention when the measure was adopted on August 16 (II, 304).

In a preface to the *Records of the Convention* which he never completed, James Madison listed the lack of uniformity among state naturalization laws as "among the defects which had been severely felt" (III, 548). In speaking to Congress on February 3, 1790, Connecticut's Roger Sherman said that the Convention had vested this power in Congress "in order to prevent particular States receiving citizens, and forcing them upon others who would not have received them in any other manner. It was therefore meant to guard against an improper mode of naturalization, rather than foreigners should be received upon easier terms than those adopted by the several States" (III, 359). Although vesting Congress with the power to provide for uniform rules of naturalization and requiring that individuals who ran for the presidency or for either house of Congress be citizens (the Constitution further required individuals running for president either to be either in the nation at the time the Constitution was adopted or to be "natural-born"), the Convention did not settle on a definition of citizenship. This eventually led to disputes over whether blacks, especially those who were free, could be citizens. The Supreme Court answered this question negatively in the *Dred Scott* decision, 60 U.S. 393 (1857), but Section 1 of the Fourteenth Amendment later reversed this decision by extending citizenship to all persons "born or naturalized in the United States and subject to the jurisdiction thereof."

See Also Congress, House of Representatives, Qualifications of Members; Congress, Senate, Qualifications; President, Qualifications

FOR FURTHER READING

Farrand, Max, ed. 1937. *The Records of the Federal Convention.* 4 vols. New Haven, CT: Yale University Press.

Horton, James Oliver. 1986. "Weevils in the Wheat: Free Blacks and the Constitution, 1787–1860." American Political Science Association, American Historical Association. *this Constitution: Our Enduring Legacy.* Washington, DC: Congressional Quarterly.

NECESSARY AND PROPER CLAUSE

See POWERS, IMPLIED

NEGATIVE ON STATE LAWS

One of the more novel provisions of the Virginia Plan, formulated by James Madison, who discussed the proposal in a number of letters prior to the Convention (Hobson 1979, 219), was a provision for a congressional negative on state laws. Section 6 of the Virginia Plan accordingly provided that Congress would have the power "to negative all laws passed by the several States, contravening in the opinion of the National Legislature the articles of Union" (Farrand 1937, I, 21). This was in addition to the negative that the proposed Council of Revision, consisting of the president and key members of the judiciary, would exercise over both congressional and state legislation, subject to congressional override (see President, Council).

Debates of June and July

Madison, who had observed state legislative excesses firsthand in the Virginia legislature, had hoped to give Congress a negative of state laws that were "improper" as well as unconstitutional (Hobson, 226). He accordingly joined Charles Pinckney of South Carolina in supporting such a widening of this veto on June 8. In proposing this motion, Pinckney observed that

> such a universality of the power was indispensably necessary to render it effectual; that the States must be kept in due subordination to the nation; that if the States were left to act of themselves in any case, it wd. be impossible to defend the national prerogative, however extensive they might be on paper; that the acts of Congress had been defeated by this means . . . that his univer-

sal negative was in fact the corner stone of an efficient national Govt. (I, 164)

Although one wonders how well the analogy would have been accepted by most members of the Convention who had once chafed under British rule, Pinckney did not flinch in comparing this mechanism to the negative that the Crown had exercised over the colonies in the colonial era. Madison argued that Pinckney's revision was "absolutely necessary to a perfect system." He cited the tendencies of the states not only to "encroach on the federal authority" but also to oppress the weak within their own states. The negative on state legislation would be preferable to coercion. In short: "This prerogative of the General Govt. is the great pervading principle that must controul the centrifugal tendency of the States; which, without it, will continually fly out of their proper orbits and destroy the order & harmony of the political system" (I, 164–165).

Such nationalistic sentiments did not equally appeal to all. North Carolina's Hugh Williamson thought that it would trench on state powers of "regulating their internal police" (I, 165). Elbridge Gerry of Massachusetts thought that such a power was unnecessary and that either a "remonstrance agst unreasonable acts of the State wd. reclaim them" or, if necessary, force could be used. Gerry thought the proposal to be overly speculative and impractical. He explained: "The States too have different interests and are ignorant of each other's interests. The negative therefore will be abused. New States too having separate views from the old States will never come into the Union" (I, 166). Connecticut's Roger Sherman thought that occasions for the exercise of such a negative required further definition. Pennsylvania's James Wilson thought that the negative would affirm common nationhood. Similarly, Delaware's John Dickinson thought that it was impossible to draw a line between occasions when Congress should exercise the veto and those when it should not. Thinking the danger that states would injure the national government to be greater than the reverse, he supported the negative. By contrast Gunning Bedford, also of Delaware, thought the provision would "strip the small States of their equal right of suffrage" (I, 167). He also offered practical objections: "How can it be thought that the proposed negative can be exercised? Are the laws of the States to be suspended in the most urgent cases until they can be sent seven or eight hundred miles, and undergo the deliberations of a body who may be incapable of Judging of them? Is the National Legislature too to sit continually in order to revise the laws of the States?" (I, 167–178).

Madison's response was elusive: "The case of laws of urgent necessity must be provided for by some emanation of the power from the Natl. Govt. into each State so far as to give a temporary assent at least" (I, 168); Madison did not explain precisely what this "emanation" might be (Hobson, 227). Madison also suggested that the Senate, rather than the full Congress, might exercise this right. The Convention rejected Pinckney's motion to expand the negative on state laws by a vote of 7-3-1, but a qualified negative remained in the report by the Committee of the Whole (I, 229).

In favoring the New Jersey Plan, which did not contain a congressional negative over state laws, over the Virginia Plan, New York's John Lansing observed on June 16 that "the States will never feel a sufficient confidence in a general Government to give it a negative on their laws" (I, 250). Not surprisingly, Madison saw things differently. Speaking on June 19, he observed that "the plan of Mr. Paterson, not giving even a negative on the Acts of the States, left them as much at liberty as ever to execute their unrighteous projects agst. each other" (I, 318). Tracking arguments he had made in his "Vices of the Political System of the United States," Madison further observed that the New Jersey Plan did not remedy "1. the multiplicity of the laws passed by the several States. 2. the mutability of their laws. 3. the injustice of them. [or] 4. the impotence of them" (I, 318–319).

Lansing was still not convinced of the merits of the Virginia Plan. He pointed to a variety of practical problems that he envisioned in regard to the veto, which he tied to the veto once exercised by the Crown (Greene 1917, 107):

It is proposed that the genl. Legislature shall have a negative on the laws of the States. Is it conceivable that there will be leisure for such a task? There will on the most moderate calculation, be as many Acts sent up from the States as there are days in the year. Will the members of the general Legislature be competent Judges? Will a gentleman from Georgia be a Judge of the expediency of a law which is to operate in N. Hamshire. Such a Negative will be more injurious than that of Great Britain heretofore was. (I, 337)

In an extended speech that he gave on June 27, Maryland's Luther Martin also argued for keeping the national government within narrow limits. One of his observations was "that the States, particularly the smaller, would never allow a negative to be exercised over their laws" (I, 438). By contrast, in arguing for proportional representation within Congress, Madison argued on the next day that the negative on state laws would make Congress "an essential branch of the State Legislatures & of course will require that it should be exercised by a body established on like principles with the other branches of those Legislatures" (I, 447).

On July 17, just one day after the Convention rejected proportional representation in both houses of Congress in favor of the Connecticut Compromise, it reconsidered the negative. Perhaps influenced in part by the diminished role that the large states would play in the reconfigured Congress, Gouverneur Morris opposed the provision on the basis that it was likely to be "terrible to the States, and not necessary, if sufficient Legislative authority should be given to the Genl. Government" (II, 27). Roger Sherman also argued that it was unnecessary; he thought that courts would invalidate any state laws that were unconstitutional. Luther Martin of Maryland rhetorically asked, "Shall all the laws of the States be sent up to the Genl. Legislature before they shall be permitted to operate?" (II, 27).

Madison continued to view the negative as "essential to the efficacy & security of the Genl. Govt." It was needed because of the state propensity to pursue individual interests at the expense of the common good. States would do harm before judges could act. State judges were often subservient to the legislatures: "A power of negativing the improper laws of the States is at once the most mild & certain means of preserving the harmony of the system" (II, 28). Again, Madison cited the operation of the British system. Again, he elusively suggested that "some emanation" of national power in the states could "give a temporary effect to laws of immediate necessity" (II, 28).

Morris remained unconvinced. Such a negative "would disgust all the states" (II, 28). Judges could set aside improper laws, or Congress could repeal them. The delegates overwhelmingly cast aside the provision by a vote of 7-3. Significantly, the Convention immediately began discussion of the supremacy clause, which can be understood at least as a partial substitute for the state negative.

Debate on August 23

On August 23, Charles Pinckney tried again to introduce a negative of state laws in cases where two-thirds or more of Congress agreed. This time, North Carolina's William Blount seconded the motion. Sherman viewed the provision as unnecessary, pointing to the supremacy clause. Madison tried to get the proposal committed to a committee where it could be refined. Mason thought it totally impractical: "Are all laws whatever to be brought up? Is no road nor bridge to be established without the Sanction of the General Legislature? Is this to sit constantly in order to receive & revise the State Laws?" (II, 390). Williamson thought the law was unnecessary, while James Wilson thought it was "the key-stone wanted to compleat the wide arch of Government we are raising." It would provide the national government with a needed defense. Moreover, "It will be better to prevent the passage of an improper law, than to declare it void when passed" (II, 391). South Carolina's John Rutledge was appalled: "If nothing else, this alone would damn and ought to damn the Constitution. Will any state ever agree to be bound hand & foot in this manner. It is worse than making mere corporations of them whose bye laws would not be subject to this shackle" (II, 391). Connecticut's Oliver Ellsworth wondered whether proponents of the negative intended for the national government to appoint state governors to oversee state legislation—an expedient that Alexander Hamilton had suggested

on June 18 (I, 293). The Convention decided by a 6-5 vote not to commit the matter to committee, and Pinckney withdrew the motion.

Other Comments

In later discussions of a provision regulating state interference with contracts, Madison supported the provision but opined "that a negative on the State laws could alone secure the effect" (II, 440). In a post-Convention letter to Thomas Jefferson, Madison continued to argue that the Constitution was defective in not adequately providing for the defense of individual rights, as the congressional negative (operated by a body representing a wider area and embracing a wider variety of interests) would have done (Hobson, 233).

Analysis

Although his goals were noble, Madison's plan for a negative of state laws was too undeveloped for delegates to know how it could operate in practice without leading to excessive delay and excessive congressional interference in state affairs. By contrast, the judicial system, reinforced by the supremacy clause, stood as a barrier against unconstitutional legislation while leaving in place laws that national authorities might consider unwise but that were not in contradiction to the Constitution.

See Also Madison, James, Jr.; Pinckney, Charles; President, Council; Presidential Veto; Supremacy Clause; Vices of the Political System of the United States

FOR FURTHER READING

Clark, Bradford R. "The Supremacy Clause as a Constraint on Federal Power." *George Washington Law Review* 71 (February 2003): 91–130.

Farrand, Max, ed. 1937. *The Records of the Federal Convention.* 4 vols. New Haven, CT: Yale University Press.

Greene, Evarts B. 1917. "American Opinion on the Imperial Review of Provincial Legislation, 1776–1787." *American Historical Review* 23 (October): 104–107.

Hobson, Charles F. 1979. " The Negative on State Laws: James Madison, the Constitution, and the Crisis of Republican Government." *William and Mary Quarterly*, 3rd ser. 36 (April): 214–235.

NEM. CON.

Readers of the Convention records compiled by James Madison will constantly encounter the expression "nem. con." after various votes. This is an abbreviation of the Latin words *Nemine contradicente*, meaning "no one contradicting" (Benton 1986, 14) and represents a unanimous state vote. Readers need to keep in mind that, consistent with the rules that the Convention adopted, votes were recorded by states rather than under the individual names of delegates, so a nem. con. notation does not necessarily mean that every *delegate* was in agreement.

On August 16, Madison recorded an initial vote for coining money as having passed "nem. con." and proposals for regulating foreign coin and for fixing the standard of weights and measures, which he records directly below the previous resolution, as having been adopted "do. do" (II, 308). The next day, he observed that the Convention voted "nem. con." to constitute inferior tribunals and then voted "do. do" to make rules for captures on land and sea (II, 315). These references appear to be abbreviations for "ditto."

See Also Rules of the Constitutional Convention

FOR FURTHER READING

Benton, Wilbourne E., ed. 1986. *1787: Drafting the U.S. Constitution*. 2 vols. College Station: Texas A and M University Press.

NEW ENGLAND CONFEDERATION

The Articles of Confederation had been preceded by a smaller confederation with a similar name. The Articles of Confederation of the New England colonies, or the New England Confederation, had been formed in 1643 and lasted roughly until 1686. Delegates from New Haven, Connecticut, Plymouth, and Massachusetts Bay formed this confederation in Boston in 1643. Three of these four colonies had authorized their representatives to enter into a binding agreement, but in a prelude to later ideas of popular sovereignty and to later referendums, Plymouth had specified that voters would have to approve any agreement reached (Long 1926, 50).

Apparently largely stimulated by fears of the Dutch (in nearby New York) and the Indians, the Articles conferred powers on the Confederation to deal with matters of war and peace, to enact laws for the benefit of its members, to levy taxes for the cost of war to be defrayed on the basis of the number of male inhabitants, and to requisition additional troops if quotas for this purpose proved to be inadequate (Long, 51–52).

Further provisions of the Articles provided for recognizing the sovereignty of each state, for prohibiting any two from uniting without the consent of the others, for admitting new colonies by unanimous consent, for acknowledging the superiority of decisions reached collectively, for extraditing criminals, and for acknowledging no superior authority (Long, 52). Much as in the case of the current U.S. Senate, under the Confederation, each of the four colonies had two representatives. Votes of six of more were immediately binding; votes by simple majorities required approval by the General Court, or Assembly, of each colony (Long, 52).

In 1686, England's King James II revoked the charters of the American colonies, and the Articles dissolved to be replaced by the brief Dominion of New England. Several features of the New England Confederation were later reflected in the Articles of Confederation and in the U.S. Constitution.

See Also Albany Plan of Union; Articles of Confederation; Dominion of New England

FOR FURTHER READING

Long, Breckinridge. 1926. *Genesis of the Constitution of the United States of America.* New York: Macmillan.

NEW HAMPSHIRE

At least as early as the 1770s, New Hampshire had been divided into three sections corresponding to three different geographical regions designated by watersheds. Those in Piscataqua near the coast, including residents of Portsmouth and Exeter, had acquired wealth through trade and wanted to keep things largely as they were. The Merrimack watershed served those in the central part of the state who had felt unrepresented in the colonial government. Those from the Connecticut River Valley were also resentful of the control by the Eastern section and had sometimes sought to separate from the rest of the state (Daniell 1988, 182).

State Government

A provincial congress had taken control when the royal governor had departed. This congress adopted a state constitution in 1776 that included a bicameral legislature consisting of a House of Representatives and a Council. It was during the tenure of this government that the state ratified the Articles of Confederation while attempting to continue to assert state sovereignty. This government also successfully prevented attempts by towns in the Connecticut River Valley to join Vermont.

The state succeeded in adopting a new constitution in 1784. It provided for a president elected by the people, a Senate composed of delegates selected by counties, and a House of Representatives primarily representing towns. Like many

other states, New Hampshire suffered economic decline during the Articles of Confederation. Although it appointed delegates to the Annapolis Convention, none attended (Daniell).

Representation at the Convention

New Hampshire's influence at the Constitutional Convention was limited by the fact that neither of its two delegates, John Langdon and Nicholas Gilman, arrived at the Convention until July 23. Both signed the Constitution. It would be interesting to speculate, although it is impossible to know with certainty, as to what effect the earlier arrival of delegates from one of the smaller states might have had on early deliberations about state representation in Congress, especially had the New Hampshire delegates been joined by delegates from Rhode Island, the least populous state and the only state that did not send delegates to the Convention.

Ratification

New Hampshire became the critical ninth state to ratify the U.S. Constitution, although had Virginia and New York not followed, it is not clear that the new government could have succeeded. In light of the ratification of neighboring Massachusetts, delegates arrived at the ratifying convention in Exeter on February 13, 1788, with the expectation that ratification would proceed fairly expeditiously. It selected John Sullivan, the state president, to preside over the convention. Sullivan found that a slim majority disfavored ratification, with many arriving from their districts with specific instructions to oppose the new document. Federalists subsequently succeeded in adjourning the convention so that delegates could return home and seek release from their instructions. In this instance, as in others during the convention, the Federalists successfully outmaneuvered their opponents.

The convention reassembled at Concord on June 18, 1788, and ratified the document four days later by a 57 to 47 majority, with four dele-

View of Portsmouth, New Hampshire from across the Piscataqua River (Library of Congress)

gates abstaining from voting. Although Federalists had initially accepted adjournment in place of the idea of accepting the Constitution with recommendatory amendments, they ultimately had to give on this point. Federalists did succeed here, as in Massachusetts, from conditioning ratification on the adoption of a specific amendment or set of amendments.

Curiously, one Antifederalist objection to the new Constitution stemmed from its prohibition of religious tests. The state constitution of 1784 had required that officeholders be "of the Protestant religion" and had made explicit provision for religious instruction. Many in the state believed that religion was indispensable to founding good government, and they doubted the propriety of a national government without such support. Fortunately, a number of clergymen who attended the state ratifying convention actually supported the prohibition of religious tests at the national

level as a positive good. Perhaps they also realized that it would not ban such tests for state officials.

Another objection to the Constitution centered on its acquiescence in the perpetuation of the institution of slavery. Although New Hampshire had never officially outlawed slavery, it was dying a natural death in the state, with only 158 slaves recorded in the state by 1790. Slavery stuck in the craw of many Antifederalists who were motivated by some of the same kinds of moral and religious sentiments that led others to favor a religious oath of office. Ultimately, however, the new Constitution did little more than the Articles in recognizing slavery as a local institution (indeed, it at least provided for a possible end to the slave trade after 1808), and those opposing the institution did not so much seek to abolish it as simply to keep the state from joining states where it was approved.

Some Antifederalists also opposed the terms of

members of the U.S. House of Representatives and the Senate. They favored annual elections like those used for both houses of the state legislature.

At the ratifying convention, a committee of eight Federalists and seven Antifederalists recommended a total of 12 amendments, most tracking those that had been previously introduced in Massachusetts. One amendment, which would prohibit Congress from enacting legislation "touching religion," appears to have been designed to protect New Hampshire's own limited establishment (Yarbrough 1989, 252).

See Also Gilman, Nicholas; Langdon, John

FOR FURTHER READING

Buffam, Francis H., ed. 1942. *New Hampshire and the Federal Constitution: A Memorial of the Sesquicentennial Celebration of New Hampshire's Part in the Framing and Ratification of the Constitution of the United States.* 2nd ed. Concord, NH: Granite State Press.
Daniell, Jere. 1988. "Ideology and Hardball: Ratification of the Federal Constitution in New Hampshire." In Patrick T. Conley and John P. Kaminski, eds. *The Constitution and the States: The Role of the Original Thirteen in the Framing and Adoption of the Federal Constitution.* Madison, WI: Madison House.
Yarbrough, Jean. 1989. "New Hampshire: Puritanism and the Moral Foundations of America." In Michael Allen Gillespie and Michael Lienesch, eds. *Ratifying the Constitution.* Lawrence: University Press of Kansas.

NEW JERSEY

Originally settled by immigrants from Sweden and Holland, the English took possession of New Jersey in 1664, and the king granted the land to Lord John Berkeley and Sir George Carteret. Politically, the state was split between the east and the west. The east, which New Englanders had primarily settled, had close ties with New York and was more republican, while the west, which Swedes and Quakers had largely settled, was closer to Pennsylvania and was more conservative.

The two areas were combined into a single royal colony in 1702. Benjamin Franklin's illegitimate son, William (from whom he was estranged), was the royal governor when the movement for independence began. At the time, New Jersey was predominately agricultural, and it boasted no town larger than 1,500 inhabitants (Murrin 1988, 58). New Jersey called a number of provincial congresses. The third of these congresses repealed previous instructions in order to authorize its congressional representatives to vote for independence. This congress also appointed a committee of 10 men who drafted a constitution, which went into effect on July 2, 1776.

State Constitution

This constitution vested government in a governor, a Legislative Council, and a General Assembly, with the general assembly being the most powerful. Freemen of property annually elected members of this bicameral body. It selected the governor and most members of the judicial branch, including judges of the Supreme Court who served for seven-year terms. The Council and the governor served as the final court of appeal. The governor, who presided over the Council, exercised his power primarily through personal influence. William Livingston, a delegate to the U.S. Constitutional Convention, held this position from 1776 until 1790. Although the New Jersey legislature was sovereign, the state's citizens were accustomed to acting not only through the legislature but through conventions and other institutions that arose outside it.

New Jersey under the Articles of Confederation

As a small middle Atlantic state with large debts from the Revolution and with no Western lands that it might sell, New Jersey was not particularly profiting from the Articles. Indeed, during the Articles, individuals sometimes likened New Jersey to a cask with a tap on each end since New York and Pennsylvania were both taxing its trade.

During the Articles of Confederation, New Jersey supported several proposals to strengthen the powers of Congress. New Jersey's lack of commercial revenue might indeed help account for its failure, which James Madison had cited in a speech at the Convention on June 19, to comply with a financial requisition from Congress (Farrand 1937, I, 315), but the state also appears to have been influenced by Congress's decision not to continue payment on the national debt, much of which was due to New Jersey creditors (Jensen 1978, 123). New Jersey had sided with the Southern states in opposing giving up rights in a treaty to navigate the Mississippi River. Significantly, New Jersey was one of five states to send delegates to the Annapolis Convention; New Jersey's Abraham Clark has been credited as being the individual who suggested using the Convention report to call for the Constitutional Convention. The College of New Jersey, today's Princeton University, educated more delegates who attended the Convention than did any other such institution.

Representation at the Convention

Five delegates represented New Jersey at the Constitutional Convention. They were David Brearly, Jonathan Dayton (who had been selected to replace Abraham Clark, who thought service at the Convention would interfere with his work as a member of Congress), William Churchill Houston, William Livingston, and William Paterson. All but Houston, who appears to have left the Convention because of illness but later signed the report of the state's delegation, signed the Constitution. The only delegate from New Jersey who made a substantial impact on the Convention was Paterson, but his work was so notable that his name is almost always associated with the New Jersey Plan, which he offered in opposition to that of Virginia.

This plan will forever be identified with the interests of the smaller states, of which New Jersey was one. It was predicated on the idea that the Articles of Confederation might be revised rather than replaced. It thus proposed to continue a national unicameral legislature in which each state would retain its equal representation, but in which congressional laws would be paramount (the plan provided the basis for the supremacy clause). Some delegates from other states thought that New Jersey was primarily concerned with maintaining its status within the new government. Thus, when the respective merits of the New Jersey and Virginia Plans were being considered on June 16, South Carolina's Charles Pinckney said, notwithstanding the other elements of its plan, that if New Jersey secured equal representation within Congress, "she will dismiss her scruples, and concur in the Natil. system" (I, 255). Nathaniel Gorham of Massachusetts observed on June 29 that New Jersey could ill afford for the Union to dissolve:

> Should a separation of the States take place, the fate of N. Jersey wd. be worst of all. She has no foreign commerce & can have but little. Pa. & N. York will continue to levy taxes on her consumption. If she consults her interest she wd. beg of all things to be annihilated. (I, 462)

In point of fact, once the Connecticut Compromise was adopted granting states equal representation in the Senate, New Jersey did become a strong supporter of the new proposal.

Ratification of the Constitution

Abraham Clark was generally regarded as the leader of republican forces in the West. Conservatives like Paterson were from the East. The story of ratification in New Jersey has been likened, as in a Sherlock Holmes mystery, to "the dog that did not bark" (Shumer 1989, 85). It was the third state to ratify the Constitution, and, despite what might have been expected based on the east/west divisions within the state, it ratified unanimously. Elections took place from November 17 through December 1. The Convention began on December 11. There was little recorded debate, and the vote of 38 to 0 took place on December 18.

Although Clark had long been an advocate of states' rights and thus might have been expected to oppose the new Constitution, he, like others in

Abraham Clark (1726–1794)

Abraham Clark served his home state of New Jersey and the nation of which it was to become a part in many ways. According to the recollection of James Madison, Clark was apparently the individual who suggested the idea of using the Annapolis Convention, to which he was a representative, to call for the Constitutional Convention that eventually met in Philadelphia to write the Constitution (Jensen 1978, III, 124).

Born in Elizabethtown, New Jersey in 1726, Clark studied surveying but ended up carrying out so much legal business that he was sometimes called "the poor man's counselor" (Garraty and Carnes 1999, IV, 908). Chosen for several positions under the colonial government of New Jersey, he joined the patriot cause serving as a member of the state's Committee of Safety and of its Provincial Congress. He held either state or congressional offices continuously between 1776 and 1789 and was one of the signers of the Declaration of Independence.

During the Articles of Confederation, he advocated the issuance of paper money. Although New Jersey selected him to serve as a delegate to the Convention, he thought it was inappropriate to serve both in this capacity and as a member of Congress, and Jonathan Dayton was selected in his stead. Clark appears to have been a tepid advocate of the new Constitution and was elected to the second and third Congresses where he served until he died in 1794.

FOR FURTHER READING

Garraty, John A., and Mark C. Carnes, eds. 1999. *American National Biography.* Vol. 4 of 24. New York: Oxford University Press.

Jensen, Merrill. 1978. *Ratification of the Constitution by the States Delaware, New Jersey, Georgia, Connecticut.* Vol. 3 of *The Documentary History of the Ratification of the Constitution.* Madison: State Historical Society of Wisconsin.

---

the state, was caught in the grip of what he considered to be economic necessity. Delegates to the ratifying convention may also have been concerned about insurrections like Shays's Rebellion. Conservatives and Republicans thus united around the new Constitution.

See Also Brearly, David; Dayton, Jonathan; Houston, William Churchill; Livingston, William; New Jersey Plan; Paterson, William

FOR FURTHER READING

Farrand, Max, ed. 1937. *The Records of the Federal Convention.* 4 vols. New Haven, CT: Yale University Press.

Jensen, Merrill, ed. 1978. *Ratification of the Constitution by the States Delaware, New Jersey, Georgia, Connecticut.* Vol. 3 of *The Documentary History of the Ratification of the Constitution.* Madison: State Historical Society of Wisconsin.

Murrin, Mary R. 1988. "New Jersey and the Two Constitutions." In Patrick T. Conley and John P. Kaminski, eds. *The Constitution and the States: The Role of the Original Thirteen in the Framing and Adoption of the Federal Constitution.* Madison, WI: Madison House, 55–75.

Shumer, Sara M. 1989. "New Jersey: Property and the Price of Republican Politics." In Michael Allen Gillespie and Michael Lienesch, eds. *Ratifying the Constitution.* Lawrence: University Press of Kansas.

NEW JERSEY PLAN

The Virginia, or Randolph, Plan dominated the first two weeks of deliberation and debate at the Constitutional Convention. On Thursday, June 14, William Paterson of New Jersey asked delegates to postpone further consideration of this plan for a day so that several delegations, particularly that of New Jersey, would have time to "contemplate the plan reported from the Committee of the Whole, and to digest one purely federal, and contradistinguished from the reported plan" (Farrand 1937, I, 240). That Friday, he subsequently proposed what has become known as the New Jersey Plan. The Committee of the Whole adjourned for consideration of the plan on the following day.

Paterson appears to have included proposals in the plan by Maryland's Luther Martin and by New York's John Lansing, but a Paterson biographer is convinced that Paterson intended for the plan primarily "to be a stalking horse for equal [state] representation" (O'Connor 1979).

The Contents of the Plan

The New Jersey Plan was contained in a total of nine resolutions, which more closely tracked the existing Articles of Confederation than had the Virginia Plan. By maintaining equal state representation in Congress, the New Jersey Plan also more clearly preserved the interests of the less populous states. Consistent with Paterson's intention to amend rather than replace the Articles of Confederation, the first resolution of the New Jersey Plan almost directly tracked the language of the Annapolis Convention: "Resd. that the articles of Confederation ought to be so revised, corrected & enlarged, as to render the federal Constitution adequate to the exigencies of Government, & the preservation of the Union" (I, 242).

Consistent with this goal, the second resolution made no attempt to alter the unicameral structure of the confederal Congress but focused instead on enlarging its powers. These included power "to pass acts for raising a revenue, by levying a duty or duties on all goods or merchandizes of foreign growth or manufactures imported into any part of the U. States"; to regulate the collection of such taxes; to alter such regulations when needed; and "to pass Acts for the regulation of trade & commerce as well with foreign nations as with each other." All controversies over such acts were to originate in state judiciaries, subject to ultimate appeal to the judiciary of the U.S.

Recognizing problems with the existing tax structure, which depended upon congressional requisitions on the states, the New Jersey Plan provided that such requisitions would be made according to the white population and three-fifths of slaves. If states refused to comply, Congress was granted the power to "pass acts directing & authorizing the same" (I, 243), subject to an unspecified supermajority of states.

Perhaps consistent with the agreement to which the Convention had come in respect to the Virginia Plan, the New Jersey Plan further specified that Congress would elect an executive to consist of an unspecified number of persons (but clearly plural in nature), to serve for a single term of unspecified years. Congress was to have the power to remove the executives "on application by a majority of the Executives of the several States," and would have the power to appoint officers not otherwise provided for. The plan prohibited the president from taking personal command of U.S. troops. Whereas the Virginia Plan called for legislative appointment of judges, the New Jersey Plan provided that the executive would appoint judges. Like the Virginia Plan, it provided that members of the judiciary would try impeachment of federal officers.

The New Jersey Plan did not make provision for a Council of Revision or a negative of state laws, but it did contain the basis for what would become known as the supremacy clause. It accordingly provided

that all Acts of the U. States in Cong. made by virtue & in pursuance of the powers hereby & by the articles of confederation vested in them, and all Treaties made & ratified under the authority of the U. States shall be the supreme law of the respective States so far forth as those Acts or Treaties shall relate to the said States or their Citizens, and that the Judiciary of the several States shall be bound thereby in their decisions, any thing in the respective laws of the Individual States to the contrary notwithstanding; and that if any State, or any body of men in any State shall oppose or prevent ye. carrying into execution such acts or treaties, the federal Executive shall be authorized to call forth ye power of the Confederated States, or so much thereof as may be necessary to enforce and compel an obedience to such Acts, or an Observance of such Treaties. (I, 245)

Although Paterson argued that his plan provided for direct action of the Congress on individuals as well as on the states (I, 251), by authorizing the use of military power against states rather than directing it specifically against individuals, this part of the plan may have been designed to preserve the confederal nature of the existing government, under which national authorities act on states but not on individuals.

The New Jersey Plan also called for a provision for admitting new states, for a common rule for naturalization, and for treating individuals who committed offenses in other states just like those individuals would be treated if they were state citizens. Matters like the amending process, which the New Jersey Plan omitted, would presumably have remained the same as under the existing Articles of Confederation.

Discussions of the Plan

New York's John Lansing, who eventually left the Convention rather than continuing its discussion of the Virginia Plan, made the first speech in defense of the New Jersey Plan. He focused not so much on the merits of the plan as on the fact that it was more in line with what the states and Congress had commissioned and that Lansing hence thought it was more likely to be adopted. Paterson himself made a similar argument, indicating that he thought his primary role was not to create "such a Governmnt. as may be best in itself, but such a one as our Constituents have authorized us to prepare, and as they will approve" (I, 250). Paterson proceeded to argue that the Articles were a type of treaty and that changes in state representation could therefore not be made without the unanimous consent of the states that agreed to it. He further argued that state sovereignty required that "the Representatives must be drawn immediately from the States, not from the people" (I, 251). Paterson was concerned both that a bicameral legislature was unnecessary and that it would be expensive.

On the day that Paterson introduced the New

Jersey Plan, Robert Yates, a colleague of New York's John Lansing, recorded in his notes that Lansing observed "that the two systems are fairly contrasted." Lansing explained that "the one now offered is on the basis of amending the federal government, and the other to be reported as a national government, on propositions which exclude the propriety of amendment [of the Articles]" (I, 246). Pennsylvania's James Wilson, who favored the Virginia Plan, drew up a more expansive list of 13 particulars in which the Virginia and New Jersey Plans differed (I, 252–253).

Analysis and Ultimate Influence

A Paterson biographer has observed:

> To the extent that the New Jersey Plan had been intended by Martin or Lansing to protect their special interests or perhaps even to break up the convention, it was a dismal failure. But to the extent that Paterson and some others (especially Dickinson, Sherman, and the Connecticut group) saw the resolutions as another attempt to convince the convention of their firmness on the matter of representation, the desired result was achieved. (O'Connor, 150)

Initially, the New Jersey Plan gained relatively little favor, and the Convention continued using the Virginia Plan as its primary template. Over time, however, the New Jersey Plan resulted in a compromise resulting in equal state representation in the Senate. Elements of the New Jersey Plan also became incorporated in the method for selecting members of the federal judiciary, with the president nominating judges, as the New Jersey Plan specified, and the Senate, to which the Virginia Plan would have entrusted appointments, confirming them. The supremacy clause also found its way into the final Constitution. In other ways, too, the New Jersey Plan indicated concern that the government proposed by the Virginia Plan was too "national" in character. It perhaps signaled the ultimate demise of the congressional negative on state laws and the creation of other limitations on congressional powers.

See Also Annapolis Convention; Articles of Confederation; Connecticut Compromise; New Jersey; Paterson, William; Supremacy Clause; Virginia Plan

FOR FURTHER READING

Birkby, Robert H. 1966. "Politics of Accommodation: The Origins of the Supremacy Clause." *Western Political Quarterly* 19 (March): 123–135.

Farrand, Max, ed. 1937. *The Records of the Federal Convention*. 4 vols. New Haven, CT: Yale University Press.

O'Connor, J. J. 1979. *William Paterson: Lawyer and Statesman, 1745–1806*. New Brunswick, NJ: Rutgers University Press.

Wolfe, Christopher. 1977. "On Understanding the Constitutional Convention of 1787." *Journal of Politics* 19 (February): 97–118.

NEW YORK

Settled by the Dutch and the British, who had wrested control from the Dutch, much of New York was sparsely settled at the time of the Constitutional Convention. British Canada posed a potential threat to the north and the Indians posed a similar threat in the West. Politically, the state was split between the Hudson River Valley area and the area around the port of New York. Dutch aristocrats, who had settled the valley area, had adopted a manorial system, whereas more densely populated areas surrounding the port of New York had become the locus of thriving commerce. Leadership by aristocratic families of Dutch descent had given place during the Revolution to leadership by men with greater popular influence. The most notable of these was Governor George Clinton, who was first selected as governor in 1777 and was still in this position at the time the U.S. Constitution was debated.

State Constitution

New York had adopted a fairly conservative constitution in April 1777, and a number of features of this constitution were later reflected in the Virginia Plan and in the U.S. Constitution. The governor served longer than in most states, with a three-year renewable term. Similarly, although members of the Assembly were elected annually, members of the Senate served for four-year terms. Judges were appointed by the governor in conjunction with four senators and served during good behavior. Together with a Council of Revision that included the chancellor and judges of the Supreme Court, the governor had the power to veto or revise all legislation, subject to a two-thirds override of both houses.

New York had suffered during the Revolutionary War, and the British remained in New York City two years after the colonial victory at Yorktown. New York had accordingly joined the New England states at the Hartford Convention in November 1780 to call for greater national powers and had initially approved the proposal for a national impost, a measure that Rhode Island had defeated. New York had subsequently profited from the weakness of the Articles of Confederation by levying a state impost on goods imported from other states and by selling lands in the West and lands confiscated from the Tories. It had accordingly withdrawn its approval of the congressional impost of 1781 and loaded its approval of a second proposal in 1783 with conditions that Congress could not accept, thus blocking this impost, as Rhode Island had blocked an earlier one.

Believing it would profit from still further trade, the state had supported the Annapolis Convention, where Alexander Hamilton and Egbert Benson had represented it and where the former had been a driving force. In early 1787 stories had appeared in New York newspapers advocating that the country be divided into three or four loosely allied confederacies (Kaminski 1985, 64). At the time of the Constitutional Convention, New York was still claiming the area of Vermont, which was seeking its independence and which was also claimed by New Hampshire and Massachusetts.

Representation at the Constitutional Convention

New York was arguably one of the most poorly represented states at the Constitutional Convention. Although its delegates were men of political experience, their attendance was woefully inadequate, and they were deeply divided. Delegates John Lansing and Robert Yates, chosen largely through the influence of Governor George Clinton to block the nationalizing influence of Alexander Hamilton, left the Convention on July 10, in part to return to judicial duties but also because the Convention had taken positions that they could not support. Hamilton, who could not cast a vote for the state in the absence of his two colleagues, in turn absented himself during much of the Convention.

Lansing and Yates became Antifederalists, opposed to the new document. Although Hamilton signed the document (since he was the only one of three delegates from New York, he signed as an individual rather than on behalf of his state), he made it clear that he did not think it went nearly far enough in strengthening the new government and making it more like the British model that he so admired. Arguably, his own support for the document grew the more he found himself in the role of promoting it as a better alternative than the Articles of Confederation.

Although its own delegation was often absent from the Constitutional Convention, there were at least two other delegates with strong ties to New York. One was the talkative Gouverneur Morris, who had been born, and would die, in the state but who was representing Pennsylvania, where he had recently moved, at the Convention. Another was the less influential William Livingston, who was from a prominent New York family and had lived in the state until the age of 49, but was serving as a delegate from New Jersey, where he was the governor. In addition, William Houston, who represented Georgia at the Convention, later moved to New York.

Mentions of New York in Convention Debates

In addition to other influences it exerted, the New York state constitution is believed to have served as a partial model for Charles Pinckney's plan of government. During Convention debates on June 18, Hamilton observed that the New York

Senate, members of which were chosen for four-year terms, had proved to be inefficient (Farrand 1937, I, 299), but his view may in part be discounted by the fact that he was pushing for a national Senate whose members would serve during good behavior. Gouverneur Morris, who was almost as attached to New York as to the state of Pennsylvania which he was representing, used the example of New York on July 17 to indicate that elections (as in those for the state governor) held over large areas were less likely to be subject to intrigue than those held in smaller districts (II, 30–31). On July 23, Nathaniel Gorham of Massachusetts cited New York's attachment to its impost as a reason not to submit the Constitution to ratification by existing state legislatures (II, 90). Gouverneur Morris further argued on September 12 that the New York example proved that a legislature should not be able to override an executive veto by a two-thirds majority (II, 585).

Even before the Convention had ended, Hamilton was publishing attacks on the Clinton Antifederalists that ensured that the debate in the state would be rancorous. The debate is, of course, best known for the publication of *The Federalist*, a series of articles published in New York newspapers and later collected into a book of two volumes which Alexander Hamilton, James Madison, and John Jay authored under the pen name Publius. It is not altogether clear that these specific essays had a significant impact on New York's eventual decision to ratify, but the essays are today regarded as one of the classic defenses, and expositions, of the U.S. Constitution. A 40-page pamphlet printed by "Federal Farmer," probably Melancton Smith, in November 1787 proved to be one of the most influential Antifederalist writings on the Constitution (Webking 1987).

Ratification of the Constitution

New York called an election for convention delegates for April 29, 1788, scheduled to begin in Poughkeepsie on June 17, 1788. It marked the first time in the state's history that all free males who were 21 or older were permitted to vote by secret ballot—the state constitution required that individuals who voted in other elections own property. Forty-six of the 65 delegates chosen were Antifederalists (most of the Federalist delegates came from the New York City area), albeit many were apparently willing to accept a new Constitution if it could be accompanied with amendments. The convention selected Governor Clinton as its president. Although the convention featured other notables, the two most outspoken delegates were Melancton Smith, who represented the Antifederalist point of view, and Alexander Hamilton, who spoke for the Federalist supporters of the new Constitution. Both sides initially agreed to debate the Constitution section by section. Apparently, neither wanted to act quickly. Antifederalists wanted to appear fair and may have hoped that disapproval by the state of Virginia would make their disapproval easier; Federalists realized that they did not have the necessary votes and may have been hoping for positive news of ratification to arrive from other states.

Apart from the debates themselves, the most significant influence on the New York convention appears to have been the news, received on June 24, that New Hampshire had ratified and, more significantly, on July 2 that Virginia had ratified. This largely shifted the debate from whether there would be a new Union to whether New York would join the new Union or not. On July 10, John Lansing led Antifederalists in proposing what has been described as "a package of explanatory, conditional, and recommendatory amendments" (Eubanks 1989, 326). Largely under the leadership of John Jay, but with the eventual acquiescence of Melancton Smith (Brooks 1967), the convention accepted the explanatory and recommendatory amendments, while rejecting those that were conditional. The convention subsequently cast a vote of 30 to 27 on July 26 to accept the new Constitution, making it the 11th state to ratify.

Federalists had already launched an elaborate celebratory federal procession (twice before delayed) on July 23 (Kaminski 1985, 112–113). Some Federalists had threatened that pro-Union forces might secede from New York and join the Union on their own if the entire state refused to do so. With New York's approval, the Constitution was almost guaranteed that it would get a fair trial, even though North Carolina and Rhode Is-

land waited some time before they gave their own approval.

Cecil Eubanks has identified several reasons for the Federalists' success in New York. He observes that both sides recognized that there was a need for some change. Moreover, the Federalists adopted better strategies, with their delays giving time to reach the convention that Virginia had ratified. Eubanks believes that Federalists were more politically skillful, and that Antifederalists proved more conciliatory than might have been expected. He also observes that the press in New York was highly favorable to the new Constitution (Eubanks, 329–330). Ultimately, those in New York who thought the state had a glorious future expanding in the West joined with those who anticipated commercial expansion in the East and ratified the Constitution. Even though the Clinton forces ultimately lost, Clinton used the ratifying convention to strengthen his own electoral base, which he would later devote chiefly to the Democratic-Republican Party.

See Also *Federalist, The;* Hamilton, Alexander; Jay, John; Lansing, John; Vermont; Yates, Robert

FOR FURTHER READING

Brooks, Robin. 1967. "Alexander Hamilton, Melancton Smith, and the Ratification of the Constitution in New York." *William and Mary Quarterly,* 3rd ser. 24 (July): 339–358.

Eubanks, Cecil L. 1989. "New York: Federalists and the Political Economy of Union." In Michael Allen Gillespie and Michael Lienesch, eds. *Ratifying the Constitution.* Lawrence: University Press of Kansas.

Farrand, Max, ed. 1937. *The Records of the Federal Convention.* 4 vols. New Haven, CT: Yale University Press.

Kaminski, John P. 1985. "New York: The Reluctant Pillar." In Stephen L. Schechter, ed. *The Reluctant Pillar: New York and the Adoption of the Federal Constitution.* Troy, NY: Russell Sage College.

———. 1988. "Adjusting to Circumstances: New York's Relationship with the Federal Government, 1776–1788." In Patrick T. Conley and John P. Kaminski, eds. *The Constitution and the States: The Role of the Original Thirteen in the Framing and Adoption of the Federal Constitution.* Madison, WI: Madison House, 225–250.

Webking, Robert H. 1987. "Melancton Smith and the Letters from the Federal Farmer." *William and Mary Quarterly*, 3rd ser. 44 (July): 510–528.

NORTH CAROLINA

North Carolina had been largely settled by immigrants from Virginia and South Carolina and was sometimes described as "the vale of humility between two mountains of conceit" (quoted in Watson 1988, 252). North Carolina had been one of the states that took the lead in the American Revolution, as was manifested by its Mechlenburg Resolves of 1775. The state deposed its royal governor in 1775 and replaced him with a provisional government.

State Constitution

The state constitution, which a Provincial Congress had written, was relatively democratic. Although it created three branches of government, it vested primary power in the state legislature. Voting was open to Protestant freemen who paid their taxes, and the constitution recognized a variety of rights.

At the time of the Convention, North Carolina was the fourth largest state and was composed of land, including today's state of Tennessee (then generally referred to as Franklin), that reached to the Mississippi River. The roughly 400,000 inhabitants were sparsely spread in this vast expanse and included fewer slaves (about 20 percent) than neighboring states. The state did not have the vast plantations of its neighbors, although there were some tensions between the more conservative east and the more radical west. Thomas Burke, who came from the latter, had been the individual most responsible at the Continental Congress for incorporating the doctrine of state sovereignty in the Articles of Confederation, and the state even then initially voted against ratification. North Carolina appointed five delegates to the Annapolis Convention, but only Hugh Williamson went, and he arrived too late for its deliberations.

Representation at the Constitutional Convention

Five delegates represented North Carolina at the Constitutional Convention; all were from the more conservative eastern part of the state. They were William Blount, William Richardson Davie, Alexander Martin, Richard Dobbs Spaight, and Hugh Williamson. Of these, Williamson was clearly the intellectual leader, and he, Blount, and Spaight were the only delegates to sign. North Carolina generally identified with the interests of other Southern states at the Convention. The state was not mentioned frequently, although during debates over whether members of Congress should be eligible for other offices, Williamson observed that in his state, he could scarcely think of "a single corrupt measure . . . which could not be traced up to office hunting" (Farrand 1937, II, 287).

Ratification of the Constitution

On August 2, 1788, the North Carolina ratifying convention meeting in Hillsboro cast a vote 184 to 83 to recommend amendments and otherwise protect the state's rights rather than to ratify the document. Willie Jones, Thomas Person, and Samuel Spencer were among the most prominent opponents of ratification. Although one New Englander accused the state of going "whoring after Strange Gods" (quoted in Lienesch 1979, 343), the state's behavior was consistent with its "politics of resistance to distant power and protection of local liberties" (Lienesch, 343), such as had been embodied within its own constitution. North Carolina's action in delaying ratification was particularly adventuresome since every other state except for Rhode Island had ratified when the convention took its vote.

Although Federalists, led by Richard Dobbs Spaight, future Supreme Court Justice James Iredell, and Governor Samuel Johnson (who presided over the proceedings), generally had the rhetorical advantage, Antifederalists greatly outnumbered Federalists at the state ratifying convention. They emphasized the importance of rights, which they tied to the state and to the region of which they were a part. By contrast, Federalists generally took a more cosmopolitan view, identifying rights with the interests of the nation as a whole. Antifederalists attempted to condition their ratification on the prior adoption of the Bill of Rights, but Federalists refused.

North Carolina was officially independent at the time the new government went into effect and thus did not cast votes in the first presidential election. However, Hugh Williamson continued effectively to represent the state's interest in Congress and to encourage the national government to pursue a conciliatory policy to woo the state back into the fold.

Antifederalists had largely conditioned their initial rejection on the absence of a bill of rights. Virginia's James Madison helped to pacify them when he indicated that he would introduce such a bill in the first Congress. Once Congress submitted this bill to the states, North Carolina called another convention. This convention met in Fayetteville, again with Governor Johnson presiding. This time it ratified the Constitution on November 21, 1789, by a vote of 194 to 77. The following month, North Carolina became the fourth state to ratify the proposed Bill of Rights.

See Also Blount, William; Davie, William Richardson; Martin, Alexander; Spaight, Richard Dobbs; Tennessee; Williamson, Hugh

FOR FURTHER READING

Craig, Burton. 1987. *The Federal Convention of 1787: North Carolina in the Great Crisis.* Richmond, VA: Expert Graphics.

Farrand, Max, ed. 1937. *The Records of the Federal Convention.* 4 vols. New Haven, CT: Yale University Press.

Lefler, Hugh T. 1947. *A Plea for Federal Union, North Carolina, 1788: A Reprint of Two Pamphlets.* Charlottesville, VA: Tracy W. McGregor Library.

Lienesch, Michael. 1979. "North Carolina: Preserving Rights." In Michael Allen Gillespie and Michael Lienesch, eds. *Ratifying the Constitution.* Lawrence: University Press of Kansas.

Messengill, Stephen E. 1988. *North Carolina Votes on the Constitution: Roster of Delegates to the State Ratification Conventions of 1788 and 1789.* Division of Archives and History. North Carolina Department of Cultural Resources.

Trenholme, Louise Irby. 1967. *The Ratification of the Federal Constitution in North Carolina.* New York: AMS Press.

Watson, Alan D. 1988. "States' Rights and Agrarianism Ascendant." In Patrick T. Conley and John P. Kaminski, eds. *The Constitution and the States: The Role of the Original Thirteen in the Framing and Adoption of the Federal Constitution.* Madison, WI: Madison House.

NORTHWEST ORDINANCE OF 1787

Historians generally recognize the Northwest Ordinance of 1787 as one of the most important acts of legislation enacted by the Articles of Confederation. Adopted by Congress on July 13, just a day after the Constitutional Convention had agreed to the three-fifths compromise (Lynd 1966, 225), the ordinance dealt not only with the issue of slavery, for which it is most generally recognized, but also with the status of new states in the West. In accepting the entry of such states on an equal status with the original 13, the Northwest Ordinance affirmed the decision that the delegates to the Constitutional Convention incorporated into Article IV, Section 3, thus arguably preventing the U.S. from becoming an imperial power early in its history and settling a problem that had led to the colonies' own independence.

Status of the Ordinance

The Northwest Ordinance replaced the ordinance of 1784, which had been adopted but never implemented. The ordinance of 1787 has 14 paragraphs, six articles, and a concluding paragraph repealing the ordinance it replaced. The ordinance became the basis for the formation of the states of Ohio, Indiana, Illinois, Michigan, and Wisconsin, and remained in effect until Wisconsin became part of the Union in 1848 (Finkelman 1996, 34).

Government under the Ordinance

The government of the Northwest Territory had three main elements: a governor, whom Congress appointed to a three-year term; a House of Representatives with a minimum of 25 members; and a Legislative Council consisting of five members. The ordinance also provided for a secretary and for judges. The governor was to serve as commander-in-chief of the militia. Members of the House of Representatives—containing one representative "for every five hundred free male inhabitants" (Frohnen 2002, 226)—served for two-year terms. This body was responsible for sending 10 names to Congress, five of whom Congress would choose as members of the Legislative Council for five-year terms. Laws required a majority vote of the House of Representatives and the Council as well as the consent of the governor. The territory was to have a representative in Congress, where states were at the time represented equally, with the power to debate but not to vote.

Rights under the Ordinance

The articles of the Northwest Ordinance contain a number of provisions similar to those later incorporated into the Bill of Rights of the U.S. Constitution. The first, anticipating the free exercise clause of the First Amendment, prevented any man from being "molested on account of his mode of worship or religious sentiments" (227). The second contained a potpourri of provisions, some foreshadowing those in the Fifth and Eighth Amendments, including a guarantee of "proportional representation," of judicial proceedings according to the common law, and of bail; prohibition of deprivation of "liberty or property, but by the judgment of his peers, or the

law of the land" and of "cruel or unusual punishments"; and provision for just compensation for any property taken by the government (227). The notable third article was designed to provide for public education by encouraging "schools and the means of education," a provision that had been given a firm foundation by the Land Ordinance of 1785, which had provided for one section of each township to be reserved for such purposes (Finkelman, 45). Article III was also designed to secure the lands and property of the Indians. The fourth article specified that the territory would forever remain "subject to the Articles of Confederation, and to such alterations therein as shall be constitutionally made"—a provision that might have been intended as at least an indirect communication from the Congress to the Constitutional Convention. Article V provided that the territories would be divided into three to five states, setting the initial population requirement for each at "sixty thousand free inhabitants" (228). As under the new Constitution, such governments were to be "republican" in nature.

Slavery under the Ordinance

Scholars have justifiably subjected Article VI of the ordinance to the closest scrutiny. It both prohibited slavery and provided, much like the new Constitution, for the return of fugitive slaves:

> There shall be neither slavery nor involuntary servitude in the said territory, otherwise than in the punishment of crimes whereof the party shall have been duly convicted: *Provided, always,* That any person escaping into the same, from whom labor or service is lawfully claimed in any one of the original States, such fugitive may be lawfully reclaimed, and conveyed to the person claiming his or her labor or service as aforesaid. (228)

This last article remains one of the most concrete public evidences of the American Founders' antipathy to slavery, but, in part because of the absence of recorded debate, it is more ambiguous than it first appears. Apparently added at the suggestion of Nathan Dane of Massachusetts relatively late in the legislative process, most state representatives who accepted this provision were from the South. There is some evidence that the provision might have been added to make the Northwest Territory more appealing to buyers from the Ohio Company, represented by Manasseh Cutler, whose purchase of a huge chunk of the territory was anticipated to relieve the government of the Articles of Confederation of much of its debt (Finkelman, 40–41). More ominously, the rejection of slavery in the Northwest Territory might have actually strengthened slavery elsewhere by suggesting that territory in the rapidly growing Southwest would not be subject to such restrictions (Finkelman, 36). Similarly, some Southern delegates may have supported the ordinance in the self-interested hope that it would cut down on competition by preventing the cultivation of tobacco and indigo in the territory (40).

Paul Finkelman has pointed to a number of additional problems with Article VI. The provision for slave abolition was inconsistent with other references to "free" inhabitants as well as to protections for private property, which may well have been thought to include slaves. The provision, seemingly based on the false assumption that slavery did not at the time exist in the territory, had no enforcement provision and did not make it clear whether it was intended to apply only to future slave importation into the area or to free those already there. If the latter were its intention, the legislation was not particularly effective. The national government did not take action against slavery in the region, and Finkelman observe that slavery lingered especially long in Indiana and Illinois; it was not until Illinois's second constitution in 1848 that slavery was finally eliminated from what had been the former territory (55). Despite its ambiguity in practice, the ordinance became a key evidence for abolitionists that the American Founders opposed slavery and did not want it to expand further.

The Ordinance and the Constitution

Just prior to adoption of the Northwest Ordinance, a number of members of men, some of whom were members of both bodies, had carried news back and forth from the Convention to the Congress. Given the ordinance's timing in relation to the adoption of the three-fifths clause, there is continuing speculation as to whether the events may have been related (see Lynd 1966; Potts 1986).

See Also Articles of Confederation; Bill of Rights; Slavery; States, Admission and Creation; Territory of the United States; Three-fifths Clause

FOR FURTHER READING

Farrand, Max. 1921. *The Fathers of the Constitution: A Chronicle of the Establishment of the Union.* New Haven, CT: Yale University Press.

Finkelman, Paul. 1996. *Slavery and the Founders: Race and Liberty in the Age of Jefferson.* Armonk, NY: M. E. Sharpe.

Frohnen, Bruce, ed. 2002. "Northwest Ordinance." *The American Republic: Primary Sources.* Indianapolis, IN: Liberty Fund, 225–228.

Lynd, Staughton. 1966. "The Compromise of 1787." *Political Science Quarterly* 81 (June): 225–250.

Onuf, Peter S. 1987. *Statehood and Union: A History of the Northwest Ordinance.* Bloomington: Indiana University Press.

Potts, Louis W. 1986. "'A Lucky Moment': The Relationship of the Ordinance of 1787 and the Constitution of 1787." *Mid-America* 68 (October): 141–151.

OATHS OF OFFICE

Article VI of the Constitution provides that members of the two branches of Congress, of the state legislatures, and those holding executive and judicial offices both in the United States and within the states "shall be bound by Oath or Affirmation, to support this Constitution." This requirement grew out of a provision in the Virginia Plan, presented to the Convention on May 29, that provided that "the Legislative Executive & Judiciary powers within the several States ought to be bound by oath to support the articles of Union" (Farrand 1937, I, 22).

Although he kept meticulous notes on just about everything, Madison simply reported that this provision was postponed on June 5 after "a short uninteresting conversation" (I, 122). The Convention resumed consideration of the proposal on June 11. Connecticut's Roger Sherman opposed the provision as "unnecessarily intruding into the State jurisdictions" (I, 203). Virginia's Edmund Randolph argued that it was necessary to prevent the "competition between the National Constitution & laws & those of the particular States, which had already been felt." He observed that states were already bound by oath to support their state constitutions, and that "a due impartiality" required that "they ought to be equally bound to the Natl. Govt." He further observed that although members of the state executive and judicial branches were technically independent of the state legislatures, "they will always lean too much to the State systems, whenever a contest arises between the two" (I, 203). Elbridge Gerry of Massachusetts argued that there was as much reason to require an oath by national officials to support state laws as vice versa. For his part, Maryland's Luther Martin moved to strike the words "within the several States"; he reasoned that if state and federal oaths were concurrent the second would be unnecessary, while if they were in conflict, the new oath would be "improper" (I, 203). The Convention rejected Martin's motion by a vote of 7-3 and accepted the provision in the Virginia Plan by a vote of 6-5.

Somewhat consistent with Elbridge Gerry's earlier observation, on June 23, North Carolina's Hugh Williamson suggested that it was appropriate for national officials to take an oath to support the states. Instead the Convention unanimously accepted Gerry's proposal to require national officers to support the Constitution. Pennsylvania's James Wilson then expressed reservations about oaths. He observed that they provided only what he described as "a left handed security." As he explained, "A good Govt. did not need them, and a bad one could not or ought not to be supported" (II, 87). He feared that oaths might serve as an obstacle to future needed changes. Nathaniel Gorham of Massachusetts did not see any inconsistency. "The oath could only require fidelity to the existing Constitution. A constitutional alteration of the Constitution,

Title page of Washington, a Biography, *by Benson J. Lossing, showing the swearing-in of George Washington as president (Library of Congress)*

could never be regarded as a breach of the Constitution, or of any oath to support it" (II, 88). Gerry agreed. The new oaths would help to guarantee that state officials no longer gave preference to their own constitutions.

The last provision in Article II, Section 1 provides for a specific oath of the president. It is the only one whose language is specified within the Constitution. On August 30, the Convention added the words "or affirmation" after "oath," without recorded debate but in apparent deference to individuals adhering to religious orders (most notably the Quakers) who thought that the Bible opposed the practice of swearing. This action arguably foreshadowed the free exercise clause of the First Amendment.

The provision for oaths is a recognition that

the U.S. Constitution and laws and treaties made under its authority are designed to be the supreme law of the land. The practice of oaths draws from a religious tradition in which certain covenants, or promises, are considered to be particularly sacred. Although the Convention rejected the idea of a national religious test, one scholarly analyst has noted that "insofar as an oath imposes a sacred obligation, an oath requirement could be characterized as a 'religious test'" (Dreisbach 1996, 289). Significantly the first law adopted by Congress and signed by President Washington dealt with oaths (Dreisbach, 291).

Despite their ubiquity, the utility of oaths can be questioned. Although Abraham Lincoln clearly interpreted this oath as mandating that he fight for the preservation of the Union, leaders in the Confederate states just as surely thought that the oaths they had taken to their state constitutions were paramount.

See Also President, Oath of Office; Religious Tests, Prohibition; Supremacy Clause

FOR FURTHER READING

Dreisbach, Daniel L. 1996. "The Constitution's Forgotten Religion Clause: Reflections on the Article VI Religious Test Ban." *Journal of Church and State* 38 (Spring): 261–296.

Farrand, Max, ed. 1937. *The Records of the Federal Convention.* 4 vols. New Haven, CT: Yale University Press.

OCCUPATIONS OF THE DELEGATES

It is rare for legislatures or other groups of representatives to be exact reflections of the population. The people typically elect individuals who are better educated and richer than themselves—wealth often provides opportunities for greater education and increased leisure, enabling such individuals to acquaint themselves more intimately with public affairs. Similarly, such individuals find themselves in a far better position to run for offices than others. Similarly, some professions—the law, in particular—are thought to provide better training and greater familiarity with the issues that such bodies are likely to face than are other careers.

Although some delegates at the Convention believed that representatives should be a direct reflection of the people, the majority view appears to have been reflected in Madison's defense of the new government in *Federalist* No. 10. There he argued that representatives in the new government would "refine and enlarge the public views by passing them through the medium of a chosen body of citizens, whose wisdom may best discern the true interest of their country and whose patriotism and love of justice will be least likely to sacrifice it to temporary or partial considerations"

(Hamilton, Madison, and Jay 1961, 82). Madison also anticipated that government over a large land area would increase the number of interests and make it less likely that any one group would dominate.

Historian Forrest McDonald has conducted one of the most thorough summaries of the professions of members of the Convention (1958). His analysis shows that 34, or a clear majority, of the 55 delegates were lawyers. Of these, McDonald believes that eight chiefly derived their incomes from work with merchants, 13 from practicing among farmers, and 10 from salaries from public office. McDonald classifies the other three, who had been trained in but did not actively practice law, as "pensioners" (86–88)–Virginia's influential James Madison was among those who today would be called a "career politician." McDonald says that at least nine of the lawyers combined their practices with farming.

Including those listed above as having dual interests, McDonald believes that 18 of the delegates were farmers. Sixteen of these, mostly from the South, conducted farming on a large scale, and two were small farmers (87). All but two of the large-scale farmers owned slaves as did at least five other delegates.

McDonald has identified 15 delegates (including eight of the lawyers) as either merchants themselves or individuals whose work led them to be heavily involved in mercantile activities. Two delegates were practicing physicians. Three, including Benjamin Franklin, were retired. A number had begun studies for the ministry, and Abraham Baldwin had served as a chaplain during the Revolutionary War.

Historian Charles Beard advanced the thesis that delegates to the Convention were often motivated by economic concerns, but he focused more on the kinds of property that he believed delegates owned than on their occupations. For the most part, delegates at the Convention appear to have more typically divided along ideological lines or according to the central interests of their state or region than according to their occupations.

See Also Beard, Charles; Education of Convention Delegates

FOR FURTHER READING

Hamilton, Alexander, James Madison, and John Jay. 1961. *The Federalist Papers.* Ed. Clinton Rossiter. New York: New American Library.

McDonald, Forrest. 1958. *We the People: The Economic Origins of the Constitution.* Chicago: University of Chicago Press.

ORATORY AND RHETORIC

From the time of the ancient Greek city-states, oratory has been connected to politics. The study of rhetoric was a component of the classical education that had shaped many of the delegates to the Constitutional Convention—education still based on the medieval "trivium" of rhetoric, logic and grammar and the "quadrivium" of arithmetic, music, geometry, and astronomy (Richard 1994, 20). In addition, most of the delegates had prior experience in legislatures and other governmental bodies.

The best-known contribution of Georgia's William Pierce to the understanding of the Constitutional Convention is a series of character sketches that he did of all 55 delegates who attended except for Maryland's John Mercer and New Jersey's William C. Houston. These sketches generally included some mention of a delegate's profession, education, and most notable characteristics, including, when they were distinctive, physical characteristics like weight and stature. Perhaps in part because of his own classical education at the College of William and Mary (for its emphasis at the time on the classics, see Richard 1994, 20), Pierce was an especially acute observer, and commentator, on the speaking abilities of the delegates.

Pierce clearly obtained some of his knowledge from personal conversations and gossip among the delegates, but he appears to have gained most of it from the observations he gleaned from Convention debates, or from his observations of delegates in other venues. Given the absence of recordings of the delegates' voices, Pierce's comments on the rhetorical styles of the delegates is especially valuable. Some of Pierce's negative observations were probably affected by unfamiliar accents from other regions of the continent and, in some cases, from nations of foreign birth.

Pierce's comments on the rhetoric of delegates are listed below under delegates' names, which have been arranged alphabetically. Notably, Pierce did not assess the rhetorical abilities of George Washington or of himself. In other cases, where Pierce made no mention of a delegate's rhetorical abilities, their names have been omitted.

Pierce's Observations

Abraham Baldwin: "joins in a public debate with great art and eloquence."

Richard Bassett: "has modesty enough to hold his Tongue."

Gunning Bedford: "a bold and nervous Speaker . . . warm and impetuous in his temper, and precipitate in his judgment."

John Blair: "no Orator, but his good sense, and most excellent principles, compensate for his other deficiencies."

William Blount: "no Speaker."

David Brearly: "As an Orator he has little to boast of."

Jacob Broom: "He is silent in public, but cheerful and conversable in private."

Pierce Butler: "as a politician or an Orator, he has no pretentions to either."

William Davie: "He was silent in the Convention, but his opinion was always respected."

Jonathan Dayton: "he speaks well, and seems desirous of improving himself in Oratory."

John Dickinson: "I have often heard that he was a great Orator, but I found him an indifferent Speaker. With an affected air of wisdom he labors to produce a trifle, —his language is irregular and correct, —his flourishes (for he sometimes attempts them), are like expiring flames, they just shew themselves and go out."

Oliver Ellsworth: "eloquent, and connected in public debate; and always attentive to his duty. He is very happy in a reply, and choice in selecting such parts of his adversary's arguments as he finds make the strongest impressions, —in order to take off the force of them, so as to admit the power of his own."

William Few: "speaks tolerably well in the Legislature."

Thomas Fitzsimmons: "speaks very well I am told, in the Legislature of Pennsylvania."

Benjamin Franklin: "he is no Speaker" but "tells a story in a style more engaging than anything I ever heard."

Elbridge Gerry: "He is a hesitating and laborious speaker; –possesses a great degree of confidence and goes extensively into all subjects that he speaks on, without respect to elegance or flower of diction. He is connected and sometimes clear in his arguments."

Nathaniel Gorham: "He is eloquent and easy in public debate, but has nothing fashionable or elegant in his style; –all he aims at is to convince."

Alexander Hamilton: "whilst he is able, convincing, and engaging in his eloquence the Heart and Head sympathize in approving him. Yet there is something too feeble in his voice to be equal to the strains of oratory; –it is my opinion that he is rather a convincing Speaker, than a blazing Orator. . . . His language is not always equal, sometimes didactic like Bolingbroke's and at others light and tripping like Stern's. His eloquence is not so defusive as to trifle with the senses, but he ambles just enough to strike and keep up the attention."

William Houston: "He has none of the talents requisite for the Orator, but in public debate is confused and irregular."

Jared Ingersoll: "speaks well, and comprehends his subject fully."

Daniel of St. Thomas Jenifer: "He sits silent in the Senate, and seems to be conscious that he is no politician."

William Samuel Johnson: "As an Orator in my opinion, there is nothing in him that warrants the high reputation which he has for public speaking. There is something in the tone of his voice not pleasing to the Ear, –but he is eloquent and clear, –always abounding with information and instruction."

Rufus King: "much distinguished for his eloquence and great parliamentary talents. . . . a sweet high toned voice. In his public speaking there is something peculiarly strong and rich in his expression, clear and convincing in his argu-

ments, rapid and irresistible at times in his eloquence but he is not always equal. His action is natural, swimming, and graceful, but there is a rudeness of manner sometimes accompanying it."

John Lansing: "He has a hesitation in his speech, that will prevent his being an Orator of any eminence."

William Livingston: "he is no Orator, and seems little acquainted with the guiles of policy."

James Madison. "tho' he cannot be called an Orator, he is a most agreeable, eloquent, and convincing Speaker. From a spirit of industry and application which he possesses in a most eminent degree, he always comes forward the best informed Man of any point in debate."

Alexander Martin: "he is not formed to shine in public debate, being no Speaker."

Luther Martin: "possesses a good deal of information, but he has a very bad delivery, and so extremely prolix, that he never speaks without tiring the patience of all who hear him."

George Mason: "able and convincing in debate."

James McClurg: "He attempted once or twice to speak, but with no great success."

James McHenry: "nor has he any of the graces of the Orator."

Thomas Mifflin: "well informed and a graceful Speaker."

Gouverneur Morris: "conspicuous and flourishing in public debate: –He winds through all the mazes of rhetoric, and throws around him such a glare that he charms, captivates, and leads away the senses of all who hear him. With an infinite stretch of fancy he brings to view things when he is engaged in deep argumentation, that render all the labor of reasoning and pleasing. But with all these powers he is fickle and inconstant, –never pursuing one train of thinking –nor ever regular."

Robert Morris: "I am told that when he speaks in the Assembly of Pennsylvania, that he bears down all before him. What could have been his reason for not speaking in the Convention I know not."

William Paterson: "an Orator; – and of a disposition so favorable to his advancement that every one seemed ready to exalt him with their praises. He is very happy in the choice of time and manner of engaging in a debate, and never speaks but when he understands his subject well."

Charles Pinckney: "He speaks with great neatness and perspicuity, and treats every subject as fully, without running into a prolixity, as it requires."

Charles C. Pinckney: "When warm in a debate he sometimes speaks well, – but he is generally considered an indifferent Orator."

Edmund Randolph: "a force of eloquence. . . . a most harmonious voice."

George Read: "his powers of Oratory are fatiguing and tiresome to the last degree; – his voice is feeble, and his articulation so bad that few can have patience to attend to him."

John Rutledge: "much framed in his own State [South Carolina] as an Orator, but in my opinion he is too rapid in his public speaking to be denominated an agreeable Orator."

Roger Sherman: "the oddity of his address, the vulgarisms that accompany his public speaking, and that strange New England cant which runs through his public as well as his private speaking make everything that is connected with him grotesque and laughable. . . . If he cannot embellish he can furnish thoughts that are wise and useful."

Caleb Strong: "As a Speaker he is feeble, and without confidence."

Hugh Williamson: "He enters freely into public debate from his close attention to most subjects, but he is no Orator."

James Wilson: "No man is more clear, copious, and comprehensive than Mr. Wilson, yet he is no great Orator. He draws the attention not by the charm of his eloquence, but by the force of his reasoning."

George Wythe: "He is a neat and pleasing Speaker."

Robert Yates: "not distinguished as an Orator."

Other References to Rhetoric

The longest speech at the Convention was that of New York's Alexander Hamilton, which he delivered on June 19. This speech, in which Hamilton presented his own plans for a new government, appears to have been about six hours in length, but its lack of influence–Dr. William Samuel Johnson observed that "though he [Hamilton] has been much praised by every body, he has been supported by none" (Farrand 1937, I, 363)– appears to have stemmed from Hamilton's ideas themselves rather than from their mode of delivery. Maryland's Luther Martin appears to have confirmed, and perhaps established, Pierce's negative observations about him by a speech that he delivered on June 27. After what appears to be an uncharacteristically short summary for such a long speech, Madison observed that after more than three hours of speaking, Martin "was too much exhausted . . . to finish his remarks, and reminded the House that he should tomorrow, resume them" (I, 438). The next day, Madison again provided a rather shortened version of Martin's remarks and observed that "This was the substance of the residue of his discourse which was delivered with much diffuseness & considerable vehemence" (I, 445).

Gunning Bedford, whom Pierce described as "warm and impetuous in his temper," appeared to confirm this judgment when on June 30 he raised the possibility that small states might confederate with foreign nations. Perhaps sensing the effect of his words, Bedford quickly added that his words were not intended "to intimidate or alarm" (I, 492), and responded to Rufus King's characterization of his "intemperance" by attributing it to "the score of passion" (I, 493). On July 5, he further attributed his speaking to "the habits of his profession [he was an attorney] in which warmth was natural & sometimes necessary" (I, 531).

There is general agreement that one of the most forceful rhetoricians in America was Virginia's Patrick Henry, who had done so much to rally sentiment against the British during the American Revolution. Although he trained all his rhetorical guns on the Constitution at the Virginia ratifying convention–on one occasion having his speeches punctuated by the thunder of a storm–James Madison and others succeeded in winning the arguments through less dramatic but more systematic and thoughtful presentations on behalf of the new document. On this occasion, as in Pierce's observations, rhetorical style was but one element in a speaker's persuasiveness.

See Also Delegates, Individual Rankings; Speeches, Number of

FOR FURTHER READING

"Constitutional Convention of 1787: William Pierce notes on Signers of New Constitution." http://franklaughter.tripod.com/cgi-bin/histprof/misc/pierce.html.

Farrand, Max, ed. 1937. *The Records of the Federal Convention.* 4 vols. New Haven, CT: Yale University Press.

Richard, Carl. J. 1994. *The Founders and the Classics: Greece, Rome, and the American Enlightenment.* Cambridge, MA: Harvard University Press.

ORIGINAL INTENT

There is general agreement that the debates about the U.S. Constitution at the Constitutional Convention, in the public press, in the state ratifying conventions, and in the first Congress are important in understanding the Constitution. One of the purposes of this book is to present such materials in a complete, systematic, and unbiased fashion that will be useful to students, scholars and general readers.

Originalists and Their Foes

However, there is vigorous debate about which set of debates is most important and what significance such debates should have in contemporary interpretations of the Constitution. Debates about original intent became particularly shrill during the administration of President Ronald Reagan when Attorney General Edwin Meese, who was upset with the liberal direction that the U.S. Supreme Court had taken on a number of issues, argued for a return to a jurisprudence of

original intent, and some scholars and a number of U.S. Supreme Court justices openly disagreed.

The idea of original intent is still being refined (see Kesavan and Paulsen 2003) so as to move away from the idea of reading the mind of individual Framers to that of attempting to ascertain, as much as possible, the objective meaning of words within the Constitution. Thus, scholars who favor interpreting the Constitution according to original intent ("originalists") also typically favor close textual interpretation that focuses specifically on what the words of the Constitution say. Thus, Vasan Kesavan and Michael Stokes Paulsen, two recent defenders of this approach, explain that

> when we use the term "originalism," it is not in reference to a theory of "original intent" or "original understanding." Rather, it is in reference to original, nonidiosyncratic meaning of words and phrases in the Constitution: how the words and phrases, and structure . . . would have been understood by a hypothetical, objective, reasonably well-informed reader of those words and phrases, in contest, at the time they were adopted, and within the political and linguistic community in which they were adopted. (Kesavan and Paulsen, 1132)

Pointing to the fact that the Constitution refers to itself as the "supreme law," these authors thus observe that "It is simply not consistent with the idea of the Constitution as binding law to adopt a hermeneutic [method of interpretation] of textualism that permits individuals to assign their own private, potentially idiosyncratic meanings to the words and phrases of the Constitution" (1130).

Scholars sometimes refer to such individuals as "interpretivists." Such interpretivists often express concern about limiting the discretion that judges bring to cases they have to decide, with original intent and textualism intended to serve as restraints on this discretion regarding issues that they think should be largely determined by democratic majorities. By contrast, others—sometimes designated as "noninterpretivists"—think it is more relevant for judges to look beyond the original intentions of the Framers and seek to adopt the Constitution to modern exigencies and to advance newly recognized rights. In addition, judges and commentators might stress the role of precedent, constitutional principles that are sometimes implicit within the text, or other interpretative approaches.

Some Problems with Originalism and the Writing of the Constitution

Although many members of the first Congress had attended the Constitutional Convention and participated in the ratification debates, many of the sources that are now available for understanding the formation of individual provisions of the U.S. Constitution were not available to those who initially had to interpret the Constitution, when critical precedents were established. The Constitutional Convention was held in secret, the official records of the Convention were not published until 1819, and James Madison's notes of the Convention, still the single most complete source of Convention debates, were not published until 1840 after he and all the other delegates who had attended the Convention were dead.

However useful it has been, the publication of Convention debates has left many matters unresolved. The Convention sometimes took votes without recorded debate, and the resulting Constitution was a collective product. It is common, but not necessarily correct, to assume that those who talked the most at the Convention had the most influence, but even someone like Madison, who is often called the Father of the Constitution, did not get his way on many points. *The Federalist* essays were, of course, available as explanations of key provisions of the Constitution, but despite their many merits, they have always been recognized as being in part a work of advocacy.

Some Problems with Originalism and the Ratification of the Constitution

Madison, himself, appeared to believe that the intentions of those who ratified the Constitution were as important as, indeed even more impor-

tant than, those who wrote it. Madison thus gave a speech on April 6, 1796, in which he observed that

> whatever veneration might be entertained for the body of men who formed our constitution, the sense of that body could never be regarded as the oracular guide in the expounding [of] the constitution. As the instrument came from them, it was nothing more than the draught of a plan, nothing but a dead letter, until life and validity were breathed into it, by the voice of the people, speaking through the several state conventions. If we were to look therefore, for the meaning of the instrument, beyond the face of the instrument, we must look for it not in the general convention, which proposed, but in the state conventions, which accepted and ratified the constitution. (Quoted in Rakove 1996, 362)

However, for a number of reasons, ascertaining the intent of the ratifiers is as problematic as, if not more so than, ascertaining the intent of the writers. There are scores of publications on both sides of the Federalist/Antifederalist debates making it difficult to assign authoritative weight to any single one of them; some states ratified the Constitution without recorded debate; and records of debates in other states are still being edited.

Historian Jack Rakove has thus observed that

> any effort to analyze this [ratifying] debate in the expectation of producing a definitive understanding of what the Constitution originally meant to Americans at the moment of its adoption must accordingly fall short of perfection. We possess neither the equation needed to convert expressions of individual opinion on particular provisions into collective understandings nor formulas to extract from the unstable compounds of hopes, fears, and expectations those elements that best predicted how the Constitution would operate in practice. Nor can one tidily graph how these perceptions shifted over time, as participants on both sides grappled with objects and counter-arguments or thought through the implications of their own positions. (1996, 134)

Such issues become even more complicated when attempts are made to apply eighteenth-century debates to issues and technologies that were unknown to the Founders.

The Continuing Value of the Framers' Arguments

Vasan Kesavan and Michael Stokes Paulsen have recently argued that the debates of the Constitutional Convention are as useful as, and in some cases more useful than, many alternate sources that are cited for an understanding of the original intent of the Constitution (2003, 1180–1214). Whatever position one takes as to the role of original intent in contemporary constitutional interpretation, it continues to provide a useful starting point. One of the exciting aspects of studying debates during the writing and ratification of the Constitution is that the Framers generally included not only *what* they wanted in the new Constitution but also recorded arguments as to *why* they favored particular provisions. Moreover, because debates were originally secret, it is not likely that the delegates were purposely playing to political audiences when they made their arguments. These arguments continue to be worthy of examination and often remain applicable even in today's context.

See Also *Federalist, The;* Madison, James, Jr.; Madison's Notes of the Convention; Ratification in the States; Secrecy

FOR FURTHER READING

Anderson, William. 1955. "The Intentions of the Framers: A Note on Constitutional Interpretation." *American Political Science Review* 49 (June): 340–352.

Bork, Robert H. 1990. *The Tempting of America: The Political Seduction of the Law.* New York: The Free Press.

Kesavan, Vasan, and Michael Stokes Paulsen. 2003. "The Interpretive Force of the Constitution's Secret Drafting History." *Georgetown Law Journal* 91 (August): 1113–1214.

Levy, Leonard W. 1988. *Original Intent and the Framers' Constitution.* New York: Macmillan.

———. 1995. *Seasoned Judgments: The American Constitution, Rights, and History.* New Brunswick, NJ: Transaction Publishers.

Nelson, Caleb. 2003. "Originalism and Interpretive Conventions." *University of Chicago Law Review* 70 (Spring): 519–598.

Patterson, Charles F. 2002. *The True Meaning of the Constitution: Ratifier Understanding.* Xenia, OH: Bentham Press.

Politics and the Constitution: The Nature and Extent of Interpretation. 1990. Washington, DC: National Legal Center for the Public Interest.

Powell, H. Jefferson. 1985. "The Original Understanding of Original Intent." *Harvard Law Review* 98 (March): 885–948.

Rakove, Jack N. 1990. *Interpreting the Constitution: The Debate over Original Intent.* Boston: Northeastern University Press.

———. 1996. *Original Meanings: Politics and Ideas in the Making of the Constitution.* New York: Alfred A. Knopf.

$\mathcal{P}$

PAINE, THOMAS (1737–1809)

Thomas Paine was one of America's most controversial Founding Fathers. He did not attend the Constitutional Convention, but he did much to help bring about the American Revolution and to plant the seeds for the development of a written Constitution.

Portrait of Thomas Paine, American Revolution–era political writer, whose works helped influence the course of American independence (Library of Congress)

Paine was born in Thetford, England, in 1737 and lived a largely undistinguished life until he met Benjamin Franklin in London and moved to Philadelphia at the age of 37. Initially the editor of the *Pennsylvania Magazine*, Paine quickly came to support the colonial cause. In January 1776, he published *Common Sense*, a highly influential pamphlet written in terms that appealed to everyday citizens questioning the British constitution and its doctrine of hereditary succession, associating kingship with war, and arguing that the colonies should declare independence and cut their ties to the mother country.

In a dramatic passage that presaged the idea of a written Constitution, Paine dramatically asked, "Where . . . is the king of America?" Proclaiming that God, and not the king, was in control, Paine continued:

> Yet that we may not appear to be defective even in earthly honors, let a day be solemnly set apart for proclaiming the charter; let it be brought forth placed on the divine law, the word of God; let a crown be placed thereon, by which the world may know that, so far as we approve of monarchy, that in America *the law is king.* (Paine 1953, 32)

Once independence was declared, Paine continued to bolster the Patriot cause with a series of pamphlets under the title *The American Crisis*. He worked in Pennsylvania to draft the state's highly democratic constitution, which remained in effect at the time of the Constitutional Convention of 1787. In December 1780, Paine also published *Public Good*, in which he advocated, among other things, the calling of a "Continental convention" to write a new Constitution strengthening the national government.

After the Revolutionary War, Paine moved first to England and then to France, where he was welcomed because of his publication of the *Rights of Man*, attempting to refute Edmund Burke's criticism of the French Revolution in his *Reflections on the Revolution in France*. Paine played a largely ineffectual part in the French Revolution, eventually being imprisoned, and weakening his support among some erstwhile American supporters with the publication of *The Age of Reason*, in which he attacked Christianity and the authority of the Bible. He later imprudently followed these attacks with attacks on the character of President Washington.

Paine returned to the United States during the presidency of Thomas Jefferson. Paine's continuing radical writings alienated him from most of his adopted countrymen. He died in relative obscurity in New York in 1809.

See Also Declaration of Independence; Franklin, Benjamin; Monarchy; Republicanism; Revolutionary War

FOR FURTHER READING

Ferguson, Robert A. 2000. "The Commonalities of Common Sense." *William and Mary Quarterly*, 3rd ser. 57 (July): 465–504.

Foner, Eric. "Paine, Thomas." American National Biography Online. http://www.anb.org/articles/16-16-01251-article.html.

Paine, Thomas. 1953. *Common Sense and Other Political Writings*. Ed. Nelson F. Adkins. New York: The Liberal Arts Press.

PARIS, TREATY OF

The Treaty of Paris was the document that officially brought an end to the Revolutionary War. The preliminary version of this treaty was signed on November 20, 1782; the final version was signed on September 2, 1783; and the Continental Congress approved it in 1784.

John Adams, Benjamin Franklin, John Jay, Henry Laurens, and Thomas Jefferson had been appointed for the negotiations, but the British had captured and imprisoned Laurens, and Jefferson did not arrive in time (Foner and Garrity 1991). The three Americans negotiated most of the terms without the knowledge of the French, and, partly as a result, they got more generous terms than they might otherwise have done. These included recognition of U.S. independence, of U.S. claims to the lands reaching to the Mississippi River, and of fishing rights in the Atlantic.

Americans, in turn, agreed to put pressure on the states to require citizens to pay their debts to English creditors and to return confiscated lands to Tories. As America proved unable to enforce its part of the agreement, the British, in turn, enacted discriminatory trade policies against U.S. goods. Britain also refused to withdraw troops from the American Northwest Territories.

James Madison listed the failure to enforce the Treaty of Paris and other treaties in his essay entitled "Vices of the Political System of the United States" (Meyers 1973, 83). In introducing the Virginia Plan on May 29, Virginia's Edmund Randolph listed as the first defect of the Articles of Confederation the fact that it could not protect against "foreign invasion" or "cause infractions of treaties or of the law of nations, to be punished" (Farrand 1937, I, 19). On May 31, Benjamin Franklin proposed to extend the proposed congressional negative of state laws to violations to "any Treaties subsisting under the authority of the union" (I, 47). Although the congressional negative on state laws was abandoned, Franklin's suggestion made its way in modified form into the supremacy clause of Article VI of the Constitution. David Hendrickson (2003) has recently highlighted the importance that this concern and other matters of foreign policy had on the Constitutional Convention.

See Also France; Franklin, Benjamin; Great Britain; Revolutionary War; Supremacy Clause

*The signing of the Treaty of Paris in 1783, which officially brought to a close the American Revolutionary War
(North Wind Picture Archives)*

FOR FURTHER READING

Farrand, Max, ed. 1937. *The Records of the Federal Convention.* 4 vols. New Haven, CT: Yale University Press.

Foner, Eric, and John A. Garraty, eds. 1991. *The Reader's Companion to American History.* Boston: Houghton Mifflin.

"For the Classroom. The Treaty of Paris, 1783." 1985. *this Constitution,* no. 8 (Fall): 36–39.

Hendrickson, David C. 2003. *Peace Pact: The Lost World of the American Founding.* Lawrence: University Press of Kansas.

Meyers, Marvin, ed. 1973. *The Mind of the Founder: Sources of the Political Thought of James Madison.* Indianapolis, IN: Bobbs-Merrill.

PARTIES, FACTIONS, AND INTERESTS

The delegates to the Constitutional Convention did not specifically mention political parties in the Constitution that they wrote. Indeed, their failure to anticipate such parties resulted in part in

the tie between Thomas Jefferson and Aaron Burr (republican electors had cast ballots for both in the belief that the former would become president and the latter would become vice president) in the presidential election of 1800 (see Weisberger 2000). This election was in turn the primary catalyst for the adoption of the Twelfth Amendment in 1804 specifying that presidential electors would cast separate votes for president and vice president.

References to Factions at the Convention

If the Framers did not anticipate the dominant two-party system that developed during the Washington administration and that, with a smattering of other parties, has continued throughout most of American history, they were certainly aware that politics involved conflict. Moreover, they recognized that regional, religious, economic, and political interests, as well as loyalty to different candidates, could lead to conflict. The Framers often used the term "faction," as, for example, Madison did in *Federalist* No. 10, to refer to what individuals today would call political parties or interest groups. The idea of creating a republic over an extended land area was based in part on the theme, which James Madison particularly emphasized, of embracing multiple factions so that no one would be able to form a permanent majority that would oppress the others. The fact that he anticipated that proponents of individual parties would often work contrary to the public interests is perhaps a foreshadowing of the view that dominated in the early history of the republic in which individuals in one party looked suspiciously on the patriotism of those in the other.

On June 6, about defending a republic over a large area, Madison observed:

> All civilized Societies would be divided into different Sects, Factions, & interests, as they happened to consist of rich & poor, debtors & creditors, the landed, the manufacturing, the commercial interest, the inhabitants of this district, or that district, the followers of this political leader or that political leader, the disciples of this religious sect or that religious sect. In all cases where a majority are united by a common interest or passion, the rights of the minority are in danger. (Farrand 1937, I, 135)

As he proceeded, Madison indicated that race could also be a basis for faction—"We have seen the mere distinction of colour made in the most enlightened period of time, a ground of the most oppressive dominion ever exercised by man over man" (I, 135). Madison concluded that "where a majority are united by a common sentiment and have an opportunity, the rights of the minor party become insecure." He then advanced his favorite remedy:

> The only remedy is to enlarge the sphere, & thereby divide the community into so great a number of interests & parties, that in the 1st place a majority will not be likely at the same moment to have a common interest separate from that of the whole or of the minority; and in the 2d. place, that in case they shd. have such an interest, they may not be apt to unite in the pursuit of it. (I, 136)

At times, Madison emphasized the importance of certain interests over others. In thus attempting to assure the small states that the primary conflicts in the new nation were not likely to be based on state size, on June 29, Madison emphasized the difference between North and South:

> The great danger to our general government *is the great southern and northern interest of the continent, being opposed to each other. Look to the votes in congress, and most of them stand divided by the geography of the country, not according to the size of the states.* (I, 476)

Charles Pinckney referred in debates of July 2 to the "real distinction [between] the Northern & Southn. interests" (I, 510); Madison argued on July 13 that "the difference of interest in the U. States lay not between the large & small, but the N. & Southn. States" (I, 601); and Gouverneur Morris argued on August 8 that the primary factor distinguishing the North and the South was the institution of slavery (II, 221–222).

In addition to numerous disputes over individual issues involving the structure of the new government, the Convention witnessed disputes between the large states and the small ones, and between those who primarily hoped to vest powers in the national government and those who favored the states. Delegates at the Convention frequently spoke of the geographical divisions between the Eastern (Northern), Middle, and Southern states as well as differences in interests between states with seaports and those without them. Delegates from the Eastern and Middle states often expressed suspicion of individuals in the West.

In opposing legislative appointment of the president on July 24, Gouverneur Morris observed:

> In all public bodies there are two parties. The Executive will necessarily be more connected with one than with the other. There will be a personal interest therefore in one of the parties to oppose as well as in the others to support him. Much had been said of the intrigues that will be practiced by the Executive to get into office. Nothing had been said on the other side of the intrigues

to get him out of office. Some leader of party will always covet his seat, will perplex his administration, will cabal with the Legislature, till he succeeds in supplanting him. (II, 104)

Morris proceeded to illustrate with examples from English history.

Federalist-Antifederalist Debates

After the Constitution was written, the nation split into two camps. Federalists supported the new Constitution, and Antifederalists opposed it. Although both groups soon agreed as to the desirability of the new Constitution (especially with the inclusion of the Bill of Rights), individuals continued to disagree as to how this document should be interpreted. Significantly, one of the first two political parties established within Congress took the Federalist name. There are also ties between the Antifederalist views expressed during the ratification debates, and in the first U.S. Congress under the new Constitution, and the philosophy later articulated by the Democratic-Republican Party (Aldrich and Grant 1993).

Subsequent Developments

Perhaps in part because the presidency creates a "winner-take-all" system, as Morris predicted, Americans have generally identified themselves with two parties. At times (the Civil War being the most prominent example), American political parties have fallen victim to larger geographical divisions. Throughout most of American history, political parties have, like the nation itself, embraced a multitude of interests, incorporating within themselves the diversity that Madison expected to find in the nation as a whole. Political scientists who focus on such interests are today designated as "pluralists"; Robert Dahl is among the most prominent of these.

See Also Antifederalists; Federalist and Democratic-Republican Parties; *Federalist, The;* Federalists; Madison, James, Jr.

FOR FURTHER READING

Aldrich, John H., and Ruth W. Grant. 1993. "The Antifederalists, the First Congress, and the First Parties." *Journal of Politics* 55 (May): 295–326.

Dahl, Robert A. 1967. *Pluralist Democracy in the United States: Conflict and Consent.* Chicago: Rand McNally.

Farrand, Max, ed. 1937. *The Records of the Federal Convention.* 4 vols. New Haven, CT: Yale University Press.

Hofstadter, Richard. 1972. *The Idea of a Party System: The Rise of Legitimate Opposition in the United States, 1780–1840.* Berkeley: University of California Press.

Main, Jackson Turner. 1973. *Political Parties before the Constitution.* New York: W. W. Norton.

Weisberger, Bernard A. 2000. *America Afire: Jefferson, Adams, and the Revolutionary Election of 1800.* New York: William Morrow.

PATENTS

See COPYRIGHTS AND PATENTS

PATERSON, WILLIAM (1745–1806)

William Paterson was born in Ireland on Christmas Eve of 1745. His father, a merchant, brought him to the U.S. when he was two years old. Paterson studied at the University of New Jersey (today's Princeton), in a building just across the street from a store that his father owned. Paterson earned two degrees, but his career languished until the American Revolution when he joined the Patriot side and went on to become the state's attorney general (Haskett 1950). Paterson became a secretary of the Provisional Congress and had a hand in drafting the New Jersey Constitution. Paterson married Cornelia Bell and lived on an estate near Raritan, New Jersey. After Cornelia died, Paterson married Euphemia White, one of her close friends. Paterson served as a delegate to the Annapolis Convention. At the Constitutional Convention, Paterson is primarily remembered as

William Paterson, delegate from New Jersey
(Pixel That)

the author of the New Jersey Plan, which both favored the smaller states and required fewer changes in the relation of the national government and the states than had the Virginia Plan.

Paterson's Views in the Opening Days of the Convention

Paterson was present for the opening day of business at the Convention on May 25. His first recorded comment, on June 5, was prophetic in that he argued for deciding how states would be represented in Congress before deciding on the adoption of a clause whereby Congress would guarantee a republican form of government to the states (Farrand 1937, I, 121). Similarly, on June 9, Paterson moved to resume discussion of the subject of representation in Congress. Soon thereafter, he indicated that he thought the idea of proportional representation threatened "the existence of the lesser States" (I, 177). He further pointed out that the Convention had been called to revise

the Articles, and he said that if the delegates exceeded this call, "we should be charged by our constituents with usurpation" (I, 178). Paterson did not think the people had given warrant to exchange a "federal" government for "a national Govt." (I, 178), and he thought the delegates were bound by the people's wishes: "We must follow the people; the people will not follow us" (I, 178).

Paterson further argued that a federal government presupposed the equality of the states, that "If we are to be considered as a nation, all State distinctions must be abolished, the whole must be thrown into hotchpot, and when an equal division is made, then there may be fairly an equality of representation" (I, 178). Likening states to individuals, Paterson said there was no more reason for states paying more money to have more votes in Congress than for rich people to have more votes. Paterson pointed to colonial resistance to the Galloway Plan on the basis that a parliament with only a third of the representatives from the New World would not have done justice to their interests. Paterson further questioned whether it was necessary that a government formed to act directly on the people necessarily had to be selected by the people (as opposed to the state legislatures). Commending the existing Articles of Confederation, Paterson argued that "No other amendments were wanting than to mark the orbits of the States with due precision, and provide for the use of coercion, which was the great point" (I, 179). Responding to Pennsylvania's James Wilson, Paterson said that if the large states chose to confederate among themselves, they were free to do so but that they had no power to compel the smaller states to do so. Paterson did not mince words. As to New Jersey, it "will never confederate on the plan before the Committee. She would be swallowed up. He had rather submit to a monarch, to a despot, than to such a fate. He would not only oppose the plan here but on his return home do everything in his power to defeat it there" (I, 179).

Whereas many delegates took positions on key issues throughout the Convention, Paterson introduced most of his ideas in the New Jersey Plan. Most of what we know about his views comes from this plan and his explanation of it.

Introduction of the New Jersey Plan

On June 14, Paterson asked the Convention for a postponement of business so that delegates from New Jersey and other states could devise and propose a purely federal plan. He presented this plan on the following day in the form of nine propositions. The first proposition advocated revising, correcting, and enlarging the Articles of Confederation, in accord with the task that had been assigned to the Convention, so "as to render the federal Constitution adequate to the exigencies of Government, & the preservation of the Union" (I, 242). The second proposition called for granting five new powers to Congress but not for altering its unicameral structure. The first three powers were all related. They included the power to levy duties or imposts, to make rules for the foregoing, and to be able to alter these rules. Paterson also proposed that Congress have power to regulate trade among the states and with foreign nations and to see that punishments for violations of such rules would be judged by the courts of the states, subject to correction by the federal judiciary (I, 243). The third proposition would have continued the existing system of requisitioning the states according to their white citizens and three-fifths of other persons with the understanding that, if the states did not comply, Congress could "direct the collection thereof in the non complying States" subject to approval by an unspecified supermajority of Congress. The fourth proposition called for a plural executive to be elected by Congress for a nonrenewable term and removable by Congress on application of a majority of state governors. The executive would have power over the military but would not be permitted personally to command troops. Paterson's fifth proposition called for the executive branch to appoint the federal judiciary (the Virginia Plan had called for appointments to be made by Congress) and included the power to hear impeachments of federal officials. The sixth proposition is recognizable as the origin of the current supremacy clause recognizing that Congress acts as the supreme law of the land. The last three propositions called for a provision to admit new states, for a uniform law regarding naturalization, and for recognition that individuals who violated the law in another state would be treated just like state citizens in the same circumstances (I, 245).

Justification for the New Jersey Plan

Paterson sought to justify the New Jersey Plan on June 16. He argued that the plan was in closer accord with both the commission of the Convention and the sentiments of the people. Indeed, Paterson observed that "Our object is not such a Governmt. as may be best in itself, but such a one as our Constituents have authorized us to prepare, and as they will approve" (I, 250). Paterson further argued that states were on equal footing under the Articles of Confederation and that no alteration could be made in these Articles without the unanimous consent of the states. He argued that "If the sovereignty of the States is to be maintained, the Representatives must be drawn immediately from the States, not from the people" (I, 251). Again Paterson suggested that the only way to "cure the difficulty" is to throw "the States into hotchpot" (I, 251).

Paterson observed that delegates had objected to the idea of coercing states, but he doubted that coercion would be any easier under the Virginia Plan than under the plan he had presented: "Its efficacy will depend on the quantum of power collected, not on its being drawn from the States, or from the individuals; and according to his plan it may be exerted on individuals as well as according that of Mr. R[andolph]" (I, 251).

Paterson further questioned the need for a bicameral Congress. Paterson thought that representatives from different states would be adequate checks on one another. He did not think that the people were complaining about the actions of Congress but simply about the inadequacy of powers in this body: "With proper powers Congs. will act with more energy & wisdom than the proposed Natl. Legislature; being fewer in number, and more secreted & refined by the mode of election" (I, 251). Paterson further projected that the Congress under the Virginia Plan could have 180 members in one house and half again as many in the other, and that it would be far too expensive to have a Congress this size.

Paterson's Role during the Rest of the Convention

The Committee of the Whole decided to proceed with the central outline of the Virginia Plan rather than with the New Jersey Plan. Interestingly, Paterson seconded a motion on June 30 urging the delegation from New Hampshire (another small state) to do its best to get to the Convention, probably hoping for the arrival of reinforcements.

The only committee on which Paterson served during the Convention was the 11-man committee, established on July 2, that came up with the Connecticut Compromise providing for representation in the House of Representatives according to population and equally in the Senate. When a subsequent committee suggested further modifications, Paterson professed to be uncertain whether he thought it important that money bills should originate in the House of Representatives but absolutely certain that "the small States would never be able to defend themselves without an equality of votes in the 2d. branch." Not surprisingly, he drew this as a line in the sand, which he did not think could be crossed: "There was no other ground of accommodation. His resolution was fixt. He would meet the large States on that Ground and no other" (I, 551).

When another committee recommended a house composed of 56 members to be apportioned among the states according to population and wealth, Paterson objected that this formula was too vague. Although his own plan had called for counting slaves in the proportion to be fixed for ascertaining taxes, Paterson objected to including them for purposes of representation in a mix of persuasive practical and theoretical considerations:

He could regard Negroes slaves in no light but as property. They are no free agents, have no personal liberty, no faculty of acquiring property, but on the contrary are themselves property, & like other property entirely at the will of the Master. Has a man in Virga. a number of votes in proportion to the number of his slaves? and if Negroes are not represented in the States to which they belong, why should they be represented in the Genl. Govt. What is the true principle of Representation? It is an expedient by which an assembly of certain individls. chosen by the people is substituted in place of the inconvenient meeting of the people themselves. If such a meeting of the people was actually to take place, would the slaves vote? they would not. Why then shd. they be represented. (II, 561)

Paterson further observed that allowing for representation of the slaves would give further encouragement to the slave trade, and pointed to the ignominy of the institution by the fact that its supporters had refused to use the term "slaves" in the Articles of Confederation (I, 561).

On July 16, the day that the Convention finally acceded to the Connecticut Compromise, Paterson, either apparently misunderstanding or purposely misconstruing (O'Connor 1979, 157, believes the latter) a motion by Edmund Randolph as a motion to adjourn sine die, or indefinitely, and not simply for the day, seconded the motion and proposed that the delegates be released from secrecy and be able to consult their constituents. He reiterated that "No conciliation could be admissible on the part of the smaller States on any other ground than that of an equality of votes in the 2d. branch" (II, 18).

On July 19, Paterson supported a proposal to grant states from one to three electors in the choice of the president (II, 56). On July 23, Paterson further supported a motion proposing that the Constitution should be referred for ratification to state legislators (II, 88).

He left that same day, the day that delegates from New Hampshire finally arrived, for New Jersey. Paterson returned in September to sign the Constitution (O'Connor 1979, 160–161).

Life after the Convention

After signing the Constitution, Paterson went on to serve as one of his state's senators (supporting Alexander Hamilton's proposals for economic reform), as the state governor, and, finally, as an associate justice of the U.S. Supreme Court, to which George Washington appointed him. Appropriately enough, Paterson had served in the first Congress to draft the Judiciary Act of 1789; as a justice, he was responsible for riding the massive Southern circuit. As governor, Paterson also issued the charter for the city named in his honor. After he was injured in a carriage accident, Paterson's health declined and he died at the home of a daughter in Albany, New York, in 1806.

See Also New Jersey; New Jersey Plan; Virginia Plan

FOR FURTHER READING

Cushman, Clare. 1995. *The Supreme Court Justices: Illustrated Biographies, 1789–1995.* Washington, DC: Congressional Quarterly.
Farrand, Max, ed. 1937. *The Records of the Federal Convention.* 4 vols. New Haven, CT: Yale University Press.
Haskett, Richard C. 1950. "William Paterson, Attorney General of New Jersey: Public Office and Private Profit in the American Revolution." *William and Mary Quarterly,* 3rd ser. 7 (January): 26–38.
O'Connor, J. J. 1979. *William Paterson: Lawyer and Statesman, 1745–1806.* New Brunswick, NJ: Rutgers University Press.

PATERSON PLAN

See NEW JERSEY PLAN

PENNSYLVANIA

Pennsylvania was founded by William Penn, a Quaker who saw the state as a haven for liberty, especially of religion and conscience, which Great Britain had denied to him and others at home. Pennsylvania was the home of the nation's largest city and was regarded as one of the Middle states (what would today be called the mid-Atlantic) and thus could potentially play a mediating role between states of the East (or North) and the South.

Government and Constitution

At the time of the Convention, Pennsylvania had one of the most democratic constitutions in the nation; indeed, critics thought that this constitution, which had been adopted in 1776, was too democratic. It provided for a unicameral legislature, annual elections, term limits, strong legislative powers, and minimal executive authority. It also contained a provision for a Council of Censors that would meet every seven years to propose constitutional amendments.

The state had divided into two factions. Those who supported the egalitarian state constitution were called "Constitutionalists," while those who favored a constitution with greater checks and balances were called "Republicans." The Constitutionalists tended to be concentrated in the western part of the states and the Republicans in the east; Constitutionalists tended to be more rural and Republicans more urban.

Delegates at the Convention

Pennsylvania was host to the Constitutional Convention just as it had been to the Second Continental Congress where the Declaration of Independence had been written. One of the three most populous states, Pennsylvania was also the best represented. Partly because of the proximity of its delegates and partly because of its size, Pennsylvania sent eight delegates to the Constitutional Convention, all from Philadelphia. Four of the delegates had signed the Declaration of Independence and all ended up signing the Constitution; in addition, Delaware's John Dickinson had previously served in the Pennsylvania Assembly. Although the contributions of George Clymer, Thomas Fitzsimons, Jared Ingersoll, Thomas Mifflin, and Robert Morris to Convention debates were fairly minimal, Benjamin Franklin was a major presence, as were James Wilson and Gouverneur Morris, who also had connections with New York. Only Virginia could boast of a comparable delegation.

References to Pennsylvania at the Convention

It was natural that delegates would refer to the example of Pennsylvania in their debates. On June 20, Virginia's George Mason pointed out that the Pennsylvania legislature and the Congress under the Articles of Confederation were the only two examples of a unicameral legislature (Farrand 1937, I, 339), although he appears to have been mistaken, as this was also true of Georgia. In attempting to refute Gouverneur Morris's proposal that Western states should not be equally represented with those of the East, Virginia's James Madison observed on July 11 that delegates cited Pennsylvania as an example of a state where "those who were possessed of the power in the original settlement, never admitted the new settlmts. to a due share of it" (I, 584). On July 21, Elbridge Gerry of Massachusetts commended the practice of Pennsylvania in getting experts to help draw up legislative bills (II, 75), and on July 25, Gouverneur Morris cited the rotation of offices within the state as a cause of instability (II, 112–113). Morris further opposed a motion to prevent the seat of the new government from being located in an existing state capital by noting that such a proposal would alienate individuals in New York City and Philadelphia who were still hoping that their city would be chosen (II, 127). James Wilson cited Pennsylvania's generous policy of allowing foreigners to have all the rights of citizens after two years of residence (II, 272), and Gouverneur Morris cited reports by the Pennsylvania Council of Censors to show that the legislative department had frequently invaded executive powers (II, 299–300).

Ratification of the Constitution

Pennsylvania was the first large state to ratify the Constitution, and, although its decision came shortly after Delaware's, the anticipation of Pennsylvania's ratification appears to have influenced the smaller state. Ratification in Pennsylvania was beset with partisan controversy, and the struggle for the hearts and minds of the people proved more difficult than the actual act of ratification. When on September 28, the state legislature was contemplating calling a ratifying convention for November 20, Constitutionalists who opposed adoption of the Constitution sought to absent themselves to prevent a quorum. A mob forcibly returned two of these legislators to the chambers where the motion was adopted.

One of the landmarks of the Pennsylvania ratification was a speech that James Wilson made on October 6 in the State House Yard. As a delegate to the Convention, Wilson knew the document better than many of its opponents. He defended the Constitution against attacks using the language of popular sovereignty that was so popular within his state. Like Franklin had done within the Convention, Wilson portrayed the document not as perfect but as the best that could be obtained.

Wilson subsequently led pro-ratification forces at the Convention. He was aided by Dr. Benjamin Rush and opposed chiefly by William Findley, John Smilie, and Robert Whitehill. Wilson argued that the Constitution would have to be accepted or rejected as a whole.

The Pennsylvania convention voted to ratify the Constitution on December 12. The vote was 46 to 23. A student of the Convention observes that although "ratification was assured . . . popular approval was far from being won" (Graham 1989, 67). Antifederalist sentiment remained strong in the state and even resulted in a riot in Carlisle, Pennsylvania, where participants burned Wilson in effigy. Mistaking "ratification for legitimation" (Graham, 68–69), Federalists, although boosted by their early success in Pennsylvania, would have to tailor future ratification battles not only to those within the Convention but also to those outside.

Not long after ratification of the U.S. Constitution, Pennsylvania adopted a state constitution that was less egalitarian and more like its national counterpart. It strengthened the powers of the governor and replaced the unicameral legislature with a bicameral one.

See Also Clymer, George; Fitzsimons, Thomas; Franklin, Benjamin; Ingersoll, Jared; Mifflin, Thomas; Morris, Gouverneur; Morris, Robert; Philadelphia; Wilson, James

FOR FURTHER READING

Doutrich, Paul. 1988. "From Revolution to Constitution: Pennsylvania's Path to Federalism." In Patrick T. Conley and John P. Kaminski, eds. *The Constitution and the States: The Role of the Original Thirteen in the Framing and Adoption of the Federal Constitution.* Madison, WI: Madison House.

Farrand, Max, ed. 1937. *The Records of the Federal Convention.* 4 vols. New Haven, CT: Yale University Press.

Graham, George J., Jr. 1989. "Pennsylvania: Representation and the Meaning of Republicanism." In Michael Allen Gillespie and Michael Lienesch, eds. *Ratifying the Constitution.* Lawrence: University Press of Kansas.

Ireland, Owen S. 1995. *Religion, Ethnicity, and Politics: Ratifying the Constitution in Pennsylvania.* University Park: Pennsylvania State University Press.

St. John, Jeffrey. 1990. *A Child of Fortune: A Correspondent's Report on the Ratification of the U.S. Constitution and Battle for a Bill of Rights.* Ottawa, IL: Jameson Books.

PENNSYLVANIA PACKET AND DAILY ADVERTISER

Although the Constitution was "embossed," or written in script, by Jacob Shallus on September 17, 1787, the *Pennsylvania Packet and Daily Advertiser* published the first printed copy of the U.S. Constitution to appear before the public on September 19, 1787. In an era of many newspapers throughout the states, this document was widely printed in the months and weeks thereafter. The *Pennsylvania Packet and Daily Advertiser* was published in Philadelphia from October 28, 1771, through December 31, 1790.

See Also Press Coverage; Shallus, Jacob

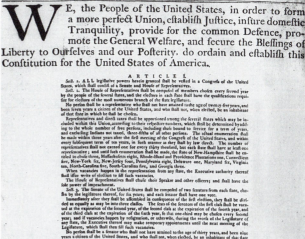

September 19, 1787: A page of the Pennsylvania Packet and Daily Advertiser *publishing the articles of the new U.S. Constitution in the month of its inauguration (MPI/Getty Images)*

FOR FURTHER READING

http://www.libraries.psu.edu/newsandmicroforms/microfinder/fullnew.htm.

PENNSYLVANIA STATE HOUSE (INDEPENDENCE HALL)

The site of the Constitutional Convention of 1787 was the Pennsylvania State House, now generally called Independence Hall. This is one of the most historic buildings in America. The building once accommodated the Library Company of Philadelphia and the American Philosophical Society. It was the host of the Second Continental Congress (the first Congress had met in nearby Carpenters' Hall). It was the place that the Second Continental Congress commissioned George Washington as commander-in-chief of America's revolutionary forces and the place where delegates signed the Declaration of Independence. It was the location not only of the debates and signing of the Constitution, but also for the calling of the Pennsylvania ratifying convention. The first U.S. Congresses met from 1790 to 1800 nearby in a newly constructed county courthouse dubbed Congress Hall while the first U.S. Supreme Court met in the nearby City Hall (Mires 2002, 31–32).

The Pennsylvania Assembly authorized the construction of the Pennsylvania State House in 1729. Famed American attorney Andrew Hamilton, who argued the historic *Peter Zenger* case involving freedom of the press (Vile 2001, I, 326) and was at the time speaker of the Pennsylvania Assembly, had a prominent role in designing the building and in choosing to place it on Chestnut Street between Fifth and Sixth Streets. At the time, this was not in the center of the city (the city had largely grown around the Delaware River several blocks away), making its location "more suburban than urban, looking more like a gentleman's country seat than a house of state" (Mires, 6).

The designs of the Italian architect Andrea Palladio, who later influenced Thomas Jefferson, also influenced the style of the red brick building. Measuring 107 by 45 feet, the State House was the largest building in the city at the time that it was built, but it originally had a cupola rather than the more distinctive steeple that was later added. Outwardly, the well-proportioned building, the construction of which was superintended by Edmund Woolley, has a Georgian simplicity. Andrew Hamilton apparently designed the interior, the first floor of which features two rooms; they measure about 40 feet square and have 20-foot ceilings, with a commodious 2-foot hallway in between. One, the East Room, where the Constitutional Convention met, was the home of the

Pennsylvania Assembly. Equipped with two marble fireplaces and a crystal chandelier (albeit not the one that is currently there), it was furnished with round tables covered with green velour and Windsor and ladderback chairs (none of the originals are known to exist) where the delegates sat facing a raised table at which Washington was seated during much of the Constitutional Convention. The other side of the first floor was designated for the provincial state court. The jury boxes (for both grand and petit jurors) and the iron cage in which defendants stood during trials serve as a continuing reminder of the influence of English common law on the U.S. judicial system.

The upstairs contained one lengthwise long room facing Chestnut Street, with "the remaining space divided into chambers for the Provincial Council and committee meetings of the Assembly" (Mires, 8). The distinctive masonry steeple was added in the 1750s, along with a staircase leading up to what is now known as the Liberty Bell, which, as most every American child knows, has a distinctive crack that developed sometime between 1817 and 1846. Almost prophetically, the bell bore the words from Leviticus 25:10: "Proclaim liberty thro' all the land to all the inhabitants thereof" (8). The original wooden steeple that adorned the top of the masonry tower deteriorated, was torn down in 1781, and was later replaced.

Philadelphia, the "City of Brotherly Love" is known for its careful layout, attributable to its founder, William Penn. Penn had originally planned five public squares for the city, but the State House became the site of a sixth (10). Suffering from neglect during the British occupation of the city during the Revolutionary War, the city had created a park in the State House yard in the 1780s. People became increasingly interested in visiting Independence Hall in 1800 and the years thereafter as the Revolutionary generation was passing away.

Philadelphia was the site of the Exposition of 1876, in effect, America's first world's fair. It has continued to be the site of numerous constitutional anniversaries, including the sesquicentennial (1937) and the bicentennial (1987), and has become an increasingly popular tourist destination. Although the city attempted to sell the Lib-

State House or Hall of Independence, Philadelphia, Pennsylvania (Historical Picture Archive/Corbis)

erty Bell for scrap in 1828, in part because of the abolitionist movement, it subsequently became a national icon and was removed from Independence Hall and enclosed in a separate glass case outside the building in 1976 (Lukacs 1987, 75). Independence Hall is largely original, but most of its furnishings are not. An exception is the beautiful Chippendale chair in which George Washington sat during much of the Convention and on the back of which is painted a sun, which Benjamin Franklin proclaimed on the final day of the Convention to be "rising" rather than "setting" on a strengthened nation. The Syng Inkstand, which the delegates used in both the signing of the Declaration of Independence and the Constitution, has also been preserved.

On July 4, 2003, the National Constitution Center opened on Independence Mall facing the State House. This museum, filled with interactive displays especially appropriate for middle and high school students, is the first museum in history devoted solely to the U.S. Constitution. The idea for the museum grew out of activities in Philadelphia celebrating the bicentennial of the U.S. Constitution of 1987. The facts that the State House is known for the signing of the nation's two most important documents and that it is designated as Independence Hall rather than Constitution Hall (see Mires) suggest that the new museum fills an important educational function.

For individuals on the West Coast who might not get to visit Philadelphia, Knott's Berry Farm theme park, near Disneyland in California, has a replica of the Pennsylvania State House (and the Liberty Bell). The exterior of the administration building at Austin Peay State University in Clarksville, Tennessee, also closely resembles that of Independence Hall.

See Also Commemorations of the Constitutional Convention; Declaration of Independence; Liberty Bell; National Constitution Center; Philadelphia; Rising Sun Chair; Syng Inkstand

FOR FURTHER READING

Bullock, Steven C. 2002. "Talk of the Past." *Common-Place* 2, no. 4 (July). http://www.common-place.org.

A Smoke-Filled Room?

It is traditional in modern politics to talk about deliberations taking place in "smoke-filled rooms." The image originated from the nomination of Warren G. Harding as the Republican presidential nominee in 1920, a period before primary elections chose most delegates to the national nominating conventions, when party bosses essentially selected the nominees behind closed doors.

There were no national political parties at the time of the Constitutional Convention of 1787, so this part of the image would not fit. Like so-called smoke-filled rooms, the Convention proceedings were secret, so this part of the image would. What about the smoke?

Surprisingly, it is relatively difficult to ascertain with any certainty whether any of the delegates smoked during the Convention or not. Tobacco was an important crop in the South, especially Maryland, Virginia, and North Carolina (as in modern-day Kentucky and Tennessee), and tobacco products appear to have been widely available. By 1794, Philadelphia alone had 27 manufacturers of tobacco products, employing more than 4,000 people (Robert 1952, 78). There was no ban on tobacco use in the Convention rules that the delegates adopted early in their proceedings (although if members of the upper class in attendance considered this an improper social norm, no such explicit rule would have been necessary), but the only mentions of tobacco occur in its role as a staple crop that might be subject to taxation. Contemporaries who did smoke used long clay pipes; the cigar was not introduced until the 1790s and the cigarette much later.

Foreign visitors often commented on the ubiquity of smoking and other forms of tobacco use in America, but some of these observations come from a later period (Larkin 1988, 166–69), while others may have been intended to put some distance between the visitors and their more rustic New World counterparts (Rozbicki 1997). Francis Hopkinson, who signed the Declaration of Independence, is known to have taken snuff (Staff, Independence National Historical Park 1970, 32), which was fairly popular, especially among elites, at the time. Snuff consisted of finely ground tobacco, which users inhaled. In addition, Congress is known to have installed spitting boxes (32), for individuals who indulged in the widely practiced practice of chewing tobacco. Unlike alcohol, tobacco (with its nicotine), along with coffee and tea, is a stimulant. If members of the Convention indulged in similar habits, their use of tobacco may have served, much like modern cigarettes or coffee, to keep delegates occupied and attentive during relatively long business sessions in which there was no break for lunch.

FOR FURTHER READING

Larkin, Jack. 1988. *The Reshaping of Everyday Life, 1790–1840.* New York: Harper and Row.

Robert, Joseph C. 1952. *The Story of Tobacco in America.* New York: Alfred A. Knopf.

Rozbicki, Michal J. 1997. "The Curse of Provincialism: Negative Perceptions of Colonial American Plantation Gentry." *Journal of Southern History* 63 (November): 727–752.

Staff, Independence National Historical Park. 1970. "Furnishing Plan for the Assembly Room, Independence Hall" (February). Provided courtesy of James W. Mueller, Chief Historian and Compliance Coordinator, Independence National Historical Park.

Delmar, Frances. 2002. "Pastimes: Shouldering Independence." *Common-Place* 2, no. 4 (July). http://www.common-place.org.

Lukacs, John. 1987. "Unexpected Philadelphia." *American Heritage,* May/June, 72–81.

Mires, Charlene. 2002. *Independence Hall in American Memory.* Philadelphia: University of Pennsylvania Press.

Neustadt, Katherine D. 1981. *Carpenters' Hall: Meeting Place of History.* Philadelphia, PA: Winchell.

Vile, John R., ed. 2001. *Great American Lawyers: An Encyclopedia.* 2 vols. Santa Barbara: ABC-CLIO. (Essay on Andrew Hamilton is in I, 325–331.)

PHILADELPHIA

Initially settled largely by Swedes, Philadelphia, meaning the "city of brotherly love," had been largely founded and planned by William Penn. He had laid the city streets out in an orderly grid pattern that impressed visitors. At the time of the Constitutional Convention, Philadelphia was the largest city not only in Pennsylvania but in all of the 13 states. It contained 28,000 citizens according to the 1790 census, with another 14,000 in the suburbs, and was thus, behind London, the second largest English-speaking city in the world. Philadel-

phia, which was fairly centrally located within the colonies, had served as the site of both the First and Second Continental Congresses, although the second such Congress had to relocate on a number of occasions, including a time of British occupation, after the writing of the Declaration of Independence. Mary Schweitzer has described the city's economy as "mercantile"; it was based primarily on trade, which was facilitated by the city's location on the Delaware River (1993, 32).

At the time of the Constitutional Convention, Philadelphia was the home of Benjamin Franklin, one of America's best-known citizens, and Robert Morris, reputed to be the nation's richest. It was also home to all of Pennsylvania's six other delegates to the Constitutional Convention. The city was the site of eight newspapers, a bustling port, a museum directed by Charles Willson Peale, an orrery (a mechanical device using balls of varied sizes to illustrate the motions and positions of

Second Street at Christ Church, Philadelphia, 1799 (Pixel That)

Contemporary Philadelphia: A Ban on Plays

Although Philadelphia boasted shopping, museums, newspapers, public gardens, and a library, theatrical productions were one form of entertainment that was not available to delegates attending the Constitutional Convention there—at least not officially. The city had adopted the prohibition during the Revolutionary War, in what has been described as partly an "economy measure" and partly a "Presbyterian gesture," and the prohibition remained in effect until 1789 (Carr 1990, 24).

Not only could plays be performed outside the city limits, but they could apparently also be "disguised as 'moral lectures' or 'spectacles'" (Carr, 24). Thus, "Shakespeare's *Richard III* was advertised as a 'series of historical lectures in five parts on the fate of tyranny' and Oliver Goldsmith's *She Stoops to Conquer* was billed as 'a lecture on the disadvantages of improper education'" (Peters 1987, 47).

FOR FURTHER READING

Carr, William G. 1990. *The Oldest Delegate: Franklin in the Constitutional Convention*. Newark, NJ: University of Delaware Press.
Peters, William. 1987. *A More Perfect Union*. New York: Crown Publishers.

various celestial bodies) constructed by David Rittenhouse, and many shops. In addition to the facilities at the State House that could accommodate meetings like the Convention, the city had an abundance of private homes, inns, and taverns that could easily house the delegates. The city was the site of the nation's first medical school, a large public library, and a number of prominent furniture-makers. It also housed a jail, relatively close to the State House, whose occupants begged passersby for money and often hurled curses and insults at those who refused to contribute. Contemporaries regarded the city, which had long practiced religious tolerance and was the site of the American Philosophic Society, as one of the most cosmopolitan in America. It was hosting a meeting of the Society of the Cincinnati as well as the Pennsylvania Anti-Slavery Society contemporaneously with hosting the Constitutional Convention.

Whatever its charms, Philadelphia was still a city of its time. In 1787, it was common for residents to throw garbage in the streets and let the pigs and cows eat it. Especially in the summer, droppings from such animals, as well as those of the horses that were used for transportation, drew biting insects and spread diseases. These periodically swept through the cities, accounting in part for the high infant mortality rates of the times (Hakim 2003, 162–163).

As was true of most Eastern port cities, supporters of the new Constitution dominated Philadelphia politics. They successfully pressed their advantage by compelling members of the opposition to attend the ratifying convention, supported by the speech in favor of the new Constitution that Benjamin Franklin had delivered on September 17 as well as by arguments by James Wilson, who had served as one of Pennsylvania's delegates to the Convention.

Although the nation's capital began in New York, it transferred back to Philadelphia from 1790 to 1800, at which time it moved to its current site in the District of Columbia. Since then, Philadelphia has been the focal point of numerous celebrations commemorating the Declaration of Independence and the Constitution (especially at centennials, sesquicentennials, and bicentennials). As of July 4, 2003, it is also the site not only of Independence Hall, the Liberty Bell, the Betsy Ross house, and other historic places, but also of the National Constitution Center, the first museum designed exclusively to commemorate the U.S. Constitution.

See Also Commemorations of the Constitutional Convention; National Constitution Center; Pennsylvania; Pennsylvania State House

FOR FURTHER READING

Hakim, Joy. 2003. *From Colonies to Country*. Book 3 of *A History of the US*. New York: Oxford University Press.

Kelley, Joseph J., Jr. 1973. *Life and Times in Colonial Philadelphia*. Harrisburg, PA: Stackpole Books.

Schweitzer, Mary M. 1993. "The Spatial Organization of Federalist Philadelphia, 1790." *Journal of Interdisciplinary History* 25 (Summer): 31–57.

Staib, Walter. 1999. *City Tavern Cookbook: 200 Years of Classic Recipes from America's First Gourmet Restaurant*. Philadelphia, PA: Running Press.

Wolf, Edwin, II. 1975. *Philadelphia: Portrait of an American City*. Philadelphia, PA: Winchell.

PIERCE, WILLIAM (1740–1789)

Believed to have been born in Virginia in 1740, Pierce studied at the College of William and Mary where he was a member of Phi Beta Kappa, today's leading college honor society. He served in the Revolution as an aide-de-camp to General Nathaniel Greene, was recognized by Congress for his valor, and received land for his service to Virginia. He subsequently headed a trade company in Savannah, married well, and was elected first to the Georgia Assembly and then to the confederal Congress. He was a member of the Society of the Cincinnati, a veterans' organization.

In a letter from New York dated May 19, 1787, before the start of the Constitutional Convention, William Pierce observed that he favored "powers equal to a prompt and certain execution, but tempered with a proper respect for the liberties of the People. I am for securing their happiness, not by the will of a few, but by the direction of the Law" (Hutson 1987, 9). In this same letter, he said that it was necessary to pay respect "to the temper of the People" and indicated that he thought this temper was incompatible with the establishment of a monarchy (9). He recorded that he opposed the exercise of "dictatorial power," and that "Unless *we* can settle down into some permanent System very shortly, our condition will be as fickle and inconsistent, as that of the Romans; and our political schemes be nothing more than chimeras and disorders" (10). Clearly, Pierce recognized that the Convention he would attend would be important. He concluded his letter, in his own idiosyncratic spelling, by observing that "the Statesman and the Phylosopher have their attention turned towards us: the oppressed and wretched look to America" (10).

Pierce was seated at the Convention on May 31. Pierce's most distinctive contribution to the Convention was a set of character sketches of all but two of the delegates that was eventually published in the *American Historical Review* (see Farrand 1937, III, 87–97) and that has been published numerous times since. These sketches reveal an individual of considerable literary accomplishment and powers of observation. He identified himself as a soldier in the Revolutionary War, spoke of his interest in the general welfare, mentioned his ambition, and spoke with pride of having sat on what he described, with perhaps a bit of hyperbole, as "the wisest Council in the World" (III, 97). On occasion, his notes are useful supplements to those of James Madison and other members.

Pierce's notes of the first day indicate that he believed it was necessary to know "how the Senate should be appointed" before deciding on how the first branch would be selected. His notes continue with his view that it would be necessary to balance the powers of the state and national governments:

It appeared clear to me that unless we established a Government that should carry at least some of its principles into the mass of the people, we might as well depend upon the present confederation. If the influence of the States is not lost in some part of the new Government we never shall have any thing like a national institution. But in my opinion it will be right to shew the sovereignty of the State in one branch of the Legislature, and that should be in the Senate. (I, 59)

Pierce followed up on these thoughts on June 6 when he said that he "was for an election by the people as to the 1st. branch & by the States as to the 2d. branch; by which means the Citizens of the States wd. be represented both *individually & collectively*" (I, 137). On June 12, Pierce successfully proposed that members of the House of Representatives should be paid out of the national Treasury (I, 216). That same day, Pierce proposed that the term of senators should be three years. At the time, the Convention was considering a seven-year term; Pierce pointed out that such a term had caused "great mischief" in Great Britain where it has been "reprobated by most of their patriotic Statesmen" (I, 218).

Pierce reiterated the need to balance state and national interest on June 29 in following up a speech by Madison. Pierce observed that members of Congress had represented the interests of their states. Pointing out that the federal government under the Articles of Confederation was "no more than a compact between states," he observed:

> We are now met to remedy its defects, and our difficulties are great, but not, I hope, insurmountable. State distinctions must be sacrificed so far as the general government shall render it necessary—without, however, destroying them altogether. Although I am here a representative from a small state, I consider myself as a citizen of the United States, whose general interest I will always support. (I, 474)

As a member of a state that needed national help in repelling Indian attacks, Pierce's position may have enabled him to take a more nationalistic view than that of delegates from states where such a dependency was less obvious.

Pierce left the Convention after he felt that "all the first principles of the new Government were established" (Hutson, 182). He then went back to Congress where he pled for national help for Georgia against Indian threats. His early departure would appear to have been a genuine loss to the Convention. Explaining to St. George Tucker in a letter of September 18, 1787, why he had not stayed at the Convention and signed the document, he referred to "a piece of business so necessary that it became unavoidable." He further indicated that he supported the document:

> I approve of its principles, and would have signed it with all my heart, had I been present. To say, however, that I consider it as perfect, would be to make an acknowledgement immediately opposed to my judgment.
>
> Perhaps it is the only one that will suit our present situation. The wisdom of the Convention was equal to something greater; but a variety of local circumstances, the inequality of states, and the dissonant interests of the different parts of the Union, made it impossible to give it any other shape or form. (III, 100–101)

Pierce helped persuade Congress to send the Constitution to the states for ratification, and he helped print the Constitution in his home state and worked for its ratification. Pierce's life took a decidedly downward turn after the Convention, when both his business and his health failed. He died shortly thereafter in 1789.

See Also Georgia; Oratory and Rhetoric; Society of the Cincinnati

FOR FURTHER READING

Bradford, M. M. 1981. *Founding Fathers: Brief Lives of the Framers of the United States Constitution.* 2nd ed. Lawrence: University Press of Kansas.

Farrand, Max, ed. 1937. *The Records of the Federal Convention.* 4 vols. New Haven, CT: Yale University Press.

Hutson, James H., ed. 1987. *Supplement to Max Farrand's* The Records of the Federal Convention of 1787. New Haven, CT: Yale University Press.

"Notes of Major William Pierce on the Federal Convention of 1787." *American Historical Review* 3 (January): 310–334.

PINCKNEY, CHARLES (1757–1824)

The reality and the myth of Charles Pinckney are somewhat difficult to separate. After Georgia delegate William Pierce incorrectly identified Pinckney (who was 29 at the time) as being the youngest man at the Convention (rather than New Jersey's Jonathan Dayton, who was 26), Pinckney made no attempt to correct the impression (Matthews 2004, 39–40). Scholars are still debating the content and the influence of the plan that he introduced just after the Virginia Plan which was later apparently considered by the Committee of Detail. It seems clear that a version of the Constitution that he claimed to have proposed was not in fact the one that he offered in the early days of the Convention, but numerous suggestions that he made at the Convention appear to have found their way into the final document. Largely on the basis of a letter (supplied to him by James Monroe) that Pinckney had written as a member of Congress to protest his handling of negotiations with Spain over navigation of the Mississippi River, James Madison formed a negative impression of Pinckney, which he kept throughout his life and appears to have conveyed to others (Matthews, 36), and which may have found its way into his notes.

Pinckney was born to the family of a lawyer and planter in Charleston, and was related to many other prominent men in the state; his cousin Charles Cotesworth Pinckney also represented South Carolina at the Constitutional Convention. Pinckney read law with his father and went on to achieve success at the South Carolina bar. Pinckney took an early lead in the movement for revolution against England, helping to serve on a three-person state executive committee and later helping to draft a new state constitution. He fought in the Revolutionary War, during which the British captured and imprisoned him for a time. The British were unable to compel him, unlike his father, who had served as state governor, to switch sides—his father's actions would lead to heavy fines on his property that would plague the son throughout most of his life. He subsequently served as a delegate to the Continental Congress, where he had argued for strengthening the national government. Princeton awarded him an honorary degree for his congressional service in 1787, an honor it bestowed that same year on Virginia's James Madison.

Charles Pinckney, delegate from South Carolina
(Library of Congress)

Pinckney was present on the opening day of the Convention, and on this day, he moved that the Convention create a Rules Committee. He was subsequently one of three individuals appointed (along with Virginia's George Wythe and New York's Alexander Hamilton) to this committee (Farrand 1937, I, 2). Wythe, the chair of the committee and the nation's first law professor, probably had the most important role on the committee, but it was nonetheless important in establishing a set of rules designed to promote reason and deliberation at the Convention.

The Pinckney Plan

Madison's notes indicate that Pinckney introduced his plan on May 29, the same day that Edmund Randolph introduced the Virginia Plan, and, perhaps because Pinckney's plan followed Randolph's proposal, it was referred along with this plan to the Committee of the Whole. As best as can be reconstructed, the plan called for a bicameral Congress consisting of a Senate and a House of Delegates. State legislatures were to select members of the House of Delegates who would in turn select senators to four-year terms either from their own ranks or from among the people at large (III, 605). The nation was to be divided into four districts for this purpose.

The Senate was to choose the president every four years. His powers would include power to correspond with state executives, execute the laws, serve as commander-in-chief of the armed forces, and convene the legislature. He was to be aided by a Council of Revision consisting of various department heads (III, 606).

Congress would have exclusive power to raise military forces, to regulate interstate and foreign trade, establish a post office, coin money, etc. The legislature would also have the power to appoint major officers and to institute a federal judicial court. Two-thirds majorities would be required for regulating trade, levying imposts, and raising revenue (III, 608). The House of Delegates would have the power of impeachment and the Senate and federal judges would judge such impeachments.

The plan further provided for the later addition of powers by the consent of an unspecified number of states. It also provided for trial by jury, freedom of the press, and a prohibition of religion tests (III, 609).

Federalism

On May 30, the day after Edmund Randolph introduced the Virginia Plan, Pinckey asked him whether he intended to abolish state governments altogether (I, 33–34). In the same vein, Pinckney expressed concern on the next day about granting Congress power "in all cases to which the State Legislatures were individually incompetent" (II, 53). Pinckney thought that this language was too vague.

On June 8, however, Pinckney indicated that he favored a congressional negative over state laws "which they shd. judge to be improper" (I, 164). Moreover, he argued:

that such a universality of the power was indispensable necessary to render it effectual; that the

States must be kept in due subordination to the nation; that if the States were left to act of themselves in any case, it wd. be impossible to defend the national prerogatives, however extensive they might be on paper; . . . that this universal negative was in fact the corner stone of an efficient national Govt. (I, 164)

Pinckney renewed his support for the negative of state laws on July 17 (II, 28), and again on August 23. On the latter occasion, he proposed that such a negative would require a two-thirds vote of both houses of Congress (II, 390). He further suggested that state governors (perhaps appointed by Congress) should be able to exercise such power and suggested that this might be done if another convention were to be called (II, 391).

On August 9, Pinckney indicated that he opposed congressional oversight of the times, places, and manner of their elections. He thought that the states should be relied on for this purpose (II, 240). He favored allowing Congress to subdue rebellion in the states without an application from their legislatures (II, 317). Pinckney thought that many state debts were so related to national purposes that they should be considered as expenditures on behalf of the nation as a whole (II, 327).

Congress

Selection of Senators

Consistent with reconstructions of Pinckney's plan, on May 31, he apparently proposed to divide the nation into four divisions, from which senators would be chosen (I, 59). On June 7, Pinckney observed that if senators were to be chosen by state legislatures, and that if each state were to have at least one, the Senate would consist of at least 80 members, which number he thought was too high (I, 150). However, he argued later in the day that members of the Senate "ought to be permanent & independent," and that appointment by state legislatures would enhance this likelihood. In a precursor to the Connecticut Compromise, he also proposed that states should be divided into three classes, granting the smallest states one senator, the medium-size states two, and the large states three (I, 155; also see I, 169). Still later he proposed a Senate of 36 persons, with states having from one to five members (II, 5).

Apportionment of Representation

Pinckney generally sided with the large states on the issue of representation. He was realistic, perhaps even skeptical of the motives of the small ones. His tone on June 16 was almost cynical: "Give N. Jersey an equal vote, and she will dismiss her scruples, and concur in the Natil. system" (I, 255). On this occasion, he further argued that the Convention had the power to go to whatever length it needed in making recommendations "to remedy the evils which produced this Convention" (I, 255).

On July 2, Pinckney said that he thought it would be "inadmissible" to grant states equal votes in the Senate. He recognized, however, that larger states "would feel a partiality for their own Citizens & give them a preference, in appointments" (I, 510). He appeared to argue that the difference between Northern and Southern states was greater than that between the large and small states. Still, he suggested, consistent with his earlier proposal to divide states into three groups, that the small states should be granted "some but not a full proportion" (I, 511).

Origination of Money Bills in the House

On July 6, he argued that the provision providing that money bills should originate in the House was of little substance (I, 545). He later argued that "if the Senate can be trusted with the many great powers proposed, it surely may be trusted with that of originating money bills" (II, 224; also see II, 263).

Method of Selection

On June 6, Pinckney opposed popular election of members of the first branch of Congress, "contending that the people were less fit Judges and

that the Legislatures would be less likely to promote the adoption of the new Government, if they were to be excluded from all share in it" (I, 132). On June 13, Pinckney argued that it was necessary to decide how the Senate would be apportioned before deciding whether the origination of money bills should be confined to the House (I, 234).

Composition of the Senate

On June 25, Pinckney delivered an extended speech to the Convention regarding the composition of the Senate. Pinckney observed that the most singular fact about the U.S. was that "there are fewer distinctions of fortune & less of rank, than among the inhabitants of any other nation" (I, 398). He expected this relative equality would continue into the foreseeable future and therefore thought that the lessons to be drawn from the British constitution, which he believed "to be the best constitution in existence," were limited (I, 398). Specifically, Pinckney doubted the propriety of using a peerage "for forming a Legislative balance between the inordinate power of the Executive and the people" (I, 399). Instead, the system to be established "must be suited to the habits & genius of the People it is to govern, and must grow out of them" (I, 402).

Pinckney believed that men in the U.S. fell into three classes—professional men, commercial men, and those with landed interests (I, 402). From this point forward, his speech is difficult to follow. It seemed, however, to call for reserving local rights to the states (II, 404). At the same time, he apparently continued to favor a congressional negative of state laws (I, 412), and he may even have introduced such a plan, although it is not included in Convention notes (I, 412). It is not at all clear exactly how Pinckney hoped that the Senate would represent the three central interests that he identified.

Representation in the House

On July 6, Pinckney opposed reexamination of the formula whereby the House of Representatives would have one representative for every 40,000 inhabitants. He thought that this measure would be better than state contributions of revenue because it would fluctuate less. He wanted blacks to be counted equally with whites for purposes of representation, but was willing to settle for the three-fifths formula (I, 542).

Qualifications of Members

On July 26, Pinckney seconded a motion by Virginia's George Mason that would have required qualifications of landed property, and the exclusion of individuals having unsettled accounts from serving in Congress (II, 121). He further hoped to extend such qualifications to all three branches of government (II, 122). Later in the day, Pinckney said that he had reconsidered the idea of excluding public debtors since it would exclude individuals who had purchased confiscated property or property in the West (II, 126).

Pinckney favored a motion raising the citizenship requirements for members of the Senate from four to 14 years. He thought there would be particular danger of foreign intrigues in this body since it was responsible for managing foreign affairs (II, 235). When this was initially rejected, he pushed for a ten-year citizenship requirement (II, 239). When some delegates objected that it would not be fair to impose citizenship requirements on those who were already in the country, Pinckney said that current laws varied widely and that the Convention was in a situation where it was appropriate to consider "first principles" (II, 271).

Pinckney was concerned when a committee failed to report property qualifications for members of Congress and left this issue to the first Congress. He feared that this body might set the qualifications so as to favor either the rich or the poor. His argument then took an interesting turn. Contending that he opposed "an undue aristocratic influence in the Constitution," he said that it was necessary for members of all three branches to possess "competent property to make them independent & respectable" (II, 248). As for him, he thought a president should have at least $100,000,

and that judges and members of Congress should have at least half this amount (II, 248). This would certainly have been a relatively substantial sum in a nation that Pinckney thought was characterized by relative equality.

Eligibility for Other Offices

Pinckney opposed making members of Congress ineligible for other offices, and made at least three arguments against this. He thought it was degrading, inconvenient, and impolitic (II, 283); he later argued that it was also contrary to state practice (II, 287). Pinckney indicated that he hoped that the Senate might especially "contain the fittest men" and "become a School of Public Ministers, a nursery of Statesmen" (II, 283). He was willing to support a clause, eventually adopted, preventing members from accepting offices for which they received pay without first resigning (II, 284). Opposing congressional ineligibility for other offices on September 3, Pinckney observed that this eligibility should be like "the policy of the Romans in making the temple of virtue the road to the temple of fame" (II, 490). He anticipated that the first Congress would "be composed of the ablest men to be found," and he did not want them excluded from other offices, like the judiciary, that would be formed during this Congress (II, 491).

Powers and Limits

Pinckney opposed vesting the power to make war in Congress as a whole. He feared that it would be too slow, that it would meet too infrequently, and that the House of Representatives would be too large for this purpose (II, 318). He thought this power would be better vested in the Senate. He did not think that equal state representation would prove deleterious in such circumstances because all states would have a stake in the survival of the nation (II, 318).

Pinckney favored congressional regulation of the militia. He had little faith in the state militia as then constituted. He further thought that over-reliance on such undertrained troops was evident in the states' "rapid approaches toward anarchy" (II, 332).

One of Pinckney's most important contributions to the Constitution may have been the idea of enumerating and limiting congressional powers. On August 20, he submitted a series of proposals for consideration by the Committee of Detail, some provisions of which, while not making it into the original Constitution, later reappeared as provisions within the Bill of Rights. These included the following provisions: each house should be judge of its own privileges and its members should have certain privileges going to and from that body (also see II, 502); the executive and each house of Congress should be able to request the Supreme Court to give its opinions on important matters of law; the writ of habeas corpus should be guaranteed; liberty of the press; a prohibition of troops in time of peace without legislative assent; military subordination to the government; a prohibition against quartering troops in private homes without consent; a prohibition on dual officeholding; a prohibition of religious tests; the designation of the U.S. as one corporate body; authorization for Congress to create a great seal of the U.S.; a provision that all commissions should be in the name of the U.S.; and the extension of judicial jurisdiction over controversies between the U.S. and states and between the U.S. and state citizens (II, 341–342).

On August 23, Pinckney introduced the resolution that provided that no individual holding public office in the United States should be able without congressional approval to accept any emolument, office, or title from foreign states (II, 389). Pinckney introduced a resolution on August 28 providing that the writ of habeas corpus should only be suspended on the most urgent occasions and then for a period not to exceed 12 months (II, 438).

On August 29, Pinckney advocated a provision, later adopted, granting Congress power to establish uniform laws on bankruptcies (II, 447). He also introduced the motion prohibiting religious oaths as a condition for public office (II, 468). On September 14, Pinckney seconded James Madison's motion to grant Congress the power to establish a national university in which no preference would be made on the basis of religious affiliation (II, 616).

On September 14, Pinckney opposed a provision limiting a standing army (II, 617). On this same day, he advocated a provision designed to guarantee freedom of the press (II, 617), a provision similar to one later incorporated into the First Amendment. Later in the day, he favored a motion providing for congressional accounting of expenditures "from time to time" rather than annually (II, 619).

Other Legislative Matters

Pinckney favored having the national capital in a place other than a state capital. However, he thought it would be appropriately located in "a large town or its vicinity" (II, 127). He did not think that it was necessary to specify congressional meeting times within the Constitution (II, 198). Pinckney seconded a motion to allow Congress to appoint the treasurer (II, 314).

On August 29, Pinckney introduced a resolution providing that two-thirds majorities of both houses of Congress would be required for regulating commerce. He identified five distinct interests corresponding to different sections of the country and including fisheries, free-grade wheat and flour, tobacco, and rice and indigo (II, 449). He argued that these interests "would be a source of oppressive regulations if no check to a bare majority should be provided" (II, 449). He also gave insight into his view of human nature by observing that "States pursue their interest with less scruple than individuals" (II, 449). Pinckney further observed that allowing Congress to regulate commerce "was a pure concession on the part of the S. States." He reasoned that "they did not need the protection of the N. States at present" (II, 449). He indicated that he considered the division between the North and South as an even greater division than the five interests he had previously identified (II, 450).

Pinckney favored allowing a two-thirds majority of both houses of Congress to override presidential vetoes. He feared that an alternative proposal for a three-fourths vote would put "a dangerous power in the hands of a few Senators headed by the President" (II, 586).

Executive

On June 1, Pinckney said that he favored "a vigorous Executive" (I, 64). However, he feared that the executive would take up the power of war and peace that the Continental Congress exercised and thought that this "would render the Executive a Monarchy, of the worst kind, to wit an elective one" (I, 65). He nonetheless seconded a motion by James Wilson to vest the executive power in a single individual (I, 65; also see I, 88). Pinckney opposed a provision granting the president power to exercise unspecified powers that were neither legislative nor judicial in nature, but he reasoned that such powers were already implicit in the power of the executive to carry into effect national laws (I, 67).

On June 1, Pinckney supported a seven-year presidential term (I, 68). On July 25, when the Convention was considering a six-year term, Pinckney proposed that no individual should be able to serve for more than six of any 12 years, thus avoiding the problems that might be created if the Congress had to decide to reelect a sitting president (II, 112).

On July 17, Pinckney favored selection of the president by Congress. He believed that legislators, being most interested in the laws they had adopted, would "be most attentive to the choice of a fit man to carry them properly into execution" (II, 30). By contrast, he thought that popular elections would "be led by a few active & designing men" and that, in such circumstances "the most populous States by combining in favor of the same individual will be able to carry their points" (II, 30). On August 24, Pinckney moved to require majority attendance in Congress when the president was being selected (II, 403). He later proposed a two-thirds attendance requirement for the Senate when that institution was being considered as the one to determine presidential elections (II, 526).

On September 4, Pinckney opposed the Electoral College on four grounds. He thought it would effectively give power to the Senate; he questioned whether electors would know the respective candidates; he feared that it would lead to executive re-eligibility, which he opposed; and he thought it would be inappropriate to involve the Senate in this mechanism, since it would have the responsibility of judging cases of presidential impeachment (II, 501). Pinckney renewed his opposition to the Electoral College on the following day, again raising four arguments that largely tracked his arguments of the previous day (II, 511).

On July 20, Pinckney opposed the impeachment of presidents while they were serving in office (II, 64). He feared that if the legislature directed such impeachments, they would be held "as a rod over the Executive and by that means effectually destroy his independence" and negate his veto power (II, 66; also see II, 551, applying this argument specifically to trials by the U.S. Senate). He further contended that presidential powers "would be so circumscribed as to render impeachments unnecessary" (II, 68).

Judiciary

On June 5, after the Committee of the Whole decided to strike the provision that the legislature would appoint judges, Pinckney notified the Convention that he hoped to restore this power to the entire Congress (I, 121). On June 13, however, after first proposing that the national legislature should make such appointments, Pinckney withdrew his motion after Madison argued in favor of appointment by the Senate (I, 233). On July 21, Pinckney argued that the Senate was to be preferred to the president in making appointments because "the Executive will possess neither the requisite knowledge of characters, nor confidence of the people for so high a trust" (II, 81). On September 7, Pinckney opposed a role for the Senate in confirming any appointments accept for ambassadors, which he did not think the president should appoint (II, 539).

Although he had originally favored a Council of Revision, Pinckney indicated on June 6 that he no longer believed that it was proper to put heads of departments on such a council since the president would already have power to call upon them (I, 139). As he later expressed this, if the delegates were to have "an able Council," then "it will thwart him" whereas if he had "a weak one," then "he will shelter himself under their sanction" (II, 329). Pinckney also indicated that he opposed including judges on such a council (I, 139). He later argued that this would "involve them in parties, and give a previous tincture to their opinions" (II, 298).

Slavery

On June 11, Pinckney seconded a resolution by Pennsylvania's James Wilson providing that representation in the House of Representatives should be apportioned according to the population of whites and free inhabitants and three-fifths of other persons (I, 201). On other occasions, he argued that blacks should count equally for purposes of state representation. On July 12, he argued that counting blacks equally with whites for purposes of representation was just because "The blacks are the labourers, the peasants of the Southern States: they are as productive of pecuniary resources as those of the Northern States. They add equally to the wealth, and considering money as the sinew of war, to the strength of the nation" (I, 596).

Pinckney did not view slavery as a moral issue. Characteristic of such a position, on August 8, he indicated that he "considered the fisheries & the Western frontier as more burdensome to the U.S. than the slaves" (II, 223).

On August 21, Pinckney said that South Carolina would never accept the Constitution if it prohibited the slave trade. He observed that "In every proposed extension of the powers of Congress, that State has expressly & watchfully excepted that of meddling with the importation of Negroes" (II, 364). He held out the prospect, however, that the state might eliminate this trade on its own, as Virginia and Maryland had already done (II, 365). The next day, Pinckney went on to argue that "If slavery is wrong, it is justified by the example of all the world" (II, 371). He observed that "In all ages one half of mankind have been

slaves" (II, 371). He again held out the prospect, however, that South Carolina might abolish the slave trade on its own and indicated that he would personally favor such a move (II, 371).

On August 28, Pinckney seconded a motion made by fellow delegate Pierce Butler and soon thereafter retracted. It was designed to require that "fugitive slaves and servants" were "to be delivered up like criminals" (II, 443).

Amending Process and Ratification

On June 5, the Committee of the Whole was debating a provision for an amending process to which the assent of Congress would not be required. Pinckney doubted the "propriety or necessity" either of the provision as a whole or, as seems more likely, of the exclusion of the legislature (I, 121). Later that day, Pinckney favored the ratification of a new Constitution by nine or more states (I, 123). On August 31, he favored using conventions for this purpose (II, 476). He wanted the Committee of Style to prepare an address to the people to accompany the Constitution (II, 564).

When George Mason announced his decision not to sign the Constitution on September 17, Pinckney said that this gave "a peculiar solemnity to the present moment." He feared however that "nothing but confusion & contrariety" could result from allowing states to propose amendments, and he thought that "Conventions are serious things, and ought not to be repeated." Like other delegates, Pinckney had concerns about the proposed Constitution. He especially "objected to the contemptible weakness & dependence of the Executive" and to the fact that a majority of Congress had power to control interstate commerce. Fearing "the danger of a general confusion, and an ultimate decision by the Sword," Pinckney decided that adoption of the Constitution was a safer and more desirable option (II, 632).

Life after the Convention

Pinckney was elected to, and appears to have had a major influence at, the South Carolina ratifying

Charles Pinckney and the Contradictions of Slavery

Charles Pinckney of South Carolina was among the delegates to the Constitutional Convention who owned slaves. A recent biographer has suggested that he may have owned as many as 200 to 300 at a time (Matthews 2004, 79). At the Convention, Pinckney observed: "If slavery is wrong, it is justified by the example of all the world" (Farrand 1937, II, 371). At the Constitutional Convention, Pinckney defended the right of Southern states to continue the importation of slaves (II, 371), and toward the end of his life, in debates that eventuated in the Missouri Compromise, Pinckney laid the groundwork for arguments that many others would repeat, claiming that slavery was of benefit to both masters and slaves and that Southern slaves were actually better off than most free blacks in the North (Matthews, 135).

Such a view clearly offended many Northerners, one of whom, Harrison Gray Otis of Massachusetts, subsequently wrote a letter to his wife claiming that a group of men, seeing a man who they thought was a robber entering an abandoned house, had surrounded it. According to Otis's account, Pinckney unsuccessfully attempted to avoid detection for being with a "mulatto wench" by jumping out a window but was caught and then released when the group recognized who he was (Matthews, 135). It is unknown whether Otis's story is true, but it shows the suspicions, and the possibilities for rumors, that the slave system bred.

Similarly, Pinckney's final will freed and provided for a slave woman named Dinah and all four of her children, including a son named Carlos, the Spanish equivalent of Charles. Pinckney's wife, Polly, like Thomas Jefferson's wife, Martha, had died at a relatively young age, and, like Jefferson, Pinckney had never remarried. This led to speculation that Pinckney may have had a long-term relationship with Dinah similar to that which many scholars now believe Jefferson had with Sally Hemmings (Matthews, 81–82). The possibility was but one unsavory feature of a system that the Framers, for all their wisdom, were unable to solve in their lifetimes.

FOR FURTHER READING

Farrand, Max, ed. 1937. *The Records of the Federal Convention.* 4 vols. New Haven, CT: Yale University Press.

Matthews, Marty D. 2004. *Forgotten Founder: The Life and Times of Charles Pinckney.* Columbia: University of South Carolina Press.

convention. Just before the convention, he married Mary Eleanor Laurens, the daughter of a wealthy Charleston merchant, Henry Laurens, who had previously served as president of the Continental Congress. Pinckney and his wife had three children, but she died in 1794. Pinckney served four times as a governor, and also served as a U.S. senator, as a state representative, and as a member of the U.S. House of Representatives. Initially a Federalist, Pinckney later supported Democratic-Republican Thomas Jefferson for the presidency. Jefferson rewarded Pinckney by appointing him as the U.S. minister to Spain. He later served in the U.S. House of Representatives, where in the dispute over the Missouri Compromise he helped develop the view that Congress could not exclude slavery, which he now defended as a positive good, from new states. Pinckney died in 1824, after decades of public service, hounded to the end by creditors for debts that he had largely inherited with his father's property.

See Also Committee of Detail; Pinckney Plan; South Carolina

FOR FURTHER READING

Bradford, M. M. 1981. *Founding Fathers: Brief Lives of the Framers of the United States Constitution.* 2nd ed. Lawrence: University Press of Kansas.

Farrand, Max, ed. 1937. *The Records of the Federal Convention*. 4 vols. New Haven, CT: Yale University Press.

Matthews, Marty D. 2004. *Forgotten Founder: The Life and Times of Charles Pinckney*. Columbia: University of South Carolina Press.

Williams, Frances Leigh. 1978. *A Founding Family: The Pinckneys of South Carolina*. New York: Harcourt Brace Jovanovich.

PINCKNEY, CHARLES COTESWORTH (1746–1825)

Charles Cotesworth Pinckney was born in 1746 to Charles and Elizabeth Lucas Pinckney. The former was an interim chief justice of South Carolina, and the latter managed her father's plantations after his death and later did the same when her husband died in 1758. Pinckney had 16 years of formal education. He was schooled at Christ Church College at Oxford College where he sat under the lectures of the great English jurist William Blackstone, at the Temple in London, and at the Royal Military Academy located in Caen, France. Upon his return to South Carolina, Pinckney entered a very successful law practice and was soon appointed as deputy to the state's attorney general. He also married Sarah Middleton, the daughter of a wealthy plantation owner, and thus became the brother-in-law to Edward Rutledge and Arthur Middleton, both of whom signed the Declaration of Independence. The Pinckneys had three children. After Sarah's death, Pinckney married Mary Stead. No children resulted from this second union.

An early supporter of colonial independence, Pinckney helped draft South Carolina's first constitution. Pinckney rose to the rank of brigadier general during the Revolutionary War. The British imprisoned him after the surrender of Charleston. He made friends with George Washington during the Revolutionary War and had his trust throughout his life. Pinckney's law practice continued to flourish after the war.

Charles Cotesworth Pinckney arrived at the

Charles Cotesworth Pinckney (1746–1825), American Revolutionary general who acted as minister to France, and was the Federalist candidate for president in 1804 and 1808 (Corbis)

Constitutional Convention on May 17 and was present on the opening day of business on May 25. He sought to protect his state's interest and participated in a fair number of debates, chiefly focusing on protecting the state's slave interest and on preventing import taxes.

Federalism

Pinckney's first recorded action at the Constitutional Convention was on May 30 when he seconded a motion by Delaware's George Read proposing an introductory motion to accompany the Virginia Plan for "a more effective government consisting of a Legislative, Judiciary, and Executive" (Farrand 1937, I, 30). Although this motion recognized the need for greater centralized powers, Read proposed it as a substitute for an earlier motion calling for the establishment of "a national government" (I, 30). It would thus appear that the resolution Pinckney supported was de-

Elizabeth Lucas Pinckney, a Founding Mother (1722–1793)

Only a handful of the mothers and wives of the Founding Fathers are as well-known as their sons and husbands, but many made contributions that warrant their classification as Founding Mothers. One such woman was Elizabeth (called Eliza) Lucas Pinckney, the mother of Charles Cotesworth Pinckney, one of the delegates who attended the Constitutional Convention from South Carolina, and Thomas Pinckney, who also played an important part in the Revolution.

Eliza's father was a British officer and she moved with her parents to South Carolina when she was 16. Extremely well educated and well versed in foreign languages and science, she is credited with planting the first successful indigo crop (used to make blue dye) on the American mainland while she managed her father's three plantations (her mother was sick), first as he went off to war and later as he served as governor of Antigua. This crop was to become one of the major stables of the state. Resisting an earlier marriage that her father had arranged–she told her father that "the riches of Peru and Chile if he had them put together could not purchase a sufficient esteem for him to make him my husband" (Roberts 2004, 3)–she married Charles Pinckney, who owned seven plantations, after he was widowed. She was 22 and he was 45 when they married, but the marriage was based not simply on Pinckney's ample property but also on love. The couple had three sons (one of whom died in infancy) and a daughter. Eliza helped manage her husband's property and arranged for the production and weaving of silk (one of her silk dresses remains). After Charles Pinckney failed to be appointed chief justice of South Carolina, the family moved to England where they stayed from 1753 until 1758. The Pinckneys left their two oldest boys in England to get an education, and Charles died shortly after they returned to South Carolina from malaria. Eliza went on successfully to manage his extensive property and set up a small hospital for those with smallpox (she had been inoculated in England), succeeding in saving 14 of 15 patients under her care (Roberts 2004, 9).

FOR FURTHER READING

Hakim, Joy. 2003. *From Colonies to Country.* Book 3 of *A History of US.* New York: Oxford University Press.
Roberts, Cokie. 2004. *Founding Mothers: The Women Who Raised Our Nation.* New York: William Morrow.

signed to give a somewhat less nationalistic cast to the proposal under consideration. Pinckney was on record the same day as doubting whether members of the Convention were authorized either by the act of Congress creating it or by their state commissions to discuss "a System founded on different principles from the federal Constitution [a reference to the government under the Articles of Confederation]" (I, 35).

On June 6, Pinckney indicated that he "wished to have a good national Govt. & at the same time to leave a considerable share of power in the States" (I, 137). He also expressed doubts about the feasibility of electing either house of Congress through popular election. He believed that the legislature typically exercised better judgment than the people and illustrated it with his experience from his home state of the former opposing, and the latter favoring, the issuance of paper money. He attributed this to the fact that members of the legislature had "some sense of character and were restrained by that consideration" (I, 137). He also believed that state governments would exercise greater jealousy of their powers and be ready "to thwart the National Govt. if excluded from a participation in it" (I, 137). On June 21, Pinckney noted that he "was for making the State Govts. a part of the General System." He further observed that, "If they were to be abolished, or lose their agency, S. Carolina & other States would have but a small share of the benefits of Govt." (I, 360).

Legislative Powers

Selection of Members

Pinckney opposed allowing the people to select members of either branch of Congress, favoring state legislative appointment of such delegates instead. Not only was this consistent with his view of federalism, but it also reflected his distrust of the people (Zahniser 1967, 92). Speaking at the Convention on June 6, General Pinckney thus observed:

> An election of either branch by the people scattered as they are in many States, particularly in S. Carolina was totally impracticable. He differed from gentlemen who thought that a choice by the people wd. be a better guard agst. bad measures, than by the Legislatures. A majority of the people of S. Carolina were notoriously for paper money as a legal tender; the Legislature had refused to make it a legal tender. The reason was that the latter had some sense of character and were restrained by that consideration. The State Legislatures also he said would be more jealous, & more ready to thwart the National Govt. if excluded from a participation in it. (I, 137)

Consistent with this view, Pinckney moved on June 21 to allow members of the House of Representatives to be selected "in such manner as the Legislature of each State should direct" (I, 358). He argued that this would allow the legislatures to "accommodate the mode to the conveniency & opinions of the people," that it would avoid undue influence by the larger counties, and that it would prevent disputed elections from having to be appealed to the legislature where it would cause trouble and expense (I, 358). The Convention defeated this motion by a vote of 6-4-1.

Origination of Money Bills

Pinckney opposed the idea of limiting the origination of money bills to the House of Representatives. He said that this distinction had been a source of controversy between the two branches

within his home state and had proven relatively easy to evade (I, 234). He later argued that this was not really a concession on the part of the small states (I, 546).

Ineligibility for Other Offices

On June 23, Pinckney opposed the provision that would have made members of the House of Representatives ineligible to accept state offices. He thought that this would prove inconvenient and that it would attain little (I, 386). Using a biblical analogy, he also suggested that such a provision would be setting up a kingdom divided against itself (I, 386).

Term Lengths

When the Convention was discussing the terms of senators on June 25, Pinckney supported terms of four years rather than six years or for good behavior. He was concerned about what today is sometimes called the "beltway syndrome," through which representatives who spend a long time in the nation's capital are thought to lose contact with their constituents:

> A longer term wd. fix them at the seat of Govt. They wd. acquire an interest there, perhaps transfer their property & lose sight of the States they represent. Under these circumstances the distant States wd. labour under great disadvantages. (I, 409)

Pinckney repeated this argument the following day (I, 421).

Pay and Property Qualifications

Pinckney revealed his aristocratic proclivities on June 26 when he proposed that senators should serve without pay. He reasoned that "as this branch was meant to represent the wealth of the Country, it ought to be composed of persons of wealth; and if no allowance was to be made the wealthy alone would undertake the service" (I, 426–427). On July 26, he further moved to extend property and citizenship qualifications not only to members of Congress but also to members of the other two branches (II, 122).

After the Convention defeated Pinckney's motion that senators should serve without pay by a 6-4 vote, Pinckney then advocated allowing states to pay the salaries of their senators and to recall them home. Notes indicate that Pinckney observed that "such a restriction would also discourage the ablest men from going into the Senate" (I, 429). This could mean that Pinckney actually hoped that the best men would remain in service at the state level. He had previously reported that he "was for making the States as much as could be conveniently done a part of the Genl. Gov't" (I, 429).

State Representation in Congress

On July 2, Pinckney reluctantly supported the appointment of a committee of a member from each state to resolve the issue of state representation in Congress (I, 511). He actually preferred a motion by Benjamin Franklin on June 30, however. It would have provided for equal state representation in one house and would have granted each state an equal vote when matters of state sovereignty were in question.

Pinckney was concerned when a committee raised the initial number of representatives in the House from 56 to 65 members, and his concern was motivated by regional considerations. He feared that the new allocation was less favorable to the Southern states. He did not expect these states to be represented equally, but he thought they needed to be brought closer to equality than the proposed allocation (I, 567). He proposed raising the number of representatives from North Carolina from five to six, those from South Carolina from five to six, and Georgia's from three to four (I, 568; also see II, 219).

Pinckney further tried on July 11 to strike the three-fifths clause so as to provide equal representation for slaves and free persons (I, 580). Pinckney wanted a specific formula, however, rather than a general reference to representation on the basis of wealth. He feared that otherwise "property in slaves" would be "exposed to danger" (I, 594).

Powers and Limits

On August 18, when the Convention was discussing whether it was appropriate to have troops in time of peace, Pinckney questioned whether the nation would have to wait until it was attacked before raising such troops (II, 330). He also favored allowing the Congress to regulate and discipline the militia, citing his own military experience to indicate that the dissimilarity among state militias "had produced the most serious mischiefs" during the Revolutionary War (II, 330). On this issue, "he saw no room for such distrust of the Genl. Govt." (II, 331; also see II, 386).

Slavery

In addition to supporting full representation for slaves, Pinckney worked in other ways to protect the institution of slavery. On July 23, he said that he would be duty-bound to vote against the Constitution if it did not provide "some security to the Southern States agst. an emancipation of slaves, and taxes on exports" (II, 95).

Pinckney discoursed more fully on the subject on August 22, just after his cousin had attempted to justify slavery by appealing to historical practice. The general observed that his influence and that of other Southern delegates would not be enough to achieve Southern ratification of the Constitution if slavery were not protected. He did not believe that his state and Georgia could do without slaves, and he argued that the only reason other Southern states were not insistent on slave importation is that they believed their own slaves would rise in value if imports ceased. Ignoring arguments about the morality or immorality of slavery, he further argued for the economic benefits of continuing importation:

The importation of slaves would be for the interest of the whole Union. The more slaves, the more produce to employ the carrying trade; The more consumption also, and the more of this, the more of revenue for the common treasury. (II, 371)

Pinckney did indicate that he thought that slaves should be subject to the same taxes as other imports, but repeated that if slave imports were prohibited, his state would not ratify the new Constitution (II, 372). Unlike his cousin, the general did not think it was likely that his state would stop such imports on its own, at least not permanently (II, 373). The general eventually succeeded in moving the prohibition of slave imports from the year 1800 to 1808 (II, 415). He somewhat cynically conceded that one reason he was willing to accept a tax on incoming slaves was that this would acknowledge that they were considered to be property (II, 416). He subsequently supported a motion designed to see that all duties and imposts were enacted uniformly throughout the U.S. (II, 418).

Although Pinckney thought it would be best for the South if there were no federal regulation of commerce, he nonetheless opposed fettering this with requirements for supermajorities. He partly based this argument on the good faith and liberality that he had observed in the Eastern states (II, 449–450).

On August 30, Pinckney supported the prohibition of religious tests as a condition for office (II, 468). On September 14, he opposed the appointment of the national treasurer by joint ballot. Appealing as he often did to his experience in South Carolina, Pinckney indicated that such a mechanism had resulted in bad appointments there but that the legislature refused to accept reports of faults of such an officer (II, 614).

Judiciary

Given Pinckney's extensive legal training, he said little at the Convention related to the judiciary, but he clearly thought judges were important. On August 27, Pinckney opposed a motion to prohibit pay raises for sitting judges. He reasoned that "the importance of the Judiciary will require

men of the first talents: large salaries will therefore be necessary, larger than the U.S. can allow in the first instance" (II, 429). He did not think it would be proper for more recently appointed judges to have higher salaries than those who had been on the bench for some time (II, 430).

Ratification

On July 16, the day of the Connecticut Compromise, Pinckney appears to have misunderstood a motion by Edmund Randolph to adjourn for the day as a motion to adjourn the Convention. He observed that he "could not think of going to S. Carolina, and returning again to this place" (II, 18). He also thought it was unlikely that, if the states were consulted, they would be able to agree to any plan before it was completed.

Life after the Convention

In 1790, Pinckney helped write a new constitution for South Carolina. He declined a number of appointments by Washington as a Supreme Court justice and as secretary of state or secretary of war, but he did agree to be an envoy to France where he was one of three American participants in the notorious XYZ Affair involving a French attempt to demand bribes as a condition for negotiation. After returning home, Pinckney was placed third in command, behind Washington and Hamilton, in preparation for a possible war with France.

Pinckney supported the Federalist Party and ran unsuccessfully as a vice presidential candidate in 1800 and as a presidential candidate in both 1804 and 1808 (he did not carry his home state in either election). Pinckney helped found the University of South Carolina and served on its board of trustees. In his later years, Pinckney served as president of the Society of the Cincinnati, a group of Revolutionary War veterans, and as president of the Charleston Bible Society. He also mounted a campaign against dueling. Pinckney died in Charleston in 1825.

See Also South Carolina

FOR FURTHER READING

Farrand, Max, ed. 1937. *The Records of the Federal Convention*. 4 vols. New Haven, CT: Yale University Press.

William, Frances Leigh. 1978. *A Founding Family: The Pinckneys of South Carolina*. New York: Harcourt Brace Jovanovich.

Zahniser, Marvin R. 1967. *Charles Cotesworth Pinckney: Founding Father*. Chapel Hill: University of North Carolina Press.

PINCKNEY PLAN

On May 29, 1787, the same day that Edmund Randolph introduced the Virginia Plan, South Carolina's Charles Pinckney also presented a plan of government. He may or may not have read the plan to the Convention (compare James Madison's and Robert Yates's accounts in Farrand 1937, I, 23 and 24) but it is not included in any of the notes of the Convention, including Madison's, which were the most comprehensive. The delegates committed Pinckney's plan, along with Randolph's, to the Committee of the Whole where it remained until being discharged without further apparent action on July 24. It was then referred to the Committee of Detail, where it appears to have been used to fill in gaps in existing proposals.

When John Quincy Adams edited the official records of the Convention in 1818, he wrote to Pinckney asking for a copy of his original plan. Pinckney in turn presented Adams with a plan, which has many similarities to the Convention's final product, and Adams published it. Given the numerous similarities between the Pinckney Plan and the Convention's final product, from time to time, scholars have attributed major influence to the Pinckney Plan. Some have even accused Madison of suppressing the important role of this delegate, who was known for his egotism and general unpopularity among fellow delegates (see especially Collier and Collier 1986, 64–74). Madison was convinced that the plan Pinckney provided to Adams was not his early draft but a document compiled toward the end of the Convention debates.

Madison appears to have been largely vindicated. Drawing from other scholarship, historian Max Farrand has presented four reasons to doubt that the plan Pinckney offered to Adams was his original. Farrand observed that the paper was not from the time of the Convention and appears to have been prepared in 1818 rather than at the time of the Convention; a number of its provisions are opposed to positions Pinckney was known to have taken at the Convention; the copy of the plan included provisions that were not reached until after weeks of dispute and compromise; and a copy of a speech Pinckney prepared for publication just before the Convention differs from the plan he presented to Adams in several significant respects (see III, Appendix D, 602). It appears that the plan that Pinckney offered to Adams was largely a summary of the report of the Committee of Detail rather than his original plan (III, 604).

It does seem clear that Pinckney came to the Convention with ideas for a strengthened national government. Pinckney's ideas can be pieced together from a report suggesting changes in the Articles of Confederation of a Grand Committee of Congress of which he had been a member, from a description that George Read of Delaware gave of a draft Pinckney had given him early in the Convention, from a pamphlet that Pinckney published after the Convention ended, and from a document later found in notes taken by James Wilson and included in the Committee of Detail (III, 603–604). Much of Pinckney's plan appears to have been taken from New York state and other contemporary state constitutions, meaning that it would have reflected ideas with which other delegates would have been familiar and some of which therefore might have been adopted without his input.

The central provisions of Pinckney's original plan appear to have called for a bicameral Congress represented according to population, with state legislatures selecting members of the House of Delegates whose members would choose the Senate from among four districts established either from among themselves or from the people. Pinckney's plan would apparently have incorporated the three-fifths formula for counting slaves (see Ohline 1971, 569). The two houses would choose the president (a single individual) for a seven-year term. As in the Virginia Plan, he would, in turn, be associated with a Council of Revision. The two houses would further have had the power to institute "a federal judicial Court." Two-thirds majorities of Congress would be required to regulate trade or to levy imposts. Many of the details are similar to those that are found within the final document.

See Also Committee of Detail; New Jersey Plan; Pinckney, Charles; Plans of Government Introduced at the Convention; Records of the Constitutional Convention; Virginia Plan

FOR FURTHER READING

Collier, Christopher, and James Lincoln Collier. 1986. *Decision in Philadelphia: The Constitutional Convention of 1787.* New York: Random House.

Farrand, Max, ed. 1937. *The Records of the Federal Convention.* 4 vols. New Haven, CT: Yale University Press.

Ohline, Howard A. 1971. "Republicanism and Slavery: Origins of the Three-fifths Clause in the United States Constitution." *William and Mary Quarterly,* 23rd ser., 8 (October): 563–584.

PIRACIES, PUNISHING

Article I, Section 8, Clause 10 provides that Congress shall have power "to define and punish Piracies and Felonies committed on the high Seas, and Offences against the Law of Nations." This power resembled that under the Articles of Confederation to appoint "courts for the trial of piracies and felonies committed on the high seas and establishing courts for receiving and determining finally appeals in all cases of captures." That provision arguably prepared the way in part for the system of lower federal courts that was established under the new Constitution. Significantly, Article III of the Constitution grants the judicial power of the United States "to all cases of admiralty and maritime Jurisdiction."

The congressional power to punish piracies, like most other enumerated powers, appears to have emerged from the report that the Committee of Detail headed by John Rutledge of South Carolina submitted to the Convention on August 6. It included the power "to declare the law and punishment of piracies and felonies committed on the high seas, and the punishment of counterfeiting the coin of the United States, and of offenses against the law of nations" (Farrand 1937, II, 182). It is not clear how offenses on the high seas became connected with counterfeiting.

The Convention debated these provisions on August 17. Madison initially moved to strike the words "and punishment" (II, 315), but records do not record his reasons for doing so. The debates that followed were quite legalistic in nature. Fellow Virginian George Mason objected that Madison's suggestion would be unwise "considering the strict rule of construction in criminal cases"; he also doubted the propriety of giving the national government exclusive jurisdiction in this area (II, 315). Gouverneur Morris thought the power over counterfeiting might have to extend further, so as, for example, to cover bills of exchange. Another unnamed delegate observed that Congress might need to punish the counterfeiting of foreign paper. Randolph doubted the efficacy of declaring the law without specifying the right to punish its violations, while James Wilson favored Madison's motion on the basis that "Strictness was not necessary in giving authority to enact penal laws; though necessary in enacting & expounding them" (II, 315). The Convention voted 7-3 to accept Madison's motion.

The Convention then voted 7-3 to accept Gouverneur Morris's motion to strike "to declare the law" and insert "punish" before "piracies." Madison and Randolph, in turn, proposed inserting "define &" before "punish." Wilson argued that the common law sufficiently defined felonies, and John Dickinson concurred. Mercer favored the amendment. Madison argued that the common law was both vague and defective. Although a statute under Queen Anne had somewhat remedied the deficiency, Madison did not think the U.S. should be bound by such foreign legislation. He further feared that if state laws were to prevail, there would be "neither uniformity nor stability in the law" (II, 316). Although Gouverneur Morris indicated that he preferred the word "designate" to the word "define," others apparently thought that the term "define" would better apply both to felonies and piracies, and the Convention adopted the motion. Oliver Ellsworth then introduced an enlarged motion giving Congress power "to define and punish piracies and felonies committed on the high seas, counterfeiting the securities and current coin of the U. States, and offenses agst. the law of Nations," which the Convention unanimously accepted (II, 316). The Committee of Style subsequently separated the provisions dealing with counterfeiting from those dealing with crimes on the high seas (compare II, 570 and 595).

See Also Committee of Detail; Congress, Power of the Purse

FOR FURTHER READING

D'Amato, Anthony. 1988. "The Alien Tort Statute and the Founding of the Constitution." *American Journal of International Law* 82 (January): 62–67.

Farrand, Max, ed. 1937. *The Records of the Federal Convention*. 4 vols. New Haven, CT: Yale University Press.

PLANS OF GOVERNMENT INTRODUCED AT THE CONVENTION

Although delegates literally introduced and debated hundreds of individual proposals, most such proposals were introduced within the contexts of larger architectonic structures, or plans. Each state had its own charter of constitution, most fairly republican in nature. However, there was an emerging consensus that such constitutions vested too much power within the state legislatures and offered too little balance on the part of the executive and judicial branches.

Existing Articles of Confederation

There was, of course, the existing system under the Articles of Confederation with which all the delegates were familiar. Delegates were almost in uniform agreement that this plan, which consisted of a single branch of government and vested primary power in the states, which were equally represented there, provided inadequate national authority. Initially, however, delegates were divided as to whether the system could be remedied simply by increasing the powers allocated to Congress or whether a whole new system was needed.

Virginia Plan

Despite the fact that the Convention had been called to revise, correct, and enlarge the Articles, Virginia's Edmund Randolph boldly introduced the Virginia Plan in the opening days of business. Scholars generally attribute this plan primarily to James Madison. The plan called for three branches of government and a bicameral Congress in which states would be represented according to population rather than equally, as under the Articles of Confederation. The plan also proposed a congressional negative of state laws. This plan set the Convention's initial agenda. After Randolph introduced it and the Convention discussed it, delegates found it almost impossible to think about the Articles of Confederation in the same way.

Pinckney Plan

It appears that Charles Pinckney of South Carolina introduced a plan on the same day that the Virginia Plan was introduced. His plan appears patterned in part after the government of New York. It would have provided for a bicameral Congress that would select the president for seven-year terms. The president would have been associated with a Council of Revision. The Virginia Plan largely preempted the Pinckney Plan, but it appears to have influenced the Committee of Detail when it put a rough draft of the Constitution together in late July and early August.

The New Jersey Plan

The central rival to the Virginia Plan was the New Jersey Plan, which William Paterson introduced on June 15. This plan more closely tracked the Articles of Confederation by providing for a unicameral Congress in which states would be equally represented. However, having been introduced after two weeks of discussion and agreement on the Virginia Plan, the New Jersey Plan incorporated a number of provisions of that plan, including the division of the national government into three branches. It also proposed the incubus of the provision that eventually became the supremacy clause of the Constitution. The differences in congressional representation between the Virginia and New Jersey Plans ultimately provided the basis for the Great Compromise which provided for representation in the U.S. House of Representatives on the basis of population and in the U.S. Senate equally.

Hamilton Plan

As delegates were considering the merits of the Virginia and New Jersey Plans, on June 18, Alexander Hamilton introduced a plan of government, largely patterned after that of Great Britain, that would have invested greater powers in the national government than either of the two other plans. It would have provided for life terms for the president and for members of the upper house of Congress. The national government would appoint state governors, who would have the power to veto state legislation. The Convention did not consider this highly nationalistic plan very seriously.

Dickinson Plan

John Dickinson of Delaware, who was the initial author of the Articles of Confederation, also prepared a plan for presentation to the Convention but apparently backed down when the Convention rejected the first proposal in this plan and he took ill. One of the most novel features of Dickinson's plan was the idea of a plural executive representing each of the three main geographical regions of the U.S.

The Virginia Plan clearly had the most influence of any plan on the Constitution. However, that document is clearly a composite product that rested on multiple visions and compromises.

See Also Articles of Confederation; Compromise; Dickinson, John; Dickinson Plan; Hamilton, Alexander; Hamilton Plan; Madison, James, Jr.; New Jersey Plan; Paterson, William; Pinckney, Charles; Pinckney Plan; Randolph, Edmund; State Constitutions; Virginia Plan

FOR FURTHER READING

Rossiter, Clinton. 1966. *1787: The Grand Convention.* New York: W. W. Norton.

POLAND

In formulating the Constitution, delegates to the Constitutional Convention drew on their knowledge of foreign governments and the problems they had faced. Delegates made about half a dozen recorded references to the government of Poland during their deliberations. Almost all were related to its selection of a chief executive.

At the time a Diet, or assembly of estates, which the landowners dominated, governed Poland, portions of which Russia, Austria, and Prussia had partitioned in 1772 (a prelude to even larger partitions of 1793 and 1795). The Diet was supreme and the king was weak. Poland was known for its onerous supermajority requirements which often made governing next to impossible (Palmer 1959, 30–32).

In discussing the selection of the chief executive on June 18, New York's Alexander Hamilton observed that in Poland the election of the monarch "is made by great rival *princes* with independent power, and ample means, of raising commotions" (Farrand 1937, I, 290). Pennsylvania's James Wilson attempted to answer arguments against popular election of the president on July 17 by attempting to answer an argument (perhaps

Picture of meeting of the Diet; king seated on throne in center surrounded by members of Diet (Time Life Pictures/Getty Images)

from Hamilton's speech, but more likely from someone else's comments that are unrecorded in the notes) drawn against such a policy based on the example of Poland. Acknowledging that elections of the chief executive in Poland had been "attended with the most dangerous commotions," he further argued that the cases were "totally dissimilar" (II, 30). He explained: "The Polish nobles have resources & dependents which enable them to appear in force, and to threaten the Republic as well as each other" (II, 30).

Also favoring popular election (at least by freeholders) on the same day, Pennsylvania's Gouverneur Morris expressed surprise that popular election of the president should be compared to the system of selection in Poland. He argued that

Poland's system of selection, utilizing the Diet, was more similar to legislative selection and would lead to similar negative consequences. He observed that "the great [apparently meaning either those who were more influential or those representing more populous areas] must be the electors in both cases, and the corruption & cabal wch are known to characterize the one would soon find their way into the other" (II, 31). Further speaking out against legislative selection of the president on July 25, Virginia's James Madison observed that although the Polish chief executive "has very little real power, his election has at all times produced the most eager interference of foreign princes, and has in fact at length slid entirely into foreign hands" (II, 110).

Although records are quite sketchy, when on June 28 Virginia's James Madison apparently asked for examples of great powers combining to oppress smaller ones, New Jersey's William Paterson apparently answered (at least in his notes), "Yes–the division of Poland" (I, 459).

In a letter written on Christmas of 1802 to the president of the New York Senate, Gouverneur Morris recalled that in formulating a mechanism to select the president, the Convention had formulated the Electoral College as "the mode least favorable to intrigue and corruption, that in which the unbiased voice of the people will be most attended to, and that which is least likely to terminate in violence and usurpation" (III, 294). He further observed:

To impress conviction on this subject, the case of Poland was not unaptly cited. Great and ambitious Princes took part in the election of a Polish King. Money, threats, and force were employed; violence, bloodshed, and oppression ensued; and now the country is parceled out among the neighboring Potentates, one of whom was but a petty Prince two centuries ago. (III, 394)

Similarly, in a speech to Congress in March 1800, South Carolina's Charles Pinckney raised the specter of foreign intrigue in presidential elections that found their way for resolution in the House of Representatives. He warned that if such election did not proceed by secret ballot (which would not be as subject to such foreign influences), "we shall soon have the scenes of Polish Diets and elections re-acted here, and in not many years the fate of Poland may be that of the United America" (III, 390).

The fact that at least two such delegates remembered and referred to Poland on subsequent occasions suggests that its example may have been influential.

See Also President, Selection

FOR FURTHER READING

Farrand, Max, ed. 1937. *The Records of the Federal Convention.* 4 vols. New Haven, CT: Yale University Press.

Ludwikowski, Rett R., and William F. Fox, Jr. 1993. *The Beginning of the Constitutional Era: A Bicentennial Comparative Analysis of the First Modern Constitutions.* Washington, DC: Catholic University of America Press.

Palmer, R. R. 1959. *The Age of the Democratic Revolution: A Political History of Europe and America, 1760–1800.* Princeton, NJ: Princeton University Press.

POLYBIUS
(CA. 198–117 B.C.)

The Roman historian Polybius, who lived from approximately 198 to 117 B.C., is one of the theorists who at least indirectly influenced the thinking of delegates to the Constitutional Convention. Believing that any simple form of government like monarchy, aristocracy, or democracy was likely to degenerate into its opposite form, Polybius advocated mixed government. He thought it would help to balance these forms and provide stability.

John Adams, who published the first volume of his *Defence of the Constitutions of Government of the United States of America* in the United States in January 1787, just months before the opening of the Convention (Chinard 1940, 42), had warmly commended Polybius's theories. The delegates to the Constitutional Convention and to subsequent state ratifying conventions made constant allusions to Greek history. They often interpreted such history through the lenses of another contemporary, the French philosopher Charles Louis de Secondat de Montesquieu. Montesquieu advocated separation of powers, an idea that along with checks and balances was incorporated into the division of the new government into three branches, the legislative, executive, and judicial. The first three articles of the Constitution reflected this division. Similarly, although it strengthened the national government, the Constitution also divided power between the national government and the states in a system now called federalism.

See Also Adams, John; Classical Allusions and Influences; Federalism; Forms of Government;

Montesquieu, Charles Louis de Secondat de; Separation of Powers

FOR FURTHER READING

Chinard, Gilbert. 1940. "Polybius and the American Constitution." *Journal of the History of Ideas* 1 (January): 38–58.

POPULATION OF THE UNITED STATES

Partly as a result of the provision in Article I, Section 2, of the new Constitution requiring that a census be conducted every 10 years, scholars have a relatively good idea of the population of the United States relatively soon after the writing of the Constitution. The first census bill was adopted on March 1, 1790, and Secretary of State Thomas Jefferson issued its report on October 24, 1791.

This census reported a total of 3,893,635 persons in 16 states or future states (including Vermont and Kentucky, which had been admitted, and Maine which had not) and an additional 35,691 in the Southwest Territory. Populations in the states ranged from a low of 59,094 in Delaware to a high of 747,610 in Virginia. The slave population ranged from none in Maine and Massachusetts to 292,627 in Virginia.

The delegates to the Convention had originally allocated representation in the U.S. House of Representatives with the hope of giving one representative for every 40,000 free inhabitants (with slaves counted as three-fifths of a person). After the initial allocation of the House was settled, this number was changed at the Convention to no more than one for every 30,000 inhabitants. Both because of this new formula and because of errors in earlier population estimates, representation accordingly increased in the House of Representatives from 65 to 106 after the first census (*Guide to Congress* 1991, 741). The change in individual state representation was most dramatic in Virginia, the most populous state, which moved from 10 to 19 seats.

See Also Census; Congress, House of Representatives, Size

FOR FURTHER READING

Guide to Congress. 1991. 4th ed. Washington, DC: Congressional Quarterly.
Return of the Whole Number of Persons within the Several Districts of the United States. 1802. Washington City: William Duane. Reprinted by New York: Arno Press, 1976.

POST OFFICES AND POST ROADS

Article I, Section 8 of the Constitution grants Congress power "to establish Post Offices and post Roads." This power is a successor to the power of Congress under the Articles of Confederation of "establishing or regulating post-offices from one state to another, throughout all the united states, and exacting such postage on the papers passing thro' the same as may be requisite to defray the expences of the said office."

The Virginia Plan, which Edmund Randolph introduced on May 29, did not specifically list the power to establish a post office. The New Jersey Plan, which William Paterson presented to the Convention on June 15, contained a provision for raising revenue whereby Congress would have power to issue "stamps on paper, vellum or parchment, and by a postage on all letters or packages passing through the general post-Office, to be applied to such federal purposes as they shall deem proper & expedient" (Farrand 1937, I, 243). Like most of the other powers enumerated in Article I, Section 8, that of establishing a post office was reported by the Committee of Detail on August 6 (II, 182), and accepted on August 16. On that date Elbridge Gerry of Massachusetts proposed adding the power to establish post roads, and

Maryland's John Mercer seconded him. The Convention accepted this addition by a vote of 6-5.

Unlike the Articles of Confederation, the Constitution does not specifically grant the government the power to issue postage stamps, but this right is easily comprehended under the doctrine of implied powers. Perhaps because he doubted the extent of such powers in other areas, Benjamin Franklin moved on September 14 (just three days before the delegates signed the Constitution) to provide "a power to provide for cutting canals where deemed necessary." Fellow Pennsylvanian James Wilson seconded the proposal, which the Convention rejected after a debate in which at least five delegates other than Franklin expressed their opinions (II, 615–616).

Like its power over interstate and foreign commerce, the congressional power to establish and operate a post office facilitates communication and commerce within the nation. The national post office arguably binds the nation more closely together than if this function were carried out by individual states.

See Also Congress, Power of the Purse

FOR FURTHER READING

Farrand, Max, ed. 1937. *The Records of the Federal Convention.* 4 vols. New Haven, CT: Yale University Press.

Hutchinson, David. 1975. *The Foundations of the Constitution.* Secaucus, NJ: University Books.

POSTERITY AND PERPETUITY

The idea of posterity has been described as "a preoccupation of American republicans" (Lienesch 1980, 4). Michael Lienesch has described the period in which delegates wrote the Constitution as a time in which American leaders moved from the idea of providing posterity with "examples to follow" to the idea of presenting them with "rules to obey" (Lienesch, 4). Like their concern for fame (Adair 1967), references at the Constitutional Convention to the perpetuity of the document and to posterity provide one indication of the seriousness with which leading delegates considered their tasks.

Article XII of the Articles of Confederation had provided that "the union shall be perpetual" (Solberg 1958, 51). This wording gave some leeway to members of the Convention. South Carolina's Pierce Butler thus observed on June 5 that "the word perpetual in the confederation meant only the constant existence of our Union, and not the particular words which compose the Articles of the union" (Farrand 1937, I, 129).

Still, delegates to the Convention undoubtedly hoped that their own creation would last longer than the government that the Articles of Confederation had created. Virginia's James Madison observed that "the government we mean to erect is intended to last for ages" (I, 431; also see I, 464). In notes for a speech he prepared, Delaware's John Dickinson observed: "We are not forming plans for a Day Month Year or Age, but for Eternity" (Hutson 1987, 129). On a sourer note, as the Convention progressed, William Blount of North Carolina wrote a letter from the Convention dated July 19, in which he said: "I still think we shall ultimately end not many Years just be separate and distinct Governments perfectly independent of each other" (Hutson, 175).

After Elbridge Gerry of Massachusetts raised concerns that the Western states might eventually dominate the Union to the detriment of the states at the Convention, Connecticut's Roger Sherman first expressed doubt that this would happen soon and then followed with a reference to the future:

Besides We are providing for our posterity, for our children & our grand Children, who would be as likely to be citizens of new Western States, as of the old States. On this consideration alone, we ought to make no such discrimination as was proposed by the motion. Accepting the premise that the delegates should look to the future, Gerry responded that it would also be necessary to provide for the interests of children who stayed behind in the original states. (II, 3)

Later opposing a provision that would disqualify debtors and those with unsettled accounts from voting, Pennsylvania's James Wilson argued that such a provision would "put too much power in the hands of the Auditors." He followed with an appeal to posterity:

> We should consider that we are providing a Constitution for future generations, and not merely for the peculiar circumstances of the moment. The time has been, and will again be when the public safety may depend on the voluntary aids of individuals which will necessarily open accts. with the public, and when such accts. will be a characteristic of patriotism. (II, 125)

When discussing the issue of representation on August 8, Madison argued that requiring one representative for every 40,000 persons could result in too large a House of Representatives. When Nathaniel Gorham of Massachusetts doubted that the nation would last this long (a period he estimated would take 150 years), Connecticut's Oliver Ellsworth pointed out that, if it did, the amending process could be utilized. That same day, in one of his most memorable, if largely ineffective, speeches at the Convention, Gouverneur Morris of Pennsylvania stated that "He would sooner submit himself to a tax for paying for all the Negroes in the U. States, than saddle posterity with such a Constitution" (II, 223). As primary author of the Preamble to the Constitution, Morris is responsible for the line that ordained the Constitution "for ourselves and our posterity."

Postscript

Although one draft of the Constitution prepared by the Committee of Detail contained the provision in Article XIII of the Articles of Confederation that the Union should be "perpetual" (II, 136), this provision did not find its way into the final product (Morris 1987, 46). Abraham Lincoln later pointed to the provision in the Preamble for "a more perfect union" (Stampp 1978, 10). Lincoln further felt bound by his oath of office to protect and defend the U.S. Constitution, which

he interpreted as denying states the right to secede without getting the consent of others. After examining the records of the Constitutional Convention on the subject, Kenneth Stampp has concluded that "the delegates never engaged in a discussion that produced a clear consensus that the Union formed by the Constitution was to have perpetual life; nor did they arrive at an understanding about the related matter of federal options if one or more states should attempt secession" (1978, 13). This matter was arguably resolved more by force of arms than by abstract theory. After the Civil War, Chief Justice Salmon Chase proclaimed in *Texas v. White* (74 U.S.) 700 (1868) that the Constitution "looks to an indestructible Union, composed of indestructible States" (725).

See Also Amending Process; Fame; Preamble

FOR FURTHER READING

Adair, Douglas. 1967. "Fame and the Founding Fathers." *Fame and the Founding Fathers.* Ed. Edmund P. Willis. Bethlehem, PA: Moravian College, 27–52.

Farrand, Max, ed. 1937. *The Records of the Federal Convention.* 4 vols. New Haven, CT: Yale University Press.

Hutson, James H., ed. 1987. *Supplement to Max Farrand's* The Records of the Federal Convention of 1787. New Haven, CT: Yale University Press.

Lienesch, Michael. 1980. "The Constitutional Tradition: History, Political Action, and Progress in American Political Thought 1787–1793." *Journal of Politics* 42 (February): 2–30.

Morris, Richard B. 1987. "A Few Parchment Pages: Two Hundred Years Later." *American Heritage* 38 (May-June): 46–51.

Solberg, Winton U., ed. 1958. *The Federal Convention and the Formation of the Union of the American States.* New York: Liberal Arts Press.

Stampp, Kenneth M. 1978. "The Concept of a Perpetual Union." *Journal of American History* 65 (June): 5–33.

POWER

Government involves the exercise of power. Although force is a component of such power, democratic governments attempt to provide legitimacy for the exercise of power by grounding it on justice and on what the Declaration of Independence referred to as "the consent of the governed." Political scientists generally describe power exercised by institutions that are recognized as being legitimate as "authority." The American Framers sought to create such a legitimate authority to replace what they regarded as the inadequate government under the Articles of Confederation. Those who wrote the U.S. Constitution sought to grant adequate powers to the new government to meet the needs that they specified in the Preamble of the new Constitution while so dividing and limiting these powers that they did not threaten individual liberty.

Increased Powers for the National Government

Delegates to the Convention were in general agreement that the government under the Articles of Confederation, which had emphasized state sovereignty, was too weak, especially in the areas of taxation, control of interstate commerce, and ability to project American power in international affairs. Both the Virginia and New Jersey Plans provided for increased powers at the national level. The Virginia Plan initially contained a general statement providing that

> the National Legislature ought to be impowered to enjoy the Legislative Rights vested in Congress by the Confederation & moreover to legislate in all cases to which the separate States are incompetent, or in which the harmony of the United States may be interrupted by the exercise of individual Legislation. (Farrand 1937, I, 21)

Building on a similar list within the Articles of Confederation, in time, the Committee of Detail opted for a detailed listing of such powers, albeit with the possibility, raised by the Necessary and Proper Clause, that Congress might also exercise implied powers.

Much of the Convention centered on who would exercise power within the new govern-

ment. In addition to the issue of which powers would be exercised by the national government and which would be exercised by the states, delegates debated the proper allocation of power within the three branches of the national government that they were establishing. Early Convention debates over representation in Congress centered largely on whether power would be exercised equally by each state, as under the Articles of Confederation, or whether large states would have greater representation; the Connecticut Compromise eventually provided for representation by population in the House of Representatives and equal state representation in the Senate. The issue of state representation was in turn related to larger sectional issues. Balancing the powers of the North and the South was affected in part by the three-fifths compromise relative to how slaves would be counted for purposes of representation and taxation. Delegates also debated whether to vest a permanent majority in the existing states or whether to allow new Western states to be admitted on an equal basis with those then in existence. James Madison hoped that the variety of interests embraced by the new republic over such a large land area would ensure that no single interest would oppress the others, but even he sought ancillary protections against such a possibility.

Fear of Governmental Powers

The Founding Fathers would have agreed with the maxim that Lord Acton (John Emerick Edward Dalberg-Acton, 1824–1902) later articulated, that "power tends to corrupt and absolute power corrupts absolutely" (quoted in Siemers 2003, 9). Antifederalists often warned against giving too much "confidence" to the new government (Siemers, 13), but they were not alone. Opposing a proposal by Gouverneur Morris of Pennsylvania that would have allowed Congress to determine future methods of representation, Virginia's James Madison thus observed on July 11 that he "was not a little surprised to hear this implicit confidence urged by a member who on all occasions, had inculcated So strongly the political depravity of men, and the necessity of checking one vice and interest by opposing to them another vice & interest" (I, 584).

Although the Founding Fathers admired individuals like George Washington who had sacrificed on behalf of the common good, they were generally suspicious of human nature and of human governors. In a lengthy speech that he delivered to the Constitutional Convention on June 18, Alexander Hamilton of New York observed that "men love power" (I, 284). He further opined: "Give all power to the many, they will oppress the few. Give all power to the few, they will oppress the many" (I, 288). Speaking at the Convention on July 11, Virginia's George Mason observed: "From the nature of man we may be sure, that those who have power in their hands will not give it up while they can retain it. On the Contrary we know they will always when they can rather increase it" (I, 578). After arguing that the Framers had designed the new government so that ambition would counter ambition, James Madison observed in *Federalist* No. 51:

> It may be a reflection on human nature that such devices should be necessary to control the abuses of government. But what is government itself but the greatest of all reflections on human nature? If men were angels, no government would be necessary. If angels were to govern men, neither external nor internal controls on government would be necessary. In framing a government which is to be administered by men over men, the great difficulty lies in this: you must first enable the government to control the governed; and in the next place oblige it to control itself. (Hamilton, Madison, and Jay 1961, 322)

If anything, Antifederalist opponents of the Constitution were even more suspicious of power, especially at the national level, than were its Federalist supporters.

Electoral and Structural Restraints on Governmental Power

The Framers of the Constitution thus sought to provide both internal and external restraints on such power. The primary restraint on government was to come from its dependence on the people. Because the Framers anticipated that the legislative branch would be the most powerful, they were particularly concerned about making it accountable. They accordingly provided that voters would choose members of the House of Representatives every two years and state legislatures would choose members of the Senate every six. The Framers also provided for a four-year term for the president, who would be indirectly selected through the Electoral College. Members of the judicial branch were chosen even more indirectly through the operation of the legislative and executive branches; although more insulated from popular opinion, they would be subject to impeachment and removal from office for conviction of specified crimes. The Framers of the Constitution did not follow those who had written the Articles of Confederation in limiting the number of terms that individuals could serve in given years, although the Twenty-second Amendment later limited the president to no more than ten years in office, or two full terms.

At the national level, the Founders devised a system of separating power among the legislative, executive, and judicial branches so that branches would serve to check and balance one another. They further divided Congress, which they believed would be the most powerful branch, into two houses and required the houses' mutual consent for the passage of legislation.

Just as the Framers divided powers horizontally among the legislative, executive, and judicial branches, so too they divided powers vertically between the national government and the states. As with separation of powers, the Framers designed a federal government to ensure that neither the national government nor the state governments overstepped their bounds.

Other Limitations on Governmental Power

In addition to structural devices, the Framers incorporated a number of specific limitations on the new government. Most such provisions limiting Congress are found in Article I, Section 9 of the

Constitution. Most provisions limiting the states (some of which are identical to limits on the national government) are found in Article I, Section 10. Antifederalist concerns that these provisions were inadequate led shortly after ratification of the Constitution to the inclusion of the Bill of Rights, which initially limited only the national government. Subsequent amendments, most notably the post–Civil War amendments (Thirteen through Fifteen), and subsequent judicial interpretations of the Bill of Rights have further limited the powers of both state and national governments.

See Also Antifederalists; Bill of Rights; Checks and Balances; Committee of Detail; Congress, Bicameralism; Congress, House of Representatives, Selection of; Connecticut Compromise; Corruption; Federalism; Federalists; Human Nature; Liberty; Separation of Powers; Three-fifths Clause

FOR FURTHER READING

Farrand, Max, ed. 1937. *The Records of the Federal Convention.* 4 vols. New Haven, CT: Yale University Press.

Hamilton, Alexander, James Madison, and John Jay. 1961. *The Federalist Papers.* Ed. Clinton Rossiter. New York: New American Library.

Read, James H. 1995. "'Our Complicated System': James Madison on Power and Liberty." *Political Theory* 23 (August): 452–475.

Siemers, David J. 2003. *The Antifederalists: Men of Great Faith and Forbearance.* Lanham, MD: Rowman and Littlefield Publishers.

POWERS, IMPLIED

The textual foundation of the doctrine of implied powers is found in the last clause (18) of Article I, Section 8. It vests Congress with the power "to make all Laws which shall be necessary and proper for carrying into Execution the foregoing Powers, and all other Powers vested by this Constitution in the Government of the United States, or in any Department or Officer thereof." This clause has been variously dubbed the "necessary and proper clause," or, in light of the flexibility that it has subsequently accorded to congressional exercises of power, the "elastic" or "sweeping" clause. This provision stands in relatively stark contrast to the provision in Article II of the Articles of Confederation. It provided that "Each state retains its sovereignty, freedom, and independence, and every Power, Jurisdiction and right, which is not by this confederation *expressly* delegated to the United States, in Congress assembled" (italics added), and which thus strictly bounded congressional powers under that plan of government.

The Virginia Plan, which Edmund Randolph introduced to the Convention on May 29, did not list the specific powers of Congress but rather vested this body with the powers of the existing Congress under the Articles of Confederation and with the power "to legislate in all cases to which the separate States are incompetent, or in which the harmony of the United States may be interrupted by the exercise of individual Legislation" (Farrand 1937, I, 21). By contrast, the New Jersey Plan subsequently proposed to give Congress a limited number of additional powers.

The necessary and proper clause emerged almost full-grown from the Committee of Detail, which reported to the Convention on August 6, and which chose to enumerate the powers of Congress (II, 182). Despite the debates that swirled about this provision when the Constitution was being ratified and after the government was established, delegates at the Convention devoted little attention to it. On August 20, the Convention voted unanimously for it after rejecting as unnecessary a motion by James Madison and Charles Pinckney that would have added the words "and establish all offices" between the words "laws" and "necessary" (II, 345).

It was not until September 10 that records indicate that Randolph listed this clause on a laundry list of provisions to which he objected (II, 563). Five days later, Elbridge Gerry also listed this clause as among those by which "the rights of Citizens" were "rendered insecure" (II, 633), but he does not appear to have offered much explanation.

Antifederalists, however, raised similar worries during the ratification debates.

Addressing concerns about both the necessary and proper clause and the supremacy clause, Alexander Hamilton argued in *Federalist* No. 33 that "it may be affirmed with perfect confidence that the constitutional operation of the intended government would be precisely the same if these clauses were entirely obliterated as if they were repeated in every article" (Hamilton, Madison, and Jay 1961, 202). Hamilton further downplayed the significance of these clauses:

> What is the power but the ability or faculty of doing a thing? What is the ability to do a thing but the power of employing the means necessary to its execution? What is a LEGISLATIVE power but a power of making LAWS? What is the power of laying and collecting taxes but a *legislative power,* or a power of *making laws* to lay and collect taxes? What are the proper means of executing such a power but *necessary* and *proper* laws? (203)

Hamilton explained that the clause had been introduced simply "for greater caution, and to guard against all caviling refinements in those who might hereafter feel a disposition to curtail and evade the legitimate authorities of the Union" (203).

When the first Congress contemplated adding the Tenth Amendment, reserving rights to the states, James Madison was among those who fought back attempts to follow the language of the Articles of Confederation and reserve to the states all powers not "expressly" delegated. Although he had downplayed the significance of the clause in *The Federalist,* as secretary of the Treasury under George Washington, Hamilton relied on the necessary and proper clause to advance the constitutionality of the national bank (Clarke and Hall 1832, 95–112), while Secretary of State Thomas Jefferson (allied with James Madison in Congress) relied on the Tenth Amendment to oppose it (1832, 91–94). Chief Justice John Marshall in turn relied on this clause in upholding the constitutionality of this bank in *McCulloch v. Maryland,* 4 Wheat. (17 U.S.) 316 (1819). Under the test that Marshall established in that case, the government must show that its exercise of an un-enumerated power is related as a means to an end to those powers that are specified and that the exercise of such a power is not directly prohibited by the Constitution.

See Also Congress, Collective Powers; Corporations; Marshall, John

FOR FURTHER READING

Beck, J. Randy. 2002. "The New Jurisprudence of the Necessary and Proper Clause." *University of Illinois Law Review* 2002: 581–649.

Clarke, M. St., and D. D. Hall. 1832. *Legislative and Documentary History of the Bank of the United States Including the Original Bank of North America.* New York: Augustus M. Kelley.

Farrand, Max, ed. 1937. *The Records of the Federal Convention.* 4 vols. New Haven, CT: Yale University Press.

Hamilton, Alexander, James Madison, and John Jay. 1961. *The Federalist Papers.* Ed. Clinton Rossiter. New York: New American Library.

PRAYER AT THE CONVENTION

Sessions of Congress begin with prayer, and so it is not surprising that many people think that sessions of the Constitutional Convention followed this example. In point of fact, no public prayers appear to have been uttered during the Convention, although it is likely that some members often had silent prayers as they struggled with the complex issues of the day.

Franklin's Speech Suggesting Prayer

On June 28, 1787, Benjamin Franklin gave a memorable address, on the subject of prayer, at a time when the Convention was grappling with the perplexing issue of state representation. Franklin, the epitome of the Enlightenment in America, noted that members of the Convention had sought guidance from both ancient and modern experience but that they continued "groping as it were in the dark to find political truth" (Farrand 1937, I, 451). In such circumstances, he found it surprising "that we have not hitherto once thought of humbly applying to the Father of lights to illuminate our understandings" (I, 451). He further recalled the prayers that the revolutionaries had uttered in the very room in which he was speaking during the war with England. Citing the favor that Providence had bestowed on them on those occasions, Franklin asked, "have we now forgotten that powerful friend? or do we imagine that we no longer need his assistance?" (I, 451).

Franklin proceeded almost as though he were an evangelical minister rather than the sage man of the world:

> I have lived, Sir, a long time, and the longer I live, the more convincing proofs I see of this truth–*that God governs in the affairs of men.* And if a sparrow cannot fall to the ground with his notice, is it possible that an empire can rise without his aid? We have been assured, Sir, in the sacred writings, that "except the Lord build the House they labour in vain that build it." I firmly believe this; and I also believe that without his concurring aid we shall succeed in this political building no better than the Builders of Babel. (I, 451)

Franklin accordingly moved, in a motion that Roger Sherman of Connecticut (whose piety was more conventional than Franklin's) seconded, "that henceforth prayers imploring the assistance of Heaven, and its blessings on our deliberations, be held in this Assembly every morning before we proceed to business, and that one or more of the Clergy of this City be requested to officiate in that service" (I, 452).

Claims about the Effect of This Speech

A letter that William Steele wrote to his son in 1825 passed on a story that Steele attributed to Jonathan Dayton, one of the Convention delegates from New Jersey. The letter, which was widely publicized, agrees in essentials with the information above but then proceeds to say that "Mr. H–," presumably Alexander Hamilton (who by the time of Steele's letter had been killed in a duel with Aaron Burr), had responded by giving a speech extolling human wisdom and the talents of the members of the Convention and suggesting that he saw no necessity for "calling in *foreign aid*" (III, 471–472). George Washington was reported to have eyed Hamilton "with a mixture of *surprise* and *indignation*" as others ignored "this impertinent and impious speech" (III, 472) to adopt Franklin's proposal. The Convention was said then to have recessed for three days, after which a chaplain opened the following sessions, and Franklin paved the way for a compromise between the large and small states.

What Actually Appears to Have Happened

In point of fact, Franklin's proposal neither led to a break in the Convention's proceedings, nor do the delegates appear to have adopted his proposal. Madison's notes do record that Hamilton disagreed with Franklin's motion, but his arguments (if not expressing complete faith in Divine Providence) were not outwardly impious or impudent. Instead, Hamilton feared that inviting a chaplain to the proceedings at this point would "1. bring on it [the Convention] some disagreeable animadversions. & 2. lead the public [which, because of the rule of secrecy that the delegates had adopted, was otherwise uninformed about the Convention's day-to-day business] to believe that the embarrassments and dissentions within the convention had suggested the measure" (III, 452).

The record does not indicate that Washington upbraided Hamilton. Rather Franklin and Sherman argued that past omission of a duty was not a proper reason for a future omission, that rejecting the proposal could "expose the Convention to unpleasant animadversions than the adoption of it" and, less understandably, that any outside alarm might be as helpful as it was harmful (although perhaps the implication was that people outside the Convention would also pray). North Carolina's Hugh Williamson observed that the real reason no chaplain had been hired was that "the Convention had no funds" (I, 452). In a letter of January 6, 1834, James Madison further noted apparent concern among the delegates of "the Quaker usage" still prominent in the area (this is not altogether clear, but might refer to the Quaker opposition to war) as well as "the discord of religious opinions within the Convention, as well as among the Clergy of the Spot" (III, 531).

Edmund Randolph suggested, as an alternative, that the Convention request a sermon for the July 4 celebrations to be thereafter followed by daily prayers in the Convention. Franklin seconded this motion, but the Convention adjourned without voting on it, and it received no further recorded mention in the Convention.

Postscript

Throughout the late eighteenth and nineteenth centuries, and even into the twentieth, some individuals have been concerned that the delegates to the Constitutional Convention did not (unless one includes the reference to "the Year of our Lord one thousand seven hundred and eighty-seven" often appended to Article VII) include a reference to God in the Constitution (Vile 2003, 64). By way of contrast, the later authors of the Constitution of the Confederate States of America did include a reference to "the favor and guidance of Almighty God."

The U.S. Constitution still includes no such direct reference to God, but issues like prayer in public schools and at public events, the posting of the Ten Commandments in public places, references to the words "under God" in the Pledge of Allegiance to the flag, and even the hiring of chaplains to pray at legislative sessions continue to agitate the public mind. Although some oppose all religious devotion out of unbelief, others continue to be concerned that public manifestations will require the state to choose among religious partisans in a society with an even greater variety of religious beliefs than that of the Framers.

See Also Biblical and Religious References at the Consstitutional Convention; Franklin, Benjamin; Hamilton, Alexander; Protestantism; Religious Affiliations of the Delegates

FOR FURTHER READING

Farrand, Max, ed. 1937. *The Records of the Federal Convention.* 4 vols. New Haven, CT: Yale University Press.

Hutson, James H. 1998. *Religion and the Founding of the American Republic.* Washington, DC: Library of Congress.

Murrin, John M. 1992. "Fundamental Values, the Founding Fathers, and the Constitution." In Herman Belz, Ronald Hoffman, and Peter J. Albert, eds. *To Form a More Perfect Union: The Critical Ideas of the Constitution.* Charlottesville: University Press of Virginia.

Vile, John R. 2003. *Encyclopedia of Constitutional Amendments, Proposed Amendments, and Amending Issues, 1789–2002.* 2nd ed. Santa Barbara: ABC-CLIO.

PREAMBLE

One of the most inspiring and most frequently quoted parts of the U.S. Constitution is the Preamble with which it begins. This provision has been likened to "a grand entranceway to some great building" (Amar 2002, 681). Although it has no independent legal authority, this provision begins with a reference to "We the People of the United States" and announces the purposes of the new government to "form a more perfect Union, establish Justice, insure domestic Tranquility, provide for the common defence, promote the general Welfare, and secure the Blessings of Liberty to ourselves and our Posterity." Delegates do not appear to have debated the Preamble on the floor of the Convention, but its evolution can be traced through the Convention's proceedings.

Delegates met in Philadelphia to "revise and enlarge" the Articles of Confederation, so it is not surprising that the Preamble makes reference to "a more perfect Union." In introducing the Virginia Plan, Edmund Randolph announced plans to

The words of the Preamble of the Constitution have come to assume iconic status. (Courtesy of John R. Vile)

provide for the "common defence, security of liberty and general welfare" (Farrand 1937, I, 20), and delegates outlined other goals during the course of the proceedings. When South Carolina's John Rutledge issued the report of the Committee of Detail on August 6, the proposed Preamble included the terms "Ourselves and our Posterity," but states were individually enumerated after the term "We the People" (II, 177). Notes in the handwriting of Virginia's Edmund Randolph indicated the belief (whether Randolph's, the committee's, or both, it is difficult to tell) that the Preamble was not the place for "designating the ends of government and human polities" or pledging mutual faith but for declaring the general inadequacy of the existing government and presenting the new Constitution as a cure (II, 137–138).

The modern Preamble emerged in full form from the report of the Committee of Style and Arrangement on September 12. Although Connecticut's Dr. Johnson chaired the committee,

Gouverneur Morris is recognized as the major stylist of this provision. By referring to "We the People of the United States," without listing individual states by name, Morris both gave the document a stronger nationalistic emphasis and avoided problems that might emerge if not all the states ratified or if, as happened, some did not ratify until after the new government was established. At least indirectly, it also made it easier for new states to enter the Union on an equal basis with the original 13.

During ratification debates a number of Antifederalists, including Virginia's Patrick Henry, cited this language as presumptuous and expressed concern that it was intended to establish a too powerful central government. By adding references to widely shared popular aspirations like justice and liberty, Morris's additions undoubtedly contributed to the document's appeal.

See Also Committee of Detail; Committee of Style and Arrangement; Morris, Gouverneur; "We the People"

FOR FURTHER READING

Amar, Akhil Reed. 2002. "Architexture +." *Indiana Law Journal* 77 (Fall): 671–700.

Brookhiser, Richard. 2003. *Gentleman Revolutionary: Gouverneur Morris—The Rake Who Wrote the Constitution.* New York: The Free Press.

Farrand, Max, ed. 1937. *The Records of the Federal Convention.* 4 vols. New Haven, CT: Yale University Press.

PRESENTMENT CLAUSE

See PRESIDENTIAL VETO

PRESIDENT, CABINET

See PRESIDENT, COUNCIL

PRESIDENT, COMMANDER IN CHIEF

The designation of presidential powers in Article II, Section 2, Clause 1, actually begins with an office. It specifies that "the President shall be Commander in Chief of the Army and Navy of the United States, and of the Militia of the several States, when called into the actual Service of the United States."

The Virginia Plan, which Edmund Randolph introduced to the Convention on May 29, did not specifically mention this authority, and delegates may have taken it for granted that Congress would continue to control the military, as under the Articles of Confederation (Nelson 2002, 31). By contrast, what appears to be the draft of the Pinckney Plan further provided that the president "shall, by Virtue of his Office, be Commander in chief of the Land Forces of U.S. and Admiral of their Navy" (Farrand 1937, II, 158).

The New Jersey Plan, which William Paterson introduced on June 15, proposed a plural executive, which had authority to "direct all military operations," but it provided a caveat specifying that no member of the executive branch should "on any occasion take command of any troops, so as personally to conduct any enterprise as General, or in other capacity" (I, 244). The plan that Alexander Hamilton introduced on June 18 provided that the president would "have the direction of war when authorized or begun" (I, 292).

On July 20, Virginia's James McClurg wondered if the Convention should, before sending matters to the Committee of Detail, decide whether the president was "to have a military force" in order to enforce national laws, or whether he would only be able to use the militia (II, 69). The Convention appears to have been content to let the committee solve this problem. Much as it had done in enumerating the powers of Congress, the committee listed a number of powers that the president would exercise. These included the power to "be commander in chief of the Army and Navy of the United States, and of the Militia of the Several States," but this was not the first of the powers to be designated (II, 185).

Portrait by Gilbert Stuart of George Washington at Dorchester Heights, 1806. In the spring of 1776, George Washington and his troops seized Dorchester Heights, placing cannon in range of Boston and causing British troops to leave Boston harbor. (National Archives)

The power to "wage" war was originally vested by the Committee of Detail in Congress. When the Convention discussed this provision on August 17, Charles Pinckney of South Carolina objected that the proceedings of this body would be too slow, it would meet too infrequently, and it was too numerous to carry out such powers (II, 318). Although Pinckney wanted to vest this power in the Senate alone, South Carolina's Pierce Butler said that the objections that Pinckney had made to congressional control also applied to the Senate, and he suggested vesting these powers in the presidency, which would be composed of a single individual. After discussion, the Convention voted to change the congressional power to that of "declaring" war. At the suggestion of Connecticut's Roger Sherman, the Convention modified the Committee of Detail's provision for presidential powers on August 27 so that the president only commanded the militia "when called into the actual service of the U-S-" (II, 426).

Congress thus declares war (and makes appropriations for it), and the president wages it. Similarly, the Constitution vests the president with the right of negotiating treaties and the Senate with the power of ratifying them. Although the division of functions is rarely absolutely clear, it arguably allows the two branches to check one another. By entrusting such powers to the legislative and executive branches, the Constitution ensures civilian control over the military, an essential element of republican government.

See Also Committee of Detail; War Powers of Congress

FOR FURTHER READING

Boylan, Timothy S. 2001. "The Law: Constitutional Understandings of the War Power." *Presidential Studies Quarterly* 31 (September): 514–528.
Farrand, Max, ed. 1937. *The Records of the Federal Convention.* 4 vols. New Haven, CT: Yale University Press.
Nelson, Michael, ed. 2002. *Guide to the Presidency.* 3rd ed. Washington, DC: Congressional Quarterly.

PRESIDENT, COMPENSATION

Article II, Section 1, Clause 7 of the Constitution provides that "the President shall, at stated Times, receive for his Services, a Compensation, which shall neither be encreased nor diminished during the Period for which he shall have been elected, and he shall not receive within that Period any other Emolument from the United States, or any of them."

This provision relates directly back to a section of the Virginia Plan that Edmund Randolph proposed on May 29. It provided that the president shall "receive punctually at stated times, a fixed compensation for the services rendered, in which no increase or diminution shall be made so as to affect the Magistracy, existing at the time of increase or diminution" (Farrand 1937, I, 21). Although the New Jersey Plan that William Paterson introduced on June 15 called for a plural executive, it used almost identical language as the Virginia Plan, adding the stipulation, which had been previously agreed to by the Committee of the Whole (I, 236), that the members of the executive should "be paid out of the federal treasury" (I, 244), thus ensuring that the president would be an agent of the nation rather than of the states.

Between the time of the Virginia and New Jersey Plans, Benjamin Franklin prepared a speech, which his colleague James Wilson delivered, in support of a motion providing that the nation would pay for the presidents' expenses but that they "shall receive no salary, stipend fee or reward whatsoever for their services" (I, 81). Clearly regarded by fellow delegates as impractical, Franklin's speech is probably most notable for its view of human nature and for his view that people had an affinity for kingship because "It gives more of the appearance of equality among Citizens, and that they like" (I, 83). Arguing that men were motivated chiefly by "ambition and avarice," Franklin hoped to eliminate one such motive in the hopes of encouraging public spiritedness (I, 82). He further thought there was a hydraulic pressure in government to increase the pay of the rulers—"there will always be a party for giving more to the rulers, that the rulers may be able in return to give more to them" (I, 83). Franklin made it clear that he was not specifically concerned with the possibility of saving governmental money (and his comments elsewhere at the Convention would indicate that he did not intend to deprecate the abilities of common people who would have been excluded from office if they could receive no salary for it) but of encouraging virtue. Although George Washington, whom Franklin commended on this account, had served as commander-in-chief of the Revolutionary forces—and would serve again as the first president—without compensation, Franklin recognized that many would regard his proposal as utopian, and they appear to have done so. Madison observed that his proposal, which Alexander Hamilton seconded, "was treated with great respect, but rather for the author of it, than from any apparent conviction of its expediency or practicability" (I, 85).

On July 20, the Convention voted 10 to 0 both to fix the compensation for the president and to provide that it would be drawn from the national Treasury (II, 69). The provision prohibiting the president from accepting emoluments from the U.S. or from any of the states was added on September 15 by a 7-4 vote of the Convention after being proposed by John Rutledge of South Carolina and Benjamin Franklin of Pennsylvania (II, 646).

The Framers wisely refused to establish a specified salary that would quickly have become antiquated. By ensuring that the president's salary would not be changed during his term of office, the delegates hoped to give the president independence. By paying him out of the public treasury, the delegates ensured that he would be a national official. Although the delegates rejected Franklin's proposal to deny the president a salary, by prohibiting outside gifts, the delegates hoped to insulate him from improper influences.

The first Congress established the presidential salary at $25,000 a year. Congress raised this salary to $50,000 in 1873, to $75,000 in 1909, to $100,000 in 1949, to $200,000 in 1969, and to $400,000 in 2001. The president also has many other perquisites, including housing and an expense allowance (Bledsoe 2002, II, 977–978).

See Also Franklin, Benjamin; New Jersey Plan; Virginia Plan

FOR FURTHER READING

Bledsoe, Craig. 2002. "Executive Pay and Perquisites." In Michael Nelson, ed. *Guide to the Presidency*. 3rd ed. 2 vols. Washington, DC: Congressional Quarterly, 977–1014.

Farrand, Max, ed. 1937. *The Records of the Federal Convention*. 4 vols. New Haven, CT: Yale University Press.

PRESIDENT, COUNCIL

Article II, Section 2 of the Constitution provides that the president "may require the Opinion, in writing, of the principal Officer in each of the executive Departments, upon any Subject relating to the Duties of their respective Offices." This provision has been the basis of the president's cabinet, consisting of the heads of key departments, upon whom the president may, but is not obligated to, call for advice. The Convention considered, but ultimately rejected, the idea of creating a specific council to whom the president would have to go for advice. This decision was, in part, linked to the decision to vest the presidency in a single individual, rather than in a plurality of persons, and to the decision to limit the president's power to appoint most governmental officers by requiring senatorial confirmation.

Virginia's Proposal for a Council of Revision

The Virginia Plan, which Edmund Randolph introduced at the Convention on May 29, did not provide for an executive council, but it did provide for a Council of Revision. This council was to be composed of the president and members of the judicial branch, who would have the power to invalidate acts of Congress or of state legislatures, subject to legislative override. This provision in turn provided the starting point for the current presidential veto power, and arguably, for the development of the power of judicial review, whereby courts can invalidate laws they believe to be unconstitutional.

When the Convention discussed the executive on June 1, and especially whether the institution should be singular or plural, Elbridge Gerry of Massachusetts indicated that he "favored the idea of annexing a Council . . . in order to give weight & inspire confidence" (Farrand 1937, I, 66). Rufus King's notes from the same day indicate that Madison took the view that "the best plan will be a single Executive of long duration wth. a Council, with liberty to depart from their Opinion at his peril" (I, 70); Pierce's notes validate that Madison took this position (I, 74).

Other Proposals for a Presidential Council

On June 4, the Convention continued to consider whether the president should be singular or plural. When Pennsylvania's James Wilson observed that most states had a single executive, Connecticut's Roger Sherman admitted that this was so but observed that some or all of the states also had "a Council of advice, without which the first magistrate could not act." Sherman said that such a council would be necessary if the institution were to be acceptable to the people, and that, even in Great Britain, the king had such a council, which "attracts the Confidence of the people" (I, 97). Wilson, who probably feared that a council, like a plural executive, might dilute executive responsibility, indicated that he did not favor this plan, and the Convention accepted the idea of a single executive before moving on to a discussion of a Council of Revision.

On July 19, Gouverneur Morris of Pennsylvania spoke out on behalf of presidential re-eligibility for office. He observed that the president should have power to appoint both "ministerial officers for the administration of public affairs" and "officers for the dispensation of Justice" (II, 52). He further observed: "There must be certain great officers of State, a minister of finance, or war, of foreign affairs &c." (II, 53–54). He believed these officers would be subject to impeachment, and he observed that "Without these ministers the Executive can do nothing of consequence" (II, 54).

As discussions continued on the Council of Revision on July 21, John Rutledge of South Carolina observed that he opposed having judges as members of such a body. He thought this role would be both improper and unnecessary. He explained that "the Executive could advise with the officers of State, as of war, finance &c. and avail himself of their information and opinions" (II, 80).

On August 18, Connecticut's Oliver Ellsworth observed that the Convention had not yet provided a presidential council and that it needed to do so. He wanted such a council to play an advisory role:

His proposition was that it should be composed of the President of the Senate—the Chief-Justice,

and the Ministers as they might be estabd. for the departments of foreign & domestic affairs, war finance, and marine, who should advise but not conclude the President. (II, 329)

South Carolina's Charles Pinckney, who was anticipating a similar proposal by Gouverneur Morris, who was not then present, wanted to delay consideration of the proposal, but observed that "his own idea was that the President shd. be authorized to call for advice or not as he might chuse. Give him an able Council and it will thwart him; a weak one and he will shelter himself under their sanction" (II, 329). Elbridge Gerry opposed allowing department heads to "have any thing to do in business connected with legislation" (II, 329). Like the chief justice, whose participation he also opposed in such matters, Gerry feared that "these men will also be so taken up with other matters as to neglect their own proper duties" (II, 329). Delaware's John Dickinson observed that if the legislature were to make key appointments, then "they might properly be consulted by the Executive—but not if made by the Executive himself" (II, 329), and the issue was postponed.

As anticipated, on August 20, Gouverneur Morris, seconded by South Carolina's Charles Pinckney, proposed an elaborate plan for a presidential council "To assist the President in conducting the Public affairs" to be submitted to the Committee of Detail for consideration (II, 342). This council was to consist of the chief justice of the Supreme Court, who would preside over the council in the president's absence, a secretary of domestic affairs, a secretary of commerce and finance, a secretary of foreign affairs, a secretary of war, a secretary of the marines, and a secretary of state, who would also serve as council secretary. The president was to submit matters to the council for discussion and for written opinions, but "shall in all cases exercise his own judgment" (II, 343).

The committee reported back on August 22 with a somewhat altered "Privy-Council" consisting of the president of the Senate, the speaker of the House of Representatives, the chief justice, and the chief officers of various departments. Following Morris's and Pinckney's original proposals, the committee specified that "their advice shall not conclude him, nor affect his responsibility for the measures which he shall adopt" (II, 367). This part of the report appears to have fallen into oblivion.

On September 7, Virginia's George Mason objected to the newly sanctioned office of vice president. He thought that this office (whose occupant was to preside over the Senate) improperly mixed legislative and executive powers. For similar reasons, he opposed vesting either branch of Congress with powers of appointment or giving such power exclusively to the president. As a solution, Mason proposed establishing a "privy Council" of six members, two from each of the three existing geographical regions (Eastern, Middle, and Southern). Senate concurrence would only be necessary in the case of the appointment of ambassadors and treaty-making. Mason believed such a council would save expense by obviating the need for "constant sessions of the Senate" (II, 537), which he distrusted as an aristocratic body. James Wilson preferred such a council to presidential appointment and Senatorial confirmation, provided that the council's "advice should not be made obligatory on the President" (II, 539). By contrast, Rufus King thought that "most of the inconveniencies charged on the Senate are incident to a Council of Advice." Taking a page out of Mason's own book, he also thought the people would "be alarmed at an unnecessary creation of New Corps which must increase the expence as well as influence of the Government" (II, 539).

As the Convention proceeded without adopting his proposal, Mason observed that it was "about to try an experiment on which the most despotic Government had never ventured–The Grand Signor himself had his Divan" (II, 541). He accordingly moved that the Committee of States consider his proposal for a Privy Council. Franklin seconded the motion believing that such a council "would not only be a check on a bad President but be a relief to a good one" (II, 542). Gouverneur Morris responded that an earlier committee had "judged that the Presidt. by persuading his Council–to concur in his wrong measures, would acquire their protection for them" (I, 542). Wilson preferred instituting a council to involving the Senate in the appointment process. Delaware's

John Dickinson also favored a council as a means of guaranteeing that measures received "some previous discussion before the President," and Madison also supported it. Nonetheless, Mason's motion failed by a vote of 8-3.

Critiques of the Convention's Actions

In a copy of comments prepared at the end of the Convention and later printed as a pamphlet, Mason (one of three remaining delegates who did not sign the Constitution) repeated earlier observations he had made at the Convention by observing that the absence of a constitutional council was "a thing unknown in any safe and regular government." Mason anticipated a number of dire possibilities: the president would "be unsupported by proper information and advice, and will generally be directed by minions and favorites; or will become a tool to the Senate–or a Council of State will grow out of the principal officers of the great departments; the worst and most dangerous of all ingredients for such a Council in a free country" (II, 638). Mason further linked this omission to the creation of the vice presidency and to the investiture of improper powers in the Senate.

John Fairlie has traced the influence of discussions of a president's council at the Convention to several constitutional provisions. He thus observed that

> in place of the suggested council of revision, the president was given the qualified power of disapproving measures passed by congress. In place of the council of appointment, the advice and consent of the senate was made necessary for appointments. And of the other plans for an advisory council the barest suggestion remained in the clause providing that the president "may require the opinion, in writing, of the principal officer in each of the executive departments, upon any subject relating to the duties of their respective offices." (1913, 31–32)

The first Congress established secretaries of treasury, state, and war as well as an attorney-general. Today there are 15 cabinet-level departments, including the Department of Homeland Security, created in the aftermath of the terrorist attacks of September 11, 2001.

See Also Council of Revision; Judicial Review; Mason, George; President, Number of; Presidential Veto

FOR FURTHER READING

Fairlie, John A. 1913. "The President's Cabinet." *American Political Science Review* 7 (February): 28–44.
Farrand, Max, ed. 1937. *The Records of the Federal Convention.* 4 vols. New Haven, CT: Yale University Press.
Thach, Charles C. 1922. *The Creation of the Presidency 1775–1789: A Study in Constitutional History.* Baltimore, MD: Johns Hopkins University Press.

PRESIDENT, DISABILITY

As early as June 18, the delegates to the Constitutional Convention anticipated the possibility of the death, resignation, or removal of the president. The Committee of Detail attempted to provide for such contingencies by designating the president of the Senate to fill in until such time as another president was chosen, the president was acquitted (the Convention had anticipated that the president might step aside during impeachment hearings), or his disability was removed (Farrand 1937, II, 172).

On August 27, Pennsylvania's Gouverneur Morris suggested that the chief justice should be the "provisional successor to the President" (II, 427). At a time before the Convention had established neither the Electoral College nor the vice presidency, Virginia's James Madison was also concerned that, if the head of the Senate were designated to fill in, the Senate might drag its feet in selecting a successor. Madison wanted the council to the president to administer the office during vacancies. Identifying an issue that would long bedevil discussions of the subject, John Dickinson, of Delaware, observed that the term

"disability" was ambiguous, and it was not clear who would make such determinations (II, 427).

The Convention agreed to the creation of a vice presidency on September 6. The next day, it provided that Congress would provide by law for presidential replacements in cases in which both the president and vice president should be disabled (II, 535). Current laws designate the speaker of the House of Representatives, the president pro tempore of the Senate, and the cabinet officers in the order of their creation as presidential replacements after the vice president (Vile 2003, 469). The Convention was apparently at odds as to whether presidents might be chosen other than every four years (II, 535) and did not resolve this specific issue.

The Convention made no provision for the replacement of vice presidents who resigned, were impeached and convicted, or who were disabled. This omission as well as the difficulty of defining disability eventually resulted in the adoption of the Twenty-fifth Amendment in 1964. This amendment provided a method whereby the vice president and cabinet officers can certify presidential disability, and it provided for the selection of a new vice president upon the nomination of the president and confirmation by a majority vote of both houses of Congress.

See Also Impeachment Clause; Vice Presidency

FOR FURTHER READING

Farrand, Max, ed. 1937. *The Records of the Federal Convention.* 4 vols. New Haven, CT: Yale University Press.
Vile, John R. 2003. *Encyclopedia of Constitutional Amendments, Proposed Amendments, and Amending Issues, 1789–2002.* Santa Barbara, CA: ABC-CLIO.

PRESIDENT, EXECUTIVE POWER

The first sentence of Article II of the Constitution vests the "executive power" in the president. Section 3 further vests the president with the power to "take Care that the Laws be faithfully executed."

Scholars continue to discuss the nature and scope of such power. Clearly, the provision reflects the Framers' view of separation of powers and indicates that they intended for the executive power to differ from the legislative and judicial powers granted respectively in Articles I and III (Calabresi 1994). Textually, there is some cause for suggesting that the grant of "executive power" is somewhat broader than the corresponding grant in Article I, Section 1 of "all legislative Powers *herein granted*" (italics added; see Thomas 2000, 541), but the Constitution does not specifically refer to the idea of executive prerogative that the English philosopher John Locke had advanced (the idea that the executive might on occasion have to go beyond, or even act contrary to, law), and members of the Convention do not appear to have used this specific term in their debates. Moreover, further provisions in the Article certainly indicate that presidential powers are granted subject to limitations (Calabresi, 1398).

The delegates to the Convention appear to have spent far more time discussing whether the presidency would be singular or plural, how the president would be selected, how long individuals could serve in this post, and whether they would be combined with a Council of Revision, than with more abstract questions about the scope of the president's power. By creating a singular executive and deciding against a Council of Revision, the Founders concentrated power and responsibility in the presidential office. By formulating an Electoral College, the Framers enabled the president to secure independence from Congress. By allowing for presidential reelection, the Framers hoped to give a president an incentive toward good behavior.

The institution of the presidency evolved at the Convention, with the institution gaining power as the Convention progressed. Early views of the executive are thus not always indicative of the Framers' final view. Nonetheless, it is interesting to observe Roger Sherman of Connecticut remarking that "he considered the Executive magistracy as nothing more than an institution for carrying the will of the Legislature into effect" (I, 65).

It should also be noted, however, that Sherman used his view of the executive to propose that Congress should appoint the individuals who carried out its will (I, 65), a position that the Convention clearly went on to reject.

Delegates did make provision for the suspension of the writ of habeas corpus in times of emergency, but this power is listed in Article I, which outlines legislative powers, rather than in Article II, which outlines the powers of the president. The Constitution vested the powers of appointing heads of executive agencies in the president, subject to the advice and consent of the Senate, but did not specify who could fire such officials. Apart from individuals thought to be carrying out quasi-legislative or quasi-judicial duties, Courts have generally vested this power in the president as part of the president's duty to execute the laws. The lead case establishing this principle is *Myers v. United States*, 272 U.S. 52 (1926).

Writing in *Federalist* No. 72, Alexander Hamilton justified presidential supervision of appointed officials as essential to his executive duties:

> The administration of government, in its largest sense, comprehends all the operations of the body politic, whether legislative, executive, or judiciary; but in its most usual and perhaps in its most precise signification, it is limited to executive details, and falls peculiarly within the province of the executive department. The actual conduct of foreign negotiations, the preparatory plans of finance, the application of disbursement of the public moneys in conformity to the general appropriations of the legislature, the arrangement of the army and navy, the direction of the operations of war—these, and other matters of a like nature, constitute what seems to be most properly understood by the administration of government. The persons, therefore, to whose immediate management these different matters are committed ought to be considered as the assistants or deputies of the Chief Magistrate, and on this account they ought to derive their offices from his appointment, at least from his nomination, and ought to be subject to his superintendence. (Hamilton, Madison, and Jay 1961, 435–446)

See Also Appointments and Confirmations; Habeas Corpus; Locke, John; Separation of Powers

FOR FURTHER READING

Calabresi, Steven G. 1994. "The Vesting Clauses as Power Grants." *Northwestern University Law Review* 88 (Summer): 1377–1405.

Hamilton, Alexander, James Madison, and John Jay. 1961. *The Federalist Papers.* Ed. Clinton Rossiter. New York: New American Library.

Patterson, C. Perry. 1949. "The President as Chief Administrator." *Journal of Politics* 11 (February): 218–235.

Thomas, George. 2000. "As Far as Republican Principles Will Admit: Presidential Prerogative and Constitutional Government." *Presidential Studies Quarterly* 30 (September): 534–552.

PRESIDENT, INAUGURATION

See PRESIDENT, OATH OF OFFICE

PRESIDENT, NUMBER OF

Few decisions more directly affected the future of the presidency than the Convention's decision to vest this office in a single individual. This decision has undoubtedly contributed to both the visibility and the power of this office as well as its power to act more decisively than had it been vested in a collective body.

Under the Articles of Confederation, the president of the Congress consisted of one man, but he had no independent authority. By contrast, the Virginia Plan, which Edmund Randolph introduced on May 29, provided for three independent branches of government. The plan did not initially specify whether a single individual would be president or whether the office would be plural in nature. It did provide that the members of "a National Executive" would "be chosen by the National Legislature" and be ineligible for a second term (Farrand 1937, I, 21).

On June 1, Pennsylvania delegate James Wilson proposed that the president should "consist of a single person" and Charles Pinckney of South Carolina seconded him (I, 65). After a "considerable pause," Nathaniel Gorham of Massachusetts, acting as chair of the Committee of the Whole, and Benjamin Franklin had to coax delegates to speak, and John Rutledge of South Carolina noted "the shyness of gentlemen on this and other subjects." Although he attributed this shyness to the fear that once they spoke, they would find it difficult to change their minds (I, 65), it is likely that delegates feared offending George Washington, whom most expected to be the first chief executive if the Constitution vested the office in a single man (Nelson 2002, 22).

In any event, South Carolina's John Rutledge said that he favored a single executive, but "not for giving him the power of war and peace." Rutledge observed that "A single man would feel the greatest responsibility and administer the public affairs best" (I, 65). Connecticut's Roger Sherman clearly had a much different view of the office. He viewed the president, much like that existing under the Articles of Confederation, "as nothing more than an institution for carrying the will of the Legislature into effect" and wanted to allow Congress to vary the number of executives at its pleasure (I, 65). By contrast, Wilson argued that a single magistrate–a term, with classical roots designating individuals exercising both political and religious authority (see Coulanges 1956), frequently used in the early debates–would give "energy[,] dispatch and responsibility to the office" (I, 65). Probably recognizing that the shadow of George III hung over the proceedings, Wilson said that "he did not consider the Prerogatives of the British Monarch as a proper guide in defining the Executive powers" (I, 65). Although not directly addressing whether the Constitution should vest the presidency in a single individual, Elbridge Gerry of Massachusetts favored "annexing a Council" to "give weight and inspire confidence" (I, 66).

Edmund Randolph emerged as one of the strongest opponents at the Convention of a single executive. He said that "he regarded it as the foe-tus [fetus] of monarchy" (I, 66) and suggested an executive consisting of three persons. By contrast, Wilson said that a single executive "would be the best safeguard against tyranny" (I, 66). When discussion resumed on June 2 and Rutledge and Pinckney proposed a single executive, Randolph continued his opposition. He argued that the people would oppose an institution that resembled a monarchy this closely; a plural executive would be equally competent; people would not have the "necessary confidence" in a single leader; and the presidency would always go to someone at the center of the nation, depriving states on the periphery of due representation (I, 88). By contrast, Pierce Butler of South Carolina (one of the states on the Union's periphery) thought that one man would be more likely to look out for the common interest than would several individuals who felt duty-bound to represent regional interests (I, 88–89).

Discussion resumed on June 4. Supporting a single executive, Wilson observed that Randolph's arguments had been less directed to the wisdom of a single executive than to its putative unpopularity. However, each of the 13 states had a single executive. A single executive would promote tranquillity: "Among three equal members, he foresaw nothing but uncontrouled, continued, & violent animosities; which would not only interrupt the public administration; but diffuse their poison thro' the other branches of Govt., thro' the States, and at length thro' the people at large" (I, 96). Sherman was willing to accept a single executive, but he thought that such an institution should have a Council attached if it were to be acceptable to the people. Wilson did not think this was necessary.

Virginia's George Mason favored an executive of three persons (intentionally or otherwise, his language is close to that which Christians use to describe the Trinity) and prepared a speech on the subject. Although he does not appear to have delivered it on June 4, it may well have reflected the sentiments of other delegates. Mason acknowledged that the executive unity furthered "the Secrecy, the Dispatch, the Vigour and Energy" of the government, but he thought that these advan-tages were "greater in Theory than in Practice" and that a single executive was likely to degenerate into monarchy (Hutson 1987, 50). He favored an executive consisting of a representative from the Northern, the Middle and the Southern sections of the nation, believing that they would "bring with them, into Office, a more perfect and extensive Knowledge of the real Interests of this great Union" (Hutson, 51). Gerry feared that an executive of three persons, especially when it came to military matters, "would be a general with three heads" (I, 97). The Convention then voted 7-3 on behalf of a single executive and subsequently focused its primary attention on how the president would be selected and whether he would be re-eligible for office.

Records of the Convention indicated that George Washington, who went on to become the first president, was among those who voted for a single executive. Richard Ellis has observed that those who are known to oppose a single executive were generally older than those who favored it. He plausibly suggests that opponents may have been more influenced by their experience during the Revolutionary War against George III while proponents of a single executive were more influenced by their experience of the weaknesses of the Articles of Confederation.

See Also Council of Revision; Washington, George; Wilson, James

FOR FURTHER READING

Coulanges, Numa Denis Fustel de. 1956. *The Ancient City: A Study on the Religion, Law, and Institutions of Greece and Rome.* Baltimore, MD: Johns Hopkins University Press.

Ellis, Richard J., ed. 1999. *Founding the American Presidency.* Lanham, MD: Rowman and Littlefield.

Farrand, Max, ed. 1937. *The Records of the Federal Convention.* 4 vols. New Haven, CT: Yale University Press.

Hutson, James H., ed. 1987. *Supplement to Max Farrand's* The Records of the Federal Convention of 1787. New Haven, CT: Yale University Press.

Nelson, Michael, ed. 2002. *Guide to the Presidency.* 3rd ed. Washington, DC: Congressional Quarterly.

PRESIDENT, OATH OF OFFICE

Article VI of the Constitution provides that members of the three branches of the national and state governments all take oaths to support the U.S. Constitution. However, the only oath that the Constitution specifically delineated is the presidential oath set forth in Article II, Section 1, Clause 8. It specifies that the president shall swear or affirm (a distinction made in apparent deference to adherents to religious groups, like the Quakers, who opposed swearing) "that I will faithfully execute the Office of President of the United States, and will to the best of my Ability, preserve, protect and defend the Constitution of the United States."

This provision originated in the report of the Committee of Detail, which included a provision in the document it submitted to the Convention on August 6 that specified that the president should take an oath or affirmation to "faithfully execute the office of President of the United States of America" (Farrand 1937, II, 185). When the Convention discussed this provision on August 27, George Mason and James Madison, both of Virginia, proposed adding the words "And will to the best of my judgment and power preserve protect and defend the Constitution of the U.S." (II, 427). Although Pennsylvania's James Wilson argued that the provision in Article VI for oaths made this addition unnecessary, the Convention voted to accept this addition by a vote of 7-1 (II, 427). The Convention appears to have substituted the word "abilities" (which later became "ability") for "judgment and power" on September 15, just two days before the delegates signed the document (II, 620).

The words "so help me God," which presidents beginning with George Washington have added to their oath, are neither required nor forbidden by the Constitution. The same is true of the practice of putting one's hand on the Bible while taking it (Nelson 2002, 313).

The inauguration of George Washington on Thursday, April 30, 1789, when he took the oath of office, was one of the most visible signs that the new government created by the Convention was going into effect (see Berkin 2002, 191–204). A reluctant recipient of the presidency who had proclaimed in a letter to Major General Henry Knox "that my movements to the chair of government will be accompanied by feelings not unlike those of a culprit, who is going to the place of his execution" (quoted in Lorant 1951, 18), Washington had received a tumultuous welcome as he traveled from his home in Mount Vernon, through Philadelphia where the Constitution had been written, to the nation's temporary capital in New York City. His inauguration served as an occasion for a display of national unity, not always evident in some of the early inaugurations that followed after the development of political parties (see Robertson 2001).

See Also Committee of Detail; Oaths of Office; Washington, George

FOR FURTHER READING

Berkin, Carol. 2002. *A Brilliant Solution: Inventing the American Constitution.* New York: Harcourt.

Farrand, Max, ed. 1937. *The Records of the Federal Convention.* 4 vols. New Haven, CT: Yale University Press.

Lorant, Stefan. 1951. *The Presidency: A Pictorial History of Presidential Elections from Washington to Truman.* New York: Macmillan.

Nelson, Michael, ed. 2002. *Guide to the Presidency.* 3rd ed. Washington, DC: Congressional Quarterly.

Robertson, Andrew W. 2001. "'Look on This Picture . . . and on This!' Nationalism, Localism, and Partisan Images of Otherness in the United States, 1787–1820." *American Historical Review* 106 (October): 1263–1280.

PRESIDENT, QUALIFICATIONS

Although the Virginia Plan, which Edmund Randolph introduced at the Convention on May 29, proposed that members of the two houses of Congress should be of a minimum, but as then unspecified, age, it contained no similar requirements for the national executive. Because the Virginia Plan called for Congress to select the president, it is likely that—as in the case of the judiciary, for which no constitutional qualifications were ever set—the authors of the plan did not think it would be as necessary to restrain legislators in making their choice as it would be to restrain the people acting directly (Vile and Perez-Reilly 1991; Nelson 1987).

The qualifications that Article II, Section 1 established for the presidency are threefold. First, the president must be either a natural-born citizen or one who was a citizen at the time the Constitution was adopted. Second, the president must be at least 35 years of age. Third, the president must have been a resident in the United States for at least 14 years.

These qualifications appear to have been established largely to balance those that were established for legislators. On June 12, the Committee of the Whole had voted to set the age of senators at 30 years, and the full Convention reaffirmed this decision on June 25. On June 22, George Mason of Virginia had suggested that members of the U.S. House should be 25 years old, and his motion had carried the day. On July 26, the Convention adopted a resolution instructing the Committee of Detail to establish qualifications of property and citizenship for members of all three branches (Farrand 1937, II, 116–117), but it does not appear to have followed this instruction in regard to the president. Charles Pinckney moved consideration of a requirement that the president have a "quantum of property" (he favored no less than 100,000 for the president and lesser amounts for judges and members of Congress), and fellow South Carolinian John Rutledge seconded him. Rutledge observed that the committee had been unable to come to an agreement on the subject, "being embarrassed by the danger on [one] side of displeasing the people by making them [high], and on the other of rendering them nugatory by making them low" (II, 249). Oliver Ellsworth of Connecticut thought that the diversity of the nation would make uniform property qualifications impossible, and Franklin objected to making property a measure of merit. Pinckney's motion was overwhelmingly rejected.

The revived Committee of Detail headed by John Rutledge proposed on August 22 that the president should be 35 years of age as well as be a U.S. citizen and an inhabitant of the U.S. for at least 21 years. The Committee on Postponed Matters reported these requirements in its report to the Convention on September 4, and on September 7, the Convention unanimously accepted them (II, 536).

Presidential scholar Michael Nelson observes that the age qualification was designed both to "foster maturity" and to provide time for candidates to establish a record for electors to examine. He sees the 14-year residence requirement as a way of eliminating from consideration both American Tories who had fled to England during the Revolution and foreign military leaders like Baron Frederick von Steuben of Prussia who had fought on the Revolutionary side. This requirement was not, however, so lengthy that it would have barred such foreign-born members of the Convention as Alexander Hamilton, Pierce Butler and James McHenry. Finally, Nelson views the modified natural-born requirement as a means of quieting fears that the Convention was considering inviting such European monarchs as Prince Henry of Prussia, or Frederick, Duke of York, the Bishop of Osnaburg (George III's second son), to become the chief executive (Nelson 2002, 35–36). In a similar vein, John Jay wrote a letter to George Washington on July 25, 1787, indicating that he feared the possibility that the commander-in-chief could devolve upon someone who was naturalized:

> Permit me to hint, whether it would not be wise & seasonable to provide a strong check to the admission of Foreigners into the administration of our national Government; and to declare expressly that the Command in chief of the American army shall not be given to, nor devolve on, any but a natural *born* citizen. (Farrand II, 61)

Two centuries after its adoption, debate continues over the continuing desirability of the natural-born requirement for the presidency. Criticism of this provision has recently been fueled by supporters of California Governor Arnold Schwarzenegger, who was born in Austria.

See Also Congress, House of Representatives, Qualifications of Members; Congress, Senate, Qualifications

FOR FURTHER READING

Farrand, Max, ed. 1937. *The Records of the Federal Convention.* 4 vols. New Haven, CT: Yale University Press.

Lohman, Christina. 2000/2001. "Presidential Eligibility: The Meaning of the Natural-Born Citizen Clause." *Gonzaga Law Review* 36: 349–374.

Nelson, Michael. 1987. "Constitutional Qualifications for the President." *Presidential Studies Quarterly* 17 (Spring): 383–399.

——, ed. 2002. *Guide to the Presidency.* 3rd ed. Washington, DC: Congressional Quarterly.

Vile, John R., and Mario Perez-Reilly. 1991. "The U.S. Constitution and Judicial Qualifications: A Curious Omission." *Judicature* 74 (December-January): 198–202.

PRESIDENT, SELECTION

One of the Constitutional Convention's most difficult issues involved the selection of the president. The Convention took more than 30 votes on the subject and discussed it on 21 different days (Slonin 1986, 35). This issue was, in turn, related to presidential eligibility for reelection and to the length of presidential terms. One commentator likens the delicate balance of these three issues to a "tripod" (Slonin, 37).

The Virginia Plan, which Edmund Randolph introduced on May 29, was the first to mention the presidency. Under this plan, the national executive was to be one of three branches of the national government. The national legislature was to select the president or presidents (this issue had yet to be decided) for a single term of unspecified length. Randolph undoubtedly reasoned that ineligibility would prevent attempts on the part of the executive(s) to "corrupt," or curry favor with, the body selecting him/them.

June Debates

On June 1, Pennsylvania's James Wilson, who favored a single executive as a means of ensuring unity and energy in the executive branch, gingerly advanced the idea—he feared that his proposal "might appear chimerical"—of allowing the people to elect the president (Farrand 1937, I, 68). When the Convention returned to this issue later in the day, Wilson defended his proposal as a way of providing for executive independence of the other two branches and of the states. Virginia's George Mason thought the idea was good but impractical and suggested that Wilson be given more time to work on it (I, 69). South Carolina's John Rutledge, in turn, proposed that the second branch of the legislature (today's Senate) select the president.

The next day, Wilson introduced the skeleton of an Electoral College. He proposed dividing states according to electoral districts, with each district electing an unspecified number of electors who were to meet and elect by ballot someone other than themselves as president (I, 80). Wilson argued that the people would be more confident in a president elected by their electors rather than by members of Congress. Elbridge Gerry of Massachusetts further observed that if Congress were to make the selections, "There would be a constant intrigue kept up for the appointment" (I, 80). Gerry did not, however, think that states would be willing to give up such power and apparently favored a plan whereby state legislatures would nominate candidates and the electors would select the president from among such nominees. North Carolina's Hugh Williamson feared that the introduction of electors would lead to "great trouble and expence" (I, 81). The Convention thus voted down Wilson's proposal by an 8-2 vote and voted for legislative selection by the same vote.

On June 9, Gerry proposed an alternative method of selection under which state governors would select the president. He thought this would lessen the chance of intrigue between the president and the Congress. Randolph offered a number of objections. He thought that this would lessen the influence of small states, that governors would have little familiarity with individuals beyond their own states, that governors would be too influenced by their state legislatures, that the plan would make it difficult to fill vacancies, and, in a colorful metaphor, that state governors "will not cherish the great Oak which is to reduce them to paltry shrubs" (I, 176). Gerry's plan did not garner a single vote, although Delaware was divided on the issue.

William Paterson introduced the New Jersey Plan on June 15 as an alternative to the Virginia Plan. This plan anticipated a plural executive. As in the Virginia Plan, the Congress (albeit a unicameral one) was to choose the president, who was to be ineligible for reelection (I, 244).

July Debates

The Convention did not resume discussion of presidential selection until July 17. This time, Pennsylvania's Gouverneur Morris advocated popular election by "the freeholders [those who owned property] of the Country" (II, 29). He observed that New York and Connecticut had managed to do this and that the people would be more likely than Congress to choose a man of "continental reputation." By contrast, legislative selection was likely to be the work of "intrigue, of cabal, and of faction" and would resemble "the election of a pope by a conclave of cardinals" in which "real merit will rarely be the title to the appointment" (II, 29).

Connecticut's Roger Sherman was unpersuaded. He thought that Congress would be better able to represent the people than the people themselves, since people "will never be sufficiently informed of characters" and would be inclined to vote for individuals from their own states, giving an unfair advantage to the large states. Wilson still favored popular election and thought that an objection against it (that the people would never agree on a candidate) could be overcome by allowing Congress to decide in such cases. If Congress were to make the selection by itself, the executive would become too dependent upon it. South Carolina's Charles Pinckney feared that the people would "be led by a few active & designing men" and would give undue weight to the most populous states. By contrast, "The Natl.

Legislature being most immediately interested in the laws made by themselves, will be most attentive to the choice of a fit man to carry them properly into execution" (II, 30). Gouverneur Morris thought the people would be less able to collaborate than would members of Congress. The people would have adequate information to make such a choice.

Mason was unconvinced: "It would be as unnatural to refer the choice of a proper character for chief Magistrate to the people, as it would, to refer a trial of colours to a blind man. The extent of the Country renders it impossible that the people can have the requisite capacity to judge of the respective pretensions of the Candidates" (II, 31). North Carolina's Hugh Williamson agreed. Although the people were at the time aware of "distinguished characters," they would not always be so; they would be too inclined to vote for individuals from their own state.

Pennsylvania, home to both Wilson and Morris, was the only state to vote for popular election. Similarly, only their home states voted for the motion, introduced by Maryland's Luther Martin and Delaware's Jacob Broom, for allowing the president to be chosen by electors selected by the state legislatures. The Convention again unanimously voted for selection by Congress. When the Convention voted on the same day, however, to accept by a 6-4 vote a motion by William Houston of Georgia to allow for presidential re-eligibility, delegates had to reassess the wisdom of allowing such a president to be dependent upon Congress for such renewal. Virginia's James McClurg stirred the debate by proposing at one point that the president should serve "during good behavior" (II, 33), in what may have been a tactical maneuver designed to show the problems with presidential re-eligibility in a system where Congress would select the individual holding this office (Riker 1984, 8–9).

Delegates resumed discussion on July 19 in connection with presidential re-eligibility for office. Delegates generally agreed that re-eligibility would give a president an incentive to good conduct, but they also feared that there was danger of intrigue if Congress were to select the president. Rufus King of Massachusetts reintroduced the idea that the people should choose electors to select the president. New Jersey's William Paterson suggested that states should have from one to three electors depending on their populations. Wilson was encouraged by the growing acceptance of the idea of immediate, or intermediate, choice by the people. Madison, who acknowledged that suffrage was more "diffuse" in the North (where slavery was not as prominent) than in the South, observed that "the substitution of electors obviated this difficulty and seemed on the whole to be liable to the fewest objections" (II, 57). Somewhat modifying an earlier suggestion, Gerry now proposed that state executives should choose presidential electors. In any event, he was most opposed to popular election, repeating arguments that the people would be "uninformed, and would be misled by a few designing men" (II, 57).

Ellsworth introduced Paterson's idea of substituting a system whereby states would be awarded from one to three electors, and Broom seconded it. Rutledge continued to favor selection by Congress for a single term. Gerry preferred Ellsworth's motion and favored a total of 25 electors. The Convention appeared to be at a turning point. It voted 6-3-1 for a system of electors. It then voted 8-2 on behalf of electors selected by the state legislatures, but it postponed a decision as to their method of allocation. Significantly, the Convention followed with an 8-2 vote deciding that the president was no longer to be ineligible for future terms.

In addressing Ellsworth's proposal to grant states from one to three votes, with three going to those with a population of over 200,000, Madison observed that if this ratio were not changed, all states would eventually get the highest number of votes. Gerry thus proposed modifying this ratio so that it only applied in the first instance. This was, in turn, changed to allocate future electors on the basis of a state's number of representatives in the lower house. On the recommendation of Gerry and Gouverneur Morris, the Convention also specified that presidential electors would neither be eligible for the office they were selecting nor members of Congress. On July 21, the Convention further voted unanimously to pay electors for their service out of the national Treasury.

On July 23, William Houston of Georgia and Richard Spaight of North Carolina expressed concern over the expense involved in having electors from all over the nation meet for the single purpose of choosing a chief executive (II, 95). The next day, Houston expressed his preference for selection of the presidency by Congress. His primary argument was that capable men from distant states would be unlikely to accept positions as electors. Gerry did not think it would be difficult to find capable electors willing to serve, and he observed that if congressional selection were reinstituted, the president would again have to be limited to a single term. By contrast, Caleb Strong of Massachusetts did not think that capable electors would emerge, and he anticipated that there would be enough turnover within Congress so as to moderate any intrigue if the president were re-eligible. Williamson now joined the plea for congressional selection and also questioned whether the presidency should be vested in a single individual.

Electoral proposals became even more complicated. Gerry proposed that state legislatures should choose electors. If no individual got a majority of votes, the House of Representatives would choose two candidates from among the top four. The Senate would then choose the president from between them (II, 101). Although King seconded this plan, the Convention overwhelmingly rejected it. This paved the way for a 7-4 vote in favor of Houston's motion for congressional selection of the president, and discussion resumed on presidential re-eligibility.

The Convention proceeded to discuss the length of presidential terms. After this discussion, Wilson proposed that electors chosen "by lot from the Natl Legislature" (II, 105) should choose the president. Gerry objected that this left "too much to chance" (II, 105), and King feared that it might give individual states inordinate influence. He too expressed the sentiment that "We ought to be governed by reason, not by chance" (II, 105–106), and the motion, which Wilson indicated he did not think was the best, was postponed.

The Convention resumed discussion of presidential selection on July 25. Ellsworth attempted to develop a compromise whereby, in cases of presidential re-eligibility for office, electors appointed by state legislatures would make the selection. Gerry offered a new twist on an old proposal. He wanted state governors to select the president with advice from their councils, or, in the absence of such councils, to allow state legislatures to choose electors for this purpose (II, 109).

Madison reviewed the possibilities that had been offered as well as some that had not. He thought that selection of the presidency by the judiciary would be "out of the question" (II, 109). Selection by the legislatures could "agitate & divide" that body, would lead to "intrigue," and would tempt foreign governments to become involved. Existing state institutions were inappropriate, with state legislatures having especially "betrayed a strong propensity to a variety of pernicious measures" (II, 110). Were governors to make the selection, they would be involved in the same kind of intrigues as Congress. This left the option of allowing the people to choose the president either directly or through electors. Choosing electors who would immediately meet and make a choice would free them from the intrigues that would be involved if Congress were involved. Madison actually preferred direct popular election, but he acknowledged two problems. State residents would likely favor individuals from their own states, and, with more free voters, the North would have an advantage over the South. He announced himself "willing to make the sacrifice" (II, 111).

Ellsworth seems to have doubted the motives of a representative of the large states; he thought that "the objection drawn from the different sizes of the States, is unanswerable" (II, 111). Ellsworth's earlier motion, however, failed by a vote of 7-4, and the Convention resumed discussion of presidential re-eligibility.

Mason favored legislative selection of the president but feared foreign influence. Butler favored election by electors chosen by state legislatures. Morris best liked election by the people and most disliked selection by Congress; he favored Wilson's earlier idea of mixing the two modes. Williamson, who favored popular election, finally moved the Convention forward. He suggested that each voter should cast three votes, two to go to an individual from another state; Morris liked the idea but suggested that each voter only needed to cast one vote for an out-of state candidate (II, 113). Madison favored this plan. By contrast, Gerry thought that "popular election" would be "radically vicious," allowing the people to be influenced by organized groups like the Revolutionary War veterans in the Society of the Cincinnati (II, 114). Dickinson liked selection by the people but added a new wrinkle by suggesting that each state choose one of its citizens, and by proposing that Congress, or electors appointed by Congress, should then choose one of these. The issue was not resolved on that day.

Mason listed seven possible methods of selection. He observed that Dickinson's motion was undesirable because "It would exclude every man who happened not to be popular within his own State; tho' the causes of his local unpopularity might be of such a nature as to recommend him to the States at large" (I, 119). He also rejected the idea of choosing the president by lottery. He favored congressional selection and presidential ineligibility, allowing the people to return to the mass of people from which he came. Much to Gouverneur Morris's expressed disappointment, the Convention agreed by a vote of 7-3-1, and then voted for the entire clause relative to the executive by another vote of 6-3-1.

August Debates

In all the discussion of legislative appointment of the president, no one had specified how Congress would vote in selecting the president. The Committee of Detail, which issued its report on August 6, simply specified that the legislature would select the president by ballot. On August 7, Nathaniel Gorham of Massachusetts proposed a "joint ballot," so as to prevent the "delay, contention & confusion" that might occur were the two branches to disagree (II, 196). Wilson agreed that "Disputes between the two Houses, during & concern[in]g the vacancy of the Executive, might have dangerous consequences" (II, 197). The Convention rejected a motion by Gouverneur Morris that would have limited the necessity for both houses to agree to cases involving "legislative acts," but the Convention moved to other matters without resolving exactly how Congress would choose the president.

When discussion of this subject resumed on August 24, Rutledge proposed a joint congressional ballot. Sherman objected that this would deprive states of their due representation in the Senate. Gorham encouraged delegates to elevate considerations of "public good" over state interests, but New Jersey's Jonathan Dayton thought that a joint ballot was equivalent to allowing the House of Representatives, where large states would have the advantage, to make the decision (II, 402). A motion by Carroll and Wilson for popular election of the president failed by a 9-2 vote. David Brearly of New Jersey opposed a joint ballot, and Wilson pointed to problems of delay that such a joint ballot might cause, later observing that the president of the Senate (then slated to succeed the president) would have an incentive for such delay. Although he thought it was against the interest of his home state of New Hampshire, John Langdon agreed. Madison said that the largest state would only have a 4-1 advantage over the smallest in the case of a joint ballot, and the proposal for such a ballot passed by a vote of 7-4. By a narrower 6-5 vote, the Convention also rejected a proposal by Dayton giving each state delegation a single vote. The Convention voted down a proposal to give the president of the Senate the deciding vote in case of a tie. Morris again expressed opposition to legislative selection of the president, and reintroduced a proposal for allowing the people to select electors for this purpose. The Convention rejected this proposal by a narrow 6-5 vote as it did a more abstract but similar proposal by Morris.

On August 31, the Convention voted 9-1-1 on a motion by Gouverneur Morris to strike a provision whereby Congress was to initiate the new government by choosing the president (II, 480). This was sufficient to put the matter into the hands of the Committee on Postponed Matters.

September Debates

This committee, which reported to the Convention on September 4, largely invented the Elec-

toral College mechanism. It provided that each state would select a number of electors equal to its total congressional delegation. The electors would meet within each state and cast two ballots, at least one of which would go to someone from out of state. States would then transmit these votes to the president of the Senate who would count them. If two candidates had more than a majority (possible because each elector cast two votes) and there were a tie, the Senate would immediately choose between them. If no one had a majority, the Senate would choose among the five highest. The persons getting the second highest number of votes would be the vice president, with the Senate again fulfilling a tie-breaking function (II, 497–498). The committee's work was extraordinary. One scholar has described its proposal as being both innovative and "quite remarkable for having combined all the salient features of the numerous plans proposed during the debates while having overcome the deficiencies of each" (Slonin, 51).

Delegates appeared to like the general tenor of the resolution but quibbled about some of the details. Gorham wanted to ensure that the Senate would choose a vice president if no one had a majority of the total votes. Sherman suggested that the Senate could choose the vice president in such instances from among the five candidates having the highest number of votes. Madison and Morris feared giving states the incentive to be more concerned about choosing the five highest candidates than choosing the president. In answer to a question by Randolph and Charles Pinckney, Morris attempted to explain the committee's proposal. The plan had been motivated by the desire to eliminate the danger and intrigue connected to legislative election, allow for presidential re-eligibility, allow the Senate to serve as a court of impeachment, overcome discontent with legislative selection, move closer to popular selection; and provide for presidential independence of the legislature (II, 500).

Mason agreed that the new plan avoided "the danger of cabal and corruption," but he feared that the Senate, "an improper body for the purpose," would generally end up making the real choice (II, 500). Charles Pinckney had additional objections. He did not think the electors would know many of the candidates; he disfavored executive re-eligibility; and he did not like the idea that the same Senate that would choose the president would also sit in cases of his impeachment (II, 501). Other delegates cited putative advantages and disadvantages of the new system. Wilson suggested that the legislature (the author cannot ascertain whether he was referring to the House of Representatives or to both houses), rather than the Senate, should make the selection, and that it should choose from fewer than five candidates. Randolph also thought the legislature was more appropriate than the Senate, although Morris responded that the committee had chosen the Senate because fewer individuals could then tell the president that he owed his appointment to them (II, 502).

On September 5, Charles Pinckney renewed his objection to the new plan, placing particular attention on the increased power of the Senate. Rutledge had similar concerns. Mason was also concerned about the role of the Senate and moved to strike out its role in the case that no candidate got a majority of electoral votes; Williamson seconded the motion. Morris did not think the Senate would end up making the choice that often, and Sherman observed that, although small states would be advantaged in making such a selection, the large states would be advantaged in selecting the nominees from which they chose. Madison responded to Wilson's proposal for replacing the word "Senate" with "Legislature" by arguing that larger states would have a greater incentive to make a clear case if they did not anticipate such selection. Randolph feared that the Senate would become a new aristocracy, and Dickinson wanted the legislature rather than the Senate to make the choice, but Wilson's motion failed by a 7-3-1 vote.

Madison and Williamson moved that the Senate would only choose among candidates when they had less than one-third of the vote, but Gerry thought this would give too much power to too few states and the motion failed by a vote of 9-2. Gerry then introduced a new wrinkle in the debate, proposing that by joint ballot Congress should choose six senators and seven representatives to make the choice. Despite attempts to fix

it, this proposal was rejected by an 8-2 vote. After further tinkering, Mason, who was an ardent opponent of aristocracy who sometimes overstated his sentiments, expressed the view that the new solution was "utterly inadmissible" and that "He would prefer the Government of Prussia to one which will put all powers into the hands of seven or eight men, and fix an Aristocracy worse than absolute monarchy" (II, 515).

When the Convention resumed discussion on September 6, the states unanimously voted to exclude members of Congress as electors. Gerry then proposed eliminating presidential dependence on the Senate by providing that the legislature would choose in cases when an incumbent executive did not get a majority. Sherman, although preferring the system agreed to, thought that if the legislature were to be substituted for the Senate, then each state should have a single vote, and Gouverneur Morris agreed. Wilson then expressed fears that the new plan was aggrandizing the Senate and that instead of being "the man of the people as he ought to be" he will be "the Minion of the Senate" (II, 523). Morris attempted to defend the new institution, but Williamson and George Clymer (Pennsylvania) agreed that it gave too much power to the Senate. Alexander Hamilton suggested that the individual getting the highest number of electoral votes should be president, whether he had a majority or not. Such a person might allow a small number to make such an appointment, but this would be little different from allowing the Senate to choose one of five candidates with the smallest number of votes.

The Convention rejected a resolution requiring that the electors meet at the seat of the general government, but it accepted a motion that the election of the president take place on the same day throughout the nation. Voting on whether the Senate should choose in cases that no individual got a majority was stopped when Madison proposed that at least two-thirds of its members had to be present during this process. Seconded by Charles Pinckney, the Convention adopted this resolution by a vote of 6-4-1. Williamson then suggested that the legislature, voting by states, should select among top candidates, and, in a motion that seems so obvious it is difficult to understand why it took so long, Sherman carried the day by proposing that the House of Representatives (but with each state having a single vote), rather than the Senate, should make this choice. Mason was satisfied that this lessened the "aristocratic" influence of the Senate, and Sherman's motion carried by a 10 to 1 vote. Morris suggested that a sitting president should only be re-eligible for election if he had a majority of the votes, and, although the Convention did not act on this motion, it did establish a quorum designed to see that the president was not chosen with less than two-thirds of the senators and one-half or more of members of the House, a motion further fine-tuned the next day.

Analysis

The Electoral College is one of the most complicated mechanisms to emerge from the Constitutional Convention. It provided for an intermediate selection of the president by the people. By creating a temporary body, the Convention was able to avoid the dangers of cabal and intrigue that delegates anticipated would occur if Congress were to make the decision directly and if the president were to be re-eligible for office. The Electoral College seemed to offer something to everyone. John Roche has thus observed that

> first, the state legislatures had the right to determine the mode of selection of the electors; second, the small states received a bonus in the Electoral College in the form of a guaranteed minimum of three votes while the big states got acceptance of the principle of proportional power; third, if the state legislatures agreed (as six did in the first presidential election), the people could be involved directly in the choice of electors; and finally, if no candidate received a majority in the College, the right of decision passed to the National Legislature with each state exercising equal strength. (Roche 1961, 810)

The Electoral College was the incubus of the vice presidency, which essentially emerged from the provision under which each elector cast two votes. The mechanism did not sufficiently anticipate the rise of political parties. Thus, in the election of 1800, Thomas Jefferson and Aaron Burr, both running as Democratic-Republicans, tied in the Electoral College, and the election had to be resolved in the House of Representatives. The Twelfth Amendment mended this flaw in 1804 by specifying that electors would cast separate votes for the top two offices, but left other flaws. James Madison was among those who would later propose changes in the Electoral College that would require that electors be selected by districts rather than statewide and that would bring it back closer to the ideal of allowing electors greater discretion over whom they chose (Dewey 1962). The trend, however, has been in the opposition direction. The Twenty-third Amendment (1961) later provided for representation in the Electoral College for the District of Columbia.

The primary criticism of the current Electoral College is that it does not equally weigh every vote in the United States, and it therefore sometimes results, as in the presidential election of 2000 (when George W. Bush defeated Al Gore, Jr.), in an electoral winner who is not the winner of the popular vote (Edwards 2004, 31–54). It appears that this happens far less than had selection been vested in one or both houses of Congress. In such a situation, the modern presidency might have fostered a system far closer to that than in modern parliamentary democracies.

See Also Committee on Postponed Matters; Corruption; Poland; President, Term, Length, and Re-eligibility; Separation of Powers; Vice Presidency

FOR FURTHER READING

Adkinson, Danny M., and Christopher Elliott. 1997. "The Electoral College: A Misunderstood Institution." *PS: Political Science and Politics* 30 (March): 77–80.

Dewey, Donald O. 1962. "Madison's Views on Electoral Reform." *Western Political Quarterly* 15 (March): 140–145.

Edwards, George C., III. 2004. *Why the Electoral College Is Bad for America.* New Haven, CT: Yale University Press.

Farrand, Max, ed. 1937. *The Records of the Federal Convention.* 4 vols. New Haven, CT: Yale University Press.

Riker, William H. 1984. "The Heresthetics of Constitution-Making: The Presidency in 1787, with Comments on Determinism and Rational Choice." *American Political Science Review* 78 (March): 1–16.

Roche, John P. 1961. "The Founding Fathers: A Reform Caucus in Action." *American Political Science Review* 55 (December): 799–816.

Slonin, Shlomo. 1986. "The Electoral College at Philadelphia: The Evolution of an Ad Hoc Congress for the Selection of a President." *Journal of American History* 73 (June): 35–58.

PRESIDENT, TERM, LENGTH, AND RE-ELIGIBILITY

When Edmund Randolph introduced the original Virginia Plan on May 29, he left a blank for the section that was to specify the term of the president or presidents. The decision as to whether there was to be a single or plural executive was also still undetermined at that time. Randolph's plan provided for Congress to select the executive, who was to be ineligible for reelection (Farrand 1937, I, 21).

Pennsylvania's James Wilson, who favored popular election of the president, made the first motion regarding the length of the presidential term, when on June 1, he proposed before the Committee of the Whole that this term should be for three years and that the president should be re-eligible for office. Roger Sherman of Connecticut supported this suggested term length as well as the notion of re-eligibility. South Carolina's Charles Pinckney favored a seven-year term, as did Virginia's George Mason; Mason also favored ineligibility for further terms as a means of discouraging the president from intriguing with Congress. Delaware's Gunning Bedford fell somewhere in between the two positions, favoring a three-year term and ineligibility for further service after three terms. The Convention narrowly voted 5-4-1 for the seven-year term. The following day, it voted for ineligibility by a more conclusive vote of 7-2-1.

On July 17, Georgia's William Houston moved to strike the rule for presidential ineligibility, and Sherman seconded him. Gouverneur Morris was the motion's most vocal supporter. He thought that ineligibility would "destroy the great motive to good behavior, the hope of being rewarded by a re-appointment" and would be the equivalent of telling the president to "make hay while the sun shines" (II, 33). The Convention voted against re-eligibility by a vote of 6-4.

Delaware's Jacob Broom thought that such re-eligibility was cause to shorten the length of the term. By contrast, James McClurg of Virginia (who may have been attempting to highlight the problem with legislative selection) proposed allowing the president to serve "during good behavior," and Gouverneur Morris seconded him (II, 33). Sherman thought that re-eligibility provided enough reward for good service. Madison was more concerned about keeping the president independent than the motion under discussion whereas Mason thought that service during good behavior was "a softer name only for an Executive for life" (II, 35). The motion for replacing the seven-year term with service during good behavior failed by a vote of 6-4.

On July 19, Luther Martin reintroduced a motion for presidential ineligibility. This prompted a long speech by Gouverneur Morris in which he advocated a two-year term and continuing eligibility. Edmund Randolph supported Martin's motion, whereas Rufus King of Massachusetts thought that it was foolish to keep a good man from being reelected. For those who feared the possibility of corruption, so much depended on how the president was to be chosen, so this discussion blended into discussion of alternate selection mechanisms (the Convention was slowly beginning to edge to the idea of independent electors).

On July 24, Williamson favored a single seven-year term for the president although he was willing to accept a term of from 10 to 12 years if the president were to be ineligible for reelection (II, 100–101). Martin and Gerry, later supported by King, wanted to reinstate the provision for presidential re-eligibility. Gerry argued that the best way to make the president independent of the legislature, which was still slated to choose him, was to give him a single term of 10 or 15, or even 20, years. Martin suggested a term of 11 years, Gerry suggested 15, King (who was probably trying to show the absurdity of such proposals) proposed 20, "the medium life of a prince," and Davie suggested 8 (II, 102), but the Convention does not appear to have voted on any such motion.

On July 25, Charles Pinckney, presumably now favoring terms of two or three or six years, proposed that legislative selection of the president be qualified by the provision that no president could serve for more than six out of 12 years (II, 112). Mason and Gerry approved. After some discussion the Convention rejected this motion by a vote of 6-5 (II, 115).

The next day, Mason reintroduced the provision that the legislature should select the president for a single seven-year term. North Carolina's William Davie seconded him. Mason's motion carried by a vote of 7-3-1, much to the dissatisfaction of Gouverneur Morris.

Ultimately, the Committee on Postponed Matters, which reported to the Convention on September 4, proposed the outline of today's Electoral College system under which presidents were to serve for four-year terms (II, 497–498). The Electoral College mechanism freed the president from dependence upon, and intrigue with, the legislature and thus allowed for re-eligibility. The decisions on term length and re-eligibility were so intertwined with one another and with the issue of presidential selection that John Roche has likened the process of sorting the relationships out to a game of "three-dimensional chess" (Roche 1961, 810).

Presidents George Washington and Thomas Jefferson subsequently established the tradition that presidents would not run for a third term. After Franklin D. Roosevelt broke with the well-established tradition limiting presidents to two terms and was elected to four consecutive terms, the Twenty-second Amendment limited presidential service to no more than two full terms, or eight years.

See Also Jefferson, Thomas; President, Selection; Washington, George

FOR FURTHER READING

Farrand, Max, ed. 1937. *The Records of the Federal Convention*. 4 vols. New Haven, CT: Yale University Press.
Nelson, Michael. 2002. *Guide to the Presidency*. 3rd ed. Washington, DC: Congressional Quarterly.
Perrin, John William. 1914. "Presidential Tenure and Reeligibility." *Political Science Quarterly* 29 (September): 423–437.
Roche, John P. 1961. "The Founding Fathers: A Reform Caucus in Action." *American Political Science Review* 55 (December): 799–816.

PRESIDENT, TITLE

On August 6, the Committee of Detail proposed that the president should be designated as "His Excellency" (Farrand 1937, II, 185), but the Convention did not adopt this designation. The Convention did designate the president as commander-in-chief of the armed forces, but this arguably referenced one of his duties rather than the office as a whole.

The first Congress of the U.S. readdressed this issue. As president of the Senate, Vice President John Adams, who wanted to attract individuals of talent and ambition to government (Hutson 1968, 36), pressed for designating the president as "his Highness the President of the United States and protector of their Liberties"; he also supported referring to senators as "Right Honourable." Washington professed annoyance at this attempt "to bedizen him with a superb but spurious title," and Adams's opponents in Congress subsequently ridiculed him (although he was only five feet, six inches tall, he weighed about 275 pounds) as "His Rotundency." The Senate concurred with the House in simply designating the chief executive as "the President of the United States" (Nelson 2002, I, 64).

See Also Adams, John; Fame; President, Commander in Chief

FOR FURTHER READING

Farrand, Max, ed. 1937. *The Records of the Federal Convention.* 4 vols. New Haven, CT: Yale University Press.

Hutson, James H. 1968. "John Adams' Title Campaign." *New England Quarterly* 41 (March): 30–39.

Nelson, Michael, ed. 2002. *Guide to the Presidency.* 2 vols. 3rd ed. Washington, DC: Congressional Quarterly.

PRESIDENT OF THE CONVENTION

There were two men at the Constitutional Convention with worldwide reputations: George Washington and Benjamin Franklin. Washington had made his mark both as the commander of U.S. military forces during the Revolutionary War–he had been selected for this position in the same building by the Second Continental Congress–and the man who, like the Roman general Cincinnatus (to whom contemporaries often compared him), went back to his farm after the war's end rather than claiming power for himself. Franklin had gained his reputation in a variety of occupations, but most notably as a Philadelphia printer and inventor–among his other discoveries was that lightning was a form of electricity–and later as a diplomat who had helped win the peace with Britain at the end of the Revolutionary War. Washington was 55 and Franklin, the oldest member present, was 81. Because of physical infirmities, Franklin often relied upon fellow delegates to give his speeches for him at the Convention.

Because of the weather (it had rained heavily the previous night) and his own frail health, Franklin was unable to attend the Convention on its first day of business on Friday, May 25. Robert Morris of Philadelphia, who played host to Washington during the Convention, nominated Washington as president with the consent of the Penn-

sylvania delegation of which Franklin was a member. Virginia's James Madison observed in his notes that "the nomination came with particular grace from Penna, as Docr. Franklin alone could have been thought of [as a competitor]" (Farrand 1937, I, 4). With such an endorsement, seconded by John Rutledge of South Carolina, the Convention unanimously chose Washington as president, which is to say by a vote of 7-0, only seven states being present on the occasion.

Immediately thereafter, Washington made one of only two recorded speeches at the Convention. He thanked the Convention for the honor it had bestowed upon him, reminded members of "the novelty of the scene," decried his own lack of qualification, and asked for indulgence as to any errors that he might make (I, 3–4). Washington is not recorded as giving another official speech until the last day of the Convention, but the very fact that he attended lent credibility to the assembly, and the gravity of his demeanor is believed to have had a salutary effect on deliberations at the Convention. Similarly, his signature on the document lent credibility in the fight for the Constitution's ratification. One of James Madison's contributions to the Constitutional Convention was his role in persuading Washington to attend the proceedings.

Convention rules adopted on May 28 provided that members would take their seats after he took his chair; that members should rise to speak, addressing the president; that the president should determine which member would be recognized if more than one rose; and that members should stand after adjournment for the president to pass (I, 11–12). Convention proceedings consistently refer to Washington as "His Excellency." In a letter dated August 2, 1787, delegate John Langdon, in trying to portray the dignity of the Convention proceedings to a friend, referred to "the Great Washington, with a Dignity peculiar to himself, taking the Chair" (Hutson 1987, 201). Convention rules capitalized on Washington's dignity by requiring that members would stand to address the chair and by specifying that members would stand and wait to leave the room at adjournment time each day until after he exited (I, 11–12).

See Also Franklin, Benjamin; Washington, George

FOR FURTHER READING

Farrand, Max, ed. 1937. *The Records of the Federal Convention.* 4 vols. New Haven, CT: Yale University Press.

Hutson, James H., ed. 1987. *Supplement to Max Farrand's* The Records of the Federal Convention of 1787. New Haven, CT: Yale University Press.

Rhodehamel, John. 1998. *The Great Experiment: George Washington and the American Republic.* New Haven, CT: Yale University Press.

PRESIDENTIAL VETO

Article I, Section 7 of the Constitution outlines the federal law-making process. Because paragraph two of this section specifies that each bill that passes both houses of Congress is then to be presented to the president, scholars sometimes refer to this clause as "the presentment clause." When presented with such a bill, the president may do nothing, sign it, or veto it. In the latter case, Congress may override this veto by a two-thirds vote of both houses, but in such cases a roll-call vote is taken and votes are recorded under individual names. The section also provides for bills to become law within 10 days if not returned by the president, unless Congress adjourns, in which case, the president's failure to sign results in what is called a "pocket veto."

Origins of the Veto

Under the original Virginia Plan, which Edmund Randolph introduced in the Convention on May 29, the Congress was to exercise power "to negative all laws passed by the several States, contravening in the opinion of the National Legislature the articles of Union" (Farrand 1937, I, 21). Moreover, the president was to be joined with "a convenient number of the National Judiciary" to "compose a council of revision with authority to examine every act of the National Legislature before it shall operate, & every act of a particular Legislature before a Negative thereon shall be final" (I, 21). Congress would, in turn, have the power to override this veto by an unspecified majority. The presidential veto emerged from these provisions, which also stimulated discussion about the power of judicial review, that is, the power subsequently confirmed and established by Chief Justice John Marshall in *Marbury v. Madison* (1803) and subsequent cases, of the judiciary to declare laws to be unconstitutional.

Should the President Exercise the Veto Power Alone or with a Council of Revision?

The Convention began examining the Council of Revision on June 4. Perhaps because delegates widely agreed on the necessity for some such check on the legislative branch, they devoted little attention to whether such a veto was necessary. Instead, they concentrated on whether to vest the president and members of the judiciary with this power jointly or whether to vest such power in the president alone.

Elbridge Gerry of Massachusetts opposed combining the executive and the judiciary since he believed that judges would have the power to decide on the constitutionality of measures in the exercise of their judicial power. Rufus King, also of Massachusetts, seconded Gerry's motion to vest this power solely in the president. He observed that "the Judges ought to be able to expound the law as it should come before them, free from the bias of having participated in its formation" (I, 98).

Discussion of an Absolute Executive Veto

Pennsylvania's James Wilson had another idea. He thought that the Council of Revision should have an "absolute" negative (I, 98), a provision that New York's Alexander Hamilton joined in favoring. By contrast, Elbridge Gerry thought that an absolute negative would give the executive too much power, and Benjamin Franklin, who later reinforced his views with examples from the history of Holland, observed that the royal governor of Pennsylvania had abused such power by extorting concessions from the legislature. Roger Sherman of New Jersey observed that "No one man could be found so far above all the rest in wisdom" (I, 99), and Virginia's James Madison argued that the conditional negative was adequate. Although Wilson defended his proposal for an absolute negative, South Carolina's Pierce Butler feared an increase in executive power, and Delaware's Gunning Bedford came close to supporting legislative sovereignty: "He thought it would be sufficient to mark out in the Constitution the boundaries to the Legislative Assembly, which would give all the requisite security to the rights of the other departments" (I, 100–101). Mason feared the power of an elective monarchy and concluded that it would be sufficient "to enable the Executive to suspend offensive laws, till they shall be coolly revised, and the objections to them overruled by a greater majority than was required in the first instance" (I, 102). Not surprisingly, the Convention unanimously rejected the executive's absolute negative.

The Proposal for Allowing the President to Suspend the Law

Butler then proposed allowing the executive to suspend legislation for a still-to-be-specified period, and Franklin seconded him. Gerry feared that such suspension "might do all the mischief dreaded from the negative of useful laws; without answering the salutary purpose of checking unjust or unwise ones," and the Convention unanimously rejected the idea while unanimously accepting the power of two-thirds majorities of Congress to override the veto (I, 104). The Convention then voted 8–2 (with Connecticut and Maryland in dissent) for Gerry's motion to vest the veto power exclusively in the executive.

Renewed Discussion of the Council of Revision

The Convention resumed discussion of the veto on June 6 when Wilson proposed reconsidering the idea of adding "a convenient number of the national Judiciary" to reinforce the president in his veto decision (I, 138). Madison seconded the motion by arguing that such an alliance would both control and support the president. Acknowledging some merit in the argument that judges who had given an initial approval to laws might be biased in expounding them, Madison thought that only a few such cases were likely to arise in a typical judge's lifetime and that much good would arise from "the perspicuity, the conciseness, and the systematic character wch. the Code of laws wd. receive from the Judiciary talents" (I, 139). He thought the objection based on separation of powers was less meritorious, since he saw no "improper mixture" in the alliance of the president and the judiciary. Gerry was not as convinced as Madison of the wisdom of judges. He rather feared that their "sophistry" would "seduce" the executive and give improper "sanction" to his actions (I, 139). Observing that the Convention had settled on a unitary executive, King thought that the creation of a Council of Revision was inconsistent with this decision. Charles Pinckney thought the president would be free to consult whomever he wanted and opposed allying the president with judges. John Dickinson thought that joining the president with judges would diminish presidential responsibility whereas Wilson thought that such responsibility would still remain unified in regard to executive functions. The Convention agreed with King, Pinckney, and Dickinson, defeating the motion to ally the president with the judiciary by a vote of 8-3.

On July 21, James Wilson renewed a proposal for allying the president with members of the judiciary in a Council of Revision, and Madison seconded him. Wilson argued that it was important for judges "to have an opportunity of remonstrating agst projected encroachments on the people as well as on themselves." Seeming to anticipate that judges would exercise the power of judicial review, Wilson anticipated that they would only exercise such power when laws were unconstitutional, whereas they should also be able to note when laws were "unjust," "unwise," "dangerous," and "destructive," without being unconstitutional (II,

72). Gorham opposed the idea of allying the president with judges. He saw no reason to think that judges would have any particular knowledge of "the mere policy of public measures" (II, 73). By contrast, Oliver Ellsworth thought that judges would "give more wisdom & firmness to the Executive" and possess a more "systematic and accurate knowledge of the laws," including "the law of Nations" (II, 74). Madison believed that such an alliance would both allow an additional opportunity for the judiciary to defend itself against "Legislative encroachments" and would inspire "additional confidence & firmness in exerting the revisionary power" (II, 74). He argued that such arrangement would not give undue power to either the president or the judiciary but would guard against the legislative tendency "to absorb all power into its vortex" (II, 74). Mason joined in supporting Madison.

Elbridge Gerry had plenty of objections. He thought it was unwisely "combining & mixing" departments that ought to be kept separate. It was attempting to make mere judges into "statesmen" and unwisely "making the Expositors of the Laws, the Legislators which ought never to be done" (II, 75). Caleb Strong, also of Massachusetts, agreed that the function of expounding the law should be kept separate from making it. Gouverneur Morris feared that the executive did not have enough weight successfully to exercise the veto, but he did not seem certain that an alliance with the judiciary would adequately supply this deficiency. Luther Martin thought an executive/judicial alliance was "a dangerous innovation." He observed that judges had no better "knowledge of mankind, and of Legislative affairs" than legislators, and thought that allowing judges to review laws both when they were written and when they were implemented was to give the judiciary "a double negative" (II, 76). Madison reiterated his arguments that such an arrangement did not violate the idea of separation of powers, arguments reiterated by Wilson and Morris, while Mason thought that the alliance would enable judges to stop not only laws that were unconstitutional but those that were unwise as well. Gerry said he would prefer to give the executive an absolute

veto than to involve him in such an alliance. Gorham reiterated the objections, and Wilson attempted to defend against them. South Carolina's John Rutledge added that a president could consult with members of his cabinet, thus leaving judges in the position of not giving their opinions of a law until such laws came before them. Connecticut, Maryland, and Virginia cast votes for the proposal, but it was narrowly voted down by Massachusetts, Delaware, North Carolina and South Carolina, with Pennsylvania and Georgia being divided.

A New Twist on an Earlier Proposal

Madison was still not willing to concede, but, in renewing discussion on August 15, he altered his proposal so that laws would now be submitted separately to the president and the judiciary. Under his plan, congressional majorities of two-thirds would be required to override the veto by one institution and majorities of three-fourths would be required to override the veto of both. Wilson seconded this motion.

Charles Pinckney reiterated earlier arguments that this would unwisely involve judges in the process at two different stages. Maryland's John Mercer approved the motion, but he did so in the belief that judges had no role to play in invalidating laws on the basis of their unconstitutionality: "laws ought to be well and cautiously made, and then to be uncontroulable" (II, 298). Gerry observed that Madison's proposal differed little from the one that the Convention had already rejected. The delegates apparently agreed, turning the new proposal down by a more conclusive 8-3 majority, with only Delaware, Maryland, and Virginia favoring it.

What Is the Appropriate Majority for Overriding a Presidential Veto?

Despite this apparent conclusiveness, Gouverneur Morris regretted the decision and suggested, as an apparent alternative, that three-fourths of the legislature should be required to adopt laws over the president's veto. Dickinson now joined Mercer's earlier observation that judges should not have the power to invalidate laws on the basis that they believed them to be unconstitutional. Apparently emboldened, Morris reintroduced the idea of an absolute presidential veto as a means of protecting against legislative excesses. Sherman could see no reason to trust one man with such an awesome power and further "disapproved of Judges meddling in politics and parties." The Convention then began to wrangle over the idea of postponement, with Rutledge complaining about "the tediousness of the proceedings" and Ellsworth saying that he and his fellow delegates were growing "more & more skeptical as we proceed" (II, 301).

On a motion offered by North Carolina's Hugh Williamson and seconded by Wilson, the Convention then adopted the motion to raise the required congressional majorities needed to override an executive veto from two-thirds to three-fourths by a vote of 6-4-1. Madison succeeded in getting language adopted to make it clear that the veto would extend to a wide variety of legislative acts. The Convention also gave the president ten, rather than seven, days to return a bill to Congress.

Discussion resumed less than a week before the end of the Convention. Williamson, who had introduced the earlier motion raising the majority in Congress to override a veto, now proposed setting it back so as not to entrust the president with too much power. Sherman agreed. He believed that "it was more probable that a single man should mistake or betray this sense [of the people] than the Legislature" (II, 585). By contrast, Morris believed that the nation had more to fear from the "excess rather than the deficiency of laws," and wanted to leave the three-fourths requirement in place (II, 595). So did Alexander Hamilton. Gerry feared that the larger majority would allow too few men seeking presidential nominations to offices to join the president in blocking needed laws. Williamson feared that the three-fourths majorities might make it too difficult to repeal bad laws, and Mason agreed. Pinckney supported Gerry's argument. Madison attempted to "compare the danger from the weakness of 2/3 with the danger from the strength of 3/4" and judged that "the former was the greater" (II, 587). Nonetheless, the Convention voted 6-4-1 to restore the two-thirds provision.

Summary

The Convention thus kept the core idea in the Virginia Plan of a veto but chose to vest this power singly in the president rather than attempting to ally him with the judicial department. Partisans and opponents of the Council of Revision indicated that they were all concerned about the doctrine of separation of powers, although they clearly interpreted it differently, with those who were especially fearful of legislative powers being willing to ally the other two branches in opposition to them. Most, but by no means all, delegates who spoke on the subject appeared comfortable that in their judicial capacity, judges would examine the constitutionality of the laws that came before them, but those who supported this power thought there was a distinction between examining laws for their constitutionality and examining them for their wisdom. Delegates rejected an absolute executive veto, but they waffled on the majority that would be necessary to override a presidential veto. Agreeing for a time to a three-fourths majority, they ultimately settled on a two-thirds majority as being adequate to protect the presidency and the people against legislative encroachments without giving too much power to a single individual, perhaps allied with a few members of the legislative branch.

Robert Spitzer, who has studied the veto, has observed that the delegates to the Constitutional Convention chose not to use the term "veto," which he describes as a "semantic ploy" that "reflected a keen awareness of the monarchical roots of this power and the resentment that its use by the king and his colonial governors had engendered in America" (Spitzer 1988, 18). He observes that the placement of this power within Article I recognized that it was a legislative power and that the Constitution imposed no limits on its use. He further believes that the Framers intended for the veto to be used as much to influence the adoption of legislation as in blocking laws (18–19).

See Also Council of Revision; Judicial Review;
Massachusetts; New York; Separation of Powers

FOR FURTHER READING

Greene, Evarts B. 1917. "American Opinion on the Imperial Review of Provincial Legislation, 1776–1787." *American Historical Review* 23 (October): 104–107.

Spitzer, Robert A. 1988. *The Presidential Veto: Touchstone of the American Presidency.* Albany: State University of New York Press.

Tillman, Seth B. 2005. "A Textualist Defense of Article I, Section 7, Clause 3: Why *Hollingsworth v. Virginia* Was Rightly Decided, and Why *INS v. Chadha* Was Wrongly Reasoned." *Texas Law Review* 83 (Spring).

PRESS, FREEDOM OF

See BILL OF RIGHTS

PRESS COVERAGE

Although the Constitutional Convention operated under a rule of secrecy, newspapers, of which there were many in the United States, played a vital part in preparing the nation for the Convention by pointing to economic, political, and diplomatic problems that required a stronger national government and by circulating favorable reports of the Convention. John Alexander, the leading student of the subject, has amassed considerable evidence that demonstrates that a solid majority of the press served as advocates of the Convention and its work, even before they knew the proposals that it would make. Most editors were more concerned with advancing what they considered to be a patriotic goal than with remaining objective. Consistent with practices of the day, favorable stories in one paper were often widely reprinted (not always with proper attribution) in others. Papers gave special prominence to stories from the Philadelphia area. As a whole, the press was much less willing to print unfavorable stories.

Five Periods of Press Coverage

Alexander divides convention coverage into five periods, during each of which stories favoring the Convention dominated. These periods dated from the publication of the congressional resolution of February 21, 1787, recommending the Convention to its opening; from the start of the Convention in May through mid-June; from June 13 through mid-July; from the third week in July through early September; and from early September forward.

During the first period, the papers focused on the need for a stronger national government and on the problems of the existing Confederation. In the second period, coverage continued to be positive. Of special importance during this time period was the publication of a letter from clergyman Richard Price of England to Benjamin Rush advocating a strengthened national government. The press continued its focus on threats to the Union and the glorification of Convention delegates.

During the period beginning on June 13, members of the press rallied to minimize the potential damage of a story published in the *Pennsylvania Herald* claiming that

> some schemes, it is said, have been projected which preserve the form, but effectually destroy the spirit of democracy; and others, more bold, which, regarding only the necessity of a strong executive power, have openly rejected even the appearance of a popular constitution. (Quoted in Alexander 1990, 89–90)

In part, the press dismissed the story by arguing that the story could not be true because of the delegates' patriotism and in part by pointing out that since they were sworn to secrecy no reports purporting to come from delegates could be true (94). Papers continued to print stories emphasizing the dangers of another Shays's Rebellion or similar uprising.

After a number of stories, including an unsigned attack by Alexander Hamilton on Governor George Clinton of New York, surfaced in the third week of July questioning the consensus among delegates that the press had conveyed, the press once again rallied to the Convention's defense. During this period (August 18) the *Pennsylvania Herald* published an authorized report from the delegates indicating that, although they could not say what they were contemplating, they could affirm that they had no plans, as had been reported, to install a son of George III, or anyone else, as king. As reports that the Convention's work would soon end began to surface, the press largely counseled the public to have faith in the wisdom and patriotism of the Convention's delegates.

In the fifth and final period, in September, Antifederalist opponents of the Constitution began to get somewhat greater coverage, but they were still largely overwhelmed by the initiative that the Federalists supporting the Constitution had already gained in press favoritism toward Convention results. Newspapers often portrayed those opposed to the Constitution as being unpatriotic and disloyal. The advantage of those who supported the Constitution arguably continued into the Federalist/Antifederalist debates during debates over ratification of the Constitution.

Although it is easy to view press coverage as though it represented some form of conspiracy, evidence suggests "that publishers acted because they thought the Union must be reformed" (Alexander, 220). In supporting a strengthened national government, the press appears to have reflected popular sentiment, especially in more urban, cosmopolitan areas where commerce was more vital and where the press was strongest.

Press Coverage after Ratification of the Constitution

Once the Constitution was established, the two parties may have viewed the role of the press somewhat differently. One observer has thus noted that "Printers were well rewarded for their services. Federalists valued the press as a conduit of 'correct intelligence' from the government to the people; Anti-Federalists and later Republicans regarded it as a 'watchman on the tower of liberty'" (Gross 2001, 273). A study of subscribers to *The New York Magazine*, established in New York in 1790, suggests that literacy was fairly widespread and that the new press attempted to reinforce republican virtues and values (Nord 1988).

A study of the London press during the first decade of American independence indicates that initial stories about America reflected bitterness, fear, concern over trade disruption, and the belief that America was either unable or unwilling to honor its treaty obligations and to treat the Tories fairly (Ritcheson 1963, 93–101). Benjamin Franklin was among those who attempted to counter such views (Crane 1958). Negative attitudes in Britain largely changed to respect when the Constitution was written, with newspapers praising both the new form of government and its first president and hoping for greater friendship between the two nations (Ritcheson, 105–106).

See Also Antifederalists; Federalists; Franklin, Benjamin; *Pennsylvania Packet and Daily Advertiser;* Ratification in the States; Secrecy

FOR FURTHER READING

Alexander, John K. 1990. *The Selling of the Constitutional Convention: A History of News Coverage.* Madison, WI: Madison House.

Crane, Verner W. 1958. "Franklin's 'The Internal State of America' (1986)." *William and Mary Quarterly,* 3rd ser. 15 (April): 214–227.

Gross, Robert A. 2001. "The Print Revolution." In Mary K. Cayton and Peter W. Williams, eds. *Encyclopedia of American Cultural and Intellectual History.* Vol. 1 of 2. New York: Charles Scribner's Sons, 271–279.

Nord, David P. 1988. "A Republican Literature: A Study of Magazine Reading and Readers in Late Eighteenth-Century New York." *American Quarterly* 40 (March): 42–64.

Ritcheson, Charles R. 1963. "The London Press and the First Decade of American Independence, 1783–1793." *Journal of British Studies* 2 (May): 88–109.

PRICE, RICHARD (1723–1791)

Dr. Richard Price was a dissenting English clergyman, a disciple of Isaac Newton, and a Platonist

(Zebrowski 1994). He had supported the American Revolution in pamphlets published in 1776 and 1777 and was a friend to many leading Americans of his day. On October 6, 1778, Congress adopted a resolution considering Price as a U.S. citizen and offering to pay his way to America—an offer he politely refused (Cone 1948, 729). In 1784, Price published a pamphlet giving advice to the new nation. Entitled *Observations on the Importance of the American Revolution; and the Means of Making it a Benefit to the World*, the essay, like a later letter supporting a strengthened national government that he wrote to Benjamin Rush in January of 1787 (see Alexander 1990, 50–51), was widely circulated in the U.S.

This pamphlet opposed the slave trade, disfavored luxury in preference for an agrarian life, urged the nation to get itself on sound financial footing and pay off its debt, favored disestablishment of religion, and advocated investing Congress with greater powers. Maryland's Luther Martin cited Price in a speech to the Constitutional Convention on June 27, noting that Price had observed "that laws made by one man or a set of men, and not by common consent, is slavery" (Farrand 1937, I, 441). Delegates at Virginia's ratifying convention also evoked Price's authority (Cone, 746).

Price was less well-known than philosophers like John Locke and the Baron de Montesquieu, but his works contributed to American thinking about the defects of the Articles of Confederation, and, arguably, to the later push for a bill of rights. Although it is difficult to gauge his precise influence, it seems likely that the Framers welcomed and considered favorably the advice they received from such a longtime national friend. A year after the Constitutional Convention, 11 delegates and the wives of two others were listed as subscribers to Price's *Sermons on the Christian Doctrine as Received by the Different Denominations of Christians* (732–733). Price's sermon of 1789, *A Discourse on the Love of Our Country* was the catalyst for Edmund Burke's *Reflections on the Revolution in France* (Zebrowski, 18).

See Also Great Britain; Whig Ideology

FOR FURTHER READING

Alexander, John K. 1990. *The Selling of the Constitutional Convention: A History of News Coverage.* Madison, WI: Madison House.

Cone, Carl B. July 1948. "Richard Price and the Constitution of the United States." *American Historical Review* 53: 726–747.

———. 1952. *Torchbearer of Freedom: The Influence of Richard Price on Eighteenth Century Thought.* Lexington: University of Kentucky Press.

Farrand, Max, ed. 1937. *The Records of the Federal Convention.* 4 vols. New Haven, CT: Yale University Press.

Robbins, Caroline. 1959. *The Eighteenth-Century Commonwealthman: Studies in the Transmission, Development and Circumstances of English Liberal Thought from the Restoration of Charles II until the War with the Thirteen Colonies.* Cambridge, MA: Harvard University Press.

Zebrowski, Martha K. 1994. "Richard Price: British Platonist of the Eighteenth Century." *Journal of the History of Ideas* 55 (January): 17–35.

PRIESTLEY, JOSEPH (1733–1804)

Although he appears to have been mentioned only once—and this by Maryland's Luther Martin on June 27 in connection to a host of other thinkers (Farrand 1937, I, 437)—Joseph Priestley, like Britain's Richard Price, influenced American political thought of the Founding period. A supporter of the American Revolution in the 1770s, Priestley was both a theologian (often credited with founding modern Unitarianism) and a scientist. The discoverer of oxygen, Priestley was a political reformer who also strongly supported the French Revolution. Within England, he was a strong advocate of parliamentary reform, and his views ultimately influenced a mob to burn down his house and laboratory in Birmingham, England in 1791. Three years later Priestley sailed to the United States and settled in Pennsylvania where he lived out his last ten years.

Priestley was friends with Benjamin Franklin, with whom he associated in London in a supper club that Franklin called the Club of Honest

Whigs (Crane 1966, 210, 224–227). He was also friends with Thomas Jefferson and Benjamin Rush. He had an almost irrepressible belief in progress and used an analogy that led contemporaries to refer to him as "Gunpowder Joe." He had opined that

> we are, as it were, laying gunpowder, grain by grain, under the old building of error and superstition, which a single spark may hereafter influence, so as to produce an instantaneous explosion; in consequence of which that edifice, the erection of which has been the work of ages, may be overturned in a moment and so effectually as that same foundation can never be built again. (Quoted in Kramnick 1986, 12)

Priestley was a strong advocate of the Lockean idea of a minimalist state, in which such governments would serve the people who had consented to form them. Not only did Priestley oppose the divine right of kings and the use of civil power to enforce spiritual beliefs, but he even doubted that the government should have a role in education, where he feared it would seek to impose its own view and stifle creativity. Priestley was a strong advocate not only of the American but also of the French Revolution, and he often came into conflict with England's Edmund Burke, who he thought unduly attempted to mystify the state and those in authority. Although Priestley was strongly opposed to state authority, Priestley appears to have taken a more utilitarian (even authoritarian) approach to the possibility of subjecting individuals to increased discipline in factories, schools, prisons, and other institutions where he hoped to make them more productive and hardworking.

See Also Franklin, Benjamin; Jefferson, Thomas; Locke, John

FOR FURTHER READING

Crane, Verner W. 1966. "The Club of Honest Whigs: Friends of Science and Liberty." *William and Mary Quarterly,* 3rd ser. 23 (April): 210–233.
Kramnick, Isaac. 1986. "Eighteenth-Century Science and Radical Social Theory: The Case of Joseph Priestley's Scientific Liberalism." *Journal of British Studies* 25 (January): 1–30.

PRINTERS

See DUNLAP AND CLAYPOOLE; *PENNSYLVANIA PACKET AND DAILY ADVERTISER*

PRIVILEGES AND IMMUNITIES CLAUSE

Article IV, Section 2 of the Constitution provides that "the Citizens of each State shall be entitled to all Privileges and Immunities of Citizens in the several States." This clause appears to be a direct descendant of the provision in the Articles of Confederation that "the free inhabitants of each of these states, paupers, vagabonds and fugitives from justice excepted, shall be entitled to all privileges and immunities of free citizens in the several states" (Solberg 1958, 43). Although the Virginia Plan contained no comparable provision, on June 19 Virginia's James Madison criticized the New Jersey Plan on the basis that it would not prevent state trespasses on one another. He observed that both Virginia and Maryland had preferred their own citizens in cases "where the Citizens [of other states] are entitled to equality of privileges by the Articles of Confederation" (Farrand 1937, I, 317).

Pinckney's plan, which was forwarded to the Committee of Detail, contained an elliptical reference to a "Community of Privileges" (II, 135). The committee report, in turn, provided in its draft of a Constitution that "the Citizens of each State shall be entitled to all privileges and immunities of citizens in the several States" (II, 187), basically copying the provision from the Articles of Confederation but deftly leaving out the word "free."

When the Convention considered this provision on August 28, Madison reported that South Carolina's General Charles Cotesworth Pinckney expressed dissatisfaction apparently, favoring some more explicit provision for "property in slaves" (II, 443). The Convention nonetheless adopted the measure by a vote of 9-1-1, with Pinckney's South Carolina the only state in dissent. A scholar of the privileges and immunities clause has observed that it "was not seriously debated during the Constitutional Convention or during the ratification process because it was a familiar provision that was generally satisfactory" (Bogen 2003, 21).

The Committee of Style made no changes in the wording of this provision. It is designed to ensure that, in enforcing their laws, states treat citizens of other states like their own. It might arguably also provide a basis for a constitutional right of travel (Bogen 1987). A similar provision, which may have been designed to guarantee fundamental rights, found its way into the Fourteenth Amendment, but was largely eviscerated by subsequent Supreme Court decisions.

See Also Articles of Confederation; Committee of Detail

FOR FURTHER READING

Bogen, David S. 2003. *Privileges and Immunities: A Reference Guide to the United States Constitution*. Westport, CT: Praeger.
———. 1987. "The Individual Liberties within the Body of the Constitution: A Symposium: The Privileges and Immunities Clause of Article IV." *Case Western Reserve Law Review* 37: 794–861.
Farrand, Max, ed. 1937. *The Records of the Federal Convention*. 4 vols. New Haven, CT: Yale University Press.
Solberg, Winton U., ed. 1958. *The Federal Convention and the Formation of the Union of the American States*. New York: Liberal Arts Press.

PRIVY COUNCIL

See PRESIDENT, COUNCIL

PROGRESS

Some civilizations take the view that there is "no new thing under the sun" or that history is largely cyclical, with periods of progress inevitably followed by periods of decay. By contrast, the Enlightenment period during which the Constitution was written was often associated with the idea of progress. In a curious example of cross-fertilization, in America this idea had apparent roots in Christian ideas of the millennium that had been advanced during the Great Awakenings (Persons 1954, 149). Just as new scientific discoveries and the spread of new inventions, like those of Benjamin Franklin, promised to spread material wealth to greater numbers of people, people hoped that refinements in the science of government, like balanced government and separation of powers, might halt what many had believed to be the near-inevitable cycle of regime changes that the ancients had identified.

Many Americans believed that the American Revolution represented the start of a new epoch of freedom. Dr. Richard Price, an Englishman who supported the Americans during the Revolution, observed in his *Observations on the Importance of the American Revolution, and the Means of Making It a Benefit to the World* that "next to the introduction of Christianity among mankind, the American revolution may prove the most important step in the progressive course of human improvement" (quoted in Boyd 1970, 2). Supporters of the Revolution hoped that it could continue to bring blessings not only on the American people but throughout the world. The generally cautious George Washington thus observed:

> The foundation of our empire was not laid in the gloomy age of ignorance and superstition; but at an epocha when the rights of mankind were better understood and more clearly defined, than at any other period. The researches of the human mind after *social happiness* have been carried to a great extent; the treasures of knowledge acquired by the labors of philosophers, sages, and legislators, through a long succession of years, are laid open for our use, and their collected wisdom may be happily applied in the establishment of

Celebrations of anniversaries of the Declaration of Independence and the U.S. Constitution often emphasize progress, with scenes of the nation at its founding and scenes at the time of the celebration. These scenes are from the centennial celebration of the Declaration of Independence in 1876. (Courtesy of John R. Vile, photographed by Paul Christensen)

our forms of government. . . . At this auspicious period, the United States came into existence as a nation; and, if their citizens should not be completely free and happy, the fault will be entirely their own. (Quoted in Corwin 1964, 1–2)

In the first essay of *The Federalist,* Alexander Hamilton observed that "It seems to have been reserved to the people of this country, by their conduct and example, to decide the important question, whether societies of men are really capable or not of establishing good government from reflection and choice, or whether they are forever destined to depend for their political constitutions on accident and force" (Hamilton, Madison, and Jay 1961, 33). Over time the idea that the United States was at an auspicious time in its own life to

bring about advances in liberty (a theory consistent with cyclical views of history, which were then widely accepted) appears to have yielded to the idea that the Enlightenment was not simply "a cyclical episode, but . . . a phase of a secular trend extending far back in history, and one which would conceivably project indefinitely into the future" (Persons, 161).

The delegates to the Constitutional Convention clearly believed it was possible to apply human reason so as to create a better government. Although the delegates to the Convention do not appear to have talked at length about progress per se, it is interesting that the official journal of the Convention reports that, as chair of the Committee of the Whole, Nathaniel Gorham of Massachusetts reported at the beginning of each day's proceedings that "the Committee had made a progress in the matter to them referred" (Farrand 1937, I, 29, 45, 62, 76, 93, 115, 130, 148, 162, 174, 192, 209, 248).

The idea of progress was at least partially incorporated into the provision for patents and copyrights in Article I, Section 8 of the Constitution, which describes the powers of Congress. In justifying such patents and copyrights, it specifically cites the power of Congress "To promote the Progress of Science and useful Arts." Perhaps significantly, such progress was to be achieved not so much by government action in and of itself as by unleasing the actions of private individuals (Goldwin 1990, 41).

In 1780, John Adams may have summarized the aspirations of the Founding Fathers for continual progress. He had observed that "I must study politics and war that my sons may have liberty to study mathematics and philosophy. My sons ought to study mathematics and philosophy, geography, natural history and naval architecture, navigation, commerce and agriculture, in order to give their children a right to study painting, poetry, music, architecture, statuary, tapestry and porcelain" (quoted in Lienesch 1980, 25). Similarly, on the last day of the Convention, Benjamin Franklin expressed his hope that the sun painted on the back of President Washington's chair was rising on a new day rather than setting on an old one (II, 648).

See Also Copyrights and Patents; Price, Richard; Reason and Experience; Rising Sun

FOR FURTHER READING

Boyd, Julian P. 1970. *Anglo-American Union: Joseph Galloway's Plans to Preserve the British Empire, 1774–1788*. New York: Octagon Books.

Corwin, Edward S. 1964. "The Progress of Constitutional Theory between the Declaration of Independence and the Meeting of the Philadelphia Convention." *American Constitutional History: Essays by Edward S. Corwin*. Ed. Alpheus T. Mason and Gerald Garvey. New York: Harper and Row, Publishers.

Farrand, Max, ed. 1937. *The Records of the Federal Convention*. 4 vols. New Haven, CT: Yale University Press.

Goldwin, Robert A. 1990. *Why Blacks, Women, and Jews Are Not Mentioned in the Constitution and Other Unorthodox Views*. Washington, DC: AEI Press.

Hamilton, Alexander, James Madison, and John Jay. 1961. *The Federalist Papers*. Ed. Clinton Rossiter. New York: New American Library.

Lienesch, Michael. 1980. "The Constitutional Tradition: History, Political Action, and Progress in American Political Thought, 1787–1793." *Journal of Politics* 42 (February): 2–30.

Persons, Stow. 1954. "The Cyclical Theory of History in Eighteenth Century America." *American Quarterly* 6 (Summer): 157–163.

PROPERTY RIGHTS

Especially since historian Charles Beard argued that the delegates to the Constitutional Convention were primarily influenced by economic factors, the Framers' views of property rights have been considered important. Jennifer Nedelsky has observed that "the value of property was apparently so widely accepted in 1787 (at least in circles of men such as the Framers), that there seemed little need to defend or articulate it" (Nedelsky 1992, 47). Many delegates would undoubtedly have agreed with South Carolina's Pierce Butler when on July 6 he said that property was "the great object of Governt: the great cause of war, the great means of carrying it on" (Farrand 1937, I, 542). Social contract thinkers like Britain's John Locke had stressed that governments were formed largely for the protection of life, liberty and property, and some delegates were explicit about this. Thus, in notes for a speech that he delivered on June 18, Alexander Hamilton of New York observed that "One great objt. of Govt. is personal protection and the security of Property" (I, 302). Similarly, on July 11 South Carolina's John Rutledge observed that "Property was certainly the principal object of Society" (I, 534).

The constitutional provisions related to property are scattered throughout a number of specific provisions, the history of each of which is described separately in these volumes. This essay is intended to provide a collective overview of these provisions.

Wealth in Government

Three provisions that were discussed at the Convention dealt with the role of wealth in government. They involved the role of wealth in allocating representation in Congress and wealth qualifications for individuals seeking to vote or to run for office.

The original Virginia Plan called for state suffrage in both houses "to be proportioned to the Quotas of contribution or to the number of free inhabitants, as the one or the other rule may seem best in different cases" (I, 20). Under terms of the Great Compromise, representation was ultimately allocated differently in the two houses with states being represented equally in the Senate and according to the population of free persons and three-fifths of slaves, designated as "other persons," in the House of Representatives. Because slaves were at the time considered to be both persons and property (a tension also reflected in provisions related to slave importation and slave fugitives), the three-fifths clause thus provided for additional weight to be given to one form of property only.

The Framers considered delineating property qualifications for voting, but ultimately rejected imposing them at the national level. They were at least partly influenced by the difficulty of arriving at a standard that would be uniform throughout the United States. Since voting qualifications for national offices were to be the same as those for members of the state legislatures, states were left free to retain their own qualifications.

As in the case of imposing uniform wealth qualifications for voters, so too the delegates to the Convention found it impossible to arrive at mutually agreed-upon uniform national standards for officeholders. The U.S. Supreme Court has since decided that standards relating to age, residency, and citizenship for members of Congress are exclusive.

Powers and Limits

The new Constitution invested Congress with powers to tax and spend but barred direct taxes unless apportioned according to population. The Constitution also granted Congress powers that it had not previously been able to exercise over interstate and foreign commerce. Although the Constitution provided that treaties would require the consent of two-thirds of the Senate, it did not, as many Southern states had hoped, require a two-thirds vote for the passage of navigation acts. Article I, Section 9, did prohibit congressional taxation of exports. In a concession to the southernmost states, one limit that the delegates imposed on the latter power was the provision limiting taxation of slave imports for twenty years. As to the institution of slavery itself, the Convention essentially left this institution where it found it.

Many delegates to the Convention were quite concerned about measures that states were taking by printing money and otherwise undermining the rights of creditors. Article I, Section 10, of the Constitution thus provided that states could not interfere with the "obligation of contracts." This section also prohibited states from coining money, from emitting bills of credit, or from making "any Thing but gold and silver Coin a Tender in Payment of Debts." Article I, Sections 9 and 10 both prohibited bills of attainder, which states had sometimes used to confiscate the property of Loyalists during the Revolutionary War.

Article VI essentially left the status of existing debts against the United States in the same position it found them. It provided that "All Debts contracted and Engagements entered into, before the Adoption of this Constitution, shall be as valid against the United States under this Constitution, as under the Confederation."

The Constitution did not specifically address the power of the national government to create corporations, although the delegates did reject adding such a provision during the debates. Alexander Hamilton and John Marshall later argued that the right to create corporations was implicit in the "necessary and proper clause" of Article I, Section 8 granting powers to Congress.

Bill of Rights

The Bill of Rights grew out of concerns about the power of the new government. Although property rights are not prominent in the Bill of Rights, the Fifth Amendment (like the Fourteenth Amendment) provides that no person shall be "deprived of life, liberty, or property, without due process of law." This amendment also anticipated the right of eminent domain by providing that private property shall not "be taken for public use, without just compensation."

Property in Early America

Individuals in America derived their wealth from different sources. As the first two political parties developed, Federalists, led by Alexander Hamilton, expressed greater solicitude for the development of commerce and manufacturing, while Democratic-Republicans, led by Thomas Jefferson and drawing on the republican and classical heritages, idealized farmers as exemplars of democratic men (Eisinger 1947).

See Also African Americans; Beard, Charles; Bill of Rights; Commerce Power; Contracts Clause; Corporations; Locke, John; Occupations of the Delegates; Republicanism; Taxes on Imports and Exports; Three-fifths Clause

FOR FURTHER READING

Anderson, Thornton. 1993. *Creating the Constitution: The Convention of 1787 and the First Congress.* University Park: Pennsylvania State University Press, 85–115.

Eisinger, Chester E. 1947. "The Freehold Concept in Eighteenth-Century American Letters." *William and Mary Quarterly,* 3rd ser. 4 (1947): 42–59.

Ely, James W., Jr. 1992. *The Guardian of Every Other Right: A Constitutional History of Property Rights.* New York: Oxford University Press.

Farrand, Max, ed. 1937. *The Records of the Federal Convention.* 4 vols. New Haven, CT: Yale University Press.

Nedelsky, Jennifer. 1992. "The Protection of Property in the Origins and Development of the American Constitution." In Herman Belz, Ronald Hoffman, and Peter J. Albert, eds. *To Form a More Perfect Union: The Critical Ideas of the Constitution.* Charlottesville: University Press of Virginia, 38–72.

Siegan, Bernard H. 2003. "Protecting Economic Liberties." *Chapman Law Review* 6 (Spring): 43–121.

Vile, John R. 1987. "The U.S. Constitution and the Teaching of Economics." *The Social Studies* 78 (November/December): 244–248.

PROTESTANTISM

There is continuing debate about the influence of religion on the American Founding Fathers in general and on those who attended the Constitutional Convention in particular. Much of this discussion has centered on the Convention's failure to accept Benjamin Franklin's suggestion to begin each day with prayer, a topic treated in a separate essay in this book.

The Document

Other discussion has centered on the relative lack of religious references in the U.S. Constitution (a contrast to the Declaration of Independence but not to the Articles of Confederation, which also omitted such mention). The only reference to God in the U.S. Constitution is the statement that is usually attached indicating that the document was written "in the year of our Lord" 1787.

The Constitution arguably at least recognizes the fact that presidents might rest and worship on Sundays by exempting Sundays from the ten-day calculation used for the president to decide whether or not to veto laws. Similarly, it allows presidents either to swear or affirm when they take their oaths, thus providing for the possibility that a Quaker could accept such an office. It also prohibits religious tests as a condition for office. Probably most importantly of all, shortly after the Constitution was adopted, the First Amendment was added prohibiting the "establishment" of religion and guaranteeing its "free exercise."

The Societal Milieu

Many of the Founding Fathers are believed to have been Deists who accepted the existence of

John Calvin [no date or artist recorded]
(Library of Congress)

God but generally denied doctrines like the divinity of Christ, the Trinity, and the idea that God continually intervened in human affairs, especially through miracles. However, almost every delegate to the Constitutional Convention was affiliated with a specific Protestant denomination (two, Daniel Carroll of Maryland and Thomas Fitzsimons of Pennsylvania, were Roman Catholics), and the citizens of the nation as a whole were clearly Christian and Protestant. Some Deists like Thomas Jefferson, convinced that they were following the true teachings of Jesus, were even comfortable calling themselves Christians. Contrary to the surmises of earlier scholars, it further appears that rates of church membership were relatively high at the time the Constitution was written (Hutson 2003, 111–132). The New England states had largely been founded by Puritans who had come to the New World in search of religious freedom. Churches had been particularly active in establishing institutions of higher learning, including Princeton University, where Jonathan Edwards and John Witherspoon had both served as presidents, the latter at a time when a number of

the future delegates to the Convention, the most notable of whom was James Madison, were studying at this institution.

Undoubtedly, there had been a long-term trend toward secularization in the United States, but ideas of covenant, compact, and contract, which had strongly influenced the Puritans (who formulated the Mayflower Compact), continued to influence American political views and especially the American idea of constitutionalism. So too did the thousands of sermons that preachers delivered in the United States. Churchmen there had played an especially active role in the American Revolution. James Madison's support for religious freedom, which found expression in his support for the First Amendment and in his support of the Virginia Statute for Religious Freedom which Jefferson had authored, was influenced in large part by the persecution that he had seen Baptists and other dissenting believers suffer at the hands of Anglicans (today's Episcopalians) in his native Virginia. There is some reason to believe that the ties between Protestantism and classical liberalism may have been stronger at the time of the American Revolution and the Constitutional Convention than at later times in U.S. history (see Kloppenberg 1987; Noll 1993).

The Influence of John Calvin and Geneva

David Hall has argued in a recent book that John Calvin, one of the leaders of the Protestant Reformation, and his followers had a much greater influence on American political thought of the time period than is generally recognized. His thought would have especially influenced both the early Puritans and Presbyterians, of which there were many, but as one of the chief expositors of Protestant theology, his work would more generally have influenced Protestant denominations of his day. Calvin had been trained as a lawyer, and his thought had a particular influence on Scotland, where Presbyterianism flourished. Hall finds parallels between American thought and Calvin's view that it was a divine duty to oppose tyranny, between the pessimistic view of human nature embraced by Calvin and the Founders, between their emphasis on separation of powers and checks and balances, between their views that governments were ordained and established to promote liberty, and between their views that government had limited functions to play.

Hall also believes that many Americans of the day would have been familiar with, and would have admired, the government that Calvin established in the city of Geneva, Switzerland. In thus reviewing famous lawgivers, Theophilus Parsons of Massachusetts observed in "The Essex Result," a response to the proposal that resulted in the Massachusetts Constitution of 1780, that "the Genevans, perhaps the most virtuous republicans now existing, thought like Rousseau. They called the celebrated Calvin to their assistance. He came, and, by their gratitude, have they embalmed his memory" (text from Frohnen 2002, 207).

On June 4, Virginia's George Mason did cite the Swiss cantons as an example of republican government (Farrand 1937, I, 112). Alexander Hamilton, by contrast, pointed to wars among the cantons (I, 285), James Madison—who at the Convention generally touted the advantages of extended republics over smaller ones—cited intrigues among them (I, 319), and James Wilson cited the Swiss confederacy as one that had been held together by external threats (I, 343). These leads are relatively few, and hardly altogether complimentary, but they further suggest that the Swiss example may have been one of the examples that the Framers considered in devising their own federal system.

Protestantism and Capitalism

In a seminal work, the German sociologist Max Weber (1864–1920) argued that there was a further connection between Protestant Christianity and the system of capitalism. The Constitution surely provided strong legal support for such a free enterprise system, or what Isaac Kramnick has called "work-ethic Protestantism" (1988, 4). In addition to the idea connecting both the U.S. Revolution and the Constitutional Convention opposing "taxation without representation" and thus vesting the power to tax within Congress, the document

contains the contract clause and the limitations on state coinage of money in Article I, Section 10 (with the due process and takings clauses of the Fifth Amendment being added shortly thereafter). Although Protestants took the position that individuals obtained salvation through the grace of God rather than through works, many also thought that outward works, and prosperity itself, were evidences of such grace. Protestants further believed that one should honor God in all aspects of life, including business dealings, and so they tended to look more positively on worldly success and material possessions than had some strands within Roman Catholic Christianity.

There are undoubtedly many other areas in which Christian thought generally, and Protestant thought in particular, directly or indirectly influenced thinking both at the Convention and in the early republic. These should be sufficient to dismiss broad statements positing either that the Convention established a Christian nation (as opposed to protecting a society where Christians could worship according to their consciences) or that the delegates were uninfluenced by the religious currents of their day.

See Also Biblical and Religious References at the Constitutional Convention; Prayer at the Convention; Property Rights; Puritanism; Religious Affiliations of the Delegates; Swiss Cantons

FOR FURTHER READING

Cousins, Norman, ed. 1958. *"In God We Trust": The Religious Beliefs and Ideas of the American Founding Fathers.* New York: Harper and Brothers.

Eidsmoe, John. 1987. *Christianity and the Constitution: The Faith of Our Founding Fathers.* Grand Rapids, MI: Baker Book House.

Engeman, Thomas S., and Michael P. Zuchert, eds. 2004. *Protestantism and the American Founding.* Notre Dame, IN: University of Notre Dame Press.

Farrand, Max, ed. 1937. *The Records of the Federal Convention.* 4 vols. New Haven, CT: Yale University Press.

Fox, Frank W. 2003. *The American Founding.* 2nd ed. Boston, MA: Pearson Custom Publishing. (See especially 36–51.)

Frohnen, Bruce, ed. 2002. *The American Republic: Primary Sources.* Indianapolis, IN: Liberty Fund.

Hall, David W. 2003. *The Geneva Reformation and the American Founding.* Lanham, MD: Lexington Books.

Holmes, David L. 2003. *The Religion of the Founding Fathers.* Charlottesville, VA: Ann Arbor, MI: Ash Lawn-Highland: Clements Library.

Hutson, James H. 2003. *Forgotten Features of the Founding: The Recovery of Religious Themes in the Early American Republic.* Lanham, MD: Lexington Books.

———. 1998. *Religion and the Founding of the American Republic.* Washington, DC: Library of Congress.

Keillor, Steven J. 1996. *This Rebellious House: American History and the Truth of Christianity.* Downers Grove, IL: InterVarsity Press.

Kessler, Sanford. 1992. "Tocqueville's Puritans: Christianity and the American Founding." *Journal of Politics* 54 (August): 776–792.

Kloppenberg, James T. 1987. "The Virtues of Liberalism: Christianity, Republicanism, and Ethics in Early American Political Discourse." *Journal of American History* 74 (June): 9–33.

Kramnick, Isaac. 1988. "The 'Great National Discussion': The Discourse of Politics in 1787." *William and Mary Quarterly,* 3rd ser. 45 (January): 3–32.

Noll, Mark A. 1993. "The American Revolution and Protestant Evangelicalism." *Journal of Interdisciplinary History* 23 (Winter): 615–638.

Sandoz, Ellis. 1991. *Political Sermons of the American Founding Era, 1730–1805.* 2 vols. Indianapolis, IN: Liberty Fund.

Shain, Barry A. 1994. *The Myth of American Individualism: The Protestant Origins of American Political Thought.* Princeton, NJ: Princeton University Press.

Walters, Kerry S. 1982. *The American Deists: Voices of Reason and Dissent in the Early Republic.* Lawrence: University Press of Kansas.

Weber, Max. 1992. (1904–1905). *The Protestant Ethic and the Spirit of Capitalism.* New York: Routledge.

PUBLIC ADMINISTRATION

See BUREAUCRACY; PRESIDENT, EXECUTIVE POWER

Contemporary Death of a "Witch"

On May 5, just weeks before the Constitutional Convention began, a number of Philadelphians attacked an elderly woman known as Korbmacher, or "basketmaker," on the south side of the city because they believed that she was a witch. Consistent with lingering superstition, they had cut her forehead to counteract any evil spells she might have cast. City papers had picked up the story, along with her pleas for protection. These pleas, however, proved unavailing when, on July 10, as the Convention was meeting, another mob formed. It carried her through the city streets, where she was vilified and pelted. Newspapers report that she died from this abuse several days later.

In a subsequent trial of one of the women who had committed violence against the alleged witch, the presiding justice derided the claim that some wizened old woman could have cast ill charms. By contrast, he made the case that Edmund Morgan describes as "the occasion for a labored exercise of tasteless wit": "If, however, some damsels that I have seen, animated with the bloom of youth, and equipped with all the grace of beauty, if such women were indicted for the offence, the charge might receive some countenance, for they are indeed calculated to *charm* and *bewitch* us" (quoted in Morgan 1983, 11).

The papers do not record the outcome of the case.

No members of the Convention are known to have commented on the story. Some may very well, however, have tucked the incident away in their minds as an example of what could happen when "the people" were enabled to act lawlessly.

FOR FURTHER READING

Morgan, Edmund S. 1983. "The Witch, & We, the People." *American Heritage* 34 (August/September): 6–11.

PUBLIC OPINION

Modern students of politics take it for granted that politicians in a representative democracy will take public opinion into account in formulating their platforms and making their appeals to the public. Public opinion polling has become a standard part of modern political campaigns, and politicians often continue to seek guidance from polls once they are elected to office. Although some opinions prove to be relatively stable over time, others fluctuate fairly widely. Similarly, pollsters have discovered that opinions often vary significantly in the intensity with which they are held (Cummings and Wise 2001, 178).

Origins of the Idea of Public Opinion

The idea of public opinion appears to have arisen chiefly from the French Enlightenment and was considered to be "the ruling authority in republican government" (Sheehan 2002, 926); John Locke and David Hume also commented on the importance of such opinion in shaping societal norms (Noelle-Neumann 1979). Significantly, James Madison was among the American Framers who apparently distinguished "between mere will and reason and between ephemeral popular passions and public opinion" (Sheehan, 947). Madison, and presumably other American Founders, believed that public leaders had the responsibility to refine and guide public opinion (948), and they distinguished the noble pursuit of fame from the baser pursuit of simple popularity (Adair 1974, 11).

The Difficulty of Ascertaining Public Opinion

One of the fascinating aspects of the Constitutional Convention of 1787 is that its members were attempting to formulate a government prior to the invention of modern scientific polling. Moreover, because the proceedings were secret, even had such polling existed, pollsters would not have been able to put specific issues under discussion at the Convention directly to the people.

Similarly fascinating is the fact that delegates referred frequently to public opinion, as they understood it, sometimes using it to justify one or another measure they were proposing and at other times suggesting that it was their duty to lead. The delegates often found themselves in the dilemma of having been called to "revise and enlarge" the Articles of Confederation but finding that they were instead considering an entirely new system, which at least one state (Delaware) had forbidden its delegates to do.

Attributions of Public Sentiments: From the General to the Specific

On a number of occasions, delegates expressed absolute assurance that they knew the mind of the people regarding one or another issue under discussion. Sometimes, the sentiments that delegates attributed to the American people dealt with what might be called temperament or attachment to general principles—Lyn Spillman has observed that the delegates often referred to the "genius," or "temper," of the American people (1996, 160)—which might be easier to gauge than stances on more specific issues. Thus, in an undelivered speech, probably penned by Jared Ingersoll of Pennsylvania around June 20, 1787, he observed that

the people of the united-States, excited to Arms by the insidious designs of the then Mother Country have become admirers of liberty warmly & passionately so—they snuff tyranny in every tainted Gale—they are jealous of their liberty—they are pleased with their present Governments, they think them as energetick as they ought to be framed, they are continually planning subdivisions of the present Governments, they are complaining of the expence of the present Governments—they are jealous of designs to introduce a Monarchy, under specious pretences & different names in the despotick empire of Rome . . . they are apprehensive of designs to abridge the liberties of the common people—to make a greater difference of Ranks than the present Government admits of. (Hutson 1987, 104–105)

More frequently, delegates pointed to one or another principle that they associated with public sentiment. George Mason thus observed that he was sure that the public mind was settled in regard both to "an attachment to Republican Government" and "to more than one branch in the Legislature" (Farrand 1937, I, 339). Edmund Randolph, also from Virginia, asserted that "the people were attached to frequency of elections" (I, 36). Elbridge Gerry of Massachusetts said that "there were not 1/1000 part of our fellow citizens who were not agst. every approach towards Monarchy" (I, 425). Similarly, Connecticut's Nathaniel Gorham was convinced that the people had long been accustomed to universal freehold suffrage "and will never allow it to be abridged" (II, 216).

Ambiguity as a Reason to Propose What Was Best

If popular sentiment seemed clear on some basic issues, it gave little guidance on others. Writing to his wife on August 18, 1787, James McHenry of Maryland observed that he was "even without the satisfaction of knowing that what I am assisting in will meet the approbation of those who sent me hither" (Hutson, 246).

For some delegates the inability to ascertain popular sentiment with precision was an invitation for delegates to craft the document that they thought was the wisest and rely on the reputations of the delegates and/or on the wisdom of their final product for getting the document ratified. After Elbridge Gerry asserted that "the people of New England will never give up the point of annual elections" (I, 214), Virginia's James Madison responded by observing that the delegates should seek to do their best and hope that enlightened public opinion would follow:

> if the opinions of the people were to be our guide, it wd. be difficult to say what course we ought to take. No member of the Convention could say what the opinions of his Constituents were at this time; much less could he say what they would think if possessed of the information

& lights possessed by the members here; & still less what would be their way of thinking 6 or 12 months hence. We ought to consider what was right & necessary in itself for the attainment of a proper Governmt. A plan adjusted to this idea will recommend itself—The respectability of this convention will give weight to their recommendation of it. Experience will be constantly urging the adoption of it, and all the most enlightened & respectable citizens will be its advocates.

Should we fall short of the necessary & profit point, this influential class of citizens will be turned against the plan, and little support in opposition to them can be gained to it from the unreflecting multitude. (I, 215)

Similarly, Pennsylvania's James Wilson observed that "With regard to the *power of the Convention*, he conceived himself authorized to *conclude nothing*, but to be at liberty to *propose any thing*" (I, 253). He elaborated:

> With *regard to the sentiments of the people*, he conceived it difficult to know precisely what they are. Those of the particular circle in which one moved, were commonly mistaken for the general voice. He could not persuade himself that the State Govts. & sovereignties were so much the idols of the people, nor a Natl. Govt. so obnoxious to them, as some supposed. (I, 253)

Gouverneur Morris, also of Pennsylvania, expressed similar views:

> Much has been said of the sentiments of the people. They were unknown. They could not be known. All that we can infer is that if the plan we recommend be reasonable & right; all who have reasonable minds and sound intentions will embrace it, notwithstanding what has been said by some Gentlemen. (I, 529–530)

In a like vein, New York's Alexander Hamilton observed that while his own views differed from both the Virginia and New Jersey Plans, "the people are gradually ripening in their opinions of government—they begin to be tired of an excess of democracy" (I, 301). In discussing whether the Constitution should specify the pay of members of the legislative branch, Edmund Randolph distinguished popular opinion from prejudice. Madison cited him as fearing we were going too far, in consulting popular prejudices. Whatever respect might be due to them, in lesser matters, or in cases where they formed the permanent character of the people, he thought it neither incumbent on nor honorable for the Convention, to sacrifice right & justice to that consideration (I, 372).

Ambiguity as a Basis for Caution

Other delegates thought that inability to know the sentiments of the people, combined with an original charge simply to "revise and enlarge" the Articles of Confederation, should caution the delegates about going too far. Elbridge Gerry thus responded to Madison's previously cited arguments for delegates to propose what they deemed best by observing that

> if the reasoning of Mr. M[adison] were just, and we supposed a limited Monarchy the best form of itself, we ought to recommend it, tho' the genius of the people was decidedly adverse to it, and having no hereditary distinctions among us, we were destitute of the essential materials for such an innovation. (I, 215)

Pointing to the unlikelihood that the people would "ratify a scheme [like that in the Virginia Plan], which they had never authorized us to propose" and "which so far exceeded what they regarded as sufficient," New York's John Lansing further observed:

> To rely on any change which is hereafter to take place in the sentiments of the people would be trusting to too great an uncertainty. We know only what their present sentiments are, and it is in vain to propose what will not accord with these. The States will never feel a sufficient confidence in a general Government to give it a negative on their laws. The Scheme is itself totally

novel. There is [no] parallel to it to be found. The authority of Congress is familiar to the people, and an augmentation of the powers of Congress will be readily approved by them. (I, 250)

Favoring the New Jersey Plan over the Virginia Plan, William Paterson argued that the former was in better accord "with the powers of the Convention" and "with the sentiments of the people." He thus reiterated Lansing's view:

> If the confederacy was radically wrong, let us return to our States, and obtain larger powers, not assume them of ourselves. I came here not to speak my own sentiments, but [the sentiments of] those who sent me. Our object is not such a Governmt. as may be best in itself, but such a one as our Constituents have authorized us to prepare, and as they will approve. (I, 250)

Similarly, Delaware's Gunning Bedford observed that "the People expect an Amendment of the Confederation–they will be surprised at our System–they are not ripe for it" (Hutson, 132).

Ratification Procedures

The delegates to the Constitutional Convention bypassed existing state legislatures (who generally lost power under the new plan) by providing in Article VII that the new document would go into effect when ratified by specially called conventions in nine or more of the states. Although this falls short of modern standards, this was probably as democratic a mechanism for ascertaining public opinion as could have been used at the time. The fact that debates over the Constitution led to the push for the adoption of the Bill of Rights is one indication that the Convention mechanism allowed for popular input.

In contrast to the system that it replaced, the people chose members of the lower house of Congress by popular election rather than being appointed by states legislatures. Similarly, delegates to the Convention provided that the executive branch would be selected by an indirect means of popular election through the Electoral College. Delegates who thought that strong leadership would ultimately sway popular opinion appear to have been proven correct.

Public Opinion as a Support for the New Constitution

It is fascinating that James Madison opposed the idea, suggested by Thomas Jefferson, of mandating periodic constitutional revisions. Madison feared that such reevaluations could destabilize public opinion and undermine faith in the Constitution. Writing in *Federalist* No. 49, Madison observed that "as every appeal to the people would carry an implication of some defect in the government, frequent appeals would, in great measure, deprive the government of that veneration which time bestows on everything, and without which perhaps the wisest and freest governments would not possess the requisite stability" (Hamilton, Madison, and Jay 1961, 314). He went on to observe:

> The reason of man, like man himself, is timid and cautious when left alone, and acquires firmness and confidence in proportion to the number with which it is associated. When the examples which fortify opinion are *ancient* as well as *numerous*, they are known to have a double effect. (315)

Noting that a "nation of philosophers" where "a reverence for the laws would be sufficiently inculcated by the voice of an enlightened reason" could disregard such a consideration, Madison further observed that

> a nation of philosophers is as little to be expected as the philosophical race of kings wished for by Plato. And in every other nation, the most rational government will not find it a superfluous advantage to have the prejudices of the community on its side. (315)

Debates over public opinion continued into the early republic. Colleen Sheehan has argued

that James Madison and the Democratic-Republican Party that he helped to establish were committed both to the sovereignty of such opinion and to broad participatory politics. By contrast, she believes that Alexander Hamilton, and the Federalist Party that he founded, put heavier reliance on elites and favored a more submissive role for the public (2004).

See Also Fame; Press Coverage; Ratification in the States; Secrecy

FOR FURTHER READING

Adair, Douglass, 1974. "Fame and the Founding Fathers." *Fame and the Founding Fathers.* Ed. Trevor Colburn. New York: W. W. Norton, 3–26.

Carr, William G. *The Oldest Delegate: Franklin in the Constitutional Convention.* Newark: University of Delaware Press.

Cummings, Milton C., Jr., and David Wise. 2001. *Democracy under Pressure: An Introduction to the American Political System.* 9th ed. Fort Worth, TX: Harcourt College Publishers.

Farrand, Max, ed. 1937. *The Records of the Federal Convention.* 4 vols. New Haven, CT: Yale University Press.

Hamilton, Alexander, James Madison, and John Jay. 1961. *The Federalist Papers.* Ed. Clinton Rossiter. New York: New American Library.

Hutson, James H., ed. 1987. *Supplement to Max Farrand's* The Records of the Federal Convention of 1787. New Haven, CT: Yale University Press.

Noelle-Neumann, Elisabeth. 1979. "Public Opinion and the Classical Tradition: A Re-evaluation." *Public Opinion Quarterly* 43 (Summer): 143–156.

Schudson, Michael. 1998. *The Good Citizen: A History of American Civic Life.* New York: The Free Press.

Sheehan, Colleen A. 2002. "Madison and the French Enlightenment: The Authority of Public Opinion." *William and Mary Quarterly,* 3rd ser. 59 (October): 925–956.

——. 2004. "Madison v. Hamilton: The Battle over Republicanism and the Role of Public Opinion." *American Political Science Review* 98 (August): 405–424.

Spillman, Lyn. 1996. "'Neither the Same Nation nor Different Nations': Constitutional Conventions in the United States and Australia." *Comparative Studies in Society and History* 38 (January): 149–181.

Young, Alfred F. 1995. "The Constitution Was Created by the Genius of the American People." In William Dudley, ed. *The Creation of the Constitution: Opposing Viewpoints*. San Diego, CA: Greenhaven Press, 267–277.

PURITANISM

The Puritans, the dissenting Protestants who had originally sought to "purify" the English Church and who settled in Massachusetts and elsewhere in New England, are among the groups who are believed to have shaped America's identity and character as it is incorporated into the U.S. Constitution. Although coming to the New World in search of religious liberty, the Calvinistic Puritans were not as willing to extend such liberty to others.

The Puritans, who were the chief impetus behind the Mayflower Compact, are known for their focus on "ordered liberty," and for their emphasis on covenants and contracts binding members of society by consent for common purposes. Puritans, who believed that all of life should be lived for the glory of God, are also associated with a strong work ethic that continued in secularized form long after much of the underlying theology had been jettisoned. Commentators often associate other characteristics of Puritan thought with strains of thought in more secular successors like Benjamin Franklin and John Adams (Conkin 1968; Morgan 1961). The Puritan concern with the sinfulness of human nature, for example, easily translated into attempts to check and limit governmental powers. Puritans and other religious influences are also associated with the idea of a common good over and apart from the pursuit of individual self-interests (Shain 1994).

A group of Puritans sit at a table with their heads bowed in prayer as a man leads the blessing at Thanksgiving dinner. From an 1867 illustration. (Kean Collection/Getty Images)

See Also Contracts Clause; Human Nature; Mayflower Compact; Protestantism

FOR FURTHER READING

Conkin, Paul K. 1968. *Puritans and Pragmatists: Eight Eminent American Thinkers.* New York: Dodd, Mead.

Kessler, Sanford. 1992. "Tocqueville's Puritans: Christianity and the American Founding." *Journal of Politics* 54 (August): 776–792.

Martinez, Fernando Rey. 2003. "The Religious Character of the American Constitution: Puritanism and Constitutionalism in the United States." *The Kansas Journal of Law and Public Policy* 12 (Spring): 459–482.

Miller, Perry. 1953. *The New England Mind: From Colony to Province.* Cambridge, MA: Harvard University Press.

———. 1939. *The New England Mind: The Seventeenth Century.* New York: Macmillan.

Morgan, Edmund S. 1961. "John Adams and the Puritan Tradition." *New England Quarterly* 34 (December): 518–529.

Shain, Barry A. 1994. *The Myth of American Individualism: The Protestant Origins of American Political Thought.* Princeton, NJ: Princeton University Press.

Q

QUORUM

The Constitutional Convention had been scheduled to meet on the second Monday in May, the 14th, but the Convention did not formally convene until it had a majority of representatives from a majority of states (seven). Delegates considered such a majority, which similar bodies recognized, as necessary to constitute a quorum. This took until Friday, May 25. At this time the seven states present unanimously selected George Washington as president of the Convention and began formulating rules that would be specific to that body.

This emphasis on rules and procedures indicates that the delegates had a history of legislative practices in Britain, the legislatures of the individual colonies, and the continental congresses from which to draw. The latter example, with its difficulty meeting quorums, its weak leadership, and its multiplicity of committees, may have been more negative than positive (Wilson and Jillson 1989). Rules are designed to promote reasoned discussion and to enhance fairness. Delegates undoubtedly recognized that their proceedings would have more legitimacy if they followed customary forms.

On May 25 the states of New York, New Jersey, Pennsylvania, Delaware, Virginia, North Carolina, and South Carolina were represented by a total of 27 delegates. There was also a single representative from Massachusetts and a single delegate from Georgia in attendance on May 25 (thus bringing the total present to 29), but votes were not recorded for these or other states until a majority of delegates arrived from them.

The delegates to the Constitutional Convention specified that a majority of each house of Congress would constitute a quorum of that body. The Constitution further allowed senators to vote individually rather than by states, thus hoping to avoid gridlock, like that often experienced under the Articles of Confederation, in cases when senators from the same state split their votes (Wilson and Jillson).

See Also Congress, Quorums; Rules of the Constitutional Convention

FOR FURTHER READING

Wilson, Rick K., and Calvin Jillson. 1989. "Leadership Patterns in the Continental Congress, 1774–1789." *Legislative Studies Quarterly* 14 (February): 5–37.

R

RANDOLPH, EDMUND
(1753–1813)

Edmund Randolph was born in 1753 near Williamsburg, Virginia to John Randolph and Ariana Jennings Randolph, members of one of Vir-

Edmund Randolph, delegate from Virginia
(Pixel That)

ginia's most prominent families. Edmund Randolph attended the College of William and Mary and studied in his father's law office before beginning practice at age 20. His uncle Peyton Randolph was president of the First Continental Congress. When Edmund Randolph's parents left for England, Edmund chose to cast his lot with the Patriot cause, serving for a time as an aide-de-camp to General Washington before having to help his aunt upon the death of his uncle.

Randolph was the youngest delegate at the Virginia state convention of 1776, the same year he was chosen as the state's attorney general and the year he married Elizabeth Nicholas, with whom he would have five children. In the years following, he served as mayor of Williamsburg, as a rector of the College of William and Mary, as a clerk of the Virginia House of Delegates, and as a member of the Continental Congress. He resigned from this Congress to pursue the practice of law, which was one of the largest in Virginia. Randolph attended the Annapolis Convention and was chosen that same year as governor of Virginia.

As state governor, Edmund Randolph headed the Virginia delegation at the Constitutional Convention. In this capacity, he presented the Virginia Plan, usually thought to be the primary brainchild of Virginia's James Madison (one of the difficulties in assessing Randolph's contribution is in attempting to ascertain how much of the Virginia Plan he accepted). Randolph arrived in Philadelphia on May 15, but was one of only three delegates who stayed to the end of the Convention and did not sign the document. Although many attributed his action (or inaction) to political ambitions, Randolph at least partially redeemed himself in the eyes of many of the Constitution's supporters when he helped in the effort for constitutional ratification in his home state.

Speech Introducing the Virginia Plan

Randolph prefaced his speech on the Virginia Plan by expressing regret that the task of introducing such a momentous plan should "fall to him, rather than those, who were of longer standing in life and political experience" (Farrand 1937, I, 18) but indicating that his fellow delegates had chosen him for the task. Randolph divided his speech—one of the few that is described in far greater detail in the Convention's official journal than in Madison's notes—into four parts. These included the properties that governments should possess, the defects of the Articles of Confederation, the dangers of the situation at hand, and the remedies. Under the first heading, Randolph argued that governments should be able to secure themselves against foreign invasions and internal dissentions, to secure blessings that states were unable to secure on their own, to protect themselves against state encroachment, and to secure their authority over state constitutions (I, 18).

Randolph did not believe it was fair to impute the problems under the Articles of Confederation to the authors of this government who had to work "in the then infancy of the science, of constitutions, & of confederacies" and prior to such time as many problems had revealed themselves. Randolph identified five varieties of problems, each corresponding to the goals that Randolph had identified governments as pursuing. He believed the Articles lacked inadequate power to protect against foreign invasion, both because its power to wage war was inadequate and because they "could not cause infractions of treaties or of the law of nations, to be punished" (I, 19). He argued that the government had shown a similar inability to deal with domestic disturbances. The nation was unable to secure the benefits that might come from

"a productive impost—counteraction of the commercial regulations of other nations—pushing of commerce ad libitum —&c &c" (I, 19). He also observed that the national government was unable to protect itself against state encroachments and that it was not paramount to state constitutions (I, 19).

Randolph identified the dangers of "anarchy" and of "the laxity of government every where" (I, 19). He believed the remedy should proceed according to "the republican principle" (I, 19). He accordingly followed by outlining the 15 provisions of the Virginia Plan.

These provisions respectively provided for:

- a "correction" and "enlargement" of the Articles so as to accomplish its purposes;
- representation in the legislature on the basis of tax contributions or the number of "free inhabitants";
- a bicameral Congress;
- selection of the first branch by the people of the states for yet-to-be-designated terms, subject to recall;
- selection of the second branch by members of the first from among nominees submitted by state legislatures;
- the power of each house to originate acts in all cases "to which the separate States are incompetent, or in which the harmony of the United States may be interrupted by the exercise of individual Legislation" (I, 21) and to veto all state laws or call forth the militia against states failing to fulfill their duties;
- a national executive chosen by the national legislature for a single term the length of which was yet to be determined;
- a Council of Revision consisting of the executive and select members of the judiciary with the power to veto acts of Congress, subject to majority override;
- a national judiciary to consist of a Supreme Court and other courts established by Congress;
- the admission of new states;
- guarantees of republican governments for the states;
- the continuation of Congress until adoption of the new government;

- oaths binding state officials to support the new government; and
- a provision for the adoption of future amendments. (I, 20–22)

Randolph ended his speech asking the delegates not to let slip "the present opportunity of establishing general peace, harmony, happiness and liberty in the U.S." (I, 23).

Randolph's introduction of the Virginia Plan undoubtedly shocked many delegates by departing so radically from the existing government under the Articles of Confederation. On the next day, Randolph introduced a resolution more accurately describing the scope of the changes he had proposed (I, 30). Randolph also introduced a proposal that the existing congressional system should be proportional "and not according to the present system" (I, 31). Asked by South Carolina's Charles Pinckney whether he meant to abolish the state governments, Randolph said "that he meant by these general propositions merely to introduce the particular ones which explained the outlines of the system he had in view" (I, 34). Similarly, when asked on May 31 to explain how many members he contemplated would be in the Senate, Randolph observed "that details made no part of the plan, and could not perhaps with propriety have been introduced." He did indicate that he thought that the second branch should be smaller than the first so as "to be exempt from the passionate proceedings to which numerous assemblies are liable" (I, 51). He further traced such defects to "the turbulence and follies of democracy" (I, 51).

Federalism

Perhaps reflecting a somewhat less nationalistic view of the subject than did Madison, when asked about the Virginia Plan, Randolph "disclaimed any intention to give indefinite powers to the national Legislature, declaring that he was entirely opposed to such inroads on the State jurisdictions, and that he did not think any considerations whatever could ever change his determination" (I, 53). Indeed, when Delaware's Gunning Bedford proposed on July 17 that Congress should be able to

legislate "in all cases for the general interests of the Union, and also in those to which the States are separately incompetent," Randolph objected that this involved "the power of violating all the laws and constitutions of the States, and of intermeddling with their police" (II, 26).

On June 11, Randolph did support a provision for state officials to take an oath to support the national Constitution (I, 203). Consistent with his criticisms of the Articles in introducing the Virginia Plan, Randolph indicated later in the Convention (July 18) that Congress needed to be able to guarantee states a "republican" form of government (II, 47); indeed, he wanted to go further and affirmatively specify that states could form no other kind (II, 48).

In a discussion of the full faith and credit clause on August 29, Randolph indicated that "there was no instance of one nation executing the judgments of the Court of another nation" (II, 448). He accordingly proposed a substitution whereby states would recognize the legal acts recorded under the seal of authority of another (II, 448). Randolph renewed objections to the full faith and credit clause on September 3, observing that one of his concerns about the Constitution was that "its definition of the power of the Government was so loose as to give it opportunities of usurping all the State powers" (II, 489).

Comparing Plans

It may well have been a simple act of courtesy, but on June 14, Randolph seconded a proposal by New Jersey's William Paterson postponing a report from the Committee of the Whole so as to give Paterson time to prepare what became known as the New Jersey Plan (I, 240). After this plan was considered, some delegates argued that the New Jersey Plan better reflected the sentiments of the people and was thus more likely to be adopted. Randolph responded that "it would be treason to our trust, not to propose what we found necessary" (I, 255). He pointed anew to the problems of the existing government, and argued that the two remedies were "coercion" and "real legislation." He believed the former was "*impracti-*

cable, expensive, [and] *cruel to individuals."* He further believed that such a plan tended "to habituate the instruments of it to shed the blood & riot in the spoils of their fellow Citizens, and consequently trained them up for the service of Ambition" (I, 256). By contrast, he favored direct control by the national government over individuals. He argued that the Congress under the Articles constituted "a mere diplomatic body" whose members were "always obsequious to the views of the States" (I, 256). He concluded that "A Natl. Govt. alone, properly constituted, will answer the purpose; and he begged it to be considered that the present is the last moment for establishing one" (I, 256).

Randolph expressed dismay over the strong language of Delaware's Gunning Bedford suggesting that the small states might seek foreign allies (I, 514). Randolph claimed that neither the small states nor the large could exist well without the other, and that such an attempt would "involve the whole in ruin" (I, 515).

When the Convention reached the Great Compromise involving representation in the two houses of Congress, one of the provisions of this compromise called for restricting the origination of money bills to the House. Although a number of large state supporters including James Madison of Virginia and James Wilson of Pennsylvania questioned the wisdom of this move, Randolph was among those who successfully supported the restoration of this provision for fear that its elimination would endanger the entire compromise (II, 230; also see II, 232; II, 234). He appears to have believed that the origination of money bills would actually provide the House of Representatives with an advantage (II, 263; also see II, 273), and he was concerned about popular opinion. He explained on August 13:

> We had numerous & monstrous difficulties to combat. Surely we ought not to increase them. When the people behold in the Senate, the countenance of an aristocracy; and in the president, the form at least of a little monarch, will not their alarms be sufficiently raised without taking from their immediate representatives, a

right which has been so long apportionment to them. (II, 278–279)

The Legislature

House of Representatives

Randolph favored terms of two years rather than three for members of the House of Representatives. He actually preferred annual elections, which he believed the people favored, but he thought that they would be inconvenient for a government the size of the United States (I, 360).

Senate

Although Randolph had been somewhat vague about the initial configuration of the U.S. Senate, he favored seven-year terms for senators (I, 218), with terms to end so that relatively equal numbers would annually come up for election (I, 408). He argued that the "democratic licentiousness of the State Legislatures proved the necessity of a firm Senate" (I, 218). He also foresaw this body as guarding against possible combinations of the executive with demagogues in the first branch (I, 218). Randolph thought that it would be difficult for an aristocratic Senate, such as Gouverneur Morris of Pennsylvania proposed, to coexist with a democratic House (I, 514). When the Convention tied in a vote over representation in the Senate, Randolph proposed a temporary adjournment (II, 17–18).

Randolph favored executive appointment in the case of senatorial vacancies. He observed that some state legislatures only met once a year and that, as a smaller body, the Senate could not afford vacancies. He believed that the executive could be trusted with such interim appointments (II, 231).

Randolph thought that a 14-year citizenship requirement for senators was too long. Prefacing his remarks with the comment that he "did not know but it might be problematical whether emigrations to this Country were on the whole useful or not," he continued by pointing to promises that the nation had extended to foreigners during the American Revolution and feared that, if these were not kept, immigrants might oppose the new system. He said he could accept no more than a seven-year citizenship requirement (II, 237), although he subsequently supported a nine-year requirement (II, 239). He favored substituting a four-year for a seven-year citizenship requirement in the House (II, 268).

Congressional Powers

When the Convention discussed whether Congress should have the power to issue paper money, Randolph expressed his "antipathy" to such a power, but he opposed an absolute bar since "he could not foresee all the occasions that might arise" (II, 310). When the Convention was discussing a provision to prohibit the taxation of incoming slaves, Randolph was among those who favored a compromise. He observed that the Convention faced a dilemma: "By agreeing to the clause, it would revolt the Quakers, the Methodists, and many others in the States having no slaves. On the other hand, two States might be lost to the Union" (II, 374). Randolph favored a provision specifying that the new government would have the power to fulfill the obligations entered into by the previous Congress (II, 376). He also favored a provision that all debts entered into under the Articles would remain valid under the new government (II, 414).

Randolph wanted to grant Congress the power to provide for uniform arming and training of the militia. He doubted that "the Militia could be brought into the field and made to commit suicide on themselves." He observed that states were currently neglecting the militia and that members of the state legislatures were courting popularity "too much to enforce a proper discipline" (II, 387).

Randolph had reservations about allowing each house of Congress to judge the privileges of its members (II, 503). On September 14, Randolph seconded Madison's motion that would have al-lowed Congress to charter corporations (II, 615). He also seconded a motion by Virginia's George Mason that would have included an admonition against standing armies in times of peace (II, 617).

Other Congressional Matters

Randolph opposed allowing states to pay members of Congress. He believed that this would lead to "a dependence . . . that would vitiate the whole System." He also believed that "the whole nation has an interest in the attendance & services of its members" and should accordingly pay them (I, 372).

Randolph disfavored allowing Congress to decide when to reapportion itself. He observed that "a pretext would never be wanting to postpone alterations, and keep the power in the hands of those possessed of it" (I, 561; also see I, 567). Randolph proposed periodic censuses for this purpose (I, 571). He observed that "If a fair representation of the people be not secured, the injustice of the Govt. will shake it to its foundations" (I, 580). Randolph wanted the formula for counting slaves as three-fifths of a person in representation for the House of Representatives specifically secured in the Constitution: "He urged strenuously that express security ought to be provided for including slaves in the ratio of Representation. He lamented that such a species of property existed. But as it did exist the holders of it would require some security" (I, 594).

Randolph and Madison supported a motion giving members of Congress the power to compel the attendance of absent members. He also favored Madison's idea that the Constitution should require a two-thirds vote to expel members of Congress (II, 254). He supported a motion by Gouverneur Morris that would allow any member to call for a roll-call vote (II, 255).

Randolph favored the clause preventing members of Congress from being able to accept offices for which the emoluments had been increased during their terms as a way of closing the door on "influence & corruption" (II, 290; also see II, 491). He was willing to make an exception for individuals who might be needed to command military forces (II, 290). Randolph and Madison favored preventing any new pay raises for Congress from going into effect until the passage of three years (II, 430).

Randolph thought that the power to declare war should be entrusted to the House rather than the Senate (II, 279).

Randolph thought that Congress should have the power to refer some federal appointments to state executives or legislatures (II, 405–406).

The Executive

Apart from the reference to the alliance of the executive and the judiciary in a Council of Revision, the Virginia Plan had been silent as to how many individuals should constitute the executive branch. Randolph came out on June 1 in opposition to a single executive, which he regarded as "the foetus of monarchy" (I, 66). Opposing Pennsylvania's James Wilson on this point, Randolph believed that an executive composed of three men could just as easily provide for "vigor, dispatch & responsibility" as one (I, 66). Randolph elaborated on his arguments the following day. He said that a single executive was adverse to the "temper" of the people, that a plurality could accomplish the same objects, that the people would not place confidence in a single executive and that a single executive (who would tend to be from the center of the nation) would leave more remote areas of the nation on an unequal footing (I, 88).

The Virginia Plan called for Congress to select the president. Randolph opposed a plan introduced by Elbridge Gerry that would have entrusted presidential selection to state governors, who would have votes in proportion to their state's population. Randolph argued that the small states would not have a chance of selecting one of their own by this procedure. He also feared that governors would not be familiar enough with individuals outside their own states to be able to make good choices. He further feared that state governors would see the president as a rival and that "they will not cherish the great Oak which is to reduce them to paltry shrubs" (I, 176). On July 2, Randolph indicated that he was willing to allow each state to have an equal voice in the selection of the president (I, 514).

Randolph had questions about the Electoral College (II, 500). He apparently preferred legislative selection. He thought that if the new system were to be adopted, the House, rather than the Senate, should make the final selection of candidates if none of them received a majority (II, 502; II, 513).

At a time (July 19) when the Convention was still contemplating legislative selection of the president, Randolph opposed allowing the president to be eligible for more than one term. He argued that "If he should be re-appointable by the Legislature, he will be no check on it. His revisionary power will be of no avail" (II, 55).

Randolph was a strong proponent of executive impeachment. He observed that "Guilt wherever found ought to be punished" (II, 67). He further feared that the executive would have "great opportunitys of abusing his power; particularly in time of war when the military force, and in some respects the public money will be in his hands. Should no regular punishment be provided, it will be irregularly inflicted by tumults & insurrections" (II, 67). At that point, Randolph was considering the possibility that state judges might serve as a forum for such impeachments or that there might be some forum that would act as a preliminary inquest (II, 67).

Randolph proposed a revised variant of the presentment clause, allowing for a presidential veto of congressional legislation, which the Convention adopted on August 16 (II, 305). He opposed allowing the vice president to serve as president of the Senate (II, 537). Randolph did not think the president should have the power to pardon treason. He observed that "the President may himself be guilty. The Traytors may be his own instruments" (II, 616).

The Judiciary

On June 13, Randolph and Madison successfully proposed that the jurisdiction of the national judiciary "should extend to cases, which respect the collection of the National revenue, impeachments of any national officers, and questions which involve the national peace and harmony" (I, 232). On July 18, he indicated that he did not think that state courts could be trusted to enforce national laws (II, 46).

On July 18, Randolph said that he favored the appointment of judges by Congress rather than by the executive (II, 43). He indicated that the hopes of receiving appointments would be more "diffusive if they depended on the Senate, the members of which wd. be diffusively known, than if they depended on a single man who could not be personally known to a very great extent; and consequently that opposition to the System, would be so far weakened" (II, 43). On July 21, however, Randolph seemed to have changed his mind.

Randolph opposed a provision that would have permitted the removal of judges by the president on a petition from Congress. He feared that the result would be that of "weakening too much the independence of the Judges" (II, 429).

Miscellaneous

When Benjamin Franklin proposed that the Convention should begin each day with prayer, Randolph proposed that the Convention request a sermon for the Fourth of July as a substitute (I, 452).

Randolph served on three committees at the Convention–the Original Apportionment of Congress Committee, the Committee of Detail, and the Committee of Interstate Comity & Bankruptcy. Among Randolph's more interesting notes from the Committee of Detail are his notations regarding drafting a Constitution. He observed that two considerations needed to be foremost:

1. To insert essential principles only, lest the operations of government should be clogged by rendering those provisions permanent and unalterable, which ought to be accommodated to times and events, and
2. To use simple and precise language, and general propositions, according to the example of the (several) constitutions of

the several states. (For the construction of a constitution of necessity differs from that of law.) (II, 137)

Amending Process and Ratification of the Constitution

On June 11, Randolph agreed with fellow Virginian George Mason that the new Constitution would prove to be defective and that it would be better to provide for a process of amending the document than, in Mason's words, "to trust to chance and violence" (I, 203). On June 20, Randolph said that it was important to refer the new document to the people for their approval (I, 336). He reiterated this idea on July 23. Randolph feared that referring the Constitution for approval to state legislatures would put power into the hands of "local demogagues who will be degraded by it from the importance they now hold" and who would accordingly "spare no efforts to impede that progress in the popular mind which will be necessary to the adoption of the plan" (II, 89). He further observed that "some of the States are averse to any change in their Constitution, and will not take the requisite steps, unless expressly called upon to refer to the question to the people" (II, 89). Randolph suggested on August 30 that nine states should be sufficient to ratify the new document (II, 469). The next day, he suggested that if the Constitution were not in a "final form" that would "permit him to accede to it," then "the State Conventions should be at liberty to propose amendments to be submitted to another General Convention which may reject or incorporate them, as shall be judged proper" (II, 479).

The Decision Not to Sign

Randolph sent the first recorded signal that he might not sign the new Constitution on August 29 when he argued that failure to adopt a provision requiring a two-thirds congressional majority for the adoption of navigation acts "would compleat the deformity of the system" (II, 452). Without going into details on his view, he indicated that "What he had in view was merely to pave the way for a declaration which he might be hereafter obliged to make if an accumulation of obnoxious ingredients should take place, that he could not give his assent to the plan" (II, 453).

On September 10, Randolph expressed renewed reservations about the Constitution. He tied them to how the Constitution would be ratified. Randolph said that he had been among those who had been convinced "that radical changes in the system of the Union were necessary" (II, 560). Believing that the Convention had subsequently departed in significant respects from the "republican" principles of the original Virginia Plan, he said that he favored allowing states to propose amendments to the Constitution, which would be considered by a second convention (II, 561). Later in the day, he listed his own specific objections, some of which he appeared to have been expressing for the first time. He disfavored the role of the Senate in sitting as a court of impeachment; he believed that a vote by three-fourths rather than two-thirds of each house should be required to override a presidential veto; he thought there were too few representatives in the House of Representatives; he thought there should be a restriction of a standing army in times of peace; he opposed the necessary and proper clause; he thought there should be further restraints on the power to enact navigation acts; he disfavored the provision related to the taxation of exports; he feared the power of Congress to intervene in state affairs on the petitions of state governors; he thought there needed to be "a more definite boundary between the General & State Legislature–and between the General and State Judiciaries"; he thought the president's power to pardon treason was too broad; and he was concerned about the ability of members of Congress to set their own compensation (II, 563–564). Having rhetorically asked whether he was "to promote the establishment of a plan which he verily believed would end in Tyranny," he then equivocated by indicating that "he must keep himself free, in case he should be honored with a Seat in the Convention of his State, to act according to the dictates of his judgment" (II, 564). He reiterated his call to allow states to either adopt the Constitution or propose

amendments, which would then be considered in yet another convention (II, 564).

Randolph repeated his concerns on September 15. Expressing the psychological pressures that he must have felt at not joining the majority of his colleagues in signing the document, he nonetheless kept his future options open.

> Mr. Randolph animadverting on the indefinite and dangerous power given by the Constitution to Congress, expressing the pain he felt at differing from the body of the Convention, on the close of the great & awful subject of their labours, and anxiously wishing for some accommodating expedient which would relieve him from his embarrassments, made a motion importing "that amendments to the plan might be offered by the State Conventions, which should be submitted to and finally decided on by another general Convention." Should this proposition be disregarded, it would he said be impossible for him to put his name to the instrument. Whether he should oppose it afterwards he would not then decide but he would not deprive himself of the freedom to do so in his own State, if that course should be prescribed by his final judgment. (II, 631)

Randolph reiterated his concerns on September 17, again indicating that his refusal to sign the document at the Convention did not mean that "he should oppose the Constitution without doors. He meant only to keep himself free to be governed by his duty as it should be prescribed by his future judgment" (II, 645). Urged by fellow members to sign in attestation to the unanimity of the states, Randolph responded that this would be the same as giving his approval: "He repeated that in refusing to sign the Constitution, he took a step which might be the most awful of his life, but it was dictated by his conscience, and it was not possible for him to hesitate, much less, to change" (II, 646). He continued to fear that giving the people an all-or-nothing option, rather than allowing them to propose amendments, "would really produce the anarchy & civil convulsions which were apprehended from the refusal of individuals to sign it" (II, 646).

Life after the Convention

Randolph surprised many observers by supporting the Constitution at the Virginia ratifying convention. He said that he would rather lose a limb than "assent to the dissolution of the Union" (Reardon 1974, 139), but partisans on both sides suspected his motives.

President Washington subsequently named him as the nation's first attorney general, where he established many important precedents. As attorney general he successfully argued the government's case in *Chisholm v. Georgia* allowing Georgia to be sued without its consent by out-of-state citizens (1793), only to see this decision overturned by the Eleventh Amendment. Randolph served less successfully as secretary of state to George Washington. After losing Washington's confidence, Randolph returned to Virginia to practice law. Although he was a highly successful practitioner, he faced increasing debts in later life, a period during which he began writing a history of Virginia that was published long after his death near Millwood, Virginia, in 1813. The Grand Lodge of Freemasons in Virginia, where Randolph had served as a grand master, built a monument in Millwood to honor Randolph in 1940.

See Also Virginia; Virginia Plan

FOR FURTHER READING

Farrand, Max, ed. 1937. *The Records of the Federal Convention.* 4 vols. New Haven, CT: Yale University Press.

Reardon, John J. 1974. *Edmund Randolph: A Biography.* New York: Macmillan.

Vile, John R., ed. 2001. *Great American Lawyers: An Encyclopedia.* 2 vols. Santa Barbara, CA: ABC-CLIO.

RANDOLPH PLAN

See VIRGINIA PLAN

RATIFICATION, CONVENTION DEBATES, AND CONSTITUTIONAL PROVISION

Article VII provides that "the Ratification of the Conventions of nine States, shall be sufficient for the Establishment of this Constitution between the States so ratifying the Same." This provision bypassed the mechanism for amending the Articles of Confederation and the Resolution of Congress of February 21, 1787, authorizing the Constitutional Convention. Both had provided for proposal (or approval) of Congress and the unanimous consent of the state legislatures. The delegates had good reasons for bypassing the amending provision of the Articles. It is generally regarded as having been overly wooden; no amendments had been successfully ratified using this procedure.

Discussions of the Virginia Plan

Section 15 of the Virginia Plan, which Edmund Randolph introduced on May 29, provided that any amendments that the Convention offered "ought at a proper time, or times, after the approbation of Congress to be submitted to an assembly or assemblies of Representatives, recommended by the several Legislatures to be expressly chosen by the people, to consider & decide thereon" (Farrand 1937, I, 22). When the Committee of the Whole first considered this provision on June 5, Connecticut's Roger Sherman argued that popular ratification through the means proposed was unnecessary since the Articles already provided a method for ratifying amendments. By contrast, Virginia's James Madison argued that the proposed provision was "essential," and that the Articles were defective. He observed that if the Articles were regarded as a treaty, some people might regard the breach of one provision as a dissolution of the whole, and that it was therefore "indispensable that the new Constitution should be ratified in the most unexceptionable form, and by the supreme authority of the people themselves" (Farrand 1937, I, 122–123). Elbridge Gerry was not all that confident in the people. He observed that the people in some of the Eastern states "had the wildest ideas of Government in the world" including abolition of the Senate in Gerry's home state of Massachusetts (I, 123).

Although Rufus King, also from Massachusetts, thought that the method specified in the Confederation was appropriate, he saw some advantages to moving to ratification by conventions. First, a convention would not have two branches; second, it would not stand, like state legislatures, to lose power under the new system (I, 123). James Wilson of Pennsylvania then introduced a new idea. He feared that the system under the Articles could allow a few states to block improvements needed by all of them, and he hoped that a system of ratification could be devised so as "to admit of such a partial union, with a door open for the accession of the rest" (I, 123). South Carolina's Charles Pinckney suggested that approval of nine states might be sufficient to start the new government, but the matter was unanimously postponed.

Arguing passionately for equal state representation in Congress on June 9, William Paterson of New Jersey reminded delegates from the large states that they might unite in a new government as they chose, but they had no authority to compel the small states to join them (I, 179). Three days later the Committee of the Whole affirmed Resolution 15 of the Virginia Plan by a vote of 6-2-2.

The New Jersey Plan

When William Paterson offered the New Jersey Plan on June 15, it proposed "that the articles of Confederation ought to be so revised, corrected & enlarged, as to render the federal Constitution adequate to the exigencies of Government, & the preservation of the Union" (I, 242). He accordingly provided for no special ratifying mechanism, undoubtedly expecting simply to rely on the method of constitutional change provided for under the Articles. In defending the New Jersey

Plan on June 16, Paterson argued that his plan was better aligned both with the purpose of the Convention that had been created and with the sentiments of the people who had authorized it. He suggested that "If the confederacy was radically wrong," then the delegates should return home to their states "and obtain larger powers," rather than "assume them of ourselves" (I, 250). In contrasting the Virginia and New Jersey Plans, Pennsylvania's James Wilson observed that ratification of the former would be "by the people themselves" and of the latter by "the legislative authorities according to the 13 art. of Confederation" (I, 253). Uncertain of the people's sentiments, but not desiring to call yet another convention, Wilson saw popular ratification as a means of getting over the difficulty of whether the existing convention had the power to propose what it was proposing.

On June 20, Oliver Ellsworth of Connecticut expressed the hope that the proposals of the Convention could "go forth as an amendment to the articles of Confederation, since under this idea the authority of the Legislatures could ratify it." He feared that "If the plan goes forth to the people for ratification several succeeding Conventions within the States would be unavoidable." He further observed that "He did not like conventions. They were better fitted to pull down than to build up Constitutions" (I, 335).

Discussions of July 23

On July 23, the Convention revisited the issue of constitutional ratification. Ellsworth proposed that state legislatures should ratify the Constitution, and Paterson seconded the motion. This time George Mason argued for the desirability of ratification by conventions. He made at least three arguments. First, he argued that the people were the source of power in free governments. Second, he observed that one set of state legislatures might try to undo what previous legislatures had done. Third, citing his home state of Virginia, Mason questioned whether all state legislatures were sufficiently "derived from the clear & undisputed authority of the people" (II, 89). Randolph supported his fellow Virginian. He feared that state legislatures, who would be losing power, would have an incentive to oppose the new government. He also feared that such legislatures would give platforms to "local demagogues" who "will spare no efforts to impede that progress in the popular mind which will be necessary to the adoption of the plan." Transferring the ratification platform to conventions would transfer it "to a field in which their efforts can be less mischievous" (II, 89).

Elbridge Gerry thought it was far too late to question the legitimacy either of the Articles of Confederation or of existing state legislatures. Just as Ellsworth had previously done, Gerry thought that "Great confusion . . . would result from a recurrence to the people. They would never agree on any thing. He could not see any ground to suppose that the people will do what their rulers will not. The rulers will either conform to, or influence the sense of the people" (II, 90).

Nathaniel Gorham took Mason's and Randolph's side in the debate. He offered five arguments for convention ratification. First, he thought that individuals chosen specifically for this purpose, and with nothing to lose, "will discuss the subject more candidly than members of the Legislature who are to lose the power which is to be given up to the Genl. Govt." Second, he observed that conventions would be more streamlined than legislatures, most of which had two branches. Third, he observed that the legislatures often excluded the most able men, including clergymen, who would be eligible to serve in ratifying conventions. Fourth, legislatures would be constantly interrupted by other business that could be used as an excuse for delay. Fifth, if provisions of the Articles were to be followed, they would require unanimous consent, which would be especially unlikely in the case of Rhode Island and possibly New York. He thought delegates should seriously consider allowing the Constitution to be ratified without unanimous state consent (II, 90).

Ellsworth continued to argue for legislative ratification: "He thought more was to be expected from the Legislatures than from the people" (II, 91). Ellsworth appeared also to note a change in opinion that scholars have subsequently documented (Wood 1969, 306–343). He observed that "a new sett of ideas seemed to have crept in since the articles of Confederation were established. Conventions of the people, or with power derived expressly from the people, were not then thought of. The Legislatures were considered as competent" (II, 91). He still believed them to be so.

North Carolina's Hugh Williamson thought that the provision under consideration would permit ratification by either state legislatures or conventions. He believed, however, that the latter mode was likely to produce abler men. Gouverneur Morris of Pennsylvania observed that if the method of the Articles were required and state legislatures did not unanimously consent, courts would not consider the ratifications to be valid. By contrast, a majority of the people would have authority to alter the existing compact (II, 92).

Although Rufus King of Massachusetts agreed that existing state legislatures had authority to ratify the new Constitution, he thought that "a reference to the authority of the people expressly delegated to Conventions" was "the most certain means of obviating all disputes & doubts concerning the legitimacy of the new Constitution; as well as the most likely means of drawing forth the best men in the States to decide on it" (II, 92). He further observed that some members of existing state legislatures might think that their oaths prevented them from approving a new Constitution. Madison argued that "it would be a novel & dangerous doctrine that a Legislature could change the constitution under which it held its existence" (II, 92–93). He further said that the difference between a government ratified by state legislatures and one ratified by the people (in convention) was the difference "between a *league* or *treaty*, and a *Constitution*" (II, 93). The Convention voted down Ellsworth's proposal for legislative proposal by a 7-3 vote, with New Hampshire, Massachusetts, and Delaware in dissent. Gouverneur Morris's subsequent proposal for the plan to be referred "to one general Convention, chosen & authorized by the people to consider, *amend*, & establish the same" failed for want of a second (II, 93). The Convention voted for the provision for ratification by state convention by a 9-1 vote with only Delaware in dissent.

Committee of Detail

When the Committee of Detail reported to the Convention on August 6, it proposed that the Convention should present the Constitution to Congress for its approval and that it should be subsequently ratified by a number of state conventions (the number still to be determined) (II, 189). In his notes of the next day, James McHenry of Maryland indicated that he thought such a mechanism might conflict with provisions in his state's constitution (II, 211).

On August 30, the Convention discussed the number of state conventions that should be required to ratify the Constitution. Wilson proposed seven as representing a majority of the states. Morris was not as specific but thought that different numbers might be required depending on whether the ratifying states were geographically contiguous. Pointing out that the Articles required unanimous consent, Sherman thought the consent of at least 10 should be required. Randolph proposed nine as "being a respectable majority of the whole, and being a number made familiar by the constitution of the existing Congress." Wilson then suggested eight, while Dickinson raised the question as to whether the consent of Congress was really essential. Given variances in population, Madison feared that seven to nine states might not represent a majority of the population. Wilson said that only the states that ratified would be bound by the Constitution. It was time to act outside the framework of the Articles: "The House on fire must be extinguished, without a scrupulous regard to ordinary rights." Pierce Butler of South Carolina favored nine and opposed the idea that one or two states ought to be able to stop the others from doing what they needed to do. Maryland's Daniel Carroll moved for unanimity, and King argued against the ability of a part to bind the whole (II, 468–469).

In accord with King's criticism, on the next day, the Convention voted 9-1, with Maryland alone in dissent, that the agreement on the new Constitution would only affect the states that voted to approve. Consistent with his earlier objection, Madison then moved that seven or more states with 33 or more votes in the House of Rep-

resentatives (the majority of 65) should be able to approve the new document. Sherman continued to think the Constitution should require unanimous state approval.

Morris moved to allow states to ratify the Constitution in whatever mode they chose, apparently thereby giving some consolation to Carroll. By contrast, King argued that giving up on ratification by conventions "was equivalent to giving up the business altogether. Conventions alone, which will avoid all the obstacles from the complicated formation of the Legislatures, will succeed, and if not positively required by the plan, its enemies will oppose that mode" (II, 476). Citing principles within state bills of rights, Madison thought that "the people were in fact, the fountain of all power, and by resorting to them, all difficulties were got over. They could alter constitutions as they pleased" (II, 476). After continued discussion, the Convention defeated Morris's resolution by a 6-4 vote. The Convention rejected a motion by Carroll and Martin, which was supported only by their home state of Maryland. After rejecting a proposal for ratification by 10 states by a 7-4 vote, the Convention settled 8-3 on the number nine (II, 477).

The same day, the delegates took up the following section of the report of the Committee of Detail and voted 8-3 on a motion by Gouverneur Morris and Charles Pinckney to strike the provision mandating that the work of the Convention would be sent to Congress "for their approbation" (II, 478). Morris and Pinckney then proposed a substitute provision specifying that the work of the Convention would "be laid before the U.S. in Congress assembled," after which it would be submitted to the states for approval in convention "as speedily as circumstances will permit" (II, 478). Martin and Gerry accused Morris of trying to get the document approved before states could discover its defects, and the Convention defeated the motion by a 7-4 vote. Mason voted to postpone the provision, indicating that "he would sooner chop off his right hand than put it to the Constitution as it now stands" (II, 479). He favored calling another grand convention, and Gouverneur Morris thought perhaps another convention might create a government with still greater firmness (probably *not* what the republican-minded Mason wanted). In any case, Randolph indicated his desire that states be able to propose amendments that would go before yet another grand convention, but by an 8-3 vote, the Convention instead reaffirmed the plan for laying the Constitution before Congress and then submitting it to state conventions.

Debates in September

The delegates resumed discussion on September 10. Gerry objected to bypassing congressional approval and, somewhat curiously, Alexander Hamilton agreed. Hamilton proposed that the Convention should send the Constitution to Congress, and, if approved by it, the state legislatures should refer the plan to conventions, "each Legislature declaring that if the convention of the State should think the plan ought to take effect among nine ratifying States, the same shd take effect accordingly" (II, 560). Gorham feared that some states would concur in the nine-state majority and others would not. Thomas Fitzsimons of Pennsylvania said that the Convention had eliminated the need for congressional approval so as to spare its members from violating their oaths. Randolph again argued that states should be able to propose amendments to the plan that would be considered in another convention. Wilson opposed Randolph's suggestion while King, later supported by Sherman, thought it was more "respectful" simply to lay the plan before Congress than to require it to approve or disapprove. He further thought that the consent of nine states should be adequate to approve the new document. Gerry, by contrast, bemoaned the "pernicious tendency of dissolving in so slight a manner, the solemn obligations of the articles of confederation" (II, 561).

Hamilton then introduced an elaborate measure, seconded by Gerry. It provided for Congress to approve the document and send it to the states, which would then call conventions. States that had agreed to allow a total of nine to approve would be therefore bound. Wilson strongly opposed resting the fate of the Convention on congressional approval. He feared that the Convention was about to throw away its summer's work. Pennsylvania's George Clymer also argued that Hamilton's proposal would "embarrass" Congress since it would be a breach of the Articles of Confederation. King and Rutledge affirmed these objections, and the Convention voted 10 to 1 against Hamilton's proposal. The Convention also unanimously rejected a simpler motion by Williamson and Gerry to reinstate the words "for the approbation of Congress" (II, 563).

Randolph followed with a critique of the Convention's work and with a proposal, seconded by Franklin, allowing state conventions to "adopt reject or amend" the proposals and send these to another grand convention "with full power to adopt or reject the alterations proposed by the State Conventions, and to establish finally the Government" (II, 564). Mason suggested that the Convention table the motion until it could ascertain how delegates would react to Randolph's criticisms, and Pinckney suggested that the Committee of Style propose an address to the people of the United States to accompany the Constitution (II, 564).

On September 15, just two days before the delegates signed the Constitution, Randolph resubmitted a motion providing that the state conventions should be able to submit amendments, which would then be presented to another grand convention. Mason joined in indicating that, although he could not consent to a "take this or nothing" approach, he could sign "with the expedient of another Convention as proposed" (II, 632). Charles Pinckney, by contrast, feared that "the Deputies to a second Convention coming together under the discordant impressions of their Constituents, will never agree. Conventions are serious things, and ought not to be repeated" (II, 632). The Convention unanimously agreed to reject Randolph's proposal and approved the Constitution as amended.

Analysis

One of the little-cited facts about the Virginia Plan, which Randolph had originally offered, is that it permitted ratification of the Constitution either by individual conventions within each of the states or by a single convention called for that purpose. The idea of allowing a single convention to approve or reject the Constitution sounds dangerously close to the idea, which James Madison and other delegates opposed, of having a second constitutional convention to propose additional amendments. It might also have left open the possibility for approving the Constitution by a majority of delegates from throughout the United States rather than requiring the individual consent of each of the states. If this had indeed ever been considered, it was probably doomed by the strong states' rights sentiments that resulted in the decision requiring equal state representation in the Senate. Although Madison's proposal for ratification of the Constitution by a majority of people in a majority of states was arguably better tailored to democratic ideals than the nine-state standard that the Convention adopted for ratification, it arguably gave too little consideration to states' rights.

The delegates to the Convention made at least four critical decisions in regard to constitutional ratification, each with important consequences. First, they decided to bypass the provision for unanimous state legislative assent to amendments that the Articles of Confederation had specified. This mechanism had served as an obstacle to all amendments under the Articles and probably would have doomed ratification of the new Constitution as well. Second, the delegates decided not to ask for congressional ratification and to provide that the Constitution would be ratified by state conventions rather than by state legislatures. This decision allowed them to bypass institutions that would be losing power under the new plan or whose members might think that ratifying the Constitution was in violation of their oath of office. Moreover, in accord with the theory of the day, this decision provided a wider democratic base, and thus greater legitimacy, for the new government. This decision also ensured that members of bodies deciding on constitutional ratification would be addressing the issue of constitutional ratification and it alone, thus making it less likely that they would be sidetracked by questions of

day-to-day governance. Third, the delegates decided to allow the Constitution to go into effect among nine or more states choosing to ratify it rather than wait for state unanimity. This prevented the majority of states from effectively being held hostage by one or more recalcitrant states (it had taken four years for the last state to ratify the Articles of Confederation), while not forcing states with objections to enter a reconfigured Union that they did not choose to join; as a matter of fact, the new government began without the initial participation of either North Carolina or Rhode Island. Fourth, the Convention rejected proposals (most notably Randolph's) for providing for yet another convention to consider amendments that the states might have offered.

Although it is not generally considered as such, there is a sense in which the first Congress (although dealing with a myriad of other issues connected with the establishment of a new government) served as a kind of constitutional convention, proposing a series of amendments that the state later ratified as the Bill of Rights. Another Convention might have accomplished this same purpose, but it might also have simply led to demands for still further conventions that would have ended in the same kind of irresolution that had preceded the meeting of 1787.

Scholars still debate the legality of the Convention's actions in calling for a new form of constitutional ratification (see, for example, Kay 1987; Ackerman and Katyal 1995). It clearly bypassed existing constitutional mechanisms. Just as clearly, it got as close to the source of popular authority as it was probably possible to get given the technology of the day. Sadly, even the Convention mechanism was inadequate to resolve future disputes over whether states had the power to withdraw from the Union without the consent of the Union of the whole, and this dispute eventually led to civil war.

Postscript

Legal scholars have recently raised the question as to when the new Constitution went into effect. In *Owings v. Speed*, 18 U.S. 420 (1820), Chief Justice

John Marshall decided that the Constitution did not become effective when the ninth state (New Hampshire) ratified the document on June 21, 1788, but on either March 4 or April 30 of 1789 when the new Congress and president were inaugurated. Gary Lawson and Guy Seidman have suggested that Marshall was mistaken and that various provisions of the Constitution became effective at different times (2001, 2002). Vasan Kesavan has disputed this view (2002).

See Also Amending Process; Articles of Confederation; Constitutional Convention Mechanism; Legality of the Convention; Ratification in the States; Resolution Accompanying the Constitution

FOR FURTHER READING

Ackerman, Bruce, and Neal Katyal. 1995. "Our Unconventional Founding." *University of Chicago Law Review* 62 (Spring): 475–573.

Farrand, Max, ed. 1937. *The Records of the Federal Convention.* 4 vols. New Haven, CT: Yale University Press.

Goldwin, Robert A. 1997. *From Parchment to Power: How James Madison Used the Bill of Rights to Save the Constitution.* Washington, DC: AEI Press.

Kay, Richard S. 1987. "The Illegality of the Constitution." *Constitutional Commentary* 4 (Winter): 57–80.

Kesavan, Vasan. 2002. "When Did the Articles of Confederation Cease to Be Law?" *Notre Dame Law Review* 78 (December): 35–82.

Lawson, Gary, and Guy Seidman. 2001. "When Did the Constitution Become Law?" *Notre Dame Law Review* 77 (November): 1–37.

——. 2002. "The First 'Establishment' Clause: Article VII and the Post-Constitutional Confederation." *Notre Dame Law Review* 78 (December): 83–100.

McGinnis, John O., and Michael B. Rappaport. 2002. "Our Supermajoritarian Constitution." *Texas Law Review* 80 (March): 703–806.

Rakove, Jack N. 1999. "The Super-Legality of the Constitution, or, a Federalist Critique of Bruce Ackerman's Neo-Federalism." *Yale Law Journal* 108 (June): 1931–1958.

Wood, Gordon S. 1969. *The Creation of the American Republic 1776–1787.* Chapel Hill: University of North Carolina Press.

RATIFICATION IN THE STATES

The process of ratifying the U.S. Constitution was almost as exciting as the process of writing it. Although the Articles of Confederation had speci-

---

The First American Novel

The year 1789, during which the U.S. Constitution went into effect, coincided with the publication of what is generally regarded as America's first novel, a book by William Hill Brown entitled *The Power of Sympathy.* The book has been described as "a tale of seduction and incest" and as "an overheated, chaotic, and scandalous piece of writing that appeals to the reader's prurience and urges him or her–more likely, her–to feel" (Gilmore 1987, 35). In short, the book was almost the complete antithesis of the style and content of the Constitution. By contrast, the Constitution seems to come much closer to the style of books by Charles Brockden Brown, who published four novels between 1798 and 1800. The best known of these was called *Wieland, or The Transformation.* An English professor, Michael Gilmore, has drawn parallels between the more measured style of these works and the U.S. Constitution (37–40).

FOR FURTHER READING

Gilmore, Michael T. 1987. "1787: The Constitution in Perspective: 'We Do Ordain and Establish': The Constitution as Literary Text: The Constitution and the Canon." *William and Mary Law Review* 29 (Fall): 35–40.

fied that the document could not be amended except through the unanimous consent of the state legislatures, the delegates decided that the new document would go into effect when ratified by special ratifying conventions called within each of the states.

Even before the Convention had ended, some delegates had returned to their states determined to oppose the document being crafted in Philadelphia, and Alexander Hamilton had joined the fray in New York by attacking the Antifederalists. Moreover, on September 17, the day that the Constitution was signed, three of the remaining delegates—Edmund Randolph and George Mason of Virginia and Elbridge Gerry of Massachusetts—refused to sign the document.

Federalists and Antifederalists

The fight for ratification divided the country almost as strongly as had the earlier fight for independence. Those who supported the new Constitution called themselves Federalists, somewhat thereby deflecting criticisms that the new government was too "national" and not "federal" enough. The supporters of the Constitution in turn designated their opponents as Antifederalists, sending the clear message that their opponents did not have a positive solution to the problems that many Americans had already recognized.

Federalists had at least three other advantages. First, leading supporters had already spent the summer together in Philadelphia and had developed faith in one another. Thus, they were far better organized than their opponents. Second, the press was highly favorable to the new Constitution. Third, supporters of the Constitution were able to evoke the venerated names of George Washington and Benjamin Franklin, both of whom had attended the Constitutional Convention and supported the new document.

Still, the process of ratification had to be fought within individual states, and the outcome, particularly in the largest states, was often precariously balanced. Moreover, populated coastal and urban areas more involved in commerce were often far more in favor of the new Constitution than were residents of the hinterlands who were sometimes underrepresented within their own state legislatures and in the ratifying conventions (Roll 1969), and were often far more distrustful of centralized authority. Such Antifederalists were particularly concerned over the absence of a bill of rights within the new Constitution. Over time, Federalists realized that just as the Constitution was the product of compromise, so too, they would have to promise to adopt a bill of rights before many of these opponents would cast their lot with the new government.

Progress of State Ratifications

The first state to ratify the new Constitution was Delaware. It ratified on December 7, 1787, by a unanimous 30 to 0 vote. This vote indicated that small states were content enough with the Great Compromise (guaranteeing them equal representation within the U.S. Senate) that the battle in some of these states might be easier than in the larger ones.

Pennsylvania had actually set the process of ratification in motion prior to Delaware, although it did not ratify until December 12. The conflict in Pennsylvania had sometimes been ugly, with Federalists forcibly bringing in some Antifederalists to the state legislature so that they would have a quorum to call a constitutional convention, and with a much closer vote of 46 to 23 within the state ratifying convention. There is generally agreement that James Wilson, soon to become a U.S. Supreme Court justice, played a major role in justifying the new Constitution, making arguments that would serve as a template for others who would argue on its behalf.

As in Delaware, the vote in New Jersey came easily. This state, which had supported equal state representation at the Convention, ratified the Constitution on December 18 by a unanimous vote of 38 to 0. Georgia added its approval by a vote to 26 to 0 on December 31. Many delegates within that state apparently hoped that the new government would help the state expand westward and would provide greater security against the threat of Indians.

Connecticut was the fifth state to ratify the Constitution. It did so on January 9, 1788, by a vote of 128 to 40. Although the vote was solid, it revealed regional differences within the state.

The Contests Become Closer

The debate in Massachusetts was bitter. With Samuel Adams and John Hancock initially on the fence, Federalists had to work hard to get their support and that of a majority of the ratifying convention. This was the state in which the Federalists originated the idea that the Constitution could be ratified, not conditionally, but while suggesting amendments for the first Congress to consider. The positive vote on behalf of the Constitution in Massachusetts was 187 to 168 and took place on February 6, 1788.

In Maryland, Federalists had to overcome the intemperate criticism of Luther Martin, one of the state's representatives at the Constitutional Convention. The Maryland ratifying convention voted in favor of ratification by a vote of 63 to 11 on April 28, 1788.

South Carolina followed on May 23 by a vote of 149 to 73 that showed tension between the state's uplands and lowlands. Debates made it fairly clear that the state probably would not have agreed to the new Union had it not made provision in the three-fifths clause for extra representation for the slave states, and, in a separate provision, for the continuing importation of slaves during the next twenty years.

New Hampshire, the Critical State

Whereas concessions to slavery helped the Federalist cause in South Carolina, they raised fears in New Hampshire, where residents worried that slavery was a compromise with evil. Some were also concerned that the provision in the new Constitution that prohibited religious oaths by national officials opened up participation within the new government to non-Christians. The state ratified the Constitution on June 21, 1788, by a vote of 57 to 47. It followed the example of Mass-achusetts by accompanying its approval with a series of proposed amendments, including proposals for religious liberty.

Additional Ratifications before Inauguration of the New Government

Although New Hampshire's ratification brought the total to the required nine, it is doubtful that the new government could have gone into effect without the participation of Virginia, the largest and most populous state. The debates in this state featured the noted orator Patrick Henry, who raised almost every conceivable objection to the new document, against James Madison, who took a far more systematic approach to explaining the virtues of the new Constitution. Richard Henry Lee, James Monroe, John Marshall, Edmund Randolph (who had switched from the opposition that he had expressed at the Convention), George Mason (who did not switch), and others joined in this debate. Although he did not attend the state convention, George Washington's known support for the Constitution proved critical. The Federalists prevailed on June 25 by a vote of 89 to 79, again with accompanying amendments.

Word from Virginia and New Hampshire eventually helped sway the results in New York where debate may have been as bitter as in Virginia. Although thousands of articles were written for and against the Constitution, the writing of *The Federalist* in New York (the joint work of Federalists Alexander Hamilton, James Madison, and John Jay under the name of Publius) was undoubtedly one of its best-known products. New York ratified the Constitution on July 26 by a narrow vote of 30 to 26.

Additional Ratifications after Inauguration of the New Government

The next two states took their time. North Carolina's first ratifying convention rejected the Constitution on August 2, 1788, by a 184 to 84 vote. That state preferred to wait until Congress proposed the Bill of Rights. Then on November 21,

Dates and Votes by Which States Ratified the U.S. Constitution

December 7, 1787   Delaware ratifies the Constitution by a vote of 30 to 0.

December 17, 1787   Pennsylvania ratifies the Constitution by a vote of 46 to 23.

December 18, 1787   New Jersey ratifies the Constitution by a vote of 38 to 0.

January 2, 1788   Georgia ratifies the Constitution by a vote of 26 to 0.

January 9, 1788   Connecticut ratifies the Constitution by a vote of 128 to 40.

February 6, 1788   Massachusetts ratifies the Constitution by a vote of 187 to 168.

April 28, 1788   Maryland ratifies the Constitution by a vote of 63 to 11.

May 23, 1788   South Carolina ratifies the Constitution by a vote of 149 to 73.

June 21, 1788   New Hampshire ratifies the Constitution by a vote of 57 to 47.

June 25, 1788   Virginia ratifies the Constitution by a vote of 89 to 79.

June 26, 1788   New York ratifies the Constitution by a vote of 30 to 27.

November 21, 1798   North Carolina ratifies the Constitution by a vote of 195 to 77.

May 29, 1790   Rhode Island ratifies the Constitution by a vote of 34 to 32.

FOR FURTHER READING

Conley, Patrick, T. and John P. Kaminski. 1988. *The Constitution and the States: The Role of the Original Thirteen in the Framing and Adoption of the Federal Constitution.* Madison, WI: Madison House, 1988.

1789, it voted to accept the Constitution by a vote of 194 to 77.

Rhode Island had not sent delegates to the Constitutional Convention, and so it is not surprising to find that it was the last to approve the new document. The state held a popular referendum rejecting the Constitution, which was followed by similar legislative rejections. Finally, after the new government threatened it with trade sanctions, it joined the Union on May 29, 1790, by a vote of 34 to 32. Critics observed that the state had used the intervening months and years to pay off its heavy state debts with depreciated currency, which it would no longer be able to issue under the new system.

Since the original ratification of the Constitution, 37 other states have joined, each thereby attesting to its acceptance of the document. New states entered the Union on an equal basis with the original 13.

See Also Antifederalists; Bill of Rights; Connecticut; Constitutional Convention Mechanism; Delaware; *Federalist, The;* Federalists; Georgia; Maryland; Massachusetts; New Hampshire; New Jersey; New York; North Carolina; Pennsylvania; Press Coverage; Ratification, Convention Debates, and Constitutional Provision; Rhode Island; Signing of the Constitution; South Carolina; Virginia

FOR FURTHER READING

Conley, Patrick T., and John P. Kaminski, eds. 1988. *The Constitution and the States: The Role of the Original Thirteen in the Framing and Adoption of the Federal Constitution.* Madison, WI: Madison House.

Gillespie, Michael Allen, and Michael Lienesch, eds. 1989. *Ratifying the Constitution.* Lawrence: University Press of Kansas.

Howard, A. E. Dick. 1993. *The Constitution in the Making: Perspectives of the Original Thirteen States.* Williamsburg, VA: National Center for State Courts.

Roll, Charles W., Jr. 1969. "We, Some of the People: Apportionment in the Thirteen State Conventions Ratifying the Constitution." *Journal of American History* 56 (June): 21–40.

Siemers, David J. 2002. *Ratifying the Republic: Antifederalists and Federalists in Constitutional Time.* Palo Alto, CA: Stanford University Press.

Smith, Craig R. 1993. *To Form a More Perfect Union: The Ratification of the Constitution and the Bill of Rights, 1787–1791.* Lanham, MD: University Press of America.

St. John, Jeffrey. 1990. *A Child of Fortune: A Correspondent's Report on the Ratification of the U.S. Constitution and Battle for a Bill of Rights.* Ottawa, IL: Jameson Books.

READ, GEORGE (1733–1798)

George Read was born in Cecil County, Maryland in 1733 of Irish immigrant parents who were planters. Read attended the Reverend Francis Alison's Academy in New London, Pennsylvania and read law before being admitted to the bar first in Pennsylvania and then in Delaware where he had moved. He was appointed attorney general for Delaware 10 years after being admitted to the bar. He served from 1765 to 1780 as a Delaware legislator and from 1774 to 1779 as a representative to the Continental Congress. There he voted against Independence but still signed the Declaration of Independence. One of the state's most powerful politicians during the Revolutionary period, he was sometimes called "Dionysius, Tyrant of Delaware" (Gillespie and Lienesch 1989, 32). Active in drawing up Delaware's constitution, he served as the state's acting president from 1777 to 1778. A judge of the Court of Appeal in Admiralty under the Articles of Confederation, which he had reluctantly supported, Read attended the Annapolis Convention prior to going to the Constitutional Convention.

Read was present on the opening day of Convention business on May 25, but he attended under a restraint, which he himself had helped to author, that did not bind all the delegates. On May 30, he accordingly moved to postpone consideration of congressional regulation since he and other Delaware delegates had been instructed not to yield the state's equal suffrage and might feel compelled to leave the Convention if the matter

George Read, delegate from Delaware
(Pixel That)

were pursued (Farrand 1937, I, 37). When Madison suggested that this matter might be resolved by sending it to committee, presumably the Committee of the Whole, Read was apparently not completely satisfied (I, 37), but he did not leave the Convention.

In a letter that Read wrote to John Dickinson on May 21, he indicated that existing plans seemed predicated on giving the smaller states a single representative in the lower house of Congress. He accordingly indicated that "I suspect it to be of importance to the small States that their deputies should keep a strict watch upon the movements and propositions from the larger States, who will probably combine to swallow up the smaller ones by addition, division, or impoverishment" (III, 26).

Federalism

After reading the above letter, it is surprising to find that Read's most distinctive contribution to the Convention was openly to question the continuing existence of the states. It is, of course, possible that Read thought that eliminating the states would also eliminate any advantages then enjoyed by the larger states. However, one observer has interpreted Read's position as "part of a rhetorical strategy designed to protect the people of his state from political impotence and to secure for them as much influence as could be acquired" (Bradford 1994, 106). Read first advanced his view that states should be diminished, if not abolished, on June 6:

> Too much attachment is betrayed to the State Governmts. We must look beyond their continuance. A national Govt. must soon of necessity swallow all of them up. They will soon be reduced to the mere office of electing the national Senate. He was agst. patching up the old federal System: he hoped the idea wd. be dismissed. It would be like putting new cloth on an old garment. The confederation was founded on temporary principles. It cannot last: it cannot be amended. If we do not establish a good Govt. on new principles, we must either go to ruin, or have the work to do over again.
>
> The people at large are wrongly suspected of being averse to a Genl. Govt. The aversion lies among interested men who possess their confidence. (I, 137)

Read reiterated this theme on June 11 when the Convention was discussing a provision for guaranteeing the territory of each state. He felt that such a provision "abetted the idea of distinct States wch. would be a perpetual source of discord" (I, 202). He further observed that "there can be [no] cure for this evil but in doing away [with the] States altogether and uniting them all into [one] great Society" (I, 202).

In a discussion of Senate terms on June 26, Read again argued that state lines should, as much as possible, be ignored. Addressing the small states, he said that "it was in their interest that we should become one people as much as possible, that State attachments shd. be extinguished as much as possible, that the Senate shd. be so con-

stituted as to have the feelings of citizens of the whole" (I, 424).

Read argued even more forcefully for his views on June 19. He said that "he shd. have no objection to the system if it were truly national, but it has too much of a federal mixture in it" (I, 463). He did not believe that the small states had much to fear; indeed, he thought the large states labored under the weakness of trying to govern areas that were too large. By contrast, "Delaware had enjoyed tranquility & he flattered himself wd. continue to do so" (I, 463). Again Read argued that the solution was to incorporate all the states into one system:

> If the States remain, the representatives of the large ones will stick together, and carry every thing before them. The Executive also will be chosen under the influence of this partiality, and will betray it in his administration. These jealousies are inseparable from the scheme of leaving the States in Existence. They must be done away. The ungranted lands also which have been assumed by particular States must also be given up. (I, 463)

Read indicated that he favored the plan that Alexander Hamilton had introduced and would rather have it than the Virginia Plan.

On August 8, Read opposed long periods of state residence as a condition to holding legislative offices. He observed that "we were now forming a *Natil* Govt. and such a regulation would correspond little with the idea that we were one people" (II, 217). On August 18, Read further opposed leaving the appointment of militia officers to the states. He argued that if such a power were to remain with the states, it should be invested in the governors rather than in state legislatures (II, 333).

Congress

On June 7, Read proposed that the president should appoint members of the Senate from nominees suggested by state legislatures. He indicated that he feared delegates would be "alarmed" at his proposal (I, 151). Instead, it simply failed to receive either a second or other support. On June 24, when other delegates were suggesting terms of from four to seven years, Read proposed that members of the Senate should serve during good behavior (I, 409). This would have given members of that body the same independence that members of the federal judiciary enjoy today. When this resolution received little support, Read advocated nine-year terms (I, 421). Read appeared to believe that this would give senators greater independence from their states.

On June 13, Read indicated that he favored the provision limiting the origination of money bills to the House of Representatives. However, he did not think this should prevent the Senate from amending such bills (I, 234). On August 9, Read said that although he did not consider the origination of money bills in the House of Representatives to be important and had previously voted for striking it, he was willing to restore it for those who thought it was an essential element of the compromise relating to state representation within Congress (II, 232–233).

On July 9, Read questioned why Delaware had only one representative and Georgia had three (I, 561). Alluding on July 10 to the fact that his state and Rhode Island would each only have one representative if the initial House had, as proposed, only 65 members, Read proposed doubling this number. He argued that states with a small number of representatives might sometimes find themselves unrepresented, and he doubted that the people would "place their confidence" in so small a number (I, 570). Consistent with his earlier support for the Hamilton Plan, Read further observed that "He hoped the objects of the Genl. Govt. would be much more numerous than seemed to be expected by some gentlemen, and that they would become more & more so" (I, 570). He further suggested that representation for new Western states might be limited by putting a cap on the whole number of representatives (I, 570). On July 13, Read said that he suspected some of the larger states were not taking their full share of representatives in order to avoid their share of taxes. He thought that both should be apportioned fairly (I, 601).

Read argued on July 11 that "the Legislature ought not to be too much shackled" (I, 582). He feared that such restraints would act like religious creeds, which embarrassed those who agreed with them and produced dissatisfaction among others (I, 582). Consistent with his view, Read supported congressional regulation over state elections, granting Congress not only the power to alter state regulations but also to provide for such regulations in cases when states failed to act on their own (II, 242).

One power that Read did not want Congress exercising was the power to issue, or emit, paper money. On August 16, he said that the exercise of such a power "would be as alarming as the mark of the Beast in Revelation" (II, 310). Similarly, on September 14, Read successfully introduced the words "or other direct tax" after "limits on capitation taxes" lest "some liberty might otherwise be taken to saddle the States with a readjustment by this rule, of past Requisitions of Congs" (II, 618).

Presidency

On August 7, Read supported an absolute presidential veto of congressional laws. He said that "He considered this . . . essential to the Constitution, to the preservation of liberty, & to the public welfare" (I, 200). Read also believed that the president, and not Congress, should have the power to appoint the national treasurer. He thought that experience in the states had demonstrated that legislatures were inappropriate institutions for making such a choice and he argued that "the Executive being responsible would make a good choice" (II, 315).

On August 24, Read offered a motion to grant the president of the Senate the right to cast the deciding vote in the case of a tie in that body for president. The Convention rejected this proposal, apparently without a state-by-state record of the vote (II, 403). On September 6, Read opposed a motion by Elbridge Gerry of Massachusetts to send the election to the House of Representatives in the case when the Senate did not reelect a candidate by a majority; he expressed his opposition to indulging individual delegates (II, 522). When the Convention contemplated allowing the House of Representatives to decide elections in which no presidential candidate obtained a majority, Read feared that states, like his own, with only one member might end up being unrepresented in the case that a member was sick or absent (II, 536).

Judiciary

On August 27, Read opposed vesting jurisdiction in cases of both law and equity, the two central divisions of English law, in the same court (II, 428). However, the record does not reveal the basis of his opposition.

Life after the Convention

Read was the only individual who signed the Constitution twice, since fellow delegate John Dickinson, a longtime friend, who had left the Convention because of illness, asked him to sign on his behalf. Read worked for ratification of the Constitution on his return to Delaware after which he was selected as one of Delaware's first two senators and aligned himself with the Federalist Party. He resigned from this post in order to take the post of chief justice of his state, a position in which he served until his death in 1798. The previous year he published a two-volume *Laws of Delaware*.

See Also Delaware

FOR FURTHER READING

Bradford, M. M. 1994. *Founding Fathers: Brief Lives of the Framers of the United States Constitution*. 2nd ed. Lawrence: University Press of Kansas.

Farrand, Max, ed. 1937. *The Records of the Federal Convention*. 4 vols. New Haven, CT: Yale University Press.

Gillespie, Michael Allen, and Michael Lienesch, eds. 1989. *Ratifying the Constitution*. Lawrence: University Press of Kansas.

REASON AND EXPERIENCE

Although most were well educated, the delegates to the Constitutional Convention are generally regarded as practical men. They included individuals with considerable experience in winning national independence and in writing and implementing state constitutions. As a group, the Framers have been credited for "their ability to synthesize experience and ideas" (Dunn 1996, 753).

The delegates to the Convention functioned during the Enlightenment period, the Age of Reason, when belief in the power of reason was prevalent. Such a belief is reflected in the "Circular Letter addressed to the Governors" that George Washington wrote on June 8, 1783. There he observed:

> The foundation of our empire was not laid in the gloomy age of ignorance and superstition; but at an epoch when the rights of mankind were better understood and more clearly defined, than at any other period. The researches of the human mind after *social happiness* have been carried to a great extent; the treasures of knowledge acquired by the labors of philosophers, sages, and legislators, through a long succession of years, are laid open for our use, and their collected wisdom may be happily applied in the establishment of our forms of government. . . . At this auspicious period, the United States came into existence as a nation; and, if their citizens should not be completely free and happy, the fault will be entirely their own. (Quoted in Corwin 1964, 1–2)

A similar spirit had motivated John Adams, writing to George Wythe in January 1776 on the eve of the Revolutionary War and the flurry of state constitution-making:

> You and I . . . have been sent into life at a time when the greatest lawgivers of antiquity would have wished to live. How few of the human race have ever enjoyed an opportunity of making an election of government, more than of air, soil, or climate, for themselves or their children! When, before the present epoch, had three millions of

people full power and a fair opportunity to form and establish the wisest and happiest government that human wisdom can contrive? (Quoted in Ranney 1976, 140–141)

The rules that the delegates to the Constitutional Convention established for governing the proceedings and the seriousness with which they made and listened to arguments not only during the Convention but also during subsequent ratification debates are testimony to their belief in the power of persuasion.

For practical men, this attitude was not inconsistent with some skepticism of abstract reason divorced from experience. More generally, Americans, often taking a cue from Scottish Enlightenment thinkers, became known for tempering more skeptical and radical aspects of Enlightenment thinking often associated with Europe and especially France (Meyer 1976; Lundberg and May 1976). At times, therefore, delegates commended reason, and at other times they appealed to experience. Americans were voracious readers of history, and they often appealed to such history for a vindication of their rights (Colbourn 1965). A scholar of the Founding has thus observed that the Founders sometimes applied reason in fairly conservative ways, melding "conclusions of reason with institutions and ideas of a traditionalist or customary cast—institutions and ideas whose strength and direction would be provided by prejudice and prescription" (Watson 2003, 75).

There is hardly a page of convention deliberations during which delegates do not refer to some aspect of either contemporary experience under the Articles of Confederation, in the states, or in contemporary nations. Similarly, they constantly cited examples, and responded with counterexamples, from the history of Greece, Rome, Great Britain, and other nations. Madison was among those who prepared for the Convention by studying and writing about the experiences of prior confederacies.

Raoul Narroll has found that the delegates are recorded as having made almost 400 historical references at the Convention. Of these about 125 references were to American history (mostly from 1763 onward) and another 100 were to British history, meaning that together such references accounted for about 55 percent. The delegates referred to continental European history about seventy times and to ancient history almost as often (Narroll 1953, 3–4). Narroll further found that, while the delegates were sometimes mistaken about such history, they rarely used the examples simply as rhetorical flourishes (11).

In discussing the Council of Revision, Virginia's George Mason referred to experience as "the best of all tests" (Farrand 1937, I, 101). When Pennsylvania's James Wilson joined Connecticut's Oliver Ellsworth in arguing that inserting a provision on ex post facto laws in the Constitution would "proclaim that we are ignorant of the first principles of Legislation" (since by his reasoning, such laws were inherently void), Maryland's John Carroll responded that "experience overruled all other calculations" and that such experience showed a need for such a prohibition because states had in fact been passing them (II, 376). In an outline for a speech that he prepared for delivery at the Convention, New Jersey's William Paterson observed that "A little practicable Virtue [is to be] preferred to Theory" (I, 186). During discussion of representation in Congress, Wilson (who favored apportioning representation by population in both houses) observed that delegates were forming a government for "*men*" rather than "for the imaginary beings called *States*" and he questioned whether the people would "be satisfied with metaphysical distinctions" (I, 483). Benjamin Franklin appealed to a similar penchant for practicality by suggesting that a compromise on the issue of representation in Congress would be like a carpenter (Franklin called him an "artist") fitting two planks for a table together by taking a "little from both" and thus making a good joint (I, 488). Rufus King of Massachusetts argued that "We ought to be governed by reason, not by chance" (II, 106). Typically, reason and experience could be expected to coincide. Thus, in favoring restrictions on officeholding by immigrants, Pennsylvania's Gouverneur Morris argued: "The lesson we are taught is that we should be governed as much by our reason, and as little by our feelings as possible.

What is the language of Reason on this subject? That we should not be polite at the expense of prudence" (II, 237–238).

Delegates did not always live up to their own standards. Morris thus ironically followed his appeal to reason with an arguably outrageous, and highly emotional, example in which he compared opening offices to immigrants to the reputed practice among Native Americans (like other delegates, he called them Indians) of sharing their wives and daughters with strangers!

Sometimes the delegates compared reason to chance. In thus urging the rejection of a proposal whereby members of Congress would be selected by lot to choose the president, Elbridge Gerry of Massachusetts observed that "this is committing too much to chance" (II, 105). Similarly, Rufus King argued that "We ought to be governed by reason, not by chance" (II, 106).

In notes for a speech that he gave on June 19, Rufus King of Massachusetts commended the Virginia Plan by observing that "the System proposed to be adopted is no scheme of a day, calculated to postpone the hour of Danger, & then leave it to fall with double ruin on our successors" (I, 332). He further observed that "it is no idle Experiment, no romantic Speculation—the measure forces itself upon wise men" (I, 332).

Perhaps the most notable comment on the subject of experience at the Convention was a speech on August 13 in which Delaware's John Dickinson was arguing for an English mechanism, a restriction of the origination of money bills in the lower house, that was proving otherwise difficult to justify. Dickinson's approach was much like that which is today associated with the English philosopher Edmund Burke who thought that institutions grew over time and should not be lightly dismantled:

Experience must be our only guide. Reason may mislead us. It was not Reason that discovered the singular & admirable mechanism of the English Constitution. It was not reason that discovered or ever could have discovered the odd & in the eye of those who are governed by reason, the absurd mode of trial by Jury. Accidents probably produced these discoveries, and experience has given sanction to them. This is then our guide. (II, 278)

Although the delegates to the Convention did not use experience as an excuse not to make changes, they clearly attempted to see that the changes they proposed were commended not only in theory but also by historical and/or contemporary practices. In justifying the new Constitution in the first of *The Federalist Papers*, Alexander Hamilton, who had served at the Convention as a delegate from New York, observed that the contest over the Constitution would "decide the important question, whether societies of men are really capable or not of establishing good government from reflection and choice, or whether they are forever destined to depend for their political constitutions on accident and force" (Hamilton, Madison, and Jay 1961, 33). Similarly, in arguing before the Pennsylvania convention for ratification of the Constitution, James Wilson observed:

Government, indeed, may yet be considered to be in its infancy; and with all its various modifications, it has hitherto been the result of force, fraud or accident. For after six thousand years since the creation of the world, America now presents the first instance of a people assembled to weigh deliberately and calmly, and to decide leisurely and peaceably, upon the form of government by which they will bind themselves and their posterity. (Schecter 1915, 723, quoting *N.Y. Daily Advertiser*, December 3, 1787)

See Also Classical Allusions and Influences; Common Law; Great Britain; Scottish Enlightenment

FOR FURTHER READING

Ahern, Gregory S. 2004. "Virtue, Wisdom, Experience, Not Abstract Rights, Form the Basis of the American Republic." Center for Constitutional Studies. http://www.nhinet.org/ccs/ccs-res.htm.

Bainton, Roland. 1968. "The Appeal to Reason and the American Constitution." In Conyers Read, ed.

The Constitution Reconsidered. New York: Harper and Row, Publishers, 121–130.

Colbourn, H. Trevor. 1965. *The Lamp of Experience: Whig History and the Intellectual Origins of the American Revolution.* Chapel Hill: University of North Carolina Press.

Corwin, Edward S. 1964. "The Progress of Constitutional Theory between the Declaration of Independence and the Meeting of the Philadelphia Convention." *American Constitutional History: Essays by Edward S. Corwin.* Ed. Alpheus T. Mason and Gerald Garvey. New York: Harper and Row, Publishers.

Dunn, Susan. 1996. "Revolutionary Men of Letters and the Pursuit of Radical Change: The Views of Burke, Tocqueville, Adams, Madison, and Jefferson." *William and Mary Quarterly,* 3rd ser. 53 (October): 729–754.

Farrand, Max, ed. 1937. *The Records of the Federal Convention.* 4 vols. New Haven, CT: Yale University Press.

Hamilton, Alexander, James Madison, and John Jay. 1961. *The Federalist Papers.* Ed. Clinton Rossiter. New York: New American Library.

Koch, Adrienne. 1961. "Pragmatic Wisdom and the American Enlightenment." *William and Mary Quarterly,* 3rd ser. 18 (July): 313–319.

Lundberg, David, and Henry F. May. 1976. "The Enlightened Reader in America." *American Quarterly* 28 (Summer): 262–293.

Meyer, D. D. 1976. "The Uniqueness of the American Enlightenment." *American Quarterly* 28 (1976): 165–186.

Narroll, Raoul Soskin. 1953. *Clio and the Constitution: The Influence of the Study of History on the Federal Constitutional Convention of 1787.* Ph.D. diss., University of California, Los Angeles.

Ranney, Austin. 1976. "'The Divine Science': Political Engineering in American Culture." *American Political Science Review* 70 (March): 140–148.

Ryn, Chaes G. 1992. "Political Philosophy and the Unwritten Constitution." *Modern Age* 34 (Summer). Center for Constitutional Studies. http://www.nhinet.org/ccs/ccs-res.htm.

Schecter, Frank I. 1915. "The Early History of the Tradition of the Constitution." *American Political Science Review* 9 (November): 707–734.

Watson, Bradley C. C. 2003. "Hume, Historical Inheritance, and the Problem of Founding." In Ronald J. Pestritto and Thomas G. West, eds. *The American Founding and the Social Compact.* Lanham, MD: Lexington Books, 75–94.

RECORDS OF THE CONSTITUTIONAL CONVENTION

Although there are scores of books and articles on the Constitutional Convention and a resulting document that students of the subject can examine, most accounts of the actual proceedings in Philadelphia are based on a relatively few primary sources. A number of delegates published information shortly after the Convention. Pennsylvania's Benjamin Franklin released the texts of some of his speeches, South Carolina's Charles Pinckney published the text of one of his prepared speeches, Maryland's Luther Martin (who had refused to sign the Constitution) published a negative report that he submitted to his state legislature, and some former delegates disclosed information about the Convention during the course of the ratification debates (Farrand 1907, 45–46). These debates have themselves been collected in two major series, the second of which has been of particular value to recent scholarship on the Constitution (Elliott 1888; Jensen 1976). These debates also featured publication of *The Federalist Papers* by Alexander Hamilton, James Madison, and John Jay, the first two of whom had been Convention delegates; both repeated and elaborated arguments they had made at the Convention.

The Official Journal

Delegates at the Constitutional Convention selected William Jackson to keep a journal. On the last day of the Convention, Rufus King of Massachusetts suggested that the journals should either be destroyed or entrusted to George Washington's custody. The second measure was adopted after the observation of Pennsylvania's James Wilson that, were they to be destroyed, it would be impossible to refuse "false suggestions" that might be "propagated" about the Convention's work (Farrand 1937, II, 648).

John Quincy Adams, then secretary of state, edited this Journal and published it in 1819. The

Journal is largely a record of motions and votes, and is not particularly accurate. Adams noted that the Journal records "were no better than the daily minutes from which the regular journal ought to have been but never was, made out" (quoted in Farrand 1907, 48).

Other Notes

Robert Yates of New York published his notes in 1821, but they end when he left the Convention on July 5, 1787. Moreover, in part because they were edited by a partisan, they do not appear to be particularly reliable (Hutson 1987a, 412). William Pierce of Georgia published his famous character sketches of the delegates in 1828. Despite numerous biographies of the Framers, narrators of the Constitutional Convention have often reproduced Pierce's sketches, which are generally memorable and seem relatively accurate, and taken them at face value, rather than comparing them with the judgments of others.

Madison's Notes

Most prominent are the notes that James Madison took at the Convention. Stationing himself near the front of the room, he did not miss a single day of the proceedings, and he made a Herculean effort to record not only his own varied contributions but those of other delegates. Madison appeared to anticipate that his notes would be published, but he did not publish them in his lifetime. Dolley Madison sold Madison's notes to the State Department after he died in 1836; they are currently housed in the manuscript division of the Library of Congress.

Madison's notes of the Convention were first published in 1840 in a three-volume set, *The Papers of James Madison,* edited by H. D. Gilpin. Madison had made a number of changes in his notes, largely on the basis of the official Journal, but because the Journal was itself faulty, not all the changes were for the better. Gilpin also appears to have made some changes. Madison's Convention debates were subsequently edited by

Gaillard Hunt and James Brown Scott and published in 1920. Historian Charles C. Tansill published important documents for Congress including Madison's notes as House Document no. 398 (see Benton 1986, 7). Ohio University Press subsequently reprinted these in 1966 (Benton, 8).

From time to time, scholars, most notably William Winslow Crosskey, have alleged that Madison doctored his notes for political reasons, but there is little evidence to support this view (Hutson 1987a, 412–415). It must, however, be recognized that Madison never purported to offer a transcription of Convention proceedings. Since he would have been unable to write and speak at the same time, his records of his own speeches might sometimes reflect what he wished he had said rather than what he actually did say. A modern scholar of the subject has estimated that he recorded about 10 percent of the proceedings of each day (Hutson 1986, 34).

Still Other Notes

Other records of the Convention were later published in the papers of Rufus King of Massachusetts and James McHenry of Maryland. Notes have also been located from William Paterson of New Jersey and Alexander Hamilton of New York, Charles Pinckney of South Carolina, and George Mason of Virginia, the latter including a copy of Randolph's report from the Committee of Detail. Although Madison's notes remain primary, other records are important in largely substantiating the accuracy of, or, on occasion, correcting or filling out, his reports.

The Notes Compiled

Historian Max Farrand compiled these accounts of the Convention in *The Records of the Federal Convention of 1787,* originally published in 1911 and revised in 1937. The first two volumes blended all of the above accounts into a day-by-day account of the Convention. The third volume supplemented these accounts with letters by members of the Convention in the time immediately before, during, and after the Convention. The original fourth volume added corrections, additions, and an index. This has subsequently been superseded by a supplement edited by James H. Hutson (1987b). In addition to newly discovered letters, this volume has entries from George Washington's diary during the Convention and from notes by John Lansing of New York, first published in 1939, after publication of Farrand's volumes.

One difficulty with following Madison's and other accounts of the Convention is that the task of tracing individual constitutional provisions through almost four months of debate can become quite complex. Arthur Prescott has rearranged Madison's notes topically (1968); Professor Wilbourn E. Benton has also published a two-volume set of records designed to trace debates on each individual Article and Section of the Constitution (1986). Professors Philip B. Kurland and Ralph Lerner have taken a similar approach, expanding their focus by including materials in addition to those of Convention records (1987). Historian Saul K. Padover has also published a volume arranging Convention debates by topic (1962). An earlier compilation by Jane Butzner focuses topically on rejected proposals at the Convention (1941). A more recent compilation focuses specifically on debates on the presidency (Ellis 1999). Many books of primary sources include outlines of the Virginia and New Jersey Plans as well as notes on noteworthy speeches at the Convention.

See Also Farrand, Max; *Federalist, The;* Jackson, William; King, Rufus; McHenry, James; Madison, James, Jr.; Martin, Luther; Pierce, William; Yates, Robert

FOR FURTHER READING

Benton, Wilbourn E. 1986. *1787: Drafting the U.S. Constitution.* 2 vols. College Station: Texas A and M University Press.

Butzner, Jane, comp. 1941. *Constitutional Chaff—Rejected Suggestions of the Constitutional Convention of 1787 with Explanatory Argument.* New York: Columbia University Press.

Elliott, Jonathan, ed. 1888. *The Debates in the Several State Constitutions on the Adoption of the Federal Constitution.* 5 vols. New York: Burt Franklin.

Ellis, Richard J., ed. 1999. *Founding the American Presidency.* Lanham, MD: Rowman and Littlefield Publishers.

Farrand, Max. October 1907. "The Records of the Federal Convention." *American Historical Review* 13: 44–65.

——, ed. 1937. Paperback ed. 1966. *The Records of the Federal Convention.* 4 vols. New Haven, CT: Yale University Press.

Hutson, James H. 1986. "The Creation of the Constitution: The Integrity of the Documentary Record." *Texas Law Review* 65 (November): 1–39.

——. 1987a. "Riddles of the Federal Constitutional Convention." *William and Mary Quarterly,* 3rd ser. 44 (July): 411–423.

——, ed. 1987b. *Supplement to Max Farrand's* The Records of the Federal Convention of 1787. New Haven, CT: Yale University Press.

Jensen, Merrill, ed. 1976. *The Documentary History of the Ratification of the Constitution.* 18 vols. Madison: State Historical Society of Wisconsin.

Kurland, Philip B., and Ralph Lerner. 1987. *The Founders' Constitution.* 5 vols. Chicago: University of Chicago Press.

Padover, Saul K. 1962. *To Secure These Blessings: The Great Debates of the Constitutional Convention of 1787, Arranged According to Topics.* New York: Washington Square Press/Ridge Press Book.

Prescott, Arthur Taylor. 1968. *Drafting the Federal Constitution: A Rearrangement of Madison's Notes Giving Consecutive Developments of Provisions in the Constitution of the United States, Supplemented by Documents Pertaining to the Philadelphia Convention and to Ratification Processes, and Including Insertions by the Compiler.* Westport, CT: Greenwood Press.

Tansill, Charles C., arranger. 1927. *Documents Illustrative of the Formation of the Union of the American States.* Washington, DC: U.S. Government Printing Office.

RELIGIOUS AFFILIATIONS OF THE DELEGATES

Commentators have often portrayed the Founding Fathers as deists who accepted the existence of a God who had implanted basic principles of morality within human beings but who did not intervene in human affairs, as with miracles. There were certainly some prominent individuals among the Framers, Thomas Jefferson, for example, who appear to fit this description. However, almost every delegate to the Constitutional Convention was associated with a particular Protestant denomination, and their religious beliefs were often quite diverse (West 1996, 11–78).

M. M. Bradford, who has authored one of the most concise summaries of the lives of the Founders, indicates that the most dominant religion, identified with 28 of the delegates, was Episcopalian. Americans thus continued to be influenced by their predominately English roots—Episcopalians were members of the American branch of the Church of England, which had split under Henry VIII from the Roman Catholic Church (Bradford 1982, iv–v). Anglicanism was particularly prominent in some states, with Bradford identifying six of the seven delegates (all but McClung, who is unclassified) from Virginia, all four South Carolinians, and two Georgians as being affiliated with this church.

Presbyterians and Congregationalists are next on the list, with the former having eight adherents and the latter having seven. Congregationalists were an offshoot of Puritanism and were mostly concentrated in the Northeast. Presbyterian affiliation predominated among the delegations from New Jersey (with Princeton University) and North Carolina. Three onetime Quakers from Pennsylvania and Delaware had all affiliated with different religions, perhaps in part because of the Quaker opposition to war. Both individuals associated with the Dutch Reformed Church were from New York, where the Dutch had originally settled. Delaware's Richard Bassett (who, along with Connecticut's Roger Sherman, probably came closest to being an Evangelical) was a Methodist as was Georgia's William Few. Pennsylvania's Thomas Mifflin (a onetime Quaker) and Delaware's Jacob Broom were Lutherans. Thomas Fitzsimons of Pennsylvania and Daniel Carroll of Maryland were the only two Roman Catholics.

Outward religious affiliation does not, of course, necessarily point to inward belief. Bradford identifies Benjamin Franklin and James Wilson (also listed as an Episcopalian) of Pennsylvania and Hugh Williamson of North Carolina (who is also listed as a Presbyterian) as deists, although in part because of his association with Thomas Jefferson, some people believe that James Madison, who was silent about his religious beliefs throughout most of his adult life, may also have been one. By contrast, Alexander Hamilton is believed to have become much more devout toward the end of his life after his son was killed in a duel.

See Also Biblical and Religious References at the Constitutional Convention; Prayer at the Convention; Protestantism; Puritanism; Religious Tests, Prohibition

FOR FURTHER READING

Bradford, M. M. 1982. *A Worthy Company: Brief Lives of the Framers of the United States Constitution.* Marlborough, NH: Plymouth Rock Foundation.

——. 1993. *Original Intentions: On the Making and Ratification of the United States Constitution.* Athens: University of Georgia Press.

Eidsmoe, John. 1987. *Christianity and the Constitution: The Faith of Our Founding Fathers.* Grand Rapids, MI: Baker Book House.

Holmes, David L. 2003. *The Religion of the Founding Fathers.* Charlottesville, VA: Ann Arbor, MI: Ash Lawn-Highland: Clements Library.

West, John G., Jr. 1996. *The Politics of Revelation and Reason: Religion and Civic Life in the New Nation.* Lawrence: University Press of Kansas.

RELIGIOUS REFERENCES AT THE CONSTITUTIONAL CONVENTION

See BIBLICAL AND RELIGIOUS REFERENCES AT THE CONSTITUTIONAL CONVENTION

RELIGIOUS TESTS, PROHIBITION

One provision of the Constitution that emerged relatively late in the Convention was the clause in Article VI providing that "no religious Test shall ever be required as a Qualification to any Office or public Trust under the United States." By way of contrast, almost all the state constitutions required religious affirmations. Delaware's constitution of 1776, for example, required officeholders to acknowledge the Trinity and the "divine inspiration" of "the holy scriptures of the Old and New Testaments" (cited in Kurland and Lerner 1987, IV, 634); others limited public offices to Christians or Protestants (Dreisbach 1999, 264–268). The prohibition on oaths has thus been called "a bold departure from the prevailing practices in Europe, as well as most of the states" (Dreisbach, 262).

Charles Pinckney of South Carolina, who may have offered a similar provision as part of a package of proposals that he presented to the Convention about 10 days earlier (Farrand 1937, II, 342), proposed the prohibition on religious tests on August 30 (II, 468). At the time, the delegates were discussing the provision that would also appear in Article VI requiring all state and national officials to affirm their support of the U.S. Constitution. Gouverneur Morris of Pennsylvania joined in supporting Pinckney's motion to prohibit religious tests. Connecticut's Roger Sherman did not think that a constitutional prohibition was needed. He argued that "the prevailing liberality" was a "sufficient security agst. such tests" (II, 468). Rather than take the chance that such liberality would continue to prevail, the Convention unanimously voted to add the prohibition.

Apparently, some members remained unconvinced that the clause was a good idea. Maryland's Luther Martin later observed in a report of November 29 to the Maryland state legislature that

> there were some members so unfashionable as to think, that a belief in the existence of a Deity, and of a state of future rewards and punishments would be some security for the good conduct of our rulers, and that, in a Christian country, it would be at least decent to hold out some distinction between the professors of Christianity and downright infidelity or paganism. (III, 227, italics omitted)

The proceedings of the Constitutional Convention were secret. Curiously, Jonas Phillips, a Jewish leader in Philadelphia, had sent a letter to George Washington, who was widely known for his liberal views toward religious liberty (Boller 1960), on September 2, just four days after the adoption of the prohibition on religious tests, in which he urged the Convention to reject them. He observed that existing state requirements requiring individuals to acknowledge the inspiration of the Old and New Testaments violated the beliefs of Jews, many of whom, like himself, had bravely fought during the Revolutionary War (St. John 1987, 194).

Many state constitutions subsequently copied the prohibition against religious oaths in the U.S. Constitution (Dreisbach, 272). The provision, which may have largely grown out of the inability to formulate a test that would apply to all of the colonies with their diverse denominations, did not of its own force invalidate existing state religious oaths. The adoption of the clause did help calm fears of a national religious establishment that opponents sometimes raised against the Constitution during ratification debates. A student of the subject observes that

> many delegates to the state conventions were unwilling to grant the new national regime authority to implement a practice (i.e., religious tests) that was common at the state level precisely because they wanted to retain the state tests and they feared a federal test might displace existing state tests. (Dreisbach, 286)

Despite subsequent interpretations that have sometimes been placed on the clause in light of the religious clauses later included in the First Amendment, such delegates, like those at the Constitutional Convention, generally appear to have been more interested in using the clause to preserve existing state institutions and establishments than to create a secular state (Dreisbach, 294).

See Also Bill of Rights; Oaths of Office

FOR FURTHER READING

Boller, Paul F. 1960. "George Washington and Religious Liberty." *William and Mary Quarterly*, 3rd ser. 17 (October): 486–506.

Bradley, Gerald V. 1987. "The Individual Liberties within the Body of the Constitution: A Symposium: The No Religious Test Clause and the Constitution of Religious Liberty: A Machine That Has Gone of Itself." *Case Western Reserve Law Review* 37: 674–747.

Dreisbach, Daniel L. 1999. "The Constitution's Forgotten Religion Clause: Reflections on the Article VI Religious Test Ban." *Journal of Church and State* 38 (Spring): 261–296.

Farrand, Max, ed. 1937. *The Records of the Federal Convention.* 4 vols. New Haven, CT: Yale University Press.

Kurland, Philip B., and Ralph Lerner, eds. 1987. *The Founders' Constitution.* Vol. 4: *Article 2, Section 2, through Article 7.* Chicago: University of Chicago Press.

St. John, Jeffrey. 1987. *Constitutional Journal: A Correspondent's Report from the Convention of 1787.* Ottawa, IL: Jameson Books.

RENDITION CLAUSE

See FUGITIVE SLAVE CLAUSE

REPUBLIC

The members of the Constitutional Convention often designated the government they created as a "republic." They did so both in order to distinguish it from governments in which monarchs or aristocrats inherited positions from birth and to distinguish it from pure democracies, which they associated with instability and injustice. Benjamin Franklin was reported to have responded to a question as to what kind of government the Convention had created by saying, "A republic, if you can keep it" (Farrand 1937, III, 85).

The terminology can be confusing because advocates of republics themselves fell into at least two camps. These included followers of John Locke, who are often called "liberals," or "classical liberals." They tended to stress the idea of limited government in which individual liberties were secured by mechanisms like separation of powers and checks and balances. By contrast, "republicans," who are often associated with the British "country" party, gave greater focus to the responsibilities of collective citizenship and the role of citizen "virtue" in supporting government. As Farber and Sherry have observed: "A republic (the type of government), then, can be either liberal or republican (depending on whether it is mostly Lockean or mostly 'Country')" (Farber and Sherry 1990, 12).

Uses of Term in Convention Debates

The delegates' preference for republican government was evident early in the Convention when, in introducing the Virginia Plan, Edmund Randolph portrayed his solution to the problems under the Articles of Confederation as being based on "the republican principle" (I, 19). One of the provisions of his plan, later incorporated into the guarantee clause in Article IV, Section 4, of the Constitution, also provided that the United States should guarantee "a Republican Government" to each state (I, 22). The fact that all 13 original states were accepted into the new government without requiring structural changes indicates that the term was inclusive enough to include governments that the Framers thought were extremely democratic as well as those, like the government they proposed, that they hoped would provide for greater stability and balance.

On June 1, Pennsylvania's James Wilson argued that the "extent" of the nation "was so great, and the manners so republican, that nothing but a great confederated Republic would do for it" (I, 66). On June 6, Virginia's George Mason further observed that although "improper elections in many instances, were inseparable from Republican Govts.," he still thought that such elections more clearly favored "the rights of the people, in favor of human nature" (I, 134). In a similar vein, on August 19, Madison opposed allowing Congress to set qualifications for voters:

> The qualifications of electors and elected were fundamental articles in a Republican Govt. and ought to be fixed by the Constitution. If the Legislature could regulate those of either, it can by degrees subvert the Constitution. A Republic may be converted into an aristocracy or oligarchy as well by limiting the number capable of being elected, as the number authorized to elect. (II, 250)

On an earlier occasion, Madison had used the fact that "we were now digesting a plan which in its operation wd. decide forever the fate of Republican Govt." as a reason for considering a nine-year Senate term, which he believed would give this government an element of "wisdom & virtue" (I, 423).

The pervasiveness of the belief in the desirability of republican government at the Convention may be indicated by a speech that Alexander Hamilton gave on June 26. Hamilton observed that although he did not himself "think favorably of Republican Government" (the plan he introduced at the Convention would have allowed both the president and members of the Senate to serve "during good behavior"), he was addressing his remarks "to those who did think favorably of it, in order to prevail on them to tone their Government as high as possible" (I, 424). Fellow New York delegate Robert Yates elaborated Hamilton's sentiments in further detail:

> We are now forming a republican government. Real liberty is neither found in despotism or the extremes of democracy, but in moderate governments.
>
> Those who mean to form a solid republican government, ought to proceed to the confines of another government. As long as offices are open to all men, and no constitutional rank is established, it is pure republicanism.

But if we incline too much to democracy, we should soon shoot into a monarchy. (I, 432)

In supporting a provision that made apportionment of congressional districts mandatory after periodic censuses, Randolph observed on July 11 that the Baron de Montesquieu had regarded matters related to suffrage as "a fundamental article in Republican Govts." (I, 580). On July 19, Pennsylvania's Gouverneur Morris further observed that "it has been a maxim in political Science that Republican Government is not adapted to a large extent of Country, because the energy of the Executive Magistracy can not reach the extreme parts of it" and used this as an argument on behalf of either allowing the executive to serve for life or allowing the people to select him (II, 52, 54).

On August 13, Virginia's George Mason argued that "notwithstanding the superiority of the Republican form over every other, it had its evils" (II, 273). He listed the two most prominent as majority oppression of the minority and "the mischievous influence of demagogues" (II, 273). He argued that the general government would provide a "cure" for such problems, but argued that the U.S. Senate should not be allowed to originate money bills (II, 274). Madison took the opposite view, but he did so while agreeing that "One of the greatest evils incident to Republican Govt. was the spirit of contention & faction" (II, 276). Madison frequently argued that a large republic would better be able to battle such problems than would the existing Confederation.

Ratification Debates

Although some scholars believe that the distinction between republican government and democratic government was relatively new (Adams 2001, 110), Federalists further advanced this distinction during the constitutional ratification debates. In *Federalist* No. 10, which is generally regarded as its most famous essay, James Madison explained that a republican government utilized a system of representation designed to enlarge and refine the public interest. Many Antifederalists had followed the arguments of the Baron Charles

Louis de Secondat de Montesquieu in arguing that republican government was only possible in governments that covered small land areas. By contrast, Madison, who drew from the writings of David Hume, argued that, by covering wider areas, republics encompassed more factions or interests, making it less likely that any single interest could dominate.

See Also Aristocracy; Democracy; *Federalist, The;* Forms of Government; Guarantee Clause; Hume, David; Liberalism; Locke, John; Madison, James, Jr.; Monarchy; Montesquieu, Charles Louis de Secondat de; Republicanism

FOR FURTHER READING

Adams, Willi Paul. 2001. *The First American Constitutions: Republican Ideology and the Making of the State Constitutions in the Revolutionary Era.* Lanham, MD: Rowman and Littlefield Publishers.

Diamond, Martin. 1981. *The Founding of the Democratic Republic.* Itasca, IL: F. F. Peacock Publishers.

Farber, Daniel A., and Suzanna Sherry. 1990. *A History of the American Constitution.* Saint Paul, MN: West Publishing.

Farrand, Max, ed. 1937. *The Records of the Federal Convention.* 4 vols. New Haven, CT: Yale University Press.

Greene, Thurston. 1991. *The Language of the Constitution: A Sourcebook and Guide to the Ideas, Terms, and Vocabulary Used by the Framers of the United States Constitution.* Westport, CT: Greenwood Press.

Hamilton, Alexander, John Jay, and James Madison. *The Federalist.* Washington, DC: Robert B. Luce.

Pocock, J. G. A. 1975. *The Machiavellian Moment: Florentine Political Thought and the Atlantic Republican Tradition.* Princeton, NJ: Princeton University Press.

Shoemaker, Robert W. 1966. "'Democracy' and 'Republic' as Understood in Late Eighteenth-Century America." *American Speech* 41 (May): 83–95.

REPUBLICANISM

A republican government is associated with democratic representation in a legislative branch. Because such governments involved the population in governing in a way that monarchical governments (involving the rule of one person) and aristocratic governments (involving the rule of a few) did not, political theorists often associated republican governments with a high level of public commitment. Republican thinkers, heirs of the English Whig tradition, emphasized this connection. John Trenchard (1662–1723) and Thomas Gordon (late seventeenth century–1750), authors of *Cato's Letters,* which were widely circulated in the American colonies prior to the U.S. Revolution, are important representatives of this school of thought, which was suspicious of entrenched power and strongly committed to civil and religious liberty.

Political thinkers associated this commitment to republican government with citizen "virtue," the willingness to subordinate individual desires to the common good. Advocates of republicanism, who also sometimes advocated widespread property ownership as a way of encouraging citizen independence, believed that republican governments fostered such virtue because, within such governments, individuals could feel like citizens, and not simply subjects. Even with mechanisms for separation of powers and checks and balances within place, without such virtue, many advocates of republicanism did not believe that popular government could long survive. Although there were undoubtedly close ties between the two schools of thought, historians and political scientists thus often contrast advocates of republican government with advocates of classical liberalism, such as is associated with the philosophy of John Locke (for an influential study of republican thought going back to Niccolo Machiavelli, see Pocock 1975). Some believe that the period from the adoption of the Declaration of Independence in 1776 to the writing of the U.S. Constitution in 1787 marks a relatively steady progression from republican to classical liberal thought (Wood 1969).

Virginia's George Mason connected republicanism to classical ideas of citizen virtue at the Constitutional Convention. In a speech opposing a single executive, which he associated with monarchy, he portrayed republican government as superior:

This invincible principle is to be found in the love, the affection, the attachment of the citizens to their laws, to their freedom, and to their country. Every husbandman will be quickly converted into a soldier when he knows and feels that he is to fight not in defence of the rights of a particular family, or a prince, but for his own. (Farrand 1937, I, 112)

Mason went on to cite examples of republican virtue:

It was this which in ancient times enabled the little cluster of Grecian republics to resist, and almost constantly to defeat, the Persian monarch.

It was this which supported the States of Holland against a body of veteran troops through a thirty year's war with Spain, then the greatest monarchy in Europe, and finally rendered them victorious. It is that which preserves the freedom and independence of the Swiss Cantons in the midst of the most powerful nations. (I, 112)

Mason associated this same spirit with the American revolutionaries and was especially fearful that the Senate might give the new government too aristocratic a tinge. Other Antifederalists would express similar fears about the powers of the judicial branch.

In addition to the confusion that is sometimes generated by the distinction between a "republican" form of government and "republicanism," additional confusion has been furthered by the development of the Democratic-Republican Party. In one of the first two American political parties, largely founded by Thomas Jefferson and James Madison of Virginia, adherents shared some elements of both liberal and republican thought.

See Also Armies, Standing; Corruption; Federalist and Democratic-Republican Parties; Locke, John; Mason, George; Republic; Society of the Cincinnati; Virtue

FOR FURTHER READING

Adams, Willi Paul. 2001. *The First American Constitutions: Republican Ideology and the Making of the State Constitutions in the Revolutionary Era*. Lanham, MD: Rowman and Littlefield Publishers.

Diamond, Martin. 1981. *The Founding of the Democratic Republic*. Itasca, IL: F. F. Peacock Publishers.

Farrand, Max, ed. 1937. *The Records of the Federal Convention*. 4 vols. New Haven, CT: Yale University Press.

Gould, Philip. 1993. "Virtue, Ideology, and the American Revolution: The Legacy of the Republican Synthesis." *American Literary History* 5 (Autumn): 564–577.

Greene, Thurston. 1991. *The Language of the Constitution: A Sourcebook and Guide to the Ideas, Terms, and Vocabulary Used by the Framers of the United States Constitution*. Westport, CT: Greenwood Press.

Hamilton, Alexander, John Jay, and James Madison. *The Federalist*. Washington, DC: Robert B. Luce.

Henretta, James A. 1987. "Society and Republicanism: America in 1787." *This Constitution* no. 15 (Summer): 21–26.

Kerber, Linda K. 1985. "The Republican Ideology of the Revolutionary Generation." *American Quarterly* 37 (Autumn): 474–495.

Pocock, J. G. A. 1975. *The Machiavellian Moment: Florentine Political Thought and the Atlantic Republican Tradition*. Princeton, NJ: Princeton University Press.

Rodgers, Daniel T. 1992. "Republicanism: The Career of a Concept." *Journal of American History* 79 (June): 11–38.

Shalhope, Robert E. 1982. "Republicanism and Early American Historiography." *William and Mary Quarterly*, 3rd ser. 39 (April): 334–356.

——. 1972. "Toward a Republican Synthesis: The Emergence of an Understanding of Republicanism and American Historiography." *William and Mary Quarterly*, 3rd ser. 29 (January): 49–80.

Trenchard, John, and Thomas Gordon. 1995. *Cato's Letters or Essays on Liberty, Civil and Religious, and Other Important Subjects*. Ed. Ronald Hamowy. 2 vols. First published in four volumes in 1755. Indianapolis, IN: Liberty Fund.

Wood, Gordon S. 1969. *The Creation of the American Republic, 1776–1787*. Chapel Hill: University of North Carolina Press.

RESERVED POWERS OF THE STATES

See STATES, POLICE POWERS

RESOLUTION ACCOMPANYING THE CONSTITUTION

The delegates to the Constitutional Convention adopted an accompanying resolution, forwarded along with the document to Congress, which specified a procedure for ratifying the document and for inaugurating the new government. Dated September 17, 1787, the most important aspect of this resolution may have been the fact that George Washington, who had presided over the Convention and whose presence at the Convention had been one of its central legitimizing aspects, signed it. It is probably also significant that while suggesting a procedure for ratifying the Constitution without direct congressional or state legislative approval, the document called upon Congress both to pass along the document to the states and to initiate the new government just as it called upon the states to issue calls for ratifying conventions.

Unlike the Preamble to the U.S. Constitution (with its generalized reference to "We the People"), the first full paragraph of the resolution listed the 12 states in attendance, following the north-to-south ordering. Because New York did not have a majority of delegates present, Hamilton got special mention–"Mr. Hamilton from New York." The delegates resolved to lay the document before Congress under the Articles of Confederation, but rather than ask officially for congressional approval, the delegates recommended that the document be submitted to delegates in state conventions called by state legislatures, notice of ratifications to proceed from the conventions back to Congress.

Consistent with Article VII, the delegates further recommended that as soon as nine states had ratified, Congress should fix a day for electors to vote for president and for the election of senators and representatives and "the Time and Place for commencing Proceedings under this Constitution" (Jensen 1976, 318). The Senate would appoint a president of that body "for the sole Purpose of receiving, opening and counting the Votes for President" (318). Then "Congress, together with the President, should, without Delay, proceed to execute this Constitution" (318). Congress responded on September 13, 1788, by resolving:

that the first Wednesday in January next be the day for appointing Electors in the several states, which before the said day shall have ratified the said Constitution; that the first Wednesday in February next be the day for the Electors to assemble in their respective states, and vote for a President; and that the first Wednesday in March next be the time, and the present seat of Congress [New York City] the place for commencing proceedings under the said Constitution. (Quoted in Lawson and Seidman 2001, 6)

Significantly, a recent treatment of the Constitutional Convention of 1787 ends with the inauguration of President Washington. This account thus emphasizes that the new government did not come into power with its ratification but with the initiation of a new government (see Berkin 2002, 191–204).

See Also Ratification in the States; Washington, George

FOR FURTHER READING

Berkin, Carol. 2002. *A Brilliant Solution: Inventing the American Constitution.* New York: Harcourt.

Jensen, Merrill, ed. 1976. *Constitutional Documents and Records, 1776–1787.* Vol. 1 of *The Documentary History of the Ratification of the Constitution.* Madison: State Historical Society of Wisconsin.

Kesavan, Vasan. 2002. "When Did the Articles of Confederation Cease to Be Law?" *Notre Dame Law Review* 78 (December): 35–82.

Lawson, Gary, and Guy Seidman. 2001. "When Did the Constitution Become Law?" *Notre Dame Law Review* 77 (November): 1–37.

REVOLUTIONARY WAR

When the delegates to the Second Continental Congress declared their independence from Great Britain in 1776, they not only legitimized a conflict that had already begun, but they also set in motion a series of reforms the impact of which continues to be felt to the present day. In 1786, just one year before the Constitutional Convention, Benjamin Rush thus decried the tendency "to confound the terms of the American revolution with those of the late American war." He further observed that "nothing but the first act of the great drama is closed. It remains yet to establish and perfect our new forms of government, and to prepare the principles, morals, and manners of our citizens, for these forms of government, after they are established and brought to perfection" (quoted in Rakove 1979, 388).

Relation between the Convention and the Revolution

Although historians of the Progressive Era often portrayed the Constitutional Convention as a conservative reaction against the more heady philosophy of the Declaration of Independence, it seems more logical to interpret these events as part of the same movement, with the proponents of a new Constitution tempered by intervening experiences but still committed to revolutionary ideals. Stanley Elkins and Eric McKitrick have thus observed that the Federalists who supported the Constitution generally tended to be about 10 to 12 years younger than those who opposed it (1961, 203). They observe that Federalists generally came to manhood and were most influenced by the events of the Revolution, while the Antifederalists tended to be influenced more by prior events.

Elkins and McKitrick believe that the Revolution was the primary influence in giving the Federalists a more "continental" perspective than a state-centered one. Significantly, 22 of the delegates who signed the Constitution, and the secretary of the Convention, who also signed, were Revolutionary War veterans (Wright and MacGregor 1987). These included George Washington, who had led the American forces during the war, as well as John Dickinson, Alexander Hamilton, Rufus King, William Livingston, Gouverneur Morris, Charles Pinckney, and Charles Cotesworth Pinckney.

The inability to enforce the Treaty of Paris, by which the Revolutionary War had been brought to an end, was among the catalysts for the Constitutional Convention. In large part, the Convention's work can be interpreted as an attempt to provide for the kind of continental unity that the government under Britain had provided for the 13 colonies and that the Articles of Confederation had not successfully achieved.

Mentions of the War at the Convention

Delegates to the Convention referred a number of times to the Revolutionary War. On June 4, Virginia's George Mason cited American victory in this conflict as a triumph of republican government "found in the love, the affection, the attachment of the citizens to their laws, to their freedom, and to their country" (Farrand 1937, I, 112). In defending the work of the Convention on June 20 before he eventually soured on its outcome, Mason further cited the treaty of peace with Great Britain as a great example of commissioners disregarding their instructions in order to achieve a higher good (I, 338). That same day, Pennsylvania's James Wilson argued that American success in the Revolution was in spite of, rather than a result of, Congress (I, 343). On June 27, Maryland's Luther Martin pointed to the contributions that his state of Maryland and New Jersey had made during the Revolution as cause for giving these state equal representation (I, 441). On August 21, Martin further argued against slavery on the basis that "it was inconsistent with the principles of the revolution and dishonorable to the American character" (II, 364). Oliver Ellsworth of Connecticut responded to Madison's criticism of Connecticut's failure to meet its tax burden under the Articles of Confederation by arguing that "the muster rolls would show she had more troops in the field than Virg." (I, 487).

The surrender of the British at Yorktown, with Rochambeau directing General Charles O'Hara to present his sword to General George Washington. By Francois Godefroy, ca. 1784. (Library of Congress)

The Convention's only official holiday was the Fourth of July, on which they celebrated American Independence. On August 7, Benjamin Franklin cited the refusal of American sailors to redeem themselves from impressments by agreeing to switch loyalties as an example of "the virtue & public spirit of our common people" (II, 204–205). Two days later, Franklin cited the contributions of foreigners to the war effort as a reason to be generous in allowing immigrants to qualify for public office (II, 236), a point that James Wilson reiterated on August 13 (II, 469).

A number of delegates to the Convention expressed sympathy for veterans of the Revolutionary War who had sold government securities at a discount. In an issue that was renewed when the new government became operational, Pierce Butler expressed concern that the new government should not, in honoring debts of previous governments, "compel payment as well to the Blood-suckers who had speculated on the distresses of others, as to those who had fought & bled for their country" (II, 392). Elbridge Gerry expressed similar concern that "the frauds on *the soldiers* ought to have been foreseen. These poor & ignorant people could not but part with their securities" (II, 413).

Reviewing such references, Lyn Spillman has connected mentions of the Revolutionary War at the Convention to "national identity." She observes that the Convention was often "mentioned in association with the lesson of particular mistakes of good government made by the British and in arguments that their part in the Revolution gives a claim to the common people, or to creditors, or a state, in the reconstitution of government" (Spillman 1996, 173).

The Revolution as a Training Ground

Not only did the Revolution serve as the source of problems that the delegates to the Constitutional Convention sought to remedy, but it had also served as a training ground for Convention delegates. One of the lessons they learned was the need to provide for peaceful means of change in order to avoid future revolution. This need was most directly addressed in the constitutional amending process in Article V of the Constitution, which provided for the initiation and ratification of such changes through the mechanisms of congressional supermajorities and approval of the state legislatures, or, in a mechanism yet to be utilized, by conventions called under the authority of the new Constitution (Tulis 2001).

See Also Amending Process; Declaration of Independence; Paris, Treaty of

FOR FURTHER READING

Banning, Lance. 1985. "From Confederation to Constitution: The Revolutionary Context of the Great Convention." *this Constitution,* no. 6 (Spring): 12–18.

Bailyn, Bernard. 1967. *The Ideological Origins of the American Revolution.* Cambridge, MA: Belknap Press of Harvard University Press.

Elkins, Stanley, and Eric McKitrick. 1961. "The Founding Fathers: Young Men of the Revolution." *Political Science Quarterly* 76 (June): 181–216.

Farrand, Max, ed. 1937. *The Records of the Federal Convention.* 4 vols. New Haven, CT: Yale University Press.

Fleming, Thomas. 1997. *Liberty! The American Revolution.* New York: Viking.

Rakove, Jack N. 1979. *The Beginning of National Politics: An Interpretive History of the Continental Congress.* New York: Alfred A. Knopf.

Spillman, Lyn. 1996. "'Neither the Same Nation nor Different Nations': Constitutional Conventions in the United States and Australia." *Comparative Studies in Society and History* 38 (January): 149–181.

Tulis, Jeffrey K. 2001. "Constitution and Revolution." In Sotirios A. Barber and Robert P. George, eds. *Constitutional Politics: Essays on Constitution Making, Maintenance, and Change.* Princeton, NJ: Princeton University Press, 116–127.

White, Morton. 1978. *The Philosophy of the American Revolution.* New York: Oxford University Press.

Wood, Gordon S. 1991. *The Radicalism of the American Revolution.* New York: Vintage Books.

Wright, Robert K., Jr., and Morris J. MacGregor, Jr. 1987. *Soldier-Statesmen of the Constitution.* Washington, DC: Center of Military History, U.S. Army.

RHETORIC

See ORATORY AND RHETORIC

RHODE ISLAND

If any state was reviled at the Constitutional Convention, it was Rhode Island, the one no-show. The least populous of the 13 states and landlocked with no Western lands, Rhode Island had a long history of independence. This dated back to its settlement by Roger Williams, who had founded the state as a haven for those, including himself, who dissented from the Puritan establishment in nearby states. Britain's King Charles II subsequently granted Rhode Island a charter in 1663. It was so conducive to religious liberty and self-government that the state kept it until 1843.

Rhode Island had ratified the Articles of Confederation in July 1778, but was thereafter often regarded with disdain by the other states for its perceived obstinacy. Shortly after adoption of the Articles of Confederation, which required states to ratify amendments unanimously, Rhode Island had been the only state that refused to accept an amendment proposed in 1781 that would have allowed Congress to impose a 5 percent import duty (Kyvig 1997, 37). Thereafter, it continued to pursue policies, most notably issuing paper money to aid state debtors, that brought it into the contempt of its neighbors, who referred to it as "Rogue" or "Rogues Island."

Rogues Island

Rhode Island was the only of the 13 states that did not send delegates to the Constitutional Convention, and it was the last to ratify the document the Convention produced. Established by Roger Williams as a haven for religious dissenters, the colony had long been looked down upon by its more orthodox neighbors. The single holdout against the amendment proposed in 1781 that would have granted Congress the power to impose a national impost, Rhode Island subsequently attempted to mitigate the financial problems of debtors by printing money, a scheme that respectable men in other colonies regarded as unjust (since the currency was not as valuable as the gold or silver that had originally been borrowed).

An excerpt from a long poem titled "Anarchiad, 1786–1787," the product of a small group of men from Connecticut called the Connecticut Wits, indicates the low esteem in which the state was held and helps explain why Rhode Island was as wary of the other states as they were of it:

> Hail! realm of rogues, renowd'd for fraud and guile,
> All hail; ye knav'ries of you little isle.
> There prowls the rascal, cloth'd with legal pow'r,

> To snare the orphan, and the poor devour;
> The crafty knave his creditor besets,
> And advertising paper pays his debts;
> Bankrupts their creditors, with rage pursue,
> No stop, no mercy from the debtor crew.
> Arm'd witjh new tests, the licens'd villain bold,
> Presents his bills, and robs them of their gold;
> Their ears, though rogues and counterfeiters lose,
> No legal robber fears the gallows noose.
>   (Quoted in Conley 1988, 284)

In addition to being called "Rogues Island," the state was sometimes referred to as "Wrong Island" (Roll 1969, 33).

FOR FURTHER READING

Conley, Patrick T. 1988. "First in War, Last in Peace: Rhode Island and the Constitution, 1786–1790." In Patrick T. Conley and John P. Kaminski, eds. *The Constitution and the States: The Role of the Original Thirteen in the Framing and Adoption of the Federal Constitution.* Madison, WI: Madison House.

Roll, Charles W., Jr. 1969. "We, Some of the People: Apportionment in the Thirteen State Conventions Ratifying the Constitution." *Journal of American History* 56 (June): 21–40.

Political Situation

Led in 1786 by a mercantile party, Rhode Island had expressed willingness to allow Congress to regulate commerce. It had even appointed delegates to the Annapolis Convention. Shortly thereafter, however, the state had taken an economic downturn, and voters replaced the mercantile party with a "country" party that suspended the collection of taxes to pay off the state's large debt and began issuing paper money. Although the state appears to have taken this action primarily to provide a means for individuals to pay their taxes, the state supplemented this legislation with a Penalty Act, making it a criminal offense for

creditors not to accept the depreciated money in payment of debts (Kaminski 1989, 371).

Not everyone in Rhode Island was pleased with the state's refusal to attend the Constitutional Convention. A Committee of Tradesmen from Providence sent a letter to the Convention in the care of James Varnum dated May 14, 1787. The tradesmen requested the Convention's consideration of a number of measures, including exempting items produced or manufactured from duties, free commerce of goods within the United States once they had paid the national impost, reservation of the carrying trade within the United States to U.S. ships, a general currency, and admission of Vermont as a separate state (Hutson 1987, 2). A separate letter also from Providence tradesmen dated May 11, 1787, referred to "the evils of the present unhappy times" and indicated that they had written with the idea of preventing "any impressions unfavorable to the Commercial Interest of this State, from taking place in our Sister States from the Circumstance of our being unrepresented in the present National Convention" (Farrand 1937, III, 19).

Mentions of Rhode Island during Convention Debates

On May 23, Delaware's Jacob Broom observed that "All the States have now appointed except Rhode Island and no good is to be expected from her" (Hutson, 16). On July 26, after two delegates finally arrived at the Convention from New Hampshire, Georgia's Abraham Baldwin observed that "all the states have sent their Representatives except Rhode Island that she may be left alone and unsupported in her disgrace" (Hutson, 193).

Although Virginia's James Madison was the delegate to speak most frequently about the dangers of factions in small states, Connecticut's Roger Williams was the one who took up this theme on June 6. In so doing, he observed that "States may indeed be too small as Rhode Island, & thereby be too subject to faction" (I, 133). On June 16, James Wilson cited the unlikelihood that Rhode Island would approve as a reason to reject the New Jersey Plan, which would have continued the provision under the Articles of Confederation requiring unanimous state consent to constitutional alterations (I, 261). Nathaniel Gorham of Massachusetts made a similar argument for opposing unanimous state ratification of the new Constitution (II, 90).

On July 17, Madison cited Rhode Island as a state in which "the Judges who refused to execute an unconstitutional law were displaced, and others substituted, by the Legislature who would be willing instruments of the wicked & arbitrary plans of their masters" (II, 28). On this occasion, Madison used this as an example proving the need for congressional invalidation of improper state laws.

On July 18, Nathaniel Gorham of Massachusetts cited the Rhode Island example as a reason to entrust the power of appointments to the president rather than to the legislative branch:

> Public bodies feel no personal responsibility and give full play to intrigue & cabal. Rh. Island is a full illustration of the insensibility to character produced by a participation of numbers, in dishonorable measures, and of the length to which a public body may carry wickedness & cabal. (II, 42)

Later in the day, Pennsylvania's Gouverneur Morris indicated that he feared to adopt the resolution guaranteeing states a republican form of government as "He should be very unwilling that such laws as exist in R. Island should be guarantied" (II, 47). In a similar vein, New Jersey's Jonathan Dayton cited the example of Rhode Island as "shewing the necessity of giving latitude to the power of the U-S." in regard to introducing troops within states to suppress domestic violence, even if the state legislature refused to request such aid (II, 467).

Ratification

When the Rhode Island state legislature received the Constitution, it refused to call a convention. It seems to have been motivated chiefly by its philosophy of states' rights and by its fear that the new Constitution would undermine the state's fiscal system (Kaminski, 378). On March 1, 1788, the legislature rejected the idea of a convention by a 42 to 12 vote. It did call a referendum for March 24, but the people overwhelmingly rejected the document by a vote of 2,711 to 239. This vote was somewhat magnified by the refusal of Federalists in some towns to participate and show their weakness. The state legislature rejected numerous subsequent calls for other ratifying conventions on April 2, but resistance weakened as the state succeeded in paying off its debts in depreciated currency and as the new Congress (which had been formed without the state's help) proposed the Bill of Rights.

Facing threats of economic sanctions by the new government, on January 17, the state legislature finally agreed to call a ratifying convention. Governor John Collins (whose party subsequently ditched him from his position) cast the deciding vote in the upper house. The ratifying convention met in Little Rest on March 1, 1790. It adjourned and later reconvened on May 24, 1790, at the Colony House in Newport. During its adjournment, the U.S. Senate threatened to boycott the state and force it to pay what it owed to the previous Congress. Antifederalists put heavy emphasis on their fear that taxes on land and polls under the new government would be exorbitant, on their fear that a distant government would threaten liberty, and on concern that the delegates had conceded too much to the slave interests, which Quakers within the state especially detested (Conley 1988, 280–283). After some members of the country party finally absented themselves, the convention narrowly ratified the Constitution on May 29, 1790, by a vote of 34 to 32, the closest vote in any of the states. A recent student of the ratifying convention has argued that the convention also adopted a bill of rights for the state, which subsequently slipped from public view (see Leitao 1996).

Rhode Island as an Example

Recalcitrant as it had proved to be, the example of Rhode Island served as a valuable source of Federalist propaganda. Historian John Kaminski has observed that Federalists used Rhode Island as an example of what could go wrong in the states without a stronger central authority. Connecticut's Oliver Ellsworth thus opined that "the little state of Rhode-Island was purposely left by Heaven to its present madness, for a general conviction in the other states, that such a system as is now proposed is our only preservation from ruin" (quoted in Kaminski, 387).

Although it did not send representatives to the Convention, Rhode Island undoubtedly served as a goad to the adoption of constitutional provisions prohibiting states from emitting money or from abridging contracts. Had the state been represented at the Convention, or had the delegates from New Hampshire arrived earlier, it is likely that the Connecticut Compromise would have been adopted earlier, although it is always possible that the delegates from Rhode Island would simply have left.

Perhaps because the state had been the last to ratify the Constitution, President George Washington scheduled a visit there in August 1790. Washington later responded to the warm welcome from members of the Jewish community that he had met in the Touro Synagogue by penning words that resonated not only with the ideals of the new nation but also with Rhode Island's long-standing commitment to religious freedom. Washington observed that "the Government of the United States, which gives to bigotry no sanction, to persecution no assistance, requires only that they who live under its protection should demean themselves as good citizens" (quoted in Conley, 291).

See Also Ratification in the States

FOR FURTHER READING

Bishop, Millman Metray. 1950. *Why Rhode Island Opposed the Federal Constitution.* Providence, RI: Roger Williams Press.

Conley, Patrick T. 1988. "First in War, Last in Peace: Rhode Island and the Constitution, 1786–1790." In Patrick T. Conley and John P. Kaminski, eds. *The Constitution and the States: The Role of the Original Thirteen in the Framing and Adoption of the Federal Constitution.* Madison, WI: Madison House.

Farrand, Max, ed. 1937. *The Records of the Federal Convention.* 4 vols. New Haven, CT: Yale University Press.

Hutson, James H., ed. 1987. *Supplement to Max Farrand's* The Records of the Federal Convention of 1787. New Haven, CT: Yale University Press.

Kaminski, John P. 1989. "Rhode Island: Protecting State Interests." In Michael Allen Gillespie and Michael Lienesch, eds. *Ratifying the Constitution.* Lawrence: University Press of Kansas.

Kyvig, David E. 1997. *Explicit and Authentic Acts: Amending the U.S. Constitution, 1776–1995.* Lawrence: University Press of Kansas.

Leitao, Kevin D. 1996. "Rhode Island's Forgotten Bill

of Rights." *Roger Williams University Law Review* 1 (Spring): 31–61.

Polishook, Irwin H. 1969. *Rhode Island and the Union, 1774–1795.* Evanston, IL: Northwestern University Press.

RIGHTS

See BILL OF RIGHTS; NATURAL RIGHTS

RISING SUN

James Madison recorded one of the most beloved and repeated stories about the Constitutional Convention in his Notes. Rather than relating a speech, it concerns Benjamin Franklin's personal comments to colleagues on the sun that a craftsman had painted on the upper back slat of the Chippendale chair that had seated George Washington as president of the Convention.

Franklin timed his anecdote to correspond with the signing of the document. This arguably helped him get in the last word which had been denied him on the Convention floor. There his persuasive speech urging all delegates at the Convention to sign the document had been followed by speeches by a number of delegates, like Virginia's Edmund Randolph, explaining why they chose not to do so.

Madison's Notes, focusing on the signing of the Constitution, require no additional commentary:

Whilst the last members were signing it Doctr. Franklin looking towards the Presidents Chair, at the back of which a rising sun happened to be painted, observed to a few members near him, that Painters had found it difficult to distinguish in their art a rising from a setting sun. I have, said he, often and often in the course of the Session, and the vicissitudes of my hopes and fears as to its issue, looked at that behind the President without being able to tell whether it was rising or

setting: But now at length I have the happiness to know that it is a rising and not a setting Sun. (Farrand 1937, II, 648)

Many depictions of the signing of the document feature the rising sun. Although the Constitution could just as easily be viewed as terminating the Articles of Confederation, most commentators have preferred to see it as initiating a new chapter in American history, what the Great Seal of the United States calls "Novus Ordo Seclorum," the New Order of the Ages.

See Also Franklin, Benjamin; Rising Sun Chair; Signing of the Constitution

FOR FURTHER READING

Farrand, Max, ed. 1937. *The Records of the Federal Convention.* 4 vols. New Haven, CT: Yale University Press.

Isaacson, Walter. 2003. *Benjamin Franklin: An American Life.* New York: Simon and Schuster.

RISING SUN CHAIR

Apart from the inkstand that the delegates used to dip their quills on signing the U.S. Constitution, there is only one existing piece of furniture known to have been in the Philadelphia State House (Independence Hall) at the time of the Constitutional Convention. It is the high-back Chippendale chair (a style that British cabinetmaker Thomas Chippendale 1718?–1779 began and that others have widely copied in America not only in the colonial era but also today) in which George Washington sat as the Convention's president.

John Folwell, who had an office on Front Street, in Philadelphia (some sources say he was from Bucks County), Pennsylvania, constructed the 60 ⅓-inch-tall chair to replace the speaker's chair that had been destroyed or misplaced when the British occupied Philadelphia during the Revolutionary War. The painted rising sun at the top of the chair, about which Benjamin Franklin com-

Congress, had sat in it (it was not yet built) when he so boldly signed the Declaration of Independence (Diethorn 1992; Giannini 1998).

A replica of the chair is preserved at the Pennsylvania capitol ("'Rising Sun' Chair").

See Also Masons; Pennsylvania State House; Rising Sun; Syng Inkstand

FOR FURTHER READING

Bjerkoe, Ethel Hall. 1978. *The Cabinetmakers of America.* Exton, PA: Schiffer.
Diethorn, Karie. 1992. "History and Description of the Chair." Belmont Technical College. November 6. http://www.belmont.cc.oh.us/bpr/herbert.htm.
Giannini, R. 1998. "Description." Belmont Technical College. January 13. http://www.belmont.cc.oh.us/bpr/herbert.htm.
"'Rising Sun' Chair." Website: "Decorative Arts and Historic Furnishings of the Capitol." http://www.legis.state.pa.us/WU01/VC/visitor_info/brown/decorative_art.htm.

The Rising Sun chair served as George Washington's seat at the Constitutional Convention of 1787, where the drafting of the U.S. Constitution took place. (ChromoSohm Inc./Corbis)

mented as fellow delegates signed the Constitution, may have reflected Masonic symbolism since Folwell was known to have been a member of the St. John's Masonic Lodge. Folwell has been called "the Thomas Chippendale of America," and he proposed to publish, but apparently did not succeed in printing, a counterpart to Chippendale's writing to be called "The Gentleman and Cabinet-maker's Assistant, Containing a Great Variety of Useful and Ornamental Household Furniture" (Bjerkoe 1978, 94).

The now-revered chair moved with the capital of the Pennsylvania state government first to Lancaster (1799) and then to Harrisburg (1812). Pennsylvania's governor returned the chair to Philadelphia in 1867, and it has remained at Independence Hall ever since. The chair has sometimes been incorrectly called the "Hancock" chair in the mistaken assumption that John Hancock of Massachusetts, the president of the Second Continental

ROME

See CLASSICAL ALLUSIONS AND INFLUENCES

RULE OF LAW

See CONSTITUTIONALISM

RULES OF THE CONSTITUTIONAL CONVENTION

The rules of procedure at the Constitutional Convention give insight into the kind of deliberation and mutual respect that the delegates were attempting to foster. In effect, the delegates were already adhering to rules before they actually convened since they delayed their scheduled meeting for Monday, May 14, 1787, until Friday, May 25, the time it took for representatives to appear from a majority of the states and thus constitute a quorum. Moreover, the meeting began with a formal motion by Pennsylvania's Robert Morris suggesting the election of a president by ballot.

Selection of a Committee

After the delegates unanimously elected George Washington and selected a secretary, a messenger, and a door-keeper, Charles Pinckney of South Carolina moved that the Convention choose a committee to draw up "standing Orders of the Convention" (Farrand 1937, I, 2). The Convention chose Pinckney, Virginia's George Wythe, and New York's Alexander Hamilton. Consciously or otherwise the delegates thus gave some representation to the Southern, the Middle, and the Eastern (or Northern) states, divisions to which the delegates would frequently allude during the course of Convention deliberations. Wythe, a lawyer who served at the College of William and Mary as the nation's first law professor, delivered the committee report on Monday, May 28, which consisted of 14 paragraphs.

Rules Adopted

The official Journal reports that two committee rules were rejected, but the only one described in Madison's Notes was the elimination of a rule that would have allowed any member to call for a roll-call vote that would be recorded under individual names. Rufus King of Massachusetts noted that delegates were not binding their constituents, as they would be were they making laws, and that they should be free to change their minds without appearing to have contradicted themselves. Virginia's George Mason seconded this objection, likewise arguing that delegates would find it more difficult to alter their positions if votes were recorded under individual names and that opponents of the Convention's results might use such votes to ill effect. Thus proposed and seconded, eliminating this rule was effected without opposition. This important innovation arguably further established the role of the Convention as a deliberative assembly, where reason was designed to prevail over strict representation of state interests and where a change of mind was to be regarded not as a sign of indecision but of effective persuasion.

The remaining rules themselves were a blend of orderly procedures and good manners. The quorum was set at seven, thus effectively acquiescing in the manner of voting (each state having a single vote) that existed under the Articles of Confederation. A majority was required on all questions other than adjournment, when fewer than seven states could be present. The rules prescribed that the minutes would be read after the president was seated, followed by orders of the day. Members were to rise when speaking, and to refrain from passing between the speaker and the president or reading materials while speakers were standing; the president would determine which of two speakers, rising simultaneously, would be first recognized. No speaker was, without special permission, to speak more than twice on the same subject. In any event, no individual was to give a second speech on a topic until everyone else who so wanted had a chance for a first. Motions were to be made, seconded, and, if necessary, repeated aloud by the secretary prior to debate; sponsors could withdraw motions before a final vote. The only motions permitted during debate were to amend, commit, or divide a motion or to postpone the debate. Any state delegation had the power to postpone debate until the next day. Long proposals were to be debated and amended provision by provision, with a final vote on the total result. The Convention provided that delegates would select committee members by ballot, with the order of nominees being used in cases of ties. Members could call one another to order or the president could do so; his judgment on such matters was not subject to appeal. Questions for adjournments would not be debated, and when adjournment occurred, all members were to stand until the president left.

Emendation of the Rules

After the Convention adopted the rules suggested by the committee on May 28, South Carolina's Pierce Butler moved that the "house provide agst. interruption of business by absence of members, and against licentious publications of this proceedings" (I, 13). To this, North Carolina's Richard Spaight added a motion, similar to that by King and Mason, providing that no vote would preclude a future tally for good cause on a previously decided issue. Spaight's goal was to balance adherence to mature judgments without precluding reconsideration as needed changes became apparent (I, 13).

The Convention forwarded both suggestions to the Rules Committee for consideration, and it, in turn, reported the next day. New rules that were added prevented the interruption of a state's representation at the Convention without permission, prohibited committees from meeting at the same time as the Convention, and precluded the inspection of the journal by non members or the taking of journal entries without Convention approval. The Convention further voted that to reconsider a motion on the day it was adopted would require unanimous consent; it would otherwise require at least one day's prior notice and be assigned to a specific day.

Rule of Secrecy

Perhaps most jarring to modern minds was the rule providing "That nothing spoken in the House be printed, or otherwise published, or communicated without leave" (I, 15). Like the intent of the resolutions rejecting individual roll-call votes and permitting revotes, the secrecy rule was designed both to allow members to speak freely without fear of outside recrimination and to allay fears that might be spread should rumors be circulated on the basis of partial information. Although not completely without breach, members generally took the idea of secrecy seriously. Washington limited diary entries throughout the Convention to comments on his social affairs, and delegates generally indicated in their correspondence that they were not at liberty to discuss specific proposals.

Effect of the Rules

Writing on August 2 to Joshua Bracket, New Hampshire's John Langdon indicated that the rules, undoubtedly aided by the perception of crisis and the consequent solemnity of the occasion, left him in awe long after the Convention had been in session:

> The Convention, well now see the Convention; Figure to yourself the Great Washington, with a Dignity peculiar to himself, taking the Chair. The Notables are seated, in a Moment and after a short Silence the Business of the day is open'd with great Solemnity and good Order. The Importance of the Business, the Dignified Character of Many, who Compose the Convention, the Eloquence of Some and the Regularity of the whole gives a Ton[e] to the proceedings which is extremely pleasing. (Hutson 1987, 201)

Langdon, who testified in the letter to his own good intentions, arguably also hinted that the occasion might have been intimidating: "Your old friend takes his Seat. Conscious of his upright Intentions, and as far as his poor Abilities will go keep his eye single to what is righteous and of good Report" (Hutson, 201).

Postscript

Article V of the Constitution provides that two-thirds of the states may petition Congress to call a convention to propose amendments. To date the nation has never used this mechanism, and there are questions about how it would be organized. Certainly, some contemporaries have wondered whether a modern convention could effectively function under the glare of constant media coverage. A modern convention might also face problems related to the sheer number of delegates it would take effectively to represent 50 states and more than 270 million people. Clearly, many states have used a convention mechanism and committee structures to good effect in revising their own state constitutions, but some elements of civility and deliberation might be more difficult in a modern context than in the more deferential environment of the late eighteenth century and in the absence of an individual like George Washington who would be the subject of almost universal respect.

See Also Committee on Rules; Secrecy; Washington, George; Wythe, George

FOR FURTHER READING

Eidelberg, Paul. 1968. *The Philosophy of the American Constitution: A Reinterpretation of the Intentions of the Founding Fathers.* New York: The Free Press.

Farrand, Max, ed. 1937. *The Records of the Federal Convention.* 4 vols. New Haven, CT: Yale University Press.

Hutson, James H., ed. 1987. *Supplement to Max Farrand's* The Records of the Federal Convention of 1787. New Haven, CT: Yale University Press.

Lansky, Dana. 2000. "Proceeding to a Constitution: A Multi-Party Negotiation Analysis of the Constitutional Convention of 1787." *Harvard Negotiation Law Review* 5 (Spring): 279–338.

John Rutledge, delegate from South Carolina
(Pixel That)

RUTLEDGE, JOHN (1739–1800)

John Rutledge was born in Charleston, South Carolina in 1739 to Dr. John Rutledge, a physician who had immigrated from Ireland, and his 15-year-old wife, Sarah Hext Rutledge, who had inherited a great deal of money. Rutledge's father died in 1740, but a clergyman educated him before he studied law under a local lawyer and then attended the Inns of Court in England. After his return, Rutledge married Elizabeth Grimke, by whom he would have 10 children, including one who would serve in the U.S. House of Representatives. By his marriage, he also became related to Angelina and Sarah Grimke, who went on in the 1830s to become prominent South Carolina abolitionists.

Elected to the First Continental Congress, Rutledge successfully exempted South Carolina rice from the embargo with England. After attending the Second Continental Congress (during which his younger brother, Edward, signed the Declaration of Independence), Rutledge helped write his state constitution, under which he served as the state's first president. He became governor under a new state constitution adopted in 1778 and tried during much of the Revolutionary War to protect his state. He was elected to the Continental Congress in 1782, and became chief judge of South Carolina's Court of Chancery. Apparently fearful that people were forgetting the importance of the union of states, Rutledge named his seventh child, a son, "States Rutledge" (Barry 1971, 308).

Rutledge arrived in Philadelphia by ship on May 18 and spent his first three weeks staying at the house of Pennsylvania's James Wilson before joining his wife at the Indian Queen when she arrived about three weeks later (Barry, 315). Rutledge was present on the opening day of Convention business on May 25 (Washington had reported his arrival on May 17), and he seconded the motion made by Robert Morris nominating George Washington as president of the Convention. In so doing he indicated that he hoped, as proved to be the case, that the vote would be unanimous and that "the presence of Genl Washington forbade any observations on the occasion which might otherwise be proper" (Farrand 1937, I, 3).

Perhaps seeking some regional balance, on May 30, the Convention selected Nathaniel Gorham of Massachusetts over Rutledge as chair of the Committee of the Whole by a vote of 7-1 (I, 29). Rutledge's nomination was itself, however, an honor, and Rutledge did his share of work on other committees. He served on the committee formed on July 2 to compromise on representation in Congress, on the committees formed on July 6 and July 9 for ascertaining and revising the initial membership of Congress and on the Committee formed on August 29 on interstate comity and bankruptcy. Most importantly, Rutledge chaired the five-member Committee of Detail, formed on July 24. One of the Convention's most important committees, it introduced the idea of enumerated powers and otherwise tilted the document in a more state-friendly direction.

Congress

Selection of Members

On June 6, Rutledge seconded a motion by fellow South Carolinian Charles Pinckney providing that the state legislatures, rather than the people, should select members of the first branch of Congress. Rutledge presumably agreed with Pinckney's explanation that states would be more likely to ratify a system in which they had such a part (I, 132). On June 21 he offered another reason. Distinguishing "between a mediate & immediate election by the people," he argued that elections by state legislatures would be more "refined" and would result in the selection of "fitter men" (I, 359). He doubted that the delegates to the Convention would be of the same character if the people, rather than the state legislatures, had selected them.

Apportionment

On June 11, Rutledge argued that apportionment in the House should "be according to the quotas of contribution" (I, 196; also see I, 201 where Rutledge supports the introduction of a motion to this effect). When the Convention was about to discuss the powers of Congress, Rutledge proposed postponing this matter until the delegates resolved the more fundamental question of how states would be represented (I, 436). On July 5, Rutledge repeated his view that the Convention should apportion seats in Congress not simply according to population but also according to property. He observed that "Property was certainly the principal object of Society" (I, 534).

When the Convention settled on 65 representatives for the House including three for New Hampshire, Rutledge proposed reducing its representation to two, but he based his justification both on his view that New Hampshire's population did not entitle it to three and that "it was a poor State" (I, 566). Rutledge seemed most concerned about the admission of Western states. On July 11 he observed that "the Western States will not be able to contribute in proportion to their numbers, [and] they shd. not therefore be represented in that proportion" (I, 582). Rutledge indicated on August 30 that he did not believe that states should be partitioned without their consent, although he did not think that either Virginia or North Carolina would try to hold on to their lands, which then included the states of Tennessee and Kentucky, beyond the mountains (II, 462).

On July 16, the decisive day on which the Convention finally voted to grant states equal representation in the Senate, as a committee on which Rutledge had served proposed, he opposed an adjournment "because he could see no chance of a compromise" (II, 19). Rutledge explained that the decision to be made was simply whether the large states would agree or not. For his part, he was willing to compromise:

he conceived that although we could not do what we thought best, in itself, we ought to do something. Had we not better keep the Govt. up a little longer, hoping that another Convention will supply our omissions, than abandon every thing to hazard. Our Constituents will be very little satisfied with us if we take the latter course. (II, 19)

In opposing a motion to double the size of the House of Representatives, Rutledge argued that existing state legislatures had too many members, that states would see that their members attended Congress, and, in what is one of the most erroneous predictions of the Convention, that he doubted that Congress would need to meet for more than six to eight weeks a year (I, 570). On August 7, Rutledge did introduce a motion specifying that Congress should meet at least once a year (II, 200).

Rutledge accused those who favored the provision limiting the origination of money bills to the House of Representatives of being inconsistent in advocating this limit because the House of Lords used it but not in also following the House of Lords in permitting the upper house to amend such bills. Using an expression popular at the time, he believed the people would regard such a concession as "a mere tub to the whale" (II, 279), that is, as a diversion. As for Rutledge, if the Constitution were to lodge an exclusive right anywhere, he thought that it should lodge it in the Senate: "The Senate being more conversant in business, and having more leisure, will digest the bills much better, and as they are to have no effect, till examined & approved by the H. of Reps there can be no possible danger" (II, 279).

Length of Terms and Salaries

On June 12, Rutledge proposed that terms for members of the U.S. House of Representatives should be for two years (I, 214), as the Convention eventually decided. On this same day, Rutledge proposed that members of the Senate should receive no salary. Had this measure been adopted, it would have presumably reserved seats only for those wealthy enough to serve without pay (I, 219), thus giving the Senate a more aristocratic cast similar to that of the House of Lords in England.

Eligibility for Other Offices

On June 23, Rutledge indicated that he favored keeping Congress "as pure as possible, by shutting the door against appointments of its own members to offices, which was one source of its corruption" (I, 386). Recognizing that evasion would be possible, he supported a provision that barred not only sitting members but also those who had served within a year (I, 390).

Qualifications

On August 8, Rutledge proposed that members of the House should be required to have at least seven years' residence in their states, but, indicative of his perception of widely different sectional interests, he seemed more concerned about immigrants from other parts of the United States than from abroad. He thus observed that "An emigrant from N. England to S.C. or Georgia would know little of its affairs and could not be supposed to acquire a thorough knowledge in less time" (II, 217). When others proposed the possibility of lowering the residency requirement to one year, Rutledge proposed three instead (II, 218). When the Convention agreed to a seven-year citizenship requirement for members of the House, Rutledge said that he thought that an even longer period should be required of senators, who would exercise greater powers (II, 239). He later favored a provision that would apply qualifications to those who had already immigrated as well as to those who would immigrate in the future. He observed that the need for precaution was as great in the former case as in the latter (II, 270).

As chair of the Committee of Detail, Rutledge said that his committee had not proposed any qualifications for members of Congress because they could not agree. He observed that there was danger of displeasing the people by making them too high or of rendering qualifications of no effect by setting them too low (II, 249). Soon thereafter, however, he proposed that the Constitution should make such qualifications the same as those for members of the state legislatures (II, 251), qualifications that would presumably vary from state to state.

Powers

On May 31, Rutledge joined Charles Pinckney in objecting to the provision in the Virginia Plan granting Congress power to legislate in all cases to which the state proved "incompetent." They thought this word was too vague (I, 53). Rutledge repeated this opposition on July 16 (II, 17). Significantly, the Committee of Detail that Rutledge chaired substituted specific grants of powers for such broad statements.

Rutledge opposed granting Congress power to guarantee states a republican form of government, but only because he thought it to be unnecessary. In his view "Congs. had the authority if they had the means to co-operate with any State in subduing a rebellion. It was & would be involved in the nature of the thing" (II, 48).

Rutledge joined Charles Pinckney in opposing congressional control over state elections. The two delegates thought that the states "could & must be relied on in such cases" (II, 240). Rutledge proposed an amendment of the supremacy clause (more forcefully emphasizing the Constitution) that the Convention accepted on August 23 (II, 389).

Rutledge did not approve of the requirement, which some fellow Southern delegates favored, to require two-thirds majorities in Congress to regulate trade. He thought that fears of abuse were overdrawn and that the Convention should make decisions with the future in view: "As we are laying the foundation for a great empire, we ought to take a permanent view of the subject and not look at the present moment only" (II, 452). He thought that navigation laws were particularly needed to gain trade with the West Indies and feared that a two-thirds requirement would make this difficult. He proposed the establishment of a committee to consider the assumption of state debts. He believed that relieving states of such debts "would conciliate them to the plan" (II, 327).

Limits on Powers

Rutledge wanted to prohibit both congressional taxation of exports and the taxation of slave im-

ports (II, 306). On August 18, Rutledge introduced a motion to prevent funds appropriated for public creditors from being diverted to other purposes (II, 326).

Rutledge supported a constitutional provision on ex post facto laws. North Carolina's Hugh Williamson had argued that such a provision had worked in his state because it gave judges something to "take hold of," but Rutledge did not address this specific issue (II, 376). Rutledge did indicate on August 28 that he favored making the provision for the writ of habeas corpus "inviolable." He did not believe "that a suspension could ever be necessary at the same time through all the States" (II, 438). On August 28, Rutledge introduced a motion prohibiting Congress from passing bills of attainder or retrospective laws (II, 440). The Convention adopted, but later modified, this motion.

Rutledge used his strongest language in opposing the idea of a congressional veto of state legislation; he indicated that this was a make-or-break issue for him. Believing that human shackles were a matter of interest rather than morality, he felt more strongly about the possibility of shackling the states: "If nothing else, this alone would damn and ought to damn the Constitution. Will any State ever agree to be bound hand & foot in this manner. It is worse than making mere corporations of them whose bye laws would not be subject to this shackle" (II, 391).

Other Legislative Matters

On August 11, Rutledge joined Virginia's James Madison in proposing to exempt the Senate from publishing its proceedings when it was not acting in its legislative capacity (II, 259). On August 24, Rutledge persuasively observed that since the Constitution was entrusting the federal judiciary with jurisdiction over disputes between the states, there would be no need for a special commission, such as had existed under the Articles of Confederation, to deal with such problems (II, 401–402). Rutledge unsuccessfully proposed on September 8 that treaties should require the consent of two-thirds of all senators, rather than two-thirds of a quorum (II, 549). Rutledge opposed a provision that would have required Congress to vote by joint ballot for the treasurer; he favored allowing this officer to be appointed, as the officer now is, in the same manner as other officers (II, 614).

Presidency

On June 1, after exhorting his colleagues, who may have been reserved because of the presence of George Washington, not to be shy about expressing their opinions, Rutledge indicated that he favored a single executive but that he did not want to give this executive the power of war and peace. Rutledge reasoned that a single executive would be preferable because "A single man would feel the greatest responsibility and administer the public affairs best" (I, 65). He and Charles Pinckney made a motion to this effect on the following day (I, 88).

On June 1 Rutledge suggested that the Senate should have the power to select the president (I, 69). On July 19, he was still advocating legislative selection of the president, believing that the Constitution could secure presidential independence with a provision making the president ineligible for reelection (II, 57). When the Convention was still considering legislative selection of the president on August 24, Rutledge argued that Congress should make such a choice by joint ballot rather than allowing each house to vote individually (II, 401). On September 5, even after an Electoral College was proposed, Rutledge continued to support a plan whereby a joint ballot of Congress would select the president to a single, seven-year term (II, 511). When it was suggested that the Senate should select the president from among the top three candidates, Rutledge supported a measure, which would have granted Congress almost complete discretion, that would have allowed it to choose from among the top 13 candidates (II, 515).

On June 5, Rutledge indicated that he did not think that the president should have the power to appoint judges. He feared that "the people will think we are leaning too much towards Monarchy" (I, 119). On September 15, Rutledge joined with Benjamin Franklin to prohibit the president

from accepting any emolument from the U.S. or the states other than his salary (II, 616).

Judiciary

In opposing presidential selection of members of the judiciary on June 5, Rutledge disfavored the establishment of lower federal courts. He believed that state courts would be adequate for hearing cases in the first instance (I, 119). Later that day he reiterated that he thought state courts would be adequate to the job and argued that the creation of federal courts was an encroachment on the states that would create "unnecessary obstacles to their adoption of the new system" (I, 124).

Rutledge opposed combining members of the judiciary with the president in a Council of Revision. He argued that this was both improper and unnecessary. As to propriety, "The Judges ought never to give their opinion on a law till it comes before them." As to necessity, the president would have cabinet officers to advise him (II, 80).

Rutledge struck a blow for judicial independence on August 27 when he opposed a motion offered by Delaware's John Dickinson that would have allowed the president to remove federal judges on the application of Congress. Rutledge suggested that the fact that federal courts would sometimes have "to judge between the U.S. and particular States" would be "an insuperable objection to the motion" (II, 428). However, on September 14, Rutledge introduced a motion to suspend individuals who were impeached from office until they could be tried, a provision that may well have threatened the independence of individuals who were charged but never convicted (II, 612).

Slavery

As a representative from a state in the Deep South, Rutledge defended the institution of slavery. When Maryland's Luther Martin objected that a prohibition on the taxation of slave imports encouraged them, posed threats to internal security, and was inconsistent with the ideas of the American Revolution, Rutledge said that there was nothing to fear from slave insurrections and that he was willing to exempt the Northern states from helping to quell them (II, 364). Rutledge further argued that the issue of slavery was one of economic interest, and that the states of the North should consider the advantages they offered:

> Religion & humanity had nothing to do with this question–Interest alone is the governing principle with Nations–The true question at present is whether the Southn. States shall or shall not be parties to the Union. If the Northern States consult their interest, they will not oppose the increase of Slaves which will increase the commodities of which they will become the carriers. (II, 364)

Rutledge was vehement in his position that the people of the Carolinas and Georgia would never give up their right to import slaves, even though they were not at the time exercising it (II, 373). He was influential near the end of the Convention (September 10) in securing a provision preventing a constitutional amendment of the right of Southern states to import slaves until the year 1808 (II, 559).

Ratification

Rutledge did not believe that it was necessary for Congress to approve the new Constitution before it could be sent to state conventions for their approval (II, 563). Perhaps anxious to leave, on September 15, Rutledge opposed composing an address to the people to accompany the Constitution. He believed that Congress could compose such an address if it proved necessary and that, in any event, delegates to the Convention could explain to their constituents what they had done (II, 623).

Attempts to Speed Convention Proceedings

On August 15, Rutledge opposed postponing a motion and "complained much of the tedious-

ness of the proceedings" (II, 301). Three days later he proposed that the Convention keep more regular hours from 10:00 A.M. to 4:00 P.M. (II, 328). Despite his weariness, Rutledge stayed to the end of the Convention and signed the Constitution.

Life after the Convention

Rutledge supported the Constitution within his state. Appointed by President Washington as an associate justice of the U.S. Supreme Court, gout prevented him from attending the Court in New York but did not stop him from riding the expansive Southern circuit. In 1791, Rutledge left the U.S. Supreme Court to become chief justice of the South Carolina Court of Common Pleas. At Rutledge's request, Washington appointed him in 1795 to an interim term as chief justice of the U.S. Supreme Court. After he imprudently spoke out against the Jay Treaty, however, the Senate rejected his nomination. Broken in spirit, Rutledge unsuccessfully attempted to drown himself and battled bouts of insanity until his death in 1800. Although he had inherited 60 slaves and battled to preserve the institution at the Convention, by the time of his death Rutledge had freed all but one of them (Hakim 2003, 182).

See Also Committee of Detail; South Carolina

FOR FURTHER READING

Barry, Richard. 1971 (1942). *Mr. Rutledge of South Carolina.* Freeport, NY: Books for Libraries Press.

Cushman, Clare, ed. *The Supreme Court Justices: Illustrated Biographies, 1789–1995.* Washington, DC: Congressional Quarterly.

Farrand, Max, ed. 1937. *The Records of the Federal Convention.* 4 vols. New Haven, CT: Yale University Press.

Hakim, Joy. 2003. *From Colonies to Country.* Book 3 of *A History of US.* New York: Oxford University Press.

S

SCOTTISH ENLIGHTENMENT

Although Lockean liberalism and classical republicanism are the two schools of thought most commonly associated with the period from the writing of the Declaration of Independence in 1776 through the writing of the U.S. Constitution in 1787, there were undoubtedly a multitude of other influences. One such influence was that of the Scottish Enlightenment, which sometimes reinforced views common to contemporary Protestantism. Like Americans the Scots displayed remarkable intellectual achievements for individuals on the periphery of the English empire; Scots and Americans were both convinced of the value of a commercial republic (Howe 1989). Scots, like American Founders, believed they had discovered a "science of politics" that would prevail over "superstition" and "enthusiasm" (Farr 1988).

Notable Scottish thinkers included Thomas Reid (1710–1796); James Watt (1736–1819), the inventor of the steam engine; Adam Smith (1723–1790), whose influential *Wealth of Nations* was published in 1776); Francis Hutcheson (1694–1746), often called the "Father of the Scottish Enlightenment"; Lord Kames (1695–1782); Adam Ferguson (1723–1816); and David Hume (1711–1776), among others. The Scots were particularly known for emphasizing "common sense" understandings of things; for advocating the idea that all men had an innate "moral sense," or conscience; and for stressing community rather than the more radical individualism that was sometimes associated with Lockean liberalism.

William Small, the professor at the College of William and Mary who taught Thomas Jefferson, was part of the Scottish movement. John Witherspoon, the president of the College of New Jersey (Princeton), was influenced by Scottish philosophy and passed along Scottish moral teachings to his students, including James Madison (Wills 1978, 176). One of the Scots who appears to have been most influential on James Madison was

Adam Smith, ca. 1805 (Library of Congress)

David Hume, from whom Madison appears to have borrowed the idea, which he presented most prominently in his *Federalist* essay No. 10, that a large republic could provide a cure for the mischiefs of faction (Adair 1951). Samuel Fleischacker has also found influences on that essay, and in the writings of other American Founders, of Adam Smith (Fleischacker 2002). Pennsylvania's James Wilson, who was educated in Edinburgh, also appears to have been deeply influenced by Scottish philosophy.

See Also Hume, David; Jefferson, Thomas; Liberalism; Locke, John; Madison, James, Jr.; Protestantism; Republicanism; Wilson, James

FOR FURTHER READING

Adair, Douglass G. 1951. "The Tenth Federalist Revisited." *William and Mary Quarterly*, 3rd ser. 8 (January): 48–67.

Buchanan, James. 2003. *Crowded with Genius: The Scottish Enlightenment: Edinburgh's Moment of the Mind.* New York: HarperCollins.

Farr, James. 1988. "Political Science and the Enlightenment of Enthusiasm." *American Political Science Review* 82 (March): 51–69.

Fehrenbacher, Don E. 1984. "Race and Slavery in the American Constitutional System: 1787–1865." *this Constitution*, no. 4 (Fall): 31–37.

Fleischacker, Samuel. 2002. "Adam Smith's Reception among the American Founders, 1776–1790." *William and Mary Quarterly*, 3rd ser. 59 (October): 897–924.

Galvin, Robert W. 2002. *America's Founding Secret: What the Scottish Enlightenment Taught Our Founding Fathers.* Lanham, MD: Rowman and Littlefield Publishers.

Howe, Daniel W. 1989. "Why the Scottish Enlightenment Was Useful to the Framers of the American Constitution." *Comparative Studies in Society and History* 31 (July): 572–587.

Kloppenberg, James T. 1987. "The Virtues of Liberalism: Christianity, Republicanism, and Ethics in Early American Political Discourse." *Journal of American History* 74 (June): 9–33.

Wills, Garry. 1978. *Inventing America: Jefferson's Declaration of Independence.* Garden City, NY: Doubleday.

SECRECY

One of the rules that the Constitutional Convention developed early in its proceedings was "That nothing spoken in the House be printed, or otherwise published, or communicated without leave" (Farrand 1937, I, 15).

Origins of the Rule

Although Richard Barry has presented such secrecy as an idea cooked up by John Rutledge and James Wilson (Barry 1971, 321), Judge John Brown has commented on "the near unanimity concerning the necessity for absolute secrecy" (1988, 905). He observes that two days before the Convention had agreed to secrecy, Virginia's George Mason had commented:

It is expected our doors will be shut, and communications upon the business of the Convention be forbidden during its sitting. This, I think, myself, a proper precaution to prevent mistakes and misrepresentation until the business shall have been completed, when the whole may have a very different complexion from that in which the several crude and undigested parts might, in their first shape, appear if submitted to the public eye. (Quoted in Brown, 905)

Similarly, North Carolina's Alexander Martin observed:

This caution was thought prudent, lest unfavourable representations might be made by imprudent printers of the many crude matters and things daily uttered and produced in this body, which are unavoidable and which in their unfinished state might make an undue impression on the too credulous and unthinking mobility. (Quoted in Brown, 906)

In an age like today's when the "leak" and the "trial balloon" are almost routine, it seems highly unlikely either that a modern convention could adopt a similar rule or that, if it did, members would heed it. However, the Constitutional Convention of 1787 was quite successful in keeping its proceedings secret, and members had to divine public opinion as best they could.

Secrecy Guarded during Convention

William Paterson of New Jersey showed that delegates often did not care to share their thinking with their constituents until the final product was completed. When during debates over congressional representation, Edmund Randolph suggested that the Convention might consider an adjournment "to deliberate on the means of conciliation," Paterson either misunderstood Randolph's intent or cleverly interpreted Randolph as saying that he wanted to adjourn the Convention permanently. He appears to have caused considerable consternation when he responded that "it was high time for the Convention to adjourn that the rule of secrecy ought to be rescinded, and that our Constituents should be consulted" (II, 18). Randolph observed that he "had never entertained an idea of an adjournment sine die; & was sorry that his meaning had been so readily & strangely misinterpreted" (II, 18).

On July 25, the Convention voted to allow members of the Committee of Detail to have copies of the proceedings to do their work. This same day, however, the Convention voted 6-5 against allowing any members of the Convention to have access to such resolutions. In his report to the Maryland Legislature on the Constitutional Convention, Luther Martin of Maryland would later object that

> I moved for liberty to be given to the different members to take correct copies of the propositions to which the Convention had then agreed, in order that during the recess of the Convention, we might have an opportunity of considering them, and if it should be thought that any alterations or amendments were necessary, that we might be prepared, against the Convention met, to bring them forward for discussion. But the same spirit which caused our doors to be shut, our proceedings to be kept secret, our Journals to be locked up and every avenue, as far as possible, to be shut to public information, prevailed also in this case, and the proposal, so reasonable and necessary, was rejected by a majority of the Convention; thereby precluding even the members themselves from the necessary means of information and deliberation on the important business in which they were engaged. (Quoted in Warren 1928, 354)

Reasons for Secrecy

There were a number of reasons that delegates may have had for such secrecy. First, the Convention was not meeting to adopt a Constitution but to make recommendations for subsequent popular approval; this was one of the reasons the delegates gave for exceeding their original mandate simply to amend and enlarge the Articles. Second, as per other Convention rules specifying that votes at the Convention would not be recorded under individual names, false starts were to be expected, and delegates were encouraged to reconsider previous votes if deliberations persuaded them of the need for such changes; publicity about votes that were later changed could have led the public to think that the delegates were being duplicitous. Third, the delegates were meeting in a state where there was fierce competition between the Constitutionalist and the Anti-Constitutionalist Parties; in a historical irony, the former actually supported the existing system under the Articles of Confederation (and would thus become Antifederalists) while the latter favored the Convention's work. In any event, there was always the possibility that local partisans, dissatisfied with what they were reading in the newspapers, could have interrupted the Convention's work. Fourth, the delegates to the Convention can be considered almost as much like national representatives to a peace conference as like representatives of what Americans today call states. It was not until the twentieth century that the principle of "open covenants openly arrived at" became popular, and the second part of this formula is so questionable that it is often breached; diplomatic conferences are still typically held in secret (see Hendrickson 2003). Fifth, absent modern mechanisms of political polling, the only real medium the delegates had for ascertaining public opinion other than word of mouth, letters, and newspapers was through voting, and such voting was not appropriate until a final product had been reported.

James Madison offered a number of explanations for the secrecy of the Convention to Jared Sparks who visited him in April of 1830. He thus observed:

> It was likewise best for the convention for forming the Constitution to sit within closed doors, because opinions were so various and at first so crude that it was necessary they should be long debated before any uniform system of opinion could be formed. Meantime the minds of the members were changing, and much was to be gained by a yielding and accommodating spirit. Had the members committed themselves publicly at first, they would have afterwards supposed consistency required them to maintain their ground, whereas by secret discussion no man felt himself obliged to retain his opinions any longer than he was satisfied of their propriety and truth, and was open to the force of argument. Mr. Madison thinks no Constitution would ever have been adopted by the convention if the debates had been public. (Farrand III, 479)

Adherence to Secrecy Rules

The delegates took the pledge of secrecy seriously. George Washington filled his diaries during this time with records of the weather and where he dined, but he included no substantive facts about the Convention. Delegates frequently cited the secrecy rule in corresponding with their friends. James Madison, the individual who kept the most extensive and accurate notes of Convention proceedings, was the last delegate who attended the Convention to die, and he specified that his notes would not be published until after his death.

An Exception to the Secrecy Requirement

On August 18 the New York *Daily Advertiser* published an article suggesting that the Constitutional Convention was considering establishing a monarchy, to be headed by the Bishop of Osnaburg, a son of Britain's George III (Farrand II, 333). In response the Convention unofficially authorized a statement in the *Pennsylvania Herald*. Citing letters that members had received that had raised this possibility, the response went on to say that, "'tho we cannot, affirmatively, tell you what we are doing; we can, negatively, tell you what we are not doing—we never once thought of a king" (Van Doren 1948, 145).

An Anecdote

One of the delegates, William Pierce, reports that on one occasion a member dropped a copy of propositions that the Convention was debating. A delegate, General Thomas Mifflin of Pennsylvania, found the document and presented it to the president. With the special gravity for which he was so known, Washington was reputed to have kept the document at his seat and addressed the body just prior to adjournment:

> I am sorry to find that some one Member of this Body, has been so neglectful of the secrets of the Convention as to drop in the State House a copy of their proceedings, which by accident was picked up and delivered to me this Morning. I must entreat Gentlemen to be more careful, lest our transactions get into the News Papers, and disturb the public repose by premature speculation. I know not whose Paper it is, but there it is [throwing it down on the table], let him who owns it take it.

Pierce reports Washington's subsequent actions as well as his own fears:

> At the same time he bowed, picked up his Hat, and quitted the room with a dignity so severe that every Person seemed alarmed; for my part I

was extremely so, for putting my hand in my pocket I missed my copy of the same Paper, but advancing up to the Table my fears soon dissipated; I found it to be in the hand writing of another Person. When I went to my lodgings at the Indian Queen, I found my copy in a coat pocket which I had pulled off that Morning. It is something remarkable that no Person ever owned the paper. (III, 86–87)

Secrecy outside the Convention

Significantly, although delegates voted to keep their own votes secret, they provided in Article I, Section 4 that

each House shall keep a Journal of its Proceedings, and from time to time publish the same, excepting such Parts as may in their Judgment require Secrecy; and the Yeas and Nays of the Members of either House on any question shall, at the Desire of one fifth of those Present, be noted in the Journal.

This indicates that the delegates conceived of what they were doing differently than the way that they perceived of congressional lawmaking, which did not require ultimate popular approval. Because delegates to the Convention expected that members of Congress, and especially the Senate, would from time to time be dealing with sensitive matters of foreign affairs involving ambassadorial appointments and the ratification of treaties, this provision did not call for complete congressional openness.

Once the delegates signed the Constitution, they made provision to circulate copies throughout the nation. The document was debated widely in pamphlets and newspapers as well as in the state ratifying conventions. Such debates made it clear that the purpose of the delegates had not been to shield their final work product from public scrutiny but rather to provide space for the delegates to debate individual components of the document freely and to arrive at appropriate compromises prior to airing it publicly.

Subsequent Records of Convention Proceedings

Shortly after the Convention, Benjamin Franklin copied a number of his speeches for distribution to friends. Charles Pinckney also published one of the speeches he had prepared for the Convention in a South Carolina newspaper. Luther Martin published a 1788 report entitled "The Genuine Information . . . relative to the Proceedings of the General Convention, lately held at Philadelphia" which was highly critical of his fellow delegates. Delegates who had attended the Convention sometimes referred to debates at the Convention during the state ratification debates as well as in subsequent service as members of Congress. Alexander Hamilton's proposed plan of government was printed in 1801 and used to discredit him, and selections from Robert Yates's notes, which had been made available to John Lansing and came into possession of E. C. Genet, the former French ambassador to the United States, were published anonymously in 1808 under the title *A Letter to the Electors of President and Vice-President of the United States* in an attempt to discredit Madison in the eyes of presidential electors (for these incidents, see Farrand 1907, 45–46). Congress authorized publication of the sketchy records of the official secretary of the Convention in 1818, with John Quincy Adams having the fairly thankless task of serving as editor of the volume which appeared the next year under the title of *Journal, Acts and Proceedings, of the Convention, . . . which formed the Constitution of the United States* (47). Yates's notes were printed in 1821, and William Pierce's character sketches of members were published in 1828. Madison's own notes, the most extensive of the Convention, were not published until 1840, four years after his death. In the early twentieth century, historian Max Farrand subsequently collected Convention notes in a four-volume set.

See Also Farrand, Max; Committee on Rules; Public Opinion; Rules of the Constitutional Convention

FOR FURTHER READING

Barry, Richard. 1971 (1942). *Mr. Rutledge of South Carolina*. Freeport, NY: Books for Libraries Press.

Brown, John R. 1988. "The Miracle of 1787: Could It? Would It? Happen Again?" *Loyola Law Review* 33: 903–920.

Farrand, Max. October 1907. "The Records of the Federal Convention." *American Historical Review* 13: 44–65.

———, ed. 1937. *The Records of the Federal Convention*. 4 vols. New Haven, CT: Yale University Press.

Hendrickson, David D. 2003. *Peace Pact: The Lost World of the American Founding*. Lawrence: University Press of Kansas.

Kesavan, Vasan, and Michael Stokes Paulsen. 2003. "The Interpretative Force of the Constitution's Secret Drafting History." *Georgetown Law Review* 91 (August): 1113–1214.

Lansky, Dana. 2000. "Proceeding to a Constitution: A Multi-Party Negotiation Analysis of the Constitutional Convention of 1787." *Harvard Negotiation Law Review* 5 (Spring): 279–338.

Van Doren, Carl. 1948. *The Great Rehearsal: The Story of the Making and Ratifying of the Constitution of the United States*. New York: Viking Press.

Warren, Charles. 1928. *The Making of the Constitution*. Boston: Little, Brown.

SECRETARY OF THE CONVENTION

The official secretary of the Constitutional Convention was William Jackson. New York's Alexander Hamilton nominated Jackson for the office on May 25, after James Wilson of Pennsylvania had placed the name of Benjamin Franklin's grandson, Temple Franklin, into nomination. Although John Beckley, the clerk of Virginia's House of Delegates, was also reported to have accompanied Governor Edmund Randolph in hopes of receiving the appointment (Hutson 1987, 1), he does not appear to have secured a nomination. Jackson won over Franklin by a vote of 5 votes to 2, much to the apparent mortification of his grandfather (Hutson, 1).

Jackson was not a good choice. He took almost no notes related to the substance of the debates, instead providing somewhat disorganized records of the individual votes at the Convention. Fortunately, Virginia's James Madison took meticulous notes that when matched with the records of Jackson and the less extensive notes of other delegates, give a relatively good view of most of the debates that transpired at the Convention. Jackson's records were released during the administration of James Monroe. Madison's notes were not published until 1840, after his death.

See Also Farrand, Max; Jackson, William; Madison, James, Jr.; Records of the Constitutional Convention

FOR FURTHER READING

Hutson, James H., ed. 1987. *Supplement to Max Farrand's* The Records of the Federal Convention of 1787. New Haven, CT: Yale University Press.

Wright, Robert K., Jr., and Morris J. MacGregor, Jr. 1987. *Soldier-Statesmen of the Constitution*. Washington, DC: Center of Military History, United States Army.

SECTIONALISM

At the time of the Constitutional Convention of 1787, observers generally classified states as falling into one of three regions. These were the East, or North, consisting of the northern New England states; the Middle states; and the South. At the time, all 13 states bordered on the Atlantic, but it would not be long before Western states, for example, Tennessee (then generally designated Franklin) and Kentucky, would also be added.

Sectional differences had evidenced themselves in the Congress under the Articles of Confederation. Delegates to the Constitutional Convention reflected the interests of both their states and of their sections. William Wiecke has thus observed the pervasiveness of sectionalism at this gathering:

Sectional divergences were a component of every problem that James Madison and other nationalists sought to remedy by drafting a new Constitution; in some ways, it was a key to all these other problems, something that had to be solved if the other issues were to be successfully resolved too. (1987, 177)

Delegates clearly had a sense of their differences. In a speech apparently prepared by Jared Ingersoll on or about June 19, he listed some of the differences he had observed, which he believed roughly divided the nation into three regions, and which he believed might argue for the continuing superiority of a confederation over the establishment of a national government:

> the Fisheries & Manufacturers of New-England, The Flour Lumber Flaxseed & Ginseng of New York New Jersey Pennsylvania & Delaware The Tobacco of Maryland & Virginia the Pitch Tar, Rice & Indigo & Cotton of North Carolina South Carolina & Georgia, can never be regulated by the same Law nor the same Legislature, nor is this diversity by any means confined to Articles of Commerce, at the Eastward Slavery is not acknowledged, with us it exists in a certain qualified manner, at the Southward in its full extent. (Hutson 1987, 103)

Proposals for Plural Executive

A plural executive was one solution to the problem of sectionalism. In arguing on June 2 for a plural executive, Virginia's Edmund Randolph feared that a single person would be more likely to be chosen from the nation's center and that "the remote parts would not be on an equal footing" (Farrand 1937, I, 88). In the draft of a speech apparently prepared for June 4, Virginia's George Mason further observed:

> If the Executive is vested in three Persons, one chosen from the northern, one from the middle, and one from the Southern States, will it not contribute to quiet the Minds of the People, and convince them that there will be proper attention paid to their respective Concerns? Will not three Men so chosen bring with them, into Office, a more perfect and extensive Knowledge of the real Interests of this great Union? (Hutson 1987, 51)

The eventual decision on behalf of a single executive does not appear to indicate that the delegates to the Convention were unconcerned with sectionalism but that they were not sure a plural executive would be a cure. South Carolina's Pierce Butler thus spoke persuasively on behalf of remote states on June 2 by observing that

> if one man should be appointed he would be responsible to the whole, and would be impartial to its interests. If three or more should be taken from as many districts, there would be a constant struggle for local advantage. In Military matters this would be particularly mischievous. (I, 88–89)

Divisions between the North and the South

Most scholars have rightfully concentrated on the division at the Convention between the most populous and least populous states—generally, although not completely accurately, designated as the large and the small. The delegates sought to resolve this issue through the Great, or Connecticut, Compromise. However, this division sometimes masked deeper regional differences.

The greatest division was, of course, between the states in the North where slavery had either been abolished or was in the process of being eliminated and those in the South where it was still flourishing. In unsuccessfully attempting to deflect attention from the division between the large and the small states, Virginia's James Madison thus observed on June 29:

> The great danger to our general government is the great Southern and northern interests of the continent, being opposed to each other. Look to the notes in congress, and most of them stand divided by the geography of the country, not according to the size of the states. (I, 476)

Madison elaborated on this division the following day. After pointing to differences in climate and in the presence of slavery, he observed:

> These two causes concurred in forming the great division of interests in the U. States. It did not lie

between the large & small States: it lay between the Northern & Southern, and if any defensive power were necessary, it ought to be mutually given to these two interests. (I, 486)

Madison repeated this argument on July 13 (I, 600). Similarly, on July 2, South Carolina's Charles Pinckney pointed to "a solid distinction as to interest between the southern and northern states" (I, 516). In what appears to be a later insertion into his notes, Madison quoted Gouverneur Morris of Pennsylvania as tracing the deleterious influence of slavery throughout the three regions of the nation:

> The moment you leave ye E. Sts. & enter N. York, the effects of the institution become visible; Passing thro' the Jerseys and entering Pa—every criterion of superior improvement witnesses the change. Proceed Southwdly, & every step you take thro' ye great regions of slaves, presents a desert increasing with ye increasing proportion of these wretched beings. (II, 221–222)

Prominent compromises between the North and the South over the issue of slavery included the three-fifths clause, dealing with representation of slaves for purposes of representation and direct taxation; the continuing importation of slavery, which Congress was not given power to regulate until 1808; and the provision, generally designated the fugitive-slave clause, to deal with slaves who attempted to secure their freedom by fleeing northward.

Although the Northern states emerged from the Constitutional Convention with a slight majority, it did not appear as though this majority would be permanent. Pierce Butler thus appeared to reflect widespread sentiment when he observed on July 13 that "the people & strength of America are evidently bearing Southwardly & S. westwdly" (I, 605).

There were, of course, other differences between North and South. The former was more deeply engaged in shipbuilding and would over time be seeking protection for its nascent industries; the latter was dependent on exports. Southern interests were in part protected by the provi-sion prohibiting the taxation of exports; both sides were protected by the provision that treaties would have to be approved by two-thirds majorities, rather than by a simple majority, of the Senate.

Divisions between the East and the West

Concerns over navigation of the Mississippi River, which was especially important to Western states, had already been reflected in the Jay-Gardoqui negotiations which had stirred conflict between Northeastern states, far more concerned with commerce on the Atlantic, and the Southern states, who generally favored the interests of the West on this matter. Opposing the three-fifths compromise, Gouverneur Morris highlighted this conflict on July 13. He even suggested that if the conflicts between the North and South were as wide as had been argued, perhaps the sections should "at once take a friendly leave of each other" (I, 604). He continued:

> There can be no end of demands for security if every particular interest is to be entitled to it. The Eastern States may claim it for their fishery, and for other objects, as the Southn. States claim it for their peculiar object [slavery]. In this struggle between the two ends of the Union, what part ought the Middle States in point of policy to take: to join their Eastern brethren according to his idea. If the Southn. States get the power into their hands, and be joined as they will be with the interior Country they will inevitably bring on a war with Spain for the Mississippi. This language is already held. The interior Country having no property nor interest exposed on the sea, will be little affected by such a war. He wished to know what security the Northn. & middle States will have agst. this danger. (I, 604)

There was considerable debate about the future admission of states from the West. Pennsylvania's Gouverneur Morris feared that Western states would be biased on behalf of liberty and against property and "thought the rule of representation ought to be so fixed as to secure to the Atlantic

States a prevalence in the National Councils" (I, 533; also see his arguments at I, 583). Nathaniel Gorham defended a committee report regarding future state representation by observing on July 9 that "the Atlantic States having ye. Govt. in their own hands, may take care of their own interest, by dealing out the right of Representation in safe proportions to the Western States" (I, 560). By contrast, Virginia's George Mason observed on July 11:

If the western States are to be admitted into the Union as they arise, they must, he wd. repeat, be treated as equals, and subjected to no degrading discriminations. They will have the same pride & other passions which we have, and will either not unite with or will speedily revolt from the Union, if they are not in all respects placed on an equal footing with their brethren. (I, 578–579)

Similarly, Pennsylvania's James Wilson argued on July 13:

The majority of people wherever found ought in all questions to govern the minority. If the interior Country should acquire this majority they will not only have the right, but will avail themselves of it whether we will or no. This jealousy misled the policy of G. Britain with regard to America.

   The fatal maxims espoused by her were that the Colonies were growing too fast, and that their growth must be stinted in time. What were the consequences? first, enmity on our part, then actual separation. Like consequences will result on the part of the interior settlements, if like jealousy & policy be pursued on ours. (I, 605)

Fortunately, such arguments eventually prevailed, avoiding the specter of the West becoming a colonial possession.

Subsequent Developments

During ratification debates between Federalists and Antifederalists over the Constitution, divisions within states (often pitting the more urban-ized eastern sections, who tended to be for ratification, against the more rural western ones, who often opposed it) were generally more visible than were divisions among geographical sections of the nation. Less fortunately, the division between the Northern and Southern regions grew in the years after the Convention, as Northern sentiment grew increasingly antislavery and Southerners became increasingly defensive about this institution and increasingly likely to describe it as a positive good rather than as a necessary evil.

   Regionalism was manifested in divisions within and between the major political parties, in recurring disputes over tariffs, in disputes about the proper balance between the powers of the national government and the states, as well as in disputes that led to the Missouri Compromise of 1820, the Compromise of 1850, and eventually in the Civil War. John C. Calhoun of South Carolina, who revived the idea of a plural executive, formulated his theory of "concurrent majorities" largely from the idea that each geographical interest should be entitled to a veto over actions of the others (Ford 1994). The ratification of the Thirteenth Amendment in 1865 brought an end to chattel slavery, and thus to the three-fifths clause and to other compromises connected to slavery. Geographical divisions remain but have been far less pronounced since the abolition of this nefarious institution.

See Also Compromise; Connecticut Compromise; Geography; Jay-Gardoqui Negotiations; Mississippi River; Parties, Factions, and Interests; President, Number of; Slave Importation; Slavery; States, Admission and Creation; Taxes on Imports and Exports; Three-fifths Clause; Treaty-Making and Ratification

FOR FURTHER READING

Davis, Joseph L. 1977. *Sectionalism in American Politics, 1774–1787.* Madison: University of Wisconsin Press.
Farrand, Max, ed. 1937. *The Records of the Federal Convention.* 4 vols. New Haven, CT: Yale University Press.
Ford, Lacy K., Jr. 1994. "Inventing the Concurrent Majority: Madison, Calhoun, and the Problem of

Majoritarianism in American Political Thought." *Journal of Southern History* 60 (February): 19–58.

Hutson, James H., ed. 1987. *Supplement to Max Farrand's* The Records of the Federal Convention of 1787. New Haven, CT: Yale University Press.

Lynd, Staughton. 1966. "The Compromise of 1787." *Political Science Quarterly* 81 (June): 225–250.

Morgan, Kenneth. 2001. "Slavery and the Debate over Ratification of the United States Constitution." *Slavery and Abolition* 22 (December): 40–65.

Ohline, Howard A. 1972. "Republicanism and Slavery: Origins of the Three-fifths Clause in the United States Constitution." *William and Mary Quarterly,* 3rd ser. 18 (October): 563–584.

Onuf, Peter S. 1986. "Liberty, Development, and Union: Visions of the West in the 1780s." *William and Mary Quarterly,* 3rd ser. 53 (April): 179–213.

Wiecke, William M. 1987. "The Witch at the Christening: Slavery and the Constitution's Origins." In Leonard W. Wevy and Dennis J. Mahoney, eds. *The Framing and Ratification of the Constitution.* New York: Macmillan.

SENTRIES

A contemporary press account of the Constitutional Convention, quoted–but not specifically cited–by historian Max Farrand, said that "sentries are planted without and within–to prevent any person from approaching near–who appear to be very alert in the performance of their duty" (1913, 58).

It seems likely that these "sentries" were, in fact, the relatively unheralded messenger Nicholas Weaver and the door-keeper Joseph Fry (Farrand 1937, I, 13), whom the Convention appointed on May 25. Whether they were these men or others, they would have been used to enforce the secrecy rule by which the Convention conducted its business. Historian Charles Warren cited an account in the *New York Journal* dated June 7 that observed that the Convention took secrecy so seriously that "all debate is suspended on the entrance of their own officers" (Warren 1928, 138).

See Also Fry, Joseph; Secrecy; Weaver, Nicholas

FOR FURTHER READING

Farrand, Max. 1913. *The Framing of the Constitution of the United States.* New Haven, CT: Yale University Press.

——, ed. 1937. *The Records of the Federal Convention.* 4 vols. New Haven, CT: Yale University Press.

Warren, Charles. 1928. *The Making of the Constitution.* Boston: Little, Brown.

SEPARATION OF POWERS

Although the Constitution does not specifically use the term, most commentators agree that it embodies the principle of separation of powers. Significantly, the first three Articles of the document begin by delineating the respective powers of the legislative, executive, and judicial branches. Although these powers sometimes overlap (as when the president exercises a veto of congressional legislation), they are distinct. The document further provides that the president shall be selected by an Electoral College rather than by members of Congress, and, although the matter is not definitively settled by the words of the Constitution, the judicial branch has long exercised the power, called judicial review, to strike down legislation that arises in cases before it that it considers to be constitutional. Unlike parliamentary systems, it is possible under the U.S. system for the president and members of the legislature to be from different political parties. Political scientists refer to such a situation as "divided government."

The idea of separation of powers is closely tied to the idea of checks and balances, which in turn is arguably connected to the idea (especially prominent in international politics) of the balance of power. Separation of powers is sometimes also associated with the idea of "mixed government," which, however, is usually based on balancing interests or classes, rather than balancing branches of government (Casper 1997, 9). The Framers of the Constitution divided powers to ensure their responsible exercise. Although lines of division are not always clear-cut, Congress was invested with the power of making laws, the president with the power of administering them, and the judiciary with the power of interpreting them. The mechanism of separation of powers stems from the idea, later defended in *The Federalist,* that the concentration of all powers in a single set of hands is the essence of tyranny, and that institutional protections for civil liberties are to be preferred to trust in an individual or institution or to attempting to select or train virtuous rulers.

Virginia and New Jersey Plans

The idea of separation of powers was implicit in the Virginia Plan's creation of three different branches of government, a principle that the New Jersey Plan reaffirmed. On June 2, the Convention was discussing a proposal introduced by John Dickinson of Delaware whereby Congress could remove the chief executive upon receiving petitions from a majority of the state legislature for such removal. Madison observed that in making his argument, Dickinson "went into a discourse of some length, the sum of which was, that the Legislative, Executive, & Judiciary departments ought to be made as independt. as possible; but that such an Executive as some seemed to have in contemplation was not consistant with a republic; that a firm Executive could only exist in a limited monarchy" (Farrand 1937, I, 86).

Council of Revision

A proposal contained in the Virginia Plan to ally the president and members of the judiciary in a Council of Revision generated discussion of the idea of separation of powers at the Convention. Some delegates opposed this alliance on the basis that it would give judges two bites at the same apple—first determining whether a law was wise and later determining whether it was constitutional—but other delegates were primarily concerned with separation-of-powers concerns. During the discussion of the subject on June 4, James Wilson of Pennsylvania observed: "If the Legislative Exetive & Judiciary ought to be distinct & indepen-

dent, The Executive ought to have an absolute negative. Without such a Self-defense the Legislature can at any moment sink it into non existence" (I, 98). In a discussion of the same mechanism on June 6, Virginia's James Madison now weighed in on behalf of the Council of Revision. Specifically attempting to answer the argument "that the Judiciary Departmt. ought to be separate & distinct from the other great Departments" (I, 138), he denied that the Council would result in any "improper mixture of these distinct powers." He observed: "In England, whence the maxim itself had been drawn, the Executive had an absolute negative on the laws; and the supreme tribunal of Justice (the House of Lords) formed one of the other branches of the Legislature" (I, 139). Later in the day, Delaware's John Dickinson repeated his argument that mixing the executive and judiciary together "involved an improper mixture of powers" (I, 140), and the Convention eventually rejected the idea of a Council of Revision on July 17.

After James Wilson and James Madison reintroduced the idea of joining the president and the judiciary in a Council of Revision on July 21, Elbridge Gerry again opposed this on the basis of separation of powers:

> The motion was liable to strong objections. It was combining & mixing together the Legislative & the other departments. It was establishing an improper coalition between the Executive & Judiciary departments. It was making Statesmen of the Judges; and setting them up as the guardians of the Rights of the people. (II, 75)

Not surprisingly, Madison disagreed:

> Mr. Madison could not discover in the proposed association of the Judges with the Executive in the Revisionary check on the Legislature any violation of the maxim which requires the great departments of power to be kept separate & distinct. On the contrary he thought it an auxiliary precaution in favor of the maxim. If a Constitutional discrimination of the departments on paper were a sufficient security to each agst. encroachments of the others, all further provisions

would indeed be superfluous. But experience had taught us a distrust of that security; and that it is necessary to introduce such a balance of powers and interests, as will guarantee the provisions on paper.

Instead therefore of contenting ourselves with laying down the Theory in the Constitution that each department ought to be separate & distinct, it was proposed to add a defensive power to each which should maintain the Theory in practice. In so doing we did not blend the departments together. We erected effectual barriers for keeping them separate. (II, 77)

He went on to argue that the Council of Revision no more violated the idea of separation of powers than did the executive veto, but again, he failed to convince fellow delegates to approve the Council of Revision.

Presidential Selection

Discussion of presidential selection often centered on the proper relation between the legislative and executive branches. On June 1, Connecticut's Roger Sherman said that he favored making the presidency "absolutely dependent" on Congress (I, 68). By contrast and consistent with republican fears of "corruption," Virginia's George Mason opposed re-eligibility for office on the basis that it would provide a basis for presidential intrigue with the legislature (I, 68). Other delegates repeated this theme throughout the Convention (see, for example, Elbridge Gerry, I, 80 and 175). In discussing a proposal to grant the president tenure "during good behavior," a proposal advanced by his friend James McClurg of Virginia, Madison launched into an extensive discussion of separation of powers on July 17 (the same day he would lose his fight for a Council of Revision). He observed:

If it be essential to the preservation of liberty that the Legisl: Execut: & Judiciary powers be separate, it is essential to a maintenance of the separation, that they should be independent of each other. The Executive could not be independent of the Legislure, if dependent on the pleasure of that branch for a re-appointment. (II, 34)

Citing Montesquieu, and undoubtedly with his prized proposal for a Council of Revision in mind, Madison argued that an alliance between the executive and legislature was more to be feared than one between the executive and the judiciary. In again discussing the selection of the presidency on July 19, James Madison, who continued to defend his now-rejected Council of Revision, repeated the same arguments:

If it be a fundamental principle of free Govt. that the Legislative, Executive & Judiciary powers should be *separately* exercised; it is equally so that they be *independently* exercised. There is the same & perhaps greater reason why the Executive shd. be independent of the Legislature, than why the Judiciary should: A coalition of the two former powers would be more immediately & certainly dangerous to public liberty. It is essential then that the appointment of the Executive should either be drawn from some source, or held by some tenure, that will give him a free agency with regard to the Legislature. (II, 56)

Eventually, the Convention designed an Electoral College mechanism freeing the presidency from dependency on the legislative branch.

Vice Presidency

In creating the Electoral College, which specified that each elector would vote for two different people for president, the Convention also created the vice presidency. Partly in order to give the vice president something to do, the Convention agreed that he would serve as president of the Senate. George Mason was among those who believed that this violated separation of powers. He argued that "it mixed too much the Legislative & Executive, which as well as the Judiciary departments, ought to be kept as separate as possible" (II, 537). His own solution, which the Convention rejected, was to create a six-person Privy Council to advise the president.

Presidential Impeachment

In a discussion of the impeachment of the president that took place on July 20, Rufus King of Massachusetts expressed concern about the impact such a mechanism might have on separation of powers:

He wished the House to recur to the primitive axiom that the three great departments of Govts. should be separate & independent: that the Executive & Judiciary should be so as well as the Legislative: that the Executive should be so equally with the Judiciary. (II, 66)

King's concern was probably mitigated in part by specifying specific bases for impeachment—treason, bribery and "other crimes and misdemeanors"—rather than allowing for impeachment on purely political grounds.

Pardon Power

During a discussion of the pardon power on September 15, just two days before the delegates signed the Constitution, Virginia's Edmund Randolph proposed withdrawing the power from the president in cases of treason. Correctly or not, fellow delegates took this to mean that the legislature would exercise the power in such cases. Rufus King objected that the exercise of such a power would violate the separation of powers:

it would be inconsistent with the Constitutional separation of the Executive & Legislative powers to let the prerogative be exercised by the latter.—A Legislative body is utterly unfit for the purpose. They are governed too much by the passions of the moment. (II, 626)

The Convention rejected Randolph's proposal.

Federalist Arguments for the Constitution

The idea of separation of powers probably became more self-conscious in debates over the Constitution than it had been during the Convention itself. In *Federalist* No. 9, Alexander Hamilton cited "the regular distribution of power into distinct departments" as one of the advances in "the science of politics" that was unknown to the authors of ancient republics (Hamilton, Madison, and Jay 1961, 72). After rejecting the idea of a Council of Censors in the previous essay, James Madison said in *Federalist* No. 51 that "the interior structure of the government" must be so contrived "as that its several constituent parts may, by their mutual relations, be the means of keeping each other in their proper places" (320). Madison went on to argue that the system must be so constructed that "Ambition must be made to counteract ambition. The interest of the man must be connected with the constitutional rights of the place" (322). Madison presented the division of power between state and national authorities and the division of power among three separate departments as providing "a double security . . . to the rights of the people" (323).

Analysis

The idea of separation of powers emerges from the structure of the Constitution delineated in the first three Articles rather than from specific words referring to the concept in the abstract. It seems clear that many delegates believed that separation of powers was a mechanism for protecting liberty. Although Supreme Court justices have not always viewed the principle in this manner (sometimes juxtaposing efficiency against liberty), scholars have also argued that the Framers viewed the separation of powers as a way of promoting governmental efficiency, by investing each branch with the powers that it could best exercise (Rossum 2001, 77).

Although the delegates supported the idea of separation of powers, they were not always clear as to how separate the notion of separation must be. In particular, Madison and a number of other delegates appeared to believe that there would be far less threat if members of the judiciary were allied with the executive branch than if members of the legislative and executive branches were mixed or if the latter were made dependent upon the former. The fact that Madison did not prevail on this point may indicate that others were not persuaded by his arguments.

See Also Checks and Balances; Council of Revision; Impeachment Clause; Judicial Review; Montesquieu, Charles Louis de Secondat de; Presidential Veto; Vice Presidency

FOR FURTHER READING

Carpenter, William Seal. 1928. "The Separation of Powers in the Eighteenth Century." *American Political Science Review* 22 (February): 32–44.

Casper, Gerhard. 1997. *Separating Power: Essays on the Founding Period.* Cambridge, MA: Harvard University Press.

Farrand, Max, ed. 1937. *The Records of the Federal Convention.* 4 vols. New Haven, CT: Yale University Press.

Goodwin, Robert A., and Art Kaufman, eds. 1986. *Separation of Powers—Does It Still Work?* Washington, DC: American Enterprise Institute for Public Policy Research.

Hamilton, Alexander, James Madison, and John Jay. 1961. *The Federalist Papers.* Ed. Clinton Rossiter. New York: New American Library.

Mason, Alpheus T. 1976. "America's Political Heritage: Revolution and Free Government—A Bicentennial Tribute." *Political Science Quarterly* 91 (Summer): 193–217.

Rossum, Ralph A. 2001. *Federalism, the Supreme Court and the Seventeenth Amendment: The Irony of Constitutional Democracy.* Lanham, MD: Lexington Books.

Utley, Robert L., Jr., ed. 1989. *Principles of the Constitutional Order: The Ratification Debates.* Lanham, MD: University Press of America.

Vile, M. J. C. 1998. *Constitutionalism and the Separation of Powers.* 2nd ed. Indianapolis, IN: Liberty Fund.

Wilson, Bradford P., and Peter W. Schramm, eds. 1994. *Separation of Powers and Good Government.* Lanham, MD: Rowman and Littlefield Publishers.

tution, has come to be the most important, but it has taken some time for it to achieve this status. Particularly during the commemoration of the centennial of the U.S. Constitution, there were questions as to whether the date of the signing should be the focus or whether celebrations should be held on the anniversary of the date (June 21, 1788) that New Hampshire, the critical ninth state, ratified the document, or perhaps even the date that George Washington was inaugurated as first president. Moreover, the writing and ratification of the Constitution has sometimes had to share the spotlight with that of the first 10 amendments, now designated as the Bill of Rights.

The controversy resembles disputes over Independence Day. July 2 was the date that the actual resolution for Independence from Great Britain was adopted. Thus, it could just as easily have become the day that Independence is celebrated as July 4, the day that the Second Continental Congress officially adopted Thomas Jefferson's amended Declaration as an explanation for its actions (Wills 1978, 336–340).

Largely through the work of the Sons and Daughters of the American Revolution, the week of September 17 has been designated as Constitution Week.

See Also Commemorations of the Constitutional Convention; Signing of the Constitution

FOR FURTHER READING

Bullock, Steven C. 2002. "Talk of the Past." *Common-Place* 2, no. 4. (July). http://www.common-place. org.

Kammen, Michael. 1987. *A Machine That Would Go of Itself: The Constitution in American Culture.* New York: Alfred A. Knopf.

Wills, Garry. 1978. *Inventing America: Jefferson's Declaration of Independence.* Garden City, NY: Doubleday.

SEPTEMBER 17, 1787

Of all the dates associated with the Constitutional Convention of 1787, September 17, the date that most of the remaining delegates signed the Consti-

SHALLUS, JACOB (1750–1796)

In "detective" work he did in connection with the sesquicentennial of the U.S. Constitution, historian John C. Fitzpatrick identified Jacob Shallus as the individual who "engrossed," or transcribed, the Constitution. Shallus was a Pennsylvanian of Dutch ancestry, who was born just a year after his father, Valentine, immigrated to Pennsylvania. He had volunteered for duty in the Revolutionary War, fought in Canada, become a quartermaster of Pennsylvania's First Battalion, helped outfit a privateer ship named the *Retrieve* to prey on British commerce, and began to accumulate property in the Philadelphia area for the taxes on which he would later find himself in debt.

By the end of the Revolutionary War, Shallus had become the assistant clerk of the Pennsylvania Assembly, which met in the Pennsylvania State House, where the Constitutional Convention assembled, and he held this position for more than a few years. The third session of the eleventh Assembly had begun meeting upstairs in the State House on September 4, 1787, while the Convention was still meeting on the ground floor, so the Convention's desire for speed would have made him the logical choice (he may even have engrossed the document within the building), and his known handwriting matches that of the Constitution. By contrast, the names of the states at the end of the document are in Alexander Hamilton's handwriting (Hamilton, IV, 274).

Congress paid Shallus $30 for his efforts in engrossing the Constitution on four sheets of vellum parchment (made of treated animal skins) approximately 28 by 23 inches. He probably used a goose quill. Shallus subsequently became a notary and a tabellion-public (an official similar to a notary but with somewhat enlarged duties) and served as the secretary of Pennsylvania's own constitutional convention of 1790. There he supported the Federalist majority and was sent to round up Antifederalist delegates to gain a quorum for a vote–a task at which Philadelphia mobs appear to have had greater success. Although he generally appears to have been a man of property, Shallus faced the possibility of debtors' prison in 1788, a fate he appears to have escaped.

Shallus died in 1796 at the age of 46. He had married Elizabeth Melchior in 1771 and they had eight children. The eldest son, Francis Shallus, who became an artistic engraver in his own right

and who enlisted in the army during the War of 1812 and compiled a book called *Chronological Tables,* may have written some of the headings as an apprentice to his father (Plotnik 1987a, 30). Neither, however, is on record as citing a role in this job.

See Also Dunlap and Claypoole; Pennsylvania State House

FOR FURTHER READING

Fitzpatrick, John C. 1941. "The Man Who Engrossed the Constitution." In Sol Bloom, director-general. *History of the Formation of the Union under the Constitution.* Washington, DC: U.S. Government Printing Office.

Hamilton, Alexander. *The Papers of Alexander Hamilton.* Ed. Harold C. Syrett. Vol. 4: *January 1787–May 1788.* New York: Columbia University Press.

Plotnik, Arthur. 1987a. "The Search for Jacob Shallus." *Pennsylvania Heritage* 13: 24–31.

——. 1987b. *The Man behind the Quill: Jacob Shallus, Calligrapher of the United States Constitution.* Washington, DC: National Archives and Records Administration.

SHAYS'S REBELLION

One of the pivotal events leading up to the Constitutional Convention of 1787 was a rebellion of farmers in western Massachusetts led by Captain Daniel Shays (1747?–1825), a veteran of the Revolutionary War. This rebellion had been presaged by revolutionary movements in the western part of the state both preceding and following the Revolutionary War. It appears to have grown out of the failure of local governmental institutions to achieve legitimacy in the aftermath of the transition from British to state rule–what one historian has called "disrupted elites and discredited political traditions" (Brooke 1989, 436)–as well as from agrarian grievances connected to taxation, debt, and the scarcity of specie with which to pay it and the desire of individuals to halt judicial enforcement of debt and tax collection.

The Scope of the Rebellion

Shays's Rebellion covered the period from August 29, 1786, when a mob seized a courthouse in Northampton, Massachusetts, extended through the intimidation of the Supreme Court that later met in Springfield, and ended in bloodshed as Shay and his men unsuccessfully attempted to capture the federal arsenal at Springfield on January 25, 1787, and the days immediately following. News of the turbulence, as well as rumors that the revolutionaries were set on creating an equal, almost communistic, system (Warren 1905, 42) that threatened property and peace, helped convince both Congress and wavering states and delegates that the Articles of Confederation were inadequate and that the call of the Annapolis Convention for a meeting in Philadelphia should be heeded (but see Feer 1969, who doubts that the event was that important). Although there is some dispute over the matter (Feer, 396–397), the event appears to have been one of the developments that persuaded George Washington to attend (Richards 2002, 2).

One of the fascinating aspects of the event is that, in the months of unrest leading up to it, the confederal Congress attempted to raise forces—which it had to do by making requests of the states—largely under the not altogether inaccurate guise that it was preparing for possible Indian attacks (Warren). The event also witnessed some ingenious reasoning by Virginia's James Madison. He had attempted to justify congressional intervention under the Articles on the highly speculative basis that the revolutionaries might have ties to the British, whom Americans still regarded as an enemy (Warren, 63).

Major-General William Shepard was responsible for the successful defense of the Springfield arsenal on January 25, 1787. After Shays's forces failed to heed an order to stop their advance, the general, whose 1,200 troops were outnumbered by the less organized insurgents, first ordered his troops to fire over their heads and then commanded them to fire a howitzer and level a volley into Shays's forces. It resulted in four deaths to Shays's forces and one serious injury to his own. General Benjamin Lincoln, commander of the Massachusetts troops

Proclamation by the state of Pennsylvania offering reward for Daniel Shays and three other rebellion ringleaders. Signed by Benjamin Franklin, May 19, 1787. (Library of Congress)

(whom Boston merchants had financed from private contributions), arrived with reinforcements on January 28, 1787, and drove Shays's troops away. He later routed them in mid-February, bringing an end to the immediate crisis, as most of the insurgents returned to their homes.

Citing accounts by the Rev. Bezaleel Howard, Richard Brown, a contemporary historian, faults both the illegal actions of Captain Shays and his men and the vindictive policies of Governor James Bowdoin, which Brown believes were typical of the era before the idea of legitimate political party opposition was accepted (1983). Bowdoin's vindictiveness included the hanging of two insurgents. This appears to have backfired when the electorate chose John Hancock, best known

Riots as Expressions of Popular Sovereignty

In a provision that accompanies the guarantee clause, Article IV of the Constitution grants Congress power to send troops at the request of a state legislature or governor to suppress domestic insurrection. This provision undoubtedly stemmed in part from concerns about anarchy that Shays's Rebellion in Massachusetts generated prior to the U.S. Constitutional Convention of 1787. Farmers and others who joined this rebellion closed down local courts that were enforcing state taxes and foreclosing mortgages at a time when economic conditions were tough and specie was in short supply.

Whereas modern attitudes toward riotous assemblies are almost uniformly negative, the colonists and their early successors did not always have such a negative view. In categorizing governments, they did not always distinguish between democracy and mob rule, and, even when they did so, actions taken by a mob on behalf of community rights might be understood to be protecting the former rather than the latter. At the time, the line between established institutions like the "hue and cry" (used by the community to apprehend felons who were on the loose), the *posse commitatus* (consisting of able-bodied men recruited by local sheriffs to handle dire situations), and even the militia (which was under state and local control), on the one hand, and extralegal means of control like riots, on the other hand, was not altogether clear (Maier 1970, 19). Proponents of liberty might further tie riotous assemblies to the wider right of revolution, which documents like the Declaration of Independence had justified as appropriate reactions to tyrannical government. Indeed, events like those leading to the Boston Massacre and the Boston Tea Party that helped precipitate the Revolutionary War are now known not to have been unique either in the U.S. or in Great Britain (Maier, 15–16). Rioters, sometimes closing down brothels, sometimes protesting undue enforcement of unjust laws, sometimes seeking to prevent the spread of contagion, and the like, often believed they were serving wider community interests. On many occasions, local leaders actually encouraged the rioters, especially when their reactions were directed to arbitrary actions of a government centered in Great Britain, after resorts to more conventional means failed.

Moreover, rioters sometimes showed remarkable direction and restraint, as when mobs dispersed after accomplishing their immediate objectives or, as in Boston, refused to riot on Saturday and Sunday evenings because they considered such times to be holy (Maier, 17). Even the Tory Thomas Hutchinson, then lieutenant governor of Massachusetts, observed in 1768 that "mobs a sort of them at least are constitutional" (27). Riots were often likened to weather-related phenomena that brought good as well as bad, often reining in governmental abuses and reminding leaders that they needed to be responsive to popular demands. Indeed, popular insurrections could point to flaws in the existing systems that needed to be corrected. Hence, Thomas Jefferson could express relative equanimity when corresponding to Abigail Adams and others about Shays's Rebellion.

With the establishment of the Constitution and its reliance on "We the People," resort to such extraconstitutional means of change became more difficult to justify, perhaps thereby obscuring the perceived legitimacy that such mechanisms often had in the period prior to the writing of the Constitution (35). Perhaps as a partial substitute, the nation has increasingly relied on broad protections of freedom of speech and press.

FOR FURTHER READING

Maier, Pauline. 1970. "Popular Uprisings and Civil Authority in Eighteenth-Century America." *William and Mary Quarterly*, 3rd ser. 17 (January): 3–35.

for signing the Declaration of Independence with such flourish, over him as governor.

Discussions at the Constitutional Convention

In introducing the Virginia Plan at the Constitutional Convention, Edmund Randolph mentioned the disturbances in Massachusetts (Farrand 1937, I, 18), and on a later occasion he cited Congress's inability to respond with decisive force as an indication of the need for a strong plan like the one he was introducing (I, 263). Madison warned that "the insurrections in Massts. admonished all the States of the danger to which they were exposed" (I, 318), and later observed, in apparent reference to the rebellion, that "symptoms of a leveling spirit . . . have sufficiently appeared in a certain quarters to give notice of the future danger" (I, 423). Elbridge Gerry of Massachusetts cited the rebellion as evidence that "the leveling spirit" had proceeded too far (I, 48). Connecticut's Oliver Ellsworth observed that Massachusetts could "not keep the peace one hundred miles from her capital, and is now forming an army for its support" (I, 406–407). In an interesting counterargument against the provision allowing Congress to subdue rebellion in the states, Gerry argued: "The States will be the best Judges in such cases. More blood would have been spilt in Massts in the late insurrection, if the Genl. authority had intermeddled" (II, 317).

In a somewhat different vein, fellow delegate Rufus King used the desire of one session of the Massachusetts assembly to hang the insurgents and the next to pardon them as an example of legislative instability and the reason that the Constitution should entrust the executive with the pardon power (II, 626–627).

Significance of Shays's Rebellion

In addition to convincing delegates and states of the need to meet, Shays's Rebellion seems specifically responsible for the provisions in Article IV of the Constitution guaranteeing each state a "re-

publican" form of government and providing for national aid in cases of domestic insurrection within the states. As King's comment above indicates, the event might also have influenced the Convention's decision to vest the pardon power in the president.

Postscript

One of the most fascinating reactions to Shays's Rebellion came from one of the most prominent Americans not attending the Convention. On hearing the news of Shays's Rebellion, Thomas Jefferson, then serving as an American ambassador in France, expressed an equanimity that was uncharacteristic of elites of his day. Expressing the hope that the government would not deal too severely with the revolutionaries, Jefferson, writing to Madison, observed:

> I hold it that a little rebellion now and then is a good thing, & as necessary in the political world as storms in the physical. Unsuccessful rebellions indeed generally establish the encroachments on the rights of the people which have produced them. An observation of this truth should render honest republican governors so mild in their punishment of rebellions, as not to discourage them too much. It is a medicine necessary for the sound health of government. (Jefferson 1905, V, 256)

Jefferson's comments in a later letter to Abigail Adams are even more shocking:

> We have had 13. states independent 11. years. There has been one rebellion.
>
> That comes to one rebellion in a century & a half for each state. What country before ever existed a century & half without a rebellion? & what country can preserve its liberties if their rulers are not warned from time to time that their people preserve the spirit of resistance? Let them take arms.
>
> The remedy is to set them right as to facts, pardon & pacify them. What signify a few lives lost in a century or two? The tree of liberty must be

refreshed from time to time with the blood of patriots & tyrants. It is its natural manure. (Jefferson, V, 456)

Jefferson's was clearly a minority view, and from the perspective of the French Revolution which would break out in two years, Shays's Rebellion was certainly not earthshaking. Still, had a majority of delegates at the Constitutional Convention shared Jefferson's views, it is unlikely that they would have worked with such perseverance to write a new Constitution.

See Also Articles of Confederation; Guarantee Clause; Jefferson, Thomas; Massachusetts

FOR FURTHER READING

Appleby, Joyce. "The American Heritage: The Heirs and the Disinherited." *Journal of American History* 74 (December): 798–813.

Brooke, John L. 1989. "To the Quiet of the People: Revolutionary Settlements and Civil Unrest in Western Massachusetts, 1774–1789." *William and Mary Quarterly,* 3rd ser. 46 (July): 425–462.

Brown, Richard D. 1983. "Shays's Rebellion and Its Aftermath: A View from Springfield, Massachusetts, 1787." *William and Mary Quarterly,* 3rd ser. 40 (October): 598–615.

"Documents Relating to Shays's Rebellion, 1787." 1897. *American Historical Review* 2: 693–699.

Farrand, Max, ed. 1937. *The Records of the Federal Convention.* 4 vols. New Haven, CT: Yale University Press.

Feer, Robert A. 1969. "Shays's Rebellion and the Constitution: A Study in Causation." *The New England Quarterly* 42 (September): 388–410.

Jefferson, Thomas. 1905. *The Works of Thomas Jefferson.* Ed. Paul Leicester Ford. New York: G. G. Putnam's Sons, Knickerbocker Press.

Minot, George R. 1970 (1910). *The History of the Insurrections in Massachusetts in the Year Seventeen Hundred and Eighty Six, and the Rebellion Consequent Thereon.* Freeport, NY: Books for Libraries Press.

Richards, Leonard L. 2002. *Shays' Rebellion: The American Revolution's Final Battle.* Philadelphia: University of Pennsylvania Press.

Warren, Joseph Parker. 1905. "The Confederation and Shays' Rebellion." *American Historical Review* 11 (October): 42–67.

SHERMAN, ROGER
(1721–1793)

The second oldest member of the Convention (Benjamin Franklin was the oldest) Connecticut's Roger Sherman was one of the rare individuals who signed the Declaration of Independence, the Articles of Confederation, and the U.S. Constitution. He was born in 1721 in Newton, Massachusetts, to a farm family and moved in 1743 to New Milford, Connecticut where he was a cobbler. Appointed two years later as a surveyor, Sherman set up a store with his brother and married Elizabeth Hartwell. They had seven children, four of whom lived to adulthood; after Elizabeth died, Sherman married Rebecca Prescott, by whom he had eight children. Sherman was admitted to the bar in 1754, served in the Connecticut legislature, became a judge in New Haven and later in the superior court of Connecticut, was a member of the governor's council, and served as treasurer of

Roger Sherman, delegate from Connecticut
(Pixel That)

Yale, as mayor of New Haven, and as a delegate to the Continental Congresses. At the Second Continental Congress, Sherman served on the five-man committee to write the Declaration of Independence (Thomas Jefferson did most of the writing) as well as on the committee responsible for writing the Articles of Confederation (John Dickinson was the primary author).

Despite a physical awkwardness reminiscent of his Puritan roots, Sherman was one of the more influential members of the U.S. Constitutional Convention, often helping to craft compromises between the large and small states and between the North and the South. He was seated on Wednesday, May 30, a day after Edmund Randolph had shocked many of the delegates by proposing the far-reaching Virginia Plan. On his first day at the Convention, Sherman indicated that he thought that Congress needed additional powers, especially over raising money. By James Madison's assessment, however, Sherman seemed not to "be disposed to Make too great inroads on the existing system" in part because he feared that the Convention might not attain anything if it sought too much (Farrand 1937, I, 35). A Sherman biographer has identified him as a "republican" who favored "a strong legislature and a strong states'-rights position" (Collier 1971, 242). Sherman was one of the major forces at the Convention behind the Great Compromise, which balanced the apportionment by population in the U.S. House of Representatives with equal state representation in the Senate.

Federalism and Congressional Powers

Consistent with his view that the Articles of Confederation required relatively minor alterations, Sherman was a strong proponent of states' rights. He indicated on June 6 that he thought the objects of the Union could be boiled down to: "1. defence agst. foreign danger. 2. agst. internal disputes & a resort to force. 3. Treaties with foreign nations 4[.] regulating foreign commerce, & drawing revenue from it" (I, 133). Sherman accordingly favored leaving states in charge of most mat-

ters and limiting the powers of the general government:

All other matters civil & criminal would be much better in the hands of the States. States may indeed be too small as Rhode Island, & thereby be too subject to faction. Some others were perhaps too large, the powers of Govt not being able to pervade them. He was for giving the General Govt. power to legislate and execute within a defined province. (I, 133)

Rufus King summarized Sherman's sentiments in this same speech: "I am agst. a Genl. Govt. and in favor of the independence and confederation of the States, with powers to regulate commerce & draw therefrom a revenue" (I, 143).

When the delegates were discussing the possibility of a congressional negative on state laws, Sherman did not initially oppose the measure but suggested that such cases should be clearly "defined" (I, 166). Later in the Convention, he argued that such a negative would be unnecessary since courts would invalidate laws in opposition to the Constitution (II, 27). In a somewhat cleverer argument, he observed that the presence of a negative might make it appear as though laws that were not negated were therefore valid (II, 28). Still later in the Convention, Sherman observed that the supremacy clause made the congressional veto of state laws unnecessary (II, 390). He cited the provision granting the courts the power to settle disputes between the states as a reason that the new Constitution did not require an elaborate mechanism, like that under the Articles of Confederation, for settling such disputes (II, 401).

When the Convention was discussing requiring state officials to take an oath of office, Sherman disfavored it "as unnecessarily intruding into the State jurisdictions" (I, 203). He thought that states should not only determine the pay of members of Congress but that they should also be responsible for providing for it (I, 373). Using a biblical analogy, he argued that making members of Congress ineligible for state offices would be setting up a kingdom at war with itself (I, 386).

Sherman was willing to defend state actions under the Articles of Confederation as flowing from lack of congressional power rather than from state delinquency (I, 349). He observed that "Cong. is not to blame for the faults of the States. Their measures have been right, and the only thing wanting has been, a further power in Congs. to render them effectual" (I, 487).

In arguing for equal representation in the Senate, Sherman observed that the measure was not so much "a security for the small States; as for the State Govts. which could not be preserved unless they were represented & had a negative in the Genl. Government" (II, 5). Sherman expressed concern that the powers entrusted to the general government needed to be more clearly defined. In proposing an alternative, he sought to provide a guarantee that exercises of congressional powers would not interfere with state police powers (II, 25). He apparently was an early proponent of enumerating congressional powers, although Convention notes do not contain his original list (II, 26).

Sherman was willing to retain the clause granting Congress power to oversee state elections of its members, but he said that "he had himself sufficient confidence in the State Legislatures" (II, 241). Sherman favored allowing Congress to tax imports but not exports except for "such articles as ought not to be exported" (II, 308). He thought that "the oppression of the uncommercial States was guarded agst. by the power to regulate trade between the States," but he feared that the addition of an export tax "would shipwreck the whole" (II, 308).

During the discussion of war powers, Sherman indicated that he believed that Congress should have the power not simply to "declare" but also to "make" war. He apparently believed that the executive function should be largely limited to repelling attack, and that the term "declare" would overly narrowly congressional powers (II, 318). Sherman's approach to national assumption of state debts was somewhat different. He was willing to "authorize" such assumption, but unwilling to specify that Congress should specifically do so (II, 327). He hoped essentially to leave this matter where it was under the Articles of Confederation (II, 356).

Sherman seconded a motion by Ellsworth designed to allow states to retain some control over their militia, in part because he did not believe states would be willing to part with such power (II, 331). He regarded the state power to call on the militia as a concurrent power, like the power of taxation, that the states should exercise in conjunction with the national government (II, 332; also see II, 386). Sherman was dead set against restricting the right of the states to appoint only lower militia officers (II, 388). He observed that the provision in the Constitution limiting Congress to appropriating money for the military for no more than two years did not prohibit it from making more frequent reports; at the same time, he indicated that he favored limiting the number of troops that could be kept during times of peace (II, 509).

Sherman opposed a provision that would have prohibited states from laying duties of tonnage for clearing harbors or erecting lighthouses. He argued that "the power of the U. States to regulate trade being supreme can controul interferences of the State regulations [when] such interferences happen; so that there is no danger to be apprehended from a concurrent jurisdiction" (II, 625).

Sherman thought it possible, however, to distinguish between treason against the United States as a whole and treason against an individual state (II, 349). Sherman opposed granting Congress power to tax exports, but it is not clear in context whether he thought that individual states should be able to exercise this power on their own (II, 361).

Sherman was a strong advocate of fiscal responsibility who favored taking away the power of states to emit, or issue, paper money. He observed that "If the consent of the Legislature could authorize emissions of it, the friends of paper money would make every exertion to get into the Legislature in order to license it" (II, 439). Sherman was willing to allow states to exercise embargo power as necessary "to prevent suffering & injury to their poor" (II, 440). He favored allowing Congress to decide when states could tax imports from neighboring states (II, 441). He did not favor the motion by Benjamin Franklin allowing Congress to cut canals; he believed that this would have local benefits and that the states should accordingly act in such cases (II, 615).

Congress

Representation

Consistent with his view that the Convention should make relatively modest changes in the Articles of Confederation, Sherman favored state legislative, rather than popular, election of members of Congress. He expressed doubts about direct democracy: "The people . . . should have as little to do as may be about the Government. They want [lack] information and are constantly liable to be misled" (I, 48). By May 31, Sherman was advocating that each state legislature should elect a single member to the U.S. Senate (I, 52), and on June 11 (in the solution eventually adopted in the Great Compromise of July 16), he suggested that states might be represented according to population in the House and equally in the Senate. Sherman was among those who argued that the small states could never accept a plan that did not give them equal representation in at least one house (I, 201).

When Pennsylvania's James Wilson argued that the Constitution should apportion Congress so as to give equal rights to all, Sherman responded that "the question is not what rights naturally belong to men; but how they may be most equally & effectually guarded in Society" (I, 450). Sherman argued that there was no more real difference between giving large and small states an equal vote than in giving an equal vote to the rich and the poor (I, 450).

Later professing to regard the slave trade as "iniquitous," Sherman felt bound to uphold the three-fifths clause as "having been Settled after much difficulty & deliberation" (II, 221). It appears, however, that Sherman tried to obscure this representation behind the formula for direct taxes:

> Mr. Sherman did not regard the admission of the Negroes into the ratio of representation, as liable to such insuperable objections. It was the freemen of the Southn. States who were in fact to be represented according to the taxes paid by

them, and the Negroes are only included in the Estimate of the taxes. (II, 223)

Later expressing disappointment with the slave trade but believing "it best to leave the matter as we find it" lest the introduction of a provision on the subject alienate some of the Southern states, Sherman observed that slavery seemed to be dying out in the United States (II, 369–370). Somewhat thereafter he observed that "it was better to let the S. States import slaves than to part with them, if they made that a sine qua non [an absolute condition for Union]" (II, 374). He added the fascinating observation that he opposed a tax on slave importation "because it implied that they were *property*" (II, 374; also see II, 416). Similarly, in opposing the fugitive slave clause, Sherman argued that he "saw no more propriety in the public seizing and surrendering a slave or servant, than a horse" (II, 443).

Sherman had an eye for details. He thus introduced the motion modifying the motion for one representative in the House for every 40,000 persons to "not exceeding" this number (II, 221).

Sherman argued that granting states equal representation in the Senate would actually increase the vigor of Congress. Sherman observed:

> If they vote by States in the 2d. branch, and each State has an equal vote, there must be always a majority of States as well as a majority of the people on the side of public measures, & the Govt. will have decision and efficacy. If this be not the case in the 2d. branch there may be a majority of the States agst. public measures, and the difficulty of compelling them to abide by the public determination, will render the Government feebler than it has ever yet been. (I, 550)

When Congress appointed a committee to come up with the initial representation in the House of Representatives, Sherman questioned how it had done so (I, 559). He was among those who supported sending the matter back to a committee with a representative from each of the states present. He served on this committee (in place of Oliver Ellsworth who was sick at the time) as well as on a later committee to discuss commercial discrimination and the Committee on Postponed Matters.

Ironically, when the committee formed to reconsider representation in the House of Representatives proposed raising the initial number of representatives from 56 to 65, Sherman said that he would have preferred a House of 50 members, believing that the travel such a position required "will make it difficult to prevail on a sufficient number of fit men to undertake the service" (I, 569). Initially opposing the requirement that Congress should have to reapportion itself at set times, Sherman observed that he "was agst. Shackling the Legislature too much. We ought to choose wise & good men, and then confide in them" (I, 578). Later in the day, however, Sherman said that arguments by Edmund Randolph and George Mason, both of Virginia, had convinced him that "the *periods* & the *rule* of revising the Representation ought to be fixt by the Constitution" (I, 582). When the Convention was discussing a proposal whereby Congress would select the U.S. treasurer, Sherman opposed a provision for a "joint" ballot in the view that it would favor the larger states (II, 314).

Selection

Sherman clearly believed that states should choose members of both the House and the Senate. On June 6, Sherman argued that proposals for popular election would effectively destroy the states (I, 133). On June 7, he supported a motion by Delaware's John Dickinson for allowing state legislatures to choose senators. He thought that this would give states an interest in supporting the general government and thus maintain "a due harmony between the two Governments" (I, 150). Later that day, he argued that state legislative selection of senators was more likely to result in the selection of "fit men" (I, 154).

Terms

On June 12, Sherman proposed that members of the House of Representatives should be elected annually (I, 214). On June 21, he indicated that he still continued to favor annual elections but could accept them biennially. The key was that "the representatives ought to return home and mix with the people. By remaining at the seat of Govt. they would acquire the habits of the place which might differ from those of their Constituents" (I, 362).

Sherman thought a term of seven years was too long for senators but supported a five-year term (I, 218). A practical man, Sherman later seconded Hugh Williamson's motion for a six-year Senate term on the basis that such a term would make rotation easier (I, 409). Sherman tied his view of term lengths to his view that governments should preserve liberties:

> Govt. is instituted for those who live under it. It ought therefore to be so constituted as not to be dangerous to their liberties. The more permanency it has the worse if it be a bad Govt. Frequent elections are necessary to preserve the good behavior of rulers. They also tend to give permanency to the Government, by preserving that good behavior, because it ensures their re-election. (I, 423)

Qualifications

When the Convention voted to require each member of the House of Representatives to be a "resident" of the state, Sherman proposed that the term "inhabitant" would be "less liable to misconstruction" (II, 216). Sherman did not believe that the United States had assured immigrants that they would enjoy equal privileges with individuals born on the continent, and he therefore saw no problem in allowing states to set requirements as to when such individuals had the right to vote (II, 270).

Origination of Money Bills

Prior to the adoption of the Connecticut Compromise, Sherman did not think it would matter whether money bills could originate in one house or the other. He observed that "as both branches must concur, there can be no danger whichever way the Senate be formed." He further opined that "We establish two branches in order to get more wisdom which is particularly needed in the finance business" (I, 234). He later considered this provision for House origination of money bills to be vital to the Compromise (II, 4).

On a related matter, Sherman wanted to tie the congressional power of laying taxes and duties to payment of debts and expenses "incurred for the common defence and general welfare" (II, 414). On this matter, he carried only his home state.

Sherman opposed supermajority requirements for navigation acts which delegates from the Southern states favored. He argued that the diversity of interests in the nation would provide security against measures directed against individual states. He further observed that the requirement that nine states give approval to key measures under the Articles of Confederation had often proved to be "embarrassing" (II, 450).

There is a story indicating that, while serving on the Committee of Style, Gouverneur Morris attempted to change the general welfare clause by setting it apart from the power to tax and spend by a semicolon rather than, as previously, by a comma. According to this story, it was Sherman who caught the change and insisted that the comma be resubstituted (Farrand 1913, 182–183). Although the story is probably apocryphal and is generally cited to highlight Morris's reputation for sharp dealing, it might just as easily point to Sherman's reputation for attention to detail.

Unicameral or Bicameral?

After the Convention decided to proceed with the discussion of the Virginia Plan over the New Jersey Plan, Sherman supported a motion by New York's John Lansing, which would simply vest the existing unicameral Congress under the Articles of Confederation with new powers. Sherman observed that "the complaints at present are not that the views of Congs. are unwise or unfaithful, but that their powers are insufficient for the execution of their views" (I, 341). Sherman repeated his view

that adding a branch elected by the people would simply lead to mischief:

> If another branch were to be added to Congs. to be chosen by the people, it would serve to embarrass. The people would not much interest themselves in the elections, a few designing men in the large districts would carry their points, and the people would have no more confidence in their new representatives than in Congs. (I, 342)

On this occasion, however, Sherman indicated that he could support a bicameral Congress as long as states were given equal representation in one house (I, 343). Reflective of his conciliating temper, on June 21 Sherman further accepted the idea of popular election of one house (I, 359).

Congressional Pay

Perhaps because he had been a cobbler, Sherman had an unusual perspective on congressional pay. At a time when others feared that Congress might abuse its power by paying too much, Sherman feared that it might pay too little and that "men ever so fit could not serve unless they were at the same time rich" (II, 291). He favored fixing a moderate allowance to be paid out of national coffers, perhaps $5 a day, and allowing states to supplement this (II, 291).

Other Issues Involving Congress

Sherman believed that members of Congress should be eligible to accept state offices (I, 386). Although he sympathized with the object behind prohibiting members from accepting other federal offices, he did not favor it (I, 388). In another context, he indicated that "the Constitution shd. lay as few temptations as possible in the way of those in power" (II, 287).

At a time when some delegates wanted to reserve control of the new government to the states that created it, Sherman believed it was important to treat new states equally with those already in the Union. Although he did not think it likely that new states would outnumber existing states in the foreseeable future, he observed that "We are providing for our posterity, for our children & our grand Children, who would be as likely to be citizens of new Western States, as of the old States. On this consideration alone, we ought to make no such discrimination" (I, 3; also see II, 454).

Sherman favored setting both the times that Congress should meet and the frequency with which it should do so. He believed that this would help avoid disputes over the subject between the two houses (II, 199). He was confident that there would be sufficient business, much of it involving the West, to require annual meetings (II, 199).

Sherman had an interesting perspective on roll-call votes in Congress. He feared that they were mischievous since "the reasons governing the voter never appear along with them" (II, 255). Sherman joined Elbridge Gerry of Massachusetts in thinking that Congress should not have to publish its proceedings when these related to treaties and military operations (II, 260). When the Convention was still anticipating allowing Congress to select the president, Sherman opposed a joint ballot on the grounds that this would take from the states the negative they were intended to have through their representation in the Senate (II, 401).

Sherman believed that the provision preventing a religious test as a condition for office was unnecessary, "the prevailing liberality being a sufficient security agst. such tests" (II, 468). However, he opposed vesting Congress with the power to adopt uniform laws on bankruptcy for fear that they might, as in England, make this offense punishable by death (II, 489).

On September 7, Sherman believed that the need for secrecy required that the Senate, rather than both houses of Congress, should ratify treaties (II, 538). The next day, Sherman suggested that some agreements should require the approval of the entire legislature (II, 548). He also did not think that the Senate should be able to approve treaties with less than a majority of its membership, but thought that a two-thirds majority could prove too "embarrassing" (II, 549).

Presidency

Selection

Sherman's initial view of the presidency was that the institution should be "nothing more than an institution for carrying the will of the Legislature into effect" (I, 65). He accordingly proposed that the person or persons occupying this position should be appointed by the legislature. He was even willing to allow Congress to decide whether the office would be singular or plural (II, 65). Somewhat later, Sherman appeared to lean in favor of a single executive, as long as an executive council supported him (I, 97). On August 15, Sherman indicated that he opposed both an absolute executive veto and an alliance between the president and the judges: "Can one man be trusted better than all the others if they all agree? This was neither wise nor safe. He disapproved of Judges meddling in politics and parties. We have gone far enough in forming the negative as it now stands" (II, 300).

On September 12, Sherman was among those who favored allowing a two-thirds, rather than a three-fourths, majority of Congress to override a presidential veto. As on previous occasions, he observed that "it was more probable that a single man should mistake or betray this sense [of the people] than the Legislature" (II, 585).

Sherman had no more faith in the popular choice of a president than in popular choice of the legislature. He observed that the people "will never be sufficiently informed of characters, and besides will never give a majority of votes to any one man" (II, 29). He further anticipated that popular election would privilege the larger states: "They will generally vote for some man in their own State, and the largest State will have the best chance for the appointment" (II, 29).

As a member of the Committee on Postponed Matters, Sherman had a role in the development and defense of the Electoral College. In defending the institution of the vice president, which emerged as part of this plan, Sherman observed that this office had been created for the person who came in second largely to keep the president independent of Congress. He did not oppose an alteration requiring that the president, like the vice president, have a majority of electoral votes (II, 499). Sherman was not troubled by the vice president's role in presiding over the Senate; indeed, he noted that without such a responsibility, "he would be without employment" (II, 537). Sherman favored the Electoral College in part because he believed that it gave due powers to both the House and the Senate (II, 512–513), and he worked to see that the proposal continued to do so (I, 522). He was influential in seeing that when the House of Representatives had to choose among the top candidates for president, it did so with each state having a single vote (II, 527).

Other Matters Pertaining to the Presidency

Sherman favored presidential re-eligibility to office (II, 33). He strongly disfavored a motion that would allow the president to serve during good behavior, that is, for life (II, 33).

Sherman identified excessive executive independence with "tyranny" (I, 68). On June 1, he indicated that he favored a three-year renewable executive term, opposing "the doctrine of rotation as throwing out of office the men best qualified to execute its duties" (I, 68). However, consistent with his view of legislative sovereignty, on the next day he further stated that he thought the Congress should have the power to remove the executive "at pleasure" (I, 84). Sherman was willing to accept the idea of a conditional, but not an absolute, veto: "we ought to avail ourselves of his [the president's] wisdom in revising the laws, but not permit him to overrule the decided and cool opinions of the Legislature" (I, 99).

Sherman wanted to limit the number of individuals that the president could appoint, especially in cases of officers in peacetime; Sherman feared that such appointments might become a source of "corruption" in the new government (II, 405). Sherman favored limiting the presidential power to grant reprieves and pardons only to such time as the Senate could concur in such measures (II, 419). He further wanted it to be clear that the president would command the militia only in cases when it was called into service of the entire nation (II, 426). Sherman opposed congressional eligibility for other offices for fear that this would "give too much influence to the Executive" in the use of his appointment power (II, 490).

Judiciary

Sherman supported a resolution by South Carolina's John Rutledge to strike the provision from the Virginia Plan providing for inferior federal courts. Sherman, who may also have feared the centralizing tendency of such courts, argued that it was too expensive to constitute federal courts when state courts could be utilized for the same purposes (I, 125). Later in the Convention, Sherman said he was willing to grant Congress the power to establish lower federal courts "but wished them to make use of the State Tribunals whenever it could be done with safety to the general interest" (II, 46). Sherman proposed on June 13 that Congress should appoint members of the U.S. Supreme Court but withdrew his motion when Madison suggested that the Constitution should vest this power exclusively in the Senate (I, 233). Sherman thought that senators were more likely than the president to spread such appointments throughout the nation (II, 41).

Sherman favored a provision that would have allowed the president to remove judges on the application of Congress. He professed to see "no contradiction of impropriety" in such a mechanism, which he believed to be similar to one in Great Britain (II, 428). Sherman did not think that it would be appropriate for members of the U.S. Supreme Court to sit in on the impeachment of the president who had appointed them (II, 551).

Miscellaneous

Sherman was among the delegates who favored Franklin's proposal that each day's proceedings at the Convention should begin with prayer (I, 452), although it seems more likely that he did so "with a devout and fervent belief in the efficacy of prayer" and not, as Franklin is generally supposed to have done, largely to engender a spirit of unity among delegates (Boyd 1932, 233). Sherman did not favor Gerry's and Mason's motion for a bill of rights. He pointed out that existing state declarations of rights would remain in effect, that it was difficult to specify some matters, like trial by jury, and that, in such cases, Congress could be trusted (II, 588). Similarly, Sherman did not think it was necessary to provide for freedom of the press under the new Constitution since "The power of Congress does not extend to the Press" (II, 618).

Sherman favored the appointment of the secretary of the Treasury by separate votes of each house of Congress (II, 614).

Amendment and Ratification

On June 5, Sherman indicated that he did not think it was necessary to ratify the Constitution in popular conventions. He favored following the provisions under the Articles of Confederation for approval by Congress and ratification by state legislatures (I, 122). On August 30, Sherman proposed that the new Constitution should not go into effect until ratified by 10 states (II, 468–469), but the next day he was openly wondering if it would be proper for it to be ratified by less than a unanimous vote (II, 475). By September 10, Sherman was willing to accept ratification by nine states but also wanted the Convention to submit the new plan to Congress (II, 561).

Sherman initiated the proposal that allowed Congress to propose constitutional amendments for state ratification (II, 558). Previously, the delegates had been considering a provision whereby Congress only had authority to propose a convention to propose amendments at the request of the states. Sherman advocated omitting the specific requirement that three-fourths of the states ratify amendments, leaving future Congresses to decide the specific majority (II, 630).

On September 15, Sherman expressed fears that three-fourths of the states might gang up on the minority to either abolish them or strip them of their equal representation in the Senate. He moved that the provision prohibiting a restriction of state importation of slaves for twenty years should be extended "to provide that no State should be affected in its internal police, or deprived of its equality in the Senate" (II, 629). He succeeded in getting the latter portion of this proposal incorporated into the Constitution, in part by moving at one point to strike out the amending process altogether (II, 630).

Life after the Convention

Sherman returned to Connecticut to advocate the ratification of the Constitution. He served as a member of the first U.S. House of Representatives and was then chosen as a U.S. senator. Initially opposed to adding a bill of rights, Sherman succeeded in seeing that these guarantees were appended to the end of the Constitution rather than integrated into the text of the document as Virginia's James Madison advocated. Sherman died in 1793.

See Also Connecticut; Connecticut Compromise

FOR FURTHER READING

Boyd, Julian. 1932. "Roger Sherman: Portrait of a Cordwainer Statesman." *The New England Quarterly* 5: 221–236.
Collier, Christopher. 1971. *Roger Sherman's Connecticut: Yankee Politics and the American Revolution.* Middleton, CT: Wesleyan University Press.
Farrand, Max. 1913. *The Framing of the Constitution of the United States.* New Haven, CT: Yale University Press.
———, ed. 1937. *The Records of the Federal Convention.* 4 vols. New Haven, CT: Yale University Press.

SIGNING OF THE CONSTITUTION

The signing of the U.S. Constitution took place in the Philadelphia State House (Independence Hall) on September 17, 1787. Of 55 delegates who had attended the Convention from May through

George Washington, delegate from Virginia, presiding at the signing of the Constitution of the United States in Philadelphia on September 17, 1787. By Christy Howard Chandler. (Library of Congress)

September, forty-one were present and Delaware's John Dickinson had left instructions for fellow delegate George Read to sign for him.

Franklin's Speech on Behalf of Unanimity

After the Constitution was read, Benjamin Franklin, speaking because of ill health through fellow Pennsylvania delegate James Wilson, gave his longest speech at the Convention. The speech was vintage Franklin, a commonsense appeal to delegates who, like himself, found that the document was not all that they hoped it would be but who believed that the new proposal would provide a better government than existed under the Articles of Confederation. Reflecting on human nature, Franklin observed that human beings tended to believe that they alone possessed the truth. He noted that the English writer Richard Steele (1672–1729), who often joined Joseph Addison (1672–1719) in writing essays, had once observed to the pope that "the only difference between our Churches in their opinions of the certainty of their doctrines is, the Church of Rome is infallible and the Church of England is never in the wrong" (Farrand 1937, II, 642).

For his part, Franklin indicated that he was going to support the Constitution, and he urged other delegates to do the same:

I agree to this Constitution with all its faults, if they are such; because I think a general Government necessary for us, and there is no form of Government but what may be a blessing to the people if well administered, and believe farther that this is likely to be well administered for a course of years, and can only end in Despotism, as other forms have done before it, when the people shall become so corrupted as to need despotic Government, being incapable of any other. (II, 642)

Initially flattering the wisdom of the assembly to which his speech was addressed, Franklin made a further observation about human nature calculated to appeal to men who understood that humans were self-interested. He noted that "when you assemble a number of men to have the advantage of their joint wisdom, you inevitably assemble with those men, all their prejudices, their passions, their errors of opinion, their local interests, and their selfish views" (II, 642). Professing to be astonished that the system under such circumstances approached "so near to perfection as it does," Franklin appealed to American nationalism by predicting that the nation's enemies "who are waiting with confidence to hear that our councils are confounded like those of the Builders of Babel; and that our States are on the point of separation" would be astonished (II, 642). Saying that "I expect no better, and . . . am not sure, that it is not the best," Franklin proceeded to ask delegates to keep their reservations to themselves, as he himself planned to do. Referring somewhat ironically to "our real or apparent unanimity," Franklin hoped that "we shall act heartily and unanimously in recommending this Constitution (if approved by Congress & confirmed by the Conventions) wherever our influence may extend, and turn our future thoughts & endeavors to the means of having it well administered" (II, 643).

Resolution Introduced

Although urging members to swallow their objections and concur unanimously, speeches on earlier days by Virginia's Edmund Randolph and George Mason as well as by Massachusetts's Elbridge Gerry made it fairly clear that however unanimity might be hoped for, it would be unlikely to be achieved. Recognizing that this was the case, Franklin introduced a resolution the authorship of which James Madison attributed to Gouverneur Morris, who hoped that Franklin's sponsorship would be more effective than his

own. It read, "Done in Convention, by the unanimous consent of *the States* present the 17th. of Septr. &c—In witness whereof we have hereunto subscribed our names" (II, 643; italics in original).

The resolution was clever in at least three ways. First, by referring to the states present, it was intended to draw attention away from Rhode Island's continuing absence from the Convention proceedings. Interestingly, although Alexander Hamilton signed the Constitution as a delegate from New York, the official journal shows no vote for that state. Because Hamilton had no authority singly to speak for a three-person delegation, the delegates did not consider the state to be "present." Second, by referring to *state* unanimity, the resolution was designed to obscure the decisions of any individuals (so long as they remained a minority within a state delegation) who decided not to sign. Third, the provision was so worded that those who signed could, if they so chose, claim that their signatures did not represent approval of the document as such but simply attested to the unanimity of the state votes at the Convention.

Last-Minute Adjustment

This motion was temporarily interrupted by a last-minute proposal for a change in the ratio of congressional representation from a maximum of one delegate for every 40,000 voters to a maximum of one for every 30,000. This change is most notable for the fact that it occurred after the document had already been engrossed and because it represents the only recorded occasion during the Convention when George Washington publicly expressed his sentiments on behalf of a proposed change (he had previously given a short acceptance speech upon being chosen as president of the Convention). Madison records that, after the delegates agreed to this change: "On the question to agree to the Constitution enrolled in order to be signed. It was agreed to all the States answering ay" (II, 644). The Convention secretary simply recorded, "The Constitution unanimously agreed to" (II, 641).

Further Interchange among the Delegates

Edmund Randolph then reiterated a point that he had made earlier in the Convention. His failure to sign the Constitution at the Convention, he said, would not—as indeed it did not—preclude him from later supporting it at the state level if, as he doubted, nine states would be so willing to ratify. Gouverneur Morris, now attempting to take full advantage of the resolution he had putatively authored, rose to state his belief that the document was the best that could be obtained and that "the signing in the form proposed related only to the fact that the *States* present were unanimous" (II, 645). Although North Carolina's Hugh Williamson "had no scruples against putting his name to it" (II, 645), he suggested that perhaps the signing should be on an attached letter, presumably putting still further distance between signing and approving the document. Acknowledging that "no man's ideas were more remote from the plan than his own were known to be" (II, 645–646), Alexander Hamilton feared that a few holdouts may "do infinite mischief by kindling the latent sparks which lurk under an enthusiasm in favor of the Convention which may soon subside" (II, 645). North Carolina's William Blount, who had been relatively silent during most of the proceedings and might therefore have reflected the views of others who did not speak out very much, indicated that the form of the Franklin-Morris proposal appealed to him, allowing him to sign not "so as to pledge himself in support of the plan," but simply to "attest the fact that the plan was the unanimous act of the States in Convention."

Franklin's earlier words had clearly stung at least Randolph and, as he would soon indicate, Gerry, so Franklin arose to assure the former that he admired him for introducing the Virginia Plan and that he had not directed his words specifically at him. Randolph then took to the floor to observe that the form of the resolution had not eased his dilemma, that he "could not but regard the signing in the proposed form, as the same with signing the Constitution" and that "the change of form therefore could make no difference with him." He recognized that "in refusing to sign the Constitution, he took a step which might be the most awful of his life, but it was dictated by his conscience, and it was not possible for him to hesitate, much less to change" (II, 646).

Further indicating the intense peer pressure that the nonsigners must have felt in the company of men of the stature of George Washington, James Madison, James Wilson, and Gouverneur Morris, Gerry followed with protestations of his own "painful feelings" and "embarrassment" at not signing but feared debates over the document could lead to civil war in Massachusetts. He said that "the proposed form made no difference with him" but that "if it were not otherwise apparent, the refusals to sign should never be known from him" (II, 647). General Pinckney of South Carolina wryly observed that "we are not likely to gain many converts by the ambiguity of the proposed form of signing," but, should there be any doubt in his own case, "he should sign the Constitution with a view to support it with all his influence, and wished to pledge himself accordingly" (II, 647).

The proceedings now took a strange turn. Franklin, who had begun with such an eloquent speech as to why he was lending his support to the Constitution even with its putative faults and encouraging others to do so, now seemed to accept the idea that had been vaguely planted in his earlier speech that the signatures in fact constituted nothing more than recognition of unanimous state approval. He thus observed that "It is too soon to pledge ourselves before Congress and our Constituents shall have approved the plan." Jared Ingersoll of Pennsylvania, whose voice, like Blount's, had been relatively quiet during the Convention proceedings, added yet another interpretation to the act of signing—for him it neither simply attested to state unanimity nor required the signers "to support the Constitution at all event" but served "as a recommendation, of what, all things considered, was the most eligible" (II, 647) .

The Signing

A vote then followed on the Franklin-Morris motion, with the vote recording the state of the four-person delegation from South Carolina divided on the issue but the other 10 states (again excluding New York with no majority present and Rhode Island with no delegates) still unanimous. After deciding to entrust the Convention journals to George Washington, all delegates present except for Randolph, Mason, and Gerry signed as did William Jackson, the Convention secretary (with George Read of Delaware signing not only for himself but also for John Dickinson, who had requested that he sign for him in his absence).

As John Hancock had done in signing the Declaration of Independence, Washington apparently signed first—as president of the Convention rather than as a representative from Virginia. His signature appeared under the words "In Witness" and began toward the right-hand side of the last page. States were listed from New Hampshire in the North (or the East, as the delegates would have said) to Georgia in the South. With eight signatures, Pennsylvania had the most signatures; Hamilton's was the solitary signature from New York, and, of course, the state of Rhode Island was not recorded.

By the time the delegates from New Hampshire through Pennsylvania had signed the document, the signatures reached the end of the page. Signatures from delegates from Delaware and from Georgia are thus recorded in another column to the left. Secretary Jackson wrote his signature (presumably the last since it was attesting to the others) to the left of these (Wright and MacGregor 1987, 38–39, 42).

The Rising Sun

During this event, the elderly Franklin pointed to the back of the president's magnificent Chippendale chair on the back of which a rising sun was painted. He noted that artists found it difficult to distinguish between a rising and a setting sun. Professing that "the vicissitudes" of his "hopes and fears" during the Convention had often led him to wonder, he professed that he now had "the happiness to know that it is a rising and not a setting sun" (II, 648).

It is interesting to speculate as to whether some delegates signed the Constitution under cover of

the Franklin-Morris resolution who might not otherwise have done so. Only Mason, Randolph, and Gerry had previously indicated that they did not plan to sign, and the resolution did not bring any of them aboard. However, if his words are taken at face value, it appears as though Blount signed merely to attest to the unanimity of the states on the subject, and that Ingersoll did not necessarily consider his vote at the Convention to bind him later on the subject. Other delegates, who did not speak on the seventeenth, might have signed with similar understandings. Unless one credits Franklin's second explanation of his vote, however, the others who spoke all appear to have regarded the document as the best that was likely to emerge from the Convention proceedings and would probably therefore have voted to sign no matter how the resolution was worded.

In his notes of the last day, Maryland's James McHenry may have reflected common sentiments. He offered three reasons for signing. The first reflected his deference to "the opinion of a majority of gentlemen whose abilities and patriotism are of the first cast." Second, he placed confidence in the new Constitution's constitutional amending process to remedy perceived defects. Finally, McHenry engaged in what economists might call cost-benefit analysis by contrasting "the inconveniencies," "the evils" and "the little good" to be expected from the Articles of Confederation "with the public evils and probable benefits and advantages promised us by the new system" (II, 649–650).

Constitution Week

As individuals who have attempted to commemorate various constitutional anniversaries have found, there are a variety of dates that can be selected for this purpose. These include the ratification of the Constitution by the ninth state (New Hampshire) on June 21, 1788; the convening of the first Congress on March 4, 1789; the inauguration of the first president on April 30, 1789; and the ratification of the Bill of Rights on December 15, 1791, by Virginia, which provided the requisite number for it to go into effect. In 1952, Congress decided to designate September 17 as Citizenship Day, to commemorate the signing of the Constitution. The Daughters of the American Revolution subsequently proposed in 1955 that this observance should extend for an entire week beginning with September 17. A congressional resolution accepted this proposal on August 2, 1955, and designated the week beginning with September 17 as Constitution Week (*Constitution Week*, 1).

Postscript

During the bicentennial celebrations of the U.S. Constitution, individual citizens who visited Independence Hall were given the opportunity to add their signatures to a long paper roll attesting to their continuing support for the Constitution. Reflections on this experience, and the challenge of signing a document that originally made no provision for the elimination of slavery or for other modern democratic reforms, served in part as the basis of reflections of a contemporary law professor, Sanford Levinson. His title *A Constitutional Faith* arguably captured the mix of reason and emotion by which thoughtful citizens from the Constitutional Convention to the present continue to view the document. Levinson, who signed the document in 1987, decided that he could no longer do so when presented with a similar opportunity at the opening of the U.S. Constitution Center in 2003; he is particularly concerned that the amending process provided in the document is inadequate. The author of this encyclopedia has addressed Levinson's concerns in two articles that appeared in October 2003 (Vile 2003).

See Also Commemorations of the Constitutional Convention; Franklin, Benjamin; Resolution Accompanying the Constitution; Rising Sun; September 17, 1787

FOR FURTHER READING

Constitution Week, September 17–23: An American Legacy. Washington, DC: Commission on the Bicentennial of the United States Constitution.

Farrand, Max, ed. 1937. *The Records of the Federal Convention.* 4 vols. New Haven, CT: Yale University Press.

Levinson, Sanford. 1988. *A Constitutional Faith.* Princeton, NJ: Princeton University Press.

——. 2003. "Why I Did Not Sign the Constitution: With a Chance to Endorse It, I Had to Decline." http://www.constitutioncenter.org/explore/Viewpoints/WhyIDidNotSigntheConstitution.shtml.

Vile, John R. 2003. "A Republic Established on Arguments and Interests: Why I Think the Constitution Is Still Worthy of Signing." October 28. http://writ.news.findlaw.com/scripts/printer_friendly.pl?page=commentary/20031028_vile.

——. 2003. "Contemporary Constitutional Scholar Missing from Signer's Hall." Posted on National Constitution Website. October 30. http://www.constitutioncenter.org/explore/Viewpoints?ContemporaryConstitutionalScholarM.

Wright, Robert K., Jr., and Morris J. MacGregor, Jr. 1987. *Soldier-Statesmen of the Constitution.* Washington, DC: Center of Military History.

SIZE OF THE CONVENTION

Altogether 78 men from 12 of the 13 states were elected to, and 55 ultimately attended, the Constitutional Convention. Some arrived late and others departed early, probably making for an average attendance of from 30 to forty individuals. Forty-two delegates (one by proxy) were in attendance on September 17, and 39 of these signed on this date.

The total number of delegates who attended the Convention was close to the number allocated for the first House of Representatives (65). The size of the initial Senate (36), which the Founders designed to be a more cautious and deliberative body, came close to the average daily attendance at the Convention. At key points in the Convention, the delegates assigned critical matters to committees, which never had more than one delegate from each state present.

In comparing the recent meeting of Europe's constitutional convention, which began in March of 2002, to the U.S. Constitutional Convention, Paul Robinson noted that, with some 200 members, the European convention was a much larger body. He observed that the atmosphere created was "neither particularly businesslike nor conducive to rigorous debate." He further observed that "Speakers have only three minutes to say what they want, and, as one delegate told me, 'Everyone just makes their speech and there's no dialogue'" (2003, 14).

Students of group dynamics might find that the size of the Convention was a key factor in its success. The rules adopted by the delegates further emphasized the need for rational deliberation and compromise.

See Also Committees at the Constitutional Convention; Congress, House of Representatives, Size; Delegates, Collective Profile; Delegates Who Did Not Attend the Constitutional Convention; Rules of the Constitutional Convention

FOR FURTHER READING

Robinson, Paul. 2003. "A Dodgy Constitution: Paul Robinson on Why Europe's Constitutional Convention Is a Bureaucrat's Dream–Unlike the Philadelphia Convention of 1787." *Spectator* 291 (February 8): 14–15.

SLAVE IMPORTATION

However it advanced human rights for white Americans, the Constitution did not immediately advance such rights for African Americans, who remained in slavery in those states that permitted the institution to exist. States from the Deep South were interested not only in perpetuating the institution of slavery but in continuing slave importation so that the price of slaves would not become prohibitive.

Committee of Detail

On July 23, General Charles Cotesworth Pinckney of South Carolina reminded the Convention that the Southern states thought it essential that there be some security against slave emancipation and against taxation of exports (Farrand 1937, II, 95). Reacting to such sentiments, the draft of the Constitution that the Committee of Detail reported to the Convention on August 6 contained a prohibition on export taxes, a prohibition on interfering with the "migration or importation of such persons as the several States shall think proper to admit," and a guarantee that such importation should not be prohibited (II, 183).

Debates over Slave Importation

During discussion of the three-fifths compromise (providing that slaves would be counted as three-fifths of a person for purposes of representation and direct taxation) on July 23, Rufus King of Massachusetts described how the admission of slaves into the formula for representation was "a most grating circumstance to his mind." He had accepted it in the hope that the general government would be strengthened, but this hope had been dimmed by the provisions related to slave importation and the taxation of exports. He questioned the reasonableness of allowing for adding to the number of slaves, who would increase the need for defending the South, while also withholding "the compensation for the burden" (II, 220). King thought that "there was so much inequality & unreasonableness in all this, that the people of the N[orthern] States could never be reconciled [to it]" (II, 220). Connecticut's conciliatory Roger Sherman agreed to the iniquity of the slave trade but thought the three-fifths compromise had been arrived at only "after much difficulty & deliberation" and did not want to upset it (II, 221). The Convention accordingly went on to other business.

Discussion resumed on August 21. This time Maryland's Luther Martin proposed to allow for either "a prohibition or tax on the importation of slaves" (II, 364). He made three arguments: by rewarding states with additional representation, the three-fifths clause would encourage further importation; slaves weakened the Union by raising the costs of defense; and slavery was "inconsistent with the principles of the revolution and dishonorable to the American character" (II, 364). South Carolina's John Rutledge responded that the three-fifths clause would encourage further importation, that there was nothing to fear from slave uprisings (he offered to exempt the North from protecting the South against them), and that "interest alone" rather than "religion & humanity" should govern policy on this matter (II, 364). Slavery would benefit the North because the products of slave labor would increase the export trade of their ships. Oliver Ellsworth of Connecticut agreed that "What enriches a part enriches the whole," and observed that the Articles of Confederation had not sought to regulate the slave trade, and neither should the new government (II, 364). Charles Pinckney of South Carolina said that South Carolina could never approve a plan that limited the slave trade, although he suggested that, if left on its own, South Carolina might follow the states of Maryland and Virginia and itself prohibit such trade.

Discussion resumed the following day. Sherman echoed Ellsworth's earlier arguments. States possessed the right to import slaves under the Articles of Confederation, and it was "best to leave the matter as we find it" (II, 369). He also anticipated that the movement for abolition of slavery would continue. Virginia's George Mason then joined the most righteous sounding of the Northern representatives, blaming the origin of the slave traffic on "the avarice of British Merchants," and pointing to a host of evils connected to the institution including that of making every master into "a petty tyrant" (I, 370). Ellsworth, who may have felt the need to defend Eastern shippers and who may further have been put off by what he apparently perceived to be the hypocrisy of a slaveholder condemning slavery, observed that "As he had never owned a slave," he "could not judge of the effects of slavery on character," but, if morality were to govern, not only should slave imports cease, but all slaves should be freed. He further observed that Maryland and Virginia had not stopped slave importation out of moral conviction but because they found it cheaper to raise them than to import them (II, 370–371). If his ar-

gument was bitter and personal, he was nonetheless for leaving things as they were. He too anticipated the eventual end of slavery:

> Slavery in time will not be a speck in our Country. Provision is already made in Connecticut for abolishing it. And the abolition has already taken place in Massachusetts. As to the danger of insurrection from foreign influence, that will become a motive to kind treatment of the slaves. (II, 371)

Both Pinckneys affirmed that their state would see any restriction on the slave trade as a serious obstacle to ratifying the Constitution. Georgia's Abraham Baldwin said that Georgia had the same opinion although it would probably put a stop to the trade on its own.

Pennsylvania's James Wilson observed that if Georgia and South Carolina were in fact contemplating abolition of the slave trade, they should hardly oppose giving it up. Elbridge Gerry of Massachusetts wanted to leave states on their own in regard to slavery but did not want to give it "any sanction." Delaware's John Dickinson thought it was "inadmissible on every principle of honor & safety that the importation of slaves should be authorized to the States by the Constitution" (II, 372). North Carolina's Hugh Williamson observed that his state did not prohibit importation but imposed an import fee. King thought it unfair to leave slaves as the only import fee exemption. New Hamphire's John Langdon wanted to give Congress power to regulate the slave trade, and Pinckney, somewhat backtracking on assurances that other Southern delegates had made, expressed doubts that South Carolina would put a permanent end to slave importations in the near future but expressed his willingness for slaves to be subject to the same tax as other imports.

The Committee of Eleven

Rutledge joined Pinckney in recommending committing the issue to a committee. Gouverneur Morris wanted all issues concerning navigation to go to the committee in hopes that the Northern and Southern states might work out a bargain. Butler said that taxing exports could never be part of such a bargain, and Sherman opposed an import tax on slaves on the basis that "it implied they were *property*" (II, 374). After continued discussion, the delegates committed the slave importation provision and the issue of navigation to a Committee of Eleven.

This committee reported back to the Convention on August 24. It proposed to allow for continuing slave importation until the year 1800, specified that such imports could be taxed at the same average rate as other imports, provided that capitation taxes would be apportioned according to the census, and suggested striking the provision that would have required two-thirds majorities of Congress for passing navigation acts.

Discussion of the Committee Report

The Convention discussed this proposal the following day. General Pinckney proposed, and Gorham seconded, a motion to replace the 1800 date with 1808. Madison feared that "twenty years will produce all the mischief that can be apprehended from the liberty to import slaves" and argued that this term "will be more dishonorable to the National character than to say nothing about it in the Constitution" (II, 415). Nonetheless, the Convention voted 7-4 for the change, with New Jersey, Pennsylvania, Delaware, and Virginia in dissent. Gouverneur Morris favored using the term "slaves" rather than "such other persons," and, apparently somewhat facetiously, proposed that the provision should specify that importation could take place in North Carolina, South Carolina, and Georgia, so that it would be clear "that this part of the Constitution was a compliance with those States" (II, 415). A number of delegates seemed willing to allow for the explicit reference to "slaves," but Morris withdrew his motion, and the Convention agreed to the compromise allowing importation until 1808 with average duties.

Sherman, later supported by Madison, feared

that this acknowledged "men to be property," while others said that this was part of the compromise. Gorham suggested that the duty could be given a more positive interpretation, namely, as a discouragement to their importation, and after some more wrangling the Convention agreed to a maximum tax of $10 "for each person," perhaps thus attempting to give some distinction between slaves and other property (II, 417). The importance of the provision allowing for the continuing importation of slaves for twenty years was indicated by the fact that the delegates entrenched it in the Article V amending clause, like the states' equal representation in the U.S. Senate, against further amendment.

Assessment of the Issue

The slave importation clause largely represented the triumph of temporary regional interests, specifically those of the Carolinas and Georgia, over both principle and the nation's long-term well-being. Although imported slaves were to be taxed along with other goods, they were officially classified as "persons." The Convention's use of a verbal circumlocution ("such other persons") indicated the delegates' continuing discomfort with the institution, but their willingness to compromise indicates that a majority probably thought concessions were necessary if the states of the Deep South were to be kept within the Union.

See Also African Americans; Committee on Slave Trade and Navigation; Slavery; Three-fifths Clause

FOR FURTHER READING

Berns, Walter. 1968. "The Constitution and the Migration of Slaves." *Yale Law Journal* 78 (December): 198–228.

Farrand, Max, ed. 1937. *The Records of the Federal Convention*. 4 vols. New Haven, CT: Yale University Press.

Freehling, William W. "The Founding Fathers and Slavery." *American Historical Review* 77 (February): 81–93.

SLAVERY

The most striking failure of the Constitutional Convention was arguably its failure to eliminate the institution of slavery. This is not altogether surprising since the Convention had not been called to deal with this issue but with the perceived weaknesses of the existing government under the Articles of Confederation. It is still tragic that the Framers, or some subsequent deliberative body, were unable to formulate a solution to a problem that would eventually be settled by force of arms.

The Slave Legacy

Slavery in America was almost exclusively linked to Africans who had been captured, purchased, and brought to the New World against their will and whose children were also considered to be slaves. The institution was in obvious tension with the affirmations within the Declaration of Independence that "all men are created equal" and that all were entitled to the rights of "life, liberty, and the pursuit of happiness." The writers of the Constitution followed the example of the Articles of Confederation by referring to slaves through euphemisms like "such other persons," rather than by name. Abraham Lincoln would later observe that slavery "is hid away in the constitution just as an afflicted man hides away a wen [cyst] or cancer which he dares not cut out at once, lest he bleed to death" (Kammen 1987, 102).

Constitutional Provisions Related to Slavery

The essay in this volume titled "African Americans" details five distinct constitutional provisions that deal with slavery. These include provisions counting slaves as three-fifths of a person for purposes of representation in the House of Representatives; providing for use of a similar ratio in designating direct taxes; permitting slave importation for an additional twenty years; en-

Notice announcing the sale of slaves, 1780s
(Library of Congress)

trenching the provisions related to slave taxation, representation and importation against further amendment; and the so-called fugitive slave clause, obligating free states to permit the return of fugitives from the states from which they escaped (Finkelman 1996). A number of these provisions demonstrated the difficulty of deciding whether slaves were to be classified primarily as persons or as property.

Delegates' Sentiments on Slavery

Seventeen to 19 delegates to the Convention had title to slaves. Those who owned them were more likely to regard the issue of slavery as a purely state matter. Significantly, however, Gouverneur Morris of Pennsylvania, who owned no slaves, and Virginia's George Mason, who probably held more than any other member, delivered the two most impassioned speeches against slavery. On August 8, Morris indicated that he considered slavery to be "a nefarious institution," the "curse of heaven on the States where it prevailed" (Farrand 1937, II, 221). Unfavorably comparing the states where slavery flourished to those where it did not, Morris tied opposition to the institution not only to the deleterious effect that he thought it had on the cultural and economic life of the two regions but on considerations of humanity:

> The admission of slaves into Representation when fairly explained comes to this: that the inhabitant of Georgia and S.C. who goes to the Coast of Africa and in defiance of the most sacred laws of humanity tears away his fellow creatures from their dearest connections & dam[n]s them to the most cruel bondages, shall have more votes in a Govt. instituted for the protection of the rights of mankind, than the Citizen of Pa or N. Jersey who views with a laudable horror, so nefarious a practice. (II, 222)

In a suggestion that no other delegate appears to have taken seriously but which might have represented a lost opportunity for enlightened statesmanship, Morris said that "He would sooner submit himself to a tax for paying for all the Negroes in the U. States than saddle posterity with such a Constitution" (II, 223).

Almost as though he were not to be outdone, George Mason launched into his own attack on slavery on August 22. Like Morris, Mason thought the institution of slavery degraded society and was immoral:

> Slavery discourages arts & manufacturers. The poor despise labor when performed by slaves. They prevent the immigration of Whites, who really enrich & strengthen a Country. They produce a most pernicious effect on manners. Every master of slaves is born a petty tyrant. They bring the judgment of heaven on a Country. As nations can not be rewarded or punished in the next world they must be in this. By an inevitable chain of causes & effects providence punishes national sins, by national calamities. (II, 370)

As passionate as was Mason's attack, neither he nor other delegates proposed eliminating slavery. Prominent Southerners of the day generally considered the institution of slavery to be a necessary evil.

Further Developments

Essentially, then, the delegates to the Convention left slavery where they found it. The subject was frequently discussed, but did not dominate state ratification debates (Kaminski 1995; Morgan 2001). The hopes of some delegates that slavery might be in the process of gradual extinction initially proved to be chimerical as the institution continued to flourish in the South and was furthered by the invention of the cotton gin. Over time, Northern opinion, stirred by abolitionists, hardened against slavery. Southerners in turn became increasingly defensive, and, in time, prominent Southern spokesmen argued that slavery was not only a necessary evil but actually a positive good; they reasoned that since blacks were inferior, they actually benefited from being enslaved and having their masters meet their needs.

It took the Civil War (1861–1865), which Lincoln initially waged chiefly to preserve the Union, to bring an end to slavery–Lincoln justified the Emancipation Proclamation as a war measure, and it applied only behind Confederate lines. The new national policy toward slavery was incorporated into three constitutional amendments. The Thirteenth Amendment (ratified in 1865) eliminated involuntary servitude except as a punishment for crime. The Fourteenth Amendment (1868) overturned the notorious *Dred Scott* decision of 1857 by declaring that all persons born or naturalized in the United States were citizens and were entitled to certain basic rights. At least on paper, the Fifteenth Amendment (1870) prohibited individuals from being denied the right to vote on the basis of race, but states adopted numerous means of restricting such voting well into the second half of the twentieth century. Scholars continue to debate whether the Framers, working within the political restraints of their day and faced with the possibility that states from the Deep South might fail to ratify the Constitution, could realistically have done more to bring an end to this nefarious institution.

See Also Congress, House of Representatives, Representation in; Declaration of Independence;

Fugitive Slave Clause; Slave Importation; Three-fifths Clause

FOR FURTHER READING

Dellinger, Walter E., III. 1987–1988. "1787: The Constitution and 'The Curse of Heaven.'" *William and Mary Law Review* 19: 145–161.

Farrand, Max, ed. 1937. *The Records of the Federal Convention.* 4 vols. New Haven, CT: Yale University Press.

Finkelman, Paul. 1996. *Slavery and the Founders: Race and Liberty in the Age of Jefferson.* Armonk, NY: M. E. Sharpe.

Freehling, William W. 1972. "The Founding Fathers and Slavery." *American Historical Review* 77 (February): 81–93.

Kaminski, John P., ed. 1995. *A Necessary Evil? Slavery and the Debates over the Constitution.* Madison, WI: Madison House.

Kammen, Michael. 1987. *A Machine That Would Go of Itself: The Constitution in American Culture.* New York: Alfred A. Knopf.

Morgan, Kenneth. 2001. "Slavery and the Debate over Ratification of the United States Constitution." *Slavery and Abolition* 22 (December): 40–65.

Walker, Juliet E. E. 1989. "Whither Liberty, Equality or Legality? Slavery, Race, Property and the 1787 American Constitution." *New York Law School Journal of Human Rights* 6 (1989): 299–352.

West, Thomas G. 1997. *Vindicating the Founders: Race, Sex, Class, and Justice in the Origins of America.* Lanham, MD: Rowman and Littlefield Publishers.

SOCIAL CONTRACT

One of the dominant themes of the American Revolutionary and Constitution-building period was that of a social contract. This theme had emerged from the thought of Thomas Hobbes (1588–1679) and John Locke (1632–1704), two English philosophers, associated with classical liberalism, who had sought to understand government by imagining what individuals would be like in a prepolitical "state of nature." The French philosopher Jean-Jacques Rousseau (1712–1778) also used the idea of a social contract as an organizing principle.

Although Hobbes's description was starker than that of Locke, both philosophers agreed that individuals in such a state would be equal. Such a stateless state would have many inconveniences. Without an individual to judge controversies between and among individuals, life, liberty, and property would all be insecure. Both philosophers therefore surmised that individuals in such a state of nature would seek to form a social contract by which they could secure these.

In arguments that had proved to be useful in the colonies during the Revolutionary War, Locke had further argued that since government was designed to secure personal safety, liberty, and happiness, when it failed to do so, the people had the right to overthrow this government and to institute new ones. Whatever other streams of thought from which it drew, this philosophy was at the heart of the Declaration of Independence.

Virginia's James Madison argued that "the idea of a compact among those who are parties to a Govt. is a fundamental principle of free Govt." (Letter to Nicholas P. Trist dated February 15, 1830, quoted in Pestritto and West 2003, 1). Delegates mentioned the idea of a social compact on a number of occasions during the Constitutional Convention.

On May 31, Madison questioned the idea of using force against states. The Virginia Plan had introduced such a provision just two days before. Madison observed that use of such force "would probably be considered by the party attacked as a dissolution of all previous compacts by which it might be bound" (Farrand 1937, I, 54).

The Articles of Confederation complicated the idea of a social compact by bringing into question whether individuals or states were the primary parties to such a contract—an issue of ultimate power, or sovereignty, that remained ambiguous under the new Constitution and eventually led to the Civil War. In introducing the New Jersey Plan on June 16, William Paterson thus observed that "a federal compact already exists," and he found equal state sovereignty to be the basis of this contract (I, 250). On June 19, Madison used the social contract analogy to suggest that the existing contract had been breeched:

> If we consider the federal union as analogous to the fundamental compact by which individuals compose one Society, and which must in its theoretic origin at least, have been the unanimous act of the component members, it cannot be said that no dissolution of the compact can be effected without unanimous consent. A breach of the fundamental principles of the compact by a part of the Society would certainly absolve the other part from their obligation to it. If the breach of *any* article by *any* of the parties, does not set the others at liberty, it is because, the contrary is *implied* in the compact itself, and particularly by that law of it, which gives an indefinite authority to the majority to bind the whole in all cases. This latter circumstance shews that we are not to consider the federal Union as analogous to the social compact of individuals, for if it were so, a Majority would have a right to bind the rest, and even to form a new Constitution for the whole, which the Gentn. from N. Jersey would be among the last to admit. (I, 314–315)

Madison continued:

> If we consider the federal union as analogous not to the social compacts among individual men: but to the conventions among individual States, What is the doctrine resulting from these conventions? Clearly, according to the Expositors of the law of Nations, that a breach of any one article, by any one party, leaves all the other parties at liberty, to consider the whole convention as dissolved, unless they choose rather to compel the delinquent party to repair the breach. (I, 315)

That same day, Luther Martin of Massachusetts argued that the Revolutionary War had "placed the 13 States in a state of nature towards each other," but that the Articles of Confederation had replaced that state and put each state on an equal footing. Pennsylvania's James Wilson questioned the idea "that when the Colonies became independent of G. Britain, they became independent also of each other" (I, 324). He thought "that they were independent, not *Individually* but *Unitedly* and that they were confederated as they were independent, States" (I, 324; also see III, 166). New York's Alexander Hamilton then joined the fray, saying that "He denied the doctrine that the States were thrown into a State of nature. He was not yet prepared to admit the doctrine that the Confederacy, could be dissolved by partial infractions of it. He admitted that the States met now on an equal footing but could see no inference from that against concerting a change of the system in this particular" (II, 324–325). Similarly, the next day, Connecticut's Oliver Ellsworth mused that it was "dangerous not to consider the Confederation as still subsisting" (I, 335).

Discussion of the state of nature resumed on June 27, when Martin observed that "to resort to the Citizens at large for their sanction to a new Governt. will be throwing them back into a State of Nature" (I, 437). Luther continued to link states, rather than individuals, to the state of nature: "tho' the States may give up this right of sovereignty, yet they had not, and ought not: that the States like individuals were in a State of nature equally sovereign & free" (I, 437). The next day, Connecticut's Roger Sherman, one of the authors of the Connecticut Compromise which resolved the issue of representation between advocates of the large states and the small ones, observed that "the question is not what rights naturally belong to men; but how they may be most equally & effectually guarded in Society" (I, 450).

Analogies to the social contract continued when, on July 23, James Madison recommended that special conventions called in the states should ratify the proposed Constitution. He observed that some states might have granted their legislatures the power "to concur in alterations of the federal Compact. But there were certainly some which had not; and in the case of these, a ratification must of necessity be obtained from the people" (II, 93). He observed that "the difference between a system founded on the Legislatures only, and one founded on the people, to be the true difference between a *league* or *treaty*, and a *Constitution*" (II, 93). He further observed: "The doctrine laid down by the law of Nations in the case of treaties is that a breach of any one article by any of the parties, frees the other parties from their engagements. In the case of a union of people under one Constitution, the nature of the pact has always been understood to exclude such an interpretation" (II, 93).

With all these references at the Convention to the social contract, it is interesting to see that James Wilson denied at the Pennsylvania ratifying convention that the members of the Convention thought they were forming a compact (III, 166). Wilson said:

> I cannot answer for what every member thought; but I believe it cannot be said that they thought they were making a contract, because I cannot discover the least trace of a compact in that system. There can be no compact unless there are more parties than one. It is a new doctrine that one can make a contract with himself. "The convention were forming compacts." With whom? I know no bargains that were made there. I am unable to conceive who the parties could be. The State governments made a bargain with one another; that is the doctrine that is endeavored to be established by gentlemen in opposition; their State sovereignties wish to be represented! But far other were the ideas of this convention, and far other are those conveyed in the system itself. (III, 166)

It is not altogether clear whether Wilson was attempting to indicate, consistent with the view he had expressed at the Convention, that Americans were already bound by a social compact and thus were not in a state or nature vis-à-vis one another or whether he was denying that the actions of the Convention were efficacious without further ratification by constitutional conventions called within the states. Whatever his view, it seems clear that the idea of the social contract was prominent in the writing of both the Declaration of Independence and of the U.S. Constitution.

Contracts are typically interpreted fairly strictly. Those who understand the Constitution as such a contract may be more inclined to interpret this document fairly strictly when the meanings of the words of a particular provision are widely understood to have been relatively fixed (see Schauer 1987).

See Also Declaration of Independence; Liberalism; Locke, John; Natural Rights; Ratification in the States; Sovereignty

FOR FURTHER READING

Farrand, Max, ed. 1937. *The Records of the Federal Convention.* 4 vols. New Haven, CT: Yale University Press.
Locke, John. 1955. *Of Civil Government: Second Treatise.* Chicago: Henry Regnery.
Pestritto, Ronald J., and Thomas G. West, eds. 2003. *The American Founding and the Social Compact.* Lanham, MD: Lexington Books.
Schauer, Frederick. 1987. "1787: The Constitution in Perspective: 'We Do Ordain and Establish': The Constitution as Literary Text: The Constitution as Text and Rule." *William and Mary Law Review* 29 (Fall): 41–51.
Tate, Thad W. "The Social Contract in America, 1774–1787: Revolutionary Theory as a Conservative Instrument." *William and Mary Quarterly,* 3rd ser. 22 (July): 375–391.

SOCIETY OF THE CINCINNATI

On the day that the Constitutional Convention had been scheduled to begin, George Washington dined with the Society of the Cincinnati. Interestingly, one of the reasons he had originally given for not wanting to attend the Constitutional Convention was that he had told the Society (which was receiving some criticism from republican-minded citizens) that he would not be attending their meeting, and he did not want to be in Philadelphia at the same time. Correspondence from Major George Turner of South Carolina, the secretary of the meeting of the Cincinnati in Philadelphia, indicated that he feared that Washington's "extreme Prudence and Circumspection (having himself much Fame to lose) may cool our laudable and necessary Ebullition with a few

Circa 400 B.C., Roman stateman and soldier Lucius Quinctus Cincinnatus is informed of his new post as dictator of Rome, whilst ploughing on his small farm. Engraving by N. Thomas, after S. D. Mirys, 1785. (Hulton Archive/Getty Images)

drops, if not a Torrent of cold water" (cited in Hutson 1987, 9).

Description

Described by a twentieth-century historian as "the first American patriotic order" and as "the precursor of all subsequent veterans' and hereditary associations" (Davies 1948, 3), the Society was founded in 1783 just before the disbanding of the Continental Army by officers who named the Society after the Roman farmer (to whom George Washington was frequently compared) who had come to the military aid of his country and then returned to his farm. One writer has traced the origins of the Society to a remark by Henry Knox, a future leader in the Society, in 1776 when he

told John Adams that he desired some token of his military service—a "ribbon to wear in his hat or his button-hole, to be transmitted to his descendants as a badge and a proof that he had fought in defense of their liberties" (quoted in Kaplan 1952, 34). Each officer contributed a month's pay into a charitable fund. Membership was to be hereditary, with the privilege passing to firstborn sons and with the possibility of honorary members.

Chapters were established among Revolutionary veterans in France as well as in all 13 American states. The Pennsylvania Chapter was founded at the City Tavern in Philadelphia in 1783. The former Northwest Dining Room on the second floor of that establishment was named the Cincinnati Room after this group helped refurbish it (Staib 1999, 17).

Opposition

A study of reactions to the formation of the Society in New England indicates that it prompted a great deal of suspicion and opposition. Initial excitement was stimulated by the congressional decisions first to grant Revolutionary War officers half pay for life and by a subsequent decision to substitute five years of pay in governmental interest-bearing securities (Davies, 4). Further concerns centered on "distrust of the officers as a class," concerns over the Society's badge (a gold eagle medallion to be hung by a blue and white ribbon), and concerns over "the hereditary features and the honorary membership" (Davies, 7). These aspects of the Society appeared to conflict with republicanism, which stressed ideas of equality and individual (as opposed to inherited) merit, and to favor aristocracy, which most of the delegates to the Convention opposed. Interestingly, criticism of the Society found its way overseas, stimulating a number of critical writings in France (Palmer 1959, 270–271).

Convention References to Society

Eleven delegates who signed the Constitution, and seven who did not, were Society members. Signing members included Abraham Baldwin, David Brearly, Jonathan Dayton, John Dickinson, Nicholas Gilman, Alexander Hamilton, William Livingston, Thomas Mifflin, Robert Morris, Charles Cotesworth Pinckney, and George Washington. Five other signers—Pierce Butler, Benjamin Franklin, Rufus King, Gouverneur Morris, and James Wilson—would later join. Other delegates to the Convention who were members included John Lansing, James McClurg, Alexander Martin, William Pierce, Edmund Randolph, and Robert Yates. Secretary William Jackson was also a member (Kilbourne 1986).

As the Society's most prominent member, George Washington urged it to abolish its hereditary and honorary memberships and correspondence with other societies. Although never adopted, these proposals helped moderate criticisms. At least two delegates voiced such criticism in debates during the Constitutional Convention. Opposing popular election of the president on July 25, Elbridge Gerry of Massachusetts feared that such election would actually serve the interests of the Cincinnati:

> The power of the people would put it in the power of some one set of men dispersed through the Union & acting in Concert to delude them into any appointment. He observed that such a Society of men existed in the Order of the Cincinnati. They were respectable, United, and influential. They will in fact elect the chief Magistrate in every instance, if the election be referred to the people.–His respect for the characters composing this Society could not blind him to the danger & impropriety of throwing such a power into their hands. (Farrand 1937, II, 114)

On the following day, Virginia's George Mason, a neighbor of George Washington, repeated concerns that "a popular election . . . would throw the appointment into the hands of the Cincinnati, a Society for the members of which he had a great respect; but which he never wished to have a preponderating influence in the Govt." (II, 119).

The provision prohibiting titles of nobility in Article I, Section 9, of the U.S. Constitution, while addressing titles conferred by the United States or by foreign governments, was undoubtedly stimulated by some of the same fears that had led to opposition to the Society of the Cincinnati. Moreover, unlike the British, the Framers created no hereditary governmental institutions, as they could have done either in the executive branch or in the Senate.

Decline of the Society

Over time, the Society became chiefly known for the conviviality of its annual reunions, typically held on the July Fourth holiday. The Society proved to be "a strong conservative force" (21), with members including General Benjamin Lincoln opposing Shays's Rebellion in Massachusetts and others becoming key members of the Federalist Party and of Washington's first administration.

Over time, the organization devoted more of its resources to charitable activities, and by the 1820s the organization had been reduced to a few members who were for the most part regarded as "a singularly innocuous order" (25).

Current Status

The Society of the Cincinnati continues to consist of descendants of commissioned officers of the Continental and French forces during the Revolutionary War. It describes itself today as "a not-for-profit organization that supports educational, cultural, and literary activities that promote the ideals of liberty and constitutional government" ("The Society of the Cincinnati"). The national headquarters of the Society is at the Anderson House on Massachusetts Avenue in Washington, D.C. It includes collections of decorative and fine arts, artifacts from the Revolutionary War and the history of the Society, and a library with an extensive collection on the Revolutionary War.

See Also Aristocracy; Republicanism; Washington, George

FOR FURTHER READING

Davies, Wallace Evan. 1948. "The Society of the Cincinnati in New England, 1783–1800." *William and Mary Quarterly,* 3rd ser. 5 (January): 3–25.

Farrand, Max, ed. 1937. *The Records of the Federal Convention.* 4 vols. New Haven, CT: Yale University Press.

Hutson, James H., ed. 1987. *Supplement to Max Farrand's* The Records of the Federal Convention of 1787. New Haven, CT: Yale University Press.

Kaplan, Sidney. 1952. "Veteran Officers and Politics in Massachusetts, 1783–1787." *William and Mary Quarterly,* 3rd ser. 9 (January): 29–57.

Kilbourne, John Dwight, Director, Library and Museum of The Society of the Cincinnati. 1986. Memorandum Re: "The Society of the Cincinnati and the Framing of the United States Constitution." April 15. Library Archives of the Independence National Historical Park, Philadelphia, PA.

Palmer, R. R. 1959. *The Age of the Democratic Revolution: A Political History of Europe and America, 1760–1800.* Princeton, NJ: Princeton University Press.

"The Society of the Cincinnati." http://xexophon group.com/mcjoynt/socpg02.htm.

Staib, Walter. 1999. *City Tavern Cookbook: 200 Years of Classic Recipes from America's First Gourmet Restaurant.* Philadelphia, PA: Running Press.

SOUTH CAROLINA

First settled as a propriety colony in 1670, South Carolina became a royal colony in 1720. It was long governed by what has been described as "a small, close-knit political oligarchy entrenched in the lower house of the legislature" (Nadelhaft 1988, 154), which largely represented the eastern part of the state. This created a division between the east and the west, or "low country" and "backcountry." In the latter frontier regions, frustrated citizens known as "Regulators" sometimes used self-help to punish lawbreakers among them (Nadelhaft, 156).

Constitution

South Carolina had adopted a state constitution in 1776 that had largely entrenched Eastern interests. Jerome Nadelhaft has described it as "more democratic in form, yet more suited to the native aristocracy, than that enjoyed or endured through the British connection" (Nadelhaft, 159). It created a large Assembly and a president elected by the legislature for two-year renewable terms and given veto powers. Members of the General Assembly elected senators from their own midst for two-year terms. Elected officials were required to be property owners.

The state adopted a somewhat more liberal constitution in 1778. It disestablished the Anglican Church in favor of the "Christian Protestant Religion." It further stripped the governor of his veto power and fixed salary and prohibited him from being immediately re-eligible for office. The constitution granted the legislature the power of impeachment and provided for the Senate to be chosen by the people rather than by the lower house

(Nadelhaft, 161–162). The new constitution provided better representation for the backcountry, but low country interests still dominated.

South Carolina was the only state in the Union in which slaves outnumbered free persons during the eighteenth century and up to the U.S. Revolution (Weir 1989, 202). Slavery had led to tremendous wealth in the lowlands of the Eeast and promised to do the same in the western upcountry. Representatives of the east, where slaves were plentiful, had been willing from time to time to suspend the slave trade to redress the state's balance of payments. Those in the west, where slaves were less plentiful and where their employment was regarded as the key to the development of wealth, were less willing to suspend this traffic.

Strongly dependent on its exports, South Carolina had succeeded in the First Continental Congress in exempting rice from the embargo against Great Britain. South Carolina delegates had succeeded in deleting references in the Declaration of Independence to the iniquity of slavery. Although the state had been willing to grant the Congress under the Articles of Confederation increased power over commerce, it had specifically exempted the slave trade (Weir 1989, 208).

Representation at the Convention

Apart from the large states, South Carolina was one of the most ably represented at the Constitutional Convention. All four delegates, Pierce Butler, Charles Pinckney, Charles Cotesworth Pinckney, and John Rutledge, contributed significantly to Convention discussions, and all four signed the document (Henry Laurens had also been appointed but had not attended the Convention). Major William Jackson, the Convention secretary, who had also been raised in South Carolina, also signed. Scholars continue to debate the role that an early plan by Charles Pinckney, largely ignored in the initial weeks of the Convention in preference to the Virginia Plan, might have had on overall deliberations.

South Carolina was a Deep South state, at the periphery of the nation. Although it was not the only state with slave interests, it was one of only three states (the others were North Carolina and Georgia) that had a continuing interest not only in the perpetuation of slavery but also in the continuing importation of slaves. Its representatives had strongly defended slavery at the Constitutional Convention, arguing that the state needed slavery to survive, that slavery was justified by historical practice, and that the matter had nothing to do with morality.

South Carolina's delegates succeeded in guaranteeing that the right to import slaves would continue until 1808, that such imports would not be subject to special taxation, and that states with slaves would be able to count them as three-fifths of a person for purposes of representation (some South Carolina delegates had pushed for full representation). The state did not succeed in seeing that all navigation matters would require a two-thirds vote by Congress, although the Constitution did specify that a two-thirds majority in the Senate would be required for ratification of treaties.

References to South Carolina during Debates

During Convention debates, General Pinckney cited his state as an example of how a provision limiting the introduction of money bills to the lower house of the legislature could lead to conflict (Farrand 1937, I, 234), and Rutledge later affirmed this observation (II, 279). On June 21, Virginia's Edmund Randolph indicated that South Carolina was the only state not to have annual elections (I, 360). Charles Pinckney argued on June 26 that his state had never opposed congressional powers and had only failed to meet congressional requisitions for money when it had none to give (I, 430).

Ratification

The South Carolina press largely favored ratification of the Constitution, but there was some opposition within the population, especially from the backcountry. One Antifederalist, Rawlins Lowndes, melodramatically expressed the view that he wished for no other epitaph for his tomb than "Here lies the man that opposed the Constitution, because it was ruinous to the liberty of America" (quoted in Weir 1989, 222). Other Antifederalists expressed fears that the new Constitution did not adequately protect state sovereignty. The state legislature nonetheless unanimously endorsed a call for a ratifying convention and further decided to hold it in Charleston.

There were more delegates from the eastern part of the state, where Federalists dominated, than from the western part, where Antifederalists appear to have had a majority. Moreover, rejected by his hometown, Antifederalist Rawlins Lowndes, who had argued so vehemently against the Constitution in the state legislature, refused to serve when elected by a neighboring parish. The convention's delegates, presided over by Governor Thomas Pinckney (brother to Charles Cotesworth Pinckney, who had represented South Carolina at the Constitutional Convention) began meeting on May 13 and voted 149 to 73 in favor of the Constitution 10 days later. South Carolina was thus the eighth state to give its consent. The convention was swayed in part by news that Maryland had recently ratified the document. In ratifying the Constitution, the convention adopted an explanatory amendment stating that "no Section of the said Constitution warrants a Construction that the States do not retain every power not expressly relinquished by them and vested in the General Government of the Union," but it did not condition its ratification of the document on acceptance of this amendment (Weir 1989, 224). Convention debates appear to have been designed as much to spread positive word about the Constitution as to ratify it. Supporters of the Constitution had to assure delegates, especially from the west, that they had adequately protected slavery, and it appears that the convention would not have adopted the document had they not been so convinced.

Post-Ratification Developments

In 1790, South Carolina adopted yet a third state constitution. It was perhaps most notable for its endorsement of full religious toleration and for its absence of religious qualifications for office. The constitution did not, however, follow the federal precedent and grant the governor veto power or permit his immediate reelection. This constitution did provide for greater representation of the backcountry than it had enjoyed under the earlier two documents.

See Also Butler, Pierce; Jackson, William; Pinckney, Charles; Pinckney, Charles Cotesworth; Pinckney Plan; Ratification in the States; Rutledge, John

FOR FURTHER READING

Farrand, Max, ed. 1937. *The Records of the Federal Convention.* 4 vols. New Haven, CT: Yale University Press.

Nadelhaft, Jerome J. 1988. "South Carolina: A Conservative Revolution." In Patrick T. Conley and John P. Kaminski, eds. *The Constitution and the States: The Role of the Original Thirteen in the Framing and Adoption of the Federal Constitution.* Madison, WI: Madison House.

Weir, Robert M. 1989. "South Carolina: Slavery and the Structure of the Union." In Michael Allen Gillespie and Michael Lienesch, eds. *Ratifying the Constitution.* Lawrence: University Press of Kansas.

——. 1988. "South Carolinians and the Adoption of the United States Constitution." *South Carolina Historical Magazine* 89 (April) 73–89.

SOVEREIGNTY

The term "sovereignty" does not appear to have been prominent at the Constitutional Convention. The most extensive discussion of the term "sovereignty" appears to have taken place on June 19 when the Convention was discussing what role the states would play within the new system. Rufus King of Massachusetts observed that the delegates appeared to be confused in their use of a number of key terms. Focusing primarily on relations with foreign states, he observed:

> The States were not "sovereign" in the sense contended for by some. They did not possess the peculiar features of sovereignty. They could not make war, nor peace, nor alliances, nor treaties.

Considering them as political Beings, they were dumb, for they could not speak to any foreign Sovereign whatever. They were deaf, for they could not hear any propositions from such Sovereign. They had not even the organs or faculties of defence or offence, for they could not of themselves raise troops, or equip vessels, for war. (Farrand 1937, I, 323)

He concluded that "if the States therefore retained some portion of their sovereignty, they had certainly divested themselves of essential portions of it" (I, 324). He further "doubted the practicability of annihilating the States; but thought that much of their power ought to be taken from them" (I, 324).

King's discussion indicates that one of the central problems with which delegates had to deal was the locus of sovereignty, or ultimate authority, under the new government. Colonial disputes over the claim of the British Parliament to be sovereign over internal affairs, chiefly taxation, related to the New World had led in large part to the Revolutionary War (Reid 1991). Under the Articles of Confederation, the states were the primary locus of sovereignty. By contrast, those who wrote and adopted the Constitution indicated in the Preamble that they were vesting sovereignty in "We the People." This formulation was not unambiguous since the people who voted to ratify the Constitution voted not in one mass, but through representatives chosen for ratifying conventions within the separate states.

The idea of sovereignty as developed by European theorists was that there was ultimately one power with final jurisdiction in each regime. This could be the monarch, the parliament, or some other body or combination of bodies, as, for example, "the king (or queen) in parliament." The U.S. Constitution complicated this scheme both by dividing the powers of the national government into three branches and by further outlining a system in which powers were shared by the national government and the states.

The delegates to the Convention proceeded from the assumption that since the people were the source of all power (the idea of popular sovereignty), they could allocate it as they chose (Mur-

rin et al. 1974, 36). Once the people adopted the Constitution, the people's wishes would be reflected through the mechanism of representative institutions. If the people did not believe these institutions were functioning properly, a supermajority of them could, in turn, use the amending process to alter these institutions and assert, or reassert, their authority.

Antifederalist critics of the new Constitution argued that it created an "imperium in imperio," that is, one sovereign power within another. Debates over sovereignty led in part to the Civil War. Although it largely brought an end to the doctrines of state nullification of federal laws and of state secession, the relationship between state and national powers continues to be an issue.

See Also Amending Process; Constitutional Convention Mechanism; Federalism; Preamble; Separation of Powers; "We the People"

FOR FURTHER READING

Farrand, Max, ed. 1937. *The Records of the Federal Convention*. 4 vols. New Haven, CT: Yale University Press.

Miller, Joshua. 1988. "The Ghostly Body Politic: The Federalist Papers and Popular Sovereignty." *Political Theory* 16 (February): 99–119.

Morgan, Edmund S. 1988. *Inventing the People: The Rise of Popular Sovereignty in England and America*. New York: W. W. Norton.

Murrin, John M., David E. Narrett, Ronald L. Hatzenbuehler, and Michael Kammen. 1974. *Essays on Liberty and Federalism: The Shaping of the U.S. Constitution*. College Station: Texas A and M University Press.

Reid, John Phillip. 1991. *The Authority to Legislate*. Part of *Constitutional History of the American Revolution*. Madison: University of Wisconsin Press.

SPAIGHT, RICHARD DOBBS (1758–1802)

Spaight was born in New Bern, North Carolina in 1758 to an Irish immigrant; his parents died when

Richard Spaight, delegate from North Carolina
(Pixel That)

he was young. He was sent to the University of Glasgow where he was attending when the Revolutionary War started. Spaight returned to defend his native homeland and served in the war as an aide-de-camp. He was subsequently elected to the North Carolina legislature, to the Congress under the Articles of Confederation, and as speaker of the North Carolina house. In the Continental Congress, Spaight was credited with helping nix Thomas Jefferson's prohibition of slavery in the Western territories. Perhaps influenced by the Virginia Plan, Spaight appears largely to have supported those at the Convention advocating greater powers for the national government.

Rules

Spaight was present for the opening day of business in Philadelphia on May 25, 1787. On May 28, Spaight introduced a motion that would have specified that, while the delegates should not be precluded from revisiting issues when they had cause to do so, they should also be cautioned against revising measures that were "the result of mature discussion" too hastily (Farrand 1937, I, 10).

Legislative Branch

On May 30, the Convention was debating how to apportion representation in Congress. The Virginia Plan had proposed that this formula be based on "the quotas of contribution, or on the number of free inhabitants"; Spaight seconded a motion by Alexander Hamilton of New York using the latter portion of the formula only (I, 35). It seems odd that, as a Southerner, Spaight would have supported such a measure.

On May 31, Spaight introduced a motion providing that state legislatures should choose senators directly, rather than, as the Virginia Plan had proposed, by allowing members of the first branch to choose them from nominees submitted by the state legislatures (I, 51). The delegates eventually settled on Spaight's method; it remained in effect until the ratification of the Seventeenth Amendment in 1913 vested this choice directly in the voters of each state. On June 12, Spaight further proposed that members of the Senate should serve for seven-year terms (I, 218). This proposal came relatively close to the term of six years that the Convention eventually adopted.

On June 23, Spaight proposed dividing the question as to whether members of Congress should be ineligible for other offices while they were serving and for one year afterward (I, 390). The immediate outcome was approval for the first part of the resolution but not for the second.

On August 11, the Convention was discussing a provision that would prohibit one house of Congress from meeting in a city other than the one where both were meeting. Spaight feared that this would permanently establish the capital in New York. He observed that the first Congress would begin there and that "they will never be able to remove; especially if the Presidt. should be [a] Northern Man" (II, 261). Pennsylvania's Gouverneur Morris immediately chided that "such a distrust is inconsistent with all Govt." (II, 261), indicating that, on this issue at least, Spaight might have been regarded as expressing too regional a perspective.

The next day, however, Spaight wrote a letter to James Iredell, a future Supreme Court justice, indicating that he was in fact taking a national perspective. Noting that he hoped the Convention would end between the first and fifteenth days of each September, Spaight went on to observe:

> It is not probable that the United States will in future be so ideal as to risk their happiness upon the unanimity of the whole; and thereby put it in the power of one or two States to defeat the most salutary propositions, and prevent the Union from rising out of that contemptible situation to which it is at present reduced. There is no man of reflection, who has maturely considered what must and will result from the weakness of our present Federal Government, and the tyrannical and unjust proceedings of most of the State governments, if longer persevered in, but must sincerely wish for a strong and efficient National Government. (Hutson 1987, 219)

Somewhat less hopefully, Spaight observed that "We may naturally suppose that all those persons who are possessed of popularity in the different States, and which they made use of, not for the public benefit, but for their private emolument, will oppose any system of this kind" (Hutson, 219).

At a time when some Southern delegates were arguing for a provision that would have required a two-thirds majority for Congress to enact any navigation measures, Spaight disagreed. He observed that if Northerners tried to hog the carrying trade, "The Southern States could . . . save themselves from oppression, by building ships for their own use" (II, 451). On September 7, however, Spaight did support a motion providing that no treaty affecting territorial rights should be made without the concurrence of two-thirds of all the members of the Senate (II, 543).

Executive Branch

On July 23, Spaight joined Georgia's William Houston in proposing reconsideration of a provision vesting the appointment of presidential electors in state legislatures. Presumably, Spaight shared Houston's concern about "the extreme inconveniency & the considerable expense, of draw-

ing together men from all the States for the single purpose of electing the Chief Magistrate" (II, 95). On September 5, Spaight and South Carolina's John Rutledge proposed allowing the Senate to choose among the top 13, rather than five, candidates for president (II, 515); this measure garnered only the votes of North and South Carolina. On the following day, Spaight proposed a seven-year term for the president (II, 525). He also proposed that it would be better for the electors to get together and choose the president in case no one got a majority than to entrust this power to the Senate (II, 526). On September 7, Spaight introduced the successful motion granting the president to fill vacancies when the Senate was in recess by granting commissions that would expire at the end of the next Senate term (II, 540).

Ratification

At the North Carolina ratifying convention Spaight argued vigorously on behalf of what the Convention had done. He observed that "it was found impossible to improve the old system without changing the very form; for by that system the three great branches of government are blended together" (III, 351). He further observed that the delegates thought that "if so great a majority as nine states should adopt it, it would be right to establish it" (III, 351). Responding to criticism, Spaight observed: "I am, for my part, conscious of having had nothing in view but the liberty and happiness of my country; and I believe every member of that Convention was actuated by motives equally sincere and patriotic" (III, 352).

Life after the Convention

After the Convention, Spaight served as a member of the North Carolina legislature and as the state's governor. He was elected to the U.S. House of Representatives and then to the state Senate. A dispute that arose in this latter body led Spaight to engage in a duel with John Stanly, his Federalist replacement in Congress. It resulted in Spaight's death in 1802.

See Also North Carolina

FOR FURTHER READING

Bradford, M. M. 1994. *Founding Fathers: Brief Lives of the Framers of the United States Constitution.* 2nd ed. Lawrence: University Press of Kansas.

Craige, Burton. 1987. *The Federal Convention of 1787: North Carolina in the Great Crisis.* Richmond, VA: Expert Graphics.

Farrand, Max, ed. 1937. *The Records of the Federal Convention.* 4 vols. New Haven, CT: Yale University Press.

Hutson, James H., ed. 1987. *Supplement to Max Farrand's* The Records of the Federal Convention of 1787. New Haven, CT: Yale University Press.

SPAIN

At the time of the Constitutional Convention of 1787, Spain was still a major continental power that posed a potential threat to the new nation. In addition to its extensive colonies in Central and South America, it occupied modern Florida and claimed a part of the lands that lie today west of Georgia. Spain also claimed the land west of the Mississippi River and sought to control commerce on the river by its control of the port of New Orleans. Like most other European powers, Spain was a monarchy, somewhat lessening its enthusiasm for the experiment being carried out in North America. In contrast to the United States, Spain was also predominately Roman Catholic.

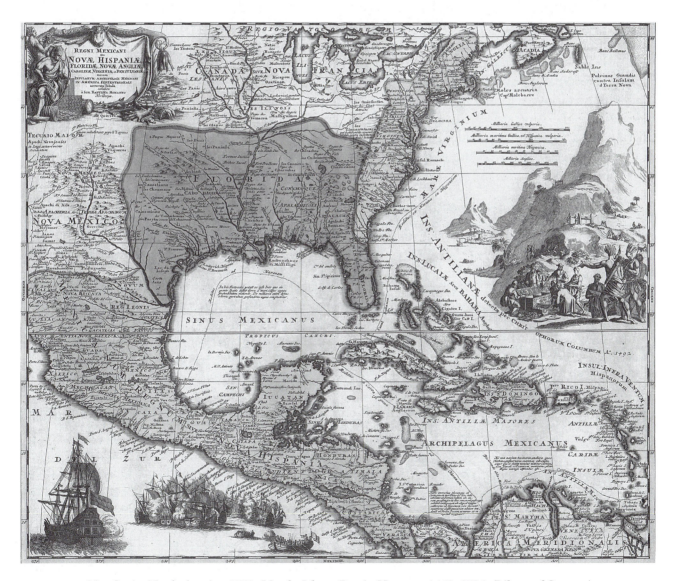

New Spain, North America, 1759. Map by Johann Baptist Homann, 1663–1724. (Library of Congress)

James Madison thus once remarked that Spain's "government, religion and manners unfit them, of all nations in Christendom for a coalition with this country" (quoted in Sheldon 2001, 42).

Although Southern states had blocked the result of negotiations between John Jay and a Spanish minister named Don Diego de Gardoqui in 1785 in which Jay considered giving up claims to navigation on the Mississippi for a time in exchange for trading and fishing rights beneficial to the Northeastern states, these negotiations had led to fears in the Southern states and the Western frontier that Northerners might be willing to sell them short. This in turn appears to have influenced the delegates' decision to require the U.S. Senate to approve treaties by two-thirds majorities. For its part, Spain appears to have engaged, at least for a time, in enticing individuals in the American West to give their allegiance to the Spanish Crown (Whitaker 1926).

The young nation eventually engaged in conflict with Spain over Florida. Spain transferred its territories in the American West to France, which in turn sold them to the United States in the Louisiana Purchase of 1803 during the presidency of Thomas Jefferson.

See Also France; Great Britain; Jay-Gardoqui Negotiations; Treaty-Making and Ratification

FOR FURTHER READING

Merritt, Eli. 1991. "Sectional Conflict and Secret Compromise: The Mississippi River Question and the United States Constitution." *American Journal of Legal History* 35 (April): 117–171.

Sheldon, Garrett Ward. 2001. *The Political Philosophy of James Madison.* Baltimore, MD: Johns Hopkins University Press.

Whitaker, A. A. 1926. "The Muscle Shoals Speculation, 1783–1789." *Mississippi Valley Historical Review* 13 (December): 365–386.

SPEECHES, NUMBER OF

One of the more elusive sources of information about the Constitutional Convention is a list, first published in an 1861 issue of the *Historical Magazine,* in which an unidentified author, or editor, relied on a reading of Madison's notes to record the number of speeches delivered at the Constitutional Convention ("Constitutional Convention, 1787" 1861, 18). Often cited without attribution in the secondary literature, the list says that delegates gave 1,782 speeches, but an accompanying list adds up to only 1,779.

According to this list, six individuals spoke more than one-hundred times. The most frequent speaker was Gouverneur Morris (PA), with 173 speeches. He was followed by James Wilson (PA) with 168, James Madison (VA) with 161, Roger Sherman (CT) with 138, George Mason (VA) with 136, and Elbridge Gerry (MA) with 119.

Six individuals are recorded as having given from 50 to 100 speeches. These were Edmund Randolph (VA), with 78; Hugh Williamson (NC) and Rufus King (MA), each with 75; Oliver Ellsworth (CT) with 73; and Nathaniel Gorham (MA) with 61.

Ten men delivered from twenty to 49 speeches. John Rutledge (SC) and Pierce Butler (SC) both gave 47. John Dickinson (DE) gave 36, Charles Cotesworth Pinckney (SC) gave 35, Luther Martin (MD) 31, George Read (DE) 27, John Langdon (NH) and Benjamin Franklin (PA) each gave 26, Daniel Carroll (MD) gave 25, and Alexander Hamilton (NY) made 23.

Five individuals spoke from 10 to 19 times. They were John Francis Mercer (MD) with 19 speeches, William Samuel Johnson (CT) with 14, Jonathan Dayton (NY) with 12, William Paterson (NJ) with 11, and Gunning Bedford (DE) with 10.

Those speaking but doing so on fewer than 10 occasions, included 16 men. Abraham Baldwin (GA) spoke 8 times; Caleb Strong (MA) and George Clymer (PA) spoke 7 times; James McHenry (MD) spoke 6 times; Jacob Broom (DE) and Thomas Fitzsimons (PA) spoke 5 times each; Richard Dobbs Spaight (NC) and William Richardson Davie (NC) each spoke 4 times; John Lansing (NY), James McClurg (VA), William Pierce (GA), William Houston (NJ), and Daniel of St. Thomas Jenifer (MD) each spoke 3 times; George Washington (VA) spoke twice; and Jared Ingersoll (PA) and William Blount (NC) spoke once.

Ten individuals were listed as not having delivered any speeches. They were Richard Bassett (DE), John Blair (VA), William Few (GA), Nicholas Gilman (NH), William C. Houston (NJ), Nicholas Gilman (NH), William Livingston (NJ), Robert Morris (PA), George Wythe (VA), and Robert Yates (NY). No mention was made of delegates David Brearly (NJ) and Alexander Martin (NC). The first spoke only on a few occasions, and the latter apparently never.

The number of speeches provides a rough measure of the influence of many members. However, there were some individuals like George Washington who spoke infrequently but are believed to have had much influence, and other individuals like Elbridge Gerry (and, to a lesser degree, Luther Martin) who spoke frequently but who sometimes alienated colleagues and ultimately ended up rejecting the work of the Convention. Also, some individuals gave longer, and more influential, speeches than others. Service on committees (or, in the case of Nathaniel Gorham and George Washington) or as chair of the Committee of the Whole or of the Convention is another measure of influence.

See Also Committees at the Constitutional Convention; Delegates, Individual Rankings; Oratory and Rhetoric

FOR FURTHER READING

"Constitutional Convention, 1787." 1861. *The Historical Magazine,* 1st ser., V (January): 18.

STABILITY

The delegates to the Constitutional Convention sought to create greater stability within the governments at both the state and national levels. In defending the Constitution in *Federalist* No. 37, Virginia's James Madison said that one of the goals of the Convention had been that of "combining the requisite stability and energy in government with the inviolable attention due to liberty and to the

republican form" (Hamilton, Madison, and Jay 1961, 226). He further observed:

Stability in government is essential to national character and to the advantages annexed to it, as well as to that repose and confidence in the minds of the people, which are among the chief blessings of civil society. An irregular and mutable legislation is not more an evil in itself than it is odious to the people; and it may be pronounced with assurance that the people of this country, enlightened as they are with regard to the nature, and interested, as the great body of them are, in the effects of good government, will never be satisfied till some remedy be applied to the vicissitudes and uncertainties which characterize the State administrations. (Hamilton, Madison, and Jay, 226–227)

Guarantees of Republican Government and against Domestic Insurrection

The concern about "domestic tranquility" that was articulated in the Preamble of the new Constitution seemed primarily designed to address the national government's ability to help states cope with situations like Shays's Rebellion, which had arisen within Massachusetts. The delegates chiefly addressed this concern through the guarantee clause in Article IV, Section 4, and the accompanying provision granting the national government the power to protect states against "domestic Violence." Strengthened congressional powers to declare war were further designed to protect states against foreign invasion. Edmund Randolph had expressed this concern when he offered the Virginia Plan for the Convention's consideration on May 29 (Farrand 1937, I, 19).

Separation of Powers, Bicameralism, and Longer Terms

The Framers were also interested in providing stability within the new government itself. Many of the state constitutions of the period incorporated the idea of legislative sovereignty (Wood 1969). By contrast, the new Constitution created three branches of government sharing powers and thus providing a brake on precipitous legislative actions.

Article V of the Articles of Confederation had provided for annual election of members of its unicameral Congress. Even during this time, representatives were subject to state recall. By contrast, the new Constitution provided for a bicameral Congress. It contained no recall mechanism. Members of the House served for two years, the president for four, and senators for six; members of the judicial behavior were to serve "during good behavior." Similarly, whereas members of Congress under the Articles of Confederation were limited to serving no more than three years out of any six, the new Constitution provided no such limits (although the Twenty-second Amendment has since limited a president to serving no more than two full terms).

The Framers appear to have envisioned an especially important role for the U.S. Senate in providing stability. In defending a seven-year term on June 12, Virginia's James Madison thus observed:

> What we wished was to give to the Govt. that stability which was every where called for, and which the enemies of the Republican form alleged to be inconsistent with its nature. He was not afraid of giving too much stability by the term of seven years. His fear was that the popular branch would still be too great an overmatch for it. (I, 218)

In further defending a nine-year term for senators on June 26, Madison observed that governments were designed "first to protect the people agst. their rulers: secondly to protect [the people] agst. the transient impressions into which they themselves might be led" (I, 421). Citing the separation of powers as one check on the transient passions of the people, Madison portrayed bicameralism as another. It was clear that longer terms were one way of providing such stability:

> It wd. next occur to such a people, that they themselves were liable to temporary errors, thro' want of information as to their true interest, and that men chosen for a short term, & employed

but a small portion of that in public affairs, might err from the same cause. This reflection wd. naturally suggest that the Govt. be so constituted as that one of its branches might have an oppy. of acquiring a competent knowledge of the public interests. (I, 422)

Although neither proposal succeeded, Madison's hope for a Council of Revision and for a congressional veto of state laws probably aimed at a similar stabilizing purpose (Rohr 1986, 23).

Presidential Re-eligibility

At the time prior to the invention of the Electoral College that delegates to the Convention were considering the possibility of congressional selection, they went so far as to consider life tenure, or service during good behavior, rather than take the chance that the president would corrupt the legislature in attempts to seek reelection (II, 33–35). Re-eligibility appeared to offer presidents, like their legislative counterparts, an incentive for good behavior. Length of service in office also appeared to offer a means of countering excessive legislative power. Gouverneur Morris of Pennsylvania thus observed on July 17: "The ineligibility proposed by the clause [then under consideration] as it stood tended to destroy the great motive to good behavior, the hope of being rewarded by re-appointment. It was saying to him, make hay while the sun shines (II, 33).

On the same day, Madison observed:

> Experience had proved a tendency in our governments to throw all power into the Legislative vortex. The Executives of the States are in general little more than Cyphers; the legislatures omnipotent. If no effective check be devised for restraining the instability & encroachments of the latter, a revolution of some kind or other would be inevitable. (II, 35)

In *Federalist* No. 71, Alexander Hamilton further tied "the energy of the executive authority" to his "duration in office" (431).

The Amending Process

The Framers did not replicate the wooden amending mechanism under the Articles of Confederation that required unanimous state consent. They did, however, formulate an amending process in Article V of the new Constitution, requiring, in the only mechanism used to date, proposal by two-thirds majorities in both houses of Congress and ratification by three-fourths of the states, which was designed to promote stability. The process thus sought to prevent precipitous change while providing a mechanism that would make future resort to force (such as had been necessitated in the American Revolution) unnecessary. In *Federalist* No. 49, Madison made a point of rejecting a mechanism for periodic constitutional reform. He observed that

> as every appeal to the people would carry an implication of some defect in the government, frequent appeals would, in great measure, deprive the government of that veneration which time bestows on everything, and without which perhaps the wisest and freest governments would not possess the requisite stability. (Hamilton, Madison, and Jay, 314)

See Also Amending Process; Articles of Confederation; Congress, House of Representatives, Terms; Congress, Senate, Terms; Guarantee Clause; Posterity and Perpetuity; President, Term, Length, and Re-eligibility; Shays's Rebellion

FOR FURTHER READING

Farrand, Max, ed. 1937. *The Records of the Federal Convention.* 4 vols. New Haven, CT: Yale University Press.

Hamilton, Alexander, James Madison, and John Jay. 1961. *The Federalist Papers.* Ed. Clinton Rossiter. New York: New American Library.

Rohr, John A. 1986. *To Run a Constitution: The Legitimacy of the Administrative State.* Lawrence: University Press of Kansas.

Wood, Gordon S. 1969. *The Creation of the American Republic, 1776–1787.* Chapel Hill: University of North Carolina Press.

STANDING ARMIES

See ARMIES, STANDING

STATE APPOINTMENT OF DELEGATES TO THE CONSTITUTIONAL CONVENTION

The delegates from the five states who gathered in September 1786 for the Annapolis Convention were the first to issue an official call for what became the Constitutional Convention. Circulated both to state executives and to Congress, the latter appointed a committee but did not ultimately approve of the Annapolis call until February 21, 1787. In the interim, six of the 12 states that ultimately attended had appointed delegates. Of the 12 states that eventually sent delegates, the largest delegation, with eight representatives, was Pennsylvania (proximity undoubtedly permitted great participation); the smallest that was appointed was New Hampshire's with two; for much of the Convention Hamilton, whose own attendance was spotty, was the only one of three representatives present from New York. Although states apportioned over seventy delegates, 55 actually attended the Convention, and some of these did not have good attendance records.

Early State Responses to the Call of the Annapolis Convention

Most prominent in responding to the call of the Annapolis Convention was the state of Virginia, whose act of November 23, 1786, was circulated by Governor Edmund Randolph to other states, which received it fairly positively. The Virginia proclamation explained that a convention would be better focused and could draw on a wider array of individuals than could the Congress under the

Articles of Confederation, whose members were limited to three out of six years of service. The resolution also observed that

> the crisis is arrived at which the good people of America are to decide the solemn question, whether they will by wise and magnanimous efforts reap the just fruits of that Independence, which they have so gloriously acquired, and of that Union, which they have cemented with so much of their common blood; or whether by giving way to unmanly jealousies and prejudices, or to partial and transitory interests, they will renounce the auspicious blessings prepared for them by the Revolution, and furnish to its enemies an eventual triumph over those by whose virtue and valour it has been accomplished. (Jensen 1976, 197)

The fact that Virginia appointed both its governor, Edmund Randolph, and George Washington as delegates undoubtedly enhanced the prestige of its call; other appointed delegates included Patrick Henry, John Blair, James Madison, George Mason, and George Wythe. The legislature eventually replaced Patrick Henry (who declined to serve and later opposed the document during the state's ratifying convention) with James McClurg.

Other states who appointed delegates prior to the congressional call included New Jersey, which made its appointments on November 23; Pennsylvania, which elected its delegates on December 30; North Carolina, which elected its delegates on January 6, 1787; Delaware, which appointed its delegates on February 3; and Georgia, which appointed its delegates on February 10. One potentially troubling development for those who wanted a free debate was that Delaware instructed its delegates that they had no authority to change the provision in the Articles of Confederation (from which it benefited as a small state) by which states were to have an equal vote in Congress.

Massachusetts, which appointed its delegates on February 22, 1787 (and probably would not have known about the resolution adopted in Congress the previous day), focused on separate reservations. The legislators wanted to ensure that their delegates would not interfere with the provisions for annual congressional elections, for congressional recalls, for limiting congressmen to serving no more than three out of six consecutive years, and with the section of the Articles of Confederation providing that members of Congress could accept no other benefits. The Massachusetts legislature subsequently repealed this part of the motion, after adding a reservation in one discarded motion that would further have cautioned delegates "not to accede to any alterations that may be proposed to be made in the present Articles of Confederation, which may appear to them, not to consist with the true republican Spirit and Genius of the Said Confederation" (Jensen, 207).

States Responding to Congressional Call for Convention

Other states appointed delegates after Congress called upon them to do so. These included New York, which did so on March 6, 1787; South Carolina, which responded on March 8; Connecticut, which acted on May 17; Maryland, which responded on May 26; and New Hampshire, which complied on June 27, well after the Convention had begun.

Rhode Island's Failure to Respond

Apart from Virginia's, the most notable state response to the call for a convention was that of Rhode Island, which was adopted on September 15, 1787, just two days before the signing of the Constitution. Noting that its conduct in not appointing delegates had been "reprobated by the illiberal" with "many severe and unjust sarcasms propagated against us," the state attributed its actions to "the love of true Constitutional liberty, and the fear we have of making innovations on the Rights and Liberties of the Citizens at large" (Jensen, 225). Ironically, the logic of the argument that the state assembly made arguably underlined the wisdom of the method that the delegates to the Constitutional Convention chose for ratifying the document. Rhode Island observed that just as the legislature thought it had no power to accede to congressional requisitions for taxes without first consulting the people, so too they thought that "as the Delegation in Convention is for the express purpose of altering a Constitution, which the people at large were only capable of appointing the Members" (226).

Rhode Island had correctly gauged that it had become the favorite whipping boy of the Constitutional Convention, whose members were disgusted by its easy money policies and referred to it in private as "Rogues Island." On the Convention floor, Nathanial Gorham thus cited the Rhode Island legislature as an example "of the length to which a public body may carry wickedness & cabal" (Farrand 1937, II, 42), and Gouverneur Morris openly questioned whether the government of the state could be regarded as republican in character (II, 476). Delegates also cited the state as an example of why the constitutional amending process, or constitutional ratification, should not require state unanimity.

Citizens of Rhode Island themselves were of at least two minds toward the Convention. A committee of 13 citizens from Providence sent a letter to the chair of the Convention on May 11, 1787, referring to "the evils of the present unhappy times" and expressing the opinion "that full power for the Regulation of the Commerce of the United States, both Foreign & Domestick ought to be vested in the National Council" (III, 18). Another committee from Providence sent a letter to James Varnun to be conveyed to the Convention indicating that they desired that all goods produced or transported within the United States be free from duties, that imported goods be subject to one duty only, that trade should be assured to U.S. vessels "on reasonable terms," and that they favored admitting Vermont as a state (Hutson 1987, 2). Still another delegation of Newport and Providence residents responded to the arguments in Rhode Island's letter of September by indicating that

it has never been thought heretofore by the Legislature of this State, or while it was a Colony, inconsistent with or any Innovation upon the Rights and Liberties of the Citizens of this State to concur with the Sister States or Colonies in

appointing Members or Delegates to any Convention proposed for the General Benefit. (Jensen, 227)

They further opined:

So our Non-compliance hath been our highest Imprudence. And therefore it would have been more Consistant with our Honor and dignity to have lamented our mistake, and decently appollogised for our Errors, than to have endeavoured to support them on ill founded reasons and indefensible principles. (228)

State Calls and Convention Action

When Congress examined the credentials from the delegates who arrived at the Convention from Delaware, they realized that they were committed to opposing any changes in the equality of state representation (I, 4). The delegates stayed on anyway, and the state, sometimes accordingly designated as "The First State," ultimately became the first to ratify the Constitution. Although Massachusetts had repealed the restrictions it had placed on its delegates, one of its members, Elbridge Gerry, was among the three remaining delegates on September 17, 1787, who refused to sign the document—the other two, George Mason and Edmund Randolph, were from the state (Virginia) that had first responded to the call of the Annapolis Convention.

See Also Annapolis Convention; Congressional Call for Constitutional Convention

FOR FURTHER READING

Farrand, Max, ed. 1937. *The Records of the Federal Convention.* 4 vols. New Haven, CT: Yale University Press.

Hutson, James H., ed. 1987. *Supplement to Max Farrand's* The Records of the Federal Convention of 1787. New Haven, CT: Yale University Press.

Jensen, Merrill. 1976. *The Documentary History of the Ratification of the Constitution.* Vol. 1: *Constitutional Documents and Records, 1776–1787.* Madison: State Historical Society of Wisconsin.

Dueling: Chapter and Verse

The place of constitutionalism in the United States is suggested in part by the early publication of compilations of constitutions that appear to have been fairly widely distributed. These were published as early as 1778 and with increased frequency throughout the nineteenth century, often in fairly portable form.

Although the U.S. Constitution did not concern itself with such domestic issues, one concern of a number of early state constitutions was that of dueling, often considered a "gentlemanly" way to solve disputes. Alexander Hamilton, who attended the Constitutional Convention from New York and who was killed in a duel with Aaron Burr, was but one of many early Americans who died from wounds received in this type of confrontation; future president Andrew Jackson was wounded but proved more successful in killing his rivals.

When Pennsylvania was debating a new constitution in 1837, delegates discussed whether to include an antidueling provision. Cognizant that compilations of state constitutions were more widely available and accessible than state statutes, one delegate suggested that including the provision within the constitution would be more effective. Marsha Baum and Christian Fritz have observed that early constitutional compilations "had something of a Bible-like quality to them: an authoritative source to be consulted and quoted when disputes arose" (2000, 213).

FOR FURTHER READING

Baum, Marsha L., and Christian G. Fritz. 2000. "American Constitution-Making: The Neglected State Constitutional Sources." *Hastings Constitutional Law Quarterly* 17 (Winter): 199–242.

STATE CONSTITUTIONS

Political science professor Donald Lutz has observed that although most books on American constitutional history focus on the national Constitution, this document is an "incomplete text" without reference to the state constitutions and other documents that preceded it and gave it context (Lutz 1980, 101). He has identified 86 "constitution-like documents" that were written by American colonists prior to 1722 and another 42 such documents that were written in England for the colonies prior to 1735 (129–132). He further counts 17 constitutions (that of Massachusetts dated to 1722; the others began in 1776) that were written prior to the U.S. Constitution (133).

The Initial Period of State Constitution-Writing

A period of active state constitution writing began in January 1776 with the action of the Congress (as the state designated its legislature) of New Hampshire in adopting a new constitution. That March, South Carolina followed by adopting a provisional constitution, which it replaced two years later with a more permanent document (Adams 2001, 66–70). Significantly, the constitution of New Hampshire and the provisional constitution of South Carolina both preceded the adoption of the Declaration of Independence.

The Second Continental Congress specifically adopted a resolution on May 10, 1776, encouraging states to draw up their own constitutions. It specified that "where no governments sufficient to the exigencies of their affairs have been hitherto established," states should "adopt such Government as shall, in the Opinion of the Representatives of the People, best conduce to the Happiness and Safety of their Constituents in particular and America in general" (quoted in Adams, 59).

Virginia's adoption of its constitution in June of 1776 was notable for its inclusion of a Declaration of Rights (largely written by George Mason), which became a model not only for that of other states but for the Bill of Rights that was later added to the U.S. Constitution. New Jersey adopted a state constitution in July. Delaware added a new feature to the adoption of such a constitution in September 1776 when it called a special convention for this purpose rather than relying simply on the state legislature to do so. Pennsylvania followed later in the month, with a constitution especially notable for its unicameral legislature. Maryland followed in November and North Carolina in December 1776. In May of 1776 and October of 1776, Rhode Island and Connecticut simply reaffirmed their existing charters, sans kings and parliament. Georgia adopted a constitution in February 1776 and New York did in August. The people of Massachusetts rejected a proposed constitution in 1778, leading to a constitutional convention that was distinct from the state legislature in 1779. This resulted in the adoption of the state constitution (largely drafted by John Adams) that is still in effect today, thus making it the world's oldest (Adams, 61–95).

In addition to the above, Vermont joined the original colonies in proposing a constitution for "New Connecticut" in July 1776. The other states did not officially recognize this government until 1791, after the new national Constitution went into effect.

Characteristics and Influences of State Constitutions

Lutz has identified five elements that most state constitutions had in common. These included: (1) an explanation of why the document is needed; (2) the creation of a people; (3) the creation of a government; (4) a self-definition of themselves as a people, their common values, rights, and interests; and (5) the specification of a form of government, which includes an outline of its institutions and the fundamental principles underlying them (Lutz, 103).

Over time the term "constitution" came primarily to embrace the last of these objectives, with most of the other functions "squeezed into a preface [preamble] and/or bill of rights" (Lutz, 121). Such a bill became particularly important in

providing the self-definition of a people and their values.

The development of early state constitutions established a recognized procedure whereby representatives of the people gathered in convention could establish fundamental law. These constitutions served for the Founders, as they continue to do today, as what Supreme Court Justice Louis Brandeis referred to as "laboratories" of democracy. The earliest state constitutions tended to emphasize legislative sovereignty and were designed to be highly democratic and responsive to the people. Although technically incorporating ideas like separation of powers and checks and balances, most early state constitutions left primary power with the legislatures, whose members often served for one-year terms, and left governors with relatively few powers. State legislatures often responded to popular demands for tax relief by issuing paper money and by engaging in schemes that leading framers of the U.S. Constitution thought were unjust to owners of property.

A number of provisions in the Constitution that was formulated in convention in 1787, most notably those in Article I, Sections 9 and 10, grew from this experience. The new Constitution was modeled more closely on constitutions, like those of Massachusetts and New York, that included checks and balances and greater executive powers than on the early constitutions under which legislatures dominated.

Significantly, although states often patterned their constitutions on those of their neighbors, Congress rejected a number of suggestions to propose a model constitution for all the states to follow (Adams, 53–54). Similarly, the U.S. Constitution provided recognition of all state constitutions that were "republican" in nature, a term that was wide enough to include each of the state constitutions then in existence.

Delegates' Experience with State Constitutions

Ten of the delegates to the Constitutional Convention had gained experience by engaging in writing constitutions at the state level, and 46 delegates had served either in the colonial or state legislatures. The delegates referred during Convention debates to their experiences not only under the existing Articles of Confederation but also under existing state constitutions. Whether they were debating the length of terms, property qualifications, or the powers of each of the three branches of government they were proposing, they had ready examples at hand to which they could refer. On some occasions—qualifications for voters, for example—the presence of wide variances in existing state constitutional requirements precluded formulation or adoption of a single uniform national standard. State constitutional experiences were not only responsible for shaping the constitutional convention mechanism for writing and ratifying such documents, but they also helped shape ratification debates (see Conley and Kaminski 1988). State constitutions also served as a source for the provisions that were incorporated into the Bill of Rights.

Subsequent Developments

Marsha Baum and Christian Fritz have observed that more than 170 constitutional conventions met in America from the time of the American Revolution through the end of the nineteenth century (2000, 200). State constitution-making was so pervasive, and interest in such constitutions was so intense, that scores of books were published for members of the general public, beginning in 1776, consisting of compilations of such constitutions, often with the U.S. Constitution, Declaration of Independence, and other national documents.

Whereas the U.S. has had a single Constitution since 1787, the only state with its original constitution is Massachusetts. State constitutions are typically much longer and more detailed than that of the U.S. States underwent particularly significant periods of rewriting their constitutions in the 1820s (Peterson 1966), during the Civil War and Reconstruction periods, and during the Progressive Era. Despite conventional wisdom on the subject, Christopher Hammons has recently ques-

tioned whether the length of state constitutions makes them inherently any less stable than the national constitution (1999).

Although the period of the Warren Court (roughly the 1950s and 1960s) witnessed major innovations in state law and criminal procedure via the application of provisions of the national Constitution to the states (largely done through the due process clause of the Fourteenth Amendment, ratified in 1868), recent years have witnessed some retrenchment as more conservative chiefs (Warren Burger and William Rehnquist) have followed. During this period, judges have sometimes instituted innovations in state law, sometimes surpassing requirements mandated by federal courts, through interpretations of state constitutional provisions (Howard 1987). The U.S. Supreme Court has generally taken the position that the Bill of Rights and other guarantees of liberty within the U.S. Constitution constitute a floor for rights rather than a ceiling. They have thus generally upheld more liberal interpretations of state law as long as these interpretations are planted clearly in the state constitutions themselves.

See Also Adams, John; Bill of Rights; Constitutional Convention Mechanism; Constitutionalism; Delegates, Collective Profile; Guarantee Clause; Mason, George; Massachusetts Constitution of 1780; Mayflower Compact; Ratification in the States; Virginia Declaration of Rights

FOR FURTHER READING

Adams, Willi Paul. 2001. *The First American Constitutions: Republican Ideology and the Making of the State Constitutions in the Revolutionary Era.* Expanded ed. Lanham, MD: Rowman and Littlefield Publishers.

Baum, Marsha L., and Christian G. Fritz. 2000. "American Constitution-Making: The Neglected State Constitutional Sources." *Hastings Constitutiional Law Quarterly* 27 (Winter): 199–242.

Conley, Patrick T., and John P. Kaminski, eds. 1988. *The Constitution and the States: The Role of the Original Thirteen in the Framing and Adoption of the Federal Constitution.* Madison, WI: Madison House.

——. 1992. *The Bill of Rights and the States: The Colonial*

and Revolutionary Origins of American Liberties. Madison, WI: Madison House.

Corwin, Edward S. 1964. "The Progress of Constitutional Theory between the Declaration of Independence and the Meeting of the Philadelphia Convention." *American Constitutional History: Essays by Edward S. Corwin*. Ed. Alpheus T. Mason and Gerald Garvey. New York: Harper and Row, Publishers.

Hammons, Christopher W. 1999. "Was James Madison Wrong? Rethinking the American Preference for Short, Framework-Oriented Constitutions." *American Political Science Review* 93 (December): 837–849.

Howard, A. A. Dick. 1987. "State Constitutions: An Essential Part of the American Constitutional System." In Robert S. Peck and Ralph S. Pollock, eds. *The Blessings of Liberty: Bicentennial Lectures at the National Archives*. Chicago, IL: ABA Press, 125–128.

Kruman, Marc W. 1997. *Between Authority and Liberty: State Constitution Making in Revolutionary America*. Chapel Hill: University of North Carolina Press.

Lutz, Donald S. 1980. "From Covenant to Constitution in American Political Thought." *Publius* 10 (Fall): 101–134.

Peterson, Merrill D. 1966. *Democracy, Liberty, and Property: The State Constitutional Conventions of the 1820's*. Indianapolis, IN: Bobbs-Merrill.

Tarr, G. Alan. 1998. *Understanding State Constitutions*. Princeton, NJ: Princeton University Press.

Wood, Gordon S. 1969. *The Creation of the American Republic, 1776–1787*. Chapel Hill: University of North Carolina Press.

STATE DELEGATIONS TO THE CONVENTION

Most scholarly attention that has focused on positions and voting records at the Constitutional Convention has centered on the 55 men who served as delegates. It is important to recognize, however, that, as under the Articles of Confederation, each state had a single vote. States, like individual delegates, had identifiable interests and their own personal dynamics.

All states except Rhode Island sent delegations to Philadelphia. The host state of Pennsylvania sent eight delegates, and Virginia, the most populous state, sent seven. New Jersey, Delaware, Maryland, and North Carolina each had a five-member delegation; Massachusetts, South Carolina, and Georgia each had a four-man delegation; Connecticut and New York each had three delegates; and New Hampshire had two. Virginia was represented on all 12 committees at the Convention, with Massachusetts and Pennsylvania being represented on 11, South Carolina and Connecticut serving on 10, New Jersey and Delaware on 7, Maryland and Georgia on 6, New York and North Carolina on 5, and New Hampshire (whose delegates arrived late) on 4 (Whitten 1961, 1285).

Dolphus Whitten, the author of the most extensive study of state delegations, has divided the delegations into four tiers of influence. He places the Virginia and Pennsylvania delegations in the top tier, largely because of the size and qualifications of their delegations. He gives Virginia a slight edge in importance due to its introduction of the highly influential Virginia Plan. He believes that the delegations from Massachusetts, South Carolina, and Connecticut were in a second bracket. He places Delaware, North Carolina, and New Jersey in the third most influential bracket, thus leaving Maryland, New York, Georgia, and New Hampshire in a fourth tier. He does not believe the Georgia delegates were especially outstanding. The Maryland and New York delegations were torn by internal dissent (when states were split or did not have a quorum, they were unable to cast votes), and the two delegates from New Hampshire arrived too late to exert significant influence (Whitten, 1286–1298).

Each state can be identified with certain key interests and principles that often corresponded to their population and size, to the importance of slavery within the state, and to the interests of the region (East, Middle, and South) of which they were a part. In addition to favoring the interests of the most populous states, Virginia supported strong national defense and congressional control over interstate commerce. The Pennsylvania delegation favored separation of powers; did not want new states created without the consent of parent states; and, as a state with immigrants, opposed onerous citizenship or residence requirements as a condition for holding public office.

Delegates from Massachusetts were concerned about stability and did not want Maine to become independent without the consent of Massachusetts. South Carolina was especially concerned with the perpetuation of slavery and opposed navigation legislation that might add to the cost of shipping. As a relatively small and weak state, Connecticut favored increased federal powers that might rescue it from its debt and often assumed the role of mediator at the Convention.

Delaware was concerned with maintaining the equal representation that it had under the Articles of Confederation. It also wanted slaves to count equally with whites for purposes of representation. North Carolina, with a large area and a growing population, often sided with Virginia on key issues and wanted to be sure that its western territories did not become states without its consent. Like Delaware, New Jersey was concerned with maintaining equal representation within Congress.

Maryland favored entrusting the federal government with power to protect its trade in tobacco and other products. New York reflected the tension between those, represented by Lansing and Yates, who thought the state was benefiting from the system under the Articles of Confederation that allowed it to impose customs duties on other states and those, represented by Alexander Hamilton, who envisioned a strong role within a strengthened Union. Georgia largely favored a stronger national government to combat the threat of Indians but wanted to preserve internal police powers. New Hampshire was driven by the need for greater security.

The interests that delegates reflected in Convention debates were often mirrored in debates over ratification of the Constitution within each of the states.

See Also Articles of Confederation; Connecticut; Delaware; Geography; Georgia; Maryland; Massachusetts; New Hampshire; New Jersey; New York; North Carolina; South Carolina; Pennsylvania; Ratification in the States; Virginia

FOR FURTHER READING

Whitten, Dolphus, Jr. 1961. *The State Delegations in the Philadelphia Convention of 1787*. 4 vols. Ph.D. diss., University of Texas, Austin.

STATE HOUSE

See PENNSYLVANIA STATE HOUSE

STATES, ADMISSION AND CREATION

With the exception of Canada, the admission of which the Articles of Confederation had optimistically provided for when it decided to accede to its government and join the other states, the Articles required nine states to consent before new states could be admitted to the Union. By contrast, Article IV, Section 3 of the U.S. Constitution provides that "New States may be admitted by the Congress into this Union; but no new State shall be formed or erected within the Jurisdiction of any other State; nor any State be formed by the Junction of two or more States, or Parts of States, without the Consent of the Legislatures of the States concerned as well as of the Congress."

The Virginia and New Jersey Plans

The Virginia Plan, which Edmund Randolph introduced to the Convention on May 29, stated "that provision ought to be made for the admission of States lawfully arising within the limits of the United States, whether from a voluntary junction of Government & Territory or otherwise, with the consent of a number of voices in the National legislature less than the whole" (Farrand 1937, I, 22). The Committee of the Whole accepted this measure on June 5. When William Paterson proposed the New Jersey Plan on June 15, it contained a much shorter section stating "that provision be made for the admission of new States into the Union" (I, 245).

Debates over Representation for the Western States

July 5

Just as the Convention was torn by debate over how to represent the small states and the large ones, so too, there was considerable disagreement as to whether new states from the West should be represented in the same ratio as those of the East. In discussing the first of three committee reports on representation on July 5, Gouverneur Morris of Pennsylvania observed that he thought representation should be based on property as well as on population. Arguing that property "ought to be one measure of the influence due to those who were to be affected by the Governmt.," he said that "the rule of representation ought to be so fixed as to secure the Atlantic States a prevalence in the National Councils" (I, 533). By way of justification, he further argued that "the new States will know less of the public interest than these, will have an interest in many respects different, in particular will be little scrupulous of involving the Community in wars the burdens & operations of which would fall chiefly on the maritime States. Provision ought therefore to be made to prevent the maritime States from being hereafter outvoted by them" (I, 534). By contrast, Virginia's George Mason thought that new states "ought to be subject to no unfavorable discriminations" (I, 534).

July 9–11

On July 9, a five-member committee, chaired by Gouverneur Morris, proposed an initial Congress of 56 members, roughly based on what was believed to be one representative for each 40,000 inhabitants. Although the committee also provided that Congress would be able to augment these numbers over time, it designed a special provision for new states:

And in case any of the States shall hereafter be divided, or any two or more States united, or any new States created within the limits of the United States, the Legislature shall possess authority to regulate the number of Representatives in any of the foregoing cases, upon the principle of their wealth and number of inhabitants. (I, 559)

The surface meaning of this provision may have differed from its first appearance. In responding to a query by Connecticut's Roger Sherman, Nathaniel Gorham of Massachusetts, who had served on the committee, thus observed that the committee had taken precaution against the eventual domination by the Western states by providing that "the Atlantic States having ye. Govt. in their own hands, may take care of their own interest, by dealing out the right of Representation in safe proportions to the Western States" (I, 560).

On July 10, Virginia's Edmund Randolph moved that Congress should periodically take a census after which it would readjust representation in Congress on the basis of "population and wealth" (I, 570). Morris continued to press for keeping power in the Eastern states. Madison reported that

he dwelt much on the danger of throwing such a preponderancy into the Western Scale, suggesting that in time the Western people wd. outnumber the Atlantic States. He wished therefore to put it in the power of the latter to keep a majority of votes in their own hands. (I, 571)

When discussion continued the following day, George Mason questioned the wisdom of sacrificing proportional representation to the desire to keep power in the hands of the existing states:

If the Western States are to be admitted into the Union as they arise, they must, he wd. repeat, be treated as equals, and subjected to no degrading discriminations. They will have the same pride & other passions which we have, and will either not unite with or will speedily revolt from the Union, if they are not in all respects placed on an equal footing with their brethren. It has been said they will be poor, and unable to make equal contributions to the general Treasury. He did not know but that in time they would be both more numerous & more wealthy than their Atlantic brethren. (I, 578–579)

Later in the day, Gouverneur Morris continued his opposition to proportional representation for the Western states. Reflecting a negative view of the frontier that was common in his day (Nobles 1989, 643–645), Morris observed that these states "would not be able to furnish men equally enlightened, to share in the administration of our common interests." He continued:

> The Busy haunts of men not the remote wilderness, was the proper School of political Talents. If the Western people get the power into their hands they will ruin the Atlantic interests. The Back members are always most averse to the best measures. He mentioned the case of Pena. formerly. The lower part of the State had ye. power in the first instance. They kept it in yr. own hands. & the country was ye. better for it. (I, 583)

This time Madison defended the Western interests. Accusing Morris of determining human character "by the points of the compass" (I, 584), he argued that England was also an example of a nation where the minority ensconced in rotten boroughs had refused to share with the majority. As to the West, "he was clear & firm [or so Madison reports!] in opinion that no unfavorable distinctions were admissible in either point of justice or policy" (I, 584). He further predicted that the West would become far more prosperous than many expected it to be. Fellow Virginian George Mason reported the common belief that in time the populations of the West and South would predominate and that they would not get their fair share of representatives unless the Constitution specifically mandated it (I, 586). Discussion then shifted focus to the issue of how slaves should be counted.

July 13–14

When on July 13 the Convention considered basing future representation in the House solely on the number of whites and on three-fifths of slaves (thus omitting wealth as a direct consideration), Gouverneur Morris again objected to the power this would in time place in the Western states. Pointing out that the interior of the nation, having "no property nor interest exposed on the sea," would be little affected by war, he asked "what security the Northn. & middle States will have agst. this danger" (I, 604).

Pennsylvania's James Wilson expressed sentiments on behalf of democracy, and illustrated the consequences of following another policy by referring to the experience of the Revolutionary War:

> The majority of people wherever found ought in all questions to govern the minority. If the interior Country should acquire this majority they will not only have the right, but will avail themselves of it whether we will or no. The jealousy misled the policy of G. Britain with regard to America. The fatal maxims exposed by her were that the Colonies were growing too fast, and that their growth must be stunted in time. (I, 605)

Debate continued the following day. This time Elbridge Gerry of Massachusetts wanted to consider the dangers of admitting Western states. He observed that "He was for admitting them on liberal terms, but not for putting ourselves into their hands. They will if they acquire power like all men, abuse it. They will oppress commerce, and drain our wealth into the Western Country" (II, 2–3). He proposed limiting the representation of the new states so that they should never be able to outnumber those bordering the Atlantic, and he proposed a specific motion to this effect that Rufus King, also of Massachusetts, seconded.

Connecticut's Roger Sherman did not think it was likely that residents of new states would ever outnumber those already in existence, and certainly not in the near future. In any case, he observed that "We are providing for our posterity, for our children & our grand Children, who would be as likely to be citizens of new Western States, as of the old States. On this consideration alone, we ought to make no such discrimination as was proposed by the motion" (II, 3). Gerry observed that, as other children would stay behind, it was incumbent on delegates also "to provide for their interests" (II, 3). Perhaps with an eye to possible Spanish influence, he also raised the specter that "foreigners" might settle in the West (II, 3). The Convention narrowly rejected Gerry's motion by a 5-4-1 vote.

Committee of Detail

The Committee of Detail, which reported on August 6, essentially followed the example of the Articles in regard to new states by requiring that the admission of new states would require a two-thirds vote of both houses of Congress. It also required the consent of the legislatures of states from which new states were formed; provided that "the new States shall be admitted on the same terms with the original States"; and specified that Congress could "make conditions with the new States, concerning the public debt which shall be then subsisting" (II, 188).

Continued Discussion

Discussion of these provisions on August 29 continued to reveal dramatic differences in the attitudes that delegates had toward Western states. Gouverneur Morris opened the discussion by moving to strike the provision admitting new states on the same basis with the older ones. By contrast, James Madison observed that Western states "neither would nor ought to submit to a Union which degraded them from an equal rank with the other States" (II, 454). Fellow Virginian George Mason observed that, as a matter of policy it might be desirable to curb westward immigration, but he observed that the people would go where they found it in their self-interest to go and that "the best policy is to treat them with that equality which will make them friends not enemies" (II, 454). Morris denied that he was seeking to discourage westward migration; he simply "did not wish . . . to throw the power into their hands" (II, 454). Connecticut's Roger Sherman could not agree to a discrimination between new states and old ones, although New Hampshire's John Lang-

don agreed that there might be circumstances "which would render it inconvenient to admit new States on terms of equality" (II, 454). North Carolina's Hugh Williamson drew an interesting distinction, indicating that existing small states were to be equally represented in the Senate because of their current status, but denying that the same rationale would apply to new states applying from the West. The Convention nonetheless rejected Morris's motion by a vote of 9-2.

Maryland's Luther Martin then joined Morris in proposing to strike the provision requiring the consent of two-thirds of the existing states to admit new states. Before it could be voted on, Morris offered a substitute for the entire provision. It provided that "New States may be admitted by the Legislature into this Union: but no new State shall be erected within the limits of any of the present States, without the consent of the Legislature of such State, as well as of the Genl. Legislature" (II, 455). Morris claimed in a letter of 1803 that this language was designed to allow the future governing of Canada and Louisiana as provinces, but he admits that had he expressed this view more openly, "a strong opposition would have been made" (III, 404), leading one to question how effective his motion would have been in securing its objectives. In any event, the Convention accepted Morris's motion through the word "Union." Martin then opposed the latter part of the provision, claiming that the "limited states," that is, those, like Maryland, without extensive expanses in the West, would be alarmed if states with large Western lands had to consent to the formation of new states within such expanses. He wondered whether Vermont, then a part of New York that had long claimed its independence (see Onuf 1985), should "be reduced by force in favor of the States claiming it?" He also wondered about Frankland (a reference to Franklin, the current state of Tennessee) and western Virginia (now Kentucky). Nonetheless, the Convention voted to accept the second portion of Morris's substitute and now considered the new section as a whole.

Sherman opposed the new provision. He thought that it was unnecessary since "The Union cannot dismember a State without its consent" (II, 455). Langdon agreed with Martin's previous criticism and feared that the new proposal would "excite dangerous opposition" (II, 455). Morris retorted that the small states should like his proposal because "it holds up the idea of dismembering the large States" (II, 455). Butler introduced a quite practical concern. If, he argued, new states could be created without the consent of the states of which they previously formed a part, demagogues would try to create such states every time the people wanted to avoid taxes. Connecticut's William Johnson observed that Congress had pledged to admit Vermont into the Union and that it should be permitted, indeed "compelled," to enter without New York's consent. Langdon thought it would injure New Hampshire if Vermont were not admitted to the Union and did not have to pay its share of taxes. Dickinson added his opposition to requiring smaller states to support larger states trying to hang on to their territory. Wilson observed that there was no obstacle to allowing a state to divide when a majority within the state wanted to do so; he said that "the aim of those in opposition to the article . . . was that the Genl. Government should abet the *minority*, & by that means divide a State against its own consent" (II, 456). Morris said that if it were the intention of the Convention to divide the large states against their will, such states would rather quickly leave.

The Convention resumed discussion of Morris's substitute motion on the following day. Carroll moved to strike the portion of the Article requiring states' consent to their division. He feared that this provision would not protect "the right of the U. States to the back lands" and proposed a clause providing that the provision did not relate to lands ceded to the United States by Britain in the treaty of peace. Rutledge said that Vermont could be provided for and that there was no need to fear that Virginia and North Carolina would attempt to hang on to their Western lands. He wanted simply to leave the matter as it was. Wilson observed that "He knew of nothing that would give greater or juster alarm than the doctrine, that a political society is to be torne asunder without its own consent" (II, 462).

After the Convention failed to commit this issue, Sherman proposed a substitute motion, designed in part to provide for Vermont's admission as a new state, which failed. Johnson then offered yet another motion inserting the words "hereafter formed" after "shall be" as a way of permitting Vermont to enter the Union without New York's consent. All states except Delaware and Maryland accepted it. The Convention accepted a similarly motivated substitution of the word "jurisdiction" [of any of the present States] for "limits" (II, 463).

Recurring Debates

The issue of Western states just would not die. Martin reiterated the "unreasonableness" of forcing western parts of existing states to get consent for their independence. He observed that "Even if they should become the majority, the majority of *Counties,* as in Virginia may still hold fast the dominion over them" (II, 463). Martin observed that Wilson, who had previously emphasized the role of popular majorities, no longer seemed to scorn states as "*political* bodies" now that the interests of the large states were at stake. Martin indicated that small states forced to keep Western states in subjection might also consider leaving the Union (II, 464). Only three states agreed to a substitute motion that Martin introduced designed to allow for the creation of new states "within as well as without the territory claimed by the several States or either of them" (II, 464). The Convention did accept Morris's amended motion by a vote of 8-3. As amended, the motion provided that "new States may be admitted by the Legislature into the Union: but no new State shall be hereafter formed or erected within the jurisdiction of any of the present States without the consent of the Legislature of such State as well as of the General Legislature" (II, 464).

Still the debate continued. Dickinson succeeded in adding a provision preventing new states from being formed by the junction of other states without their consent or that of Congress. Carroll, in turn, pressed for a motion designed to see that this provision did not affect vacant lands ceded to the U.S. by the treaty of peace with England. Wilson preferred that the Constitution simply leave this matter as it was. Madison also opposed Carroll's motion, believing that federal courts would have jurisdiction over this issue, but suggesting that if it were to be included, it should be worded so as not to affect the claims of existing states either. Baldwin addressed the interest of Georgia, and Rutledge objected that it was wrong to insert a provision "where there was nothing which it could restrain, or on which it could operate" (II, 465).

Carroll then offered a motion vesting the decision of such claims in the Supreme Court. Morris succeeded in getting this postponed to consider a provision that

> the Legislature shall have power to dispose of and make all needful rules and regulations respecting the territory or other property belonging to the U. States; and nothing in this constitution contained, shall be so construed as to prejudice any claims either of the U-S–or of any particular State. (II, 466)

Martin, in turn, tried unsuccessfully to amend Morris's motion with a proviso for Supreme Court resolution of such issues, and the Convention agreed to Morris's motion with only Maryland in dissent. The Committee of Style effected minor changes in wording but did not further alter the substance of this provision (compare II, 578 with II, 602).

Analysis

The U.S. Constitution differs from that of the Articles by not requiring a supermajority vote in Congress in order to admit new states. Despite strong and continuing arguments for retaining power in the existing states, Convention delegates wisely avoided the creation of a Western empire by providing that new states would enter the Union on an equal basis with the old. This decision has enabled the nation to grow from 13 to fifty states, with the most populous, and hence the most heavily represented in Congress, no longer being from the East. Although the delegates devoted a lot of attention to the subject, examples of state attempts to break off from others against their will (the example of West Virginia,

which separated from Virginia during the Civil War, probably comes the closest) have not been significant.

See Also Kentucky; Tennessee; Vermont

FOR FURTHER READING

Farrand, Max, ed. 1937. *The Records of the Federal Convention.* 4 vols. New Haven, CT: Yale University Press.
Nobles, Gregory H. 1989. "Breaking into the Backcountry: New Approaches to the Early American Frontier, 1750–1800." *William and Mary Quarterly,* 3rd ser. 46 (October): 641–670.
Onuf, Peter S. 1982. "From Colony to Territory: Changing Concepts of Statehood in Revolutionary America." *Political Science Quarterly* 97 (Autumn): 447–459.
——. 1986. "Liberty, Development, and Union: Visions of the West in the 1780s." *William and Mary Quarterly,* 3rd ser. 53 (April): 179–213.
——. 1985. "Virginia, Vermont, and the Origins of the Federal Republic." *this Constitution,* no. 7 (Summer): 4–10.

STATES, LEGISLATURES

In the period from the beginning of the American Revolution in 1775 and 1776, when most states began formulating their constitutions, to the Constitutional Convention of 1787, most states had formulated systems of government in which state legislative power dominated over that of the other two branches (Wood 1969). State legislatures had appointed delegates to the Mount Vernon Conference and the Annapolis Convention, and they had in turn appointed the delegates to the Constitutional Convention. Forty-one or more of the delegates to the Convention had served in their respective state legislatures and another forty had served in the Continental Congress (Beach et al. 1997), so they were well aware of, and in some cases critical of, the powers that state legislatures exercised.

Concerns about State Legislative Powers under the Articles

At times the delegates disagreed about whether the problems under the Articles stemmed from the power of the people or that of the states. Connecticut's Roger Sherman thus argued on May 31 for the selection of members of Congress by the state legislatures rather than by the people. He observed that "the people . . . should have as little to do as may be about the Government. They want [lack] information and are constantly liable to be misled" (Farrand 1937, I, 48). Agreeing with Sherman, Elbridge Gerry of Massachusetts observed that "the evils we experience flow from the excess of democracy. The people do not want virtue; but are the dupes of pretended patriots" (I, 48). By contrast, Virginia's George Mason and Pennsylvania's James Wilson argued for popular election.

Wilson observed that it was

> wrong to increase the weight of the State Legislatures by making them the electors of the national Legislature. All interference between the general and local Governmens. should be obviated as much as possible. On examination it would be found that the opposition of States to federal measures had proceded much more from the Officers of the States, than from the people at large. (I, 49)

Madison supported Wilson, fearing that if elections were intermediate "the people would be lost sight of altogether; and the necessary sympathy between them and their ruler and officers, too little felt" (I, 50). Moreover, in a speech on July 21 favoring associating judges with the executive to veto legislative acts, Virginia's James Madison thus observed: "Experience in all the States had evinced a powerful tendency in the Legislature to absorb all power into its vortex. This was the real source of danger to the American Constitutions" (II, 74).

Virginia and New Jersey Plans

Under the Articles of Confederation, state legislatures had been responsible for selecting and paying state representatives to the unicameral Congress, in which states were represented equally. The Virginia Plan, which Edmund Randolph introduced on May 29, proposed instead that Congress be bicameral and that the people of the states would elect members of the first branch of the legislature and that this branch would then select members of the second branch from among "a proper number of persons nominated by the individual Legislatures" (I, 20). Representation in both houses was to be according to population. Moreover, the powers of the Congress were to be balanced against those of a strong executive and judicial branch.

The Virginia Plan had at least two other provisions related to state legislatures. They were that Congress should have the power "to negative all laws passed by the several States, contravening in the opinion of the National Legislature the articles of Union" (I, 21). And that the executive and select members of the judiciary should comprise a Council of Revision with power to examine and invalidate acts both of Congress and of the state legislatures (I, 21). This council would apparently have the power to overturn a congressional negative, but Congress would have power to override this veto (I, 21).

In time, of course, delegates significantly modified the Virginia Plan, especially after the New Jersey Plan proposed retaining a unicameral Congress for which state legislatures would presumably continue to select members of Congress and in which states would continue to be represented equally. After elements of these plans were combined, the people assembled in districts retained the right, as proposed in the Virginia Plan, to select members of the House of Representatives, but state legislatures retained the power to appoint members of the U.S. Senate. State legislatures retained this power until they ratified the Seventeenth Amendment in 1913, which vested it in the voters. State legislatures retained significant control in the constitutional amending process. The Constitution grants two-thirds majorities of the states the power to petition Congress to call a constitutional convention to revise the Constitution. The amending Article further requires three-fourths of such legislatures (or conventions called within the states) to ratify amendments proposed by Congress. The proposals in the Virginia Plan for a congressional negative on state laws and for a Council of Revision were dropped, although judicial review of state legislation arguably provided more effective remedies.

Control over the President

On June 2, Delaware's John Dickinson proposed that Congress should have the power to remove the executive "on the request of a majority of the Legislatures of individual States" (I, 85). This proposal appears to have been motivated less by a concern to grant increased powers to state legislatures than a concern with seeing that the president simply did not become a congressional pawn (I, 86).

Providing Salaries for Members of Congress

On June 12, James Madison proposed that the national government should pay the salaries of members of Congress. Madison observed that state payments "would create an improper dependence" (I, 216). Mason expressed additional concerns about state legislative payments:

> 1. the different States would make different provision for their representatives, and an inequality would be felt among them, whereas he thought they ought to be in all respects equal. 2. the parsimony of the States might reduce the provision so low as that as had already happened in choosing delegates to Congress, the question would be not who were most fit to be chosen, but who were most willing to serve. (I, 216)

This debate was renewed on a number of occasions. Thus, on June 22 Oliver Ellsworth proposed that states should pay members of Congress. He observed "that the manners of different States were very different in the Stile of living and in the profits accruing from the exercise of like talents" (I, 371). North Carolina's Hugh Williamson expressed further concern that new Western states might burden existing Eastern states (I, 372).

Nathaniel Gorham of Massachusetts thought that states had been too miserly with such salaries, and Randolph said that "If the States were to pay the members of the Natl. Legislature, a dependence would be created that would vitiate the whole System" (I, 372). The debate was renewed on a number of occasions (see, for example, I, 427–428; II, 290–292), but in time the delegates decided to allow for the national provision of such salaries.

Presidential Selection

Delegates to the Constitutional Convention largely devised the Electoral College mechanism in order to avoid executive dependence on Congress. Although such electors are today chosen by popular vote, the system as devised by the Framers originally allowed for state legislatures to make such selections, and, as the presidential election of 2000 showed, states legislatures continue to share some power in this area.

Limits on State Legislative Powers

The Constitutional Convention imposed a number of limits on the power of state legislatures. Mostly found in Article I, Section 10, many of these limits involve powers, like treaty and war-making, that the Constitution entrusts specifically to the national government. Article I, Section 10 prohibits state legislatures, as it prohibits Congress, from adopting ex post facto laws or bills of attainder. In addition, it prohibits state legislatures from coining money or from impairing the obligation of contracts. Many of the Framers associated these two policies with injustices under the Articles of Confederation.

Section 4 of Article IV guaranteed each state "a republican form of government." It further granted Congress power to protect states against invasions or domestic insurrections. In debates on this provision on July 18, Gouverneur Morris of Pennsylvania wondered whether the Convention should agree to protect "such laws as exist in R. Island," which delegates associated with partisan legislation on behalf of debtors (II, 47). Other delegates persuasively argued that the national government should have power to protect the states.

On August 17, delegates resumed debate over the circumstances in which Congress should act. In discussing a provision to limit such aid to circumstances in which state legislatures requested it, some delegates wished to add requests for help by state governors. Maryland's Luther Martin feared that the introduction of force without state legislative consent would give Congress "a dangerous & unnecessary power." He explained that "the consent of the State ought to precede the introduction of any extraneous force whatever" (II, 317). Similarly, Elbridge Gerry of Massachusetts expressed concern about "letting loose the myrmidons of the U. States on a State without its own consent" (II, 317). In time, the Convention agreed that Congress could accept requests on behalf of state governors when state legislatures were not in session.

Delegates to the Convention recognized that there would continue to be tension between state and national interests. In addition to providing that the Constitution, and laws and treaties made under its authority, would be the supreme law of the land, Article VI of the Constitution further provided that "members of the several State Legislatures" would join members of Congress and other state and federal officers in taking oaths "to support this Constitution."

Ratification of the Constitution

The Articles had required that constitutional amendments receive the unanimous consent of the state legislatures. Not only did the Convention provide for a different amending process, but it also proposed that the new Constitution would be ratified not by state legislatures, but by special conventions called within the states. Delegates not only realized that existing state legislatures might be reluctant to vote for a system in which their powers would not be as strong vis-à-vis the new Congress as they were under the Articles of Confederation but also hoped that ratification by conventions would give the new government a more popular foundation. Still, the Constitution remained dependent on the willingness of state legislatures to call ratifying conventions.

Constitutional Theory

Both at the Convention and in later arguments that he advanced in *Federalist* No. 10, James Madison argued that the central problem of republican government was injustices spawned by factions. He suggested that such problems could be managed by extending the sphere of government and by reliance on representatives from larger districts, who would be moderate minority interests. Significantly, the number of people in the initial Congress was often smaller than the numbers of state legislatures of the day. The U.S. Senate was and remains a comparatively small body.

Responding to concerns that Antifederalists raised, Madison and others eventually supported a bill of rights. Madison remained convinced that state legislatures would pose greater threats to civil liberties than would Congress, but he did not succeed in getting approval for an amendment that would have limited the powers of the states. Moreover, Madison (who would argue against the doctrine of nullification that John C. Calhoun of South Carolina later advanced) secretly joined Jefferson in authoring the Virginia and Kentucky Resolutions in 1798 in attempts to use interposition by state legislatures to stop what both men regarded as congressional violations of civil liberties in the adoption of the Alien and Sedition Acts of the same year (Koch and Ammon 1948).

In time, the Civil War put a virtual end to the doctrines of state nullification of federal law and of state secession. Moreover, state legislatures (some under duress) ratified the Fourteenth Amendment in 1868 protecting citizens of the United States against abridgements of their privileges and immunities, their rights to due process and their right to equal protection of the laws by state governments as well. The due process clause has, in turn, become the vehicle by which the Supreme Court in the twentieth century applied most of the guarantees in the Bill of Rights to state governments as well as to Congress.

See Also Amending Process; Attainder, Bills of; Bill of Rights; Congress, House of Representatives, Selection of; Congress, House of Representatives, Size; Congress, Senate, Selection; Congress, Senate, Size; Connecticut Compromise; Contracts Clause; Federalism; *Federalist, The;* Guarantee Clause; Money, State Coining and Emissions of; Oaths of Office; President, Selection; Ratification, Convention Debates, and Constitutional Provision; State Appointment of Delegates to the Constitutional Convention; States, Limits on; Supremacy Clause

FOR FURTHER READING

Beach, John C., et al. 1997. "State Administration and the Founding Fathers during the Critical Period." *Administration and Society* 28 (February): 511.

Corwin, Edward S. 1964. "The Progress of Constitutional Theory between the Declaration of Independence and the Meeting of the Philadelphia Convention." *American Constitutional History: Essays by Edward S. Corwin.* Ed. Alpheus T. Mason and Gerald Garvey. New York: Harper and Row Publishers.

Farrand, Max, ed. 1937. *The Records of the Federal Convention.* 4 vols. New Haven, CT: Yale University Press.

Hobson, Charles F. 1979. "The Negative on State Laws: James Madison, the Constitution, and the Crisis of Republican Government." *William and Mary Quarterly,* 3rd ser. 36 (April): 214–235.

Koch, Adrienne, and Harry Ammon. 1948. "The Virginia and Kentucky Resolutions: An Episode in Jefferson's and Madison's Defense of Civil Liberties." *William and Mary Quarterly,* 3rd ser. 5 (April): 145–176.

Lerche, Charles O., Jr. 1949. "The Guarantee of a Republican Form of Government and the Admission of New States." *Journal of Politics* 11 (August): 578–604.

Wood, Gordon. 1969. *The Creation of the American Republic, 1776–1787.* Chapel Hill: University of North Carolina Press.

STATES, LIMITS ON

Article I, Section 9 limits the powers of Congress, and Article I, Section 10 limits the powers of the states. The latter section is divided into three paragraphs.

Limits on the States Alone

The Constitution grants certain powers exclusively to the national government. The states are therefore prohibited from legislating in regard to them. The first and third paragraphs of Article I, Section 10 prohibit the states from exercising such powers. The first paragraph prohibits states from entering into treaties, granting letters of marque and reprisal (used to authorize pirates during time of war), coining money or emitting bills of credit, or making anything but gold or silver payment of debts. Similarly, the third paragraph prohibits states, without the consent of Congress, from laying duties of tonnage, keeping troops or ships in time of peace, entering into interstate compacts or compacts with foreign nations, or engaging in war except when they are invaded or in imminent danger.

Limits on Both State and National Governments

In attempting to protect liberty, the delegates to the Convention wanted to prohibit any government from exercising some powers. Thus the first paragraph of Article I, Section 10 also contains limits on bills of attainder, ex post facto laws, or grants of titles of nobility, each of which the Constitution also applied to Congress in Article I, Section 9. This paragraph contains an additional limitation on impairing the obligation of contracts, undoubtedly stemming from the Framers' belief that state abuse would be more likely in this area than abuse by Congress.

Additional Limits on the States

Concern by the delegates for promoting commerce and prohibiting discriminatory state regulations is manifested in the second paragraph of Article I, Section 10. It prohibits states from taxing imports or exports.

During debates over the adoption of the Constitution, Antifederalists expressed concern that the document did not contain a bill of rights.

This led to the adoption of the first 10 amendments. Early court decisions, most notably *Barron v. Baltimore,* 32 U.S. 243 (1833), established that these amendments limited the national government but not the states. After the Fourteenth Amendment was ratified in 1868, some advocates and scholars believed that it was designed to apply the provision in the Bill of Rights to the states. Although the U.S. Supreme Court did not initially accept this conclusion, over time it has applied most of the provisions in these amendments to both state and national governments, a process known as "incorporation."

See Also Attainder, Bills of; Bill of Rights; Contracts Clause; Ex Post Facto Laws; Liberty; Money, State Coining and Emissions of; Taxes on Imports and Exports; Titles of Nobility

FOR FURTHER READING

Amar, Akhil Reed. 1998. *The Bill of Rights: Creation and Reconstruction.* New Haven, CT: Yale University Press.

Goldwin, Robert A. 1997. *From Parchment to Power: How James Madison Used the Bill of Rights to Save the Constitution.* Washington, DC: AEI Press.

Schweitzer, Mary M. 1989. "State-Issued Currency and the Ratification of the U.S. Constitution." *Journal of Economic History* 49 (June): 311–322.

STATES, POLICE POWERS

Scholars often refer to the powers that states continue to exercise in the federal system as "police powers." Scholars sometimes also call these "reserved powers" because the Constitution has not delegated them to the national government. In addition to law enforcement, these powers include, but are not limited to, legislation directed to the health, safety, welfare, education, and morality of the citizens (for fuller description, see Lieberman 1992, 382–383).

It is not altogether clear how many such rights would have remained with the states under the Virginia Plan that Edmund Randolph introduced before the Convention on May 29. This plan proposed to vest Congress with the fairly broad power "to legislate in all cases to which the separate States are incompetent, or in which the harmony of the United States may be interrupted by the exercise of individual Legislation" (Farrand 1937, I, 21). In addition, the plan proposed granting Congress power "to negative all laws passed by the several States, contravening in the opinion of the National Legislature the articles of Union" (I, 21). Over time, however, neither provision remained in the Constitution; the Committee of Detail substituted a list of enumerated powers that Congress would exercise.

On July 17, the day after the Convention adopted the Connecticut Compromise and a week before the Convention appointed the Committee of Detail, Connecticut's Roger Sherman proposed to substitute a motion relative to the powers of Congress putting greater emphasis on the limitations of congressional power. It would have provided that Congress would have power:

To make laws binding on the People of the United States in all cases which may concern the common interests of the Union: but not to interfere with the government of the individual States in any matters of internal police which respect the government of such States only, and wherein the general welfare of the United States is not concerned. (II, 21)

In introducing the resolution, Sherman observed "that it would be difficult to draw the line between the powers of the Genl. Legislatures, and those to be left with the States" (II, 25). Surprisingly, Pennsylvania's James Wilson, generally a friend of national powers, seconded the motion "as better expressing the general principle" (II, 26). Fellow Pennsylvanian Gouverneur Morris pointed to cases where a state's "internal police" ought to be infringed, "as in the case of paper money & other tricks by which Citizens of other States may be affected" (II, 26).

At this point, the debate appears to have become a bit testy. Sherman apparently read an enumeration of congressional powers (perhaps similar to those later proposed by the Committee of Detail) that included power to levy taxes on trade but apparently did not include the power of direct taxation. Morris pressed the advantage by suggesting that this would force the general government into "quotas & requisitions, which are subversive of the idea of Govt." (II, 26). Sherman acknowledged that he had not yet worked out this "deficiency," and the Convention rejected his motion by a vote of eight to two.

Although Sherman did not get what he called for, the Committee of Detail arguably addressed his concerns by deciding to enumerate the powers of Congress rather than leaving them as indistinct as they were in the Virginia Plan. In a second report by the Committee of Detail on August 22, it proposed to add a provision specifying that Congress should be able

to provide, as may become necessary, from time to time, for the well managing and securing the common property and general interests and welfare of the United States in such manner as shall not interfere with the Governments of individual States in matters which respect only their internal Police, or for which their individual authorities may be competent. (II, 367)

It does not appear that the Convention debated this provision, but Sherman reintroduced a similar concern on September 15 in discussions of the constitutional amending process. On that date, he proposed annexing a provision to the amending clause specifying "that no State shall without its consent be affected in its internal police, or deprived of its equal suffrage in the Senate" (II, 630). The Convention rejected this proposal by an 8-3 vote after Virginia's James Madison opined that if the Convention began with such "special provisos," then "every State will insist on them, for their boundaries, exports &c." (II, 630).

Defeated here, Sherman's concern arguably found expression in the Tenth Amendment (the last amendment in the Bill of Rights). It specified that "the powers not delegated to the United States by the Constitution, nor prohibited by it to the states, are reserved to the states respectively,

or to the people." Like earlier formulations that recognized that Congress would sometimes be exercising implied powers (generally supported by the "necessary and proper clause" in Article I, Section 8), this formulation is better at expressing the recognition that states retained certain powers than at specifying what they are. It thus still leaves the boundaries of state and national powers largely to be resolved by political forces and patrolled by the U.S. Supreme Court. The Eleventh Amendment (ratified in 1798) strengthened the idea that states were immunized from some suits, and the Fourteenth Amendment (ratified in 1868) further guaranteed individual rights against state abridgement.

See Also Amending Process; Bill of Rights; Committee of Detail; Congress, Collective Powers; Federalism; Sherman, Roger; Virginia Plan

FOR FURTHER READING

Farrand, Max, ed. 1937. *The Records of the Federal Convention.* 4 vols. New Haven, CT: Yale University Press.

Lieberman, Jethro K. 1992. *The Evolving Constitution.* New York: Random House.

Murrin, John M., David E. Narrett, Ronald L. Hatzenbuehler, and Michael Kammen. 1988. *Essays on Liberty and Federalism: The Shaping of the U.S. Constitution.* College Station: Texas A and M University Press.

Vile, M. J. C. 1961. *The Structure of American Federalism.* London: Oxford University Press.

STATESMANSHIP

The term "statesmen," or the contemporary "statespersons," is often used to distinguish individuals in government—sometimes distinguished from mere "politicians"—who look beyond their and their constituents' immediate self-interest toward longer-term goals. Although not losing sight of such interests, such individuals also attempt to keep larger principles in view, even when they find it necessary to compromise.

Through much of the nineteenth century, the Constitution was revered, and historians like Charles Bancroft portrayed delegates to the Constitutional Convention as demigods. Progressive historians, most notably Charles Beard, tended to stress more prosaic concerns, including the delegates' economic interests, but historian Forrest McDonald and others have called his studies into question. Political scientist John Roche has stressed what good politicians many of the delegates were and how ably they compromised on key issues, like those involving state representation in the two houses of Congress and the selection of the president through the Electoral College. Bernard Bailyn and Gordon Wood are among those who have reiterated the role that ideas (sometimes portrayed as ideologies) played in the decisions of the Framers.

There is general consensus, but far from unanimity, among writers about the Constitutional Convention that many of the key Framers—especially men like George Washington, Benjamin Franklin, James Madison, James Wilson, George Mason, Alexander Hamilton, and Roger Sherman—can clearly be classified as statesmen of the highest order. The rules of the Convention, including the secrecy of the proceedings, were designed to promote deliberation, and George Washington's presence as president of the proceedings lent them a special gravity. The delegates met with a sense that the nation was undergoing a crisis that required attention, and they recognized that they were not simply enacting policies for their day but formulating governmental structures for the future. Moreover, they often justified their proposals both in the Convention and in subsequent writings, like *The Federalist*, for the public, in fairly sophisticated terms. Quite often they were constructing structures, the effects on specific issues of which they could not accurately predict in advance (Nelson 1987).

The status of the Founding Fathers as statesmen has been furthered by the fact that the document continues to serve the nation long after it was adopted. Most of the delegates at the Convention arrived with prior service to the nation, and many went on to serve in key positions within the new government.

In justifying the new government in *The Federalist*, Essay No. 10, James Madison both recognized the possibility of statesmanship and warned against relying upon it to secure justice on a day-to-day basis. In thus outlining the manner in which he thought that an extended republic would help mitigate the problems of factions that had beset previous democracies, Madison opined:

> It is vain to say that enlightened statesmen will be able to adjust these clashing interests and render them all subservient to the public good. Enlightened statesmen will not always be at the helm. Nor, in many cases, can such an adjustment be made at all without taking into view indirect and remote considerations, which will rarely prevail over the immediate interest which one party may find in disregarding the rights of another or the good of the whole. (Hamilton, Madison, and Jay 1961, 80)

See Also Beard, Charles; Compromise; Constitutional Moments; Delegates, Collective Assessments; Founding; Motives of the Founding Fathers; Rules of the Constitutional Convention

FOR FURTHER READING

Hamilton, Alexander, James Madison, and John Jay. 1961. *The Federalist Papers*. Ed. Clinton Rossiter. New York: New American Library.

Nelson, William E. 1987. "Reason and Compromise in the Establishment of the Federal Constitution, 1787–1801." *William and Mary Quarterly*, 3rd ser. 44 (July): 458–484.

Roche, John P. 1961. "The Founding Fathers: A Reform Caucus in Action." *American Political Science Review* 55 (December): 799–816.

Scheef, Robert W. 2001. "'Public Citizens' and the Constitution: Bridging the Gap between Popular Sovereignty and Original Intent." *Fordham Law Review* 69 (April): 2201–2251.

Storing, Herbert J. 1981. "The Federal Convention of 1787: Politics, Principles, and Statesmanship." In Ralph A. Rossum and Gary L. McDowell, eds. *The American Founding: Politics, Statesmanship, and the Constitution*. Port Washington, NY: Kennikat Press, 12–28.

STRONG, CALEB (1746–1815)

Caleb Strong was born to the family of a tanner in Northampton, Massachusetts in 1746. After earning a degree at Harvard, he studied law with Joseph Hawley and was admitted to the bar. He served on Northampton's Committee of Safety and was a delegate to the Massachusetts Constitutional Convention. He also served on the Massachusetts Council and as a member of the state senate before being chosen as one of the state's four delegates to the Constitutional Convention. Strong did not serve on any committees during the Convention, and he was not a frequent speaker, but he did have something to say about the makeup of each of the three branches of the new government.

Caleb Strong, delegate from Massachusetts
(Pixel That)

Congress

Strong began attending the Constitutional Convention on May 28. The first official action he was recorded as taking was on May 31 when the Convention was discussing whether the first branch of Congress should be selected by the people. Pierce somewhat ambiguously recorded that Strong "would agree to the principle, provided it would undergo a certain modification, but pointed out nothing" (Farrand 1937, I, 58).

On June 21 Strong seconded a motion of Connecticut's Oliver Ellsworth favoring yearly elections to the U.S. House of Representatives at a time when the Convention was considering terms of two or three years (I, 361)–at the Massachusetts ratifying convention, Strong later portrayed the two-year term as a compromise between those who favored annual elections and those who wanted a longer term (III, 247). On June 12, Strong and Gerry split the Massachusetts delegation by voting against a seven-year term for senators while fellow delegates King and Gorham voted for it (I, 219). On July 2, Strong further favored the commitment of the issue of representation to a committee. At that time, however, he indicated that if the two branches "should be established on different principles, contentions would prevail and there would never be a concur-

rence in necessary measures" (I, 515). On July 14, Strong further indicated his support for the Great Compromise which this committee had formulated. He believed that the Convention faced either the prospect of accepting this report or ending in failure: "It is agreed on all hands that Congress are nearly at an end. If no Accommodation takes place, the Union itself must soon be dissolved" (II, 7).

Strong poured cold water on the idea that the large states could come up on their own with a plan to which the small states would agree. He further argued that the small states had made a concession in agreeing to allow money bills to be introduced in the House of Representatives, and he thought the larger states were also duty-bound to make their own compromise on representation. Strong appeared to reiterate the importance of this provision on August 9 when he seconded a motion by Virginia's Edmund Randolph to postpone consideration of Senate representation until it was decided whether this provision would remain (II, 232). Similarly, on August 15, Strong proposed a motion reinstating the provision limiting the origination of money bills to the House of Representatives but allowing the Senate to propose or concur in amendments to the same (II, 297).

On August 14, Strong proposed that members of Congress should be granted $4 a day for their services (II, 293). He would, however, have allowed for states to supplement this amount.

Presidency

On July 24, Strong indicated that he did not think that congressional selection of the president would require that the president be limited to a single term. He anticipated that there would be sufficient legislative turnover so that the second election would be based on a different set of men than the first and that executive corruption of the legislature would not be a major concern. He did not believe that the president would be unduly bound to the legislature through gratitude and feared that an Electoral College would be too complex. He also feared "that the first characters in the States would not feel sufficient motives to undertake the office of Electors" (II, 100).

Judiciary

On July 21, Strong went on record against allying the judiciary with the executive in forming a Council of Revision to invalidate congressional laws. He argued that "the power of making ought to be kept distinct from that of expounding the laws. No maxim was better established. The Judges in exercising the function of expositors might be influenced by the part they had taken, in framing the laws" (II, 75).

Life after the Convention

Strong left the Convention in August because of an illness in the family but later served in the Massachusetts ratifying convention. In defending the Constitution there, Strong disputed accusations that the proposed Constitution was too ambiguous and defended those who had written it: "I think the whole of it is expressed in the plain, common language of mankind. If any parts are not so explicit as they could be, it cannot be attributed to any design; for I believe a great majority of the men who formed it were sincere and honest men" (III, 248). Strong also explained the reasons for the Connecticut Compromise and for other decisions that the Convention had made.

Elected to the U.S. Senate, where he served from 1789 to 1796, Strong helped draft the Judiciary Act of 1789 and supported the Federalist Party. He was elected governor in 1800, and was returned to this position in 1812. During the War of 1812, Strong opposed allowing the U.S. government to call out the militia. He supported the Hartford Convention of 1814 and may have actually favored withdrawal from the Union by the New England states. Strong died in Northampton in 1815. He and his wife, Sara Hooker, had nine children.

See Also Massachusetts

FOR FURTHER READING

Bradford, M. M. 1994. *Founding Fathers: Brief Lives of the Framers of the United States Constitution.* 2nd ed. Lawrence: University Press of Kansas.
Farrand, Max, ed. 1937. *The Records of the Federal Convention.* 4 vols. New Haven, CT: Yale University Press.

SUFFRAGE

One of the Convention's most striking omissions was arguably its failure to designate uniform requirements for voting in national elections. Delegates addressed the issue on a number of occasions, most involving qualifications in voting for members of one or both houses of Congress or for the presidency. They ultimately finessed the issue by providing in Article I, Section 2 that "the Electors in each State shall have the Qualifications requisite for Electors of the most numerous

Women Voters in New Jersey

Early New Jersey provided a fascinating exception to the rule established elsewhere limiting voting rights to men. From the adoption of a state constitution in 1776 through the adoption of a law in 1807, New Jersey permitted women who were worth "fifty pounds" or more to vote. Since married women were covered by the doctrine of coverture by which their husbands were understood to control the property, the right to suffrage extended to unmarried adult women or to those who had been widowed.

In a study of the New Jersey law, Judith Apter Klinghoffer and Lois Elkins have concluded that the constitutional provision permitting women to vote was not an oversight but "simply stood at the cutting edge of the political continuum, and its laws represented the furthest reach of possibilities for female citizenship during the revolutionary period" (1992, 163). There is some indication that Quakers may have played a special part in securing the franchise for women of property, but such a privilege was consistent with the desire of revolutionaries to secure support for their opposition to Great Britain by as many groups as possible.

It appears that relatively few men or women voted after the Revolution was won, but this changed in 1789 when politics heated up in the state. New Jersey Federalists weakened in their support for women's suffrage the more closely it became associated with the revolutionary view of the sexes that was coming out of the French Revolution (Klinghoffer and Elkins, 175), but they were unsuccessful in repealing it, and both parties appealed to potential women voters.

By contrast, Republicans, who were also coming to doubt the reliability of the women's vote and to fear that "the petticoat faction's a dangerous thing" (quoted from a contemporary newspaper in Klinghoffer and Elkins, 177), ultimately proved successful in rescinding it by an arguably unconstitutional law in 1807. Restrictions of the right to vote also were extended to aliens and to free blacks in an apparent attempt to effect compromise among a group of moderate and more liberal Republicans (187–188). Surprisingly, women do not appear to have challenged this action in court. Klinghoffer and Elkins have speculated that their reluctance may have stemmed in part from a preference to lose their right to suffrage "rather than re-enfranchise those [aliens and free blacks] they considered inferior to themselves" (190).

The U.S. Constitution of 1787, of course, does not bar women from voting; it simply leaves the issue of their enfranchisement to the states. In time, states in the West, beginning with Wyoming, extended the right to vote for women, and this movement ultimately culminated in the ratification of the Nineteenth Amendment in 1920, which now prohibits states from withholding the right to vote on account of sex.

FOR FURTHER READING

Klinghoffer, Judith Apter, and Lois Elkins. 1992. "'The Petticoat Electors': Women's Suffrage in New Jersey, 1776–1807." *Journal of the Early Republic* 12 (Summer): 159–193.

Branch of the State Legislature," and by specifying that state legislatures would select U.S. senators and special electors would choose presidents.

Developments in the States

Marc Kruman has established that early state constitutions placed great emphasis on the right to

vote. Although some states required that adult white males (to whom such voting was often limited) own a certain amount of property deemed sufficient to grant them a "stake" in society, these requirements were rarely onerous in a society where property ownership was fairly widespread. Moreover, some states had moved to the idea that all taxpayers should be able to vote (1997, 94). Operating from similar rationales, other states

Woodcut of women casting votes in New Jersey, ca. 1850–1899 (Bettmann/Corbis)

had lifted the bans that once applied to those who were not Protestant Christians (96–97). Still, property qualifications varied from one state to another.

Influence of State Variation on Convention Debates

Such differences account for the Convention's ultimate solution. New York's Alexander Hamilton observed on June 29 that

> individuals forming political Societies modify their rights differently, with regard to suffrage. Examples of it are found in all the States. In all of them some individuals are deprived of the right altogether, not having the requisite qualification of property. In some of the States the right of suffrage is allowed in some cases and refused in others. To vote for a member in one branch, a certain quantum of property, to vote

for a member in another branch of the Legislature, a higher quantum of property is required. In like manner States may modify their right of suffrage differently, the larger exercising a larger, the smaller a smaller share of it. (Farrand 1937, I, 465–466)

Similarly, in discussing the possibility of popular election of the president on July 19, Virginia's James Madison observed that

> there was one difficulty . . . of a serious nature attending an immediate choice by the people. The right of suffrage was much more diffusive in the Northern than the Southern States; and the latter could have no influence in the election on the score of the Negroes. (II, 57)

He went on to observe that "the substitute of electors obviated this difficulty and seemed on the whole to be liable to the fewest objections" (II, 57). Further commenting on this problem on

July 25, Madison expressed the hope that the "disproportion" between the number of voters in the Northern and Southern states "would be continually decreasing under the influence of the Republican laws introduced in the S. States, and the more rapid increase of their population" (II, 111).

Discussion of Proposal by Committee of Detail

On August 6, the Committee of Detail submitted a draft Constitution providing that "the qualification of the electors shall be the same, from time to time, as those of the electors in the several States, of the most numerous branch of their own legislatures" (II, 178). The next day, Gouverneur Morris moved to "restrain the right of suffrage to freeholders" (II, 201) and was seconded by fellow Pennsylvanian Thomas Fitzsimons. Hugh Williamson of North Carolina opposed the change, and James Wilson of Pennsylvania attempted to justify leaving states to determine the matter:

This part of the Report was well considered by the Committee, and he did not think it could be changed for the better. It was difficult to form any uniform rule of qualifications for all the States. Unnecessary innovation he thought too should be avoided. It would be very hard & disagreeable for the same persons, at the same time, to vote for representatives in the State Legislature and to be excluded from a vote for those in the Natl. Legislature. (II, 201)

Morris saw no significant problem:

Such a hardship would be neither great nor novel. The people are accustomed to it and not dissatisfied with it, in several of the States.

In some the qualifications are different for the choice of the Govr. & Representatives; in others for different Houses of the Legislature.

Another objection agst. the clause as it stands is that it makes the qualifications of the Natl. Legislature depend on the will of the States, which he thought not proper. (II, 201)

By contrast, Connecticut's Oliver Ellsworth thought that an attempt to dictate national standards was likely to stir up trouble:

The right of suffrage was a tender point, and strongly guarded by most of the [State] Constitutions. The people will not readily subscribe to the Natl. Constitution, if it should subject them to be disenfranchised. The States are the best Judges of the circumstances and temper of their own people. (II, 201)

Virginia's George Mason reinforced this argument: "The force of habit is certainly not attended to by those gentlemen who wish for innovations on this point. Eight or nine States have extended the right of suffrage beyond the freeholders. What will the people there say, if they should be disfranchised" (II, 201–202).

Mason went on to make the additional argument, consistent with republican fears of government, that "A power to alter the qualifications would be a dangerous power in the hands of the Legislature" (II, 202). Pierce Butler of South Carolina argued that "there is no right of which the people are more jealous than that of suffrage," and he observed that the legislature in Holland had used its power to abridge voting to create an aristocracy (II, 202).

The advocates of freehold suffrage were not yet willing to concede. Delaware's John Dickinson offered a strong defense on its behalf:

He considered them [the freeholders] as the best guardians of liberty; And the restriction of the right to them as a necessary defence agst. the dangerous influence of those multitudes without property & without principle, with which our Country like all others, will in time abound. As to the unpopularity of the innovation it was in his opinion chimerical. The great mass of our Citizens is composed at this time of freeholders, and will be pleased with it. (II, 202)

Ellsworth raised practical concerns. He asked, "How shall the freehold be defined?" (II, 202). He further raised the idea that a freehold might unfairly discriminate against merchants. In a theme reminiscent of the Revolutionary War, he affirmed that "taxation and representation ought to go together" (II, 202).

Gouverneur Morris demonstrated in his response how different ideas in the eighteenth century could be from those of the present. At a time when citizens would have cast their votes publicly, Morris observed that the House could birth an aristocracy if voters for its members had no property qualifications:

> Give the votes to people who have no property, and they will sell them to the rich who will be able to buy them. We should not confine our attention to the present moment. The time is not distant when this Country will abound with mechanics & manufacturers who will receive their bread from their employers. Will such men be the secure & faithful Guardians of liberty? . . . The man who does not give his vote freely is not represented. (II, 202–203)

Morris went on to observe that children do not vote "because they want [lack] prudence" and "have no will of their own." He contended that "the ignorant & the dependent can be as little trusted with the public interest" (II, 203).

Mason cautioned the Convention not to get sidetracked by English precedents. Although the freehold served as a qualification there, Mason thought that the true qualification should not turn on whether one owned property. Rather the delegates should proceed from the principle that "every man having evidence of attachment to & permanent common interest with the Society ought to share in all its rights & privileges" (II, 203). By such a standard, he rhetorically asked: "Ought the merchant, the monied man, the parent of a number of children whose fortunes are to be pursued in their own [Country], to be viewed as suspicious characters, and unworthy to be trusted with the common rights of their fellow Citizens?" (II, 203).

Fellow Virginian James Madison responded with an apparent sop to both sides. He observed that "the right of suffrage is certainly one of the fundamental articles of republican Government, and ought not to be left to be regulated by the Legislature," which could so adjust it as to create an aristocracy (II, 203). As a matter of theory, Madison appeared to favor a freehold. He thus observed that "viewing the subject in its merits alone, the freeholders of the Country would be the safest depositories of Republican liberty" (II, 203). He explained:

> In future times a great majority of the people will not only be without landed, but any other sort of, property. These will either combine under the influence of their common situation; in which case, the rights of property & the public liberty, [will not be secure in their hands] or which is more probable, they will become the tools of opulence & ambition, in which case there will be equal danger on another side. (II, 204)

However, Madison knew that theory might not work in practice: "Whether the Constitutional qualification ought to be a freehold, would with him depend much on the probable reception such a change would meet with in States where the right was now exercised by every description of people" (II, 203).

Benjamin Franklin feared that the delegates were underestimating "the virtue & public spirit of our common people" that he believed they had displayed during the Revolutionary War (II, 204). He strongly opposed giving the elected the right to "narrow the privileges of the electors" (II, 205). In apparent answer to Madison's concerns about how the people would accept a freehold requirement, he observed that such a restriction "would give great uneasiness in the populous States" (II, 205). He cited the example of "The sons of a substantial farmer, not being themselves freeholders," who he thought "would not be pleased at being disfranchised" and added that "there are a great many persons of that description" (II, 205).

Coming at the issue from a very different angle, Maryland's John Mercer objected to the whole idea of letting the people select members of the House. He was especially concerned that members of the towns could always outvote those in the country (II, 205). South Carolina's John Rutledge ended the discussion by arguing that restricting the suffrage to freeholders would be "unadvised" since "It would create division among the people & make enemies of all those who should be excluded" (II, 205). The Convention thus rejected Morris's idea of doing this by a vote of 7-1, with an additional state divided (II, 206).

Analysis and Subsequent Developments

The delegates thus decided that it would be better to leave existing state qualifications in place than to try to impose a single nationwide qualification. Although the pattern was not uniform, the nineteenth century witnessed a broadening of the suffrage in most states (see Keyssar 2000). Significantly, the U.S. Constitution still does not specify who can vote, but amendments have subsequently specified the grounds on which neither state nor national governments can exclude a person from voting. Such grounds now include race (the Thirteenth Amendment, ratified in 1870), sex (the Nineteenth Amendment, ratified in 1920), failure to pay a poll tax (the Twenty-fourth Amendment, ratified in 1964), and ages 18 or above (the Twenty-sixth Amendment, ratified in 1971). Additional amendments, most notably the Twelfth (ratified in 1804) and the Twenty-third (ratified in 1961), have modified the Electoral College mechanism for selecting the president. Most significantly, the Seventh Amendment (ratified in 1913) provided that voters would thenceforth select U.S. senators rather than having them selected by members of the state legislatures.

See Also Committee of Detail; Congress, House of Representatives, Qualifications of Voters for; Congress, House of Representatives, Selection of

FOR FURTHER READING

Farrand, Max, ed. 1937. *The Records of the Federal Convention.* 4 vols. New Haven, CT: Yale University Press.
Keyssar, Alexander. 2000. *The Right to Vote: The Contested History of Democracy in the United States.* New York: Basic Books.
Kruman, Marc W. 1997. *Between Authority and Liberty: State Constitution Making in Revolutionary America.* Chapel Hill: University of North Carolina Press.

SUMPTUARY LEGISLATION

One of the more fascinating, and seemingly antiquated, suggestions at the Constitutional Convention was a proposal that Virginia's George Mason made on August 20, 1787, to give Congress authority "to enact sumptuary laws" (Farrand 1937, II, 344). Consistent with republican ideology of the day, such laws were designed to regulate excessive displays of wealth and clothing but could even reach what foods and drinks were appropriate to individuals (see Goodrich 1998; also see McDonald 1985, 15–16). Mason explained his own proposal as follows:

No Government can be maintained unless the manners be made consonant to it. Such a discretionary power may do good and can do no harm. A proper regulation of excises & trade may do a great deal but it is best to have an express provision. It was objected to sumptuary laws that they were contrary to nature. This was a vulgar error. The love is distinction it is true in natural; but the object of sumptuary laws is not to extinguish this principle but to give it a proper direction. (II, 344)

A number of delegates responded to Mason's suggestion. Connecticut's Oliver Ellsworth argued that the best remedy for luxury was "to enforce taxes & debts." Gouverneur Morris of Pennsylvania thought that such legislation tended to "fix in the great-landholders and their posterity their present possessions." Elbridge Gerry of Massachusetts noted that "the law of necessity is the best sumptuary law" (II, 344). The Convention thus rejected this suggestion by a vote of 8-3.

Mason renewed his proposal on September 13, just four days before the Constitution was signed. This time, he tied his desire for such legislation to "the extravagance of our manners, the excessive

Gunston Hall, Virginia. Illustration in Appleton's Journal, *April 4, 1872. (Library of Congress)*

consumption of foreign superfluities, and the necessity of restricting it, as well with economical as republican views" (II, 606). In a motion seconded by Connecticut's Dr. William Samuel Johnson, the Convention formed a committee consisting of Mason and Johnson, Benjamin Franklin, John Dickinson, and William Livingston to deal with this issue (II, 607), but there is no evidence in the record that it filed a report or that the issue of sumptuary laws received any further notice.

It seems fascinating that Mason, a plantation owner with a beautiful house (Gunston Hall) and considerable wealth, would have favored sumptuary legislation at all much less than that he would propose vesting such power in Congress rather than in the states. In this case, his concern for "republicanism" apparently was more important than these other considerations. Significantly, Mason was among three delegates who remained at the Convention on September 17, 1787, who did not sign the document.

Mason's proposals probably fell on hard times in part because the Convention took place at a time in history when conceptions widely held by republicans regarding luxury were changing. Goods once viewed as luxuries were increasingly recognized as necessary creature comforts. Moreover, political theorists increasingly regarded the production of items once believed to be ostentatious as providing employment and bringing other economic benefits (Crowley 2001, 152–153).

See Also Aristocracy; Mason, George; Republicanism

FOR FURTHER READING

Crowley, John E. 2001. *The Invention of Comfort: Sensibilities and Design in Early Modern Britain and Early*

America. Baltimore, MD: Johns Hopkins University Press.

Farrand, Max, ed. 1937. *The Records of the Federal Convention*. 4 vols. New Haven, CT: Yale University Press.

Goodrich, Peter. 1998. "Signs Taken for Wonders: Community, Identity, and a History of Sumptuary Law." *Law and Social Inquiry* 23 (Summer): 707–725.

Matson, Cathy, and Peter Onus. 1985. "Toward a Republican Empire: Interest and Ideology in Revolutionary America." *American Quarterly* 37 (Autumn): 496–531.

McDonald, Forrest. 1985. *Novus Ordo Seclorum: The Intellectual Origins of the Constitution*. Lawrence: University Press of Kansas.

SUPERMAJORITIES

The Articles of Confederation required the concurrence of nine of the 13 states on most key matters. It also required unanimous state consent for constitutional amendments.

Constitutional Provisions For

Although the Convention did not follow either of these supermajority requirements, it enacted a number of its own. John O. McGinnis and Michael B. Rappaport have identified seven such supermajority requirements in the Constitution. These include the two-thirds majority required in the Senate to convict someone of impeachment charges, the two-thirds requirement to ratify treaties, the two-thirds requirement to expel someone from a house of Congress, the two-thirds vote of both houses of Congress required to override a presidential veto, the two-thirds quorum required for the House to select a president in cases when the Electoral College has not done so, the requirement that nine of 13 states would have to ratify the Constitution before it went into effect, and the provision requiring that constitutional amendments required a two-thirds vote of both houses of Congress (or requests from two-thirds of the states to call a constitutional convention) to propose amendments and ratifica-

tion by three-fourths of the states (McGinnis and Rappaport 2002, 712–713). The establishment of a bicameral Congress, and the provision for presidential signature or veto, further pose obstacles to simple majority rule.

For the most part, delegates appeared to accept the utility of supermajorities in certain situations. Much of their debate on the subject focused on how large the majorities should be. Thus, on August 10, Virginia's James Madison observed that the right of expelling members of Congress "was too important to be exercised by a bare majority of a quorum: and in emergencies of faction might be dangerously abused" (II, 254). Similarly, in *Federalist* No. 43, Madison defended the majorities required to amend the Constitution as guarding "equally against that extreme facility, which would render the Constitution too mutable; and that extreme difficulty which might perpetuate its discovered faults" (Hamilton, Madison, and Jay 1961, 278). Brett King has argued that Madison was the most consistent supporter of supermajority requirements at the Convention (1998, 394).

Rejected Supermajority Provisions

In addition to the supermajorities that the Convention proposed, the delegates considered a number of such provisions that they did not adopt. North Carolina's Hugh Williamson thus proposed on June 6 that the Convention consider a requirement that Congress adopt all legislation by two-thirds majorities, in place of the Council of Revision that it was then considering (Farrand 1937, I, 140). On July 18, after toying with a majority formula (II, 42), James Madison suggested a kind of reverse majority by proposing that the president should be able to appoint judges subject to a veto by two-thirds of the Senate (II, 44). The Committee of Detail proposed that it should take a two-thirds majority vote of existing states in order to admit new ones (II, 188). The Convention did not alter this provision until August 29 (II, 446); it settled instead on a provision prohibiting existing states from being carved up without their consent (the Convention also came close to adopting a unanimity requirement by adopting a provision prohibiting any state from being deprived of its equal suffrage in the Senate without its consent). Similarly reflecting concern about the protection of regional economic interests, the Committee of Detail had proposed that two-thirds majorities of both houses of Congress should be required for the adoption of any navigation acts (II, 183).

Functions of Supermajority Provisions

Supermajorities arguably serve to prevent actions, especially those influenced by transient passions, that simple majorities favor, or those favored by well-organized special interests, which might be able to overcome simple majorities. Supermajorities can be desirable in protecting strongly held regional interests or fundamental rights. Supermajorities that are too rigorous might encourage a search for alternate methods to accomplishing the same objects, as in cases when judicial interpretations serve as substitutes for constitutional amendments or executive agreements take the place of formal treaties. The majorities required to propose and ratify amendments are close to the majority (nine of 13 states) that the Convention required for the new Constitution to go into effect.

Debates over the Constitution helped result in the Bill of Rights. This bill further entrenched fundamental rights, some of which delegates had included in the original constitutional text, against popular majorities.

See Also Amending Process; Articles of Confederation; Bill of Rights; Committee of Detail; Congress, Expulsion of Members; Congress, Impeachment Clause; Council of Revision; President, Selection; Presidential Veto; Quorums; Ratification, Convention Debates, and Constitutional Provision; Sectionalism; States, Admission and Creation; Treaty-Making and Ratification

FOR FURTHER READING

Farrand, Max, ed. 1937. *The Records of the Federal Convention.* 4 vols. New Haven, CT: Yale University Press.
Hamilton, Alexander, James Madison, and John Jay.
1961. *The Federalist Papers.* Ed. Clinton Rossiter. New York: New American Library.
King, Brett W. 1998. "The Use of Supermajority Provisions in the Constitution: The Framers, the Federalist Papers and the Reinforcement of a Fundamental Principle." *Seton Hall Constitutional Law Journal* 8 (Spring): 363–414.
McGinnis, John O., and Michael B. Rappaport. 2002. "Our Supermajoritarian Constitution." *Texas Law Review* 80 (March): 703–806.

SUPREMACY CLAUSE

Clause 2 of Article VI of the Constitution contains the supremacy clause. It provides, in full, that

> this Constitution, and the Laws of the United States which shall be made in Pursuance thereof; and all Treaties made, or which shall be made, under the Authority of the United States, shall be the supreme Law of the Land; and the Judges in every State shall be bound thereby, any Thing in the Constitution or Laws of any State to the Contrary notwithstanding.

The adoption of this provision by the Constitutional Convention needs to be understood against the background of at least two alternate provisions—the use of force against the states and a congressional negative of state laws (Clark 2003, 92).

The Virginia Plan

The Virginia Plan, which Edmund Randolph introduced on May 29, initially contained both mechanisms. Article VI thus provided that Congress would have power

> to negative all laws passed by the several States, contravening in the opinion of the National Legislature the articles of Union; and to call forth the force of the Union agst. any member of the Union failing to fulfill its duty under the articles thereof. (Farrand 1937, I, 21)

Although Virginia's James Madison clung to his hope for a negative of state laws long after the Convention rejected the proposal on July 17, within two days of the introduction of the Virginia Plan, he expressed doubts about the use of force against the states. He observed:

The use of force agst. a State, would look more like a declaration of war, than an infliction of punishment, and would probably be considered by the party attacked as a dissolution of all previous compacts by which it might be bound. He hoped that such a system would be framed as might render this recourse unnecessary, and moved that the clause be postponed. (I, 54)

Similarly, in supporting a widening of the negative of state laws (to include not only laws that contravened the Union but all laws that Congress considered to be "improper") suggested by South Carolina's Charles Pinckney, Madison argued for the superiority of this mechanism to the use of coercion:

Was such a remedy elegible? was it practicable? Could the national resources, if exerted to the utmost enforce a national decree agst. Massts. abetted perhaps by several of her neighbours? It wd. not be possible. A small proportion of the Community in a compact situation, acting on the defensive, and at one of its extremities might at any time bid defiance to the National authority. Any Govt. for the U. States formed on the supposed practicability of using force against the [unconstitutional proceedings] of the States, wd. prove as visionary & fallacious as the Govt. of Congr. The negative wd. render the use of force unnecessary. (I, 164–165)

When the Committee of the Whole issued its report on June 13, it omitted the proposal for the use of force.

The New Jersey Plan

Curiously, however, when William Paterson presented his alternative New Jersey Plan on June 15,

which provided for continuing state equality in congressional representation, he included both the incubus of the current supremacy clause *and* a provision for coercion. His plan:

Resd. that all Acts of the U. States in Congs. made by virtue & in pursuance of the powers hereby & by the articles of confederation vested in them, and all Treaties made & ratified under the authority of the U. States shall be the supreme law of the respective States so far forth as those Acts or Treaties shall relate to the said States or their Citizens, and that the Judiciary of the several States shall be bound thereby in their decisions, any thing in the respective laws of the Individual States to the contrary notwithstanding; and that if any State, or any body of men in any State shall oppose or prevent ye. carrying into execution such acts or treaties, the federal Executive shall be authorized to call forth ye. power of the Confederated States, or so much thereof as may be necessary to enforce and compel an obedience to such Acts, or an Observance of such Treaties. (I, 245)

In defending his plan, Paterson seemed to forget that the provision for direct coercion against the states had been dropped from the Virginia Plan. He thus observed: "It will be objected that Coercion will be impracticable. But will it be more so in one plan than the other? Its efficacy will depend on the quantum of power collected, not on its being drawn from the States, or from the individuals" (I, 251).

It is possible that the version of the supremacy clause in the New Jersey Plan, which had made no provision for lower federal courts, was purposely designed to allow states to evade provisions of federal laws and treaties that were contrary to state constitutions, since the plan specifically mentioned violations of state laws but not of state constitutions, some of which provided for payment of foreign debts in state currency (O'Connor 1979, 147). This is, at least, the interpretation that Maryland's Luther Martin later gave to the original proposal (see Clarkson and Jett 1970, 114–116). In defending the Virginia Plan over the New Jersey alternative, Virginia's James Madison certainly argued that, like the existing Articles, the New Jersey Plan would not prevent states from violating such treaties (I, 316). Significantly, the version that made its way into the Constitution mentioned both state constitutions and state laws.

Comparisons and Further Developments

In examining the respective merits of the Virginia and New Jersey Plans, the former of which still contained a provision for a congressional negative of state laws, Edmund Randolph observed that they presented the alternatives of "coercion" or "real legislation." Randolph was strongly opposed to the former:

Coercion he pronounced to *be impracticable, expensive, cruel to individuals.* It tended also to habituate the instruments of it to shed the blood & riot in the spoils of their fellow Citizens, and consequently trained them up for the service of Ambition. We must resort therefore to a national *Legislation over individuals,* for which Congs. are unfit. (I, 256)

Similarly, in his long speech proposing a much more nationalistic alternative to both the Virginia and New Jersey Plans, New York's Alexander Hamilton sagely observed that it would be "impossible" to exercise force on the states acting collectively. Not only would this amount "to a war between the parties," but it would encourage foreign intervention (I, 285).

The Convention proceeded with the Virginia Plan, albeit acting on July 17, the day after it settled on the Connecticut Compromise, to strip it of the provision for a congressional negative of state laws. Not coincidentally, the Convention immediately and unanimously proceeded to adopt Luther Martin's motion for a new version of the supremacy clause. It provided:

that the Legislative acts of the U.S. made by virtue & in pursuance of the articles of Union, and all treaties made & ratified under the authority of the U.S. shall be the supreme law of the re-

spective States, as far as those acts or treaties shall relate to the said States, or their Citizens and inhabitants–& that the Judiciaries of the several States shall be bound thereby in their decisions, any thing in the respective laws of the individual States to the contrary notwithstanding. (II, 29)

Curiously, Martin's reference to "the articles of Union" tracked the earlier language of the provision in the New Jersey Plan and incorrectly appeared to indicate that the new government was simply enhancing the powers of the existing government rather than creating a new one. The Committee of Detail changed this provision to read as follows:

The Acts of the Legislature of the United States made in pursuance of this Constitution, and all treaties made under the authority of the United States shall be the supreme law of the several States, and of their citizens and inhabitants; and the judges in the several States shall be bound thereby in their decisions; anything in the Constitutions or laws of the several States to the contrary notwithstanding. (II, 283)

On August 23, John Rutledge of South Carolina introduced language changing the first sentence so that it referred to "This Constitution & the laws of the U.S. made in pursuance thereto" (II, 389). The Committee of Style and Arrangement in turn transformed this clause into its current language (II, 603).

Analysis

Today, the supremacy clause serves, along with parallel language in Article III dealing with the judiciary, as one of the primary justifications for the power of judges to invalidate legislation, including that in the states, that they believe to be in conflict with the U.S. Constitution. The apparent irony of the clause is that it originated in a plan, the New Jersey Plan, that proposed strengthening the government under the Articles of Confederation rather than creating a new one. It also seems ironic that it was originally bundled in this same plan along with a provision for coercive sanction against the states that the Committee of the Whole had already rejected.

One seasoned scholar has traced the supremacy clause to the desire of representatives from the small states "To prove that they wished the common government well" (Rossiter 1966, 176). It is possible that Paterson and other advocates of the small states thought that open resort to force against recalcitrant states would be less intrusive, and far less likely to be exercised, than the constant congressional negative of state laws. Perhaps Paterson favored a confederal plan, even if coercive, that dealt directly with the states rather than acting directly on individual citizens. Perhaps Paterson also counted on equal state representation in Congress and the mere threat of force to prevent actual resort to such force.

Because American courts typically only hear cases involving real controversies, the supremacy clause does not, as the negative of state laws might have, prevent the adoption of unconstitutional laws. The clause does, however, provide a mechanism whereby such laws can be overruled and it does so through a branch that typically professes not to be enforcing its own will (as Congress might do) but simply to be enforcing constitutional mandates.

See Also Judicial Review; Negative on State Laws; New Jersey Plan; Virginia Plan

FOR FURTHER READING

Clark, Bradford R. 2003. "The Supremacy Clause as a Constraint on Federal Power." *George Washington Law Review* 72 (February): 91–130.

Clarkson, Paul S., and R. Samuel Jett. 1970. *Luther Martin of Maryland.* Baltimore, MD: Johns Hopkins University Press.

Farrand, Max, ed. 1937. *The Records of the Federal Convention.* 4 vols. New Haven, CT: Yale University Press.

O'Connor, J. J. 1979. *William Paterson: Lawyer and Statesman, 1745–1806.* New Brunswick, NJ: Rutgers University Press.

Rossiter, Clinton. 1966. *1787: The Grand Convention.* New York: W. W. Norton.

SUPREME COURT

The U.S. Supreme Court, the highest court in the land, is also the only court specifically mentioned by name in Article III of the U.S. Constitution. When the British controlled the colonies, the Privy Council had authority to disavow their laws. This arguably provided something of a precedent for the power of the modern court to void legislation that it considers to be unconstitutional. Under the Articles of Confederation, a court heard prize cases from 1780 to 1786 (Steamer 1962, 562). Similarly, Congress created an ad hoc mechanism to hear boundary disputes between states, a role the Constitution later assigned to the Supreme Court.

Virginia and New Jersey Plans

When Edmund Randolph proposed the Virginia Plan, he suggested that "a National Judiciary be established to consist of one or more supreme tribunals, and of inferior tribunals to be chosen by the National Legislature, to hold their offices during good behavior; and to receive punctually at stated times fixed compensation for their services" (Farrand 1937, I, 21–22). The "supreme tribunal" (now treated as a single institution) was "to hear and determine in the dernier [last] resort, all piracies & felonies on the high seas, captures from an enemy; cases in which foreigners or citizens of other States applying to such jurisdictions may be interested, or which respect the collection of the National revenue; impeachments of any National officers, and questions which may involve the national peace and harmony" (I, 22). The Virginia Plan also called for including members of the national judiciary, presumably including any supreme court that might be established, in a Council of Revision that would have power to veto acts of the national legislature. Although the delegates eventually rejected it, this proposal resurfaced on a number of occasions throughout Convention deliberations.

On June 4, the Committee of the Whole voted to accept a judiciary "to consist of One supreme tribunal, and of one or more inferior tribunals" (I,

95). The following day, it further accepted the idea that members of the judiciary would serve during good behavior and receive fixed compensation. On June 5, Pennsylvania's James Wilson further proposed that the executive, rather than the legislature, should appoint members of the judicial branch.

Significantly, despite many differences between the two plans, the New Jersey Plan, which William Paterson introduced on June 15, contained an almost identical provision regarding the Supreme Court as had the Virginia Plan, except that it followed Wilson's suggestion in proposing that the executive, rather than the legislature, should appoint its members (I, 244). In proposing his own outline of a plan on June 18, Alexander Hamilton apparently sidestepped the issue of who would appoint members of the judicial branch but further distinguished the original and appellate jurisdiction of such a court by specifying that "the Court [is] to have original jurisdiction in all causes of capture, and an appellative jurisdiction in all causes in which the revenues of the general Government or the citizens of foreign nations are concerned" (I, 292).

Further Treatments

On July 18, the Convention voted unanimously to establish "a Natl. Judiciary . . . to consist of one supreme tribunal" (II, 41). Consistent with the differences in the provisions of the Virginia and New Jersey Plans, the main discussion that followed focused on how members of the judiciary would be appointed.

When the Convention appointed the Committee of Detail on July 24, it had tentatively decided that the Senate would appoint all members of the national judiciary, including the Supreme Court (II, 132). The outlines, and indeed most of the details, of the modern judicial system are clearly evident in the committee's report of August 6. The report clearly focused on "one Supreme Court" and such inferior courts as Congress might establish; judges were to hold their offices during good behavior and receive fixed compensation for their services, the jurisdiction of the Supreme Court

was fairly well specified (most of it being appellate, rather than original), criminal trials were to be by jury, and judges were to be subject to impeachment and conviction (II, 186–187). Although some elaborations were added, there is not much difference between the report of the Committee of Detail and the issues that were later referred to the Committee of Style.

Curiosities

Curiously, the Constitution mentions a chief justice not within Article III, the judicial article, but in specifying who would preside over presidential impeachments—a case where it would be inappropriate for the vice president, designated as president of that body, to preside. The Constitution makes no mention of the size of the Supreme Court, which has been set at nine since just after the end of the Civil War, and which last became a major issue with Franklin D. Roosevelt's 1937 to "pack" the Court. Similarly, although a number of delegates discussed the issue, the Constitution does not specifically mention the Court's power of judicial review, that is, its power to declare laws to be unconstitutional.

Analysis

The judicial branch is the only one of the three specified within the Constitution whose members are not elected. Like the Senate, members of which the state legislatures originally appointed, it thus arguably introduces something of an aristocratic element within the Constitution, albeit one not based on birth. The mechanism of presidential appointment and Senate confirmation has not insulated the branch, and especially not the members of its highest court, from politics. The Court is recognized as having a special role in constitutional interpretation that makes it at least something like a continuing constitutional convention.

See Also Chief Justice of the United States; Council of Revision; Hamilton Plan; Judicial Jurisdiction;

Judicial Organization and Protections; Judicial Review; New Jersey Plan; Virginia Plan

FOR FURTHER READING

Abraham, Henry J. 1998. *The Judicial Process.* 7th ed. New York: Oxford University Press.

Farrand, Max, ed. 1937. *The Records of the Federal Convention.* 4 vols. New Haven, CT: Yale University Press.

O'Brien, David M. 2003. *Storm Center: The Supreme Court in American Politics.* New York: W. W. Norton.

Steamer, Robert J. 1962. "The Legal and Political Genesis of the Supreme Court." *Political Science Quarterly* 77 (December): 546–569.

SWISS CANTONS

Although scholars generally regard American federalism—the system by which the state and national governments are linked—as a unique creation, it clearly had origins elsewhere. The Swiss cantons, with which delegates to the Constitutional Convention were familiar, provided one such precedent (Elazar 1980, 21). Delegates also regarded the cantons as an incubus of republican virtue.

In a speech apparently prepared for June 4, Virginia's George Mason observed that republican virtue had enabled the Swiss cantons to preserve their freedom and independence "in the midst of the most powerful nations" (Farrand 1937, I, 112). By contrast, New York's Alexander Hamilton cited the cantons in his lengthy speech of June 18 as an example of "scarce any Union at all," which he linked to fighting among them (I, 285–286). Virginia's James Madison cast the Swiss confederation in a similar light on the next day when he cited the intrigues in its affairs of "Austria, France & the less neighouring Powers" (I, 319). Pennsylvania's James Wilson chimed in on June 20 by observing that the Swiss confederacies had been "held together not by any vital principle of energy but by the incumbent pressure of formidable neighbouring nations" (I, 343).

Maryland's Luther Martin, who ultimately opposed ratification of the new system, took a somewhat different tack on June 28 when he cited the Swiss confederacy as being among other confederacies in demonstrating "the freedom and the independency of the states composing it" (I, 454). Cautioning the larger states who were demanding representation according to population and/or wealth, he rhetorically asked, "Has Holland or Switzerland ever complained of the equality of the states which compose their respective confederacies?" and responded by saying that "Bern and Zurich are larger than the remaining eleven cantons . . . and yet their governments are not complained of" (I, 454). Martin reiterated this point during the ratification debates (III, 184).

In *Federalist* No. 19, Madison and Hamilton cited the cantons as "scarcely" amounting to a confederacy. They describe them as being held together "by the peculiarity of their topographical position; by their individual weakness and insignificancy; by the fear of powerful neighbors" and the like (Hamilton, Madison, and Jay 1961, 133). Madison cited Switzerland in *Federalist* No. 42 as an illustration of "the necessity of a superintending authority over the reciprocal trade of confederated States" (268). Madison used the Swiss in *Federalist* No. 43 as an example of a system that, divided as it was, still made provision for suppression of insurrections in member governments (276).

Although the Framers' knowledge of the Swiss cantons arguably deserves greater scholarly attention (perhaps tracing additional references during the ratification debates), there is arguably a pattern here that is probably akin to delegates' references to other leagues, that of Holland for example. Delegates generally displayed cursory knowledge of the Swiss cantons and tended to cite them as illustrations of principles that they had probably generally gleaned from experiences much closer to home (Riker 1957).

See Also Federalism; Holland; Protestantism

FOR FURTHER READING

Elazar, Daniel J. 1980. "The Biblical Theory of Covenant: Biblical Origins and Modern Developments." *Publius* 10 (Fall): 3–30.

Farrand, Max, ed. 1937. *The Records of the Federal Convention*. 4 vols. New Haven, CT: Yale University Press.

Hamilton, Alexander, James Madison, and John Jay. 1961. *The Federalist Papers*. Ed. Clinton Rossiter. New York: New American Library.

Riker, William H. 1957. "Dutch and American Federalism." *Journal of the History of Ideas* 18 (October): 495–521.

SYNG INKSTAND

The events surrounding the movement for American Independence and the creation of the U.S. Constitution are so important that the objects surrounding these events have come to have almost a sacred quality. Apart from the building itself and the Liberty Bell that it once housed, the only two objects known to exist from the Constitutional Convention are the Chippendale chair with a painting of a rising sun where George Washington sat as he presided over the Convention, which is displayed in the East Room of Independence Hall, and an elegant silver inkstand made by Philip Syng, Jr. (1703–1789) of Philadelphia in 1752. Syng is believed to have come with his family from Ireland to Philadelphia in 1714. The delegates to both the Second Continental Congress, who signed the Declaration of Independence, and the Constitutional Convention are believed to have dipped their quill pens into this inkwell prior to signing one or both historic documents.

The Pennsylvania Assembly originally owned the Syng inkstand, which it moved to Harrisburg when the state capital relocated there. Recognizing the importance of this object for U.S. history, the Assembly returned the object to Philadelphia at the centennial of the signing of the Declaration of Independence in 1876. The inkwell is now on display in a fire-resistant case along with copies of the Declaration of Independence and the U.S. Constitution at the Independence National Historical Park (*Great Essentials* 2003).

In 2003, Syng's grave marker was discovered buried in the burial ground at Christ Church in Philadelphia. The marker indicates that his body was buried next to that of his wife and seven of his 13 children. At the time the marker was discovered, Syng's descendants were preparing a new stone to celebrate Syng's accomplishments. A prominent Philadelphian, Syng was a friend of Benjamin Franklin, who helped him found the Library Company of Philadelphia and today's University of Pennsylvania (Stoiber 2003).

See Also Liberty Bell; Pennsylvania State House; Philadelphia; Rising Sun Chair

FOR FURTHER READING

Great Essentials: An Exhibition of Democracy at Independence National Historical Park. Pamphlet obtained at Independence Hall, August 30, 2003.

Stoiber, Julie. 2003. "Discovery of Stone Uncovers Syng Plot." May 18. http://www.philly.com/mld/inquirer/2003/05/18/news/local/5884858.htm?lc.

T

TAXES

See THREE-FIFTHS CLAUSE

TAXES ON IMPORTS AND EXPORTS

Congress exercises the "power of the purse." The first clause in Article I, Section 8, accordingly vests Congress with the power to "lay and collect Taxes, Duties, Imposts, and Excises." However, Article I, Section 9 prohibits Congress from laying any "Tax or Duty" on exports while Article I, Section 10 limits states from laying "Imposts or Duties on Imports or Exports, except what may be absolutely necessary for executing its inspection laws." It further provides that "the net Produce of all Duties and Imposts, laid by a State on Imports or Exports, shall be for the Use of the Treasury of the United States; and all such Laws shall be subject to the Revision and Controul of the Congress."

Interstate taxation had been a major problem under the Articles of Confederation. States like Pennsylvania and New York with ports thus taxed goods coming into the state for export from states like New Jersey, which contemporaries jokingly likened to a keg with a tap on both ends, without

such ports. Such taxes had a negative impact on interstate commerce.

Early Discussions at the Convention

A provision of the New Jersey Plan, which William Paterson introduced on June 15, specified that Congress should be "authorized to pass acts for raising a revenue, by levying a duty or duties on all goods or merchandizes of foreign growth or manufacture, imported into any part of the U. States, by Stamps on paper, vellum or parchment, and by a postage on all letters or packages passing through the general post-Office" (Farrand 1937, I, 243). On June 18, New York's Alexander Hamilton had further suggested that national revenue might be drawn from export taxes (I, 286), but the issue received little attention until July 12. After proposing that taxation should be proportioned according to representation, Gouverneur Morris of Pennsylvania indicated that he intended for this formula to apply only to forms of direct taxation and not to taxes "on *exports* & imports & on consumption" (I, 592). Approving Morris's idea of linking taxation and representation, General Charles Cotesworth Pinckney of South Carolina was nonetheless concerned about the idea of taxing exports as he was by Morris's opposition, expressed the previous day, to counting slaves in the representation formula. Pinckney calculated that South Carolina exported goods valued at about

600,000 pounds sterling a year, "which was the fruit of the labor of her blacks." If the state were not to be represented by blacks, then neither should it be taxed according to their labor. Accordingly, he expressed the hope that "a clause would be inserted in the system restraining the Legislature from taxing Exports" (I, 592).

When on July 23 the Convention discussed establishing a Committee of Detail, the General said that he would vote against any report that did not limit such taxes (II, 95). The committee report allowed Congress to lay "taxes, duties, imposts and excises," but contained a prohibition on Congress against levying any "tax or duty" laid "on articles exported from any State" and required congressional consent to any such state impositions (II, 181, 183, 187).

Debates in August

On August 16, a question arose as to the difference between "duties" and "imposts." Pennsylvania's James Wilson suggested that "duties" was the broader term, extending to some objects like stamp duties that were not specifically in commerce (II, 305). Wilson expressed concern that the Convention should not ratify congressional power over the former without a guarantee that it would not tax exports: "He was unwilling to trust to its being done in a future article. He hoped the Northn. States did not mean to deny the Southern this security. It would hereafter be as desirable to the former when the latter should become the most populous" (II, 305). Connecticut's Roger Sherman and South Carolina's John Rutledge did not oppose such a provision, but they thought it properly belonged under the section limiting the powers of Congress.

By contrast, Gouverneur Morris thought that a provision was "radically objectionable"; he thought there were cases when it would be inequitable to tax imports without also taxing exports and that taxes on exports would often be "the most easy and proper of the two" (II, 306). Virginia's James Madison agreed. He observed that export taxes could often be used as a means

of leveraging foreign markets. Raising an issue that did not appear to be under discussion (namely *state* imposition of export taxes that were forbidden in another section), Madison said that he would be "unjust" to allow states to tax exports produced in neighboring states. He also said that it would not be improper if the South paid more export taxes since they were most in need of naval protection.

Delegates began to line up on two sides. North Carolina's Hugh Williamson thought the prohibition against taxing exports was "reasonable and necessary" (II, 307). Connecticut's Oliver Ellsworth agreed but was content to leave the restriction elsewhere in the Constitution. Pennsylvania's James Wilson, like Madison, opposed a restriction on congressional imposition of export taxes but denounced state taxation of exports of other states. Elbridge Gerry of Massachusetts feared that Congress could "ruin the Country" if it had the power to tax exports (II, 307). Morris reiterated his view that there were occasions when taxing exports would be "highly politic" (I, 307). Such taxes would be preferable to direct taxes.

Maryland's John Mercer opposed allowing Congress to tax exports, but he did so in the apparent belief that this would allow states to exercise the power; he further denied that the South contributed more to the need for national defense. Almost always the conciliator, Connecticut's Roger Sherman thought the Convention had already arrived at the conclusion that imports could be taxed but exports not. Export taxes were only appropriate on "such articles as ought not to be exported," and "A power to tax exports would shipwreck the whole" (II, 308). The Convention voted to leave the restriction on taxing exports where it was. When the Convention voted on allowing Congress the power to collect taxes and levy imposts, only Elbridge Gerry dissented.

When the Convention resumed discussion of the congressional prohibition against taxing exports on August 21, New Hampshire's John Langdon objected that this left the states at liberty to do so. He wanted to require supermajority approval from Congress in such cases (II, 359). Ellsworth thought that states would be protected by the congressional power to regulate interstate trade. He went on to argue that Congress should be restrained from taxing exports since such taxes would discourage industry, would be "partial & unjust," and "would engender incurable jealousies" (II, 360). Williamson said that his state could never agree to such a power, and Sherman later agreed that all such congressional powers should be prohibited. Gerry feared that congressional powers over commerce could allow the national government to oppress the states, and Mason connected this fear to that of taxing states differentially (II, 362–363).

By contrast Gouverneur Morris continued to favor national taxation of exports. Without such a power, he doubted that Congress could levy embargoes. Such taxes might further encourage U.S. manufacturers (II, 360). Delaware's John Dickinson later argued that although such taxes might be "inconvenient at present," it would be unwise to prohibit them for all times (II, 361). Madison agreed, also fearing that a restriction might affect future embargoes. Ellsworth, however, did not think the section restricted the embargo power, and Maryland's James McHenry thought that embargoes fell under the war power. Wilson thought that it was foolish to deny Congress power over half of trade and thought that export taxes could be helpful in obtaining "beneficial treaties of commerce" (II, 362).

Hearkening back to a distinction that the colonists had sometimes made in regard to parliamentary powers prior to the Revolutionary War, George Clymer of Pennsylvania proposed that Congress should be able to tax for the purpose of regulating trade but not for the purpose of revenue. His motion failed by a vote of 7-3. Madison and Wilson then suggested substituting a two-thirds majority requirement for the absolute prohibition on taxing exports. The Convention rejected this proposal by a vote of 6-5. It then adopted the motion for prohibiting all such congressional-imposed taxes by a vote of 7-4.

When the Convention continued discussion of taxation of imported slaves on the next day, Gouverneur Morris resolved to commit the clauses related to taxes on exports to the committee. He expressed the hope that "these things may form a bargain among the Northern & Southern States" (II, 374). Butler observed that he would never "agree to the power of taxing exports" (II, 374).

On August 28, Madison proposed that the prohibition against state taxation of imports should be absolute, and Williamson seconded him. Sherman thought that Congress should retain power to allow for such taxation, and Mason observed that states might want to keep such taxes as a means of encouraging products, like hemp, for which they had a natural advantage. Madison responded that this was exactly why such a prohibition was needed, lest it "revive all the mischiefs experienced from the want of a Genl. Government over commerce" (II, 441), but his motion failed by a 7-4 vote.

The Convention proceeded to extend the prohibition of state taxation of state imports without congressional consent to exports as well, and the Convention agreed by a vote of 6-5. It then voted 9-5 to require that any such taxes would go into the common Treasury, arguably defeating any incentive for it.

September Debates

On September 12, Mason recommended that the prohibition against state taxation of exports not be interpreted to prevent "the incidental duties necessary for the inspection & safe-keeping of the produce." Madison seconded him. Gouverneur Morris had no objection, although Jonathan Dayton of New Jersey, Nathaniel Gorham of Massachusetts and John Langdon of New Hampshire all expressed fears that this might provide a subterfuge for states to tax their neighbors. Madison responded that the Supreme Court would prevent this, although he continued to press for the idea of granting Congress a negative on state laws. The Convention adopted Mason's motion on September 13, and accordingly adjusted the language of the Constitution on September 15, with only Virginia dissenting (II, 624).

The Convention handled the taxation on the importation of slaves in a separate clause of Article I, Section 9. It permitted such importation until 1808 and limited taxation to $10 per person.

Analysis

Perhaps the greatest irony of the debates on export taxes is that, for all the attempts of the states, especially those of the South, to protect themselves against taxes on exports, tariffs (taxes on imports) became a major cause of division in the early republic. Southern states had to import almost all manufactured goods. Southern states found that tariffs designed to foster industrial development in the Northeast raised consumer prices in the South. Many undoubtedly regretted that they had not incorporated a provision in the Constitution that would either have required supermajorities to adopt such tariffs or prohibited them altogether. It is difficult to know, however, how the national government would have raised money in the days before the income tax had there been such a prohibition.

See Also Commerce, Power; Slave Importation

FOR FURTHER READING

Brown, Roger H. 1993. *Redeeming the Republic: Federalists, Taxation, and the Origin of the Constitution.* Baltimore, MD: Johns Hopkins University Press.
Farrand, Max, ed. 1937. *The Records of the Federal Convention.* 4 vols. New Haven, CT: Yale University Press.
Taylor, George R., ed. *The Great Tariff Debate, 1820–1830.* Boston: D. D. Heath, 1993.

TEMPERATURES IN THE SUMMER OF 1787

Delegates to the Constitutional Convention wrote a number of letters in which they commented on the weather—a not altogether unexpected development given the secrecy to which the delegates were sworn on matters of political substance. Summer is the hottest of the four seasons. It is therefore not surprising that writers about the Convention have frequently focused on comments like those of Elbridge Gerry of Massachusetts to his wife postmarked August 14, 1787, in which he observed that "The City is now and has been for several Days excessive hot" (Hutson 1987, 223), and generalized that the summer must have been an especially hot one. James H. Hutson has observed that "the heroic stature of the framers seems to require them to have conquered the elements as well as the political crisis in the nation" (325).

Hutson gathered information from a Philadelphia brewer, Thomas Morris; from Jacob Hiltzheimer, a Philadelphia livery stable owner and businessman; and from Peter Legaux, a farmer who lived about 13 miles north of the city. All give day-to-day records of most of the period during which the Convention met. This information indicates fairly normal summer patterns of both heat and rainfall. David M. Ludlum of the American Weather History Center concluded that "in general terms Philadelphia enjoyed a cool summer in 1787" (unpublished paper cited in Hutson, 326). Specifically, his analysis showed temperatures averaged 62.0 degrees Fahrenheit in May, 70.7 in June, 72.4 in July, 74.5 in August, and 64.7 in September. These temperatures were respectively +0.7, +1.0, −4.1, −0.4, and −1.7 degrees above or below average. Temperatures ranged from a minimum of 34.1 to a maximum of 80.1 in May, from 45.0 to 93.8 in June, from 45.7 to 96.0 in July, from 50.0 to 95.0 in August, and from 36.5 to 93.9 in September (Hutson, 326).

Temperatures were undoubtedly hotter in the close confines of the Convention, and would have seemed less bearable as the proceedings dragged on for four months. Moreover, as in most summers, there were certainly hot days. The average temperatures Legaux reported close to the time that Gerry wrote his letter were as follows: 73.8 on August 11, 79.2 on August 12, 78.3 on August 13, and 82 on August 14 (Hutson, 334). This would make it quite likely that temperatures may have reached into the 90s during this time.

Moreover, however useful it is to know average Philadelphia temperatures, delegates who wrote home were not commenting on the temperatures in Philadelphia compared to previous summers *in Philadelphia* but as compared to summers to which they were accustomed. For the most part, one would expect that delegates from south of Philadelphia, where temperatures would generally be hotter, would be less likely to complain than delegates like Gerry who were from northern areas, which are generally somewhat cooler.

See Also Geography; Philadelphia

FOR FURTHER READING

Hutson, James H., ed. 1987. *Supplement to Max Farrand's* The Records of the Federal Convention of 1787. New Haven, CT: Yale University Press.

TENNESSEE

At the time of the Constitutional Convention, today's state of Tennessee was part of North Carolina. In June of 1784, North Carolina had ceded this land to the national government, but it subsequently had a change of heart and rescinded its action that November. This brought to an end the movement organized in Jonesborough to establish a new state to be named Franklin, in honor of Benjamin Franklin (see Alden 1903). In December 1789, North Carolina again ceded its Western claims to the U.S. with the proviso that slavery would be recognized within the territory called the Territory of the United States South of the River Ohio, known as the Southwest Territory (Van West 1998, 374). After a referendum indicating that the growing population of this area desired statehood, Territorial Governor William Blount, a former delegate to the U.S. Constitutional Convention, called for a convention that met in 1796 and drew up a new constitution. This state was admitted into the Union on June 2, 1796, becoming the sixteenth state.

At the Constitutional Convention of 1787, the delegates referred to the current state of Tennessee as Franklin. Nathaniel Gorham of Massachusetts indicated on July 23 that he anticipated that Kentucky, Vermont, Maine, and Franklin would join the Union as independent states (Farrand 1937, II, 94). On August 30, John Rutledge of South Carolina said that there was no reason to fear that Virginia and North Carolina would try to hold on to their Western lands beyond the mountains. North Carolina's Hugh Williamson said that his state was "well disposed to give up her Western lands" but that he opposed compulsion on this point (II, 462). In a letter written in 1832, James Madison of Virginia observed that delegates to the Convention knew that the residents of Tennessee were anticipating statehood (III, 519).

See Also Blount, William; North Carolina; States, Admission and Creation

FOR FURTHER READING

Alden, George Henry. 1903. "The State of Franklin." *American Historical Review* 8 (January): 271–289.

Farrand, Max, ed. 1937. *The Records of the Federal Convention.* 4 vols. New Haven, CT: Yale University Press.

Turner, Frederick Jackson. 1895. "Western State-Making in the Revolutionary Era I." *American Historical Review* 1 (October): 70–86.

———. 1896. "Western State-Making in the Revolutionary Era II." *American Historical Review* 2 (January): 251–269.

Van West, Carroll, ed. 1998. *The Tennessee Encyclopedia of History and Culture.* Nashville: Tennessee Historical Society/Rutledge Hill Press.

TERRITORY OF THE UNITED STATES

Article IV, Section 3 of the Constitution grants Congress the power "to dispose of and make all needful Rules and Regulations respecting the Territory or other Property belonging to the United

States." It further provides that "nothing in this Constitution shall be construed as to Prejudice any Claims of the United States, or of any particular State."

When Edmund Randolph proposed the Virginia Plan to the Convention on May 29, it contained a provision whereby the United States was to guarantee a republican government "& the territory of each State" (Farrand 1937, I, 22). The Committee of the Whole affirmed this provision on June 11 (I, 202).

The Convention devoted considerable time to discussing the admission and creation of new states. Small landlocked states on the East Coast who feared domination by larger states with extensive Western land claims were particularly concerned that these states would neither provide adequate representation for, nor allow those in the western parts of the states to form, their own governments. During the course of this discussion on August 30, Pennsylvania's Gouverneur Morris, one of the most adamant among the delegates against giving new Western states equal representation in Congress, proposed the provision that, with slight emendations, would become the current clause. He proposed that

> the Legislature shall have power to dispose of and make all needful rules and regulations respecting the territory and other property belonging to the U. States; and nothing in this constitution contained, shall be so construed as to prejudice any claims either of the U-S—or of any particular State. (II, 466)

After rejecting a provision that would have explicitly recognized the right of the U.S. Supreme Court to adjudicate such claims (a majority of delegates thought such a provision would be unnecessary), the Convention accepted the proposal.

The idea that the national authority should govern U.S. territories was hardly new. One of the most heralded accomplishments of the Articles of Confederation, actually enacted during the meeting of the Constitutional Convention, was the Northwest Ordinance Act of 1787. It provided for the governing of the West and for the eventual admission of territories in this area as states.

See Also District of Columbia; Northwest Ordinance of 1787; States, Admission and Creation

FOR FURTHER READING

Farrand, Max, ed. 1937. *The Records of the Federal Convention.* 4 vols. New Haven, CT: Yale University Press.
Onuf, Peter S. 1982. "From Colony to Territory: Changing Concepts of Statehood in Revolutionary America." *Political Science Quarterly* 97 (Autumn): 447–459.
———. 1986. "Liberty, Development, and Union: Visions of the West in the 1780s." *William and Mary Quarterly,* 3rd ser. 53 (1986): 179–213.

THREE-FIFTHS CLAUSE

One of the most antiquated and embarrassing provisions of the U.S. Constitution, which the Fourteenth Amendment subsequently voided, is the three-fifths clause, which is found in Article I, Section 2, Clause 3. It specifies that "Representatives and direct Taxes" shall be apportioned among the states "according to their respective Numbers." These, in turn, were to "be determined by adding to the whole Number of free Persons, including those bound to Service for a Term of Years, and excluding Indians not taxed, three fifths of all other Persons." The reference to "all other persons" is a euphemistic reference to slaves, who are clearly distinguished from indentured servants or those "bound to Service for a Term of Years."

Virginia and New Jersey Plans

The Virginia Plan, which Edmund Randolph introduced at the Convention on May 29, provided that members "of the National Legislature ought to be proportioned to the quotas of contribution, or to the number of free inhabitants, as the one or the other rule may seem best in different cases" (Farrand 1937, I, 31). Although designed to replace the Articles of Confederation, under which states had been equally represented in Congress, with a more national government, this proposal rather clearly looked back to procedures under the Articles whereby the national government raised taxes by requisitioning the states, rather than by taxing individual citizens. The apportionment of direct taxation remained part of the formula, but the primary concern that this provision of the Virginia Plan addressed was whether to substitute representation according to population in Congress for state equality, and, if so, how to count African American slaves.

Prior to mention of the three-fifths formula, the Convention had proposed "an equitable ratio of representation" (I, 200). On June 11, James Wilson of Pennsylvania and Charles Pinckney of South Carolina then proposed to follow these words with "in proportion to the whole number of white & other free Citizens & inhabitants of every age sex & condition including those bound to servitude for a term of years and three fifths of all other persons not comprehended in the foregoing description, except Indians not paying taxes, in each State" (201). Referring to an amendment that had proposed sharing expenses according to population, which Congress had proposed on April 18, 1783, but the states had failed to ratify (see Jensen 1976, 148–150; Wills 2003, 53), the authors of this motion observed that 11 states had agreed to the three-fifths formula under the Articles of Confederation. Although Elbridge Gerry of Massachusetts protested that blacks, who were considered by Southerners to be property, had no more business being represented than "cattle & horses in the North," the Convention agreed to the formula with no recorded additional discussion by a vote of 9-2.

New Jersey's William Paterson introduced the New Jersey Plan on June 15. Although this plan was based on equal state representation in a unicameral Congress, it provided for requisitions of the states in accord with the three-fifths formula that Wilson and Pinckney had previously introduced (I, 243). The Convention decided to proceed with the Virginia Plan, but it continued to wrestle with the conflicting plans for representation that the Virginia and New Jersey Plans had proffered.

Moreover, the Virginia Plan continued to embody possible tension between representation based on population alone and that based on population and some measure of property or tax contributions. On July 6, South Carolina's Charles Pinckney argued that "the number of inhabitants appeared to him the only just & practicable rule," but he added that although he thought the blacks ought to stand on an equality with whites [for representation purposes] he would "agree to the ratio settled by Cong." (I, 542). By contrast, on July 9, Paterson opposed combining "the rule of numbers of wealth" as being too "vague" (I, 561). He also delivered a fairly powerful salvo against using the three-fifths formula for representation:

He could regard Negro slaves in no light but as property. They are no free agents, have no personal liberty, no faculty of acquiring property, but on the contrary are themselves property, & like other property entirely at the will of the Master. Has a man in Virga. a number of votes in proportion to the number of Slaves? and if Negroes are not represented in the States to which they belong, why should they be represented in the Genl. Govt. (I, 561)

Paterson continued:

What is the true principle of Representation? It is an expedient by which an assembly of certain individls. chosen by the people is substituted in place of the inconvenient meeting of the people themselves. If such a meeting of the people was actually to take place, would the slaves vote? they would not.

Why then shd. they be represented. He was also agst. such an indirect encouragemt. of the slave trade; observing that Congs. in their act relating to the change of the 8 art: of Confedn. had been ashamed to use the term "Slaves" & had substituted a description. (I, 561)

Virginia's James Madison, the primary author of the Virginia Plan, responded with the fairly biting observation that if Paterson's observations on representation were correct, then they "must for ever silence the pretension of the small States to an equality of votes with the large ones" (I, 562). Perhaps as a way of further discomfiting Paterson, whose state had few slaves, Madison suggested that he was willing to agree to a compromise whereby states would be represented in one branch according to their number of free inhabitants and in the second by this number plus the number of slaves (I, 562). South Carolina's Pierce Butler followed by urging the importance of considering "wealth" (presumably slaves) in apportioning representatives, and Rufus King of Massachusetts observed that a concession would be needed if the wealthier Southern states were expected to join with the North, favorably citing the agreement by 11 of 13 states under the Articles to use the three-fifths formula.

Discussions in July

This formula became the topic of discussion again on July 11, supplementing the larger debate between the large and small states. Butler and Charles Cotesworth Pinckney, both of South Carolina, argued that blacks should count equally toward representation with whites. Elbridge Gerry argued that three-fifths represented a maximum. Nathaniel Gorham, who observed the ratio's previous use as a formula in tax policy, at which time Southern states had argued that slaves were "still more inferior to freemen," thought that the three-fifths formula "was pretty near the just proportion" (I, 580).

Butler now gave his rationale for full representation. It stemmed from his belief that slave labor was "as productive & valuable as that of a freeman," that "wealth was the great means of defence and utility to the Nation," and that a government designed to protect property and resting on it should provide equal representation. Virginia's George Mason thought equal representation would be unjust. Although slaves added to national assets, slaves "were not equal to freemen" (I, 581). Hugh Williamson of North Carolina felt compelled to respond to Gorham by indicating that, when it came to the apportionment of taxation, the Northern states had argued for slave

equality. Butler's argument for equal representation failed 7-3, with Delaware, South Carolina, and Georgia being the only states voting in its favor.

The delegates continued to bicker about whether to consider wealth in the apportionment of representation in the House of Representatives. During this debate Gouverneur Morris observed that he objected to including blacks in the census because "the people of Pena. would revolt at the idea of being put on a footing with slaves" (I, 583). When the delegates resumed discussion of the three-fifths clause, King observed that he thought counting blacks along with whites "would excite great discontents among the States having no slaves," and added that he thought the delegates had granted the Southern states more representatives than they were entitled to under this formula (586).

James Wilson of Pennsylvania now questioned the whole idea of representation for slaves: "Are they admitted as Citizens? Then why are they not admitted on an equality with White Citizens? Are they admitted as property? Then why is not other property admitted into the computation?" (I, 587).

Despite concerns, he was still willing to compromise. Gouverneur Morris was not, at least not then. He feared that the three-fifths formula would encourage the slave trade. Apparently, others shared these fears, because the Convention voted 6-4 against the three-fifths clause, with Connecticut, Virginia, North Carolina, and Georgia voting in the minority.

On July 12, Gouverneur Morris proposed adding the idea of proportioning taxes according to representation. Butler again contended for fully including blacks in representation. Morris was willing to limit his proposal to direct taxes, and the Convention approved a proposal to do this.

North Carolina's William Davie said that his state "would never confederate" on terms that did not at least count the slaves according to a three-fifths ratio (I, 593). Gouverneur Morris was equally convinced that the people of Pennsylvania could never agree to such representation. Ellsworth proposed a provisional solution whereby the three-fifths clause should be used in apportioning direct taxes, but although he professed to lament the institution of slavery, Randolph "urged strenuously that express security ought to be provided for including slaves in the ratio of Representation" (I, 594). Wilson hoped to admit slaves into representation indirectly, by allowing them in the formula for taxation and then apportioning representation on this measure. Likening blacks to "the labourers, the Peasants of the Southern states," Charles Pinckney wanted them counted fully for purposes of representation, but the states rejected his motion by an 8-2 vote, with only South Carolina and Georgia voting affirmatively. The Convention voted on the same day to accept the three-fifths formula for representation and taxation by a vote of 6-2-2, with New Jersey and Delaware voting no and Massachusetts and South Carolina divided.

Discussion of the three-fifths clause resumed on July 13—the day on which Congress adopted the Northwest Ordinance (Lynd 1966, 225). At that time, Randolph suggested that delegates should use this formula to adjust future representation in the House of Representatives, not on the basis of population and "wealth" but by counting whites as whole persons and slaves as three-fifths of a person. Again Gouverneur Morris pointed to contradictions:

If Negroes were to be viewed as inhabitants, and the revision was to proceed on the principle of numbers of inhabt. they ought to be added in their entire number, and not in the proportion of 3/5. If as property, the word wealth was right, and striking it out would produce the very inconsistency it was meant to get rid of. (II, 604)

Nonetheless, the Convention voted to accept the compromise by a 9-0 vote. Three days later, the Convention approved the Connecticut Compromise, which provided for representation in the House according to population (counting slaves as three-fifths of a person) and giving states equal representation in the Senate.

Debates of August and September

Discussion resumed on August 8. After the Convention voted explicitly to tie the ratio of representation to that of direct taxation, King expressed deep concern about so embedding slavery within the Constitution. He thought the Convention should have to make a choice between representing slaves and taxing exports, a prohibition that the Southern states had already obtained. Sherman thought the issue of representation had been firmly settled, but, shortly thereafter, Gouverneur Morris moved to limit representation to "free" inhabitants, and gave an impassioned speech against the institution of slavery. Again, Sherman proposed moderation and tied representation and taxation together: "It was the freemen of the Southn. States who were in fact to be represented according to the taxes paid by them, and the Negroes are only included in the Estimate of the taxes" (II, 223). Only New Jersey voted for Morris's proposal.

When on September 13, John Dickinson and James Wilson questioned the placement of a provision in Article I, Section 2 relating to direct taxes, Gouverneur Morris observed that

the insertion here was in consequence of what had passed on this point; in order to exclude the appearance of counting the Negroes in the Representation—the including of them may now be referred to the object of direct taxes, and incidentally only to that of Representation. (II, 607)

As obfuscating as it appeared, the provision was retained. Elbridge Gerry subsequently cited the three-fifths clause as one reason for objecting to the new Constitution (II, 635), but, odious as it was, the clause had at least temporarily bridged the gap between Northern and Southern interests.

Analysis

Although the three-fifths clause is often portrayed as a clause that permitted the South to count slaves for purposes of representation and the North to count them for purposes of taxation, there is little evidence that much of a trade took place. Instead, the three-fifths formula, which had been suggested under the Articles of Confederation as a means of assessing taxes, was now applied to the selection of representatives. The Convention was so unsure what "direct taxation" included that when Rufus King of Massachusetts asked on August what it was, no one responded (see II, 350). The delegates do not appear to have contemplated that such taxes would be used extensively, if at all. The familiarity of the three-fifths clause arguably made it less offensive than it might otherwise have been, but the real compromise appears to have been between those primarily in the South who wanted to include the slaves in whole or in part in calculating representation and those primarily in the North who wanted to exclude them altogether. The link to taxation seems to have been used more to obscure the peculiar nature of the provision than to provide the basis for it (Finkelman 1996, 9).

In a recent book, historian Garry Wills has highlighted the impact that the three-fifths clause had in the early republic on giving the South more representation than it would otherwise have had. He thinks the ratio was particularly important in the closely contested election of 1800, when Thomas Jefferson's Democratic-Republican Party replaced John Adams's Federalist Party (Wills; also see Simpson 1941). Jefferson's opponents highlighted the role of the three-fifths clause in electing Jefferson by referring to him as the "Negro President," and some, including former president John Quincy Adams, who was serving in the U.S. House of Representatives, introduced amendments in Congress to repeal this provision.

See Also African Americans; Indentured Servants; Slavery

FOR FURTHER READING

Farrand, Max, ed. 1937. *The Records of the Federal Convention.* 4 vols. New Haven, CT: Yale University Press.

Finkelman, Paul. 1996. *Slavery and the Founders: Race and Liberty in the Age of Jefferson.* Armonk, NY: M. E. Sharpe.

Jensen, Merrill, ed. 1976. *Constitutional Documents and Records, 1776–1787.* Vol. 1 of *The Documentary History of the Ratification of the Constitution.* Madison: State Historical Society of Wisconsin.

Lynd, Staughton. 1966. "The Compromise of 1787." *Political Science Quarterly* 81 (June): 225–250.

Ohline, Howard A. 1971. "Republicanism and Slavery: Origins of the Three-fifths Clause in the United States Constitution." *William and Mary Quarterly,* 3rd ser. 28 (October): 563–584.

Simpson, Albert F. 1941. "The Political Significance of Slave Representation, 1787–1821." *Journal of Southern History* 7 (August): 315–342.

Wills, Garry. 2003. *"Negro President": Jefferson and the Slave Power.* Boston: Houghton Mifflin.

Woodson, Carter G. 1918. "Documents: What the Framers of the Federal Constitution Thought of the Negro." *Journal of Negro History* 8 (January): 381–434.

TIMING

One of the factors that has led to the view that what the delegates to the Constitutional Convention accomplished was a "miracle" was the fact that those who acted to secure the Constitution acted, consciously or unconsciously, with an almost uncanny sense of timing. Delegates to the Constitutional Convention proposed the new document as a substitute for the Articles of Confederation, which had recognized state sovereignty. The experience of the Articles, as well as the experience at the state level, served as laboratories of sorts for leading figures to recognize the weaknesses of government. The propitious timing of Shays's Rebellion in the winter of 1786–1787, after the Annapolis Convention had already called for the Constitutional Convention, further helped persuade Congress to approve all but one of the undecided states to send delegates. George Washington, the military commander of the American Revolution whose integrity and public spiritedness were almost universally recognized, was still alive to preside over the proceedings and lend his support to ratification, and there was a large pool of experienced politicians and constitution writers to carry on the day-to-day proceedings at a time when the nation was not directly threatened with war.

Men like James Madison and Alexander Hamilton, whose views were distinct, nonetheless worked with relative harmony (especially in their defense of the new Constitution in *The Federalist Papers* and in the state ratifying conventions) at the Convention, but soon split into rival camps as political parties developed during the nation's first administration. Two years after the Convention, revolution rocked France. This event further divided partisans of the French and the English in the United States and led to increased party divisions. A recent writer has observed that, while "in historical memory, the founding fathers appear united in their wisdom and venerable in their concordance," in truth, the "meeting of the minds" that they achieved "in one brief shining moment" was ultimately "deceptive," in that this agreement was followed by "one long descent into a witches' brew of venomous accusation, kindled by a deep conviction of mutual betrayal" (Hendrickson 2003, 251). Another writer, who focused in part on how those favoring a stronger government attended the Convention and prominent future opponents of the Constitution chose not to, has observed that "the key conditions were all present in a pattern that virtually guaranteed for the meeting an optimum of effectiveness" (Elkins and McKitrick 1961, 212).

See Also Articles of Confederation; Federalist and Democratic-Republican Parties; Shays's Rebellion

FOR FURTHER READING

Elkins, Stanley, and Eric McKitrick. 1961. "The Founding Fathers: Young Men of the Revolution." *Political Science Quarterly* 76 (June): 181–216.
Hendrickson, David C. 2003. *Peace Pact: The Lost World of the American Founding*. Lawrence: University Press of Kansas.

1937, II, 183). The Convention voted unanimously for this provision on August 23, signaling the delegates' commitment to republicanism and their opposition to hereditary aristocracy. Immediately thereafter, Charles Pinckney of South Carolina proposed that no person "holding any office of profit or trust" under the U.S. shall "accept of any present, emolument, office or title of any king whatever, from any King, Prince, or foreign State" (II, 389). Pinckney argued that the provision was necessary to preserve "foreign Ministers & other officers of the U.S. independent of external influence" (II, 389), and the states unanimously agreed.

The concerns that motivated the prohibition against titles of nobility did not end with the ratification of the Constitution. In 1810, Philip Reed of Maryland introduced an amendment, which the necessary majorities of Congress ratified, specifying that individuals who accepted such honors without congressional approval would forfeit their citizenship and their right to hold public offices in the United States. The requisite number of states did not ratify this amendment, which is sometimes dubbed the "Phantom Amendment" (Vile 2003, 454–455).

See Also Aristocracy; Republicanism; Society of the Cincinnati

FOR FURTHER READING

Farrand, Max, ed. 1937. *The Records of the Federal Convention*. 4 vols. New Haven, CT: Yale University Press.
Vile, John R. 2003. *Encyclopedia of Constitutional Amendments, Proposed Amendments, and Amending Issues, 1789–2002*. Santa Barbara, CA: ABC-CLIO.

TITLES OF NOBILITY

A provision in the report of the Committee of Detail on August 6 stated that the United States should not "grant any title of Nobility" (Farrand

TRANSCRIBING THE CONSTITUTION

See SHALLUS, JACOB

TREASON

Article 3, Section 3 of the Constitution provides that "treason against the United States, shall consist only in levying War against them, or in adhering to their Enemies, giving them Aid and Comfort. No Person shall be convicted of Treason unless on the Testimony of two Witnesses to the same overt Act, or on Confession in open Court." The clause also gives Congress power to punish treason, but, with a view to abuses in Great Britain, limits "Corruption of Blood, or Forfeiture except during the Life of the Person attainted."

The Committee of Detail

The first mention of treason at the Convention appears to be in the plan that New York's Alexander Hamilton proposed on June 18. In this plan, he proposed exempting the president from pardoning this offense "without the approbation of the Senate" (Farrand 1937, I, 292). A document belonging to the Committee of Detail, which scholars believe to be an outline of the Pinckney Plan, also provided that Congress would "have the exclusive Power of declaring what shall be Treason and Misp. of Treason agt. U.S." (II, 136).

The primary provisions of the current clause emerged in the report of the Committee of Detail on August 6, where the provisions related to treason were treated under the powers of Congress. The committee defined treason as levying war or adhering to the enemies of the United States collectively or individually. It vested Congress with the power to punish treason. It further provided that conviction would require the testimony of two witnesses, and it limited corruption of blood and forfeiture to the life of the individual convicted (II, 182).

Debates over the Provision

The first actual debate over this provision occurred on August 20. In what seems to be a fairly uncharacteristic position for an individual so con-

Attorney William Wirt prosecutes Aaron Burr for treason in 1807. The trial resulted in increased judicial independence and further rights for criminal defendants. (Corbis)

cerned about protecting individual rights, Virginia's James Madison thought that the existing language defined the offense too narrowly, and he favored giving Congress greater latitude. He observed that the power would be as safe there as it was in the hands of the state legislatures, and "it was inconvenient to bar a discretion which experience might enlighten, and which might be applied to good purposes as well as be abused" (II, 345). George Mason of Virginia suggested using the language of Edward III, to which Madison had previously alluded. Fellow Virginian Edmund Randolph later agreed, noting that the British had extended treason not only to "adhering to" but also to giving aid and comfort to the enemy, which he thought "had a more extensive meaning" (II, 345). Connecticut's Oliver Ellsworth thought the provision was already like that of Britain, whereas Gouverneur Morris of Pennsylvania did not. Pennsylvania's James Wilson thought the provision relating to giving aid and comfort was "explanatory, not operative words" that it was better to omit. Delaware's John Dickinson agreed that the additional language was unnecessary, but he was concerned that the testimony of two witnesses should be limited to a specific overt act.

In the meantime, Gouverneur Morris had initiated discussion of a different concern. He wanted to give Congress "an exclusive right to declare what shd. be treason." He observed that in contests between the national government and the states, the people would "under the disjunctive terms of the clause, be traitors to [one] or the other authority" (II, 345). Madison observed that since the definition in the Constitution only included treason against the United States, it appeared to leave states with "a concurrent power so far as to define & punish treason particularly agst. themselves; which might involve double punishmt." (II, 346). Wilson and Johnson suggested a motion striking out "or any of them," and the Convention agreed. Madison was still concerned that individuals could be punished for treason both at the state and national levels, and discussion continued over the implications of divided sovereignty on this question. After continued discussion, the delegates voted to strike out the words "against the United States" (II, 348).

After an unnamed delegate introduced a provision limiting conviction to cases when two witnesses testified to the same overt act, a provision that dated back to a statute from the reign of Edward VI in 1552 (St. John 1987, 170), Pennsylvania's Benjamin Franklin indicated that he favored this amendment as a means to prevent injustice: "prosecutions for treason were generally virulent; and perjury too easily made use of against innocence" (II, 348). Wilson could see arguments on both sides. He thus observed that "treason may sometimes be practiced in such a manner, as to render proof extremely difficult," but the Convention still accepted the provision (II, 348).

Consistent with earlier discussions as to whether treason could take place against both the nation and the states, Rufus King of Massachu-setts proposed adding the word "sole" so that only Congress would have this power, and Delaware's Jacob Broom seconded him. The delegates defeated this motion. Extensive discussion on the issue of divided sovereignty then led to a reinstatement of the words "United States." Madison expressed continued concern that individuals might end up being prosecuted under both state and national laws. Mason successfully moved to add the words "giving them aid and comfort" as restricting "adhering to their Enemies." Maryland's Luther Martin succeeded in adding a provision permitting conviction for treason in cases when individuals admitted to treason in open court (II, 350).

Luther Martin's Concern

Official records do not record another motion that Martin later told the Maryland state legislature that he had supported. According to Martin's later account, his motion would have qualified the treason clause by providing

> that no act or acts done by one or more of the States against the United States, or by any citizen of any one of the United States, under the authority of one or more of the said States, shall be deemed treason, or punished as such; but, in case of war being levied by one or more of the States against the United States, the conduct of each party towards the other, and their adherents respectively, shall be regulated by the laws of war and of nations. (III, 223; italics omitted here and in following quotation)

Luther rendered a fairly partisan interpretation of this proposal's rejection:

> But this provision was not adopted, being too much opposed by the great object of many of the leading members of the convention, which was, by all means to leave the States at the mercy of the general government, since they could not succeed in their immediate and entire abolition. (III, 223)

Work of the Committee of Style and Arrangement

On September 8, the Convention appointed a Committee of Style and Arrangement to put the finishing touches on the resolutions that had been adopted and to arrange them into a document. In its report of September 12, the committee moved the provisions relative to treason from the section of the Constitution relating to congressional powers to those dealing with the judiciary. Psychologically speaking, such placement emphasized the degree to which the provisions relative to treason were designed as restraints on legislative powers rather than as additions to them.

Treason and the President's Pardon Power

Two days before the Constitution was signed, delegates discussed the president's pardon power. As in Hamilton's earlier set of proposals, Virginia's Edmund Randolph suggested that this power should not extend to cases of treason when the president might himself be guilty, and Mason supported him. Apparently, there was general agreement that some provision needed to be made for pardons in all cases. Morris thus expressed the view that it would be better to entrust such power in the president than to Congress. Wilson thought that presidents involved in treasonable conduct could be impeached, and the Constitution does list this as one of three impeachable offenses. Madison suggested that he would prefer associating the president with a Council of Advice in such situations. Randolph and Mason expressed fears that the Senate was already too strong, but the Convention rejected Randolph's motion to exclude the president from pardoning treasonable offenses by a vote of 8-2-1. Although he had opposed associating the president and the Senate in granting certain pardons, in listing his reasons for opposing the Constitution, Mason nonetheless observed that the president's unrestricted power in pardoning treason "may be sometimes exercised to screen from punishment those whom he had secretly instigated to commit the crime, and thereby prevent a discovery of his own guilt" (II, 639).

Analysis

The Convention clearly borrowed heavily from British experience with treason. It used the language of British statutes to define this offense and attempted to profit from the example of British abuses both by setting tough standards for proving treason and by limiting the punishment to actual offenders and not continuing to visit such punishment on their descendants. A commentator has observed that the Framers "carefully weighted the definitional scope of treason with the historical record of its application" and "sought language that would prevent political disagreements from escalating into charges of treason and the abuses of treason law as practiced by British authorities" (Hall 2002, 809).

Discussions of whether states could also prosecute treasonous offenses indicated continuing confusion over exactly where the Constitution drew the line between state and national authority. Largely because it could not come up with a suitable alternative, the Convention allowed the president to pardon treasonous offenses, presumably in the hope that impeachment could be wielded against a president who abused this privilege to shield his own conduct or that of his co-conspirators.

Prosecutions for treason have been relatively rare in U.S. history, but such cases—that of Aaron Burr, for example—have often been dramatic. The language of the Constitution has largely succeeded in ensuring that individuals are convicted only for overt acts and that they are not convicted of treason simply for their disagreements with governmental policies. Cases like *Pennsylvania v. Nelson*, 350 U.S. 497 (1956), which overturned a state law against the knowing advocacy of violent overthrow of the government as conflicting with federal law (the Smith Act) related to the same subject, indicate that the Convention did not fully sort out the relation between state and national authorities on this subject.

See Also Federalism

FOR FURTHER READING

Farrand, Max, ed. 1937. *The Records of the Federal Convention*. 4 vols. New Haven, CT: Yale University Press.
Hall, Kermit L. 2002. *The Oxford Companion to American Law*. New York: Oxford University Press.
Leek, J. J. 1951. "Treason and the Constitution." *Journal of Politics* 13 (November): 604–622.
St. John, Jeffrey. 1987. *Constitutional Journal: A Correspondent's Report from the Convention of 1787*. Ottawa, IL: Jameson Books.

TREASURY, SECRETARY OF THE

The secretary of the Treasury was one of three initial cabinet positions; the others were the attorney general and the secretary of state. In authorizing the Treasury Department, the first Congress anticipated a closer relationship with it than with either the State or War Department (Galloway 1958, 466). The first secretary, Alexander Hamilton, exercised wide powers. Like other members of the cabinet, the president appoints the secretary of the Treasury with the advice and consent of the Senate.

The first apparent mention of the treasurer at the Constitutional Convention was contained in the report that the Committee of Detail sent to the Convention on August 6. Perhaps with a view to the congressional power of the purse, the Committee proposed granting power to Congress "to appoint a Treasurer by ballot" (Farrand 1937, II, 182). By contrast, it proposed that the Senate would appoint ambassadors and Supreme Court judges (II, 183), with the president being granted power to "appoint officers in all cases not otherwise provided for by this Constitution" (II, 185).

When the Convention first discussed the Treasury position on August 17, it amended the report of the Committee of Detail by inserting the word "joint" before "ballot," to make it clear that both houses of Congress would have a share in the treasurer's appointment (II, 315). Although the Convention had vested the appointment of other officers in the president with the advice and consent of the Senate (II, 574), the report of the Committee of Style to the Convention on September 12 continued to vest appointment of the treasurer in Congress (II, 594).

The Convention discussed this provision on September 14, just three days before the signing of the Constitution. At this time, South Carolina's John Rutledge proposed striking the provision so that the treasurer would be chosen like other federal officers. Nathaniel Gorham and Rufus King of Massachusetts both opposed this motion arguing that the people were accustomed to congressional appointment of the treasurer and that changing this would increase opposition to the new Constitution (II, 614). Gouverneur Morris of Pennsylvania responded that the legislature would more closely watch, and be more likely to impeach, an officer appointed by another institution. By contrast, Connecticut's Roger Sherman thought it was appropriate for the institution that appropriated money to make such appointment; however, he favored separate votes by the two houses (II, 614). South Carolina's General Pinckney observed that South Carolina appointed its treasurer by joint ballot with the result that bad appointments were made and that "the Legislature will not listen to the faults of their own officer" (II, 614). After this surprisingly short exchange, the Convention voted 8-3 (with Massachusetts, Pennsylvania, and Virginia in dissent) to strike this clause, and it did not make it into the final draft of the Constitution.

Although the Constitution thus vests the power to appoint the treasurer, like other cabinet officials, in the president, the document is silent about the power of removal of such officers. With some exceptions for quasi-legislative and quasi-judicial positions, the U.S. Supreme Court has generally extended broad removal power of executive officials to the president on the basis that the power of removal corresponds more closely to the power of appointment than to the power of confirmation—see *Myers v. United States*, 272 U.S. 52 (1926). James Madison was, however, among those who thought the president's power to fire the secretary of the Treasury, who he thought would not be a "purely executive" officer, should be distinguished from his power over other officers (see O'Brien 2003, 319).

See Also Bureaucracy; Committee of Detail; Hamilton, Alexander

FOR FURTHER READING

Farrand, Max, ed. 1937. *The Records of the Federal Convention*. 4 vols. New Haven, CT: Yale University Press.

Fisher, Louis. 1983. "Congress and the Removal Power." *Congress and the Presidency* 10: 63.

Galloway, George B. 1958. "Precedents Established in the First Congress." *Western Political Quarterly* 22 (September): 454–468.

O'Brien, David M. 2003. *Struggles for Power and Governmental Accountability*. Vol. 1 of *Constitutional Law and Politics*. 5th ed. New York: W. W. Norton.

TREATY-MAKING AND RATIFICATION

Article II, Section 2 of the Constitution provides that the president "shall have Power, by and with the Advice and Consent of the Senate, to make Treaties, provided two thirds of the Senators present concur." Under the Articles of Confederation, treaties were negotiated on behalf of Congress, in which each state had a single vote. Such treaties required approval of nine or more states. The Virginia Plan did not mention treaties, presumably indicating that it intended to leave such powers with Congress (Tansill 1924, 459). The New Jersey Plan did provide for the Supreme Court to have a role in the interpretation of all treaties. Significantly, when the New Jersey Plan first introduced the supremacy clause, it provided for the supremacy of treaties along with "all Acts of the U. States in Congs." (Farrand 1937, II, 245).

Agreement on Senate Negotiation of Treaties

When the Committee of Detail drew up the first draft of the Constitution, which it presented to the Convention on August 6, it provided that "the Senate of the United States shall have power to make treaties, and to appoint Ambassadors, and Judges of the supreme Court" (II, 183). On August 15, Virginia's George Mason, in supporting the origination of money bills in the House of Representatives, observed, in a probable reference to John Jay's plans under the Articles of Confederation to give up temporary claims to American rights to navigate the Mississippi River, that the Senate "could already sell the whole Country by means of Treaties" (II, 297). This prompted Maryland's John Mercer to observe "that the Senate ought not to have the power of treaties." He went on to say that treaties "would not be final so as to alter the laws of the land, till ratified by legislative authority" (II, 297). Mason expressed further fears that "the Senate by means of treaty might alienate territory &c. without legislative sanction" (II, 297).

Discussion of treaty-making resumed on August 23. In line with the changes brought about by the Connecticut Compromise, Virginia's James Madison "observed that the Senate represented the States alone, and that for this as well as for other obvious reasons it was proper that the President should be an agent in Treaties" (II, 392). Although he was unsure whether the Senate should negotiate treaties, Gouverneur Morris of Pennsylvania proposed that treaties should be ratified by law (possibly thus involving the president's veto). Nathaniel Gorham of Massachusetts suggested that this would create all kinds of practical problems. Morris responded that this would be good, forcing foreign governments to send their ministers to the U.S. He further observed that "he was not solicitous to multiply & facilitate Treaties," and that "the more difficulty in making treaties the more value will be set upon them" (II, 393). Pennsylvania's James Wilson observed that the English king had to resort to Parliament for the enforcement of treaties and that without some kind of legislative approval, "the Senate alone can make a Treaty, requiring all the Rice of S. Carolina to be sent to some one particular port" (II, 393). Although Delaware's John Dickinson realized that, as a small state representative, he might be taking a stance against his own interest, he too favored legislative ratification (that is, ratification by both houses) of treaties. Connecticut's William Samuel Johnson thought that it was unusual to require a "minister with plenipotentiary powers from one Body" to "depend for ratification on another Body" (II, 393). By contrast, Gorham thought it was necessary to guard against negotiators being "seduced." After a motion to postpone failed, the Convention rejected Morris's motion for full legislative ratification of treaties by a vote of 8-1-1. Madison suggested that delegates might consider allowing the president and the Senate to make treaties of limited alliance and leave others to approval by both houses.

Changes Initiated by
the Committee on Postponed Matters

As in the case of appointments, which it switched from senatorial to presidential hands, the Committee on Postponed Matters initiated a major change on September 4. At that time it proposed that "the President by and with the advice and consent of the Senate shall have power to make treaties," but also provided that treaties should require approval by two-thirds of the members who were present (II, 495). The Convention discussed this proposal on September 7. It seems likely that the Convention proposed this majority as a way of guarding sectional interests, most notably the right to navigate the Mississippi River, which the South and West so valued, and the rights to Newfoundland fisheries, which the Northeast so valued (McClendon 1931, 768).

Wilson wanted to require the consent of both houses of Congress to treaties, because having the "operation of laws, they ought to have the sanction of laws also" (II, 538). Connecticut's Roger Sherman thought that the Senate could be trusted, and he feared that requiring approval from both houses would make secrecy impossible. Thomas Fitzsimons of Pennsylvania nonetheless seconded Wilson's motion, which the Con-

vention overwhelmingly rejected by a 10 to 1 vote, with only Wilson's Pennsylvania supporting the motion.

Later that same day, the Convention discussed the propriety of the two-thirds Senate majority to ratify treaties. Wilson feared that this would give undue power to the minority, and Rufus King of Massachusetts concurred. Madison moved to exempt peace treaties from this requirement, and the Convention agreed without dissent.

Madison further proposed that two-thirds of the Senate should be able to make peace treaties without presidential approval. Madison feared that presidents might otherwise be tempted to prolong wars to increase their importance, and South Carolina's Pierce Butler agreed, seconding his motion. Gorham pointed out that "the means of carrying on the war would not be in the hands of the President, but of the Legislature," and Gouverneur Morris observed that "no peace ought to be made without the concurrence of the President, who was the general Guardian of the National interests" (II, 541). Pierce Butler of South Carolina continued to think the provision to be "a necessary security against ambitious & corrupt Presidents" (II, 541). Fearing that treaties could become occasions upon which "the extremities of the Continent" might be sacrificed, Elbridge Gerry of Massachusetts thought that treaties of peace might actually require greater majorities, whereas North Carolina's Hugh Williamson favored the same majorities in the case of these treaties as of others. The states rejected Madison's motion by an 8-3 vote, and the same majority approved the amended resolution. Hugh Williamson and Richard Spaight, also of North Carolina, then proposed "that no Treaty of Peace affecting Territorial rights shd be made without the concurrence of two thirds of the [members of the Senate present]." King suggested that this limitation should extend to "all present rights of the U. States," but neither suggestion was approved (II, 543).

The following day the Convention resumed discussion of treaties. Just as the Convention had previously voted to exempt peace treaties from the two-thirds requirement, James Wilson wanted to go even further. He proposed allowing the Senate to approve all treaties by majority vote—"If the majority cannot be trusted, it was a proof . . . that we were not fit for one Society" (II, 548).

Morris wanted to keep the exception for peace treaties. Indicating that "the Fisheries" and "the Mississippi" were "the two great objects of the Union," he indicated that without such an exemption, the nation might otherwise be unwilling to go to war when necessary (II, 548). Moreover, if a majority of the Senate favored peace, they might simply achieve it by cutting off war supplies. Williamson observed that a majority of the Senate, where states were to be represented equally regardless of population, might not contain a majority of the people and that an even smaller quorum should not be able to decide on the "conditions of peace" (II, 548). Wilson feared that if two-thirds majorities were required for peace, "the minority might perpetuate war, against the sense of the majority" (II, 548). Gerry feared that such a small number of senators might be "corrupted by foreign influence" (II, 548). Sherman proposed that no rights under the Treaty of Paris should be ceded "without the sanction of the Legislature," and Gouverneur Morris seconded him. Madison observed that it had been "too easy" to make treaties under the Articles of Confederation, even with the concurrence of two-thirds of the states.

After voting 8-3 to reject the exemption of treaties of peace from the two-thirds requirement, the Convention further rejected a proposal by Wilson and New Jersey's Jonathan Dayton to strike the two-thirds requirement for all treaties by a vote of 9-1-1. John Rutledge of South Carolina and Gerry then proposed that no treaties be made without the consent of two-thirds of all senators, rather than of those simply in attendance. Gorham pointed out that under the Articles, presidential consent was not required, and the motion was defeated by a vote of 8-3. Sherman then moved that no treaty should be made without a majority of the whole number of senators, and Gerry seconded him. North Carolina's Hugh Williamson said that this would provide less security than the two-thirds requirement, and Sherman retorted that it would be "less embarrassing" (II, 549). The measure failed by a 5-6 vote. The Convention also rejected a motion by Madison to require two-thirds of the Senate for a quorum by

a 5-6 vote. The Convention further voted down a requirement for giving prior notice to senators of treaty votes by a 5-6 vote. The Convention then affirmed the two-thirds requirement for treaties, with only the states of Pennsylvania, New Jersey, and Georgia in dissent.

In assessing the reasons he was not going to sign the Convention, George Mason observed on September 15:

> By declaring all treaties supreme laws of the land, the Executive and the Senate have, in many cases, an exclusive power of legislation; which might have been avoided by proper distinctions with respect to treaties, and requiring the assent of the House of Representatives, where it could be done with safety. (II, 639)

Although there would later be controversy about what role the House of Representatives might play in implementing treaties, there is no evidence that his concern was widely shared by other Convention delegates.

Analysis

The primary debates over treaties at the Convention focused on whether the president or the Senate should negotiate them, what majority of the Senate was appropriate for approving them, whether treaties of peace should be treated differently from other treaties, and whether both houses should have to concur in treaties. The Convention ultimately made a relatively clear break with the Articles of Confederation in shifting initial responsibility for negotiating treaties to the president. However, the continuing requirement for confirmation by two-thirds of the Senate, where states would be represented equally, came closer to ratification by the Congress under the Articles than it would have had the delegates either entrusted this power to the House of Representatives or shared it between the two branches of Congress.

Despite apparent visions that the president would actually consult with the Senate while he was negotiating treaties (Tansill has observed, at page 461, a distinction between the president's exclusive power to nominate ambassadors, judges, and other officers, whom the Senate would confirm, and his power to make treaties "with the advice and consent of the Senate" and subject to two-thirds of the Senate's concurrence), this process broke down when George Washington first tried it. The Senate has subsequently "played more of a 'consent' role than an 'advice' role (Nelson 2002, 1331). From time to time, most notably during discussions after World War I about American entry into the League of Nations, which President Woodrow Wilson had advocated, critics have questioned the requirement for a two-thirds majority of the Senate to ratify treaties. Similarly, continuing controversy over executive agreements, which do not require senatorial approval, and proposals like the Bricker Amendment, designed to ensure that treaties conform to constitutional restrictions (Vile 2003, 51–52), indicate that Mason's expressed concern that rights might be forfeited by the president and Senate acting in concert continue to remain an issue. Moreover, although the Constitution does not require House confirmation of treaties, the House has at least an indirect role in providing funding for treaties that require it.

See Also Committee of Detail; Committee on Postponed Matters; Jay-Gardoqui Negotiations; Mississippi River; Supremacy Clause

FOR FURTHER READING

Farrand, Max, ed. 1937. *The Records of the Federal Convention.* 4 vols. New Haven, CT: Yale University Press.

McClendon, R. Earl. 1931. "Origin of the Two-Thirds Rule in Senate Action upon Treaties." *American Historical Review* 36 (July): 768–772.

Merritt, Eli. 1991. "Sectional Conflict and Secret Compromise: The Mississippi River Question and the United States Constitution." *American Journal of Legal History* 35 (April): 117–171.

Nelson, Michael. 2002. *Guide to the Presidency.* 3rd ed. Washington, DC: Congressional Quarterly.

Reveley, W. Taylor, III. 1974. "Constitutional Allocation of the War Powers between the President and the Congress: 1787–1788." *Virginia Journal of International Law* (Fall): 73–147.

Tansill, Charles C. 1924. "The Treaty-Making Powers of the Senate." *American Journal of International Law* 18 (July): 459–482.

Vile, John R. 2003. *Encyclopedia of Constitutional Amendments, Proposed Amendments, and Amending Issues, 1789–2002.* Santa Barbara, CA: ABC-CLIO.

UNITARY GOVERNMENT

Political scientists generally recognized three forms of government based on the allocation of power between the national government and geographic subdivisions, which Americans designate as states. A unitary government, like that of Great Britain or France, has no such permanent, or sovereign, entities with fixed boundaries. In such a system, the national government acts directly on individuals without such intermediaries. By contrast, confederal and federal governments divide power between national and subnational entities, both of which exercise elements of sovereignty. In confederal governments, like that under the Articles of Confederation, states are sovereign; the national entity, often designated as a treaty or league, must go through states in acting on individual citizens. In federal governments, like the delegates to the Constitutional Convention created, the national authority may act directly on the states or directly on individuals. In a federal government, the national authority is thus stronger than it is under a confederation.

Although the Framers were familiar with unitary governments from their knowledge of the British and other European systems, the idea of a federal government was in the making and their terminology was thus different from that of today. The Framers thus generally referred to governments that modern political scientists would call unitary governments as "national" governments. Similarly, since the federal government they were inventing was new, they generally referred to a confederal government as a "federal," or "foederal" government. Thus, when he introduced the Virginia Plan to the Convention on May 29, Edmund Randolph proposed "that a union of the States, merely federal [meaning, in modern terminology, merely confederal], will not accomplish the objects proposed by the articles of confederation" (Farrand 1937, I, 30). After the Convention ended, Madison subsequently described the new government in *Federalist* No. 39 as neither "wholly national nor wholly federal" (Hamilton, Madison, and Jay 1961, 246).

Objecting to the new government as being too much like that of Great Britain, Maryland's Luther Martin, an Antifederalist opponent of the new document, later expressed exasperation with the changing terminology and critiqued his fellow delegates (who were at the time calling themselves "Federalists") for being less than candid:

> Afterwards the word "*national*" was struck out by them, because they thought the word might tend to *alarm;* and although, *now,* they who *advocate* the system pretend to call themselves *federalists,* in convention the distinction was quite the reverse; those who *opposed* the system were there considered and styled the *federal party,* those who advocated it, the *antifederal.* (III, 195)

Although the Virginia Plan was far more nationalistic than the existing government under the Articles of Confederation, delegates at the Constitutional Convention expressed little sentiment for abolishing states, and they deleted some of the more nationalistic provisions—like the Council of Revision and the negative of state laws—of the Virginia Plan as they proceeded. The result was thus an amalgam of the previous "national" and "federal" forms. The Framers arguably made a virtue of necessity by pointing to the advantages both for safeguarding liberty and for administering a large nation that they thought the newly devised system would have over a purely "national" or unitary system.

See Also Articles of Confederation; Confederal Government; Federalism; Forms of Government; Great Britain; Sovereignty

FOR FURTHER READING

Farrand, Max, ed. 1937. *The Records of the Federal Convention*. 4 vols. New Haven, CT: Yale University Press.

Hamilton, Alexander, James Madison, and John Jay. 1961. *The Federalist Papers*. Ed. Clinton Rossiter. New York: New American Library.

Murrin, John M., David E. Narrett, Ronald L. Hatzenbuehler, and Michael Kammen. 1988. *Essays on Liberty and Federalism: The Shaping of the U.S. Constitution*. College Station: Texas A and M University Press.

Vile, M. J. C. 1961. *The Structure of American Federalism*. London: Oxford University Press.

UNITED COLONIES OF NEW ENGLAND

Students of the Articles of Confederation and of the U.S. Constitution have long tied these constitutions to earlier covenants and compacts, with the former idea being especially linked to biblical ideas. It seems to be more than mere coincidence that the Articles of Confederation actually bore the same name of an agreement, "Articles of Confederation," that bound a union of states created in 1643 among four of the New England colonies but that was usually referred to as the United Colonies of New England. Although lasting on paper through 1684 or 1685 (the original agreement was revised in 1672), the main work of this union appears to have taken place during the first twenty years or so of its existence.

The 12 articles of this union contain many similarities to the Articles of Confederation and a number to the U.S. Constitution. Rather than being continental in scope, the Articles created a regional confederation of Massachusetts, Plymouth, New Haven, and Connecticut. They united "for themselves and their posterities" into "a firme and perpetual league of frendship and amytie for offence and defence, mutuall advice and succour," with special concern for waging "just warrs whether offensive or defensive" (Ward 1961, 384–385). To this end, each jurisdiction was authorized to send two commissioners who would meet at least once a year, rotating their meetings in different towns within each. The consent of six to eight commissioners was typically required in order to requisition troops by a preestablished ratio; absent such a supermajority, their suggestions were to be referred to general courts within each jurisdiction. Commissioners in turn elected a president.

Like the Articles of Confederation, contemporaries referred to the agreement between the United Colonies as a "treaty" (Ward, 389). Initially written by delegates of Massachusetts, New Haven, and Connecticut, the agreement did not embrace Plymouth until its delegates agreed to it in August 1643. John Winthrop, the governor of Massachusetts, was among the signers of the Articles. Scholars have suggested that the Pilgrims involved, a number of whom had spent time in Holland prior to migrating to America, may have been influenced in their work by the Union of Utrecht (Matthews 1914, 396), and that this plan may in turn have influenced Benjamin Franklin when he wrote the Albany Plan of Union.

See Also Albany Plan of Union; Articles of Confederation; Constitutionalism; Franklin, Benjamin; Puritanism

FOR FURTHER READING

Lutz, Donald S. 1988. *The Origins of American Constitutionalism.* Baton Rouge: Louisiana University Press.

Matthews, L. L. 1914. "Benjamin Franklin's Plans for a Colonial Union, 1750–1775." *American Political Science Review* 8 (August): 393–412.

Ward, Harry M. 1961. *The United Colonies of New England–1643–1690.* New York: Vantage Press.

De Grazia, Sebastian. 1977. *A Country with No Name: Tales from the Constitution.* New York: Pantheon Books.

Farrand, Max, ed. 1937. *The Records of the Federal Convention.* 4 vols. New Haven, CT: Yale University Press.

Hutchinson, David. 1975. *The Foundations of the Constitution.* Secaucus, NJ: University Books.

Nettels, Curtis P. 1947. "A Link in the Chain of Events Leading to American Independence." *William and Mary Quarterly,* 3rd ser. 3 (January): 36–47.

Willard, Simon, Jr. 1815. *The Columbian Union . . .* Albany, NY: printed for the author.

UNITED STATES, NAME

The term "United States" appears to have been patterned on previous uses of the term "United Colonies," which the Continental Congress and writings by other contemporary writers had employed (Hutchinson 1975, 11). Jefferson used this term in the Declaration of Independence, and the Articles of Confederation declared in Article I that "the Stile of this confederacy shall be 'The United States of America'" (Hutchinson, 11).

At the Constitutional Convention, the Committee of Detail incorporated this name into the proposed Article I of the new Constitution on August 6 (Farrand 1937, II, 177). The Committee of Style later transferred this phrase to the Preamble where a reference to "We, the People of the United States," left open the possibility that not all states would ratify before the new Constitution went into effect.

The term "United States" reflects the idea of federalism by combining a singular with a collective term. In the early years of the Republic, there were some unsuccessful attempts to rename the nation Columbia, in honor of Christopher Columbus (see Willard 1815).

See Also Articles of Confederation; Committee of Detail; Committee of Style and Arrangement; Declaration of Independence

FOR FURTHER READING

Burnett, Edmund C. 1925. "The Name 'United States of America.'" *American Historical Review* 31 (October): 79–81.

U.S. CONSTITUTION

The most obvious product of the Constitutional Convention of 1787 is the written document called the U.S. Constitution, which outlined a new government with expanded, but still limited, powers. Even when the signatures of the signers are included, the original document had a scant 4,543 words, and was thus much shorter than most state constitutions of the day or afterwards (Hammons 1999).

The idea of such a document was not new (Lutz 1988). It grew out of a long history of prior compacts, contracts, charters, and state constitutions, which had the dual purposes of both recognizing (or granting) power and limiting it. The idea of "constituting" a government through words is similar to the idea of "founding" or "framing" such a government.

Constitution versus Constitution

The U.S. written Constitution (capital "C") neither specified all governmental practices when it was written nor has it since done so. Such a constitution thus fits against a larger constitution (small "c"), or set of practices, some of which were already in place when the document was written and others of which have developed since that time (Murphy et al. 2003, 103). Although defenders of British liberties could point to major documents dating back to the Magna Carta and earlier, the British did not have a single written document that they identified as the constitution (the British are thus said, not altogether accurately, to have an "unwritten constitution"). In part because Americans did not believe that this government had not adequately protected colonial liberties, they believed such a written document was necessary. Such a document may also have been more necessary in a system that attempted to divide powers between a central authority and various state subdivisions than in a unitary system of government like that in England without such sovereign subdivisions.

At the time that the Constitutional Convention of 1787 was meeting, a constitution, known as the Articles of Confederation, was in effect—this document entrusted far greater powers to the states than the government that the Convention would create. It would have been difficult, if not impossible, to move from a written document like the Articles of Confederation back to an unwritten constitution such as the colonists associated with Britain. Unwritten constitutions necessarily grow from the womb of time and through accretion rather than from a distinctive convention, like that which wrote the U.S. Constitution.

Evolution of the Document at the Convention

The delegates who introduced plans at the Convention introduced them as a series of written propositions designed to alter or enhance existing constitutional provisions. The Virginia Plan, which James Madison largely wrote and Edmund Randolph presented to the Convention on May 29, consisted of a series of 15 such provisions (Farrand 1937, I, 20–22). After about two weeks of discussion by the Committee of the Whole, the Convention had expanded this plan by June 13 to 19 resolutions (I, 228–32). The New Jersey Plan, which William Paterson introduced on June 15, contained nine such sections (I, 242–45), albeit many of them were longer than those of the Virginia Plan. Although it received less attention, Alexander Hamilton introduced a plan on June 18 with eleven sections (I, 291–93).

The Convention voted on June 19 to continue with its discussion of the modified Virginia Plan, but this plan continued to undergo alterations throughout the compromises that delegates agreed to during the course of Convention proceedings. The most drastic alteration of the text of the document occurred through the work of the Committee of Detail. The document it presented to the Convention on August 6 contained 23 articles, including a much-lengthened article enumerating the powers of Congress in much greater detail than previous versions.

Edmund Randolph, who served on this committee, appeared to reflect more general sentiments when he observed that drafting such a document required adherence to two guidelines. These were:

1. To insert essential principles only, lest the operations of government should be clogged by rendering those provisions permanent and unalterable, which ought to be accommodated to times and events, and
2. To use simple and precise language, and general propositions, according to the example of the (several) constitution of the several states. (II, 137)

The Committee of Style and Arrangement, which issued its report on September 12, followed a similar approach. It sparingly arranged the document into its current seven articles (II, 590–603). Gouverneur Morris of Pennsylvania was the most influential member of this committee, which was largely responsible for articulating the lofty set of purposes contained in the Preamble to the document. Whereas many other entries in this encyclopedia trace debates and decisions on individual provisions of the Constitution (and should thus be consulted about matters of detail), this concentrates on presenting a brief outline and analysis of the document as a whole.

Outline and Central Provisions of the Document

The Constitution that emerged from the Constitutional Convention consists of a Preamble and seven articles. The Preamble begins with the words "We the People" and lists the purposes of the document. It self-referentially refers to "this Constitution for the United States of America."

The Distributing Articles

Consistent with the doctrine of separation of powers, the first three Articles of the Constitution outline the respective powers of the three branches of government. Article I outlines the legislative branch. This was the only branch of government under the Articles of Confederation. The delegates discussed it first and most frequently at the Constitutional Convention, and they designed it to be the closest to the people.

As proposed by the Virginia Plan, the Convention created a bicameral Congress. The Virginia Plan had proposed that both houses be apportioned according to population; the New Jersey Plan had proposed continuing with a unicameral Congress in which states were represented equally. Consistent with the Connecticut Compromise, the Constitution apportions members of the House of Representatives to the states according to population (with slaves initially counting as three-fifths of a person for purposes of representation), and grants each state, regardless of its population, two senators. The delegates designed the House to be closer to the people. Its minimal qualifications were the lowest set that the Constitution set for any office whose qualifications it specified. The Constitution further tethered the members of the House to short two-year terms. By contrast, members of the Senate, which state legislatures chose until the Seventeenth Amendment (1913) shifted such a choice directly to the people, served six-year terms.

The Constitution designates each house with the responsibility for selecting its own officers. The Constitution vests the House of Representatives with the power to impeach public officials for certain designated offenses. The Constitution further designates the Senate to try such individuals, specifying that it can only convict and remove them from office by the vote of a two-thirds majority.

Article I, Section 7 designated the lawmaking process. Bills had to pass both houses in identical form (with all revenue-raising bills originating in the House of Representatives), and be sent to the president for approval. If Congress wanted to override such a veto, it had to muster two-thirds majorities in both houses to do so.

Article I, Section 8 designated, or enumerated, the powers of Congress. These included power such as the regulation of interstate commerce that the Congress under the Articles of Confederation had not exercised. In contrast to the Congress under the Articles, the Constitution vested Congress with the power to operate directly on individual citizens, as in raising taxes, without going through the states. In a clause that was little debated at the Convention, but which has subsequently become the central support for the doctrine of implied powers, the last clause provided that Congress would have power "To make all Laws which shall be necessary and proper for carrying into Execution the foregoing Powers."

Just as Article I, Section 8 grants powers to Congress, so too, Article I, Section 9 limits such powers. The Convention forbade Congress from prohibiting the migration of slaves for 20 years. It further limited occasions when Congress could suspend the writ of habeas corpus, prohibited bills of attainder and ex post facto laws, limited direct taxes, prohibited taxes on exports or preference for some ports over others, required accounting procedures for government appropriations, and prohibited Congress from conferring titles of nobility.

Article I, Section 10, further limited the states. It prohibited them from exercising powers, like entering into treaties or coining money, that the Constitution entrusted to Congress. In addition to being bound by most of the restraints that had bound Congress and with a view to perceived contemporary abuses, this section prohibited the states from impairing the obligations of contracts.

Article II outlined the powers of the executive branch. It vested this power in a single individual, to be chosen by an Electoral College—whose members were apportioned among the states according to their total number of U.S. representatives and senators. Presidents were to serve for four-year terms, to which they could be reelected. The Constitution also granted the Electoral College the power to choose a vice president. Although this individual had the power to preside over the Senate and to cast tie-breaking votes, the vice president's main function was that of serving, in cases of presidential death or disability, as a successor to the president.

The president is responsible for enforcing the laws and for serving as symbolic head of state as well as the day-to-day head of government. The Constitution designates the president as "Commander in Chief" of the nation's military. It also vested the president with power to make treaties subject to approval by two-thirds of the Senate and to appoint ambassadors, judges, and other public officials with the "advice and consent" of that body. The Constitution subjected the president, like other executive officials, to conviction and removal for impeachable offenses.

Article III outlined the powers of the judicial branch. It vested such powers "in one supreme Court, and in such inferior Courts as the Congress may from time to time ordain and establish." In contrast to members of the two elected branches, members of the judiciary were to serve "during good Behaviour." Section 2 specified the cases to which the judicial power extended, and provided for jury trials in criminal cases. Curiously, it did not specifically endorse the power of judicial review, whereby such courts have voided legislation that they consider to be unconstitutional in cases that arise for their consideration. Section 3 did define treason in a limited fashion, designed to prevent prosecutions for mere political differences.

The Rest of the Document

Just as the first three articles focus on the separation of powers among the three branches of government, Article IV delineates the division of power, known as federalism, between the national government and the states. The article obligates states to give "full faith and credit" to the acts of other states, ensures that citizens shall have "all privileges and immunities" in all the states, and provides for the extradition of criminals and the return of fugitive slaves (although here, as elsewhere in the document, the text avoids using the term "slave"). Article IV further provides for the admission of new states and for federal governance of the territories. It obligates the national government to guarantee to each state a "republican" form of government and to protect it against invasion and domestic violence.

Article V outlines processes for formally amending the Constitution. The process has two parts. Two-thirds majorities of both houses of Congress can propose amendments. Alternatively, two-thirds of the states can request that Congress call a convention for proposing such amendments. By congressional specification, amendments must then be ratified either by three-fourths of the state legislatures or by conventions called within three-fourths of the states. Article V entrenches the Connecticut Compromise by specifying that no state can be deprived of its equal representation in the Senate without its consent.

Article VI sweeps within its ambit various provisions that do not appear to fit comfortably elsewhere within the document. It specifies that debts against the United States will be as valid under the new Constitution as under the old. It provides for the supremacy of the Constitution and laws and treaties made under it to state laws, and it binds both state and federal officials by oath to support the Constitution.

Article VII further specified that "this Constitution" would become effective if conventions in nine or more states ratified it. In specifying such a procedure, the Constitution effectively bypassed the mechanism requiring unanimous state consent for amending the Constitution under the Articles of Confederation.

The Convention sent the Constitution to Congress accompanied by a letter, signed by George Washington. He recommended it as an improvement over the Articles of Confederation. He further observed that "the Constitution, which we now present, is the result of a spirit of amity, and of that mutual deference and concession which the peculiarity of our political situation rendered indispensable (II, 667).

Subsequent Alterations

In part because the written Constitution is embedded within a larger unwritten constitution, not all changes in constitutional interpretation have waited on constitutional amendments. Exercising the power of judicial review of both state and congressional legislation, the judiciary has played a particularly important role in interpreting the document. Congressional and presidential practices, as well as extraconstitutional developments like the rise of political parties, the democratization of the Electoral College, and the like, have also played important roles.

To date, although members of Congress have introduced thousands of amending proposals, only 27 formal amendments have been added to the Constitution. The first ten amendments, known as the Bill of Rights, emerged from the debate between Federalist proponents and Antifederalist opponents of the new Constitution, the latter of whom were especially fearful of the increased powers that the new Constitution was entrusting to the national government. Initially designed to limit this national government, the Supreme Court has subsequently used the adoption of the Fourteenth Amendment to apply most of these provisions as limits on the states as well. Key rights include those of religion, speech, press, assembly, and petition, outlined in the First Amendment; the elusive right to bear arms, outlined in the Second Amendment; the provision against unreasonable searches and seizures, in the Fourth Amendment; provisions related to the rights of criminal defendants and individuals who are on trial, in the Fifth, Sixth, and Seventh Amendments; the right to reimbursement for property taken by the government, in the Fifth Amendment; the provision against cruel and unusual punishments, in the Eighth Amendment; and the more elusive designation of rights reserved to the people and the states, respectively referenced in the Ninth and Tenth Amendments,

the last of which ends, as the Preamble begins, with an evocation of "the people."

The nation has often adopted key amendments within relatively short time periods. In addition to the first ten amendments, which were collectively adopted in 1791, the Thirteenth through Fifteenth Amendments were respectively ratified between 1865 and 1870, and amendments sixteen through nineteen were adopted between 1913 and 1920. The first set of amendments, proposed and ratified in the immediate aftermath of the Civil War, ranks in importance with the Bill of Rights. It respectively prohibited involuntary servitude, defined citizenship as applying to all persons born or naturalized in the United States and extended rights to all Americans, and prohibited discrimination in voting on the basis of race. The second set of amendments, adopted during the Progressive era, respectively approved the income tax, provided for direct election of senators, initiated national alcoholic prohibition (a measure that the Twenty-first Amendment later repealed), and prohibited denying the right to vote to women.

Four amendments have overturned Supreme Court decisions. The Eleventh Amendment thus limited occasions in which courts could hear suits against the states. The Fourteenth Amendment overturned the *Dred Scott* decision of 1857 by declaring that African Americans were citizens of the United States. The Sixteenth Amendment overturned a ruling that had invalidated the national income tax, and the Twenty-sixth Amendment prohibited states from limiting the vote to those who were 18 years of age or older.

Most other amendments have dealt with relatively minor matters. The Twelfth and Twenty-third Amendments made minor adjustments to the Electoral College; the Twentieth Amendment adjusted the times that new presidents and Congresses were inaugurated; the Twenty-second Amendment limited presidential service to two consecutive terms; the Twenty-fourth Amendment eliminated poll taxes in national elections; and the Twenty-fifth Amendment further provided for cases of presidential disability. The most recent amendment, the Twenty-seventh (originally proposed as part of the Bill of Rights but

---

Child of Fortune

On the day after the Constitution was signed and George Washington prepared to return home, he wrote a letter to Marquis de Lafayette, the Frenchman who had joined Americans in the Revolutionary War. In this letter Washington referred to the Constitution as "a Child of fortune, to be fostered by some and buffeted by others" (quoted in St. John 1987, 224). Although Washington did not, in this letter, comment favorably or unfavorably on the document, his support was quite influential in getting the document ratified.

FOR FURTHER READING

St. John, Jeffrey. 1987. *Constitutional Journal: A Correspondent's Report from the Convention of 1787.* Ottawa, IL: Jameson Books.

---

not putatively ratified by Congress until 1992), limited the timing of congressional pay raises.

Other Points

The U.S. Constitution is the oldest such document that continues to be an effective instrument of national government (the Massachusetts Constitution of 1780 is the oldest document of its kind). In contrast to many modern constitutions, the U.S. Constitution largely focused on guaranteeing individual political rights (often negatively) rather than on guaranteeing social and economic rights, like those that the national government has increasingly provided from the time of the New Deal forward. In part because of the desire of James Madison and other Federalists who were seeking to avoid a second constitutional convention that might undo the work of the first, the Bill of Rights established that the precedent of congressional proposal and state ratification of amendments. Only the Twenty-first Amendment has been ratified, by congressional specification, by state conventions.

To date, the mechanism whereby two-thirds of the states can request Congress to call a special convention to propose amendments has been often threatened but never utilized. The Confederate States did use a convention mechanism in Montgomery, Alabama in March 1861 to debate a constitution, which a committee of twelve men had written and which Congress and the states that made up the Confederacy subsequently ratified (Vile 2003, 84). The victory of the Union in the Civil War brought this constitution to an end.

FOR FURTHER READING

Amar, Akhil Reed. 2002. "Architexture +." *Indiana Law Journal* 77 (Fall): 671–700.

Farrand, Max, ed. 1937. *The Records of the Federal Convention.* 4 vols. New Haven, CT: Yale University Press.

Ferguson, Robert A. 1987. "1787: The Constitution in Perspective: 'We Do Ordain and Establish': The Constitution as Literary Text." *William and Mary Law Review* 19 (Fall): 2–25.

Hammons, Christopher W. 1999. "Was James Madison Wrong? Rethinking the American Preference for Short, Framework-Oriented Constitutions." *American Political Science Review* 93 (December): 837–849.

Lutz, Donald S. 1988. *The Origins of American Constitutionalism.* Baton Rouge: Louisiana State University Press.

Murphy, Walter F., James F. Fleming, Sotirious A. Barber, and Stephen Macedo. 2003. *American Constitutional Interpretation.* 3rd ed. New York: Foundation Press.

Vile, John R. 2001. *A Companion to the United States Constitution and Its Amendments.* 3rd ed. Westport, CT: Praeger.

——. 2003. *Encyclopedia of Constitutional Amendments, Proposed Amendments, and Amending Issues, 1789–2002.* 2nd ed. Santa Barbara, CA: ABC-CLIO.

V

VERMONT

Led by Ethan and Ira Allen and the Green Mountain Boys, the inhabitants of today's Vermont adopted a constitution at a convention held in July 1777. In so doing, Vermont asserted its independence from the states of New York and New Hampshire. Although both were claiming authority over it, New York's claim was clearly stronger. Willi Paul Adams has cited the example of Vermont as the first case in which "the inhabitants of a newly settled territory adopted a constitution as a means of substantiating their claim to recognition as an independent entity" (Adams 2001, 91). However, in yet another demonstration of the weaknesses of the Articles of Confederation, as of the time of the Constitutional Convention of 1787, it had not acted to recognize Vermont. The government that the Constitutional Convention created admitted Vermont as the fourteenth state in 1791. By this time, New York had concluded that it was in its own interest to give up claims to govern the area.

Delegates mentioned Vermont on a number of occasions during the Convention. William Paterson of New Jersey included references to Vermont and Kentucky in notes prepared on June 9 for a speech (Farrand 1937, I, 188). In arguing for limiting the number of senators from each state to two or three, Nathaniel Gorham of Massachusetts cited Kentucky and Vermont, as well as Maine and Franklin (Tennessee), as new states that were likely to be added (II, 94). In questioning a provision that would prevent new states from being formed from existing states without the consent of the latter, Maryland's Luther Martin asked on August 29 whether Vermont should "be reduced by force in favor of the States claiming it" (II, 455). On the same day, Connecticut's William Johnson feared that the clause requiring state consent for dismemberment would leave Vermont subject to New York "contrary to the faith pledged by Congress." He added that he thought "that Vermont ought to be compelled to come into the Union" (II, 456).

John Rutledge of South Carolina responded in part to this concern the next day when he observed, with an eye on discussions that had already been held regarding Vermont under the Articles of Confederation, that "the case of Vermont will probably be particularly provided for." He further observed that "there could be no room to fear, that Virginia or N– Carolina would call on the U. States to maintain their Government over the Mountains" (II, 462). Just to be sure, Johnson successfully introduced a motion the next day inserting the words "hereafter formed" so as to prevent Vermont from being dependent upon the consent of New York for entry into the Union (II, 463).

In what is arguably one of the Convention's most far-sighted measures, delegates provided that new states, like Vermont, would enter the Union on an equal basis with the old. Opponents of this proposal had wanted to keep power concentrated within the Eastern states.

See Also Kentucky; New Hampshire; New York; States, Admission and Creation; Tennessee

FOR FURTHER READING

Adams, Willi Paul. 2001. *The First American Constitutions: Republican Ideology and the Making of the State Constitutions in the Revolutionary Era.* Lanham, MD: Rowman and Littlefield Publishers.

Farrand, Max, ed. 1937. *The Records of the Federal Convention.* 4 vols. New Haven, CT: Yale University Press.

Onuf, Peter S. 1981. "State-Making in Revolutionary America: Independent Vermont as a Case Study." *Journal of American History* 67 (March): 797–815.

——. 1985. "Virginia, Vermont, and the Origins of the Federal Republic." *this Constitution* no. 7 (Summer): 4–10.

VETO

See PRESIDENTIAL VETO

VICE PRESIDENCY

Delegates to the Constitutional Convention devoted relatively little discussion to the vice presidency. The Virginia and New Jersey Plans, which Edmund Randolph and William Paterson introduced early in the Convention, did not even mention such an office. In the plan of government that New York's Alexander Hamilton had introduced on June 18, he had proposed that the president of the Senate would act as president until a successor could be appointed (Farrand 1937, I, 292). The Committee of Detail incorporated this idea into its report which it prepared in early August (II, 172).

Creation

The vice presidency emerged from the creation of the Electoral College mechanism for selecting the president. North Carolina's Hugh Williamson seems to have been correct in observing "that such an officer as vice-president was not wanted. He was introduced only for the sake of a valuable mode of election which required two to be chosen at the same time" (II, 537). In order to ensure that large states would not completely dominate the process, the Convention provided that each elector would cast two votes. The individual with the highest number of votes would become president, and the individual with the second highest would become vice president. In the aftermath of the election of 1800 in which republican electors cast a tie vote for Thomas Jefferson and Aaron Burr, the Twelfth Amendment, which specified that electors would cast separate votes for president and vice president, altered this provision.

Perhaps because it appeared unwise to create and pay an officer whose only purpose was to be ready to succeed the president, the Committee of Eleven built on Hamilton's earlier motion by providing that the vice president would be president of the Senate. The Constitution grants this vice president the right to preside in all cases other than the trials of presidential impeachments and the right to cast a deciding vote in the case of a tie (II, 495).

Concerns Raised at the Convention

Vesting the vice president with power to preside over the Senate appeared to be in tension with the idea of separation of powers, and some delegates opposed it. Elbridge Gerry of Massachusetts argued that the Convention "might as well put the President himself at the head of the Legislature" given the close intimacy that was likely to exist between the two, and he recorded his opposition to even have a vice president (II, 536–537). By contrast, Gouverneur Morris of Pennsylvania argued that "the vice president then will be the first heir apparent that ever loved his father" (II, 537). Morris observed that if there were to be no vice president, the president of the Senate would take over in the case of the president's death and would thus be the de facto vice president "which would amount to the same thing" (II, 537). Connecticut's Roger Sherman saw a need for some sort of vice presidential appointment: "If the vice-President were not to be President of the Senate, he would be without employment, and some member by being made President must be deprived of his vote" (II, 537). Edmund Randolph joined Gerry in opposing having the president preside over the Senate, and fellow Virginian George Mason specifically linked this provision to a violation of the idea of unduly mixing legislative and executive powers, which "ought to be kept as separate as possible" (II, 537). Moreover, Mason hoped that the Senate itself would not have to be kept in frequent session, preferring a Privy Council of six members. Nonetheless, the Convention voted to allow the vice president to preside over the Senate, with only New Jersey and Massachusetts casting negative votes.

Omissions

In notes that he eventually circulated as a pamphlet, Virginia's George Mason, one of only three remaining delegates who did not sign the Constitution at the Convention on September 17, severely criticized the fact that the Convention did not create a constitutional council to restrain the presidency. Mason went on to criticize the vice presidency:

> Hence also sprung that unnecessary (and dangerous) officer the Vice-President, who for want of other employment is made president of the Senate, thereby dangerously blending the executive and legislative powers, besides always giving to some one of the States an unnecessary and unjust preeminence over the others. (II, 639)

Mason's position was unusual. Professor Michael Nelson has observed that "the Constitutional Convention showed little concern for the vice presidency in general and for vice-presidential removal in particular." Apart from a unanimous decision on September 8 to include the vice president among those officials who could be impeached (II, 545), Nelson goes on to note that the Convention neither discussed nor made provi-

sion for "the death, resignation, or disability of the vice president" (Nelson 2002, I, 465). The Twenty-fifth Amendment partly remedied this omission.

See Also President, Disability; President, Selection; Separation of Powers

FOR FURTHER READING

Farrand, Max, ed. 1937. *The Records of the Federal Convention.* 4 vols. New Haven, CT: Yale University Press.
Nelson, Michael, ed. 2002. *Guide to the Presidency.* 3rd ed. 2 vols. Washington, DC: Congressional Quarterly.

VICES OF THE POLITICAL SYSTEM OF THE UNITED STATES

Because of his role as primary author of the Virginia Plan, James Madison's views of the defects of the Articles of Confederation are particularly important and make a useful supplement to Edmund Randolph's speech introducing the Virginia Plan at the Constitutional Convention on May 29. Randolph had identified five major defects in the Articles. These focused on the documents inability to provide security against foreign invasion (tied both to the government's inability to provide adequate revenue and to enforce treaties), to check quarrels among the states or rebellions within them, to provide for a uniform system of commercial regulation, to protect itself against state encroachments, and to establish its paramount authority over the states. Madison had developed a more extensive list of 11 failures of the Articles of Confederation in an essay authored in April 1787 entitled "Vices of the Political System of the United States." He repeated these themes in speeches throughout the Convention as well as during subsequent ratification debates.

Madison first identified the "failure of the states to comply with constitutional requisitions"; he believed this flaw was "uniformly exemplified in every similar Confederacy" (Madison 1973, 83). Madison next singled out "encroachments by the states on the federal authority," specifically citing Georgia's wars with the Indians, unlicensed compacts among the states, and troops raised by Massachusetts (83). Third, Madison singled out "violations of the law of nations and of treaties," pointing to violations of treaties with Great Britain, France, and Holland (83). Madison next cited "trespasses of the states on the rights of each other." He was specifically concerned with state decisions to issue paper money and restrict commerce with other states, which "though not contrary to the federal articles, is certainly adverse to the spirit of the Union, and tends to beget retaliating regulations" (84–85). Madison's fifth, somewhat overlapping, indictment was that there was a "want [lack] of concert in matters where common interest requires it" (85). Interestingly, for one who would later veto bills because he believed the new Constitution also failed to grant such powers, Madison pointed to the central government's inability to give "grants of incorporation for national purposes," including "canals and other works of general utility" (85). Madison's sixth indictment against the Articles of Confederation was that under this system there was a "want of guaranty to the states of their constitutions & laws against internal violence" (85). Madison was particularly concerned that a minority with military power could sometimes rule over a majority without it, and observed that "where slavery exists the republican Theory becomes still more fallacious" (85).

In moving to the second half of his indictments, Madison pointed to the "want of sanction to the laws, and of coercion in the government of the confederacy" (85). Although he appears to have changed his mind about the efficacy of attempting to use force directly against states rather than proceeding against private citizens, in his April 1787 essay, Madison argued that "A sanction is essential to the idea of law, as coercion is to that of Government" (85). Madison attributed this weakness to overoptimism about "the justice, the good faith, the honor, [and] the sound policy, of the several state assemblies" prior to the lessons of experience (86). Noting that every act of the general union "must necessarily bear unequally hard on some particular member or members," Madison feared that there would always be "causes & pretexts" for the states to dispute national authority.

Madison's eighth criticism of the Articles was that they had not been ratified by the people. This left states to assert the supremacy of their own laws and gave them the pretext of absolving themselves from their obligations under it. Madison next pointed to the "multiplicity of laws in the several states" (87). He associated this "luxuriancy of legislation" with instability and believed that the states could compress existing laws into "one tenth of the compass" (88).

Madison's last two criticisms related to the last. He focused both on the "mutability" and the "injustice of the laws of the states" (88). He observed that laws were being repealed "before any trial can have been made of their merits, and even before a knowledge of them can have reached the remoter districts within which they were to operate" (88). Similarly, in pointing to the injustices of state laws, he found that motives of "ambition" and "personal interest" were prevailing over those of the "public good" (88). In a theme that he made familiar both during Convention deliberations and during the ratification of the new Constitution, he pointed to the division of the population in numerous factions and the proclivity of the majority faction to impose its will on the minority. Here Madison pointed to the solution of enlarging the sphere of government so as to embrace enough factions that no single one would be able to dominate.

From time to time, modern political scientists are accused of overemphasizing the defects of the Articles of Confederation over their accomplishments. If this proclivity does indeed exist, perhaps it is because prescient men like Madison, who perceived the need for a stronger government, were more focused on such defects than on whatever merits the Articles had in transitioning the former colonies from British rule to a new Constitution.

See Also Articles of Confederation; Madison, James, Jr.; Randolph, Edmund; Virginia Plan

John Adams on George Washington

Of all the delegates who attended the Constitutional Convention, none was more revered than George Washington, the former commander-in-chief of the Revolutionary forces who was selected as president of the Convention and as the first president of the new nation. Although John Adams respected Washington, under whom he would serve for two terms as vice president, Adams was never admired like Washington, and he feared that Washington's reputation would overshadow his own.

Writing in 1807 to Benjamin Rush, Adams offered ten reasons, a mixture of frank assessment and satire, to explain Washington's reputation. He thus observed that he had

1. An handsome face. That this is a talent, I can prove by the authority of a thousand instances in all ages. . . . 2. A tall stature, like the Hebrew sovereign [King Saul] chosen because he was taller by the head than the other Jews. . . . 3. An elegant form. 4. Graceful attitudes and movements. 5. A large, imposing fortune. . . . There is nothing, except bloody battles and splendid

victories, to which mankind bow down with more reverence than to great fortune. . . . 6. Washington was a Virginian. This is equivalent to five talents. Virginian geese are all swans. . . . 7. Washington was preceded by favorable anecdotes. . . . 8. He possessed the gift of silence. This I esteem as one of the most precious talents. 9. He had great self-command. . . . 10. Whenever he lost his temper as he did sometimes, either love or fear in those about him induced them to conceal his weakness from the world. (Miroff 1986, 129, quoting from Schultz and Adair 1966, 97–98)

FOR FURTHER READING

Miroff, Bruce. 1986. "John Adams: Merit, Fame, and Political Leadership." *Journal of Politics* 48 (February): 116–132.

Schultz, John A., and Douglass Adair, eds. 1966. *The Spur of Fame: Dialogues of John Adams and Benjamin Rush, 1805–1813.* San Marion, CA: Huntington Library.

FOR FURTHER READING

Madison, James. 1973. "Vices of the Political System of the United States. April 1787." *The Mind of the Founder: Sources of the Political Thought of James Madison.* Ed. Marvin Meyers. Indianapolis, IN: Bobbs-Merrill.

VIRGINIA

Virginia, which at the time included present-day Kentucky and West Virginia, was the largest and most populous of the original 13 colonies, and European settlers had come there the earliest. The colony was one of the first to oppose British colonial rule. After Lord Dunmore, the governor, dissolved the long-standing House of Burgesses, the delegates called the first of at least four revolutionary conventions, which in turn appointed delegates to the Continental Congresses. The fifth such convention appointed a 36-man committee to write the state's constitution. George Mason, one of the members, was largely responsible for drafting the Declaration of Rights and a plan of government. The convention ratified this constitution on June 29, 1776, chose Patrick Henry as the new governor, and created a Council of State.

Constitution

In addition to articulating rights, the new constitution was significant because it was based on the separation of powers. The Constitution divided the General Legislature into a House of Delegates and a Senate, with members of the latter body selected to four-year terms. Joint sessions of the legislature elected the governor, who could serve no more than three successive terms, annually. He was aided by an eight-member Council of State and could issue pardons but did not have the power to veto legislation.

The judiciary consisted of several different courts including a Supreme Court of Appeals. The General Assembly appointed judges for indefinite service. Local county courts, which operated at the local level, exercised legislative, executive, and executive powers (Kaminski and Saladino 1988).

Virginia under the Articles of Confederation

Virginians owed significant debts to the British, and disputes over these payments provided one of the pretexts for the British refusal to uphold the Treaty of Paris and withdraw troops from the American Northwest. Although it initially accepted depreciated paper money to pay for taxes and debts, the Virginia legislature subsequently refused to print such money. Under the Articles of Confederation, Virginia extended to the Mississippi River, and the state was adamant about preserving the right to navigate that river. The state adamantly opposed the proposed treaty that John Jay reached with Don Diego de Gardoqui in 1785 to give up rights to navigate the Mississippi in exchange for certain other trade advantages. The state's concern over this attempted bargain, which Virginia and other states had been able to block under the Articles of Confederation, appears largely responsible for the constitutional provision that treaties be approved by two-thirds majorities.

Virginia initially supported a proposal in 1781 to grant Congress power to levy a five percent impost on imports, but when Rhode Island refused to agree, the state changed its mind and withdrew its approval. Virginia did agree to a similar plan in 1783, but this time New York was able to block the plan since the Articles of Confederation required unanimous state approval.

Delegates from Maryland and Virginia met at Mount Vernon, in what is generally considered to be a prelude to the Annapolis Convention, to discuss common matters of navigation. In September 1786, the state was one of five represented at the Annapolis Convention. A circular letter on the part of the Virginia governor helped persuade other states to send delegates to Philadelphia.

Virginia at the Convention

With the possible exception of Pennsylvania, the Old Dominion was arguably the best represented at the Constitutional Convention. Its delegation included George Washington, who would serve as the Convention's president; James Madison, who is often called the "Father" of the Constitution; Edmund Randolph, the popular state governor who introduced the Virginia Plan; George Mason, famed author of the Virginia Declaration of Rights; George Wythe, the nation's first professor of law; John Blair; and Dr. James McClurg. In addition, Maryland's John Mercer had previously served in the Virginia state legislature. However, his wife's serious illness called Wythe home; Blair never spoke; McClurg left early, clearly feeling inferior to the rest of his delegation; and Mason and Randolph refused to sign the document.

Virginia's Thomas Jefferson, the chief author of the Declaration of Independence, was serving at the time as an American diplomat to France, but his longtime friend James Madison was there to represent his views. Jefferson had supplied Madison with books on government from France, which Madison had studied in preparation for the Convention. More ominously, the popular former governor, Patrick Henry, who was a guardian of states' rights, had refused to attend because he "smelt a rat." Similarly, Richard Henry Lee, who would become an Antifederalist, had thought that his role as a delegate to the Continental Congress would make service at the Convention inappropriate, and Thomas Nelson, Jr., who had been appointed to replace Henry, had also declined.

As the largest and most populous state in the Union, Virginia was also the natural leader of the Southern states. Consistent with its opposition to the Jay-Gardoqui negotiations, it also regarded itself as a defender of the West, from which the state of Kentucky would soon be birthed.

Virginia gave its name to the bold plan that Edmund Randolph introduced in the first days of the Convention. This plan was most notable for proposing a stronger bicameral Congress where states would be represented in both branches according to population in place of the weak unicameral Congress under the Articles where each state had been represented equally. Virginia was a slave state, and so it supported the three-fifths compromise, but states south of Virginia, rather than the Old Dominion itself, were insistent on, and ultimately responsible for, allowing the importation of slaves until 1808. Although the new Constitution did not specify the location, it permitted the new capital eventually to be located on the Potomac River on land previously owned by Maryland and Virginia.

Ratification

Unbeknownst to Virginia, New Hampshire had become the critical ninth state to ratify the Constitution even before Virginia's ratifying convention began. Given the size and importance of the state, however, it is not clear that the new nation would have actually come into existence without Virginia's acquiescence (had it not joined, George Washington could not have served as the nation's first president), and this acquiescence in turn appears to have been influential in inducing New York to join. The struggle in Virginia was thus worthy of the care that the delegates spent on it. Debates pitted the powerful oratory of Patrick Henry and allies like George Mason, James Monroe, and Richard Henry Lee on one side against the less powerful speaking skills but more subtle arguments of James Madison, John Marshall (the future chief justice of the U.S. Supreme Court who would do so much to interpret the new document), and, ultimately, Edmund Randolph, on the other. Although he did not attend, George Washington's known support for the document also undoubtedly played a part.

The ratifying convention chose to debate the Constitution clause by clause. Antifederalists who were not sure whether they had votes to reject the new Constitution initially proposed this strategy. It ultimately worked to the advantage of James Madison and others who were better at thoughtfully justifying each provision of the Constitution than at responding to the shotgun criticisms and exaggerated fears that the oratorically gifted Henry and other opponents mustered against it.

Ultimately, Madison's rationality prevailed. Whatever possible dangers Henry and others could imagine, it seemed clear that the existing government had not been able to provide the security and defense that Virginia and the rest of the nation needed. Pointing to the fact that he had opposed the Constitution in Philadelphia, Randolph would say that "the accession of eight states reduced our deliberations to the single question of Union or no Union. . . . When I see safety on my right, and destruction on my left, . . . I cannot hesitate to decide in favor of the former" (quoted in Banning 1989, 286). Federalists succeeded in Virginia, as in other states, in blocking an Antifederalist proposal that would have conditioned ratification on the adoption of specific amendments. Virginia ratified the Constitution on June 25 by a vote of 89 to 79 and then went on to vote on a number of recommendatory amendments. Although the relationship between Madison and Henry had been permanently ruptured, Mason seems to have been pacified by the later addition of the Bill of Rights, and Henry magnanimously pledged to support the new government.

Virginia and the New Constitution

Representative of its size and influence, as well as its reputation for leadership, four of the nation's first five presidents (Washington, Jefferson, Madison, and Monroe) came from Virginia, and each served for two terms. Of these, Washington largely favored the agenda of the Federalist Party as outlined in the financial program of his secretary of the Treasury, Alexander Hamilton. Many of the concerns for states' rights and fear of centralized power that Henry and other Antifederalists articulated in the Virginia ratifying convention were eventually incorporated into the political philosophy of the Democratic-Republican Party which Jefferson and Madison helped to found. They also proclaimed this philosophy in the Virginia and Kentucky Resolutions (the first authored by Madison and the second by Jefferson) of 1798 in opposition to the Alien and Sedition Acts.

Significantly, Virginia's John Marshall, who served on the U.S. Supreme Court from 1801 to 1835, proved to be one of the staunchest supporters of the Federalist vision of a strong central government. He articulated the principle of judicial review providing that courts could void unconstitutional congressional legislation in the path-breaking case of *Marbury v. Madison* (1803), when ruling that the Judiciary Act of 1789 could not grant the Court original jurisdiction in a case asking for a writ of mandamus against then Secretary of State James Madison. Marshall has arguably had as great an influence on the interpretation of the Constitution as any man who attended the Convention.

See Also Annapolis Convention; Bill of Rights; Blair, John, Jr.; Henry, Patrick; Jefferson, Thomas; Kentucky; Madison, James; Marshall, John; Mason, George; McClurg, James; Monroe, James; Mount Vernon Conference; Randolph, Edmund; Virginia Plan; Washington, George; Wythe, George

FOR FURTHER READING

Banning, Lance. 1989. "Virginia: Sectionalism and the General Good." In Michael Allen Gillespie and Michael Lienesch, eds. *Ratifying the Constitution.* Lawrence: University Press of Kansas.

Briceland, Alan V. 1988. "Virginia: The Cement of the Union." In Patrick T. Conley and John P. Kaminski, eds. *The Constitution and the States: The Role of the Original Thirteen in the Framing and Adoption of the Federal Constitution.* Madison, WI: Madison House, 201–223.

Kaminsky, John P., and Gaspare J. Saladino, eds. 1988. *Ratification of the Constitution by the States: Virginia.* Vol. 8 of *The Documentary History of the Ratification of the Constitution.* Madison: State Historical Society of Wisconsin.

Risjord, Norman K. 1974. "Virginians and the Constitution: A Multivariant Analysis." *William and Mary Quarterly,* 3rd ser. 31 (October): 613–632.

VIRGINIA DECLARATION OF RIGHTS

Virginia delegate George Mason and other Antifederalists criticized the Constitution as reported by the Constitutional Convention for not containing a bill of rights. This issue was especially important to Mason because he had been the primary author of the Virginia Declaration of Rights which his state had adopted on June 12, 1776, just a few weeks before the Continental Congress adopted the Declaration of Independence. The Virginia Declaration of Rights is generally regarded as a precursor not only to many state bills of rights but also to the Bill of Rights that the first Congress added to the Constitution.

The Virginia Declaration is divided into 16 sections. The first section is similar to the opening lines of the Declaration of Independence in declaring "That all men are by nature equally free and independent, and have certain inherent rights" which include "the enjoyment of life and liberty, with the means of acquiring and possessing property, and pursuing and obtaining happiness and safety" (Kendall and Carey 1970, 161). Similarly, the second section resembles the opening words of the Constitution, "We the People," in declaring that "all power is vested in, and consequently derived from, the people" (161). Section 3 goes on to identify the purpose of government as that of securing the happiness of the people and also recognizes the right of the people "to reform, alter, or abolish" existing governments (161–162).

The next several sections embody principles that are later incorporated into the structure not only of the Virginia state constitution but also of the government of the U.S. Consistent with the critique of monarchy that Thomas Paine authored in *Common Sense,* Section 4 says that no positions within government should be hereditary. Section 5 advocates separation of powers among the legislative, executive, and judicial branches as well as periodic elections. Section 6 goes beyond the original national Constitution in advocating widespread suffrage; consistent with the opposition to parliamentary taxation that fueled the Revolutionary War, it also makes the case against depriving individuals of their property for public use without their consent. Section 7 opposes the suspension of laws, presumably by the king or colonial governors.

The remainder of the Virginia Declaration consists of rights similar to those guaranteed in the U.S. Bill of Rights. The provisions of Section 8 resemble those of the U.S. Sixth Amendment for protecting the rights–like the right to confrontation, the right to a jury, and the right against self-incrimination–of individuals on trial. Section 9 resembles the Eighth Amendment in opposing excessive bail, excessive fines, and cruel and unusual punishments. Section 10 resembles the Fourth Amendment in opposing general warrants that do not specify the person or place to be searched. Section 11, like the later Seventh Amendment, deals with the right to jury trials in civil cases. Section 12, like the later First Amendment, deals with freedom of the press. Section 13, like the later Second Amendment, deals with the need for "a well-regulated militia" and says that standing armies are to be avoided.

Section 14 prohibits the establishment of rival governments within the state. Section 15 somewhat resembles the Preamble to the U.S. Constitution in seeking to encourage "a firm adherence to justice, moderation, temperance, frugality, and virtue" as means to encourage "free government" and "the blessings of liberty." Section 16, like the First Amendment to the U.S. Constitution, protects "the free exercise of religion, according to the dictates of conscience" (163).

Consistent with other early statements of its type, the Virginia Declaration most frequently listed rights in terms of "oughts" rather than as outright prohibitions. Thus, Section 10 specifies that general warrants "ought not to be granted," and Section 11 says that the right to trial by jury "is preferable . . . and ought to be held sacred"

(163). As such the provisions in the Declaration appear as directed to guiding the people on the nature of the polity as to providing mechanisms that judges are expected to enforce in courts.

See Also Bill of Rights; Constitutionalism; Declaration of Independence; Mason, George; State Constitutions; Virginia

FOR FURTHER READING

Friedman, Dan. "Tracing the Lineage: Textual and Conceptual Similarities in the Revolutionary-Era State Declarations of Rights of Virginia, Maryland, and Delaware." *Rutgers Law Journal* 33 (Summer): 929–1028.

Kendall, Willmoore, and George W. Carey. 1970. *The Basic Symbols of the American Political Tradition.* Baton Rouge: Louisiana State University Press.

Rutland, Robert Allen. 1962. *The Birth of the Bill of Rights, 1776–1791.* New York: Collier Books.

VIRGINIA PLAN

One of the most significant developments at the Constitutional Convention may have been the fact that most states were not present on Monday, May 14, the day the Convention was scheduled to convene. George Mason reported to his son in a letter dated May 20, 1787, that "the Virginia deputies (who are all here) meet and confer together two or three hours every day, in order to form a proper correspondence of sentiments." (Farrand 1937, III, 23)

Origins of the Virginia Plan

James Madison later explained in a letter to Noah Webster that

> when the convention as recommended at Annapolis took place at Philadelphia, the deputies from Virginia supposed, that as that state had been first in the successive steps leading to a revi-

sion of the federal system, some introductory proposition might be expected from them. They accordingly entered into consultation on the subject, immediately on their arrival in Philadelphia, and having agreed among themselves on the outline of a plan, it was laid before the convention by Mr. Randolph, at that time governor of the state, as well as member of the convention. (II, 409)

As the state with the largest population, Virginia was expected to play a leading part, and four of its members, namely George Washington, James Madison, George Mason, and Edmund Randolph, played particularly prominent roles. Although Randolph, as Virginia's governor, introduced the plan (and scholars accordingly sometimes refer to it as the Randolph Plan), its ideas appear to correspond most closely to those of James Madison. Evidence for this thesis can be gleaned from parallels between provisions of the Virginia Plan and ideas that Madison had suggested in letters to friends prior to the convening of the Convention (see Rutland 1987, 25–28).

The Annapolis Convention had called upon the states to call a convention for the purpose of revising and enlarging the Articles of Confederation. Although, as discussed below, the Virginia delegation tried to put such a window-dressing on its plan in its first resolution, the plan took a much different path. For all practical purposes, it proposed to replace rather than to enlarge or amend the existing government. This plan, which Randolph introduced on behalf of his state delegate on Tuesday, May 29, 1787, dominated discussion of the Convention (organized as a Committee of the Whole) until Friday, June 15. At that time, William Paterson introduced the New Jersey Plan. By then, it is reasonable to assume, and elements of the New Jersey Plan confirm, that many delegates, who might otherwise have considered themselves bound to limiting themselves to revising or enlarging the Articles, had now conceived that a replacement might be necessary. The Virginia Plan thus set the agenda of the Convention in a direction that it otherwise might have been unlikely to take.

Randolph's Justification of the Virginia Plan

The outline of Randolph's speech, written in his own hand, is available in Madison's notes and, consistent with the time that he and fellow delegates had to put into it, was well structured. Beginning with a deferential notice of the fact that others at the Convention "were of longer standing in life and political experience" than he (I, 18), Randolph further observed Virginia's role in originating the Convention and the fact that his Virginia colleagues had imposed the obligation to present the plan on him.

Randolph divided his speech into four parts. He focused first on "the properties, which such a government ought to possess," and second on "the defects of the confederation." He then examined "the danger of our situation" and what he conceived to be "the remedy" (I, 18):

> The character of the government necessitated that it be able to attain five goals. These involved both foreign and domestic concerns. Government needed to: secure the nation "against foreign invasion"; to guard against "dissentions" between the states and "seditions from within them"; to secure blessings that the states could not achieve individually; to "be able to defend itself against incroachment; and to "be paramount to the state constitutions." (I, 18)

In assessing the defects of the Articles, Randolph wanted to cast no aspersions on the Patriots who created it. Its defects came from "the then infancy of the science, of constitutions, & of confederations," and from the lack of experience in the defects that had shown themselves. Randolph identified five such defects, each related to the properties Randolph had identified in a proper government. The first accordingly related to foreign policy. The confederation had been unable to provide "security agai[nst] foreign invasion," had been unable to enforce treaties, and had been unable to provide for sufficient revenues to protect the states. Second, the Articles had been unable to check quarrels between the states and rebellions within them. Third, existing government had been unable to impose a uniform system of commercial regulation. Fourth, the government had been unable to defend itself against state encroachments. Fifth, it had not proven to be paramount to the state constitutions.

The Resolution Introducing the Virginia Plan

The chief danger presented by these defects was the danger of "anarchy from the laxity of government every where" (I, 19). Randolph set forth the remedy in 15 resolutions that comprised the Virginia Plan. Significantly, William Paterson observed that Randolph presented his plan as being "founded on republican Principles" (I, 27). Because it was designed to track the call of the Annapolis Convention, the first resolution was arguably the least candid as to the breadth of the changes the Virginia Plan was advocating:

> Resolved that the articles of Confederated ought to be so corrected & enlarged as to accomplish the objects proposed by their institution; namely, "common defence, security of liberty, and general welfare." (I, 20)

Perhaps other delegates chided Randolph and the Virginia delegation about the discrepancy between his resolution and those that followed, or perhaps Randolph had intended to modify it from the beginning. In any event, as soon as the Convention met as a Committee of the Whole on the next day, Randolph, seconded by Gouverneur Morris, proposed that his first resolution, proposing to correct and enlarge the Articles, be altered to say:

> Resolved that an union of the States, merely federal, will not accomplish the objects proposed by the articles of confederation, namely "common defence, security of liberty, and general welfare." (I, 30)

Curiously, Pierce Butler then introduced a resolution, seconded by Randolph, to postpone this resolution for yet another, which as slightly modified, and after refusing to postpone the new resolution for yet another, of like consequence, read:

> Resolved that it is the opinion of this Committee that a national government ought to be established consisting of a supreme Legislative, Judiciary, and Executive. (I, 30–31)

Since the Articles essentially consisted of a single branch of government, this last resolution more effectively indicated the far-reaching nature of the Virginia Plan than did the one that Randolph initially presented.

The Contents of the Virginia Plan

The Legislative Branch

Resolutions 2 through 6 of the Virginia Plan outlined a new legislative branch. The second resolution called for representation in the national legislature to be based on "the Quotas of contribution, or to the number of free inhabitants" (I, 20). The larger states, like Virginia, had been unsuccessful in obtaining this goal under the Articles of Confederation. Representation became a key bone of contention with smaller states. The New Jersey Plan favored equal state representation like that under the Articles of Confederation, and the Convention ultimately resolved the issue by adopting the Great Compromise providing for representation by population in the House of Representatives and equal state representation in the Senate. The third resolution called for a bicameral, rather than a unicameral, Congress. The fourth resolution outlined provisions for selecting the first branch of the legislature by the people of the states for a term yet to be specified. Legislators were to be incapable of holding other offices during their terms of service or their immediate aftermath, incapable of reelection for an unspecified time period, and subject, as under the Articles of Confederation, to recall. The fifth resolution, addressing the second branch of Congress, provided for election by the first house from among nominees of the states. Members were to be ineligible for other offices during their terms and for an unspecified period following the same. The sixth resolution provided that both houses would have the power to originate acts, and that, in addition to powers exercised under the Articles of Confederation, they should be able "to legislate in all cases to which the separate States are incompetent, or in which the harmony of the States may be interrupted by the exercise of individual Legislation" (I, 29). This resolution also contained a provision known through records of subsequent debates to have been particularly important to James Madison, namely a power "to negative all laws passed by the several States, contravening in the opinion of the National Legislature the articles of Union" (see Hobson 1979). The Virginia Plan also proposed to entrust Congress "to call forth the force of the Union" against any states that did not fulfill their duties.

The Executive Branch

Resolutions 7 and 8 dealt with the executive branch. The legislature was to choose an executive, which the plan also called "the Magistracy," for an unspecified number of years of service. He was to be ineligible for a second term. The executive was to have "a general authority to execute the National laws" and "the Executive rights vested in Congress by the Confederation" (I, 21). The executive was to be joined with "a convenient number of the National Judiciary" to compose "a council of revision," which would have the power to negate both national and state laws, unless, in the case of the former, they were passed by an unspecified majority of each branch.

Other Provisions

Resolution 9 dealt with the judicial branch. It was to consist of one or more supreme and other inferior tribunals chosen by Congress with specified jurisdiction. Its power would include the trial of "impeachments of any National officers" (I, 22).

Resolution 10 provided for the admission of new states. Resolution 11 provided for the guarantee of a "Republican Government" to each state (I, 22). The next resolution provided that the existing Congress would continue in effect until the new government was instituted.

Resolution 13 provided for incorporating future amendments without congressional consent. Resolution 14 specified that members of all three branches would be bound by oath, and Resolution 15 specified that, once Congress approved the Convention's proposals, they should be submitted to "an assembly or assemblies of Representatives, recommended by the several Legislatures to be expressly chosen by the people, to consider & decide thereon" (I, 22).

Having presented this major departure from the Articles, Randolph exhorted his fellow delegates. He said that they should not allow "the present opportunity of establishing generally peace, harmony, happiness and liberty in the U.S. to pass away unimproved" (I, 23).

Report of the Committee of the Whole on the Virginia Plan

On Wednesday, June 13, the Committee of the Whole reported the results of two weeks of discussion and debate over the Virginia Plan. The committee had arranged the plan somewhat differently in a total of 19 resolutions. The first consisted of the substitute motion, accepted on the first day of debate on the Virginia Plan, specifying that a "National" government should be established consisting of three branches.

Resolutions 2 through 8 dealt with the legislative branch. The second resolution (the previous third) specified that Congress would be bicameral. The third provision, relating to the first branch of the legislature, specified that its members would serve for three-year terms, be paid out of "the National Treasury," and be ineligible for office during their terms and for one year afterwards. The committee specified that members of the second branch would be "chosen by the individual [state] Legislatures" rather than, as under the original plan, by members of the first branch from among their nominees. Members of the second house had similar limitations to those of the first, with a minimum age of 30 specified and a term of seven years. As in the original plan, both branches would be able to originate money bills. The powers of Congress remained as specified in the original plan, with a continuing provision for the negative of state laws, significantly expanded to include a veto of laws inconsistent with any U.S. treaties. Representation for both branches was to be "according to some equitable ration of representation, namely, in proportion to the whole number of white & other free citizens & inhabitants, of every age sex and condition, including those bound to servitude for a term of years, & three fifths of all other persons," excluding Indians (Farrand I, 236), thus specifying a partial representation for African Americans not delineated in the original Virginia Plan.

Provisions 9 and 10 related to the executive. The first specified that there would be a single executive who would serve a seven-year nonrenewable term. It further specified that he could veto acts subject to an override by two-thirds majorities of both houses. Significantly, although the issue would later reemerge, the delegates had decided to eliminate the Council of Revision.

Provisions 11 through 13 related to the judicial branch. The revised plan stipulated that the second house of Congress would choose judges. The judiciary continued to have the power to try impeachments of national officials. Other provisions continued to provide for the admission of new states, for the continuation of Congress until the new system went into effect, for the guarantee of a republican government to the states, for constitutional amendments (albeit omitting the statement that legislative assent should no longer be required), for state officials to be bound by oath to support the Constitution, and for submission of Convention results to conventions within the states.

For the most part, then, the Virginia Plan was refined and enlarged (with details like the terms of office being added) but contained most of its initial structure after the first two weeks of debate. The basic scheme for three branches of government, for representation in a bicameral Congress based on population, and for a veto of conflicting

acts remained in place. The report from the Committee of the Whole, however, prompted William Paterson to introduce the New Jersey Plan with a very different approach to the problems of the Confederation.

The Importance of the Virginia Plan

The most important aspect of the Virginia Plan was probably its role in setting the Convention's initial agenda. Max Farrand observed:

It is altogether possible, if the New Jersey plan had been presented to the convention at the same time as the Virginia plan . . . and if without discussion a choice had then been made between the two, that the former would have been selected. It would seem as if the New Jersey plan more nearly represented what most of the delegates supposed that they were sent to do. But in the course of the two weeks' discussions, many of the delegates had become accustomed to what might well have appeared to them at the outset as somewhat radical ideas. (Farrand 1913, 89)

The Virginia Plan was an audacious remedy for what was perceived to be radical defects in the Articles of Confederation. Despite its accomplishments, the Confederation was a weak league of states, consisting essentially of a single branch of government, with a unicameral Congress with limited powers. Moreover, under the Articles, states were represented equally by delegates, which state legislatures appointed to Congress. The Virginia Plan proposed to replace this with a new arrangement between the nation and the states (at the Convention generally called "national," now generally called "federal") in which the national government would have the power to veto state legislation. Under the new plan, the national government was to consist of three branches, the first of which would be chosen directly by the people, would exercise significant new powers, and in which states would be represented equally.

Nothing short of a general perception of crisis could justify such a departure from the existing

Agenda-Setting

Students of the actions of collective bodies recognize that the initial agenda of such bodies can prove extremely important in influencing the outcomes of such bodies. One of the reasons that scholars put so much emphasis on the Virginia Plan is that it played such an important role in setting the agenda of a Convention that had been initially called simply to revise and enlarge the existing government under the Articles of Confederation. Instead, the Virginia Plan called for a completely new form of government, with a bicameral Congress apportioned according to population rather than a unicameral body where states would be represented equally, and with three branches of the national government rather than one.

Although Governor Edmund Randolph introduced the Virginia Plan, James Madison, who had spent months reading in preparation for the Convention and who arrived early to draw up a plan and rally fellow delegates behind it, is generally understood to have been its central author. Largely because of this role, he is credited with being the single most important person in setting the agenda of the Constitutional Convention (Lansky 2000, 320). Clearly, Madison did not accomplish everything that he desired. Just as clearly, the Convention is unlikely to have developed as strong a departure from the existing Articles of Confederation had Madison not formulated and rallied his colleagues around the Virginia Plan.

FOR FURTHER READING

Lansky, Dana. 2000. "Proceeding to a Constitution: A Multi-Party Negotiation Analysis of the Constitutional Convention of 1787." *Harvard Negotiation Law Review* 5 (Spring): 279–338.

system, and nothing but wisdom and a spirit of compromise would enable its proponents to know which parts of the new plan were key to providing a government for posterity and which parts could be discarded. Significantly, although the next day witnessed controversy over the wording of the first resolution of the Virginia Plan, delegates did not, at that time, object that the plan went beyond the Convention's mandate.

See Also Articles of Confederation; Committee of the Whole; Connecticut Compromise; Madison, James, Jr.; Negative on State Laws; New Jersey Plan; Randolph, Edmund; also see individual branches of government

FOR FURTHER READING

Farrand, Max. 1913. *The Framing of the Constitution of the United States.* New Haven, CT: Yale University Press.
———, ed. 1937. *The Records of the Federal Convention.* 4 vols. New Haven, CT: Yale University Press.

Hobson, Charles F. 1979. "The Negative on State Laws: James Madison, the Constitution and the Crisis of Republican Government." *William and Mary Quarterly,* 3rd ser. 36 (April): 215–235.

Maier, Pauline. 1987. "The Philadelphia Convention and the Development of American Government: From the Virginia Plan to the Constitution." *this Constitution,* no. 15 (Summer): 13–19.

Rutland, Robert A. 1984. "The Virginia Plan of 1787: James Madison's Outline of a Model Constitution." *this Constitution,* no. 4 (Fall): 23–30.

VIRTUE

The U.S. Constitution does not use the term "virtue." However, the idea of citizen virtue was a key concept of republicanism, and delegates discussed virtue on several occasions at the Convention.

References to Virtue at the Convention

Thus, on May 31, Elbridge Gerry of Massachusetts observed that "the people do not want [lack] virtue; but are the dupes of pretended patriots" (Farrand 1937, I, 48). On June 16, Pennsylvania's James Wilson said that the only check on a unicameral legislature was "the inadequate one, of the virtue & good sense of those who compose it" (I, 254). On June 26, Virginia's James Madison commended the establishment of a Senate "sufficiently respectable for its wisdom & virtue" (I, 423). That same day, Gerry expressed hope that "there would be a sufficient sense of justice & virtue for the purpose of Govt." (I, 425). On July 2, Gouverneur Morris said that "*Abilities* and *virtue*, are equally necessary in both branches" (I, 512), and on August 7, Benjamin Franklin urged his fellow delegates not to underestimate "the virtue & public spirit of our common people" (II, 204).

Meaning of Virtue

Such references should make it clear that although the term "virtue" is often used to describe individual moral or religious qualities, delegates to the Convention also understood the term to encompass what Daniel Farber and Suzanna Sherry call a "willingness to sacrifice private interests to the public good" (1990, 13). They illustrate this point of view with a quotation from John Adams from 1776:

Public virtue is the only foundation of republics. There must be a positive passion for the public good, the public interest, honor, power, and glory, established in the minds of the people, or there can be no republican government, nor any real liberty; and this public passion must be superior to all private passions. Men must be ready, they must pride themselves, and be happy to sacrifice their private pleasures, passions, and interests, nay, their private friendships and dearest connections, when they stand in competition with the rights of society. (1990, 13)

Tensions between Republican and Liberal Thought

Although scholars generally acknowledge that there were many intellectual influences on the American Founders, scholars of the intellectual foundations of the United States often split between those who believe that these foundations are based chiefly on classical republican thought, with its emphasis on the need for citizen virtue and participation, and those who believe it was established chiefly on principles associated with classical liberalism, which puts greater emphasis on designing governmental structures to convert selfish behavior into public good. Historian Gordon Wood has been among those who have suggested that there may have been a shift in thinking from republicanism, which he believes dominated during the Revolutionary War period, to liberalism, which he believes became more prominent at the time of the writing of the U.S. Constitution (1969).

The fact that delegates did not incorporate the term "virtue" into the Constitution does not necessarily mean that they considered it unimportant. Indeed, no less a delegate than James Madison emphasized the importance of virtue at the Virginia state ratifying convention when he responded to Antifederalist charges that Congress would abuse its power:

But I go on this great republican principle: that the people will have virtue and intelligence to select men of virtue and wisdom. Is there no virtue among us? If there be not, we are in a wretched situation. No theoretical checks, no form of government, can render us secure. To suppose that any form of government will secure liberty or happiness without any virtue in the people is a chimerical idea. (Quoted in Banning 1988, 73–74)

Reasons the Constitution May Not Mention Virtue

This does not mean that the Framers were necessarily inconsistent when they omitted references to virtue within the text of the Constitution.

Many early Americans appear to have believed that, although government depended upon citizen virtue, it could not effectively create it. Richard Vetterli and Gary C. Bryner have observed that "government itself was not the source of public virtue: instead, the promotion of virtue was a function of the primary institutions of society—family, schools, communities, and churches" (1988, 92).

In a related vein, some American leaders believed that citizen interest in preserving the government rested chiefly on independent citizens who had a concrete interest in society, such as was made possible by widespread property ownership. Thomas Jefferson thus observed:

> Those who labor in the earth are the chosen people of God, if ever He had a chosen people, whose breast He has made His peculiar deposit for substantial and genuine virtue. It is the focus in which he keeps alive that sacred fire, which otherwise might escape from the face of the earth. Corruption of morals in the mass of cultivators is a phenomenon of which no age or nation has furnished an example. It is the mark set on those, who, not looking to heaven, to their own soil and industry, as does the husbandman, for their subsistence, depend for it on casualties and caprice of customers. (Jefferson 1964, 157)

To the extent that the Framers thought they had created mechanisms for the widespread acquisition and possession of property, they might have thought they had created a substantial basis for citizen virtue.

Similarly, the Framers of the U.S. Constitution recognized that they were not replacing all governments, but simply overlaying existing state governments with what they hoped would be an improved national superstructure. Delegates may have expected state governments to fulfill traditional functions, later recognized with the adoption of the Tenth Amendment, that are today subsumed under the term "police powers." States are generally regarded as having powers, under this rubric, to provide for the health, safety, and morals of their citizens. The establishment clause of the First Amendment, which (like the similar provision within the Constitution requiring religious oaths of *national* officials) prohibited *Congress* from adopting laws respecting an establishment of religion, may serve as an additional indication that most Framers wanted the national government to keep out of the business of recognizing or establishing a national religion, but they were, at the time, relatively content to allow states (some of which would continue to recognize an official church until the early part of the nineteenth century) to decide on how they thought churches, and other institutions that might instill virtue, might best flourish at the state level.

Moralists often cited the lives of the Founding Fathers, and especially of George Washington, as examples of selfless statesmanship and as examples of virtue (see Bennett 1997) for modern citizens to emulate.

See Also Corruption; Federalism; Liberalism; Republicanism; Statesmanship

FOR FURTHER READING

Banning, Lance. 1988. "1787 and 1776: Patrick Henry, James Madison, the Constitution, and the Revolution." In Neil L. York, ed. *Toward a More Perfect Union: Six Essays on the Constitution.* Provo, UT: Brigham Young University, 59–90.

Bennett, William J., ed. 1997. *Our Sacred Honor: Words of Advice from the Founders in Stories, Letters, Poems, and Speeches.* New York: Simon and Schuster.

Crowe, Charles. 1964. "Bishop James Madison and the Republic of Virtue." *Journal of Southern History* 30 (February): 58–70.

Farber, Daniel A., and Suzanna Sherry. 1990. *A History of the American Constitution.* Saint Paul, MN: West Publishing.

Farrand, Max, ed. 1937. *The Records of the Federal Convention.* 4 vols. New Haven, CT: Yale University Press.

Jefferson, Thomas. 1964. *Notes on the State of Virginia.* New York: Harper and Row, Publishers.

Kramnick, Isaac. 1988. "The 'Great National Discussion': The Discourse of Politics in 1787." *William and Mary Quarterly,* 3rd ser. 45 (January): 3–32.

Savage, James D. 1994. "Corruption and Virtue at the Constitutional Convention." *Journal of Politics* 56 (February): 174–186.

Trees, Andrew S. 2004. *The Founding Fathers and the Pol-*

itics of Character. Princeton, NJ: Princeton University Press.

Vetterli, Richard, and Gary C. Bryner. 1988. "Religion, Public Virtue, and the Founding of the American Republic." In Neil L. York, ed. *Toward a More Perfect Union: Six Essays on the Constitution.* Provo, UT: Brigham Young University.

Wood, Gordon S. 1969. *The Creation of the American Republic, 1776–1787.* Chapel Hill: University of North Carolina Press.

VOTING AT THE CONVENTION

Under the Articles of Confederation, each state had a single vote. According to James Madison's Notes, the Pennsylvania delegation, and, in particular, Gouverneur Morris and Robert Morris, were prepared to challenge this equality at the very outset of the Convention (Farrand 1937, I, 10–11). Madison further records that the delegates from Virginia urged them not to press the point at this early stage lest it "beget fatal altercations between the large & small States." The Virginia delegates further argued that it would be "easier to prevail on the latter, in the course of the deliberations, to give up their equality for the sake of an effective Government" than to compel them to do so at the outset (I, 10–11).

The result was that notes of the debates record votes by states, with the largest total possible being 12, since delegates from Rhode Island never attended. Moreover, the delegates from New Hampshire did not arrive until late in the Convention proceedings, about the time that the New York delegates had left (two permanently and one to return at Convention's end). Delegates from 11 states thus decided many issues. On the opening day, only seven states had a majority of their delegations present, and only they could vote.

When states had equal numbers of representatives, their vote was recorded as split. It is thus not uncommon to see a voting record like 5-4-2. Such a vote indicates that 5 states approved a motion, 4 states opposed, two were split, one had not

yet arrived, and another would never do so. The Constitution was signed on September 17, 1787, by all the states present, but not only was Rhode Island not present, but New York was represented only by one of three delegates and thus did not have a quorum. Although Alexander Hamilton signed the document, he thus did so in his individual capacity rather than on behalf of his state. The vote for the Constitution was thus recorded as 11 to 0. There were a total of 569 recorded votes during the Constitutional Convention.

The equal weight given to the states both in Congress and at the Convention does much to explain the intensity of debate over representation in Congress. Since the delegates from Delaware arrived with specific instructions not to alter the system of state representation, it seems unlikely that they would have stayed at a convention, the work of which they later ratified, had they initially been denied the equal suffrage to which they were accustomed.

See Also Quorum; Rules of the Constitutional Convention; Signing of the Constitution

FOR FURTHER READING

Farrand, Max, ed. 1937. *The Records of the Federal Convention.* 4 vols. New Haven, CT: Yale University Press.

Lansky, Dana. 2000. "Proceeding to a Constitution: A Multi-Party Negotiation Analysis of the Constitutional Convention of 1787." *Harvard Negotiation Law Review* 5 (Spring): 279–338.

VOTING BLOCS

See COALITIONS

VOTING QUALIFICATIONS

See SUFFRAGE

W

WAR POWERS OF CONGRESS

No society can be safe if its government does not have the authority to protect it. This power is so critical that it arguably could be assumed to be inherent in national sovereignty if the Constitution did not specifically grant it. In a government with different branches, however, it is necessary to specify which branch has which powers. Article I, Section 8, Clause 11, accordingly specifies that Congress shall have power "To declare War, grant letters of Marque and Reprisal, and make Rules concerning Captures on Land and Water." This clause needs to be understood in the context of Article II, Section 2, which specified that the president is commander-in-chief of the armed forces. Consistent with constitutional silence on the subject, the judicial branch rarely intervenes in matters related to national defense, especially in cases when U.S. power is directed abroad.

Early Plans

Under the Articles of Confederation, Congress had "the sole and exclusive right and power of determining on peace and war." Congress had the further right to appoint officers of land and sea forces and to agree on their number, but it requisitioned states for their quota of troops rather than raising them directly (see Articles VI and IX). The first of the defects that Edmund Randolph identified in the Articles of Confederation when he presented the Virginia Plan to the Convention on May 29 was that it "produced no security agai[nst] foreign invasion; congress not being permitted to prevent a war nor support it by th[eir] own authority" (Farrand 1937, I, 19).

The Virginia Plan proposed vesting the national government with all powers, presumably including war, to which the states were individually incompetent. The New Jersey Plan proposed that a plural executive would "direct all military operations," but it provided that none of them would "take command of any troops, so as personally to conduct any enterprises as General, or in other capacity" (I, 244). In a provision that came quite close to the Convention's ultimate resolution of the subject, Alexander Hamilton proposed in the plan that he presented to the Convention on June 18 that the executive should "have the direction of war when authorized or begun" (I, 292).

Committee of Detail

The Committee of Detail originally vested Congress with the power "to make war" (II, 182). In discussions on August 17, South Carolina's Charles Pinckney questioned whether this power should be vested in the legislature. He feared that it would act slowly and that it would not be in session frequently enough. He favored granting the power specifically to the Senate, which, with its power to ratify treaties, would have power to make peace and should therefore also have the power to make war. Pierce Butler, also of South Carolina, thought that the reasons that would argue against war-making by the entire Congress would equally apply to the Senate. He favored vesting this power in the president.

This discourse was the apparent catalyst for a proposal that James Madison of Virginia offered, and Elbridge Gerry of Massachusetts seconded, substituting the word "declare" for "make" and thus more clearly giving the president the right to repel attacks (II, 318), and, arguably, for directing day-to-day operations (Levy 1997, 2, however, doubts that the change of language was significant; also see Reveley 1974, 103–104). Connecticut's Roger Sherman liked the existing language, thinking that the proposed substitute would unduly narrow congressional powers. Gerry thought that it was unrepublican to think of the president declaring war while Ellsworth argued that the powers of making war and making peace should not be placed on the same footing. Virginia's George Mason feared giving the power to make war to the executive and did not think that the Senate was appropriately constituted to deal with it. He preferred the word "declare" to "make." The Convention agreed by a vote of 7-2-1, continuing to keep this power vested in Congress as a whole rather than specifically in the Senate.

The Convention overwhelmingly proceeded to reject a motion by Charles Pinckney to strike out the clause granting Congress the power to declare war. Butler then proposed granting the legislature the same power over peace that it had over war, and thus taking the power to ratify treaties away from the Senate. Gerry seconded the motion in the belief that the entire legislature was less likely to be corrupted than was the Senate. The Convention, however, rejected Butler's motion by a vote of 10-0. While vesting the power to declare war in the national government, the Convention specified in Article I, Section 10 that states could not "keep troops, or Ships of War in time of peace . . .

or engage in War, unless actually invaded, or in such imminent Danger as will admit of no delay."

Analysis

In examining the debates, which largely focus on the respective allocations of power between the president and the Congress, it is easy to lose sight of the fact that every plan that the Convention considered—whether vesting power in Congress as a whole, in the Senate, in the president, or in some combination of the above—was designed to subordinate military to civil authorities. The idea of essentially vesting Congress with the power to declare war (as well as with the power of financing it), the president with the power to wage it, and the president and the Senate with the power to confirm treaties ending a war works best in situations when there is a declared war, but many conflicts in U.S. history have not been declared to be such. The War Powers Act of 1973 is but one indication of the continuing tension between the powers of the legislative and executive branches in this area.

See Also Armies, Standing; President, Commander in Chief

FOR FURTHER READING

Farrand, Max, ed. 1937. *The Records of the Federal Convention.* 4 vols. New Haven, CT: Yale University Press.

Huntington, Samuel P. 1956. "Civilian Control and the Constitution." *American Political Science Review* 50 (September): 676–699.

Levy, Leonard W. 1997. "Foreign Policy and War Powers: The Presidency and the Framers." *American Scholar* 66 (Spring): 271–275.

Moore, John Allphin, Jr. 1993. "Empire, Republicanism, and Reason: Foreign Affairs as Viewed by the Founders of the Constitution." *The History Teacher* 26 (May): 297–315.

Reveley, W. Taylor, III. 1974. "Constitutional Allocation of the War Powers between the President and the Congress: 1787–1788." *Virginia Journal of International Law* 15 (Fall): 73–147.

Treanor, William Michael. 1997. "Fame, the Founding, and the Power to Declare War." *Cornell Law Review* 82: 695–772.

WASHINGTON, GEORGE (1732–1799)

Scholars generally agree that George Washington was the "father of the country" and that his attendance at the Constitutional Convention, his support for the document, and his service for two terms as president were indispensable to the new republic. Addressed as "His Excellency" during the Convention, state delegations unanimously elected him as the Convention's president on May 25. His only possible rival for the post was the ailing Benjamin Franklin, with whom he had dined shortly after arriving in Philadelphia. With the approval of Franklin, who was unable to attend that day because of illness, fellow Pennsylvanian Robert Morris placed Washington's name in nomination.

Life Prior to the Convention

Born in Westmoreland County, Virginia, the handsome Washington, who grew to six feet, two inches in height, began his career in surveying. With Washington's service first in the French and Indian War and then as commander-in-chief of America's revolutionary forces, he had a far more continental perspective than many of the delegates. His father died in Washington's youth, and he inherited property not only from him but also later from his older half brother, Lawrence. He further increased his wealth in 1759 when he married Martha Dandridge Custis, a wealthy widow. He was elected to the Continental Congress in 1774 after having previously served in the Virginia House of Burgesses. With his military record (it also helped that he was from the South at a time when New England states were taking the lead),

Portrait of George Washington, delegate from Virginia and first president of the United States (1789–1796) (Library of Congress)

he was a logical choice for commander-in-chief to which position Congress unanimously elected him. As his anguished letters demonstrated, he was particularly aware of the difficulty that the Congress had in fulfilling its obligations to his troops. After the war, Washington had set an example that will forever be honored in republican governments by renouncing any attempts to crown him as king. He further dissuaded unpaid troops from marching on Congress to demand their rights by force of arms, and by returned to his beloved plantation at Mount Vernon (Schwartz 1983). Sometimes cash poor, Washington was one of the wealthiest men in the nation.

Increasingly pessimistic about the nation's prospects under the Articles of Confederation, Washington's house served as the gathering place for Virginia and Maryland delegates discussing navigation on the Potomac River. This meeting was in turn the launching pad for the Annapolis Convention, which issued the call for the Convention in Philadelphia.

Washington's Role at the Convention

In 1787, the 55-year-old Washington had a world-wide reputation that he was reluctant to hazard at a Convention the prospects of which were so uncertain. Fellow Virginian James Madison played a particularly active role in convincing him that his presence was necessary to rescue the government, and he reluctantly came, arriving early and spending the following months at the home of Robert Morris, who had proved so helpful in financing the Revolutionary War. Washington attended every day of the Convention, after which he returned to Mount Vernon.

In resolutions adopted on the next day of business after Washington was selected as Convention president, members agreed on a series of formalities that played to Washington's strengths. Members would not take their seats until he had taken his. Each member who wanted to speak would address the president, and while a delegate spoke, "none shall pass between them, or hold discourse with another, or read a book, pamphlet or paper, printed or manuscript" (Farrand 1937, I, 11). When the Convention adjourned at the end of each day, each member was required to stand until Washington had left the room (I, 12). The symbolism must have been impressive. John Langdon, a New Hampshire delegate, attempted to convey the scene in a letter to a friend on August 1, 1787:

> Figure to yourself the Great Washington, with a Dignity peculiar to himself, taking the Chair. The Notables are seated, in a Moment and after a short Silence the Business of the day is open'd with great Solemnity and good Order. The Importance of the Business, the Dignified Character of Many, who Compose the Convention, the Eloquence of Some and the Regularity of the whole gives a Ton[e] to the proceedings which is extreamly pleasing. (Hutson 1987, 201)

Washington's role as president is believed to have had a sobering influence on the Convention. Georgia's William Pierce reported that on one occasion during the Convention when he found that a delegate had dropped notes of the proceedings in the State House, Washington addressed his fellows:

> I am sorry to find that some one Member of this Body, has been so neglectful of the secrets of the Convention as to drop in the State House a copy of their proceedings, which by accident was picked up and delivered to me this Morning. I must entreat Gentlemen to be more careful, lest

---

Civilian Control of the Military

Long before the Constitution embodied the idea of civil control of the military by making the president, an elected official, commander-in-chief of the military, the nation had been given a sterling example of military deference to military control by George Washington. Gordon Wood has described Washington's act of resignation as commander-in-chief of the U.S. military in 1783 as "the greatest act of his life, the one that gave him the greatest fame" (1991, 205). Contemporaries likened Washington to Cincinnatus, the legendary Roman who left his field to assume command of the nation's armed forces and then returned to his fields again. Wood cites England's George III as predicting that if Washington retired to his farm, "he will be the greatest man in the world" (206). King George III repeated similar sentiments when Washington later retired again from the presidency (Lipset 1988, 24).

FOR FURTHER READING

Lipset, Seymour Martin. 1988. "George Washington and the Founding of Democracy." *Journal of Democracy* 9, no. 4: 24–38.
Wood, Gordon S. 1991. *The Radicalism of the American Revolution.* New York: Vintage Books.

our transactions get into the News Papers, and disturb the public repose by premature speculations. I know not whose Paper it is, but there it is (throwing it down on the table), let him who owns it take it. At the same time he bowed, picked up his Hat, and quitted the room with a dignity so severe that every Person seemed alarmed. (III, 86–87)

Pierce reported that he himself was extremely alarmed and was only reassured when he examined the document and discovered that it was not in his handwriting. He returned to his lodging at the Indian Queen and found his own copy. He also reports that no one ever stepped forward to claim the missing papers.

Although his letters testify that Washington was far more adept at written words than many contemporary politicians, he was a reluctant speaker who gained power more from his actions than from his speeches. He is only recorded as giving two formal speeches during the Convention. The first was an acceptance speech, which he delivered after delegates chose him as president of the Convention and Robert Morris and John Rutledge escorted him to the raised dais. His speech was undoubtedly longer than Madison's summary, but the summary adequately conveys the quiet dignity that the general was able to project:

he thanked the Convention for the honor they had conferred on him, reminded them of the novelty of the scene of business in which he was to act, lamented his want of [better qualifications], and claimed the indulgence of the House towards the involuntary errors which his inexperience might occasion. (I, 3–4)

Apart from rulings that he had to make in his role as president, he then fell largely silent until the final day of the Convention when he spoke in favor of permitting one representative for every 30,000 residents, rather than for every 40,000 (II, 644), and when, later in the day, he asked the delegates what they wanted him to do with the Convention's journals. Commenting on Washington's intervention in the seemingly trivial matter of the number of individuals each U.S. representative

would represent, one author has observed: "The size of the districts was not a major issue. By breaking his silence to endorse a minor change, Washington was signifying to the delegates that no major changes needed to be made" (Brookhiser 1996, 68).

Glenn Phelps, a student of Washington's constitutional philosophy who has attempted to analyze Washington's positions at the Convention drawing from Madison's records of the votes of the Virginia delegation, says that Washington pursued two major concerns. First, he consistently supported an energetic executive. Second, with the exception of opposing the power to emit paper money, Washington consistently favored stronger powers for the national government (Phelps 1993, 134). Phelps further notes that "the Constitution addressed nearly every major concern that he had raised in the previous six or seven years and did so in ways that fit well with his avowed goals" (116).

Washington's prestige undoubtedly aided in the initial reception that the Convention provided to the Virginia Plan. Washington appears to have encouraged fellow delegates to consider not simply what they thought the people would adopt but what they needed. At the outset of the Convention, Washington thus observed:

It is possible that no plan we suggest will be adopted. Perhaps another dreadful conflict is to be sustained. If, to please the people, we offer what we ourselves disapprove, how can we afterwards defend our work? Let us raise a standard to which the wise and honest can repair; the event is in the hands of God. (Lee 1932, 25)

There is evidence that the widespread anticipation that he would serve as the nation's first chief executive made delegates more willing to vest this institution in a single individual and give it greater powers than they might otherwise have been willing to entrust to it. South Carolina's Pierce Butler thus observed that members had "cast their eyes towards General Washington as President; and shaped their ideas of the Powers to be given a President, by their opinions of his Virtue" (quoted in Rhodehamel 1998, 109). In unsuccessfully arguing that the president should not receive a salary, Benjamin Franklin pointed on June 2 to Washington's laudable example when serving as commander-in-chief of the Revolutionary forces (I, 84). Two days later, Franklin observed that "the first man, put at the helm will be a good one. No body knows what sort may come afterwards" (I, 103).

Consistent with the rule of secrecy that the Convention adopted, Washington's diaries do not give the substance of the events that transpired at the Convention, but they show that he engaged in an active social life, where his behind-the-scene interactions with other delegates and comments on their work may very well have been influential. He also used a break in Convention proceedings to revisit Valley Forge, where he and his troops had spent such a miserable winter during the Revolutionary War.

Washington is the further source of a number of anecdotes, not all of which can be verified, but each of which illuminates one or another aspect of his character. Pierce's description of Washington's alleged comments after discovering a copy of the proceedings has been noted above. Gouverneur Morris of Pennsylvania further told how he responded to a bet by New York's Alexander Hamilton that he could not slap the general on the shoulder in a public gathering and won only after receiving considerable mortification by Washington's icy response (III, 85), a sign of his perceived preeminence. Washington was later alleged to have poured coffee into a saucer and blown over it to explain to Thomas Jefferson why the Convention had agreed on a bicameral rather than a unicameral Congress (III, 359), with the Senate "cooling" the passions of the House. In discussions about prohibiting a standing army of any more than 3,000 troops, Washington was reputed to have whispered to a fellow delegate that "no foreign enemy should invade the United States at any time, with more than three thousand troops" (Hutson 1987, 229). When Alexander Hamilton was alleged to have opposed Franklin's motion that each day begin with prayer on the basis that the Convention should not ask for foreign aid, Washington was reported to have "fixed his eye upon the speaker, with a mixture of *surprise*

and *indignation*, while he uttered this impertinent and impious speech, and then looked around to ascertain in what manner it affected others" (III, 472). Even the president's chair became the subject of comment, when on the Convention's last day, Benjamin Franklin professed to believe that the sun painted on the back slat was rising on a new day.

Some true, some apocryphal, and some a mixture of both, these stories (like Parson Weems's later embellishments of Washington's life, as in his story of Washington chopping down a cherry tree) illustrated the quiet dignity of a man whose very presence could call out the best behavior in those around him. It is perhaps significant that the idea of breaking the Convention into a Committee of the Whole presided over by Nathaniel Gorham rather than by Washington was abandoned when debates over the respective merits of the proposals for state representation in the Virginia and New Jersey Plans got serious.

Life after the Convention

After the Convention, Washington carefully followed the progress of ratification, maintaining a vigorous correspondence and using his personal influence wherever possible in the Constitution's favor. One sad result of the Convention was that the long friendship between Washington and his neighbor George Mason came to an end with the latter's refusal to sign the Constitution. The support of the Constitution by both Washington and Franklin was a major argument that Federalists made in its favor. Washington authorized Madison to signal his support at the Virginia ratifying convention.

Washington remains the only president ever unanimously selected by the Electoral College to the presidency. Although he had mixed feelings about accepting yet another position that might further hazard the reputation he had so assiduously cultivated, he proceeded to his inauguration in triumph cheered by 20,000 citizens in Philadelphia and greeted by a banner in Trenton, where he had previously fought a battle, that read: "THE DEFENDER OF THE MOTHERS WILL

BE THE PROTECTOR OF THE DAUGHTERS"
(Brookhiser 1996, 73). He was inaugurated at Federal Hall in New York City on April 30, 1789, where Chancellor Robert Livingston of that state administered his oath. In his Inaugural Address, Washington thanked God for guiding the steps of the new nation through its recent deliberations:

Every step by which they [the people] have advanced to the character of an independent nation seems to have been distinguished by some token of providential agency; and in the important revolution just accomplished in the system of their united government the tranquil deliberations and voluntary consent of so many distinct communities from which the event has resulted cannot be compared with the means by which most governments have been established without some return of pious gratitude, along with an humble anticipation of the future blessings which the past seems to presage. (Quoted in Hunt 1997, 4–5)

Commending the idea of adding provisions like those being considered for the Bill of Rights, Washington avoided specific recommendations while encouraging general action:

I assure myself that whilst you carefully avoid every alteration which might endanger the benefits of an united and effective government, or which ought to await the future lessons of experience, a reverence for the characteristic rights of freemen and a regard for the public harmony will sufficiently influence your deliberations on the question how far the former can be impregnably fortified or the latter be safely and advantageously promoted. (Hunt, 6)

As the first president under the new government, Washington attempted, with only partial success, to rise above the conflicts that quickly developed in his government between Federalists led by his secretary of the Treasury, Alexander Hamilton, and Democratic-Republicans, who were led by his secretary of state, Thomas Jefferson, and by James Madison. Washington acted with knowledge that almost everything he did in office would be considered to be a precedent.

During his first administration, he gave his quiet support to adoption of the Bill of Rights. Washington supported the ambitious programs of his secretary of the Treasury, including the establishment of a national bank. Washington helped secure the establishment of the nation's capital, which the nation named after him, established in its current location on the Potomac River down from his own plantation. In his Farewell Address, Washington renewed his concern about the prevalence of party spirit and recommended a policy of avoiding foreign alliances, a policy that served the nation particularly well in its early years.

One of Washington's most important contributions may have been his decision not to seek reelection after his first two terms. He had actually toyed with the idea of retiring after his first term, but proponents of both emerging parties had persuaded him to stay. His decision to retire after his second term set a precedent that lasted until President Franklin D. Roosevelt and that has subsequently been incorporated into the Twenty-second Amendment.

In Adams's administration, Washington accepted the president's request to take military command of American forces in anticipation of a war with France that, fortunately, did not materialize. Washington died at Mount Vernon in 1799 and was famously eulogized by Virginia's Richard Henry Lee who called him "first in war, first in peace, and first in the hearts of his countrymen." Washington, who had long owned slaves and long regretted the institution of slavery, provided that his slaves would be freed upon his death (Wienek 2003).

See Also Federalist and Democratic-Republican Parties; Mount Vernon Conference; President of the Convention; Virginia; Virginia Plan

FOR FURTHER READING

Brookhiser, Richard. 1996. *Founding Father: Rediscovering George Washington.* New York: The Free Press.

Ellis, Joseph. 2004. *His Excellency: George Washington.* New York: Alfred A. Knopf.

Farrand, Max, ed. 1937. *The Records of the Federal Convention.* 4 vols. New Haven, CT: Yale University Press.

Hunt, John Gabriel, ed. 1997. *The Inaugural Addresses of the Presidents.* New York: Gramercy Books.

Hutson, James H., ed. 1987. *Supplement to Max Farrand's* The Records of the Federal Convention of 1787. New Haven, CT: Yale University Press.

Lee, Howard B. 1932. *The Story of the Constitution.* Charlottesville, VA: Michie.

Liebiger, Stuart. 1999. *Founding Friendship: George Washington, James Madison, and the Creation of the American Republic.* Charlottesville: University of Virginia Press.

Nordham, George Washington. 1987. *George Washington: President of the Constitutional Convention.* Chicago: Adams Press.

Phelps, Glenn A. 1993. *George Washington and American Constitutionalism.* Lawrence: University Press of Kansas.

Rhodehamel, John. 1998. *The Great Experiment: George Washington and the American Republic.* New Haven, CT: Yale University Press.

Schwartz, Barry. 1987. *George Washington: The Making of an American Symbol.* New York: The Free Press.

——. 1983. "George Washington and the Whig Conception of Heroic Leadership." *American Sociological Review* 48 (February): 18–33.

Watson, Henry B. 1983. *George Washington: Architect of the Constitution.* Daytona Beach, FL: Patriotic Education.

Wienek, Henry. 2003. *An Imperfect God: George Washington, His Slaves, and the Creation of America.* New York: Farrar, Straus and Giroux.

"WE THE PEOPLE"

The first three words of the Constitution, which are found in the Preamble and refer to "We the People," are probably the most quoted and the most symbolic. They underline the fact that the Constitution intended to create a government that is intended to be accountable to the people, who are considered to be the ultimate sovereigns. Scholars generally refer to such a government as a democracy or a republic. The words "We the People" emerged from the Committee of Style and Arrangement and are primarily attributable to the pen of Gouverneur Morris of Pennsylvania, who was a member of that committee.

The words, and those that follow, "We the People of the United States," leave considerable room for ambiguity. Nationalists have most frequently emphasized the words "We the People" and "United" whereas advocates of states' rights have more frequently emphasized the "States." This ambiguity is accentuated by the federal nature of the government that the Constitution created.

Prior to reaching the Committee of Style and Arrangement, the Preamble listed the names of each individual state, which would have given a still further states' rights spin to the document. It appears that the committee eliminated the names of the states not only for stylistic reasons but also because it was not altogether clear which states would ratify the document, which was slated to go into effect when nine or more approved.

A number of groups have used the moniker "We the People" in support of various educational or political causes. The Center for Civic Education, located in Calabasas, California, thus sponsors a widely known program called "We the People. . . The Citizen and the Constitution." The center supports a series of regional, state, and national mock congressional hearings in which classes of school students demonstrate their knowledge of the Constitution before educator and practitioner judges. In addition to other activities, the center prints texts for students and sponsors summer seminars for high school teachers. The words "We the People" are displayed on the right side of the front entrance of the new National Constitution Center in Philadelphia.

See Also Committee of Style and Arrangement; Federalism; Forms of Government; Morris, Gouverneur; National Constitution Center; Preamble; Ratification in the States; Sovereignty

FOR FURTHER READING

Morgan, Edmund S. 1988. *Inventing the People: The Rise of Popular Sovereignty in England and America.* New York: W. W. Norton.

"We the People: The Citizen and the Constitution." http://www.civiced.org/wethepeople.php

WEAVER, NICHOLAS

Records of the federal Convention indicate that delegates appointed Nicholas Weaver as their messenger on May 25, the same day that they designated Joseph Fry as door-keeper (Farrand 1937, I, 2). Congress paid Weaver $100 for his services. Officials calculated this amount at four months of service for a job that paid $300 a year (Hutson 1987, 277).

A man named Nicholas Weaver, who may or may not have been the same man, served in the First Volunteer Corps of Pennsylvania which was raised in 1765 under the command of Richard Peters ("The First Volunteer Corps of Philadelphia"). The diary of Jacob Hiltz-Heimer of Philadelphia from October 26 of 1786 says that a Nicholas Weaver was elected on this date as sergeant at arms of the Pennsylvania State Assembly. Since the Constitutional Convention met in the same building (the State House, or Independence Hall) as the Pennsylvania Assembly, it is likely that this is the same individual.

See Also Fry, Joseph; Pennsylvania State House; Sentries

FOR FURTHER READING

Farrand, Max, ed. 1937. *The Records of the Federal Convention.* 4 vols. New Haven, CT: Yale University Press.

"The First Volunteer Company of Philadelphia, Raised by Richard Peters, A.D. 1765." *The Military Magazine and Record of the Volunteers of the City and County of* . . . July 1839: 1, 5: APS Online. Supplied for the author by Sheridan Harvey of the Library of Congress.

Hiltz-Heimer, Jacob. "Extracts from the Diary of Jacob Hiltz-Heimer, of Philadelphia, 1768–1798." Supplied for the author by Sheridan Harvey of the Library of Congress in May 2004.

Hutson, James H., ed. 1987. *Supplement to Max Farrand's* The Records of the Federal Convention of 1787. New Haven, CT: Yale University Press.

WHIG IDEOLOGY

Among the strains of thought that influenced those who fought the American Revolution and wrote the U.S. Constitution was that of Whig ideology. Whig was the name of the party within the English Parliament that had resisted the Stuart monarchs, Charles I and James II. Whigs were often identified with the English "Country," or opposition, Party.

Whigs were passionately committed to the idea of liberty and convinced that English liberties went all the way back to Saxon times and that such liberties had been reaffirmed in the Magna Carta (Colbourn 1965, 25–32) and in colonial charters. Because of their origins, the Whigs typically favored legislative over executive powers, often seeing liberty as something that the people needed to defend against their rulers (Lokken 1974, 92). Whigs generally espoused republican principles, with their emphasis on the need for citizen virtue and the dangers of corruption; they often associated citizenship with both the right and the responsibility of serving in the militia and opposed large standing armies, which they feared could be used by the executive to oppress the people (Cress 1979).

Allen Guelzo has described the principles of Whiggery that were influential in the American Revolutionary and Founding periods as follows:

1. Liberty is natural, and cannot be a gift of a monarch.
2. Liberty, however, can be destroyed, normally by the corrupt elite who strive to concentrate power in themselves and corrupt others.
3. Liberty therefore requires an alliance with virtue for protection from corruption and power, whether in the form of the natural virtues (like modesty, productive work, or self restraint), or religious ones (such as would be found in strict Protestant moralism).
4. Because Whigs prefer virtue to power, they are most often the "country" party, and are found outside the centers of power. (Guelzo 2001, I, 197)

This ideology clearly overlaps with that of both liberalism and republicanism.

Just as one of the first two American political parties appropriated the term "Federalist," so too the party that arose in the 1820s out of the Federalist demise in opposition to Andrew Jackson's broad exercise of executive authority appropriated the Whig moniker (Holt 1999). Kentucky's Henry Clay was the most prominent leader of this party, which at one time included Abraham Lincoln as a member and which survived until the early 1850s, when the Republican Party succeeded it. The Whig Party modified a number of tenets of original Whig thinking. Changes include what has been described as "the substitution of economic mobility for physical location in the 'country'"; the "definition of virtue as self-improvement, whether through commerce, thrift, or religious transformation"; and "the relocation of power and Whig nationalism" (see Guelzo, I, 200–201, italics omitted).

See Also Corruption; Court and Country Parties; Liberalism; Protestantism; Republicanism; Virtue

FOR FURTHER READING

Bradley, James E. 1975. "Whigs and Nonconformists: 'Slumbering Radicalism' in English Politics, 1739–1789." *Eighteenth-Century Studies* 9 (Autumn): 1–27.

Colbourn, H. Trevor. 1965. *The Lamp of Experience: Whig History and the Intellectual Origins of the American Revolution.* Chapel Hill: University of North Carolina Press.

Cress, Lawrence Delbert. 1979. "Radical Whiggery on the Role of the Military: Ideological Roots of the American Revolutionary Militia." *Journal of the History of Ideas* 40 (Jan.-Mar.): 43–60.

Guelzo, Allen C. 2001. "Whig Ideology." In Mary K. Cayton and Peter W. Williams, eds. *Encyclopedia of American Cultural and Intellectual History.* Vol. 1 of 2. New York: Charles Scribner's Sons, 197–204.

Holt, Michael F. 1999. *The Rise and Fall of the American Whig Party: Jacksonian Politics and the Outset of the Civil War.* New York: Oxford University Press.

Lokken, Roy N. 1974. "The Political Theory of the American Revolution: Changing Interpretations." *The History Teacher* 8 (November): 81–95.

Robbins, Caroline. 1959. *The Eighteenth-Century Commonwealthman: Studies in the Transmission, Development and Circumstance of English Liberal Thought from the Restoration of Charles II until the War with the Thirteen Colonies.* Cambridge, MA: Harvard University Press.

Wood, Gordon S. 1969. *The Creation of the American Republic 1776–1787.* Chapel Hill: University of North Carolina Press.

WILLIAMSON, HUGH (1735–1819)

Hugh Williamson was born in West Nottingham, Pennsylvania in 1735 to merchant parents who had immigrated to the United States from Ireland. After attending a private academy at New London, Pennsylvania, Williamson attended the College of Philadelphia, today's University of Pennsylvania. After earning an undergraduate degree, he returned for theological study, was licensed to preach as a Presbyterian minister, and picked up a master's degree in mathematics. Williamson later attended the University of Edinburgh and the University of Utrecht from which he earned a medical degree.

Also interested in astronomy, Williamson published scientific papers and later became a trustee of what became the University of Delaware. A witness to the Boston Tea Party, Williamson traveled to England where he obtained incriminating correspondence from Massachusetts governor Thomas Hutchinson, which, with Benjamin Franklin's help, he published. Since Philadelphia fell to the British, Williamson moved to North Carolina where he served as the surgeon general of the state's militia. Before being selected to attend the Constitutional Convention, he had served in the North Carolina legislature, in the Congress under the Articles of Confederation where he was active in drafting legislation related to the admission of new Western states, and as a delegate to the Annapolis Convention. He had, however, arrived too late to participate in the latter.

established on July 9, the committee on state debts and regulation of the militia which was created on August 18, the Committee on Slave Trade and Navigation which was formed on August 22, the Committee on Commercial Discrimination which was formed on August 25, and the Committee on Postponed Matters which was created on August 31. Williamson did not chair any of these bodies.

Congress

Representation and Size

On June 9, Williamson attempted to defend representation in Congress on the basis of population by noting that such methods were used in most of the states for representing counties, and that if it was appropriate in the latter case then it should also be appropriate for the former (Farrand 1937, I, 180). He returned to this theme on June 28. He suggested, "if any political truth could be grounded on mathematical demonstration, it was that if the states were equally sovereign now, and parted with equal proportions of sovereignty, that they would remain equally sovereign" (I, 445).

Williamson feared that if small states had equal votes with the large ones, the former would attempt to put their burdens on the latter. He feared that this problem might be compounded by the addition of Western states (I, 446). On July 9, Williamson suggested that the idea of apportioning representatives according to population should not equally apply to the West where he anticipated that property values would be lower (I, 560). On August 29, Williamson argued that the reason for granting existing states equal representation within the Senate would not apply to new states that were admitted into the Union (II, 454).

When a committee proposed that the initial House of Representatives should consist of 65 delegates, Williamson observed that the Northern states had a majority, and he thought that this posed a danger to the Southern states (I, 567). Whereas some delegates wanted to leave it to Congress to decide when to redistrict, Williamson

Hugh Williamson, delegate from North Carolina
(Pixel That)

Williamson was present on the first day of Convention business on May 25 and he stayed to the end. He had the advantage of serving in a delegation that was united. He observed in a letter of July 19 that "there has not in a single important Question been a Division in our Representation nor so much as one dissenting Voice" (Hutson 1987, 175). Little noticed in many histories of the Convention, Williamson was the most outspoken member of the North Carolina delegation. He delivered his views on a wide variety of subjects, but his comments were often briefer than those of better-known delegates. Williamson may be best known for introducing the motion that terms of senators would be for six years. Seeds of ideas that he planted appear, sometimes somewhat reconfigured, in a number of provisions that the delegates incorporated into the Constitution, and especially in the Electoral College mechanism.

Williamson served on five different committees during the Convention. These included the committee designed to reconsider the initial representation in the House of Representatives which was thought that the Constitution needed to make it explicit when it should do so (I, 579). Williamson favored the three-fifths compromise which counted slaves as three-fifths of a person in allocating representation in the U.S. House of Representatives (I, 581). He proposed reducing New Hampshire's representation in the House of Representatives from three members to two, arguing that the state, delegates from which had not yet arrived at the Convention, might not want to pay the extra direct taxes that would be apportioned on the basis of this representation (I, 601), but perhaps also being pleased to think of an expedient that would also reduce Northern representation. On September 5, however, Williamson argued that Rhode Island should be given more than one member. He also said that he thought that the initial House of Representatives would be too small if it were confined to 65 members (II, 511; also see II, 553). On September 14, Williamson wanted to increase the House by half its size, making sure that the smallest states had at least two members (II, 612).

By July 2, Williamson was ready for some compromise on the issue of representation. He thus favored establishing a committee for this purpose. He observed that "If we do not concede on both sides, our business must soon be at an end" (I, 515). When one of the compromises that emerged was to restrict the origination of money bills in the lower house, however, Williamson suggested that the Convention had things backwards. He reasoned that the people would more closely watch what the Senate did than they would watch the branch that had "most of the popular confidence" (I, 544). On August 9, a day after the Convention had struck out the provision regarding the origination of money bills, however, Williamson joined Virginia's Edmund Randolph in asking for a reconsideration of this issue (II, 230). He indicated that he thought this was one of the conditions on which North Carolina, and other small states, had agreed to the Great Compromise (II, 233; also see II, 263 and II, 287). On August 15 he observed that since some thought the restriction on money bills was critical and others thought it only unimportant, the delegates should prefer the former over the latter (II, 297). He

further observed that many delegates would be unwilling to strengthen the Senate unless the Convention reinstituted the prohibition on money bills.

When Virginia's George Mason objected that granting each state three senators would make that body too numerous, Williamson added that it would be more difficult for distant states to send this number than for those that were nearer (II, 94). On this same occasion, he indicated that he supported "per capita," or individual, voting in the Senate, rather than by state delegation.

Compensation

On June 22 Williamson argued that states should pay the salaries of their own members of Congress. He feared that new Western states would be poor and would have different interests from those in the East, and he did not think that existing states should have to pay the salaries of individuals "who would be employed in thwarting their measures & interests" (I, 372). In the discussion of June 28, cited above, Williamson feared that new states in the West would be poor and would be tempted to burden the commerce and consumption of the Eastern states (I, 446).

Williamson proposed that members of Congress should be compensated "for the devotion of their time to the public Service" (I, 427). The purpose appears to have been to eliminate the term "fixed" so as to provide greater flexibility in the future.

Qualifications and Voting

On August 7, Williamson opposed making a freehold a condition for voting, but notes of the Convention do not record his reasons (II, 201). The next day, he opposed requiring a number of years of residency before an individual could run for Congress. He observed that "New residents if elected will be the most zealous to Conform to the will of their constituents, as their conduct will be watched with a more jealous eye" (II, 218). After the Convention voted to accept a requirement that members of the House of Representatives should be citizens for at least seven years, however, Williamson believed the delegates should establish a similar or longer period for the Senate. He observed that "Bribery & Cabal can be more easily practiced in the choice of the Senate which is to be made by the Legislatures composed of a few men, than in the House of Represents. who will be chosen by the people" (II, 239). On August 13, Williamson suggested that nine years of residency, rather than seven, should be required for members of the House. He observed: "He wished this Country to acquire as fast as possible national habits. Wealthy emigrants do more harm by their luxurious examples, than good, by the money, they bring with them" (II, 268).

On August 10, Williamson opposed allowing members of Congress to set the amount of property that individuals should own in order to become members. He feared that if members of a single profession (he cited lawyers) dominated Congress, members of this profession might secure the election of other members (II, 250).

Williamson indicated on August 14 that he supported a provision making members of Congress ineligible for other offices. He observed that "He had scarcely seen a single corrupt measure in the Legislature of N– Carolina, which could not be traced up to office hunting" (II, 287). On September 3, however, Williamson indicated that he did not think members should be ineligible for vacancies in offices that occurred while they were serving (II, 490; also see II, 492).

Powers and Limits on Powers

On August 16, Williamson supported prohibiting congressional taxation of exports (II, 307), and on August 28, he favored an absolute limit on state taxation of imports (II, 441). On August 22, Williamson supported a prohibition on ex post facto clauses. He observed that in his own state, a similar provision had worked because it had given judges something to take hold of (II, 376). This suggests that he probably favored the power of judicial review, by which judges invalidate legislation that they believe to be unconstitutional in cases that litigants bring before them. Williamson thought that the congressional veto of state legislation was "unnecessary" (II, 391). On August 27, Williamson indicated that he thought the Constitution should grant Congress power to designate presidential successors (II, 427).

On August 29, Williamson supported a provision, which Southern states favored, to require two-thirds majorities of Congress to enact regulations of commerce. He did not believe the requirement for nine votes had defeated any needed measure under the Articles of Confederation (II, 450). Interestingly, Williamson said he favored the measure not because he thought it was actually needed to provide security for Southern states, which he believed could build their own ships if commercial regulations grew too heavy, but because he thought it would allay Southern fears. Similarly, on August 30, Williamson said that he thought that his state was disposed to give up its Western lands, which now included the state of Tennessee, but that he did not think the Constitution should compel it to do so (II, 462).

On September 7, at a time when some delegates were arguing that Congress should be able to enact treaties of peace more easily than other kinds of treaties, Williamson indicated that he favored similar majorities for these treaties as with others (II, 541; also see II, 543 and II, 549). Williamson was apparently concerned that, without such majorities, the interests of the distant states might be sacrificed to others (II, 548). This concern appears to have been important. Williamson went on to propose that the Senate should not be able to enter into treaties without giving its members "previous notice" and "a reasonable time for their attending" (II, 550).

Other Legislative Matters

On June 25, Williamson proposed the current six-year senatorial term. He offered a very practical reason, namely, that it would be easier to provide "rotation" for such a term than for the term of seven years that had been proposed (I, 409). As observed below, Williamson also pressed unsuccessfully for longer presidential terms.

On August 9, Williamson supported a motion by Virginia's Edmund Randolph allowing governors to appoint senators in cases of vacancy. Williamson thought that this was necessary since there would be cases when senators would resign or not accept their selection by the legislatures (II, 231).

Presidency

Number of Persons

On June 1, Williamson argued that there was little difference between having an executive and a council (presumably the proposed Council of Revision) and having a plural executive of three or more persons (I, 7; also see I, 97). On July 24, Williamson indicated that he personally favored a plural executive consisting of three men "taken from three districts into which the States should be divided" (II, 100). He thought that the veto power would make it especially problematic to invest powers in an individual from a single section. He also feared that a unitary executive would pave the way for a monarchy:

> Another objection agst. a single Magistrate is that he will be an elective king, and will feel the spirit of one. He will spare no pains to keep himself in for life, and will then lay a train for the succession of his children. It was pretty certain he thought that we should at some time or other have a King; but he wished no precaution to be omitted that might postpone the event as long as possible. (II, 101)

If the Convention were to stick with a unitary executive, Williamson thought that he should be ineligible to run again. Under such circumstances, he was willing to allow the president to serve for as long as 10 or 12 years (II, 101).

Selection

On June 2, Williamson said that he could see nothing but "trouble and expense" from selecting the president through a series of electors rather than allowing their representatives in Congress to do this (I, 81). On July 17, Williamson likened the selection of the president by the people to selection "by lot" (I, 32). He reasoned that in time most people would know few leaders outside their own state and that candidates in the largest states would therefore be the only ones elected (II, 32). Williamson did not think congressional selection would result in overdependency since the presidential salary would be fixed and presidents would not be eligible for a second term (II, 32). When on July 19 the Convention tentatively settled on a system of electors, Williamson seconded a motion to keep the president from being eligible for another term. He expressed his lack of confidence in the electors and his fears that "they would be liable to undue influence" (II, 58).

Williamson appears to have proposed one aspect of the current Electoral College when on July 20 he proposed that after the first elections, each state should have a number of electors equal to its membership in the House of Representatives (II, 64); the Convention eventually combined this number with the number of U.S. senators. The next day, Williamson proposed that the national government should provide compensation for the presidential electors (II, 73).

Williamson advanced the seed of another provision of the Electoral College on July 25 when he proposed that each elector should vote for three candidates (they would eventually vote for two), with the hope that only the first candidate would be from his own state (II, 113). When the Convention was discussing the possibility that the Senate should select the president in cases when none received a majority, Williamson objected that this might give this body too much power and suggested that it should have to choose between the top two candidates (II, 501). Williamson was particularly concerned that allowing the Senate too much choice "lays a certain foundation for corruption & aristocracy" (II, 512). In a speculation that has been emulated by scores of later observers, he pointed out that, with each state having a single vote, and a simple majority of the Senate being necessary to make such a choice, it is possible that a choice might be made by senators representing no more than one-sixth of the people (II, 514). He later supported the provision moving the power to choose presidents in cases when none had a majority of the Electoral College from the Senate to the U.S. House of Representatives (II, 522). He feared that choice by the Senate in such cases would tilt the government in an aristocratic direction (II, 524). When the Convention decided to allow the House to make this decision, Williamson successfully proposed that it should make such a choice by states, rather than per capita (II, 527).

Powers and Privileges

On June 2 Williamson proposed that the president should be removeable by conviction of impeachment for "mal-practice or neglect of duty" (I, 88). On June 6 he advocated that a conditional veto, one that two-thirds majorities of Congress could override, was preferable to entrusting an absolute veto in the president and a Council of Revision (I, 140). On June 8 he expressed further reservations about any veto system "that might restrain the States from regulating their internal police (I, 165). On August 7, Williamson introduced a motion to limit executive vetoes to "legislative acts" (II, 196).

On August 15, Williamson proposed that it should take a congressional majority of three-fourths, rather than two-thirds, to override a presidential veto (II, 301). At this time, he also advocated vesting the veto solely in the president rather than in the president and members of the judiciary, whom he did not think should have a hand in legislation. However, on September 12, Williamson moved to reconsider the provision requiring three-fourths of Congress to override a presidential veto in favor of the current two-thirds. Observing that he had changed his mind on the subject, he now argued that "the former puts too much in the power of the President" (II, 585). Subsequently saying that he was "less afraid of too few than of too many laws," he indicated that he feared the three-fourths requirement would make unnecessary laws too difficult to repeal (II, 586).

Length of Term

On July 19, Williamson advocated a six-year presidential term. He argued both that more frequent elections would prove to be too expensive and that if elections were too often repeated, "the best men will not undertake the service and those of an inferior character will be liable to be corrupted" (II, 59). In apparent support of an effort to go back to legislative selection of the president rather than selection by electors, Williamson supported a seven-year term on July 24 (II, 100). On September 6, Williamson unsuccessfully proposed presidential terms of seven years and six years in place of the four-year term that the Convention had by then adopted (II, 525).

Vice Presidency

On September 7, Williamson expressed his opposition to the creation of the vice presidency. He observed that "He was introduced only for the sake of a valuable mode of election which required two to be chosen at the same time" (II, 537).

Judiciary

On August 24, Williamson indicated that he wanted to postpone, rather than strike, a complicated procedure designed to settle land disputes between states. He suggested that such a provision might be needed "in cases where the Judiciary were interested or too closely connected with the parties" (II, 401).

Slavery

On August 22 Williamson probably helped pave the way for a compromise on slavery by observing that his home state permitted duties on slave imports. Williamson did not think his state would join the new government if it were to be prohibited from importing slaves, and he thought "it was wrong to force any thing down, not absolutely necessary, and which any State must disagree to" (II, 373).

On August 25, Williamson further clarified his views. After Gouverneur Morris of Pennsylvania proposed that the Constitution should limit slave importation to the two Carolinas and Georgia, thus subjecting them to special scrutiny, Williamson objected. Noting that "both in opinion & practice he was, against slavery," he added that he "thought it more in favor of humanity, from a view of all circumstances, to let in S-C & Georgia on those terms, than to exclude them from the Union" (II, 415–416).

Other Matters

During the discussion as to whether the Convention should begin each day with prayer, Williamson rather pragmatically observed that the real reason the Convention had not made provision for doing so was that "the Convention had no funds" (I, 452). When the Convention was discussing a provision to bind state officials by oath to support the U.S. Constitution, Williamson proposed that national officers should take a reciprocal oath to support the constitutions of the states (II, 87).

On July 26, Williamson favored a provision to bar the national capital from being established in a city with a state capitol, but he feared that putting such a provision within the Constitution would stir opposition in such capitals and might be evaded by a state later moving its capital to the national capital (II, 127). He later expressed the fear that the capital would never leave New York City (II, 262), a city quite distant from his own state.

Ratification

On July 23, Williamson expressed support for a provision whereby either state legislatures or state conventions could ratify the Constitution. He preferred the latter, believing that they were "more likely to be composed of the ablest men in the States" (II, 91). On September 10, Williamson indicated that he thought the Constitution should first be sent to Congress for its approval (II, 563). When the delegates were preparing to sign the Constitution on September 17, Williamson suggested that perhaps there would be greater unanimity if they would instead sign the accompanying letter. As for him, "he did not think a better plan was to be expected and had no scruples against putting his name to it" (II, 645).

Life after the Convention

Williamson left the Convention for Congress where he helped get the Constitution reported to the states. Although he missed North Carolina's first ratification convention because of his congressional service, he attended the next one and argued for its ratification. Married to Maria Apthorpe in 1789, when Williamson was 53, the couple had two sons, but Maria died delivering the second child, and both sons died in early manhood. Elected to Congress, he retired in 1793. He spent the rest of his life in New York where he died in 1819.

See Also North Carolina

FOR FURTHER READING

Craige, Burton. 1987. *The Federal Convention of 1787: North Carolina in the Great Crisis.* Richmond, VA: Expert Graphics.

Farrand, Max, ed. 1937. *The Records of the Federal Convention.* 4 vols. New Haven, CT: Yale University Press.

Hutson, James H., ed. 1987. *Supplement to Max Farrand's* The Records of the Federal Convention of 1787. New Haven, CT: Yale University Press.

Whitney, David C. 1974. *Founders of Freedom in America: Lives of the Men Who Signed the Constitution of the United States and So Helped to Establish the United States of America.* Chicago: J. J. Ferguson Publishing.

WILSON, JAMES (1742–1798)

James Wilson was a distinguished delegate in a state delegation (from Pennsylvania) of distin-

James Wilson, delegate from Pennsylvania and one of the first associate justices of the U.S. Supreme Court (1789–1798) (Collection of the Supreme Court of the United States)

guished delegates. A 41-year-old, foreign-born lawyer with heavy spectacles who later became a U.S. Supreme Court justice, Wilson was a strong proponent of popular election of both members of Congress and the presidency. He was a consistent advocate of a single executive and allied on many matters with James Madison. At the Convention, Wilson often read speeches for his ailing friend, Benjamin Franklin.

Born to a farm family near St. Andrews, Scotland on September 14, 1742, Wilson attended the University of St. Andrews in Scotland before immigrating to Pennsylvania in 1765. Initially employed as a Latin teacher at the College of Philadelphia, today's University of Pennsylvania, he subsequently studied law under John Dickinson. He established a legal practice in Reading, and later in Carlisle, Pennsylvania. He married Rachel Bird in 1769 and they had six children. Wilson married Hannah Gray in 1793, after the death of his first wife, but the only child of this second union did not survive.

Wilson was active in public affairs. He chaired the Carlisle Committee of Correspondence and served as a member of the Pennsylvania provincial convention. In 1768 Wilson published a manuscript entitled "Considerations on the Nature and Extent of the Legislative Authority of the British Parliament." As a delegate to the Continental Congress from 1775 to 1777, Wilson signed the Declaration of Independence (one of six signers of the U.S. Constitution to have done so). He also served from 1779 to 1782 as the advocate-general for France in the United States, and was appointed in 1782 as a director of the Bank of North America. Wilson served as a Pennsylvania delegate to the Congress under the Articles of Confederation from 1785 to 1787. Wilson was strongly opposed to the constitution that Pennsylvania had adopted in 1776, believing that it was too democratic in character, and he was involved in a number of partisan battles over this document; militiamen actually fired at a crowd from his house in what has been called the Fort Wilson Riot. Wilson was closely allied with fellow delegate Robert Morris and was a strong supporter of the national bank. Only Gouverneur Morris is recorded as having spoken more frequently at the Convention than Wilson.

Congress

Powers and Limits

Wilson's first recorded comment at the U.S. Constitutional Convention indicates both his belief in democratic accountability and his hope for a stronger government. He thus observed on May 31, in defending the idea of popular election of members of the House of Representatives, that

> he was for raising the federal pyramid to a considerable altitude, and for that reason wished to give it as broad a basis as possible. No government could long subsist without the confidence of the people. In a republican Government this confidence was peculiarly essential. He also thought it wrong to increase the weight of the State Legislatures by making them the electors of the national Legislature. (Farrand 1937, I, 49)

Wilson thought that "it will have a most salutary influence on the credit of the U. States to remove the possibility of paper money" (II, 310). Although he thought that states had abused the power of taxing exports (II, 307), he believed that to deny this power to the general government would be unwisely "to take from the Common Govt. half the regulation of trade" (II, 362). Wilson apparently seconded a motion by Madison to allow a two-thirds majority of Congress to enact such taxes in the belief that such a power would be better than none at all (II, 363), but generally opposed such supermajorities (II, 375). He observed that "if every particular interest was to be secured, *unanimity* ought to be required" (II, 451). Wilson opposed the provision limiting congressional power to control slave importation (II, 372). He favored a motion by Benjamin Franklin to grant Congress the power to cut canals, believing they could become a source of governmental revenue (II, 615). Somewhat naively, Wilson, who had been one of the directors of the national bank, did not believe that listing a power to establish banks "would excite the prejudices & parties apprehended" (II, 616). He believed that the government would have the power to create "mercantile monopolies" as part of its "power to regulate trade" (II, 616). He also favored a motion by James Madison and Charles Pinckney granting Congress the power to establish a national university (II, 616).

The lawyerly side of Wilson was quite evident in his discussion of ex post facto laws. Apparently believing that such laws were legally invalid on their face, he professed that to insert such a prohibition would be to "proclaim that we are ignorant of the first principles of Legislation, or are constituting a Government which will be so" (II, 376). He further observed that such prohibitions had not been effective in state constitutions and that "both sides will agree to the principle & will differ as to its application" (II, 376). When Gouverneur Morris proposed that Congress should be able to suspend the writ of habeas corpus in cases of rebellion or invasion, Wilson doubted the necessity for such an exception in the belief that judges would be able to decide whether "to keep in Gaol or admit to Bail" (II, 438). Wilson did favor a re-

striction on state interference in private contracts (II, 440). He also seemed to question the propriety of the fugitive slave clause by observing that "this would oblige the Executive of the State to do it, at the public expence" (II, 443). On another occasion, in which the Convention was considering a measure to grant Congress power to punish offenses against the law of nations, Wilson, again reflecting his background as an attorney, observed that "to pretend to *define* the law of nations which depended on the authority of all the Civilized Nations of the World, would have a look of arrogance, that would make us ridiculous" (II, 615).

House of Representatives

In defending popular election of the House of Representatives on June 6, Wilson observed:

> The Govt. ought to possess not only 1st. the *force* but 2ndly, the *mind* or *sense* of the people at large. The Legislature ought to be the most exact transcript of the whole Society. Representation is made necessary only because it is impossible for the people to act collectively. (I, 133)

Wilson went on to argue that he thought that the people "would be rather more attached to the national Govt. than to the State Govts. as being more important in itself, and more flattering to their pride" (I, 133). He thought there would be less to fear from large districts, where it would be less possible for wicked men to practice intrigue, than in small ones (I, 133). On June 21, Wilson observed that he "considered the election of the 1st. branch by the people not only as the corner Stone, but as the foundation of the fabric: and that the difference between a mediate and immediate election was immense" (I, 359). Wilson favored annual election of members of the House of Representatives (I, 361). He opposed setting a fixed salary for its members or allowing state governments to fix such salaries (I, 373).

Consistent with his democratic leanings, Wilson said that he "was agst. abridging the rights of election in any shape" (I, 375). This included setting a minimum age of 25 for members of the

House (I, 375). Similarly, Wilson opposed establishing a long residency requirement for members of the House (II, 217), favoring three years over seven (II, 230–231; also see II, 251) and four over seven (II, 268); he similarly supported reducing the requirements for citizenship in the Senate (II, 272). As an immigrant, Wilson admitted that he was influenced by his own situation:

> Mr. Wilson said he rose with feelings which were perhaps peculiar; mentioning the circumstances of his not being a native, and the possibility, if the ideas of some gentlemen should be pursued, of his being incapacitated from holding a place under the very Constitution which he had shared in the trust of making. He remarked that an illiberal complexion which the motion would give to the System and the effect which a good system would have in inviting meritorious foreigners among us, and the discouragement & mortification they must feel from the degrading discrimination, now proposed. (II, 237)

He observed that "to be appointed to a place may be a matter of indifference. To be incapable of being appointed, is a circumstance grating, and mortifying" (II, 237). Later in the Convention, Wilson observed that foreign monarchs would use residency requirement for officeholding to discourage their subjects from emigrating to the U.S. (II, 272). On September 3, Wilson also observed that excluding members of Congress from other political offices "would be odious to those who did not wish for office, but did not wish either to be marked by so degrading a distinction" (II, 491).

Wilson further feared that making members of Congress ineligible to accept other offices would have precluded Congress from appointing George Washington as commander-in-chief (I, 376). Wilson favored solving the problem of legislative partiality to its members by taking all appointment powers out of its hands (I, 387). Wilson further argued that if members of Congress were ineligible for other offices, it would fail to attract individuals with the requisite talents. He observed that "the ambition which aspired to Offices of dignity and trust" was not "ignoble or culpable" (II, 288).

Consistent with the direct election of representatives, Wilson believed that states should receive proportional representation in the House of Representatives. He posed rhetorical questions: "Are not the citizens of Pena. equal to those of N. Jersey? does it require 150 of the former to balance 50 of the latter?" (I, 180). Observing that "We have been told that each State being sovereign, all are equal," Wilson responded, "So each man is naturally a sovereign over himself, and all men are therefore naturally equal" (I, 180). Acknowledging that "a new partition of the States is desirable," Wilson recognized that this was "evidently & totally impracticable" (I, 180). Despite such rhetoric, Wilson expressed an early willingness to accept the three-fifths clause, "this being the rule in the Act of Congress agreed to by eleven States, for apportioning quotas of revenue on the States" (I, 201). Wilson, however, wanted to make it clear that this concession was purely one of expediency:

> Are they admitted as Citizens? Then why are they not admitted on an equality with White Citizens? Are they admitted as property? then why is not other property admitted into the computation? These were difficulties however which he thought must be overruled by the necessity of compromise. (I, 587)

Wilson did, however, seek to cover the implications of this provision by observing that "less umbrage would perhaps be taken agst. an admission of the slaves into the Rule of representation, if it should be so expressed as to make them indirectly only an ingredient in the rule, by saying that they should enter into the rule of taxation: and as representation was to be according to taxation, the end would be equally attained" (I, 595).

After William Paterson had offered the New Jersey Plan as an alternative to the Virginia Plan, Wilson summarized the differences between the two plans. He concluded that "with regard to the power of the Convention, he conceived himself authorized to *conclude nothing*, but to be at liberty to *propose any thing*" (I, 253). He indicated that the nation needed new powers, but that he was among those who were reluctant to grant such powers to the Congress as currently configured, and that, for this and other reasons, he continued to favor the Virginia Plan. He later observed that "He had been 6 years in the 12 since the commencement of the Revolution, a member of Congress and had felt all its weaknesses" (I, 343) and observed that states had been given equal representation in the Articles "of necessity not of choice" (I, 343).

Wilson argued that it was necessary to keep the provision requiring that Congress publish a record of its proceedings. The people had a right to know what their government was doing. Moreover, if the delegates eliminated a requirement, which the Articles contained, people would be suspicious of the new government (II, 260).

The Senate

Early in the Convention, Wilson indicated that he favored popular election of both branches of Congress (also see I, 69). He proposed that members of the second branch could be chosen from larger districts, which would apparently have further undermined state sovereignty by crossing state lines (I, 52; also see I, 151). Wilson strongly opposed state legislative selection of senators. He feared that "the election of the 2d. branch by the Legislatures, will introduce & cherish local interests & local prejudices" (I, 406). Wilson continued to present a view of national citizenship: "The Genl. Govt. is not an assemblage of States, but of individuals for certain political purposes—it is not meant for the States, but for the individuals composing them: the *individuals* therefore not the *States,* ought to be represented in it" (I, 406).

Wilson seconded Nathaniel Gorham's motion for a six-year Senate term. Because he envisioned the Senate as dealing with some matters of foreign policy, Wilson thought that its members needed "to be made respectable in the eyes of foreign nations" (I, 426). To this end, he also supported the idea of nine-year Senate terms. Later in the Convention, Wilson argued that the Constitution should require the consent of both houses of Congress for the ratification of treaties (II, 538); he also feared that the requirement for ratification

by a two-thirds majority "puts it in the power of a minority to controul the will of a majority" (II, 540; also see II, 548–549).

Wilson continued to oppose equal state representation in the Senate. Like Madison, Wilson believed the issue was one of principle. Faced with threats that some of the small states might leave the Union, Wilson said, "the question will be shall less than ¼ of the U. States withdraw themselves from the Union, or shall more than ¾ renounce the inherent, indisputable, and unalienable rights of men, in favor of the artificial systems of States. If issue must be joined, it was on this point he would chuse to join it" (I, 482). Wilson reiterated that the Constitution was to be for the benefit of "*men,*" and not "for the imaginary beings called *States*" (I, 483). Governments could do too much or too little, and the problem with the Articles was that it was doing too little. States were valuable, but they should not be sovereign (I, 484).

Faced with the argument that a small Senate where states were represented proportionally might leave some states without any representation, Wilson suggested on June 30 that smaller states might be guaranteed one senator (I, 488). On July 14, he further supported a motion that Charles Pinckney of South Carolina introduced proposing that states have from one to five representatives in the Senate for a total of 36 (II, 5). Wilson feared that a malapportionment in the original Senate would simply grow with time: "A vice in the Representation, like an error in the first concoction, must be followed by disease, convulsions, and finally death itself" (II, 10). Moreover, Wilson linked the current infirmities of the Articles of Confederation to such state equality (II, 10).

Like Madison, Wilson did not believe that the "concession" offered on behalf of the smaller states by which money bills would originate in the House amounted to anything significant (I, 544; also see II, 4). Asked to compromise, Wilson said that he "was not deficient in a conciliating temper, but firmness was sometimes a duty of higher obligation" (I, 550). He later opposed the provision for originating money bills by observing that "with regard to the pursestrings, it was to be observed that the purse was to have two strings, one of which was in the hands of the H. of Reps. the other in those of the Senate. Both houses must concur in untying, and of what importance could it be which untied first, which last" (II, 275).

Representation of the Western States

On a day (July 13) when Gouverneur Morris was expressing reservations about the power that Western states would claim if they were represented like those in the East, Wilson declared that since "all men wherever placed have equal rights and are equally entitled to confidence, he viewed without apprehension the period when a few States should contain the superior number of people. The majority of people wherever found ought in all questions to govern the minority" (I, 605). Drawing upon a powerful analogy, he argued that jealousy over the growth of the Western states would prove no more productive than British jealousy over the growth of the colonies (I, 605). Whereas others were arguing about the correlation between the growth of population and the generation of wealth and suggesting that representation should be based partly on the latter, Wilson argued that

> he could not agree that property was the sole or the primary object of Governt. & Society. The cultivation & improvement of the human mind was the most noble object. With respect to this object, as well as to other *personal* rights, numbers were surely the natural & precise measure of Representation. (I, 605)

Presidency

Wilson had a major impact on the construction of the U.S. presidency. He proposed on June 2 that the executive branch should consist of a single individual (I, 65). He believed that a single magistrate would give "energy[,] dispatch and responsibility to the office" (I, 65). He apparently also favored a single executive as being more likely to keep secrets (see King's notes, I, 70). Wilson associated executive powers with "executing the laws,

and appointing officers" not appointed by Congress (I, 66), and he seconded a motion that James Madison made to this effect (I, 67). Wilson understood that the idea of a single executive would remind some delegates of a monarchy, but he observed that many states already had a single governor, and that these governors had not been kingly. Wilson argued that a government headed by a single man would be more tranquil than one in which three individuals fought for control (I, 96). Similarly, Wilson observed that an executive council might be more likely "to cover, than prevent malpractices" (I, 97). On June 16, Wilson futher observed that "In order to controul the Legislative authority, you must divide it. In order to controul the Executive you must unite it" (I, 254).

Wilson favored "an absolute negative" by the executive on congressional legislation as an appropriate means of "self-defense," but he was willing to accept Madison's proposal to give this power jointly to the executive and members of the judiciary (I, 98; also see I, 104 and I, 138). He believed that the mere threat of such a veto would often be effective and that, if legislators realized that the president had such power, it "would refrain from such laws, as it would be sure to defeat" (I, 100). After the Convention rejected the idea of an absolute veto, Wilson argued that Congress should have to muster a majority of three-fourths of its members, rather than a mere two-thirds, to override such vetoes (I, 301).

Just as he believed the people should select members of Congress, so too, Wilson favored the direct election of the president by the people. Acknowledging that some might think such a proposal to be "chimerical," Wilson believed that experience in New York and Massachusetts had demonstrated that this could be both "a convenient & successful mode" (I, 68). Wilson believed that if the people selected both branches of Congress and the president, all would have sufficient independence (I, 69). Although he favored direct election, Wilson appears to have been the first at the Convention to have proposed a kind of Electoral College. He first advanced this idea on June 2 (I, 80). On July 17, Wilson was still defending popular election of the president, suggesting that the legislature could choose among candidates in the case that none received a majority of the votes (II, 30). On another occasion, Wilson suggested that a select number of congressmen, chosen by lot, might select the president (II, 103, 105). Wilson was on record as stating that the method of choosing the president was "the most difficult of all on which we have had to decide" (II, 501). He feared that the initial committee proposal for the Electoral College was too aristocratic in giving the power to choose the president when no majority was reached in the Senate. His objections helped shift this responsibility to the House (II, 522–523).

Judges

Consistent with his view of a strong presidency, Wilson favored executive, rather than legislative, appointment of judges (I, 119; also see II, 389), but was willing to accept presidential nomination and senatorial confirmation as a second best alternative (II, 41). He also favored the establishment of lower federal courts and thought they would be essential in admiralty cases (I, 124–125).

Wilson proposed on July 21 that the Constitution should associate members of the judiciary with the executive in a Council of Revision. He accepted the idea that judges would have power to invalidate legislation, the power known today as judicial review, in the course of examining cases, but he did not think this would be adequate:

> There was weight in this observation; but this power of the Judges did not go far enough. Laws may be unjust, may be unwise, may be danger-ous, may be destructive; and yet not be so uncon-stitutional as to justify the Judges in refusing to give them effect. Let them have a share in the Re-visionary power, and they will have an opportu-nity of taking notice of these characters of a law, and of counteracting, by the weight of their opin-ions the improper views of the Legislature. (II, 73)

In defending a Council of Revision, Wilson ar-gued that "the separation of the departments does not require that they should have separate objects but that they should act separately tho' on the same objects" (II, 78). He further argued that "the joint weight of the two departments was necessary to balance the single weight of the Legislature" (II, 79). Wilson was still making this argument on August 14. Drawing from the practice of parlia-mentary sovereignty in Britain, Wilson observed that "after the destruction of the King in Great Britain, a more pure and unmixed tyranny sprang up in the parliament than had been exercised by the monarch." He further insisted that the Coun-cil of Revision was an appropriate defensive power against legislative tyranny (II, 301). He thought that a council would be a more appropri-ate body to confirm presidential appointees than would the Senate (II, 542).

Wilson strongly opposed a provision allowing the president to remove judges on the application of Congress. He observed that "the Judges would be in a bad situation if made to depend on every gust of faction which might prevail in the two branches of our Govt." (II, 429).

Federalism

Wilson was clearly less attached to state govern-ments than to the national government that he envisioned, but when Delaware's George Read suggested the possible abolition of the states, Wil-son said that "He saw no incompatability be-tween the national & State Govts. provided the latter were restrained to certain local purposes" (I, 137). He further argued that past confederacies had demonstrated a greater tendency by the parts to swallow the whole than vice versa (I, 137; also see I, 355). Wilson often had to defend his inten-tions in regard to the states. On June 7, he re-sponded to John Dickinson by observing that

> he did not see the danger of the States being de-voured by the Nationl. Govt. On the contrary, he wished to keep them from devouring the na-tional Govt. He was not however for extinguish-ing these planets as was supposed by Mr. D.—nei-ther did he on the other hand, believe that they would warm or enlighten the Sun. (I, 153)

As on previous occasions, he favored election of members of Congress from large districts, which, it would appear, would not necessarily have been restricted to existing state lines (I, 153–154).

On June 8, Wilson attempted further to explain his view of the relation between the state and national governments, in defending a congressional negative over state laws:

Federal liberty is to States, what civil liberty, is to private individuals. And States are not more unwilling to purchase it, by the necessary concession of their political sovereignty, than the savage is to purchase Civil liberty by the surrender of the personal sovereignty, which he enjoys in a State of nature. (I, 166)

In this same speech, Wilson hearkened back to the First Continental Congress, observing that "among the first sentiments expressed . . . was that Virga. is no more. That Massts. is no [more], that Pa. is no more &c. We are now one nation of brethren" (I, 166).

On June 19, Wilson again found himself having to explain that he did not favor a national government that "would swallow up the State Govt's as seemed to be wished by some gentlemen" (I, 322). He argued that every large government needed subdivisions and that the states might not "only subsist but subsist on friendly terms" (I, 322). Citing the Declaration of Independence, Wilson argued that when the colonies declared their independence, they declared their independence "not Individually but Unitedly and that they were confederated as they were independent, States" (I, 324).

Wilson favored the guarantee clause as a way of securing the states "agst. dangerous commotions, insurrections and rebellions" (II, 47). He was responsible for a rewording of the clause that made it more palatable to fellow delegates (II, 49).

Wilson evidenced his nationalism in his support for a congressional veto of state laws. Arguing that this was "the key-stone wanted to compleat the wide arch of Government we are raising," he stated that such a veto would give the national government the necessary means of self-defense. Still anticipating judicial invalidation of unconstitutional legislation, Mason argued that

"It will be better to prevent the passage of an improper law, than to declare it void when passed" (II, 391).

Wilson favored a motion whereby states could not be forced to divide unless a majority in the state wanted to do so (II, 456; II, 462). He wanted to leave state claims to Western lands as they were under the Articles (II, 465).

Miscellaneous

Wilson was one of the few delegates to express reservations about the efficacy of binding members of the government through oaths. He observed that "he was never fond of oaths, considering them as a left handed security only" (II, 87). He explained that "A good Govt. did not need them, and a bad one could not or ought not to be supported" (II, 87). He also feared that individuals might feel so bound to an existing government that they would prove unwilling to make necessary changes.

Wilson was one of five delegates to serve on the influential Committee of Detail, which the Convention commissioned on July 24, and he later also served on the Committee on Interstate Comity and Bankruptcy, which the Convention formed on August 29. In defending the decision of the first committee not to formulate a uniform suffrage requirement, Wilson observed that the committee had found it difficult to come up with such a uniform rule and that it was important to avoid "unnecessary innovations." He explained: "It would be very hard & disagreeable for the same persons, at the same time, to vote for representatives in the State Legislature and to be excluded from a vote for those in the Natl. Legislature" (II, 201).

Wilson is believed to have influenced the provision in the Constitution related to treason. His statements on the subject indicated that he could see the advantages and disadvantages of allowing both the nation and the states to prosecute treason as well as the provision providing that conviction of treason should require the testimony of two or more witnesses to an overt act (II, 348).

Ratification and Amendment

Less than two weeks into Convention deliberations, Wilson was proposing that the new Constitution might go into effect when ratified by a plurality of the states, "with a door open for the accession of the rest" (I, 123). Responding on August 30 to suggestions that nine or 10 states might ratify the Constitution, he suggested that eight states would be an appropriate number to ratify the Constitution (II, 469). Consistent with his belief in democracy, Wilson subsequently supported Madison's unsuccessful motion for ratification by a majority of people in a majority of the states (II, 477).

Wilson strongly opposed the idea of allowing Congress to decide whether or not to approve the new Constitution. When such a measure was being considered, he opined that "After spending four or five months in this laborious & arduous task of forming a Government for our Country, we are ourselves at the close throwing insuperable obstacles in the way of its success" (II, 562). Wilson was the delegate who proposed ratification of constitutional amendments by three-fourths of the states after losing a similar proposal for ratification by two-thirds (II, 558–559).

Life after the Convention

In the month following the Constitutional Convention, Wilson gave a speech in support of the new document; Wilson's words, including arguments as to why he did not think a bill of rights was necessary, were widely reprinted. Wilson was the only delegate who attended the Constitutional Convention from Pennsylvania who was also selected to serve in the state ratifying convention, where he provided distinguished service. Wilson subsequently became the chief author of the new Pennsylvania Constitution, which included a number of features of the new Constitution, including the institution of a bicameral legislature.

Wilson served from 1789 to 1798 as an associate justice of the United States Supreme Court, writing one of the decisions for the majority in

Chisholm v. Georgia (1793), which the Eleventh Amendment overturned. From 1790 to 1791 he was the first professor of law to teach at the University of Philadelphia, where he delivered lectures, attended by George Washington and other notables, on the new government he had helped to create.

Long involved in speculation in Western lands, as well as a variety of other entrepreneurial activities, Wilson's land speculations ultimately bankrupted him. He ultimately resettled in New Jersey, and then fled to North Carolina (where he was imprisoned for a time) to avoid his creditors. He died at the home of fellow justice James Iredell at Edenton, North Carolina on August 21, 1798. Originally buried in North Carolina, his remains were moved to Christ Church in Philadelphia in 1906 in a ceremony that several members of the U.S. Supreme Court attended.

See Also Pennsylvania

FOR FURTHER READING

Conrad, Stephen A. 1985. "Polite Foundation: Citizenship and Common Sense in James Wilson's Republican Theory." In Philip B. Kurland, Gerhard Casper, and Dennis J. Hutchinson, eds. *The Supreme Court Review, 1984.* Chicago: University of Chicago Press, 359–388.

Cushman, Clare, ed. 1995. *The Supreme Court Justices: Illustrated Biographies, 1789–1995.* Washington, DC: Congressional Quarterly.

Farrand, Max, ed. 1937. *The Records of the Federal Convention.* 4 vols. New Haven, CT: Yale University Press.

Ferris, Robert G. 1976. *Signers of the Constitution.* Washington, DC: United States Department of the Interior, National Park Service.

Linder, Douglas D. 1985. "The Two Hundredth Reunion of Delegates to the Constitutional Convention (Or, 'All Things Considered, We'd Really Rather Be in Philadelphia')." *Arizona State Law Review* 1985: 823–863.

McLaughlin, Andrew C. 1897. "James Wilson in the Philadelphia Convention." *Political Science Quarterly* 12 (March): 1–20.

Seed, Geoffrey. 1978. *James Wilson.* Millwood, NY: kto press.

Smith, Charles Page. 1956. *James Wilson: Founding Father, 1742–1798.* Chapel Hill: University of North Carolina Press.

Wills, Garry. 1987. "Interview with a Founding Father." *American Heritage* 38 (May/June): 83–88.

WOMEN

Delegates did not specifically discuss women's rights (at least, not as distinct from the rights of other persons) at the Constitutional Convention, and no delegate appears to have suggested that women might one day occupy public offices. Thus, the Constitution contains no specific mention of women or women's rights. In contrast to the Declaration of Independence, however (with its words "all men are created equal"—words that might very well be understood to include all persons), the language of the Constitution is largely gender-neutral, with the term "person" or "persons" used instead of "man" or "men." However, the Constitution occasionally used the male pronoun "he" to refer to the president.

The term "sex" was used at the Convention to designate both men and women in a resolution that Pennsylvania's James Wilson first offered on June 11. In describing how he thought the House of Representatives should be equitably apportioned, Wilson, in a motion that South Carolina's Charles Cotesworth Pinckney seconded, proposed that this representation be made

> in proportion to the whole number of white & other free Citizens & inhabitants of every age sex & condition including those bound to servitude for a term of years and three fifths of all other persons not comprehended in the foregoing description, except Indians not paying taxes, in each State. (Farrand 1937, I, 201)

The Committee of the Whole voted to accept this motion by a 9-2 vote (I, 201; also see II, 227, 237). The Convention eventually forwarded it to the Committee of Style and Arrangement (II, 571). This committee, in turn, compressed the language into its ultimate form, which referred to "the whole number of free persons, including those bound to servitude for a term of years, and excluding Indians not taxed, three fifths of all other persons" (II, 590).

Jan Lewis, a close scholar of the subject, has observed, however, that whereas the delegates had previously voted both to delete the word "white" as superfluous (II, 350) and to replace the word "servitude" for "service" (II, 607), they had adopted no such change in the language regarding "sex" (Lewis 1999, 116–117). She thus concludes that the committee change was intended to be merely a stylistic one that did not change Wilson's original inclusion of women in the polity (Lewis, 117). She further concludes that the Constitution did intend to include women. Indeed, she argues that the acceptance of Wilson's motion represented the first occasion in what any government had considered basing representation "upon inhabitants rather than taxpayers or adult men" (Lewis, 118). She further observes, however, that the Founders chiefly anticipated that women's chief citizenship would be in the civil rather than in the political realm (Lewis, 129).

Similarly, Rosemarie Zagarri has concluded that early Americans often applied an individualistic Lockean view of rights to men and the view often associated with the Scottish Enlightenment (tying rights to duties, often of a domestic nature) to women. She further observes that Mary Wollstonecraft's *Vindication of the Rights of Woman*, which pushed thinking about women closer to the Lockean view, was not published until 1792 (Zagarri 1998).

Much to the chagrin of women like Susan B. Anthony (1820–1906) and Elizabeth Cady Stanton (1815–1902), who had worked for the emancipation of American blacks and who had often tied this cause to their own desire for suffrage, the word "male" finally entered the Constitution not with the Founding Fathers, but with the authors of the Fourteenth Amendment (ratified in 1868), who intended to penalize states that denied the right to vote to "male" inhabitants (see Vile 2003, 202). The U.S. Constitution neither extended the right to vote to women nor denied the vote to them; instead, it provided that the qualifications

"Remember the Ladies"

One of the most quoted discussions of women's rights in early U.S. history comes from the period that marks the Revolutionary War rather than that which marks the writing of the Constitution. The discussion is unique because it involves a husband and wife who were among the most thoughtful in America.

As John Adams was working at the Second Continental Congress, his devoted wife, Abigail, wrote to him expressing the hope that

> you would Remember the Ladies, and be more generous and favourable to them than your ancestors. Do not put such unlimited power into the hands of the Husbands. Remember all Men would be tyrants if they could. If particular care and attention is not paid to the Ladies we are determined to foment a Rebellion, and will not hold ourselves bound by any Laws in which we have no voice, or Representation. (Quoted in Dolbeare 1984, 81)

For all the attention the letter has received, John Adams appears to have taken it to be more of a joke than a serious request. Observing that "I cannot but laugh," he said:

> We have been told that our Struggle has loosened the bands of Government every where. That Children and Apprentices were disobedient—that schools and Colledges were grown turbulent—that Indians slighted their Guardians and Negroes grew insolent to their Masters. But your Letter was the first Intimation that another

Tribe more numerous and powerfull than all the rest were grown discontented. (Dolbeare, 81)

Although indicating that he was not about to surrender political power to women, John Adams indicated that he still thought they would have their sway in a democracy through the influence they exerted on their husbands. He thus continued:

> Depend upon it. We know better than to repeal our Masculine systems. Altho they are in full Force, you know they are little more than Theory. We dare not exert our Power in its full Latitude. We are obliged to go fair, and softly, and in Practice you know We are the subjects. We have only the Name of Masters, and rather than give up this, which would completely subject us to the Despotism of the Petticoat, I hope General Washington and all our brave Heroes would fight. (81–82)

It would take more than a century before the Constitution provided in the Nineteenth Amendment that individuals could not be denied the right to vote on the basis of gender.

FOR FURTHER READING

Dolbeare, Kenneth M. 1984. *American Political Thought.* Rev. ed. Chatham, NJ: Chatham House Publishers.

---

to vote in national elections would be the same as they were in state elections. At the time, no state had granted women the right to vote except New Jersey, where those with property were permitted to vote from 1776 to 1807. The U.S. Constitution did not prohibit discrimination in voting on the basis of sex until the ratification of the Nineteenth Amendment in 1920 (Vile, 324–327).

The Framers undoubtedly anticipated that most issues involving the rights of women would

be addressed at the state rather than the national level. Under the common law, such matters would largely have fallen into the area of domestic law, which was at the time almost solely supervised by state courts. Today the equal protection clause of the Fourteenth Amendment is the primary legal mechanism used to protect women's rights in federal courts. Although such an amendment failed at the national level, many states have also adopted equal rights amendments.

See Also African Americans; Suffrage

FOR FURTHER READING

Baker, Paula. 1984. "The Domestication of Politics: Women and American Political Society, 1780–1920." *American Historical Review* 89 (June): 620–647.

Belz, Herman. 1992. "Liberty and Equality for Whom: How to Think Inclusively about the Constitution and the Bill of Rights." *The History Teacher* 25 (May): 263–277.

Bingham, Marjorie Wall. 1990. *Women and the Constitution: Student Textbook.* Atlanta, GA: Communicorp.

Farrand, Max, ed. 1937. *The Records of the Federal Convention.* 4 vols. New Haven, CT: Yale University Press.

Goldwin, Robert A. 1990. *Why Blacks, Women, and Jews Are Not Mentioned in the Constitution, and Other Unorthodox Views.* Washington, DC: AEI Press.

Hoff-Wilson, Joan. 1989. *The History Teacher* 22 (February): 145–176.

Kerber, Linda K. 1985. "'Ourselves and Our Daughters Forever': Women and the Constitution, 1787–1876." *this Constitution*, no. 6 (Spring): 25–34.

Kerber, Linda K., et. al. 1989. "Beyond Roles, beyond Spheres: Thinking about Gender in the Early Republic." *William and Mary Quarterly*, 4th ser. (July): 565–585.

Lewis, Jan. 1999. "'Of Every Age Sex & Condition': The Representation of Women in the Constitution." In Edward Countryman, ed. *What Did the Constitution Mean to Early Americans?* Boston: Bedford/St. Martin's.

——. 1987. "The Republican Wife: Virtue and Seduction in the Early Republic." *William and Mary Quarterly*, 3rd ser. 44 (October): 689–721.

Schwarzenbach, Sibyl A., and Particia Smith, eds. 2003. *Women and the United States Constitution: History, Interpretation, and Practice.* New York: Columbia University Press.

Vile, John R. 2003. *Encyclopedia of Constitutional Amendments, Proposed Amendments, and Amending Issues, 1789–2002.* 2nd ed. Santa Barbara: ABC-CLIO.

West, Thomas G. 1997. *Vindicating the Founders: Race, Sex, Class, and Justice in the Origins of America.* Lanham, MD: Rowman and Littlefield Publishers.

Zagarri, Rosemarie. 1998. "The Rights of Man and Woman in Post-Revolutionary America." *William and Mary Quarterly*, 3rd ser. 55 (April): 203–230.

WYTHE, GEORGE (1726–1806)

George Wythe was born in Elizabeth City County, Virginia in 1726 to a planter family. His father died when he was three years old, but his gifted mother helped in his education, which was furthered by an apprenticeship to his uncle Stephen Dewey, who was an attorney. Wythe married Ann Lewis who died within eight months, and then moved to Williamsburg where he respectively served as acting attorney general, mayor, vestryman, and clerk of the House of Burgesses. Wythe gained such a reputation for integrity that he was sometimes likened to Aristides "the Just" of ancient Greece.

In colonial Williamsburg, Wythe established a residence with a new wife, Elizabeth Taliaferro (the house is still a tourist site); he also inherited a plantation from an older brother. In Williamsburg, Wythe served as a mentor to many young lawyers including Thomas Jefferson, St. George Tucker (who went on to become a prominent legal scholar), and later, Henry Clay. An early advocate of independence, Wythe was elected to serve in the Continental Congress where he signed the Declaration of Independence. He later helped re-

George Wythe, delegate from Virginia
(Pixel That)

vise the laws of Virginia. In 1779, he became the first professor of law in America (and only the second after Britain's William Blackstone, in the English-speaking world) with an appointment to the College of William and Mary. His students there included John Marshall, a cousin of James Madison with the same name, James Monroe, Spencer Roane, and others.

Wythe at the Convention

Wythe was present for the opening day of business at the Constitutional Convention on May 25 and chaired the Convention's first committee, the three-man Committee on Rules. There is a general consensus that this committee set forth orderly procedures that furthered debate and deliberation at the Convention.

On May 30, Wythe proposed that the Convention vote on one of the Randolph Resolutions to establish a government of three branches, but South Carolina's Pierce Butler said that it was not yet ready to do so (Farrand 1937, I, 41). On the next day, Wythe agreed with fellow Virginian James Madison in observing "that it would be right to establish general principles before we go into detail, or very shortly Gentlemen would find themselves in confusion, and would be obliged to have recurrence to the point from whence they sat out" (I, 60).

By June 10, Wythe was called home by his wife's sickness, an illness that resulted in her death shortly after his return. Madison recorded that Wythe had left a proxy vote in favor of establishing a single executive on June 4. Wythe subsequently resigned from the Convention (Hutson 1987, 121).

Life after the Convention

Wythe played a major role in the Virginia ratifying convention where he served as president of the Committee of the Whole and supported the new Constitution. Wythe continued in his role as a chancellor of Virginia (a role that often led to conflict with Edmund Pendleton), later moving to Richmond. Sadly, a nephew whom he had befriended, but who had gotten into debt, poisoned Wythe who died in 1806, after both forgiving and disinheriting his nephew. Wythe appears to have died embracing Christianity. His last reported words were "Let me die righteous!" (Dill 1979, 81). Today the William and Mary law school is named in honor of fellow Virginians John Marshall and George Wythe; a statue of the pair stands in front of the school's entrance.

See Also Committee on Rules; Rules of the Constitutional Convention; Virginia

FOR FURTHER READING

Dill, Alonzo. 1979. *George Wythe: Teacher of Liberty.* Williamsburg, Virginia Independence Bicentennial Commission.

Farrand, Max, ed. 1937. *The Records of the Federal Convention.* 4 vols. New Haven, CT: Yale University Press.

Hutson, James H., ed. 1987. *Supplement to Max Farrand's* The Records of the Federal Convention of 1787. New Haven, CT: Yale University Press.

Vile, John R. 2003. *Great American Judges: An Encyclopedia.* Vol. 2 of 2. Santa Barbara, CA: ABC-CLIO.

——, ed. 2001. *Great American Lawyers: An Encyclopedia.* Vol. 2 of 2. Santa Barbara, CA: ABC-CLIO.

YATES, ROBERT
(1738–1801)

Robert Yates was born in Schenectady, New York in 1738. After being educated in New York City, he read law under William Livingston, a future New Jersey governor who also attended the Constitutional Convention, and moved to Albany. He successively served as a city alderman, as a member of the Committee of Safety, as a member of the Provincial Congress, and as a justice of the New York State Supreme Court. He sat on the court from 1777 until 1798, serving as chief during his last eight years.

Actions at the Convention

Yates was seated on the opening day of the Convention on May 25. Like fellow delegate John Lansing, whom the state legislature had selected along with Yates, through the influence of New York's Governor George Clinton, Yates was in constant conflict with Alexander Hamilton, also from New York. Thus, on May 30 Yates and Hamilton split their votes, with Hamilton voting to establish a national government consisting of three branches, and Yates opposing the motion (Farrand 1937, I, 35). On May 31, Yates reports in notes that are a helpful supplement to those taken by James Madison of Virginia and some other delegates—but that were apparently compromised by partisan editing (see Hutson 1987, 412)—that he voted to accept a proposal for a bicameral Congress. He recorded that "As a previous resolution had already been agreed to, to have a supreme legislature, I could not see any objection to its being in two branches" (I, 55).

In notes that Yates made on June 9, it appears as though he added to a speech made by Paterson, probably reflecting his own sentiments on the subject. The paragraph in question upholds the equality of votes of states in a confederation and says that, without them, "there is an end to liberty" (I, 183). Yates further observed that "As long therefore as state distinctions are held up, this rule must invariably apply; and if a consolidated national government must take place, then state distinctions must cease, or the states must be equalized" (I, 183).

The delegates appointed Yates on July 2 to the committee that was responsible for formulating the Great Compromise. Delegates subsequently appointed him to a committee on July 9 to reconsider the original allocation of votes in the U.S. House of Representatives. He left the Convention the next day. Luther Martin later reported that Yates and Lansing "had uniformly opposed the system, and, I *believe*, despairing of getting a *proper one* brought forward, or of *rendering any real service*, they returned no more" (III, 190).

Report to the Governor

Yates and Lansing offered a similar assessment in a report to New York governor George Clinton. In this report, they focused on two issues—what they believed to be the lack of authority on the part of the Convention to propose a new system rather than revising and amending the old one and their opposition to consolidated government. They suggested that the Convention could have fixed the system by granting to the existing government "the monies arising from a general system of revenue," power to regulate commerce, power to enforce treaties, and "other necessary matters of less moment" (III, 246). In arguments that Antifederalists frequently repeated, they argued that a consolidated government over a large territory would be likely to lead to oppression and expense. Once they recognized that the Convention was pursuing such an object, they indicated that they thought that further attendance "would be fruitless and unavailing" (III, 247).

Opposition to Ratification of the Constitution

Yates may have authored letters in the *New York Journal* in opposition to the new Constitution under the name of "Brutus." He went on to lead the Antifederalist opposition to the new Constitution at the ratifying convention in Poughkeepsie. He seriously underestimated the opposition, which was aided by the momentum of ratifications from other states and by eventual Federalist willingness to report the Constitution with a series of proposed amendments.

Subsequent Actions

Yates did later support the Constitution. In a notable charge to a grand jury after ratification of the Constitution, Yates observed:

> The proposed form of government for the Union has at length received the sanction of so many of the States as to make it the supreme law of the land, and it is not therefore any longer a question, whether or not its provisions are such as they ought to be in all their different branches.
>
> We, as good citizens, are bound implicitly to obey them, for the united wisdom of America has sanctioned and confirmed the act, and it would be little short of treason against the republic to hesitate in our obedience and respect to the Constitution of the United States of America. Let me therefore exhort you, Gentlemen, not only in your capacity as grand jurors, but in your more durable and equally respectable character as citizens, to preserve inviolate this charter of our national rights and safety, a charter second only in dignity and importance to the Declaration of our Independence. We have escaped, it is true, by the blessing of Divine Providence, from the tyranny of a foreign foe, but let us now be equally watchful in guarding against worse and far more dangerous enemies,—domestic broils and intestine divisions. (Quoted in *Secret Proceedings* 1838, 334)

Yates twice ran unsuccessfully for state governor. He died in 1801. At the time, he had little money, but he was proud of his refusal to profit from estates that the government had confiscated from Tories during the Revolutionary War.

See Also Antifederalists; Hamilton, Alexander; Lansing, John; Livingston, William; New York

FOR FURTHER READING

Bradford, M. M. 1994. *Founding Fathers: Brief Lives of the Framers of the United States Constitution.* 2nd ed. Lawrence: University Press of Kansas.

Farrand, Max, ed. 1937. *The Records of the Federal Convention.* 4 vols. New Haven, CT: Yale University Press.

Hutson, James H. 1987. "Riddles of the Federal Constitutional Convention." *William and Mary Quarterly,* 3rd ser. 44 (July): 411–423.

Secret Proceedings and Debates of the Convention Assembled at Philadelphia, in the Year 1787, for the Purpose of Forming the Constitution of the United States of America. 1838. Cincinnati: Alston Mygatt.

Appendix A: Materials Prior to the Constitutional Convention

THE MAYFLOWER COMPACT

In the name of God, Amen. We, whose names are underwritten, the Loyal Subjects of our dread Sovereign Lord, King *James*, by the Grace of God, of *Great Britain, France and Ireland*, King, *Defender of the Faith*, &c.

Having undertaken for the Glory of God, and Advancement of the Christian Faith, and the Honour of our King and Country, a Voyage to plant the first colony in the northern Parts of Virginia; Do by these Presents, solemnly and mutually in the Presence of God and one of another, covenant and combine ourselves together into a civil Body Politick, for our better Ordering and Preservation, and Furtherance of the Ends aforesaid; And by Virtue hereof to enact, constitute, and frame, such just and equal Laws, Ordinances, Acts, Constitutions, and Offices, from time to time, as shall be thought most meet and convenient for the general Good of the Colony; unto which we promise all due Submission and Obedience.

In Witness whereof we have hereunto subscribed our names at *Cape Cod* the eleventh of *November,* in the Reign of our Sovereign Lord, King *James* of *England, France,* and *Ireland,* the eighteenth, and of *Scotland* the fifty-fourth. *Anno Domini,* 1620

Mr. John Carver,
Mr. William Bradford,
Mr Edward Winslow,
Mr. William Brewster,
Isaac Allerton,
Myles Standish,
John Alden,
John Turner,
Francis Eaton,

James Chilton,
John Craxton,
John Billington,
Joses Fletcher,
John Goodman,
Mr. Samuel Fuller,
Mr. Christopher Martin,
Mr. William Mullins,
Mr. William White,
Mr. Richard Warren,
John Howland,
Mr. Steven Hopkins,
Digery Priest,
Thomas Williams,
Gilbert Winslow,
Edmund Margesson,
Peter Brown,
Richard Britteridge,
George Soule,
Edward Tilly,
John Tilly,
Francis Cooke,
Thomas Rogers,
Thomas Tinker,
John Ridgdale,
Edward Fuller,
Richard Clark,
Richard Gardiner,
Mr. John Allerton,
Thomas English,
Edward Doten,
Edward Liester

_____

Source: The Avalon Project, Yale Law School, http://

ALBANY PLAN OF UNION

It is proposed that humble application be made for an act of Parliament of Great Britain, by virtue of which one general government may be formed in America, including all the said colonies, within and under which government each colony may retain its present constitution, except in the particulars wherein a change may be directed by the said act, as hereafter follows.

1. That the said general government be administered by a President-General, to be appointed and supported by the crown; and a Grand Council, to be chosen by the representatives of the people of the several Colonies met in their respective assemblies.

2. That within __ months after the passing such act, the House of Representatives that happen to be sitting within that time, or that shall be especially for that purpose convened, may and shall choose members for the Grand Council, in the following proportion, that is to say,

   Massachusetts Bay 7
   New Hampshire 2
   Connecticut 5
   Rhode Island 2
   New York 4
   New Jersey 3
   Pennsylvania 6
   Maryland 4
   Virginia 7
   North Carolina 4
   South Carolina 4
   48

3. —who shall meet for the first time at the city of Philadelphia, being called by the President-General as soon as conveniently may be after his appointment.

4. That there shall be a new election of the members of the Grand Council every three years; and, on the death or resignation of any member, his place should be supplied by a new choice at the next sitting of the Assembly of the Colony he represented.

5. That after the first three years, when the proportion of money arising out of each Colony to the general treasury can be known, the number of members to be chosen for each Colony shall, from time to time, in all ensuing elections, be regulated by that proportion, yet so as that the number to be chosen by any one Province be not more than seven, nor less than two.

6. That the Grand Council shall meet once in every year, and oftener if occasion require, at such time and place as they shall adjourn to at the last preceding meeting, or as they shall be called to meet at by the President-General on any emergency; he having first obtained in writing the consent of seven of the members to such call, and sent duly and timely notice to the whole.

7. That the Grand Council have power to choose their speaker; and shall neither be dissolved, prorogued, nor continued sitting longer than six weeks at one time, without their own consent or the special command of the crown.

8. That the members of the Grand Council shall be allowed for their service ten shillings sterling per diem, during their session and journey to and from the place of meeting; twenty miles to be reckoned a day's journey.

9. That the assent of the President-General be requisite to all acts of the Grand Council, and that it be his office and duty to cause them to be carried into execution.

10. That the President-General, with the advice of the Grand Council, hold or direct all Indian treaties, in which the general interest of the Colonies may be concerned; and make peace or declare war with Indian nations.

11. That they make such laws as they judge necessary for regulating all Indian trade.

12. That they make all purchases from Indians, for the crown, of lands not now within the bounds of particular Colonies, or that shall not be within their bounds when some of them are reduced to more convenient dimensions.

13. That they make new settlements on such purchases, by granting lands in the King's name, reserving a quitrent to the crown for the use of the general treasury.

14. That they make laws for regulating and governing such new settlements, till the crown shall think fit to form them into particular governments.

15. That they raise and pay soldiers and build forts for the defence of any of the Colonies, and equip vessels of force to guard the coasts and protect the trade on the ocean, lakes, or great rivers; but they shall not impress men in any Colony, without the consent of the Legislature.

16. That for these purposes they have power to make laws, and lay and levy such general duties, imposts, or taxes, as to them shall appear most equal and just (considering the ability and other circumstances of the inhabitants in the several Colonies), and such as may be collected with the least inconvenience to the people; rather discouraging luxury, than loading industry with unnecessary burdens.

17. That they may appoint a General Treasurer and Particular Treasurer in each government when necessary; and, from time to time, may order the sums in the treasuries of each government into the general treasury; or draw on them for special payments, as they find most convenient.

18. Yet no money to issue but by joint orders of the President-General and Grand Council; except where sums have been appropriated to particular purposes, and the President-General is previously empowered by an act to draw such sums.

19. That the general accounts shall be yearly settled and reported to the several Assemblies.

20. That a quorum of the Grand Council, empowered to act with the President-General, do consist of twenty-five members; among whom there shall be one or more from a majority of the Colonies.

21. That the laws made by them for the purposes aforesaid shall not be repugnant, but, as near as may be, agreeable to the laws of England, and shall be transmitted to the King in Council for approbation, as soon as may be after their passing; and if not disapproved within three years after presentation, to remain in force.

22. That, in case of the death of the President-General, the Speaker of the Grand Council for the time being shall succeed, and be vested with the same powers and authorities, to continue till the King's pleasure be known.

23. That all military commission officers, whether for land or sea service, to act under this general constitution, shall be nominated by the President-General; but the approbation of the Grand Council is to be obtained, before they receive their commissions. And all civil officers are to be nominated by the Grand Council, and to receive the President-General's approbation before they officiate.

24. But, in case of vacancy by death or removal of any officer, civil or military, under this constitution, the Governor of the Province in which such vacancy happens may appoint, till the pleasure of the President-General and Grand Council can be known.

25. That the particular military as well as civil establishments in each Colony remain in their present state, the general constitution notwithstanding; and that on sudden emergencies any Colony may defend itself, and lay the accounts of expense thence arising before the President-General and General Council, who may allow and order payment of the same, as far as they judge such accounts just and reasonable.

Source: "Basic Readings in U.S. Democracy," U.S. Department of State, http://usinfo.state.gov/usa/infousa/facts/democrac/4.htm. State cites: Leonard W. Labaree, ed. 1959. *Papers of Benjamin Franklin.* New Haven, CT: Yale University Press. Vol. 5, 387–392.

VIRGINIA DECLARATION OF RIGHTS

A DECLARATION OF RIGHTS made by the representatives of the good people of Virginia, assembled in full and free convention which rights do pertain to them and their posterity, as the basis and foundation of government.

Section 1. That all men are by nature equally free and independent and have certain inherent rights, of which, when they enter into a state of society, they cannot, by any compact, deprive or divest their posterity; namely, the enjoyment of life and liberty, with the means of acquiring and possessing property, and pursuing and obtaining happiness and safety.

Section 2. That all power is vested in, and consequently derived from, the people; that magistrates are their trustees and servants and at all times amenable to them.

Section 3. That government is, or ought to be, instituted for the common benefit, protection, and security of the people, nation, or community; of all the various modes and forms of government, that is best which is capable of producing the greatest degree of happiness and safety and is most effectually secured against the danger of maladministration. And that, when any government shall be found inadequate or contrary to these purposes, a majority of the community has an indubitable, inalienable, and indefeasible right to reform, alter, or abolish it, in such manner as shall be judged most conducive to the public weal.

Section 4. That no man, or set of men, is entitled to exclusive or separate emoluments or privileges from the community, but in consideration of public services; which, nor being descendible, neither ought the offices of magistrate, legislator, or judge to be hereditary.

Section 5. That the legislative and executive powers of the state should be separate and distinct from the judiciary; and that the members of the two first may be restrained from oppression, by feeling and participating the burdens of the people, they should, at fixed periods, be reduced to a private station, return into that body from which they were originally taken, and the vacancies be supplied by frequent, certain, and regular elections, in which all, or any part, of the former members, to be again eligible, or ineligible, as the laws shall direct.

Section 6. That elections of members to serve as representatives of the people, in assembly ought to be free; and that all men, having sufficient evidence of permanent common interest with, and attachment to, the community, have the right of suffrage and cannot be taxed or deprived of their property for public uses without their own consent or that of their representatives so elected, nor bound by any law to which they have not, in like manner, assembled for the public good.

Section 7. That all power of suspending laws, or the execution of laws, by any authority, without consent of the representatives of the people, is injurious to their rights and ought not to be exercised.

Section 8. That in all capital or criminal prosecutions a man has a right to demand the cause and nature of his accusation, to be confronted with the accusers and witnesses, to call for evidence in his favor, and to a speedy trial by an impartial jury of twelve men of his vicinage, without whose unanimous consent he cannot be found guilty; nor can he be compelled to give evidence against himself; that no man be deprived of his liberty except by the law of the land or the judgment of his peers.

Section 9. That excessive bail ought not to be required, nor excessive fines imposed, nor cruel and unusual punishments inflicted.

Section 10. That general warrants, whereby an officer or messenger may be commanded to search suspected places without evidence of a fact committed, or to seize any person or persons not named, or whose offense is not particularly described and supported by evidence, are grievous and oppressive and ought not to be granted.

Section 11. That in controversies respecting property, and in suits between man and man, the ancient trial by jury is preferable to any other and ought to be held sacred.

Section 12. That the freedom of the press is one of the great bulwarks of liberty, and can never be restrained but by despotic governments.

Section 13. That a well-regulated militia, composed of the body of the people, trained to arms, is the proper, natural, and safe defense of a free state; that standing armies, in time of peace, should be avoided as dangerous to liberty; and that in all cases the military should be under strict subordination to, and governed by, the civil power.

Section 14. That the people have a right to uniform government; and, therefore, that no government separate from or independent of the government of Virginia ought to be erected or established within the limits thereof.

Section 15. That no free government, or the blessings of liberty, can be preserved to any people but by a firm adherence to justice, moderation, temperance, frugality, and virtue and by frequent recurrence to fundamental principles.

Section 16. That religion, or the duty which we owe to our Creator, and the manner of discharging it, can be directed only by reason and conviction, not by force or violence; and therefore all men are equally entitled to the free exercise of religion, according to the dictates of conscience; and that it is the mutual duty of all to practise Christian forbearance, love, and charity toward each other.

Source: National Archives, www.archives.gov/national_archives_experience/virginia_declaration_of_rights.html.

THE DECLARATION OF INDEPENDENCE

IN CONGRESS, July 4, 1776.

The unanimous Declaration of the thirteen united States of America,

When in the Course of human events, it becomes necessary for one people to dissolve the political bands which have connected them with another, and to assume among the powers of the earth, the separate and equal station to which the Laws of Nature and of Nature's God entitle them, a decent respect to the opinions of mankind requires that they should declare the causes which impel them to the separation.

We hold these truths to be self-evident, that all men are created equal, that they are endowed by their Creator with certain unalienable Rights, that among these are Life, Liberty and the pursuit of Happiness.—That to secure these rights, Governments are instituted among Men, deriving their just powers from the consent of the governed,—That whenever any Form of Government becomes destructive of these ends, it is the Right of the People to alter or to abolish it, and to institute new Government, laying its foundation on such principles and organizing its powers in such form, as to them shall seem most likely to effect their Safety and Happiness. Prudence, indeed, will dictate that Governments long established should not be changed for light and transient causes; and accordingly all experience hath shewn, that mankind are more disposed to suffer, while evils are sufferable, than to right themselves by abolishing the forms to which they are accustomed. But when a long train of abuses and usurpations, pursuing invariably the same Object evinces a design to reduce them under absolute Despotism, it is their right, it is their duty, to throw off such Government, and to provide new Guards for their future security.— Such has been the patient sufferance of these Colonies; and such is now the necessity which constrains them to alter their former Systems of Government. The history of the present King of Great Britain is a history of repeated injuries and usurpations, all having in direct object the establishment of an absolute Tyranny over these States. To prove this, let Facts be submitted to a candid world.

He has refused his Assent to Laws, the most wholesome and necessary for the public good.

He has forbidden his Governors to pass Laws of immediate and pressing importance, unless suspended in their operation till his Assent should be obtained; and when so suspended, he has utterly neglected to attend to them.

He has refused to pass other Laws for the accommodation of large districts of people, unless those people would relinquish the right of Representation in the Legislature, a right inestimable to them and formidable to tyrants only.

He has called together legislative bodies at places unusual, uncomfortable, and distant from the depository of their public Records, for the sole purpose of fatiguing them into compliance with his measures.

He has dissolved Representative Houses repeatedly, for opposing with manly firmness his invasions on the rights of the people.

He has refused for a long time, after such dissolutions, to cause others to be elected; whereby the Legislative powers, incapable of Annihilation, have returned to the People at large for their exercise; the State remaining in the mean time exposed to all the dangers of invasion from without, and convulsions within.

He has endeavoured to prevent the population of these States; for that purpose obstructing the Laws for Naturalization of Foreigners; refusing to pass others to encourage their migrations hither, and raising the conditions of new Appropriations of Lands.

He has obstructed the Administration of Justice, by refusing his Assent to Laws for establishing Judiciary powers.

He has made Judges dependent on his Will alone, for the tenure of their offices, and the amount and payment of their salaries.

He has erected a multitude of New Offices, and sent hither swarms of Officers to harrass our people, and eat out their substance.

He has kept among us, in times of peace, Standing Armies without the Consent of our legislatures.

He has affected to render the Military independent of and superior to the Civil power.

He has combined with others to subject us to a jurisdiction foreign to our constitution, and unacknowledged by our laws; giving his Assent to their Acts of pretended Legislation:

For Quartering large bodies of armed troops among us:

For protecting them, by a mock Trial, from punishment for any Murders which they should commit on the Inhabitants of these States:

For cutting off our Trade with all parts of the world:

For imposing Taxes on us without our Consent:

For depriving us in many cases, of the benefits of Trial by Jury:

For transporting us beyond Seas to be tried for pretended offences:

For abolishing the free System of English Laws in a neighbouring Province, establishing therein an Arbitrary government, and enlarging its Boundaries so as to render it at once an example and fit instrument for introducing the same absolute rule into these Colonies:

For taking away our Charters, abolishing our most valuable Laws, and altering fundamentally the Forms of our Governments:

For suspending our own Legislatures, and declaring themselves invested with power to legislate for us in all cases whatsoever.

He has abdicated Government here, by declaring us out of his Protection and waging War against us.

He has plundered our seas, ravaged our Coasts, burnt our towns, and destroyed the lives of our people.

He is at this time transporting large Armies of foreign Mercenaries to compleat the works of death, desolation and tyranny, already begun with circumstances of Cruelty & perfidy scarcely paralleled in the most barbarous ages, and totally unworthy the Head of a civilized nation.

He has constrained our fellow Citizens taken Captive on the high Seas to bear Arms against their Country, to become the executioners of their friends and Brethren, or to fall themselves by their Hands.

He has excited domestic insurrections amongst us, and has endeavoured to bring on the inhabitants of our frontiers, the merciless Indian Savages, whose known rule of warfare, is an undistinguished destruction of all ages, sexes and conditions.

In every stage of these Oppressions We have Petitioned for Redress in the most humble terms: Our repeated Petitions have been answered only by repeated injury. A Prince whose character is thus marked by every act which may define a Tyrant, is unfit to be the ruler of a free people.

Nor have We been wanting in attentions to our British brethren. We have warned them from time to time of attempts by their legislature to extend an unwarrantable jurisdiction over us. We have reminded them of the circumstances of our emigration and settlement here. We have appealed to their native justice and magnanimity, and we have conjured them by the ties of our common kindred to disavow these usurpations, which, would inevitably interrupt our connections and correspondence. They too have been deaf to the voice of justice and of consanguinity. We must, therefore, acquiesce in the necessity, which denounces our Separation, and hold them, as we hold the rest of mankind, Enemies in War, in Peace Friends.

We, therefore, the Representatives of the united States of America, in General Congress, Assembled, appealing to the Supreme Judge of the world for the rectitude of our intentions, do, in the Name, and by Authority of the good People of these Colonies, solemnly publish and declare, That these United Colonies are, and of Right ought to be Free and Independent States; that they are Absolved from all Allegiance to the British Crown, and that all political connection between them and the State of Great Britain, is and ought to be totally dissolved; and that as Free and Independent States, they have full Power to levy War, conclude Peace, contract Alliances, establish Commerce, and to do all other Acts and Things which Independent States may of right do. And for the support of this Declaration, with a firm reliance on the protection of divine Providence, we mutually pledge to each other our Lives, our Fortunes and our sacred Honor.

Source: National Archives.

CONSTITUTION OF MASSACHUSETTS, 1780

PREAMBLE

The end of the institution, maintenance, and administration of government is to secure the existence of the body-politic, to protect it, and to furnish the individuals who compose it with the power of enjoying, in safety and tranquillity, their natural rights and the blessings of life; and whenever these great objects are not obtained the people have a right to alter the government, and to take measures necessary for their safety, prosperity, and happiness.

The body politic is formed by a voluntary association of individuals; it is a social compact by which the whole people covenants with each citizen and each citizen with the whole people that all shall be governed by certain laws for the common good. It is the duty of the people, therefore, in framing a constitution of government, to provide for an equitable mode of making laws, as well as for an impartial interpretation and a faithful execution of them; that every man may, at all times, find his security in them.

We, therefore, the people of Massachusetts, acknowledging, with grateful hearts, the goodness of the great Legislator of the universe, in affording us, in the course of His providence, an opportunity, deliberately and peaceably, without fraud, violence, or surprise, of entering into an original, explicit, and solemn compact with each other, and of forming a new constitution of civil government for ourselves and posterity; and devoutly imploring His direction in so interesting a design, do agree upon, ordain, and establish the following declaration of rights and frame of government as the constitution of the commonwealth of Massachusets.

PART THE FIRST

A Declaration of the Rights of the Inhabitants of the Commonwealth of Massachusetts.

Article I. All men are born free and equal, and have certain natural, essential, and unalienable rights; among which may be reckoned the right of enjoying and defending their lives and liberties; that of acquiring, possessing, and protecting property; in fine, that of seeking and obtaining their safety and happiness.

Art. II. It is the right as well as the duty of all men in society, publicly and at stated seasons, to worship the Supreme Being, the great Creator and Preserver of the universe. And no subject shall be hurt, molested, or restrained, in his person, liberty, or estate, for worshipping God in the manner and season most agreeable to the dictates of his own conscience, or for his religious profession or sentiments, provided he doth not disturb the public peace or obstruct others in their religious worship.

Art. III. As the happiness of a people and the good order and preservation of civil government essentially depend upon piety, religion, and morality, and as these cannot be generally diffused through a community but by the institution of the public worship of God and of the public instructions in piety, religion, and morality: Therefore, To promote their happiness and to secure the good order and preservation of their government, the people of this commonwealth have a right to invest their legislature with power to authorize and require, and the legislature shall, from time to time, authorize and require, the several towns, parishes, precincts, and other bodies-politic or religious societies to make suitable provision, at their own expense, for the institution of the public worship of God and for the support and maintenance of public Protestant teachers of piety, religion, and morality in all cases where such provision shall not be made voluntarily.

And the people of this commonwealth have also a right to, and do, invest their legislature with authority to enjoin upon all the subject an attendance upon the instructions of the public teachers aforesaid, at stated times and seasons, if there be any on whose instructions they can conscientiously and conveniently attend.

Provided, notwithstanding, That the several towns, parishes, precincts, and other bodies-politic, or religious societies, shall at all times have the exclusive right of electing their public teachers and of contracting with them for their support and maintenance.

And all moneys paid by the subject to the support of public worship and of public teachers aforesaid shall, if he require it, be uniformly applied to the support of the public teacher or teachers of his own religious sect or denomination, provided there be any on whose instructions he attends; otherwise it may be paid toward the support of the teacher or teachers of the parish or precinct in which the said moneys are raised.

And every denomination of Christians, demeaning themselves peaceably and as good subjects of the commonwealth, shall be equally under the protection of the law; and no subordination of any sect or denomination to another shall ever be established by law.

Art. IV. The people of this commonwealth have the sole and exclusive right of governing themselves as a free, sovereign, and independent State, and do, and forever hereafter shall, exercise and enjoy every power, jurisdiction, and right which is not, or may not hereafter be, by them expressly delegated to the United States of America in Congress assembled.

Art. V. All power residing originally in the people, and being derived from them, the several magistrates and officers of government vested with authority, whether legislative, executive, or judicial, are the substitutes and agents, and are at all times accountable to them.

Art. VI. No man nor corporation or association of men have any other title to obtain advantages, or particular and exclusive privileges distinct from those of the community, than what rises from the consideration of services rendered to the public, and this title being in nature neither hereditary nor transmissible to children or descendants or relations by blood; the idea of a man born a magistrate, lawgiver, or judge is absurd and unnatural.

Art. VII. Government is instituted for the common good, for the protection, safety, prosperity, and happiness of the people, and not for the profit, honor, or private interest of any one man, family, or class of men; therefore the people alone have an incontestable, unalienable, and indefeasible right to institute government, and to reform, alter, or totally change the same when their protection, safety, prosperity, and happiness require it.

Art. VIII. In order to prevent those who are vested with authority from becoming oppressors, the people have a right at such periods and in such manner as they shall establish by their frame of government, to cause their public officers to return to private life; and to fill up vacant places by certain and regular elections and appointments.

Art. IX. All elections ought to be free; and all the inhabitants of this commonwealth, having such qualifications as they shall establish by their frame of government, have an equal right to elect officers, and to be elected, for public employments.

Art. X. Every individual of the society has a right to be protected by it in the enjoyment of his life, liberty, and property, according to standing laws. He is obliged, consequently, to contribute his share to expense of this protection; to give his personal service, or an equivalent, when necessary; but no part of the property of any individual can, with justice, be taken from him, or applied to public uses, without his own consent, or that of the representative body of the people. In fine, the people of this commonwealth are not controllable by any other laws than those to which their constitutional representative body have given their consent. And whenever the public exigencies require that the property of any individual should be appropriated to public uses, he shall receive a reasonable compensation therefor.

Art. XI. Every subject of the commonwealth ought to find a certain remedy, by having recourse to the laws, for all injuries or wrongs which he may receive in his person, property, or character. He ought to obtain right and justice freely, and without being obliged to purchase it; completely, and without any denial; promptly, and without delay, conformably to the laws.

Art. XII. No subject shall be held to answer for any crimes or no offence until the same if fully and plainly, substantially and formally, described to him; or be compelled to accuse, or furnish evidence against himself; and every subject shall have a right to produce all proofs that may be favorable to him; to meet the witnesses against him face to face, and to be fully heard in his defence by himself, or his counsel at his election. And no subject shall be arrested, imprisoned, despoiled, or deprived of his property, immunities, or privileges, put out of the protection of the law, exiled or deprived of his life, liberty, or estate, but by the judgment of his peers, or the law of the land.

And the legislature shall not make any law that shall subject any person to a capital or infamous punishment, excepting for the government of the army and navy, without trial by jury.

Art. XIII. In criminal prosecutions, the verification of facts, in the vicinity where they happen, is one of the greatest securities of the life, liberty, and property of the citizen.

Art. XIV. Every subject has a right to be secure from all unreasonable searches and seizures of his person, his houses, his papers, and all his possessions. All warrants, therefore, are contrary to this right, if the cause or foundation of them be not previously supported by oath or affirmation, and if the order in the warrant to a civil officer, to make search in suspected places, or to arrest one or more suspected persons, or to seize their property, be not accompanied with a special designation of the persons or objects of search, arrest, or seizure; and no warrant ought to be issued but in cases, and with the formalities, prescribed by the laws.

Art. XV. In all controversies concerning property, and in all suits between two or more persons, except in cases in which it has heretofore been otherways used and practised, the parties have a right to a trial by jury; and this method of procedure shall be held sacred, unless, in causes arising on the high seas, and such as relate to mariners' wages, the legislature shall hereafter find it necessary to alter it.

Art. XVI. The liberty of the press is essential to the security of freedom in a State; it ought not, therefore, to be restrained in this commonwealth.

Art. XVII. The people have a right to keep and to bear arms for the common defence. And as, in time of peace, armies are dangerous to liberty, they ought not to be maintained without the consent of the legislature; and the military power shall always be held in an exact subordination to the civil authority and be governed by it.

Art. XVIII. A frequent recurrence to the fundamental principles of the constitution, and a constant adherence to those of piety, justice, moderation, temperance, industry, and frugality, are absolutely necessary to preserve the advantages of liberty and to maintain a free government. The people ought, consequently, to have a particular attention to all those principles, in the choice of their officers and representatives; and they have a right to require of their lawgivers and magistrates an exact and constant observation of them, in the formation and execution of the laws necessary for the good administration of the commonwealth.

Art. XIX. The people have a right, in an orderly and peaceable manner, to assemble to consult upon the common good; give instructions to their representatives, and to request of the legislative body, by the way of addresses, petitions, or remonstrances, redress of the wrongs done them, and of the grievances they suffer.

Art. XX. The power of suspending the laws, or the execution of the laws, ought never to be exercised but by the legislature, or by authority derived from it, to be exercised in such particular cases only as the legislature shall expressly provide for.

Art. XXI. The freedom of deliberation, speech, and debate, in either house of the legislature, is so essential to the rights of the people, that it cannot be the foundation of any accusation or prosecution, action or complaint, in any other court of place whatsoever.

Art. XXII. The legislature ought frequently to assemble for address of grievances, for correcting, strengthening, and confirming the laws, and for making new laws, as the common good may require.

Art. XXIII. No subsidy, charge, tax, impost, or duties, ought to be established, fixed, laid, or levied, under any pretext whatsoever, without the consent of the people, or their representatives in the legislature.

Art. XXIV. Laws made to punish for actions done before the existence of such laws, and which have not been declared crimes by preceding laws, are unjust, oppressive, and inconsistent with the fundamental principles of a free government.

Art. XXV. No subject ought, in any case, or in any time, to be declared guilty of treason or felony by the legislature.

Art. XXVI. No magistrate or court of law shall demand excessive bail or sureties, impose excessive fines, or inflict cruel or unusual punishments.

Art. XXVII. In time of peace, no soldier ought to be quartered in any house without the consent of the owner; and in time of war, such quarters ought not be made but by the civil magistrate, in a manner ordained by the legislature.

Art. XXVIII. No person can in any case be subjected to law-martial, or to any penalties or pains, by virtue of that law, except those employed in the army or navy, and except the militia in actual service, but by authority of the legislature.

Art. XXIX. It is essential to the preservation of the rights of every individual, his life, liberty, property, and character, that there be an impartial interpretation of the laws, and administration of justice. It is the right of every citizen to be tried by judges as free, impartial, and independent as the lot of humanity will admit. It is, therefore, not only the best policy, but for the security of the rights of the people, and of every citizen, that the judges of the supreme judicial court should hold their offices as long as they behave themselves well, and that they should have honorable salaries ascertained and established by standing laws.

Art. XXX. In the government of this commonwealth, the legislative department shall never exercise the executive and judicial powers, or either of them; the executive shall never exercise the legislative and judicial powers, or either of them; the judicial shall never exercise the legislative and executive powers, or either of them; to the end it may be a government of laws, and not of men.

PART THE SECOND

The Frame of Government

The people inhabiting the territory formerly called the province of Massachusetts Bay do hereby solemnly and mutually agree with each other to form themselves into a free, sovereign, and independent body-politic or State, by the name of the commonwealth of Massachusetts.

CHAPTER I.—THE LEGISLATIVE POWER

Section 1.—The General Court

Article I. The department of legislation shall be formed by two branches, a senate and house of representatives; each of which shall have a negative on the other.

The legislative body shall assemble every year on the last Wednesday in May, and at such other times as they shall judge necessary; and shall dissolve and be dissolved on the day next preceding the said last Wednesday in May; and shall be styled the *General Court of Massachusetts.*

Art. II. No bill or resolve of the senate or house of representatives shall become a law, and have force as such, until it shall have been laid before the governor for his revisal; and if he, upon such revision, approve thereof, he shall signify his approbation by signing the same. But if he have any objection to the passing such bill or resolve, he shall return the same, together with his objections thereto, in writing, to the senate or house of representatives, in whichsoever the same shall have originated, who shall enter the objections sent down by the governor, at large, on their records, and proceed to reconsider the said bill or resolve; but if, after such reconsideration, two-thirds of the said senate or house of representatives shall, notwithstanding the said objections, agree to pass the same, it shall, together with the objections, be sent to the other branch of the legislature, where it shall also be reconsidered, and if approved by two-thirds of the members present, shall have the force of law; but in all such cases, the vote of both houses shall be determined by yeas and nays; and the names of the persons voting for or against the said bill or resolve shall be entered upon the public records of the commonwealth.

And in order to prevent unnecessary delays, if any bill or resolve shall not be returned by the governor within five days after it shall have been presented, the same shall have the force of law.

Art. III. The general court shall forever have full power and authority to erect and constitute judicatories and courts of record or other courts, to be held in the name of the commonwealth, for the hearing, trying, and determining of all manner of crimes, offences, pleas, processes, plaints, actions, matters, causes, and things whatsoever, arising or happening within the commonwealth, or between or concerning persons inhabiting or residing, or brought within the same; whether the same be criminal or civil, or whether the said crimes be capital or not capital, and whether the said pleas be real, personal, or mixed; and for the awarding and making out of execution thereupon; to which courts and judicatories are hereby given and granted full power and authority, from time to time, to administer oaths or affirmations, for the better discovery of truth in any matter in controversy, or depending before them.

Art. IV. And further, full power and authority are hereby given and granted to the said general court from time to time, to make, ordain, and establish all manner of wholesome and reasonable orders, laws, statutes, and ordinances, directions and instructions, either with penalties or without, so as the same be not repugnant or contrary to this constitution, as they shall judge to be for the good and welfare of this commonwealth, and for the government and ordering thereof, and of the subjects of the same, and for the necessary support and defence of the government thereof; and to name and settle annually, or provide by fixed laws, for the naming and settling all civil officers within the said commonwealth, the election, and constitution of whom are not hereafter in this form of government otherwise provided for; and to set forth the several duties, powers, and limits of the several civil and military officers of this commonwealth, and the forms of such oaths or affirmations as shall be respectively administered unto them for the execution of their several offices and places, so as the same be not repugnant or contrary to this constitution; and to impose and levy proportional and reasonable assessments, rates, and taxes, upon all the inhabitants of, and persons resident, and estates ly-

ing, within the said commonwealth; and also to impose and levy reasonable duties and excises upon any produce, goods, wares, merchandise, and commodities whatsoever, brought into, produced, manufactured, or being within the same; to be issued and disposed of by warrant, under the hand of the governor of this commonwealth, for the time being, with the advice and consent of the council, for the public service, in the necessary defence and support of the government of the said commonwealth, and the protection and preservation of the subjects thereof, according to such acts as are or shall be in force within the same.

And while the public charges of government, or any part thereof, shall be assessed on polls and estates, in the manner that has hitherto been practised, in order that such assessments may be made with equality, there shall be a valuation of estates within the commonwealth, taken anew once in every ten years at least, and as much oftener as the general court shall order.

CHAPTER I

Section 2.–Senate

Article I. There shall be annually elected, by the freeholders and other inhabitants of this commonwealth, qualified as in this constitution is provided, forty persons to be councillors and senators, for the year ensuing their election; to be chosen by the inhabitants of the districts into which the commonwealth may from time to time be divided by the general court for that purpose; and the general court, in assigning the numbers to be elected by the respective districts, shall govern themselves by the proportion of the public taxes paid by the said districts; and timely make known to the inhabitants of the commonwealth the limits of each district, and the number of councillors and senators to be chosen therein: *Provided,* That the number of such districts shall never be less than thirteen; and that no district be so large as to entitle the same to choose more than six senators.

And the several counties in this commonwealth shall, until the general court shall determine it necessary to alter the said districts, be districts for the choice of councillors and senators, (except that the counties of Dukes County and Nantucket shall form one district for that purpose,) and shall elect the following number for councillors and senators, viz:

Suffolk	Six
Essex	Six

Middlesex	Five
Hampshire	Four
Plymouth	Three
Barnstable	One
Bristol	Three
York	Two
Dukes County and Nantucket	One
Worcester	Five
Cumberland	One
Lincoln	One
Berkshire	Two.

Art. II. The senate shall be the first branch of the legislature; and the senators shall be chosen in the following manner, viz: There shall be a meeting on the first Monday in April, annually, forever, of the inhabitants of each town in the several counties of this commonwealth, to be called by the selectmen, and warned in due course of law, at least seven days before the first Monday in April, for the purpose of electing persons to be senators and councillors; and at such meetings every male inhabitant of twenty-one years of age and upwards, having a freehold estate of the value of sixty pounds, shall have a right to give in his vote for the senators for the district of which he is an inhabitant. And to remove all doubts concerning the meaning of the word "inhabitant," in this constitution, every person shall be considered as an inhabitant, for the purpose of electing and being elected into any office or place within this State, in that town, district, or plantation where he dwelleth or hath his home.

The selectmen of the several towns shall preside at such meetings impartially, and shall receive the votes of all the inhabitants of such towns, present and qualified to vote for senators, and shall sort and count them in open town meeting, and in presence of the town clerk, who shall make a fair record, in presence of the selectmen, and in open town meeting, of the name of every person voted for, and of the number of votes against his name; and a fair copy of this record shall be attested by the selectmen and the town clerk, and shall be sealed up, directed to the secretary of the commonwealth, for the time being, with a superscription expressing the purport of the contents thereof, and delivered by the town clerk of such towns to the sheriff of the county in which such town lies, thirty days at least before the last Wednesday in May, annually; or it shall be delivered into the secretary's office seventeen days at least before the said last Wednesday in May; and the sheriff of each county shall deliver all such certificates, by him received, into the secretary's office seventeen days before the said last Wednesday in May.

And the inhabitants of the plantations unincorporated, qualified as this constitution provides, who are or shall be empowered and required to assess taxes upon themselves toward the support of government, shall have the same privilege of voting for councillors and senators, in the plantations where they reside, as town inhabitants have in their respective towns; and the plantation meetings for that purpose shall be held annually, on the same first Monday in April, at such place in the plantations, respectively, as the assessors thereof shall direct; which assessors shall have like authority for notifying the electors, collecting and returning the votes, as the selectmen and town clerks have in their several towns by this constitution. And all other persons living in places unincorporated, (qualified as aforesaid,) who shall be assessed to the support of government by assessors of an adjacent town, shall have the privilege of giving in their votes for councillors and senators in the town where they shall be assessed, and be notified of the place of meeting by the selectmen of the town where they shall be assessed, for that purpose, accordingly.

Art. III. And that there may be a due convention of senators, on the last Wednesday in May, annually, the governor, with five of the council, for the time being, shall, as soon as may be, examine the returned copies of such records; and fourteen days before the said day he shall issue his summons to such persons as shall appear to be chosen by a majority of voters to attend on that day, and take their seats accordingly: *Provided, nevertheless,* That for the first year the said returned copies shall be examined by the president and five of the council of the former constitution of government; and the said president shall, in like manner, issue his summons to the persons so elected, that they may take their seats as aforesaid.

Art. IV. The senate shall be the final judge of the elections, returns, and qualifications of their own members, as pointed out in the constitution; and shall, on the said last Wednesday in May, annually, determine and declare who are elected by each district to be senators by a majority of votes; and in case there shall not be the full number of senators returned, elected by a majority of votes for any district, the deficiency shall be supplied in the following manner, viz: The members of the house of representatives, and such senators as shall be declared elected, shall take the names of such persons as shall be found to have the highest number of votes in such district, and not elected, amounting to twice the number of senators wanting, if there be so many voted for, and out of these shall elect by ballot a number of senators sufficient to fill up the vacancies in such district; and in this manner all such vacancies shall be filled up in every district of the commonwealth; and in like manner all vacancies in the senate, arising by death, removal out of the State or otherwise, shall be supplied as soon as may after such vacancies shall happen.

Art. V. *Provided, nevertheless,* That no person shall be capable of being elected as a senator who is not seized in his own right of a freehold within this commonwealth, of the value of three hundred pounds at least, or possessed of personal estate to the value of six hundred pounds at least, or of both to the amount of the same sum, and who has not been an inhabitant of this commonwealth for the space of five years immediately preceding his election, and, at the time of his election, he shall be an inhabitant in the district for which he shall be chosen.

Art. VI. The senate shall have power to adjourn themselves; provided such adjournments do not exceed two days at a time.

Art. VII. The senate shall choose its own president, appoint its own officers, and determine its own rules of proceedings.

Art. VIII. The senate shall be a court, with full authority to hear and determine all impeachments made by the house of representatives, against any officer or officers of the commonwealth, for misconduct and maladministration in their offices; but, previous to the trial of every impeachment, the members of the senate shall, respectively, be sworn truly and impartially to try and determine the charge in question, according to the evidence. Their judgment, however, shall not extend further than to removal from office, and disqualification to hold or enjoy any place of honor, trust, or profit under this commonwealth; but the part so convicted shall be, nevertheless, liable to indictment, trial, judgment, and punishment, according to the laws of the land.

Art. IX. Not less than sixteen members of the senate shall constitute a quorum for doing business.

CHAPTER I.

Section 3.—House of Representatives

Article I. There shall be, in the legislature of this commonwealth, a representation of the people, annually elected, and founded upon the principle of equality.

Art. II. And in order to provide for a representation of the citizens of this commonwealth, founded upon the principle of equality, every corporate town containing one hundred and fifty ratable polls, may elect one representative; every corporate town containing three hundred and seventy-five ratable polls, may elect two representatives; every corporate town containing six hundred ratable polls, may elect three representatives; and proceeding in that manner, making two hundred and twenty-five ratable polls the mean increasing number for every additional representative.

Provided, nevertheless, That each town now incorporated, not having one hundred and fifty ratable polls, may elect one representative; but no place shall hereafter be incorporated with the privilege of electing a representative, unless there are within the same one hundred and fifty ratable polls.

And the house of representatives shall have power, from time to time, to impose fines upon such towns as shall neglect to choose and return members of the same, agreeably to this constitution.

The expenses of travelling to the general assembly and returning home, once in every session, and no more, shall be paid by the government out of the public treasury, to every member who shall attend as seasonably as he can, in the judgment of the house, and does not depart without leave.

Art. III. Every member of the house of representatives shall be chosen by written votes; and, for one year at least next preceding his election, shall have been an inhabitant of, and have been seized in his own right of a freehold of the value of one hundred pounds, within the town he shall be chosen to represent, or any ratable estate to the value of two hundred pounds; and he shall cease to represent the said town immediately on his ceasing to be qualified as aforesaid.

Art. IV. Every male person being twenty-one years of age, and resident in any particular town in this commonwealth, for the space of one year next preceding, having a freehold estate within the same town, of the annual income of three pounds, or any estate of the value of sixty pounds, shall have a right to vote in the choice of a representative or representatives for the said town.

Art. V. The members of the house of representatives shall be chosen annually in the month of May, ten days at least before the last Wednesday of that month.

Art. VI. The house of representatives shall be the grand inquest of this commonwealth; and all impeachments made by them shall be heard and tried by the senate.

Art. VII. All money bills shall originate in the house of representatives; but the senate may propose or concur with amendments, as on other bills.

Art. VIII. The house of representatives shall have

power to adjourn themselves; provided such adjournments shall not exceed two days at a time.

Art. IX. Not less than sixty members of the house of representatives shall constitute a quorum for doing business.

Art. X. The house of representatives shall be the judge of the returns, elections, and qualifications of its own members, as pointed out in the constitution; shall choose their own speaker, appoint their own officers, and settle the rules and order of proceeding in their own house. They shall have authority to punish by imprisonment every person, not a member, who shall be guilty of disrespect to the house, by any disorderly or contemptuous behavior in its presence; or who, in the town where the general court is sitting, and during the time of its sitting, shall threaten harm to the body or estate of any of its members, for anything said or done in the house; or who shall assault any of them therefor; or who shall assault or arrest any witness, or other person, ordered to attend the house, in his way in going or returning; or who shall rescue any person arrested by the order of the house.

And no member of the house of representatives shall be arrested, or held to bail on mesne process, during his going unto, returning from, or his attending the general assembly.

Art. XI. The senate shall have the same powers in the like cases; and the governor and council shall have the same authority to punish in like cases; *Provided,* That no imprisonment, on the warrant or order of the governor, council, senate, or house of representatives, for either of the above-described offences, be for a term exceeding thirty days.

And the senate and house of representatives may try and determine all cases where their rights and privileges are concerned, and which, by the constitution, they have authority to try and determine, by committees of their own members, or in such other way as they may, respectively, think best.

CHAPTER II.–EXECUTIVE POWER

Section 1.–Governor

Article I. There shall be a supreme executive magistrate, who shall be styled "The governor of the commonwealth of Massachusetts;" and whose title shall be "His Excellency."

Art. II. The governor shall be chosen annually; and no person shall be eligible to this office, unless, at the time of his election, he shall have been an inhabitant of this commonwealth for seven years next preceding; and unless he shall, at the same time, be seized, in his own right, of a freehold, within the commonwealth, of the value of one thousand pounds; and unless he shall declare himself to be of the Christian religion.

Art. III. Those persons who shall be qualified to vote for senators and representatives, within the several towns of this commonwealth, shall, at a meeting to be called for that purpose, on the first Monday of April, annually, give in their votes for a governor to the selectmen, who shall preside at such meetings; and the town clerk, in the presence and with the assistance of the selectmen, shall, in open town meeting, sort and count the votes, and form a list of the persons voted for, with the number of votes for each person against his name; and shall make a fair record of the same in the town books, and a public declaration thereof in the said meeting; and shall, in the presence of the inhabitants, seal up copies of the said list, attested by him and the selectmen, and transmit the same to the sheriff of the county, thirty days at least before the last Wednesday in May; and the sheriff shall transmit the same to the secretary's office, seventeen days at least before the said last Wednesday in May; or the selectmen may cause returns of the same to be made, to the office of the secretary of the commonwealth, seventeen days at least before the said day; and the secretary shall lay the same before the senate and the house of representatives, on the last Wednesday in May, to be by them examined; and in case of an election by a majority of all the votes returned, the choice shall be by them declared and published; but if no person shall have a majority of votes, the house of representatives shall, by ballot, elect two out of four persons, who had the highest number of votes, if so many shall have been voted for; but, if otherwise, out of the number voted for; and make return to the senate of the two persons so elected; on which the senate shall proceed, by ballot, to elect one, who shall be declared governor.

Art. IV. The governor shall have authority, from time to time, at his discretion, to assemble and call together the councillors of this commonwealth for the time being; and the governor, with the said councillors, or five of them at least, shall and may, from time to time, hold and keep a council, for the ordering and directing the affairs of the commonwealth, agreeably to the constitution and the laws of the land.

Art. V. The governor, with advice of council, shall have full power and authority, during the session of the general court, to adjourn or prorogue the same at any time the two houses shall desire; and to dissolve the same on the day next preceding the last Wednesday in May; and, in the recess of the said court, to prorogue the same from time to time, not exceeding ninety days in any one recess; and to call it together sooner than the time to which it may be adjourned or prorogued, if the welfare of the commonwealth shall require the same; and in case of any infectious distemper prevailing in the place where the said court is next at any time to convene, or any other cause happening, whereby danger may arise to the health or lives of the members from their attendance, he may direct the session to be held at some other the most convenient place within the State.

And the governor shall dissolve the said general court on the day next preceding the last Wednesday in May.

Art. VI. In cases of disagreement between the two houses, with regard to the necessity, expediency, or time of adjournment or prorogation, the governor, with advice of the council, shall have a right to adjourn or prorogue the general court, not exceeding ninety days, as he shall determine the public good shall require.

Art. VII. The governor of this commonwealth, for the time being, shall be the commander-in-chief of the army and navy, and of all the military forces of the State, by sea and land; and shall have full power, by himself or by any commander, or other officer or officers, from time to time, to train, instruct, exercise, and govern the militia and navy; and, for the special defence and safety of the commonwealth, to assemble in martial array, and put in warlike posture, the inhabitants thereof, and to lead and conduct them, and with them to encounter, repel, resist, expel, and pursue, by force of arms, as by sea as by land, within or within the limits of this commonwealth; and also to kill, slay, and destroy, if necessary, and conquer, by all fitting ways, enterprises, and means whatsoever, all and every such person and persons as shall, at any time hereafter, in a hostile manner, attempt or enterprise the destruction, invasion, detriment, or annoyance of this commonwealth; and to use and exercise over the army and navy, and over the militia in actual service, the law-martial, in time of war or invasion, and also in time of rebellion, declared by the legislature to exist, as occasion shall necessarily require; and to take and surprise, by all ways and means whatsoever, all and every such person or persons, with their ships, arms, and ammunition, and other goods, as shall, in a hostile manner, invade, or attempt the invading, conquering, or annoying this commonwealth; and that the governor be intrusted with all these and other powers incident to the offices of captain-general and commander-in-chief,

and admiral, to be exercised agreeably to the rules and regulations of the constitution and the laws of the land, and not otherwise.

Provided, That the said governor shall not, at any time hereafter, by virtue of any power by this constitution granted, or hereafter to be granted to him by the legislature, transport any of the inhabitants of this commonwealth, or oblige them to march out of the limits of the same, without their free and voluntary consent, or the consent of the general court; except so far as may be necessary to march or transport them by land or water for the defence of such part of the State to which they cannot otherwise conveniently have access.

Art. VIII. The power of pardoning offences, except such as persons may be convicted of before the senate, by an impeachment of the house, shall be in the governor, by and with the advice of council; but no charter or pardon, granted by the governor, with the advice of the council, before conviction, shall avail the party pleading the same, notwithstanding any general or particular expressions contained therein, descriptive of the offence or offences intended to be pardoned.

Art. IX. All judicial officers, the attorney-general, the solicitor-general, all sheriffs, coroners, and registers of probate, shall be nominated and appointed by the governor, by and with the advice and consent of the council; and every such nomination shall be made by the governor, and made at least seven days prior to such appointment.

Art. X. The captains and subalterns of the militia shall be elected by the written votes of the train-band and alarm-list of their respective companies, of twenty years of age and upwards; the field-officers of regiments shall be elected by the written votes of the captains and subalterns of their respective regiments; the brigadiers shall be elected, in like manner, by the field-officers of their respective brigades; and such officers, so elected, shall be commissioned by the governor, who shall determine their rank.

The legislature shall, by standing laws, direct the time and manner of convening the electors, and of collecting votes, and of certifying to the governor the officers elected.

The major-generals shall be appointed by the senate and house of representatives, each having a negative upon the other; and be commissioned by the governor.

And if the electors of brigadiers, field-officers, captains, or subalterns shall neglect or refuse to make such elections, after being duly notified, according to the laws for the time being, then the governor, with the advice of council, shall appoint suitable persons to fill such offices.

And no officer, duly commissioned to command in the militia, shall be removed from his office, but by the address of both houses to the governor, or by fair trial in court-martial, pursuant to the laws of the commonwealth for the time being.

The commanding officers of regiments shall appoint their adjutants and quartermasters; the brigadiers, their brigade-majors; and the major-generals, their aids; and the governor shall appoint the adjutant-general.

The governor, with the advice of council, shall appoint all officers of the Continental Army, whom, by the Confederation of the United States, it is provided that this commonwealth shall appoint, as also all officers of forts and garrisons.

The divisions of the militia into brigades, regiments, and companies, made in pursuance of the militia-laws now in force, shall be considered as the proper divisions of the militia in this commonwealth, until the same shall be altered in pursuance of some future law.

Art. XI. No moneys shall be issued out of the treasury of this commonwealth and disposed of, except such sums as may be appropriated for the redemption of bills of credit or treasurer's notes, or for the payment of interest arising thereon, but by warrant under the hand of the governor for the time being, with the advice and consent of the council for the necessary defence and support of the commonwealth, and for the protection and preservation of the inhabitants thereof, agreeably to the acts and resolves of the general court.

Art. XII. All public boards, the commissary-general, all superintending officers of public magazines and stores, belonging to this commonwealth, and all commanding officers of forts and garrisons within the same, shall, once in every three months, officially and without requisition, and at other times, when required by the governor, deliver to him an account of all goods, stores, provisions, ammunition, cannon, with their appendages, and small-arms with their accoutrements, and of all other public property whatever under their care, respectively; distinguishing the quantity, number, quality, and kind of each, as particularly as may be; together with the condition of such forts and garrisons; and the said commanding officer shall exhibit to the governor, when required by him, true and exact plans of such forts, and of the land and sea, or harbor or harbors, adjacent.

And the said boards, and all public officers, shall communicate to the governor, as soon as may be after receiving the same, all letters, dispatches, and intelligences of a public nature, which shall be directed to them respectively.

Art. XIII. As the public good requires that the governor should not be under the undue influence of any of the members of the general court, by a dependence on them for his support; that he should, in all cases, act with freedom for the benefit of the public; that he should not have his attention necessarily diverted from that object to his private concerns; and that he should maintain the dignity of the commonwealth in the character of its chief magistrate, it is necessary that he should have an honorable stated salary, of a fixed and permanent value, amply sufficient for those purposes, and established by standing laws; and it shall be among the first acts of the general court, after the commencement of this constitution, to establish such salary by law accordingly.

Permanent and honorable salaries shall also be established by law for the justices of the supreme judicial court.

And if it shall be found that any of the salaries aforesaid, so established, are insufficient, they shall, from time to time, be enlarged, as the general court shall judge proper.

CHAPTER II.

Section 2.—Lieutenant-Governor

Article I. There shall be annually elected a lieutenant-governor of the commonwealth of Massachusetts, whose title shall be "His Honor;" and who shall be qualified, in point of religion, property, and residence in the commonwealth, in the same manner with the governor; and the day and manner of his election, and the qualification of the electors, shall be the same as are required in the election of a governor. The return of the votes for this officer, and the declaration of his election, shall be in the same manner; and if no one person shall be found to have a majority of all the votes returned, the vacancy shall be filled by the senate and house of representatives, in the same manner as the governor is to be elected, in case no one person shall have a majority of the votes of the people to be governor.

Art. II. The governor, and in his absence the lieutenant-governor, shall be president of the council; but shall have no voice in council; and the lieutenant-governor shall always be a member of the council, except when the chair of the governor shall be vacant.

Art. III. Whenever the chair of the governor shall be vacant, by reason of his death, or absence from the commonwealth, or otherwise, the lieutenant-governor, for the time being, shall, during such vacancy perform all the duties incumbent upon the governor, and shall have and exercise all the powers and authorities which, by this constitution, the governor is vested with, when personally present.

CHAPTER II.

Section 3.—Council, and the Manner of Settling Elections by the Legislature

Article I. There shall be a council, for advising the governor in the executive part of the government, to consist of nine persons besides the lieutenant-governor, whom the governor, for the time being, shall have full power and authority, from time to time, at this discretion, to assemble and call together; and the governor, with the said councillors, or five of them at least, shall and may, from time to time, hold and keep a council, for the ordering and directing the affairs of the commonwealth, according to the laws of the land.

Art. II. Nine councillors shall be annually chosen from among the persons returned for councillors and senators, on the last Wednesday in May, by the joint ballot of the senators and representatives assembled in one room; and in case there shall not be found, upon the first choice, the whole number of nine persons who will accept a seat in the council, the deficiency shall be made up by the electors aforesaid from among the people at large; and the number of senators left shall constitute the senate for the year. The seats of the persons thus elected from the senate, and accepting the trust, shall be vacated in the senate.

Art. III. The councillors, in the civil arrangements of the commonwealth, shall have rank next after the lieutenant-governor.

Art. IV. Not more than two councillors shall be chosen out of any one district in this commonwealth.

Art. V. The resolutions and advice of the council shall be recorded in a register and signed by the members present; and this record may be called for, at any time, by either house of the legislature; and any member of the council may insert his opinion, contrary to the resolution of the majority.

Art. VI. Whenever the office of the governor and lieutenant-governor shall be vacant by reason of death, absence, or otherwise, then the council, or the major part of them, shall, during such vacancy, have full power and authority to do and execute all and every such acts, matters, and things, as the governor or the lieutenant-governor might or could, by virtue of this constitution, do or execute, if they, or either of them, were personally present.

Art. VII. And whereas the elections appointed to be made by this constitution on the last Wednesday in May annually, by the two houses of the legislature, may not be completed on that day, the said elections may be adjourned from day to day, until the same shall be completed. And the order of elections shall be as follows: The vacancies in the senate, if any, shall first be filled up; the governor and lieutenant-governor shall then be elected, provided there should be no choice of them by the people; and afterwards the two houses shall proceed to the election of the council.

CHAPTER II.

Section 4.—Secretary, Treasurer, Commissary, etc.

Article I. The secretary, treasurer, and receiver-general, and the commissary-general, notaries public, and naval officers, shall be chosen annually, by joint ballot of the senators and representatives, in one room. And, that the citizens of this commonwealth may be assured, from time to time, that the moneys remaining in the public treasury, upon the settlement and liquidation of the public accounts, are their property, no man shall be eligible as treasurer and receiver-general more than five years successively.

Art. II. The records of the commonwealth shall be kept in the office of the secretary, who may appoint his deputies, for whose conduct he shall be accountable; and he shall attend the governor and council, the senate and house of representatives in person or by his deputies, as they shall respectively require.

CHAPTER III.

Judiciary Power

Article I. The tenure that all commission officers shall by law have in their offices shall be expressed in their respective commissions. All judicial officers, duly appointed, commissioned, and sworn, shall hold their offices during good behavior, excepting such concerning whom there is different provision made in this constitution: *Provided, nevertheless,* The governor, with consent of the council, may remove them upon the address of both houses of the legislature.

Art. II. Each branch of the legislature, as well as the governor and council, shall have authority to require the opinions of the justices of the supreme judicial court upon important questions of law, and upon solemn occasions.

Art. III. In order that the people may not suffer from the long continuance in place of any justice of the peace, who shall fail of discharging the important duties of his office with ability or fidelity, all commissions of justices of the peace shall expire and become void in the term of seven years from their respective dates; and, upon the expiration of any commission, the same may, if necessary, be renewed, or another person appointed, as shall most conduce to the well-being of the commonwealth.

Art. IV. The judges of probate of wills, and for granting letters of administration, shall hold their courts at such place or places, on fixed days, as the convenience of the people shall require; and the legislature shall, from time to time, hereafter, appoint such times and places; until which appointments the said courts shall be holden at the times and places which the respective judges shall direct.

Art. V. All causes of marriage, divorce, and alimony, and all appeals from the judges of probate, shall be heard and determined by the governor and council until the legislature shall, by law, make other provision.

CHAPTER IV.

Delegates to Congress

The delegates of this commonwealth to the Congress of the United States shall, some time in the month of June, annually, be elected by the joint ballot of the senate and house of representatives assembled together in one room; to serve in Congress for one year, to commence on the first Monday in November, then next ensuing. They shall have commissions under the hand of the governor, and the great seal of the commonwealth; but may be recalled at any time within the year, and others chosen and commissioned, in the same manner, in their stead.

CHAPTER V.—THE UNIVERSITY AT CAMBRIDGE, AND ENCOURAGEMENT OF LITERATURE, ETC.

Section 1.—The University

Article I. Whereas our wise and pious ancestors, so early as the year one thousand six hundred and thirty-

six, laid the foundation of Harvard College, in which university many persons of great prominence have, by the blessing of God, been initiated in those arts and sciences which qualified them for the public employments, both in church and State; and whereas the encouragement of arts and sciences, and all good literature, tends to the honor of God, the advantage of the Christian religion, and the great benefit of this and the other United States of America, it is declared, that the president and fellows of Harvard College, in their corporate capacity, and their successors in that capacity, their officers and servants, shall have, hold, use, exercise, and enjoy all the powers, authorities, rights, liberties, privileges, immunities, and franchises which they now have, or are entitled to have, hold, use, exercise, and enjoy; and the same are hereby ratified and confirmed unto them, the said president and fellows of Harvard College, and to their successors, and to their officers and servants, respectively, forever.

Art. II. And whereas there have been, at sundry times, by divers persons, gifts, grants, devises of houses, lands, tenements, goods, chattels, legacies, and conveyances heretofore made, either to Harvard College in Cambridge, in New England, or to the president and fellows of Harvard College, or to the said college, by some other description, under several charters successively, it is declared, that all the said gifts, grants, devises, legacies, and conveyances are hereby forever confirmed unto the president and fellows of Harvard College, and to their successors, in the capacity aforesaid, according to the true intent and meaning of the donor or donors, grantor or grantors, devisor or devisors.

Art. III. And whereas by an act of the general court of the colony of Massachusetts Bay, passed in the year one thousand six hundred and forty-two, the governor and deputy governor for the time being, and all the magistrates of that jurisdiction, were, with the President, and a number of the clergy, as the said act described, constituted the overseers of Harvard College; and it being necessary, in this new constitution of government, to ascertain who shall be deemed successors to the said governor, deputy governor, and magistrates, it is declared that the governor, lieutenant-governor, council, and senate of this commonwealth are, and shall be deemed, their successors; who, with the president of Harvard College, for the time being, together with the ministers of the congregational churches in the towns of Cambridge, Watertown, Charlestown, Boston, Roxbury and Dorchester, mentioned in the said act, shall be, and hereby are, vested with all the powers and authority belonging, or in any way appertaining, to the overseers of Harvard College: *Provided,* that nothing herein shall be construed to prevent the legislature of this commonwealth from making such alterations in the government of the said university as shall be conducive to its advantage, and the interest of the republic of letters, in as full a manner as might have been done by the legislature of the late province of the Massachusetts Bay.

CHAPTER V.

Section 2.—The Encouragement of Literature, etc.

Wisdom and knowledge, as well as virtue, diffused generally among the body of the people, being necessary for the preservation of their rights and liberties; and as these depend on spreading the opportunities and advantages of education in the various parts of the country, and among the different orders of the people, it shall be the duty of legislatures and magistrates, in all future periods of this commonwealth, to cherish the interests of literature and the sciences, and all seminaries of them; especially the university at Cambridge, public schools, and grammar-schools in the towns; to encourage private societies and public institutions, rewards and immunities, for the promotion of agriculture, arts, sciences, commerce, trades, manufactures, and a natural history of the country; to countenance and inculcate the principles of humanity and general benevolence, public and private charity, industry and frugality, honesty and punctuality in their dealings; sincerity, and good humor, and all social affections and generous sentiments, among the people.

CHAPTER VI.

Oaths and Subscriptions; Incompatibility of and Exclusion from Offices; Pecuniary Qualifications; Commissions; Writs; Confirmation of Laws; Habeas Corpus; The Enacting Style; Continuance of Officers; Provision for a Future Revisal of the Constitution, etc.

Article I. Any person chosen governor, lieutenant-governor, councillor, senator, or representative, and accepting the trust, shall, before he proceed to execute the duties of his place or office, make and subscribe the following declaration, viz:

"I, A.B., do declare that I believe the Christian religion, and have a firm persuasion of its truth; and that I am seized and possessed, in my own right, of the property required by the constitution, as one qualification for the office or place to which I am elected."

And the governor, lieutenant-governor, and councillors shall make and subscribe the said declaration, in the presence of the two houses of assembly; and the senators and representatives, first elected under this constitution, before the president and five of the council of the former constitution; and forever afterwards, before the governor and council for the time being.

And every person chosen to either of the places or offices aforesaid, as also any persons appointed or commissioned to any judicial, executive, military, or other office under the government, shall, before he enters on the discharge of the business of his place or office, take and subscribe the following declaration and oaths or affirmations, viz:

"I, A.B., do truly and sincerely acknowledge, profess, testify, and declare that the commonwealth of Massachusetts is, and of right ought to be, a free, sovereign, and independent State, and I do swear that I will bear true faith and allegiance to the said commonwealth, and that I will defend the same against traitorous conspiracies and all hostile attempts whatsoever; and that I do renounce and abjure all allegiance, subjection, and obedience to the King, Queen, or government of Great Britain, (as the case may be,) and every other foreign power whatsoever; and that no foreign prince, person, prelate, state, or potentate hath, or ought to have, any jurisdiction, superiority, preeminence, authority, dispensing or other power, in any matter, civil, ecclesiastical, or spiritual, within this commonwealth; except the authority and power which is or may be vested by their constituents in the Congress of the United States; and I do further testify and declare that no man, or body of men, hath, or can have, any right to absolve or discharge me from the obligation of this oath, declaration, or affirmation; and that I do make this acknowledgment, profession, testimony, declaration, denial, renunciation, and abjuration heartily and truly, according to the common meaning and acceptation of the foregoing words, without any equivocation, mental evasion, or secret reservation whatsoever: So help me, God."

"I, A.B., do solemnly swear and affirm that I will faithfully and impartially discharge and perform all the duties incumbent on me as————, according to the best of my abilities and understanding, agreeably to the rules and regulations of the constitution and the laws of the commonwealth: So help me, God."

Provided always, That when any person, chosen and appointed as aforesaid, shall be of the denomination of people called Quakers, and shall decline taking the said oaths, he shall make his affirmation in the foregoing form, and subscribe the same, omitting the words,

"I do swear," "and abjure," "oath or," "and abjuration," in the first oath; and in the second oath, the words, "swear and," and in each of them the words, "So help me, God;" subjoining instead thereof, "This I do under the pains and penalties of perjury."

And the said oaths or affirmations shall be taken and subscribed by the governor, lieutenant-governor, and councillors, before the president of the senate, in the presence of the two houses of assembly; and by the senators and representatives first elected under this constitution, before the president and five of the council of the former constitution; and forever afterwards before the governor and council for the time being; and by the residue of the officers aforesaid, before such persons and in such manner as from time to time shall be prescribed by the legislature.

Art. II. No governor, lieutenant-governor, or judge of the supreme judicial court shall hold any other office or place, under the authority of this commonwealth, except such as by the constitution they are admitted to hold, saving that the judges of the said court may hold the office of the justices of the peace through the State; nor shall they hold any other place or office, or receive any pension or salary from any other State, or government, or power, whatever.

No person shall be capable of holding or exercising at the same time, within this State, more than one of the following offices, viz: judge of probate, sheriff, register of probate, or register of deeds; and never more than any two offices, which are to be held by appointment of the governor, or the governor and council, or the senate, or the house of representatives, or by the election of the people of the State at large, or of the people of any county, military offices, and the offices of justices of the peace excepted, shall be held by one person.

No person holding the office of judge of the supreme judicial court, secretary, attorney-general, solicitor-general, treasurer or receiver-general, judge of probate, commissary-general, president, professor, or instructor of Harvard College, sheriff, clerk of the house of representatives, register of probate, register of deeds, clerk of the supreme judicial court, clerk of the inferior court of common pleas, or officer of the customs, including in this description naval officers, shall at the same time have a seat in the senate or house of representatives; but their being chosen or appointed to, and accepting the same, shall operate as a resignation of their seat in the senate or house of representatives; and the place so vacated shall be filled up.

And the same rule shall take place in case any judge of the said supreme judicial court or judge of probate shall accept a seat in council, or any councillor shall accept of either of those offices or places.

And no person shall ever be admitted to hold a seat in the legislature, or any office of trust or importance under the government of this commonwealth, who shall in the due course of law have been convicted of bribery or corruption in obtaining an election or appointment.

Art. III. In all cases where sums or money are mentioned in this constitution, the value thereof shall be computed in silver, at six shillings and eight pence per ounce; and it shall be in the power of the legislature, from time to time, to increase such qualifications, as to property, of the persons to be elected to offices as the circumstances of the commonwealth shall require.

Art. IV. All commissions shall be in the name of the commonwealth of Massachusetts, signed by the governor, and attested by the secretary or his deputy, and have the great seal of the commonwealth affixed thereto.

Art. V. All writs, issuing of the clerk's office in any of the courts of law, shall be in the name of the commonwealth of Massachusetts; they shall be under the seal of the court from when they issue; they shall bear test of the first justice of the court to which they shall be returned who is not a party, and be signed by the clerk of such court.

Art. VI. All the laws which have heretofore been adopted, used, and approved in the province, colony, or State of Massachusetts Bay, and usually practiced on in the courts of law, shall still remain and be in full force, until altered or repealed by the legislature, such parts only excepted as are repugnant to the rights and liberties contained in this constitution.

Art. VII. The privilege and benefit of the writ of *habeas corpus* shall be enjoyed in this commonwealth, in the most free, easy, cheap, expeditious, and ample manner, and shall not be suspended by the legislature, except upon the most urgent and pressing occasions, and for a limited time, not exceeding twelve months.

Art. VIII. The enacting style, in making and passing all acts, statutes, and laws, shall be, *"Be it enacted by the senate and house of representatives in general court assembled, and by authority of the same."*

Art. IX. To the end there may be no failure of justice or danger arise to the commonwealth from a change in the form of government, all officers, civil and military, holding commissions under the government and people of Massachusetts Bay, in New England, and all other officers of the said government and people, at the time this constitution shall take effect, shall have, hold, use, exercise, and enjoy all the powers and authority to them granted or committed until other persons shall be appointed in their stead; and all courts of law shall proceed in the execution of the business of their respective departments; and all the executive and legislative officers, bodies, and powers shall continue in full force, in the enjoyment and exercise of all their trusts, employments, and authority, until the general court, and the supreme and executive officers under this constitution, are designated and invested with their respective trusts, powers, and authority.

Art. X. In order the more effectually to adhere to the principles of the constitution, and to correct those violations which by any means may be made therein, as well as to form such alterations as from experience shall be found necessary, the general court which shall be in the year of our Lord one thousand seven hundred and ninety-five shall issue precepts to the selectmen of the several towns, and to the assessors of the unincorporated plantations, directing them to convene the qualified voters of their respective towns and plantations, for the purpose of collecting their sentiments on the necessity or expediency of revising the constitution in order to make amendments.

And if it shall appear, by the returns made, that two-thirds of the qualified voters throughout the State, who shall assemble and vote in consequence of the said precepts, are in favor of such revision or amendment, the general court shall issue precepts, or direct them to be issued from the secretary's office, to the several towns to elect or direct them to be issued from the secretary's office, to the several towns to elect delegates to meet in convention for the purpose aforesaid.

And said delegates to be chosen in the same manner and proportion as their representatives in the second branch of the legislature are by this constitution to be chosen.

Art. XI. This form of government shall be enrolled on parchment and deposited in the secretary's office, and be a part of the laws of the land, and printed copies thereof shall be prefixed to the book containing the laws of this commonwealth in all future editions of the said laws.

JAMES BOWDOIN, President
Samuel Barrett, Secretary

Source: Legislature of the State of Massachusetts, www.mass.gov/legis/const.htm.

ARTICLES OF CONFEDERATION

To all to whom these Presents shall come, we the undersigned Delegates of the States affixed to our Names send greeting.

Articles of Confederation and perpetual Union between the states of New Hampshire, Massachusetts-bay Rhode Island and Providence Plantations, Connecticut, New York, New Jersey, Pennsylvania, Delaware, Maryland, Virginia, North Carolina, South Carolina and Georgia.

I.

The Stile of this Confederacy shall be **"The United States of America."**

II.

Each state retains its sovereignty, freedom, and independence, and every power, jurisdiction, and right, which is not by this Confederation expressly delegated to the United States, in Congress assembled.

III.

The said States hereby severally enter into a firm league of friendship with each other, for their common defense, the security of their liberties, and their mutual and general welfare, binding themselves to assist each other, against all force offered to, or attacks made upon them, or any of them, on account of religion, sovereignty, trade, or any other pretense whatever.

IV.

The better to secure and perpetuate mutual friendship and intercourse among the people of the different States in this Union, the free inhabitants of each of these States, paupers, vagabonds, and fugitives from justice excepted, shall be entitled to all privileges and immunities of free citizens in the several States; and the people of each State shall free ingress and regress to and from any other State, and shall enjoy therein all the privileges of trade and commerce, subject to the same duties, impositions, and restrictions as the inhabitants thereof respectively, provided that such restrictions shall not extend so far as to prevent the removal of property imported into any State, to any other State, of which the owner is an inhabitant; provided also that no imposition, duties or restriction shall be laid by any State, on the property of the United States, or either of them.

If any person guilty of, or charged with, treason, felony, or other high misdemeanor in any State, shall flee from justice, and be found in any of the United States, he shall, upon demand of the Governor or executive power of the State from which he fled, be delivered up and removed to the State having jurisdiction of his offense.

Full faith and credit shall be given in each of these States to the records, acts, and judicial proceedings of the courts and magistrates of every other State.

V.

For the most convenient management of the general interests of the United States, delegates shall be annually appointed in such manner as the legislatures of each State shall direct, to meet in Congress on the first Monday in November, in every year, with a power reserved to each State to recall its delegates, or any of them, at any time within the year, and to send others in their stead for the remainder of the year.

No State shall be represented in Congress by less than two, nor more than seven members; and no person shall be capable of being a delegate for more than three years in any term of six years; nor shall any person, being a delegate, be capable of holding any office under the United States, for which he, or another for his benefit, receives any salary, fees or emolument of any kind.

Each State shall maintain its own delegates in a meeting of the States, and while they act as members of the committee of the States.

In determining questions in the United States in Congress assembled, each State shall have one vote.

Freedom of speech and debate in Congress shall not be impeached or questioned in any court or place out of Congress, and the members of Congress shall be protected in their persons from arrests or imprisonments, during the time of their going to and from, and attendance on Congress, except for treason, felony, or breach of the peace.

VI.

No State, without the consent of the United States in Congress assembled, shall send any embassy to, or re-

ceive any embassy from, or enter into any conference, agreement, alliance or treaty with any King, Prince or State; nor shall any person holding any office of profit or trust under the United States, or any of them, accept any present, emolument, office or title of any kind whatever from any King, Prince or foreign State; nor shall the United States in Congress assembled, or any of them, grant any title of nobility.

No two or more States shall enter into any treaty, confederation or alliance whatever between them, without the consent of the United States in Congress assembled, specifying accurately the purposes for which the same is to be entered into, and how long it shall continue.

No State shall lay any imposts or duties, which may interfere with any stipulations in treaties, entered into by the United States in Congress assembled, with any King, Prince or State, in pursuance of any treaties already proposed by Congress, to the courts of France and Spain.

No vessel of war shall be kept up in time of peace by any State, except such number only, as shall be deemed necessary by the United States in Congress assembled, for the defense of such State, or its trade; nor shall any body of forces be kept up by any State in time of peace, except such number only, as in the judgement of the United States in Congress assembled, shall be deemed requisite to garrison the forts necessary for the defense of such State; but every State shall always keep up a well-regulated and disciplined militia, sufficiently armed and accoutered, and shall provide and constantly have ready for use, in public stores, a due number of field pieces and tents, and a proper quantity of arms, ammunition and camp equipage.

No State shall engage in any war without the consent of the United States in Congress assembled, unless such State be actually invaded by enemies, or shall have received certain advice of a resolution being formed by some nation of Indians to invade such State, and the danger is so imminent as not to admit of a delay till the United States in Congress assembled can be consulted; nor shall any State grant commissions to any ships or vessels of war, nor letters of marque or reprisal, except it be after a declaration of war by the United States in Congress assembled, and then only against the Kingdom or State and the subjects thereof, against which war has been so declared, and under such regulations as shall be established by the United States in Congress assembled, unless such State be infested by pirates, in which case vessels of war may be fitted out for that occasion, and kept so long as the danger shall continue, or until the United States in Congress assembled shall determine otherwise.

VII.

When land forces are raised by any State for the common defense, all officers of or under the rank of colonel, shall be appointed by the legislature of each State respectively, by whom such forces shall be raised, or in such manner as such State shall direct, and all vacancies shall be filled up by the State which first made the appointment.

VIII.

All charges of war, and all other expenses that shall be incurred for the common defense or general welfare, and allowed by the United States in Congress assembled, shall be defrayed out of a common treasury, which shall be supplied by the several States in proportion to the value of all land within each State, granted or surveyed for any person, as such land and the buildings and improvements thereon shall be estimated according to such mode as the United States in Congress assembled, shall from time to time direct and appoint.

The taxes for paying that proportion shall be laid and levied by the authority and direction of the legislatures of the several States within the time agreed upon by the United States in Congress assembled.

IX.

The United States in Congress assembled, shall have the sole and exclusive right and power of determining on peace and war, except in the cases mentioned in the sixth article—of sending and receiving ambassadors—entering into treaties and alliances, provided that no treaty of commerce shall be made whereby the legislative power of the respective States shall be restrained from imposing such imposts and duties on foreigners, as their own people are subjected to, or from prohibiting the exportation or importation of any species of goods or commodities whatsoever—of establishing rules for deciding in all cases, what captures on land or water shall be legal, and in what manner prizes taken by land or naval forces in the service of the United States shall be divided or appropriated—of granting letters of marque and reprisal in times of peace—appointing courts for the trial of piracies and felonies com-

mited on the high seas and establishing courts for receiving and determining finally appeals in all cases of captures, provided that no member of Congress shall be appointed a judge of any of the said courts.

The United States in Congress assembled shall also be the last resort on appeal in all disputes and differences now subsisting or that hereafter may arise between two or more States concerning boundary, jurisdiction or any other causes whatever; which authority shall always be exercised in the manner following. Whenever the legislative or executive authority or lawful agent of any State in controversy with another shall present a petition to Congress stating the matter in question and praying for a hearing, notice thereof shall be given by order of Congress to the legislative or executive authority of the other State in controversy, and a day assigned for the appearance of the parties by their lawful agents, who shall then be directed to appoint by joint consent, commissioners or judges to constitute a court for hearing and determining the matter in question: but if they cannot agree, Congress shall name three persons out of each of the United States, and from the list of such persons each party shall alternately strike out one, the petitioners beginning, until the number shall be reduced to thirteen; and from that number not less than seven, nor more than nine names as Congress shall direct, shall in the presence of Congress be drawn out by lot, and the persons whose names shall be so drawn or any five of them, shall be commissioners or judges, to hear and finally determine the controversy, so always as a major part of the judges who shall hear the cause shall agree in the determination: and if either party shall neglect to attend at the day appointed, without showing reasons, which Congress shall judge sufficient, or being present shall refuse to strike, the Congress shall proceed to nominate three persons out of each State, and the secretary of Congress shall strike in behalf of such party absent or refusing; and the judgement and sentence of the court to be appointed, in the manner before prescribed, shall be final and conclusive; and if any of the parties shall refuse to submit to the authority of such court, or to appear or defend their claim or cause, the court shall nevertheless proceed to pronounce sentence, or judgement, which shall in like manner be final and decisive, the judgement or sentence and other proceedings being in either case transmitted to Congress, and lodged among the acts of Congress for the security of the parties concerned: provided that every commissioner, before he sits in judgement, shall take an oath to be administered by one of the judges of the supreme or superior court of the State, where the cause shall be tried, "well and truly to hear and determine the matter in question, according to the best of his judgement, without favor, affection or hope of reward": provided also, that no State shall be deprived of territory for the benefit of the United States.

All controversies concerning the private right of soil claimed under different grants of two or more States, whose jurisdictions as they may respect such lands, and the States which passed such grants are adjusted, the said grants or either of them being at the same time claimed to have originated antecedent to such settlement of jurisdiction, shall on the petition of either party to the Congress of the United States, be finally determined as near as may be in the same manner as is before prescribed for deciding disputes respecting territorial jurisdiction between different States.

The United States in Congress assembled shall also have the sole and exclusive right and power of regulating the alloy and value of coin struck by their own authority, or by that of the respective States—fixing the standards of weights and measures throughout the United States—regulating the trade and managing all affairs with the Indians, not members of any of the States, provided that the legislative right of any State within its own limits be not infringed or violated—establishing or regulating post offices from one State to another, throughout all the United States, and exacting such postage on the papers passing through the same as may be requisite to defray the expenses of the said office—appointing all officers of the land forces, in the service of the United States, excepting regimental officers—appointing all the officers of the naval forces, and commissioning all officers whatever in the service of the United States—making rules for the government and regulation of the said land and naval forces, and directing their operations.

The United States in Congress assembled shall have authority to appoint a committee, to sit in the recess of Congress, to be denominated "A Committee of the States", and to consist of one delegate from each State; and to appoint such other committees and civil officers as may be necessary for managing the general affairs of the United States under their direction—to appoint one of their members to preside, provided that no person be allowed to serve in the office of president more than one year in any term of three years; to ascertain the necessary sums of money to be raised for the service of the United States, and to appropriate and apply the same for defraying the public expenses—to borrow money, or emit bills on the credit of the United States, transmitting every half-year to the respective States an account of the sums of money so borrowed

or emitted—to build and equip a navy—to agree upon the number of land forces, and to make requisitions from each State for its quota, in proportion to the number of white inhabitants in such State; which requisition shall be binding, and thereupon the legislature of each State shall appoint the regimental officers, raise the men and cloath, arm and equip them in a solid-like manner, at the expense of the United States; and the officers and men so cloathed, armed and equipped shall march to the place appointed, and within the time agreed on by the United States in Congress assembled. But if the United States in Congress assembled shall, on consideration of circumstances judge proper that any State should not raise men, or should raise a smaller number of men than the quota thereof, such extra number shall be raised, officered, cloathed, armed and equipped in the same manner as the quota of each State, unless the legislature of such State shall judge that such extra number cannot be safely spread out in the same, in which case they shall raise, officer, cloath, arm and equip as many of such extra number as they judge can be safely spared. And the officers and men so cloathed, armed, and equipped, shall march to the place appointed, and within the time agreed on by the United States in Congress assembled.

The United States in Congress assembled shall never engage in a war, nor grant letters of marque or reprisal in time of peace, nor enter into any treaties or alliances, nor coin money, nor regulate the value thereof, nor ascertain the sums and expenses necessary for the defense and welfare of the United States, or any of them, nor emit bills, nor borrow money on the credit of the United States, nor appropriate money, nor agree upon the number of vessels of war, to be built or purchased, or the number of land or sea forces to be raised, nor appoint a commander in chief of the army or navy, unless nine States assent to the same: nor shall a question on any other point, except for adjourning from day to day be determined, unless by the votes of the majority of the United States in Congress assembled.

The Congress of the United States shall have power to adjourn to any time within the year, and to any place within the United States, so that no period of adjournment be for a longer duration than the space of six months, and shall publish the journal of their proceedings monthly, except such parts thereof relating to treaties, alliances or military operations, as in their judgement require secrecy; and the yeas and nays of the delegates of each State on any question shall be entered on the journal, when it is desired by any delegates of a State, or any of them, at his or their request shall be furnished with a transcript of the said journal, except such parts as are above excepted, to lay before the legislatures of the several States.

X.

The Committee of the States, or any nine of them, shall be authorized to execute, in the recess of Congress, such of the powers of Congress as the United States in Congress assembled, by the consent of the nine States, shall from time to time think expedient to vest them with; provided that no power be delegated to the said Committee, for the exercise of which, by the Articles of Confederation, the voice of nine States in the Congress of the United States assembled be requisite.

XI.

Canada acceding to this confederation, and adjoining in the measures of the United States, shall be admitted into, and entitled to all the advantages of this Union; but no other colony shall be admitted into the same, unless such admission be agreed to by nine States.

XII.

All bills of credit emitted, monies borrowed, and debts contracted by, or under the authority of Congress, before the assembling of the United States, in pursuance of the present confederation, shall be deemed and considered as a charge against the United States, for payment and satisfaction whereof the said United States, and the public faith are hereby solemnly pledged.

XIII.

Every State shall abide by the determination of the United States in Congress assembled, on all questions which by this confederation are submitted to them. And the Articles of this Confederation shall be inviolably observed by every State, and the Union shall be perpetual; nor shall any alteration at any time hereafter be made in any of them; unless such alteration be agreed to in a Congress of the United States, and be afterwards confirmed by the legislatures of every State.

And Whereas it hath pleased the Great Governor of the World to incline the hearts of the legislatures we respectively represent in Congress, to approve of, and to authorize us to ratify the said Articles of Confedera-

tion and perpetual Union. Know Ye that we the undersigned delegates, by virtue of the power and authority to us given for that purpose, do by these presents, in the name and in behalf of our respective constituents, fully and entirely ratify and confirm each and every of the said Articles of Confederation and perpetual Union, and all and singular the matters and things therein contained: And we do further solemnly plight and engage the faith of our respective constituents, that they shall abide by the determinations of the United States in Congress assembled, on all questions, which by the said Confederation are submitted to them. And that the Articles thereof shall be inviolably observed by the States we respectively represent, and that the Union shall be perpetual.

In Witness whereof we have hereunto set our hands in Congress. Done at Philadelphia in the State of Pennsylvania the ninth day of July in the Year of our Lord One Thousand Seven Hundred and Seventy-Eight, and in the Third Year of the independence of America.

Agreed to by Congress 15 November 1777
In force after ratification by Maryland, 1 March 1781

———

Source: Documents Illustrative of the Formation of the Union of the American States. Edited by Charles C. Tansill. 69th Cong., 1st sess. House Doc. No. 398. Washington, DC: U.S. Government Printing Office, 1927.

RESOLUTION FROM ANNAPOLIS CONVENTION: SEPTEMBER 14, 1786

To the Honorable, the Legislatures of Virginia, Delaware, Pennsylvania, New Jersey, and New York—

The Commissioners from the said States, respectively assembled at Annapolis, humbly beg leave to report.

That, pursuant to their several appointments, they met, at Annapolis in the State of Maryland, on the eleventh day of September Instant, and having proceeded to a Communication of their powers; they found that the States of New York, Pennsylvania, and Virginia, had, in substance, and nearly in the same terms, authorised their respective Commissioners "to meet such Commissioners as were, or might be, appointed by the other States in the Union, at such time and place, as should be agreed upon by the said Commissioners to take into consideration the trade and Commerce of the United States, to consider how far an uniform system in their commercial intercourse and regulations might be necessary to their common interest and permanent harmony, and to report to the several States such an Act, relative to this great object, as when unanimously ratified by them would enable the United States in Congress assembled effectually to provide for the same."

That the State of Delaware, had given similar powers to their Commissioners, with this difference only, that the Act to be framed in virtue of those powers, is required to be reported "to the United States in Congress assembled, to be agreed to by them, and confirmed by the Legislatures of every State."

That the State of New Jersey had enlarged the object of their appointment, empowering their Commissioners, "to consider how far an uniform system in their commercial regulations and *other important matters,* might be necessary to the common interest and permanent harmony of the several States," and to report such an Act on the subject, as when ratified by them "would enable the United States in Congress assembled, effectually to provide for the exigencies of the Union."

That appointments of Commissioners have also been made by the States of New Hampshire, Massachusetts, Rhode Island, and North Carolina, none of whom however have attended; but that no information has been received by your Commissioners, of any appointment having been made by the States of Connecticut, Maryland, South Carolina or Georgia.

That the express terms of the powers to your Commissioners supposing a deputation from all the States, and having for object the Trade and Commerce of the United States, Your Commissioners did not conceive it advisable to proceed on the business of their mission, under the Circumstance of so partial and defective a representation.

Deeply impressed however with the magnitude and importance of the object confided to them on this occasion, your Commissioners cannot forbear to indulge an expression of their earnest and unanimous wish, that speedy measures may be taken, to effect a general meeting, of the States, in a future Convention, for the same, and such other purposes, as the situation of public affairs, may be found to require.

If in expressing this wish, or in intimating any other sentiment, your Commissioners should seem to exceed the strict bounds of their appointment, they entertain a full confidence, that a conduct, dictated by

an anxiety for the welfare, of the United States, will not fail to receive an indulgent construction.

In this persuasion, your Commissioners submit an opinion, that the Idea of extending the powers of their Deputies, to other objects, than those of Commerce, which has been adopted by the State of New Jersey, was an improvement on the original plan, and will deserve to be incorporated into that of a future Convention; they are the more naturally led to this conclusion, as in the course of their reflections on the subject, they have been induced to think, that the power of regulating trade is of such comprehensive extent, and will enter so far into the general System of the foederal government, that to give it efficacy, and to obviate questions and doubts concerning its precise nature and limits, may require a correspondent adjustment of other parts of the Foederal System.

That there are important defects in the system of the Foederal Government is acknowledged by the Acts of all those States, which have concurred in the present Meeting; That the defects, upon a closer examination, may be found greater and more numerous, than even these acts imply, is at least so far probable, from the embarrassments which characterise the present State of our national affairs, foreign and domestic, as may reasonably be supposed to merit a deliberate and candid discussion, in some mode, which will unite the Sentiments and Councils of all the States. In the choice of the mode, your Commissioners are of opinion, that a Convention of Deputies from the different States, for the special and sole purpose of entering into this investigation, and digesting a plan for supplying such defects as may be discovered to exist, will be entitled to a preference from considerations, which will occur, without being particularised.

Your Commissioners decline an enumeration of those national circumstances on which their opinion respecting the propriety of a future Convention, with more enlarged powers, is founded; as it would be an useless intrusion of facts and observations, most of which have been frequently the subject of public discussion, and none of which can have escaped the penetration of those to whom they would in this instance be addressed. They are however of a nature so serious, as, in the view of your Commissioners to render the situation of the United States delicate and critical, calling for an exertion of the united virtue and wisdom of all the members of the Confederacy.

Under this impression, Your Commissioners, with the most respectful deference, beg leave to suggest their unanimous conviction, that it may essentially tend to advance the interests of the union, if the

States, by whom they have been respectively delegated, would themselves concur, and use their endeav-
ours to procure the concurrence of the other States, in
the appointment of Commissioners, to meet at
Philadelphia on the second Monday in May next, to
take into consideration the situation of the United
States, to devise such further provisions as shall appear
to them necessary to render the constitution of the
Foederal Government adequate to the exigencies of
the Union; and to report such an Act for that purpose
to the United States in Congress assembled, as when
agreed to, by them, and afterwards confirmed by the
Legislatures of every State, will effectually provide for
the same.

Though your Commissioners could not with propriety address these observations and sentiments to
any but the States they have the honor to Represent,
they have nevertheless concluded from motives of respect, to transmit Copies of this Report to the United
States in Congress assembled, and to the executives of
the other States.

By order of the Commissioners.

———

*Source: Documents Illustrative of the Formation of the Union
of the American States.* Edited by Charles C. Tansill.
69th Cong., 1st sess. House Doc. No. 398. Washington, DC: U.S. Government Printing Office, 1927.

REPORT OF PROCEEDINGS IN CONGRESS: FEBRUARY 21, 1787

The report of a grand comee. consisting of Mr. Dane
Mr. Varnum Mr. S. M. Mitchell Mr. Smith Mr. Cad-
wallader Mr. Irwine Mr. N. Mitchell Mr. Forrest Mr.
Grayson Mr. Blount Mr. Bull & Mr. Few, to whom was
referred a letter of 14 Septr. 1786 from J. Dickinson
written at the request of Commissioners from the
States of Virginia Delaware Pensylvania New Jersey &
New York assembled at the City of Annapolis together
with a copy of the report of the said commissioners to
the legislatures of the States by whom they were appointed, being an order of the day was called up &
which is contained in the following resolution viz

"Congress having had under consideration the letter of John Dickinson esqr. chairman of the Commissioners who assembled at Annapolis during the last
year also the proceedings of the said commissioners
and entirely coinciding with them as to the ineffi-

ciency of the federal government and the necessity of
devising such farther provisions as shall render the
same adequate to the exigencies of the Union do
strongly recommend to the different legislatures to
send forward delegates to meet the proposed convention on the second Monday in May next at the city of
Philadelphia."

The delegates for the state of New York thereupon
laid before Congress Instructions which they had received from their constituents, & in pursuance of the
said instructions moved to postpone the farther consideration of the report in order to take up the following proposition to wit.

"That it be recommended to the States composing
the Union that a convention of representatives from
the said States respectively be held at—on—for the purpose of revising the Articles of Confederation and perpetual Union between the United States of America
and reporting to the United States in Congress assembled and to the States respectively such alterations and
amendments of the said Articles of Confederation as
the representatives met in such convention shall judge
proper and necessary to render them adequate to the
preservation and support of the Union."

On the question to postpone for the purpose above
mentioned the yeas & nays being required by the delegates for New York.

Massachusetts	*ay*
Mr. King	ay
Mr. Dane	ay
Connecticut	*d*
Mr. Johnson	ay
Mr. S. M. Mitchell	no
New York	*ay*
Mr. Smith	ay
Mr. Benson	ay
New Jersey	*no*
Mr. Cadwallader	ay
Mr. Clarke	no
Mr. Schurman	no
Pennsylvania	*no*
Mr. Irwine	no
Mr. Meredith	ay
Mr. Bingham	no
Delaware	*x*
Mr. N. Mitchell	no

Maryland	*x*
Mr. Forest	no
Virginia	*ay*
Mr. Grayson	ay
Mr. Madison	ay
North Carolina	*no*
Mr. Blount	no
Mr. Hawkins	no
South Carolina	*no*
Mr. Bull	no
Mr. Kean	no
Mr. Huger	no
Mr. Parker	no
Georgia	*d*
Mr. Few	ay
Mr. Pierce	no

So the question was lost.

A motion was then made by the delegates for Massachusetts to postpone the farther consideration of the report in order to take into consideration a motion which they read in their place, this being agreed to, the motion of the delegates for Massachusetts was taken up and being amended was agreed to as follows.

Whereas there is provision in the Articles of Confederation & perpetual Union for making alterations therein by the assent of a Congress of the United States and of the legislatures of the several States; And whereas experience hath evinced that there are defects in the present Confederation, as a means to remedy which several of the States and particularly the State of New York by express instructions to their delegates in Congress have suggested a convention for the purposes expressed in the following resolution and such convention appearing to be the most probable means of establishing in these states a firm national government.

Resolved that in the opinion of Congress it is expedient that on the second Monday in May next a Convention of delegates who shall have been appointed by the several states be held at Philadelphia for the sole and express purpose of revising the Articles of Confederation and reporting to Congress and the several legislatures such alterations and provisions therein as shall when agreed to in Congress and confirmed by the states render the federal constitution adequate to the exigencies of Government & the preservation of the Union.

———

Source: Documents Illustrative of the Formation of the Union of the American States. Edited by Charles C. Tansill. 69th Cong., 1st sess. House Doc. No. 398. Washington, DC: Government Printing Office, 1927.

Appendix B: Materials from the Convention Debates and after the Convention

JAMES MADISON'S PREFACE TO DEBATES IN THE CONVENTION

A Sketch Never Finished nor Applied.

As the weakness and wants of man naturally lead to an association of individuals, under a common authority whereby each may have the protection of the whole against danger from without, and enjoy in safety within, the advantages of social intercourse, and an exchange of the necessaries & comforts of life: in like manner feeble communities, independent of each other, have resorted to a Union, less intimate, but with common Councils, for the common safety agst powerful neighbors, and for the preservation of justice and peace among themselves. Ancient history furnishes examples of these confederal associations, tho' with a very imperfect account, of their structure, and of the attributes and functions of the presiding Authority. There are examples of modern date also, some of them still existing, the modifications and transactions of which are sufficiently known.

It remained for the British Colonies, now United States, of North America, to add to those examples, one of a more interesting character than any of them: which led to a system without an example ancient or modern, a system founded on popular rights, and so combining, a federal form with the forms of individual Republics, as may enable each to supply the defects of the other and obtain the advantages of both.

Whilst the Colonies enjoyed the protection of the parent Country as it was called, against foreign danger; and were secured by its superintending controul, against conflicts among themselves, they continued independent of each other, under a common, tho' limited dependence, on the parental Authority. When however the growth of the offspring in strength and in wealth, awakened the jealousy and tempted the avidity of the parent, into schemes of usurpation & exaction, the obligation was felt by the former of uniting their counsels and efforts to avert the impending calamity.

As early as the year 1754, indications having been given of a design in the British Government to levy contributions on the Colonies, without their consent; a meeting of Colonial deputies took place at Albany, which attempted to introduce a compromising substitute, that might at once satisfy the British requisitions, and save their own rights from violation. The attempt had no other effect, than by bringing these rights into a more conspicuous view, to invigorate the attachment to them, on one side; and to nourish the haughty & encroaching spirit on the other.

In 1774, the progress made by G. B. in the open assertion of her pretensions and in the apprehended purpose of otherwise maintaining them than by Legislative enactments and declarations, had been such that the Colonies did not hesitate to assemble, by their deputies, in a formal Congress, authorized to oppose to the British innovations whatever measures might be found best adapted to the occasion; without however losing sight of an eventual reconciliation.

The dissuasive measures of that Congress, being without effect, another Congress was held in 1775, whose pacific efforts to bring about a change in the views of the other party, being equally unavailing, and the commencement of actual hostilities having at length put an end to all hope of reconciliation; the

Congress finding moreover that the popular voice began to call for an entire & perpetual dissolution of the political ties which had connected them with G. B., proceeded on the memorable 4th of July, 1776 to declare the 13 Colonies, Independent States.

During the discussions of this solemn Act, a Committee consisting of a member from each colony had been appointed to prepare & digest a form of Confederation, for the future management of the common interests, which had hitherto been left to the discretion of Congress, guided by the exigences of the contest, and by the known intentions or occasional instructions of the Colonial Legislatures.

It appears that as early as the 21st of July 1775, A plan entitled "Articles of Confederation & perpetual Union of the Colonies" had been sketched by Docr Franklin, the plan being on that day submitted by him to Congress; and tho' not copied into their Journals remaining on their files in his handwriting. But notwithstanding the term "perpetual" observed in the title, the articles provided expressly for the event of a return of the Colonies to a connection with G. Britain.

This sketch became a basis for the plan reported by the Come on the 12 of July, now also remaining on the files of Congress, in the handwriting of Mr Dickinson. The plan, tho' dated after the Declaration of Independence, was probably drawn up before that event; since the name of Colonies, not States is used throughout the draught. The plan reported, was debated and amended from time to time, till the 17th of November 1777, when it was agreed to by Congress, and proposed to the Legislatures of the States, with an explanatory and recommendatory letter. The ratifications of these by their Delegates in Congs. duly authorized took place at successive dates; but were not compleated till March 1, 1781, when Maryland who had made it a prerequisite that the vacant lands acquired from the British Crown should be a Common fund, yielded to the persuasion that a final & formal establishment of the federal Union & Govt. would make a favorable impression not only on other foreign Nations, but on G. B. herself.

The great difficulty experienced in so framing the fedl. system as to obtain the unanimity required for its due sanction, may be inferred from the long interval, and recurring discussions, between the commencement and completion of the work; from the changes made during its progress; from the language of Congs. when proposing it to the States, wch dwelt on the impracticability of devising a system acceptable to all of them; from the reluctant assent given by some; and the various alterations proposed by others; and by a tardiness in others again which produced a special address to them from Congs. enforcing the duty of sacrificing local considerations and favorite opinions to the public safety, and the necessary harmony: Nor was the assent of some of the States finally yielded without strong protests against particular articles, and a reliance on future amendments removing their objections.

It is to be recollected, no doubt, that these delays might be occasioned in some degree, by an occupation of the public Councils both general & local, with the deliberations and measures, essential to a Revolutionary struggle; But there must have been a balance for these causes, in the obvious motives to hasten the establishment of a regular and efficient Govt; and in the tendency of the crisis to repress opinions and pretensions, which might be inflexible in another state of things.

The principal difficulties which embarrassed the progress, and retarded the completion of the plan of Confederation, may be traced to 1. the natural repugnance of the parties to a relinquishment of power: 2 a natural jealousy of its abuse in other hands than their own: 3 the rule of suffrage among parties unequal in size, but equal in sovereignty. 4 the ratio of contributions in money and in troops, among parties, whose inequality in size did not correspond with that of their wealth, or of their military or free population. 5 the selection and definition of the powers, at once necessary to the federal head, and safe to the several members.

To these sources of difficulty, incident to the formation of all such Confederacies, were added two others one of a temporary, the other of a permanent nature. The first was the case of the Crown lands, so called because they had been held by the British Crown, and being ungranted to individuals when its authority ceased, were considered by the States within whose charters or asserted limits they lay, as devolving on them; whilst it was contended by the others, that being wrested from the dethroned authority, by the equal exertion of all, they resulted of right and in equity to the benefit of all. The lands being of vast extent and of growing value, were the occasion of much discussion & heart-burning; & proved the most obstinate of the impediments to an earlier consummation of the plan of federal Govt. The State of Maryland the last that acceded to it held out as already noticed, till March 1, 1781, and then yielded only to the hope that by giving a stable & authoritative character to the Confederation, a successful termination of the Contest might be accelerated. The dispute was happily compromised by successive surrenders of portions of the territory by the States having exclusive claims to it, and acceptances of them by Congress.

The other source of dissatisfaction was the peculiar situation of some of the States, which having no convenient ports for foreign commerce, were subject to be taxed by their neighbors, thro whose ports, their commerce was carried on. New Jersey, placed between Phila & N. York, was likened to a cask tapped at both ends; and N. Carolina, between Virga & S. Carolina to a patient bleeding at both arms. The Articles Of Confederation provided no remedy for the complaint: which produced a strong protest on the part of N. Jersey: and never ceased to be a source of dissatisfaction & discord until the new Constitution, superseded the old.

But the radical infirmity of the "arts. Of Confederation" was the dependence of Congs. on the voluntary and simultaneous compliance with its Requisitions, by so many independant Communities, each consulting more or less its particular interests & convenience and distrusting the compliance of the others. Whilst the paper emissions of Congs. continued to circulate they were employed as a sinew of war, like gold & silver. When that ceased to be the case, the fatal defect of the political System was felt in its alarming force. The war was merely kept alive and brought to a successful conclusion by such foreign aids and temporary expedients as could be applied; a hope prevailing with many, and a wish with all, that a state of peace, and the sources of prosperity opened by it, would give to the Confederacy in practice, the efficiency which had been inferred from its theory.

The close of the war however brought no cure for the public embarrassments. The States relieved from the pressure of foreign danger, and flushed with the enjoyment of independent and sovereign power; (instead of a diminished disposition to part with it,) persevered in omissions and in measures incompatible with their relations to the Federal Govt. and with those among themselves.

Having served as a member of Congs. through the period between Mar. 1780 & the arrival of peace in 1783, I had become intimately acquainted with the public distresses and the causes of them. I had observed the successful opposition to every attempt to procure a remedy by new grants of power to Congs. I had found moreover that despair of success hung over the compromising provision of April 1783 for the public necessities which had been so elaborately planned, and so impressively recommended to the States Sympathizing, under this aspect of affairs, in the alarm of the friends of free Govt, at the threatened danger of an abortive result to the great & perhaps last experiment in its favour, I could not be insensible to the obliga-

tion to co-operate as far as I could in averting the calamity. With this view I acceded to the desire of my fellow Citizens of the County that I should be one of its representatives in the Legislature, hoping that I might there best contribute to inculcate the critical posture to which the Revolutionary cause was reduced, and the merit of a leading agency of the State in bringing about a rescue of the Union and the blessings of liberty staked on it, from an impending catastrophe.

It required but little time after taking my seat in the House of Delegates in May 1784 to discover that, however favorable the general disposition of the State might be towards the Confederacy the Legislature retained the aversion of its predecessors to transfers of power from the State to the Govt. of the Union; notwithstanding the urgent demands of the Federal Treasury; the glaring inadequacy of the authorized mode of supplying it, the rapid growth of anarchy in the Fedl. System, and the animosity kindled among the States by their conflicting regulations.

The temper of the Legislature & the wayward course of its proceedings may be gathered from the Journals of its Sessions in the years 1784 & 1785.

The failure however of the varied propositions in the Legislature for enlarging the powers of Congress, the continued failure of the efforts of Cons to obtain from them the means of providing for the debts of the Revolution; and of countervailing the commercial laws of G. B., a source of much irritation & agst. which the separate efforts of the States were found worse than abortive; these Considerations with the lights thrown on the whole subject, by the free & full discussion it had undergone led to an general acquiescence in the Resoln. passed, on the 21 of Jany. 1786, which proposed & invited a meeting of Deputies from all the States to insert the Resol I.

The resolution had been brought forward some weeks before on the failure of a proposed grant of power to Congress to collect a revenue from commerce, which had been abandoned by its friends in consequence of material alterations made in the grant by a Committee of the whole. The Resolution tho introduced by Mr Tyler an influencial member, who having never served in Congress, had more the ear of the House than those whose services there exposed them to an imputable bias, was so little acceptable that it was not then persisted in. Being now revived by him, on the last day of the Session, and being the alternative of adjourning without any effort for the crisis in the affairs of the Union, it obtained a general vote; less however with some of its friends from a confidence in the success of the experiment than from a hope that it might prove a step to a more comprehensive & adequate provision for the wants of the Confederacy.

It happened also that Commissioners who had been appointed by Virga. & Maryd. to settle the jurisdiction on waters dividing the two States had, apart from their official reports recommended a uniformity in the regulations of the 2 States on several subjects & particularly on those having relation to foreign trade. It apeared at the same time that Maryd. had deemed a concurrence of her neighbors Pena. & Delaware indispensable in such a case, who for like reasons would require that of their neighbors. So apt and forceable an illustration of the necessity of a uniformity throughout all the States could not but favour the passage of a Resolution which proposed a Convention having that for its object.

The commissioners appointed by the Legisl: & who attended the Convention were E. Randolph the Attorney of the State, St. Geo: Tucker & J. M. The designation of the time & place for its meeting to be proposed and communicated to the States having been left to the Comrs they named for the time early September and for the place the City of Annapolis avoiding the residence of Congs. and large Commercial Cities as liable to suspicions of an extraneous influence.

Altho' the invited Meeting appeared to be generally favored, five States only assembled; some failing to make appointments, and some of the individuals appointed not hastening their attendance, the result in both cases being ascribed mainly, to a belief that the time had not arrived for such a political reform, as might be expected from a further experience of its necessity.

But in the interval between the proposal of the Convention and the time of its meeting such had been the advance of public opinion in the desired direction, stimulated as it had been by the effect of the contemplated object, of the meeting, in turning the general attention to the Critical State of things, and in calling forth the sentiments and exertions of the most enlightened & influencial patriots, that the Convention thin as it was did not scruple to decline the limited task assigned to it and to recommend to the States a Convention with powers adequate to the occasion. Nor was it unnoticed that the commission of the N. Jersey Deputation, had extended its object to a general provision for the exigencies of the Union. A recommendation for this enlarged purpose was accordingly reported by a Come to whom the subject had been referred. It was drafted by Col H. and finally agreed to unanimously in the following form. Insert it.

The recommendation was well recd. by the Legislature of Virga. which happened to be the *first* that *acted*

on it, and the example of her compliance was made as conciliatory and impressive as possible. The Legislature were unanimous or very nearly so on the occasion and as a proof of the magnitude & solemnity attached to it, they placed Genl. W. at the head of the Deputation from the State; and as a proof of the deep interest he felt in the case he overstepped the obstacles to his acceptance of the appointment.

The law complying with the recommendation from Annapolis was in the terms following:

A resort to a General Convention to remodel the Confederacy, was not a new idea. It had entered at an early date into the conversations and speculations of the most reflecting & foreseeing observers of the inadequacy of the powers allowed to Congress. In a pamphlet published in May 81 at the seat of Congs. Pelatiah Webster an able tho' not conspicuous Citizen, after discussing the fiscal system of the U. States, and suggesting among other remedial provisions including a national Bank remarks that "the Authority of Congs. at present is very inadequate to the performance of their duties; and this indicates the necessity of their calling a Continental Convention for the express purpose of ascertaining, defining, enlarging, and limiting, the duties & powers of their Constitution,"

. . .

In 1785, Noah Webster whose pol. & other valuable writings had made him known to the public, in one of his publications of American policy brought into view the same resort for supplying the defects of the Fedl. System.

The proposed & expected Convention at Annapolis the first of a general character that appears to have been realized, & the state of the public mind awakened by it had attracted the particular attention of Congs. and favored the idea there of a Convention with fuller powers for amending the Confederacy.

It does not appear that in any of these cases, the reformed system was to be otherwise sanctioned than by the Legislative authy. of the States; nor whether or how far, a change was to be made in the structure of the Depository of Federal powers.

The act of Virga. providing for the Convention at Philada. was succeeded by appointments from other States as their Legislatures were assembled, the appointments being selections from the most experienced & highest standing Citizens. Rh. I. was the only exception to a compliance with the recommendation from Annapolis, well known to have been swayed by an obdurate adherence to an advantage which her position gave her of taxing her neighbors thro' their consumption of imported supplies, an advantage which it was foreseen would be taken from her by a revisal of the Articles of Confederation.

As the pub. mind had been ripened for a salutary Reform of the pol. System, in the interval between the proposal & the meeting, of Comrs. at Annapolis, the interval between the last event, and the meeting of Deps. at Phila. had continued to develop more & more the necessity & the extent of a Systematic provision for the preservation and Govt. of the Union; among the ripening incidents was the Insurrection of Shays, in Massts. against her Govt; which was with difficulty suppressed, notwithstanding the influence on the insurgents of an apprehended interposition of the Fedl. troops.

At the date of the Convention, the aspect & retrospect of the pol. condition of the U.S. could not but fill the pub. mind with a gloom which was relieved only by a hope that so select a Body would devise an adequate remedy for the existing and prospective evils so impressively demanding it.

It was seen that the public debt rendered so sacred by the cause in which it had been incurred remained without any provision for its payment. The reiterated and elaborate efforts of Con. to procure from the States a more adequate power to raise the means of payment had failed. The effect of the ordinary requisitions of Congress had only displayed the inefficiency of the authy. making them: none of the States having duly complied with them, some having failed altogether or nearly so; and in one instance, that of N. Jersey a compliance was expressly refused; nor was more yielded to the expostulations of members of Congs. deputed to her Legislature, than a mere repeal of the law, without a compliance.

The want of authy. in Congs. to regulate Commerce had produced in Foreign nations particularly G. B. a monopolizing policy injurious to the trade of the U. S. and destructive to their navigation; the imbecility and anticipated dissolution of the Confederacy extinguishg. all apprehensions of a Countervailing policy on the part of the U. States.

The same want of a general power over Commerce, led to an exercise of the power separately, by the States, wch. not only proved abortive, but engendered rival, conflicting and angry regulations. Besides the vain attempts to supply their respective treasuries by imposts, which turned their commerce into the neighbouring ports, and to co-erce a relaxation of the British monopoly of the W. Inda. navigation, which was attempted by Virga. the States having ports for foreign commerce, taxed & irritated the adjoining States, trading thro' them, as N. Y., Pena, Virga, & S. Carolina. Some of the States, as Connecticut, taxed imports as

from Massts higher than imports even from G. B. of wch Massts complained to Virga. and doubtless to other States. In sundry instances as of N. Y. N. J. Pa & Maryd. the navigation laws treated the Citizens other States as aliens.

In certain cases the authy. of the Confederacy was disregarded, as in violations not only of the Treaty of peace; but of Treaties with France & Holland, which were complained of to Congs.

In other cases the Fedl. Authy. was violated by Treaties & wars with Indians, as by Geo: by troops raised & kept up witht. the consent of Congs. as by Massts by compacts witht. the consent of Congs. as between Pena. and N. Jersey, and between Virga. & Maryd. From the Legisl: Journals of Virga. it appears, that a vote refusing to apply for a sanction of Congs. was followed by a vote agst. the communication of the Compact to Congs.

In the internal administration of the States a violation of Contracts had become familiar in the form of depreciated paper made a legal tender, of property substituted for money, of Instalment laws, and of the occlusions of the Courts of Justice; although evident that all such interferences affected the rights of other States, relatively creditor, as well as Citizens Creditors within the State.

Among the defects which had been severely felt was that of a uniformity in cases requiring it, as laws of naturalization, bankruptcy, a Coercive authority operating on individuals and a guaranty of the internal tranquility of the States.

As natural consequences of this distracted and disheartening condition of the union, the Fedl. Authy. had ceased to be respected abroad, and dispositions shown there, particularly in G. B., to take advantage of its imbecility, and to speculate on its approaching downfall; at home it had lost all confidence & credit; the unstable and unjust career of the States had also forfeited the respect & confidence essential to order and good Govt. involving the general decay and confidence & credit between man & man. It was found moreover, that those least partial to popular Govt., or most distrustful of its efficacy were yielding to anticipations, that from an increase of the confusion a Govt. might result more congenial with their taste or their opinions; whilst those most devoted to the principles and forms of Republics, were alarmed for the cause of liberty itself, at stake in the American Experiment, and anxious for a system that wd avoid the inefficacy of a mere confederacy without passing into the opposite extreme of a consolidated govt. it was known that there were individuals who had betrayed a bias toward Monarchy and there had always been some not unfavorable to a partition of the Union into several Confederacies; either from a better chance of figuring on a Sectional Theatre, or that the Sections would require stronger Govts., or by their hostile conflicts lead to a monarchical consolidation. The idea of a dismemberment had recently made its appearance in the Newspapers.

Such were the defects, the deformities, the diseases and the ominous prospects, for which the Convention were to provide a remedy, and which ought never to be overlooked in expounding & appreciating the Constitutional Charter the remedy that was provided.

As a sketch on paper, the earliest perhaps of a Constitutional Govt. for the Union (organized into the regular Departments with physical means operating on individuals) to be sanctioned by the people of the States, acting in their original & sovereign character, was contained in a letter of Apl. 8. 1787 from J. M. to Govr. Randolph, a copy of the letter is here inserted.

The feature in the letter which vested in the general Authy. a negative on the laws of the States, was suggested by the negative in the head of the British Empire, which prevented collisions between the parts & the whole, and between the parts themselves. It was supposed that the substitution, of an elective and responsible authority for an hereditary and irresponsible one, would avoid the appearance even of a departure from the principle of Republicanism. But altho' the subject was so viewed in the Convention, and the votes on it were more than once equally divided, it was finally & justly abandoned as, apart from other objections, it was not practicable among so many states, increasing in number, and enacting, each of them, so many laws instead of the proposed negative, the objects of it were left as finally provided for in the Constitution.

On the arrival of the Virginia Deputies at Phila. it occurred to them that from the early and prominent part taken by that State in bringing about the Convention some initiative step might be expected from them. The Resolutions introduced by Governor Randolph were the result of a Consultation on the subject; with an understanding that they left all the Deputies entirely open to the lights of discussion, and free to concur in any alterations or modifications which their reflections and judgments might approve. The Resolutions as the Journals shew became the basis on which the proceedings of the Convention commenced, and to the developments, variations and modifications of which the plan of Govt. proposed by the Convention may be traced.

The curiosity I had felt during my researches into the History of the most distinguished Confederacies, particularly those of antiquity, and the deficiency I found in the means of satisfying it more especially in what related to the process, the principles, the reasons, & the anticipations, which prevailed in the formation of them, determined me to preserve as far as I could an exact account of what might pass in the Convention whilst executing its trust, with the magnitude of which I was duly impressed, as I was with the gratification promised to future curiosity by an authentic exhibition of the objects, the opinions & the reasonings from which the new System of Govt. was to receive its peculiar structure & organization. Nor was I unaware of the value of such a contribution to the fund of materials for the History of a Constitution on which would be staked the happiness of a people great even in its infancy, and possibly the cause of Liberty throught. the world.

In pursuance of the task I had assumed I chose a seat in front of the presiding member, with the other members on my right & left hands. In this favorable position for hearing all that passed, I noted in terms legible & in abreviations & marks intelligible to myself what was read from the Chair or spoken by the members; and losing not a moment unnecessarily between the adjournment & reassembling of the Convention I was enabled to write out my daily notes during the session or within a few finishing days after its close in the extent and form preserved in my own hand on my files.

In the labour & correctness of doing this, I was not a little aided by practice, and by a familiarity with the style and the train of observation & reasoning which characterized the principal speakers. It happened, also that I was not absent a single day, nor more than a casual fraction of an hour in any day, so that I could not have lost a single speech, unless a very short one.

It may be proper to remark, that, with a very few exceptions, the speeches were neither furnished, nor revised, nor sanctioned, by the speakers, but written out from my notes, aided by the freshness of my recollections. A further remark may be proper, that views of the subject might occasionally be presented in the speeches and proceedings, with a latent reference to a compromise on some middle ground, by mutual concessions. The exceptions alluded to were,–first, the sketch furnished by Mr. Randolph of his speech on the introduction of his propositions, on the twenty-ninth day of May; secondly, the speech of Mr. Hamilton, who happened to call on me when putting the last hand to it, and who acknowledged its fidelity, without suggesting more than a very few verbal alterations which were made; thirdly, the speech of Gouverneur Morris on the second day of May, which was communicated to him on a like occasion, and who acquiesced in it without even a verbal change. The correctness of his language and the distinctness of his enunciation were particularly favorable to a reporter. The speeches of Doctor Franklin, excepting a few brief ones, were copied from the written ones read to the Convention by his colleague, Mr. Wilson, it being inconvenient to the Doctor to remain long on his feet.

Of the ability & intelligence of those who composed the Convention, the debates & proceedings may be a test; as the character of the work which was the offspring of their deliberations must be tested by the experience of the future, added to that of the nearly half century which has passed.

But whatever may be the judgment pronounced on the competency of the architects of the Constitution, or whatever may be the destiny, of the edifice prepared by them, I feel it a duty to express my profound & solemn conviction, derived from my intimate opportunity of observing & appreciating the views of the Convention, collectively & individually, that there never was an assembly of men, charged with a great & arduous trust, who were more pure in their motives, or more exclusively or anxiously devoted to the object committed to them, than were the members of the Federal Convention of 1787, to the object of devising and proposing a constitutional system which would best supply the defects of that which it was to replace, and best secure the permanent liberty and happiness of their country.

Source: James Madison's Preface to Debates in the Convention, The American Memory Project, Library of Congress. May be found at "This Nation," http://www.thisnation.com/library/madison/Intro.html, or in Max Farrand, ed. 1937. *The Records of the Federal Convention.* 4 vols. New Haven, CT: Yale University Press, 539–551. Both appear to have taken it from the *Documentary History of the Constitution of the United States of America, 1786–1870.* Department of State: Washington, DC: 1901.

THE DEBATES IN THE FEDERAL CONVENTION OF 1787 REPORTED BY JAMES MADISON, MAY 29: THE VIRGINIA PLAN

Mr. RANDOLPH then opened the main business. He expressed his regret, that it should fall to him, rather than those, who were of longer standing in life and po-

litical experience, to open the great subject of their mission. But, as the convention had originated from Virginia, and his colleagues supposed that some proposition was expected from them, they had imposed this task on him. He then commented on the difficulty of the crisis, and the necessity of preventing the fulfilment of the prophecies of the American downfal. He observed that in revising the foederal system we ought to inquire 1. into the properties, which such a government ought to possess, 2. the defects of the confederation, 3. the danger of our situation & 4. the remedy.

1. The Character of such a government ought to secure 1. against foreign invasion: 2. against dissentions between members of the Union, or seditions in particular states: 3. to procure to the several States, various blessings, of which an isolated situation was incapable: 4. to be able to defend itself against incroachment: & 5. to be paramount to the state constitutions.

2. In speaking of the defects of the confederation he professed a high respect for its authors, and considered them, as having done all that patriots could do, in the then infancy of the science, of constitutions, & of confederacies,—when the inefficiency of requisitions was unknown—no commercial discord had arisen among any states—no rebellion had appeared as in Massts.—foreign debts had not become urgent—the havoc of paper money had not been foreseen—treaties had not been violated—and perhaps nothing better could be obtained from the jealousy of the states with regard to their sovereignty.

He then proceeded to enumerate the defects:

1. that the confederation produced no security against foreign invasion; congress not being permitted to prevent a war nor to support it by their own authority—Of this he cited many examples; most of which tended to shew, that they could not cause infractions of treaties or of the law of nations, to be punished: that particular states might by their conduct provoke war without controul; and that neither militia nor draughts being fit for defence on such occasions, inlistments only could be successful, and these could not be executed without money.

2. that the foederal government could not check the quarrels between states, nor a rebellion in

any, not having constitutional power nor means to interpose according to the exigency:

3. that there were many advantages, which the U. S. might acquire, which were not attainable under the confederation–such as a productive impost–counteraction of the commercial regulations of other nations–pushing of commerce ad libitum–&c &c.

4. that the foederal government could not defend itself against the incroachments from the states.

5. that it was not even paramount to the state constitutions, ratified, as it was in many of the states.

6. He next reviewed the danger of our situation, appealed to the sense of the best friends of the U. S.–the prospect of anarchy from the laxity of government every where; and to other considerations. He proposed as conformable to his ideas the following resolutions, which he explained one by one.

RESOLUTIONS PROPOSED BY MR. RANDOLPH IN CONVENTION: MAY 29

1. Resolved that the Articles of Confederation ought to be so corrected & enlarged as to accomplish the objects proposed by their institution; namely, "common defence, security of liberty and general welfare."

2. Resd. therefore that the rights of suffrage in the National Legislature ought to be proportioned to the Quotas of contribution, or to the number of free inhabitants, as the one or the other rule may seem best in different cases.

3. Resd. that the National Legislature ought to consist of two branches.

4. Resd. that the members of the first branch of the National Legislature ought to be elected by the people of the several States every––for the term of––; to be of the age of––years at least, to receive liberal stipends by with they may be compensated for the devotion of their time to public service; to be ineligible to any office established by a particular State, or under the authority of the United States, except those peculiarly belonging to the functions of the first branch, during the term of service, and for the space of––after its expiration; to be incapable of reelection for the space of––after the

expiration of their term of service, and to be subject to recall.

5. Resold. that the members of the second branch of the National Legislature ought to be elected by those of the first, out of a proper number of persons nominated by the individual Legislatures, to be of the age of––years at least; to hold their offices for a term sufficient to ensure their independency; to receive liberal stipends, by which they may be compensated for the devotion of their time to public service; and to be ineligible to any office established by a particular State, or under the authority of the United States, except those peculiarly belonging to the functions of the second branch, during the term of service, and for the space of––after the expiration thereof.

6. Resolved that each branch ought to possess the right of originating Acts; that the National Legislature ought to be impowered to enjoy the Legislative Rights vested in Congress by the Confederation & moreover to legislate in all cases to which the separate States are incompetent, or in which the harmony of the United States may be interrupted by the exercise of individual Legislation; to negative all laws passed by the several States, contravening in the opinion of the National Legislature the articles of Union; and to call forth the force of the Union agst. any member of the Union failing to fulfill its duty under the articles thereof.

7. Resd. that a National Executive be instituted; to be chosen by the National Legislature for the term of––years, to receive punctually at stated times, a fixed compensation for the services rendered, in which no increase or diminution shall be made so as to affect the Magistracy, existing at the time of increase or diminution, and to be ineligible a second time; and that besides a general authority to execute the National laws, it ought to enjoy the Executive rights vested in Congress by the Confederation.

8. Resd. that the Executive and a convenient number of the National Judiciary, ought to compose a Council of revision with authority to examine every act of the National Legislature before it shall operate, & every act of a particular Legislature before a Negative thereon shall be final; and that the dissent of the said Council shall amount to a rejection, unless the

THE NEW JERSEY PLAN

Act of the National Legislature be again passed, or that of a particular Legislature be again negatived by——of the members of each branch.

9. Resd. that a National Judiciary be established to consist of one or more supreme tribunals, and of inferior tribunals to be chosen by the National Legislature, to hold their offices during good behaviour; and to receive punctually at stated times fixed compensation for their services, in which no increase or diminution shall be made so as to affect the persons actually in office at the time of such increase or diminution, that the jurisdiction of the inferior tribunals shall be to hear & determine in the first instance, and of the supreme tribunal to hear and determine in the dernier resort, all piracies & felonies on the high seas, captures from an enemy; cases in which foreigners or citizens of other States applying to such jurisdictions may be interested, or which respect the collection of the National revenue; impeachments of any National officers, and questions which may involve the national peace and harmony.

10. Resolvd. that provision ought to be made for the admission of States lawfully arising within the limits of the United States, whether from a voluntary junction of Government & Territory or otherwise, with the consent of a number of voices in the National legislature less than the whole.

11. Resd. that a Republican Government & the territory of each State, except in the instance of a voluntary junction of Government & territory, ought to be guarantied by the United States to each State.

12. Resd. that provision ought to be made for the continuance of Congress and their authorities and privileges, until a given day after the reform of the articles of Union shall be adopted, and for the completion of all their engagements.

13. Resd. that provision ought to be made for the amendment of the Articles of Union whensoever it shall seem necessary, and that the assent of the National Legislature ought not to be required thereto.

14. Resd. that the Legislative Executive & Judiciary powers within the several States ought to be bound by oath to support the articles of Union.

15. Resd. that the amendments which shall be

offered to the Confederation, by the Convention ought at a proper time, or times, after the approbation of Congress to be submitted to an assembly or assemblies of Representatives, recommended by the several Legislatures to be expressly chosen by the people, to consider & decide thereon.

He concluded with an exhortation, not to suffer the present opportunity of establishing general peace, harmony, happiness and liberty in the U. S. to pass away unimproved. It was then Resolved—That the House will tomorrow resolve itself into a Committee of the Whole House to consider of the state of the American Union.—and that the propositions moved by Mr. Randolph be referred to the said Committee.

————

Source: The American Memory Project, Library of Congress, http://memory.loc.gov/ammem/amlaw/lwfr.html.

Max Farrand, ed. 1937. *The Records of the Federal Convention of 1787.* 4 vols. New Haven, CT: Yale University Press. Vol. I, Randolph's Speech, 18–19; Virginia Plan, 21–23.

THE NEW JERSEY PLAN: JUNE 15, 1787

The propositions from N. Jersey moved by Mr. Patterson were in the words following.

1. Resd. that the articles of Confederation ought to be so revised, corrected & enlarged, as to render the federal Constitution adequate to the exigences of Government, & the preservation of the Union.

2. Resd. that in addition to the powers vested in the U. States in Congress, by the present existing articles of Confederation, they be authorized to pass acts for raising a revenue, by levying a duty or duties on all goods or merchandizes of foreign growth or manufacture, imported into any part of the U. States, by Stamps on paper, vellum or parchment, and by a postage on all letters or packages passing through the general post-Office, to be applied to such federal purposes as

they shall deem proper & expedient; to make rules & regulations for the collection thereof; and the same from time to time, to alter & amend in such manner as they shall think proper: to pass Acts for the regulation of trade & commerce as well with foreign nations as with each other: provided that all punishments, fines, forfeitures & penalties to be incurred for contravening such acts rules and regulations shall be adjudged by the Common law Judiciarys of the State in which any offence contrary to the true intent & meaning of such Acts rules & regulations shall have been committed or perpetrated, with liberty of commencing in the first instance all suits & prosecutions for that purpose in the superior Common law Judiciary in such State, subject nevertheless, for the correction of all errors, both in law & fact in rendering judgment, to an appeal to the Judiciary of the U. States.

3. Resd. that whenever requisitions shall be necessary, instead of the rule for making requisitions mentioned in the articles of Confederation, the United States in Congs. be authorized to make such requisitions in proportion to the whole number of white & other free citizens & inhabitants of every age sex and condition including those bound to servitude for a term of years & three fifths of all other persons not comprehended in the foregoing description, except Indians not paying taxes; that if such requisitions be not complied with, in the time specified therein, to direct the collection thereof in the non complying States & for that purpose to devise and pass acts directing & authorizing the same; provided that none of the powers hereby vested in the U. States in Congs. shall be exercised without the consent of at least States, and in that proportion if the number of Confederated States should hereafter be increased or diminished.

4. Resd. that the U. States in Congs. be authorized to elect a federal Executive to consist of persons, to continue in office for the term of years, to receive punctually at stated times a fixed compensation for their services, in which no increase or diminution shall be made so as to affect the persons composing the Executive at the time of such increase or diminution, to be paid out of the federal treasury; to be incapable of holding any other office or appointment during their time of service and

for years thereafter; to be ineligible a second time, & removeable by Congs. on application by a majority of the Executives of the several States; that the Executives besides their general authority to execute the federal acts ought to appoint all federal officers not otherwise provided for, & to direct all military operations; provided that none of the persons composing the federal Executive shall on any occasion take command of any troops, so as personally to conduct any enterprise as General, or in other capacity.

5. Resd. that a federal Judiciary be established to consist of a supreme Tribunal the Judges of which to be appointed by the Executive, & to hold their offices during good behaviour, to receive punctually at stated times a fixed compensation for their services in which no increase or diminution shall be made, so as to affect the persons actually in office at the time of such increase or diminution; that the Judiciary so established shall have authority to hear & determine in the first instance on all impeachments of federal officers, & by way of appeal in the dernier resort in all cases touching the rights of Ambassadors, in all cases of captures from an enemy, in all cases of piracies & felonies on the high seas, in all cases in which foreigners may be interested, in the construction of any treaty or treaties, or which may arise on any of the Acts for regulation of trade, or the collection of the federal Revenue: that none of the Judiciary shall during the time they remain in Office be capable of receiving or holding any other office or appointment during their time of service, or for thereafter.

6. Resd. that all Acts of the U. States in Congs. made by virtue & in pursuance of the powers hereby & by the articles of confederation vested in them, and all Treaties made & ratified under the authority of the U. States shall be the supreme law of the respective States so far forth as those Acts or Treaties shall relate to the said States or their Citizens, and that the Judiciary of the several States shall be bound thereby in their decisions, any thing in the respective laws of the Individual States to the contrary notwithstanding; and that if any State, or any body of men in any State shall oppose or prevent ye. carrying into execution such acts or treaties, the federal Executive shall be authorized to call forth ye power of the Confederated States, or so

much thereof as may be necessary to enforce and compel an obedience to such Acts, or an Observance of such Treaties.

7. Resd. that provision be made for the admission of new States into the Union.

8. Resd. the rule for naturalization ought to be the same in every State.

9. Resd. that a Citizen of one State committing an offence in another State of the Union, shall be deemed guilty of the same offence as if it had been committed by a Citizen of the State in which the Offence was committed.

SPEECH OF JAMES PATERSON ON NEW JERSEY PLAN IN THE FEDERAL CONVENTION ON JUNE 16, 1787

As I had the honor of proposing a new system of government for the union, it will be expected that I should explain its principles.

1st. The plan accords with our own powers.

2d. It accords with the sentiments of the people.

But if the subsisting confederation is so radically defective as not to admit of amendment, let us say so and report its insufficiency, and wait for enlarged powers. We must, in the present case, pursue our powers, if we expect the approbation of the people. I am not here to pursue my own sentiments of government, but of those who have sent me; and I believe that a little practical virtue is to be preferred to the finest theoretical principles, which cannot be carried into effect. Can we, as representatives of independent states, annihilate the essential powers of independency? Are not the votes of this convention taken on every question under the idea of independency? Let us turn to the 5th article of confederation—in this it is mutually agreed, that each state should have one vote—It is a fundamental principle arising from confederated governments. The 13th article provides for amendments; but they must be agreed to by every state—the dissent of one renders every proposal null. The confederation is in the nature of a compact; and can any state, unless by the consent of the whole, either in politics or law, withdraw their powers? Let it be said by Pennsylvania, and the other large states, that they, for the sake of peace, assented to the confederation; can she now resume her original right without the consent of the donee?

And although it is now asserted that the larger states reluctantly agreed to that part of the confederation which secures an equal suffrage to each, yet let it be remembered, that the smaller states were the last who approved the confederation.

On this ground, representation must be drawn from the states to maintain their independency, and not from the people composing those states.

The doctrine advanced by a learned gentleman from Pennsylvania, that all power is derived from the people, and that in proportion to their numbers they ought to participate, equally in the benefits and rights of government, is right in principle, but unfortunately for him, wrong in the application to the question now in debate.

When independent societies confederate for mutual defence, they do so in their collective capacity; and then each state for those purposes must be considered as one of the contracting parties. Destroy this balance of equality, and you endanger the rights of the lesser societies by the danger of usurpation in the greater.

Let us test the government intended to be made by the Virginia plan on these principles. The representatives in the national legislature are to be in proportion to the number of inhabitants in each state. So far it is right upon the principles of equality, when state distinctions are done away; but those to certain purposes still exist. Will the government of Pennsylvania admit a participation of their common stock of land to the citizens of New-Jersey? I fancy not. It therefore follows, that a national government, upon the present plan, is unjust, and destructive of the common principles of reciprocity. Much has been said that this government is to operate on persons, not on states. This, upon examination, will be found equally fallacious; for the fact is, it will, in the quotas of revenue, be proportioned among the states, as states; and in this business Georgia will have 1 vote, and Virginia 16. The truth is both plans may be considered to compel individuals to a compliance with their requisitions, although the requisition is made on the states.

Much has been said in commendation of two branches in a legislature, and of the advantages resulting from their being checks to each other. This may be true when applied to state governments, but will not equally apply to a national legislature, whose legislative objects are few and simple.

Whatever may be said of congress, or their conduct on particular occasions, the people in general, are pleased with such a body, and in general wish an increase of their powers, for the good government of the union. Let us now see the plan of the national government on the score of expense. The least the second branch of the legislature can consist of is 90 members— The first branch of at least 270. How are they to be paid in our present impoverished situation? Let us therefore fairly try whether the confederation cannot be mended, and if it can, we shall do our duty, and I believe the people will be satisfied.

———

Source: The American Memory Project, Library of Congress, http://memory.loc.gov/ammem/amlaw/lwfr.html. From Max Farrand, ed. 1937. *The Records of the Federal Convention.* 4 vols. New Haven, CT: Yale University Press. Vol. 1, 242–245 (NJ Plan); 258–260 (Paterson speech).

SPEECH AND PROPOSAL OF ALEXANDER HAMILTON AT FEDERAL CONVENTION: JUNE 18, 1787

Mr. Hamilton, had been hitherto silent on the business before the Convention, partly from respect to others whose superior abilities age & experience rendered him unwilling to bring forward ideas dissimilar to theirs, and partly from his delicate situation with respect to his own State, to whose sentiments as expressed by his Colleagues, he could by no means accede. The crisis however which now marked our affairs, was too serious to permit any scruples whatever to prevail over the duty imposed on every man to contribute his efforts for the public safety & happiness. He was obliged therefore to declare himself unfriendly to both plans. He was particularly opposed to that from N. Jersey, being fully convinced, that no amendment of the confederation, leaving the States in possession of their sovereignty could possibly answer the purpose. On the other hand he confessed he was much discouraged by the amazing extent of Country in expecting the desired blessings from any general sovereignty that could be substituted.—As to the powers of the Convention, he thought the doubts started on that subject had arisen from distinctions & reasonings too subtle. A *federal* Govt. he conceived to mean an association of independent Communities into one. Different Confederacies have different powers, and exercise them in different ways. In some instances the powers are exercised over collective bodies; in others over individuals, as in the German Diet—& among ourselves in cases of piracy. Great latitude therefore must be given to the signification of the term. The plan last proposed departs itself from the *federal* idea, as understood by some, since it is to operate eventually on individuals. He agreed moreover with the Honbl. gentleman from Va. (Mr. R.) that we owed it to our Country, to do on this emergency whatever we should deem essential to its happiness. The States sent us here to provide for the exigences of the Union. To rely on & propose any plan not adequate to these exigences, merely because it was not clearly within our powers, would be to sacrifice the means to the end. It may be said that the *States* can not *ratify* a plan not within the purview of the article of Confederation providing for alterations & amendments. But may not the States themselves in which no constitutional authority equal to this purpose exists in the Legislatures, have had in view a reference to the people at large. In the Senate of N. York, a proviso was moved, that no act of the Convention should be binding until it should be referred to the people & ratified; and the motion was lost by a single voice only, the reason assigned agst. it, being that it might possibly be found an inconvenient shackle.

The great question is what provision shall we make for the happiness of our Country? He would first make a comparative examination of the two plans—prove that there were essential defects in both—and point out such changes as might render a *national one,* efficacious.—The great & essential principles necessary for the support of Government, are 1. an active & constant interest in supporting it. This principle does not exist in the States in favor of the federal Govt. They have evidently in a high degree, the esprit de corps. They constantly pursue internal interests adverse to those of the whole. They have their particular debts—their particular plans of finance &c. all these when opposed to, invariably prevail over the requisitions & plans of Congress. 2. the love of power, Men love power. The same remarks are applicable to this principle. The States have constantly shewn a disposition rather to regain the powers delegated by them than to part with more, or to give effect to what they had parted with. The ambition of their demagogues is known to hate the controul of the Genl. Government. It may be remarked too that the Citizens have not that anxiety to prevent a dissolution of the Genl. Govt as of the particular Govts. A dissolution of the latter would be fatal: of the former would still leave the purposes of Govt. attainable to a considerable degree. Consider what such a State as Virga. will be in a few years, a few compared with the life of nations. How strongly will it feel its importance & self-sufficiency? 3. an habitual attachment of the people. The whole force of this tie is on the side of the State Govt. Its sovereignty is immediately before the eyes of the people: its protection is immediately enjoyed by them. From its hand distributive justice, and all those acts which familiarize & endear Govt. to a people, are dispensed to them. 4. *force* by which may be understood a *coertion of laws* or *coertion of arms*. Congs. have not the former except in few cases. In particular States, this coercion is nearly sufficient; tho' he held it in most cases, not entirely so. A certain portion of military force is absolutely necessary in large communities. Massts. is now feeling this necessity & making provision for it. But how can this force be exerted on the States collectively. It is impossible. It amounts to a war between the parties. Foreign powers also will not be idle spectators. They will interpose, the confusion will increase, and a dissolution of the Union ensue. 5. *influence.* he did not mean corruption, but a dispensation of those regular honors & emoluments, which produce an attachment to the Govt. almost all the weight of these is on the side of the States; and must continue so as long as the States continue to exist. All the passions then we see, of avarice, ambition, interest, which govern most individuals, and all public bodies, fall into the current of the States, and do not flow in the stream of the Genl. Govt. The former therefore will generally be an overmatch for the Genl. Govt. and render any confederacy, in its very nature precarious. Theory is in this case fully confirmed by experience. The Amphyctionic Council had it would seem ample powers for general purposes. It had in particular the power of fining and using force agst. delinquent members. What was the consequence. Their decrees were mere signals of war. The Phocian war is a striking example of it. Philip at length taking advantage of their disunion, and insinuating himself into their Councils, made himself master of their fortunes. The German Confederacy affords another lesson. The authority of Charlemagne seemed to be as great as could be necessary. The great feudal chiefs however, exercising their local sovereignties, soon felt the spirit & found the means of, encroachments, which reduced the imperial authority to a nominal sovereignty. The Diet has succeeded, which tho' aided by a Prince at its head, of great authority independently of his imperial attributes, is a striking illustration of the weakness of Confederated Governments. Other examples instruct us in the same truth. The Swiss cantons have scarce any Union at all, and have been more than once at war with one another—How then are all these evils to be avoided? only by such a compleat sovereignty in the general Govermt. as will turn all the strong principles & passions above mentioned on its side. Does the scheme of N. Jersey pro-

duce this effect? does it afford any substantial remedy whatever? On the contrary it labors under great defects, and the defect of some of its provisions will destroy the efficacy of others. It gives a direct revenue to Congs. but this will not be sufficient. The balance can only be supplied by requisitions; which experience proves can not be relied on. If States are to deliberate on the mode, they will also deliberate on the object of the supplies, and will grant or not grant as they approve or disapprove of it. The delinquency of one will invite and countenance it in others. Quotas too must in the nature of things be so unequal as to produce the same evil. To what standard will you resort? Land is a fallacious one. Compare Holland with Russia: France or Engd. with other countries of Europe. Pena. with N. Carolia. Will the relative pecuniary abilities in those instances, correspond with the relative value of land. Take numbers of inhabitants for the rule and make like comparison of different countries, and you will find it to be equally unjust. The different degrees of industry and improvement in different Countries render the first object a precarious measure of wealth. Much depends too on *situation.* Cont. N. Jersey & N. Carolina, not being commercial States & contributing to the wealth of the commercial ones, can never bear quotas assessed by the ordinary rules of proportion. They will & must fail (in their duty.) Their example will be followed, and the Union itself be dissolved. Whence then is the national revenue to be drawn? from Commerce, even from exports which not-withstanding the common opinion are fit objects of moderate taxation, from excise, &c &c. These tho' not equal, are less unequal than quotas. Another destructive ingredient in the plan, is that equality of suffrage which is so much desired by the small States. It is not in human nature that Va. & the large States should consent to it, or if they did that they shd. long abide by it. It shocks too much the ideas of Justice, and every human feeling. Bad principles in a Govt. tho slow are sure in their operation, and will gradually destroy it. A doubt has been raised whether Congs. at present have a right to keep Ships or troops in time of peace. He leans to the negative. Mr. P.s plan provides no remedy.—If the powers proposed were adequate, the organization of Congs. is such that they could never be properly & effectually exercised. The members of Congs. being chosen by the States & subject to recall, represent all the local prejudices. Should the powers be found effectual, they will from time to time be heaped on them, till a tyrannic sway shall be established. The general power whatever be its form if it preserves itself, must swallow up the State powers, otherwise it will be swallowed up by them. It is agst. all the principles of a good Government to vest the requisite powers in such a body as Congs. Two Sovereignties can not co-exist within the same limits. Giving powers to Congs. must eventuate in a bad Govt. or in no Govt. The plan of N. Jersey therefore will not do. What then is to be done? Here he was embarrassed. The extent of the Country to be governed, discouraged him. The expence of a general Govt. was also formidable; unless there were such a diminution of expence on the side of the State Govts. as the case would admit. If they were extinguished, he was persuaded that great oeconomy might be obtained by substituting a general Govt. He did not mean however to shock the public opinion by proposing such a measure. On the other hand he saw no *other* necessity for declining it. They are not necessary for any of the great purposes of commerce, revenue, or agriculture. Subordinate authorities he was aware would be necessary. There must be district tribunals: corporations for local purposes. But cui bono, the vast & expensive apparatus now appertaining to the States. The only difficulty of a serious nature which occurred to him, was that of drawing representatives from the extremes to the center of the Community. What inducements can be offered that will suffice? The moderate wages for the 1st. branch, would only be a bait to little demagogues. Three dollars or thereabouts he supposed would be the Utmost. The Senate he feared from a similar cause, would be filled by certain undertakers who wish for particular offices under the Govt. This view of the subject almost led him to despair that a Republican Govt. could be established over so great an extent. He was sensible at the same time that it would be unwise to propose one of any other form. In his private opinion he had no scruple in declaring, supported as he was by the opinions of so many of the wise & good, that the British Govt. was the best in the world: and that he doubted much whether any thing short of it would do in America. He hoped Gentlemen of different opinions would bear with him in this, and begged them to recollect the change of opinion on this subject which had taken place and was still going on. It was once thought that the power of Congs was amply sufficient to secure the end of their institution. The error was now seen by every one. The members most tenacious of republicanism, he observed, were as loud as any in declaiming agst. the vices of democracy. This progress of the public mind led him to anticipate the time, when others as well as himself would join in the praise bestowed by Mr. Neckar on the British Constitution, namely, that it is the only Govt. in the world "which unites public strength with individual security."—In every community where industry is encouraged, there will be a division of it into the few & the many. Hence separate interests will arise. There will be debtors & Creditors &c. Give all power to the many, they will oppress the few. Give all power to the few they will oppress the many. Both therefore ought to have power, that each may defend itself agst. the other. To the want of this check we owe our paper money—instalment laws &c. To the proper adjustment of it the British owe the excellence of their Constitution. Their house of Lords is a most noble institution. Having nothing to hope for by a change, and a sufficient interest by means of their property, in being faithful to the National interest, they form a permanent barrier agst. every pernicious innovation, whether attempted on the part of the Crown or of the Commons. No temporary Senate will have firmness en'o' to answer the purpose. The Senate (of Maryland) which seems to be so much appealed to, has not yet been sufficiently tried. Had the people been unanimous & eager, in the late appeal to them on the subject of a paper emission they would have yielded to the torrent. Their acquiescing in such an appeal is a proof of it.—Gentlemen differ in their opinions concerning the necessary checks, from the different estimates they form of the human passions. They suppose Seven years a sufficient period to give the Senate an adequate firmness, from not duly considering the amazing violence & turbulence of the democratic spirit. When a great object of Govt. is pursued, which seizes the popular passions, they spread like wild fire, and become irresistable. He appealed to the gentlemen from the N. England States whether experience had not there verified the remark. As to the Executive, it seemed to be admitted that no good one could be established on Republican principles. Was not this giving up the merits of the question; for can there be a good Govt. without a good Executive. The English model was the only good one on this subject. The Hereditary interest of the King was so interwoven with that of the Nation, and his personal emoluments so great, that he was placed above the danger of being corrupted from abroad—and at the same time was both sufficiently independent and sufficiently controuled, to answer the purpose of the institution at home. One of the weak sides of Republics was their being liable to foreign influence & corruption. Men of little character, acquiring great power become easily the tools of intermedling neibours. Sweeden was a striking instance. The French & English had each their parties during the late Revolution which was effected by the predominant influence of the former. What is the inference from all these observations? That we ought to go as far in order to attain stability and permanency, as republican principles will admit. Let one branch of the Legislature hold their places for life or at least during good-behaviour. Let the Executive also be for life. He appealed to the feelings of the members present whether a term of seven years, would induce the sacrifices of private affairs which an acceptance of public trust would require, so as to ensure the services of the best Citizens. On this plan we should have in the Senate a permanent will, a weighty interest, which would answer essential purposes. But is this a Republican Govt. it will be asked? Yes, if all the Magistrates are appointed, and vacancies are filled, by the people, or a process of election originating with the people. He was sensible that an Executive constituted as he proposed would have in fact but little of the power and independence that might be necessary. On the other plan of appointing him for 7 years, he thought the Executive ought to have but little power. He would be ambitious, with the means of making creatures; and as the object of his ambition wd. be to *prolong* his power, it is probable that in case of a war, he would avail himself of the emergence, to evade or refuse a degradation from his place. An Executive for life has not this motive for forgetting his fidelity, and will therefore be a safer depositary of power. It will be objected probably, that such an Executive will be an *elective Monarch,* and will give birth to the tumults which characterise that form of Govt. He wd. reply that *Monarch* is an indefinite term. It marks not either the degree or duration of power. If this Executive Magistrate wd. be a monarch for life—the other propd. by the Report from the Committee of the whole, wd. be a monarch for seven years. The circumstance of being elective was also applicable to both. It had been observed by judicious writers that elective monarchies wd. be the best if they could be guarded agst. the *tumults* excited by the ambition and intrigues of competitors. He was not sure that tumults were an inseparable evil. He rather thought this character of Elective Monarchies had been taken rather from particular cases than from general principles. The election of Roman Emperors was made by the *Army.* In *Poland* the election is made by great rival *princes* with independent power, and ample means, of raising commotions. In the German Empire, The appointment is made by the Electors & Princes, who have equal motives & means, for exciting cabals & parties. Might not such a mode of election be devised among ourselves as will defend the community agst. these effects in any dangerous degree? Having made these observations he would read to the Committee a sketch of a plan which he shd. prefer to either of those under consideration.

He was aware that it went beyond the ideas of most members. But will such a plan be adopted out of doors? In return he would ask will the people adopt the other plan? At present they will adopt neither. But he sees the Union dissolving or already dissolved—he sees evils operating in the States which must soon cure the people of their fondness for democracies—he sees that a great progress has been already made & is still going on in the public mind. He thinks therefore that the people will in time be unshackled from their prejudices; and whenever that happens, they will themselves not be satisfied at stopping where the plan of Mr. R. wd. place them, but be ready to go as far at least as he proposes. He did not mean to offer the paper he had sketched as a proposition to the Committee. It was meant only to give a more correct view of his ideas, and to suggest the amendments which he should probably propose to the plan of Mr. R. in the proper stages of its future discussion. He read his sketch in the words following: to wit

I. "The Supreme Legislative power of the United States of America to be vested in two different bodies of men; the one to be called the Assembly, the other the Senate who together shall form the Legislature of the United States with power to pass all laws whatsoever subject to the Negative hereafter mentioned.

II. The Assembly to consist of persons elected by the people to serve for three years.

III. The Senate to consist of persons elected to serve during good behaviour; their election to be made by electors chosen for that purpose by the people: in order to this the States to be divided into election districts. On the death, removal or resignation of any Senator his place to be filled out of the district from which he came.

IV. The supreme Executive authority of the United States to be vested in a Governour to be elected to serve during good behaviour—the election to be made by Electors chosen by the people in the Election Districts aforesaid—The authorities & functions of the Executive to be as follows: to have a negative on all laws about to be passed, and the execution of all laws passed, to have the direction of war when authorized or begun; to have with the advice and approbation of the Senate the power of making all treaties; to have the sole appointment of the heads or chief officers of the departments of Finance, War and Foreign Affairs; to have the nomination of all other officers (Ambassadors to foreign Nations included) subject to the approbation or rejection of the Senate; to have the power of pardoning all offences except Treason; which he shall not pardon without the approbation of the Senate.

V. On the death resignation or removal of the Governour his authorities to be exercised by the President of the Senate till a Successor be appointed.

VI. The Senate to have the sole power of declaring war, the power of advising and approving all Treaties, the power of approving or rejecting all appointments of officers except the heads or chiefs of the departments of Finance War and foreign affairs.

VII. The Supreme Judicial authority to be vested in Judges to hold their offices during good behaviour with adequate and permanent salaries. This Court to have original jurisdiction in all causes of capture, and an appellative jurisdiction in all causes in which the revenues of the general Government or the citizens of foreign nations are concerned.

VIII. The Legislature of the United States to have power to institute Courts in each State for the determination of all matters of general concern.

IX. The Governour Senators and all officers of the United States to be liable to impeachment for mal- and corrupt conduct; and upon conviction to be removed from office, & disqualified for holding any place of trust or profit—all impeachments to be tried by a Court to consist of the Chief or Judge of the Superior Court of Law of each State, provided such Judge shall hold his place during good behavior, and have a permanent salary.

X. All laws of the particular States contrary to the Constitution or laws of the United States to be utterly void; and the better to prevent such laws being passed, the Governour or president of each state shall be appointed by the General Government and shall have a negative upon the laws about to be passed in the State of which he is Governour or President.

XI. No State to have any forces land or Naval; and the Militia of all the States to be under the sole and exclusive direction of the United States, the officers of which to be appointed and commissioned by them.

———

Source: Documents Illustrative of the Formation of the Union of the American States. Edited by Charles C. Tansill. 69th Cong., 1st sess. House Doc. No. 398. Washington, DC: U.S. Government Printing Office, 1927.

SPEECH OF BENJAMIN FRANKLIN DELIVERED TO CONSTITUTIONAL CONVENTION: SEPTEMBER 17, 1787

The engrossed Constitution being read,

Docr. FRANKLIN rose with a speech in his hand, which he had reduced to writing for his own conveniency, and which Mr. Wilson read in the words following.

Mr. President

I confess that there are several parts of this constitution which I do not at present approve, but I am not sure I shall never approve them: For having lived long, I have experienced many instances of being obliged by better information, or fuller consideration, to change opinions even on important subjects, which I once thought right, but found to be otherwise. It is therefore that the older I grow, the more apt I am to doubt my own judgment, and to pay more respect to the judgment of others. Most men indeed as well as most sects in Religion, think themselves in possession of all truth, and that wherever others differ from them it is so far error. Steele a Protestant in a Dedication tells the Pope, that the only difference between our Churches in their opinions of the certainty of their doctrines is, the Church of Rome is infallible and the Church of England is never in the wrong. But though many private persons think almost as highly of their own infallibility as of that of their sect, few express it so naturally as a certain french lady, who in a dispute with her sister, said "I don't know how it happens, Sister but I meet with no body but myself, that's always in the right—Il n'y a que moi qui a toujours raison."

In these sentiments, Sir, I agree to this Constitution with all its faults, if they are such; because I think a general Government necessary for us, and there is no form of Government but what may be a blessing to the people if well administered, and believe farther that this is likely to be well administered for a course of years, and can only end in Despotism, as other forms have done before it, when the people shall become so corrupted as to need despotic Government, being incapable of any other. I doubt too whether any other Convention we can obtain, may be able to make a better Constitution. For when you assemble a number of men to have the advantage of their joint wisdom, you inevitably assemble with those men, all their prejudices, their passions, their errors of opinion, their local interests, and their selfish views. From such an assembly can a perfect production be expected? It therefore astonishes me, Sir, to find this system approaching so near to perfection as it does; and I think it will astonish our enemies, who are waiting with confidence to hear that our councils are confounded like those of the Builders of Babel; and that our States are on the point of separation, only to meet hereafter for the purpose of cutting one another's throats. Thus I consent, Sir, to this Constitution because I expect no better, and because I am not sure, that it is not the best. The opinions I have had of its errors, I sacrifice to the public good. I have never whispered a syllable of them abroad. Within these walls they were born, and here they shall die. If every one of us in returning to our Constituents were to report the objections he has had to it, and endeavor to gain partizans in support of them, we might prevent its being generally received, and thereby lose all the salutary effects & great advantages resulting naturally in our favor among foreign Nations as well as among ourselves, from our real or apparent unanimity. Much of the strength & efficiency of any Government in procuring and securing happiness to the people, depends, on opinion, on the general opinion of the goodness of the Government, as well as of the wisdom and integrity of its Governors. I hope therefore that for our own sakes as a part of the people, and for the sake of posterity, we shall act heartily and unanimously in recommending this Constitution (if approved by Congress & confirmed by the Conventions) wherever our influence may extend, and turn our future thoughts & endeavors to the means of having it well administred.

On the whole, Sir, I can not help expressing a wish that every member of the Convention who may still have objections to it, would with me, on this occasion doubt a little of his own infallibility, and to make manifest our unanimity, put his name to this instrument.—

He then moved that the Constitution be signed by the members and offered the following as a convenient form viz. "Done in Convention by the unanimous consent of the States present the 17th. of Sepr. &c—In Witness whereof we have hereunto subscribed our names."

This ambiguous form had been drawn up by Mr. G. M. in order to gain the dissenting members, and put into the hands of Docr. Franklin that it might have the better chance of success.

Source: Documents Illustrative of the Formation of the Union of the American States. Edited by Charles C. Tansill. 69th Cong., 1st sess. House Doc. No. 398. Washington, DC: U.S. Government Printing Office, 1927.

RESOLUTION OF FEDERAL CONVENTION TO CONTINENTAL CONGRESS

In Convention
Monday September 17th. 1787
Present
The States of
New Hampshire, Massachusetts, Connecticut, Mr. Hamilton from New York, New Jersey, Pennsylvania, Delaware, Maryland, Virginia, North Carolina, South Carolina and Georgia.
Resolved,

That the preceding Constitution be laid before the United States in Congress assembled, and that it is the Opinion of this Convention, that it should afterwards be submitted to a Convention of Delegates, chosen in each State by the People thereof, under the Recommendation of its Legislature, for their Assent and Ratification; and that each Convention assenting to, and ratifying the Same, should give Notice thereof to the United States in Congress assembled.

Resolved, That it is the Opinion of this Convention, that as soon as the Conventions of nine States shall have ratified this Constitution, the United States in Congress assembled should fix a Day on which Electors should be appointed by the States which shall have ratified the same, and a Day on which the Electors should assemble to vote for the President, and the Time and place for commencing Proceedings under this Constitution. That after such Publication the Electors should be appointed, and the Senators and Representatives elected: That the Electors should meet on the Day fixed for the Election of the President, and should transmit their votes certified signed, sealed and directed, as the Constitution requires, to the Secretary of the United States in Congress assembled, that the Senators and Representatives should convene at the Time and Place asigned; that the Senators should appoint a President of the Senate, for the sole Purpose of receiving, opening and counting the Votes for President; and, that after he shall be chosen, the Congress, together with the President, should, without Delay, proceed to execute this Constitution.

By the Unanimous Order of the Convention

Go. Washington Presidt.
W. Jackson Secretary

Source: Documents Illustrative of the Formation of the Union of the American States. Edited by Charles C. Tansill.

69th Cong., 1st sess. House Doc. No. 398. Washington, DC: U.S. Government Printing Office, 1927.

LETTER OF THE PRESIDENT OF THE FEDERAL CONVENTION, DATED SEPTEMBER 17, 1787, TO THE PRESIDENT OF CONGRESS, TRANSMITTING THE CONSTITUTION

In Convention, September 17, 1787.

Sir,

We have now the honor to submit to the consideration of the United States in Congress assembled, that Constitution which has appeared to us the most adviseable.

The friends of our country have long seen and desired, that the power of making war, peace, and treaties, that of levying money and regulating commerce, and the correspondent executive and judicial authorities should be fully and effectually vested in the general government of the Union: But the impropriety of delegating such extensive trust to one body of men is evident—Hence results the necessity of a different organization.

It is obviously impracticable in the federal government of these states, to secure all rights of independent sovereignty to each, and yet provide for the interest and safety of all: Individuals entering into society, must give up a share of liberty to preserve the rest. The magnitude of the sacrifice must depend as well on situation and circumstance, as on the object to be obtained. It is at all times difficult to draw with precision the line between those rights which must be surrendered, and those which may be reserved; and on the present occasion this difficulty was encreased by a difference among the several states as to their situation, extent, habits, and particular interests.

In all our deliberations on this subject we kept steadily in our view, that which appears to us the greatest interest of every true American, the consolidation of our Union, in which is involved our prosperity, felicity, safety, perhaps our national existence. This important consideration, seriously and deeply impressed on our minds, led each state in the Convention to be less rigid on points of inferior magnitude, than might have been otherwise expected; and thus the Constitution, which we now present, is the result of a spirit of amity, and of that mutual deference and concession which the peculiarity of our political situation rendered indispensible.

That it will meet the full and entire approbation of every state is not perhaps to be expected; but each will doubtless consider, that had her interest been alone consulted, the consequences might have been particularly disagreeable or injurious to others; that it is liable to as few exceptions as could reasonably have been expected, we hope and believe; that it may promote the lasting welfare of that country so dear to us all, and secure her freedom and happiness, is our most ardent wish.

With great respect, We have the honor to be, Sir,
Your Excellency's most obedient and humble servants,
GEORGE WASHINGTON, President.
By unanimous Order of the Convention.
His Excellency the PRESIDENT of CONGRESS.

Source: Documents Illustrative of the Formation of the Union of the American States. Ed. Charles C. Tansill. 69th Cong., Washington, DC: U.S. Government Printing Office, 1927.

THE CONSTITUTION OF THE UNITED STATES

We the People of the United States, in Order to form a more perfect Union, establish Justice, insure domestic Tranquility, provide for the common defense, promote the general Welfare, and secure the Blessings of Liberty to ourselves and our Posterity, do ordain and establish this Constitution for the United States of America.

Article. I.

Section. 1.

All legislative Powers herein granted shall be vested in a Congress of the United States, which shall consist of a Senate and House of Representatives.

Section. 2.

The House of Representatives shall be composed of Members chosen every second Year by the People of the several States, and the Electors in each State shall have the Qualifications requisite for Electors of the most numerous Branch of the State Legislature.

No Person shall be a Representative who shall not have attained to the Age of twenty five Years, and been seven Years a Citizen of the United States, and who shall not, when elected, be an Inhabitant of that State in which he shall be chosen.

Representatives and direct Taxes shall be apportioned among the several States which may be included within this Union, according to their respective Numbers, which shall be determined by adding to the whole Number of free Persons, including those bound to Service for a Term of Years, and excluding Indians not taxed, three fifths of all other Persons. The actual Enumeration shall be made within three Years after the first Meeting of the Congress of the United States, and within every subsequent Term of ten Years, in such Manner as they shall by Law direct. The Number of Representatives shall not exceed one for every thirty Thousand, but each State shall have at Least one Representative; and until such enumeration shall be made, the State of New Hampshire shall be entitled to chuse three, Massachusetts eight, Rhode-Island and Providence Plantations one, Connecticut five, New-York six, New Jersey four, Pennsylvania eight, Delaware one, Maryland six, Virginia ten, North Carolina five, South Carolina five, and Georgia three.

When vacancies happen in the Representation from any State, the Executive Authority thereof shall issue Writs of Election to fill such Vacancies.

The House of Representatives shall chuse their Speaker and other Officers; and shall have the sole Power of Impeachment.

Section. 3.

The Senate of the United States shall be composed of two Senators from each State, chosen by the Legislature thereof for six Years; and each Senator shall have one Vote.

Immediately after they shall be assembled in Consequence of the first Election, they shall be divided as equally as may be into three Classes. The Seats of the Senators of the first Class shall be vacated at the Expiration of the second Year, of the second Class at the Expiration of the fourth Year, and of the third Class at the Expiration of the sixth Year, so that one third may be chosen every second Year; and if Vacancies happen by Resignation, or otherwise, during the Recess of the Legislature of any State, the Executive thereof may make temporary Appointments until the next Meeting of the Legislature, which shall then fill such Vacancies.

No Person shall be a Senator who shall not have attained to the Age of thirty Years, and been nine Years a Citizen of the United States, and who shall not, when elected, be an Inhabitant of that State for which he shall be chosen.

The Vice President of the United States shall be President of the Senate, but shall have no Vote, unless they be equally divided.

The Senate shall chuse their other Officers, and also a President pro tempore, in the Absence of the Vice President, or when he shall exercise the Office of President of the United States.

The Senate shall have the sole Power to try all Impeachments. When sitting for that Purpose, they shall be on Oath or Affirmation. When the President of the United States is tried, the Chief Justice shall preside: And no Person shall be convicted without the Concurrence of two thirds of the Members present.

Judgment in Cases of Impeachment shall not extend further than to removal from Office, and disqualification to hold and enjoy any Office of honor, Trust or Profit under the United States: but the Party convicted shall nevertheless be liable and subject to Indictment, Trial, Judgment and Punishment, according to Law.

Section. 4.

The Times, Places and Manner of holding Elections for Senators and Representatives, shall be prescribed in each State by the Legislature thereof; but the Congress may at any time by Law make or alter such Regulations, except as to the Places of chusing Senators.

The Congress shall assemble at least once in every Year, and such Meeting shall be on the first Monday in December, unless they shall by Law appoint a different Day.

Section. 5.

Each House shall be the Judge of the Elections, Returns and Qualifications of its own Members, and a Majority of each shall constitute a Quorum to do Business; but a smaller Number may adjourn from day to day, and may be authorized to compel the Attendance of absent Members, in such Manner, and under such Penalties as each House may provide.

Each House may determine the Rules of its Proceedings, punish its Members for disorderly Behaviour, and, with the Concurrence of two thirds, expel a Member.

Each House shall keep a Journal of its Proceedings, and from time to time publish the same, excepting such Parts as may in their Judgment require Secrecy; and the Yeas and Nays of the Members of either House on any question shall, at the Desire of one fifth of those Present, be entered on the Journal.

Neither House, during the Session of Congress, shall, without the Consent of the other, adjourn for more than three days, nor to any other Place than that in which the two Houses shall be sitting.

Section. 6.

The Senators and Representatives shall receive a Compensation for their Services, to be ascertained by Law, and paid out of the Treasury of the United States. They shall in all Cases, except Treason, Felony and Breach of the Peace, be privileged from Arrest during their Attendance at the Session of their respective Houses, and in going to and returning from the same; and for any Speech or Debate in either House, they shall not be questioned in any other Place.

No Senator or Representative shall, during the Time for which he was elected, be appointed to any civil Office under the Authority of the United States, which shall have been created, or the Emoluments whereof shall have been encreased during such time; and no Person holding any Office under the United States, shall be a Member of either House during his Continuance in Office.

Section. 7.

All Bills for raising Revenue shall originate in the House of Representatives; but the Senate may propose or concur with Amendments as on other Bills.

Every Bill which shall have passed the House of Representatives and the Senate, shall, before it become a Law, be presented to the President of the United States: If he approve he shall sign it, but if not he shall return it, with his Objections to that House in which it shall have originated, who shall enter the Objections at large on their Journal, and proceed to reconsider it. If after such Reconsideration two thirds of that House shall agree to pass the Bill, it shall be sent, together with the Objections, to the other House, by which it shall likewise be reconsidered, and if approved by two thirds of that House, it shall become a Law. But in all such Cases the Votes of both Houses shall be determined by yeas and Nays, and the Names of the Per-

sons voting for and against the Bill shall be entered on the Journal of each House respectively. If any Bill shall not be returned by the President within ten Days (Sundays excepted) after it shall have been presented to him, the Same shall be a Law, in like Manner as if he had signed it, unless the Congress by their Adjournment prevent its Return, in which Case it shall not be a Law.

Every Order, Resolution, or Vote to which the Concurrence of the Senate and House of Representatives may be necessary (except on a question of Adjournment) shall be presented to the President of the United States; and before the Same shall take Effect, shall be approved by him, or being disapproved by him, shall be repassed by two thirds of the Senate and House of Representatives, according to the Rules and Limitations prescribed in the Case of a Bill.

Section. 8.

The Congress shall have Power To lay and collect Taxes, Duties, Imposts and Excises, to pay the Debts and provide for the common Defence and general Welfare of the United States; but all Duties, Imposts and Excises shall be uniform throughout the United States;

To borrow Money on the credit of the United States;

To regulate Commerce with foreign Nations, and among the several States, and with the Indian Tribes;

To establish an uniform Rule of Naturalization, and uniform Laws on the subject of Bankruptcies throughout the United States;

To coin Money, regulate the Value thereof, and of foreign Coin, and fix the Standard of Weights and Measures;

To provide for the Punishment of counterfeiting the Securities and current Coin of the United States;

To establish Post Offices and post Roads;

To promote the Progress of Science and useful Arts, by securing for limited Times to Authors and Inventors the exclusive Right to their respective Writings and Discoveries;

To constitute Tribunals inferior to the supreme Court;

To define and punish Piracies and Felonies committed on the high Seas, and Offences against the Law of Nations;

To declare War, grant Letters of Marque and Reprisal, and make Rules concerning Captures on Land and Water;

To raise and support Armies, but no Appropriation of Money to that Use shall be for a longer Term than two Years;

To provide and maintain a Navy;

To make Rules for the Government and Regulation of the land and naval Forces;

To provide for calling forth the Militia to execute the Laws of the Union, suppress Insurrections and repel Invasions;

To provide for organizing, arming, and disciplining, the Militia, and for governing such Part of them as may be employed in the Service of the United States, reserving to the States respectively, the Appointment of the Officers, and the Authority of training the Militia according to the discipline prescribed by Congress;

To exercise exclusive Legislation in all Cases whatsoever, over such District (not exceeding ten Miles square) as may, by Cession of particular States, and the Acceptance of Congress, become the Seat of the Government of the United States, and to exercise like Authority over all Places purchased by the Consent of the Legislature of the State in which the Same shall be, for the Erection of Forts, Magazines, Arsenals, dock-Yards, and other needful Buildings;—And

To make all Laws which shall be necessary and proper for carrying into Execution the foregoing Powers, and all other Powers vested by this Constitution in the Government of the United States, or in any Department or Officer thereof.

Section. 9.

The Migration or Importation of such Persons as any of the States now existing shall think proper to admit, shall not be prohibited by the Congress prior to the Year one thousand eight hundred and eight, but a Tax or duty may be imposed on such Importation, not exceeding ten dollars for each Person.

The Privilege of the Writ of Habeas Corpus shall not be suspended, unless when in Cases of Rebellion or Invasion the public Safety may require it.

No Bill of Attainder or ex post facto Law shall be passed.

No Capitation, or other direct, Tax shall be laid, unless in Proportion to the Census or enumeration herein before directed to be taken.

No Tax or Duty shall be laid on Articles exported from any State.

No Preference shall be given by any Regulation of Commerce or Revenue to the Ports of one State over those of another; nor shall Vessels bound to, or from, one State, be obliged to enter, clear, or pay Duties in another.

No Money shall be drawn from the Treasury, but in Consequence of Appropriations made by Law; and a regular Statement and Account of the Receipts and Expenditures of all public Money shall be published from time to time.

No Title of Nobility shall be granted by the United States: And no Person holding any Office of Profit or Trust under them, shall, without the Consent of the Congress, accept of any present, Emolument, Office, or Title, of any kind whatever, from any King, Prince, or foreign State.

Section. 10.

No State shall enter into any Treaty, Alliance, or Confederation; grant Letters of Marque and Reprisal; coin Money; emit Bills of Credit; make any Thing but gold and silver Coin a Tender in Payment of Debts; pass any Bill of Attainder, ex post facto Law, or Law impairing the Obligation of Contracts, or grant any Title of Nobility.

No State shall, without the Consent of the Congress, lay any Imposts or Duties on Imports or Exports, except what may be absolutely necessary for executing its inspection Laws: and the net Produce of all Duties and Imposts, laid by any State on Imports or Exports, shall be for the Use of the Treasury of the United States; and all such Laws shall be subject to the Revision and Controul of the Congress.

No State shall, without the Consent of Congress, lay any Duty of Tonnage, keep Troops, or Ships of War in time of Peace, enter into any Agreement or Compact with another State, or with a foreign Power, or engage in War, unless actually invaded, or in such imminent Danger as will not admit of delay.

Article. II.

Section. 1.

The executive Power shall be vested in a President of the United States of America. He shall hold his Office during the Term of four Years, and, together with the Vice President, chosen for the same Term, be elected, as follows:

Each State shall appoint, in such Manner as the Legislature thereof may direct, a Number of Electors, equal to the whole Number of Senators and Representatives to which the State may be entitled in the Congress: but no Senator or Representative, or Person holding an Office of Trust or Profit under the United States, shall be appointed an Elector.

The Electors shall meet in their respective States, and vote by Ballot for two Persons, of whom one at least shall not be an Inhabitant of the same State with themselves. And they shall make a List of all the Persons voted for, and of the Number of Votes for each; which List they shall sign and certify, and transmit sealed to the Seat of the Government of the United States, directed to the President of the Senate. The President of the Senate shall, in the Presence of the Senate and House of Representatives, open all the Certificates, and the Votes shall then be counted. The Person having the greatest Number of Votes shall be the President, if such Number be a Majority of the whole Number of Electors appointed; and if there be more than one who have such Majority, and have an equal Number of Votes, then the House of Representatives shall immediately chuse by Ballot one of them for President; and if no Person have a Majority, then from the five highest on the List the said House shall in like Manner chuse the President. But in chusing the President, the Votes shall be taken by States, the Representation from each State having one Vote; A quorum for this purpose shall consist of a Member or Members from two thirds of the States, and a Majority of all the States shall be necessary to a Choice. In every Case, after the Choice of the President, the Person having the greatest Number of Votes of the Electors shall be the Vice President. But if there should remain two or more who have equal Votes, the Senate shall chuse from them by Ballot the Vice President.

The Congress may determine the Time of chusing the Electors, and the Day on which they shall give their Votes; which Day shall be the same throughout the United States.

No Person except a natural born Citizen, or a Citizen of the United States, at the time of the Adoption of this Constitution, shall be eligible to the Office of President; neither shall any Person be eligible to that Office who shall not have attained to the Age of thirty five Years, and been fourteen Years a Resident within the United States.

In Case of the Removal of the President from Office, or of his Death, Resignation, or Inability to discharge the Powers and Duties of the said Office, the Same shall devolve on the Vice President, and the Congress may by Law provide for the Case of Removal, Death, Resignation or Inability, both of the President and Vice President, declaring what Officer

shall then act as President, and such Officer shall act accordingly, until the Disability be removed, or a President shall be elected.

The President shall, at stated Times, receive for his Services, a Compensation, which shall neither be increased nor diminished during the Period for which he shall have been elected, and he shall not receive within that Period any other Emolument from the United States, or any of them.

Before he enter on the Execution of his Office, he shall take the following Oath or Affirmation:—"I do solemnly swear (or affirm) that I will faithfully execute the Office of President of the United States, and will to the best of my Ability, preserve, protect and defend the Constitution of the United States."

Section. 2.

The President shall be Commander in Chief of the Army and Navy of the United States, and of the Militia of the several States, when called into the actual Service of the United States; he may require the Opinion, in writing, of the principal Officer in each of the executive Departments, upon any Subject relating to the Duties of their respective Offices, and he shall have Power to grant Reprieves and Pardons for Offences against the United States, except in Cases of Impeachment.

He shall have Power, by and with the Advice and Consent of the Senate, to make Treaties, provided two thirds of the Senators present concur; and he shall nominate, and by and with the Advice and Consent of the Senate, shall appoint Ambassadors, other public Ministers and Consuls, Judges of the supreme Court, and all other Officers of the United States, whose Appointments are not herein otherwise provided for, and which shall be established by Law: but the Congress may by Law vest the Appointment of such inferior Officers, as they think proper, in the President alone, in the Courts of Law, or in the Heads of Departments.

The President shall have Power to fill up all Vacancies that may happen during the Recess of the Senate, by granting Commissions which shall expire at the End of their next Session.

Section. 3.

He shall from time to time give to the Congress Information of the State of the Union, and recommend to their Consideration such Measures as he shall judge necessary and expedient; he may, on extraordinary Occasions, convene both Houses, or either of them, and in Case of Disagreement between them, with Respect to the Time of Adjournment, he may adjourn them to such Time as he shall think proper; he shall receive Ambassadors and other public Ministers; he shall take Care that the Laws be faithfully executed, and shall Commission all the Officers of the United States.

Section. 4.

The President, Vice President and all civil Officers of the United States, shall be removed from Office on Impeachment for, and Conviction of, Treason, Bribery, or other high Crimes and Misdemeanors.

Article. III.

Section. 1.

The judicial Power of the United States shall be vested in one supreme Court, and in such inferior Courts as the Congress may from time to time ordain and establish. The Judges, both of the supreme and inferior Courts, shall hold their Offices during good Behaviour, and shall, at stated Times, receive for their Services a Compensation, which shall not be diminished during their Continuance in Office.

Section. 2.

The judicial Power shall extend to all Cases, in Law and Equity, arising under this Constitution, the Laws of the United States, and Treaties made, or which shall be made, under their Authority;—to all Cases affecting Ambassadors, other public Ministers and Consuls;—to all Cases of admiralty and maritime Jurisdiction;—to Controversies to which the United States shall be a Party;—to Controversies between two or more States;—between a State and Citizens of another State;—between Citizens of different States;—between Citizens of the same State claiming Lands under Grants of different States, and between a State, or the Citizens thereof, and foreign States, Citizens or Subjects.

In all Cases affecting Ambassadors, other public Ministers and Consuls, and those in which a State shall be Party, the supreme Court shall have original Jurisdiction. In all the other Cases before mentioned, the supreme Court shall have appellate Jurisdiction,

both as to Law and Fact, with such Exceptions, and under such Regulations as the Congress shall make.

The Trial of all Crimes, except in Cases of Impeachment, shall be by Jury; and such Trial shall be held in the State where the said Crimes shall have been committed; but when not committed within any State, the Trial shall be at such Place or Places as the Congress may by Law have directed.

Section. 3.

Treason against the United States, shall consist only in levying War against them, or in adhering to their Enemies, giving them Aid and Comfort. No Person shall be convicted of Treason unless on the Testimony of two Witnesses to the same overt Act, or on Confession in open Court.

The Congress shall have Power to declare the Punishment of Treason, but no Attainder of Treason shall work Corruption of Blood, or Forfeiture except during the Life of the Person attainted.

Article. IV.

Section. 1.

Full Faith and Credit shall be given in each State to the public Acts, Records, and judicial Proceedings of every other State. And the Congress may by general Laws prescribe the Manner in which such Acts, Records and Proceedings shall be proved, and the Effect thereof.

Section. 2.

The Citizens of each State shall be entitled to all Privileges and Immunities of Citizens in the several States.

A Person charged in any State with Treason, Felony, or other Crime, who shall flee from Justice, and be found in another State, shall on Demand of the executive Authority of the State from which he fled, be delivered up, to be removed to the State having Jurisdiction of the Crime.

No Person held to Service or Labour in one State, under the Laws thereof, escaping into another, shall, in Consequence of any Law or Regulation therein, be discharged from such Service or Labour, but shall be delivered up on Claim of the Party to whom such Service or Labour may be due.

Section. 3.

New States may be admitted by the Congress into this Union; but no new State shall be formed or erected within the Jurisdiction of any other State; nor any State be formed by the Junction of two or more States, or Parts of States, without the Consent of the Legislatures of the States concerned as well as of the Congress.

The Congress shall have Power to dispose of and make all needful Rules and Regulations respecting the Territory or other Property belonging to the United States; and nothing in this Constitution shall be so construed as to Prejudice any Claims of the United States, or of any particular State.

Section. 4.

The United States shall guarantee to every State in this Union a Republican Form of Government, and shall protect each of them against Invasion; and on Application of the Legislature, or of the Executive (when the Legislature cannot be convened), against domestic Violence.

Article. V.

The Congress, whenever two thirds of both Houses shall deem it necessary, shall propose Amendments to this Constitution, or, on the Application of the Legislatures of two thirds of the several States, shall call a Convention for proposing Amendments, which, in either Case, shall be valid to all Intents and Purposes, as Part of this Constitution, when ratified by the Legislatures of three fourths of the several States, or by Conventions in three fourths thereof, as the one or the other Mode of Ratification may be proposed by the Congress; Provided that no Amendment which may be made prior to the Year One thousand eight hundred and eight shall in any Manner affect the first and fourth Clauses in the Ninth Section of the first Article; and that no State, without its Consent, shall be deprived of its equal Suffrage in the Senate.

Article. VI.

All Debts contracted and Engagements entered into, before the Adoption of this Constitution, shall be as valid against the United States under this Constitution, as under the Confederation.

This Constitution, and the Laws of the United States which shall be made in Pursuance thereof; and all Treaties made, or which shall be made, under the Authority of the United States, shall be the supreme Law of the Land; and the Judges in every State shall be bound thereby, any Thing in the Constitution or Laws of any State to the Contrary notwithstanding.

The Senators and Representatives before mentioned, and the Members of the several State Legislatures, and all executive and judicial Officers, both of the United States and of the several States, shall be bound by Oath or Affirmation, to support this Constitution; but no religious Test shall ever be required as a Qualification to any Office or public Trust under the United States.

Article. VII.

The Ratification of the Conventions of nine States, shall be sufficient for the Establishment of this Constitution between the States so ratifying the Same.

The Word, "the," being interlined between the seventh and eighth Lines of the first Page, the Word "Thirty" being partly written on an Erazure in the fifteenth Line of the first Page, The Words "is tried" being interlined between the thirty second and thirty third Lines of the first Page and the Word "the" being interlined between the forty third and forty fourth Lines of the second Page.

Attest William Jackson Secretary

Done in Convention by the Unanimous Consent of the States present the Seventeenth Day of September in the Year of our Lord one thousand seven hundred and Eighty seven and of the Independence of the United States of America the Twelfth In witness whereof We have hereunto subscribed our Names,

Go. Washington
Presidt and deputy from Virginia
New Hampshire
John Langdon
Nicholas Gilman
Massachusetts
Nathaniel Gorham
Rufus King
Connecticut
Wm. Saml. Johnson
Roger Sherman
New York
Alexander Hamilton
New Jersey

Wil. Livingston
David Brearly
Wm. Paterson
Jona. Dayton
Pennsylvania
B Franklin
Thomas Mifflin
Robt. Morris
Geo. Clymer
Thos. Fitzsimons
Jared Ingersoll
James Wilson
Gouv Morris
Delaware
Geo. Read
Gunning Bedford jun
John Dickinson
Richard Bassett
Jaco. Broom
Maryland
James McHenry
Dan of St Thos. Jenifer
Danl. Carroll
Virginia
John Blair
James Madison Jr.
North Carolina
Wm. Blount
Richd. Dobbs Spaight
Hu Williamson
South Carolina
J. Rutledge
Charles Cotesworth Pinckney
Charles Pinckney
Pierce Butler
Georgia
William Few
Abr Baldwin

THE BILL OF RIGHTS

Congress of the United States
    begun and held at the City of New-York, on
    Wednesday the fourth of March, one thousand
seven hundred and eighty nine.

    THE Conventions of a number of the States, having at the time of their adopting the Constitution, expressed a desire, in order to prevent misconstruction or abuse of its powers, that further declaratory and re-
strictive clauses should be added: And as extending the ground of public confidence in the Government, will best ensure the beneficent ends of its institution.

    RESOLVED by the Senate and House of Representatives of the United States of America, in Congress assembled, two thirds of both Houses concurring, that the following Articles be proposed to the Legislatures of the several States, as amendments to the Constitution of the United States, all, or any of which Articles, when ratified by three fourths of the said Legislatures, to be valid to all intents and purposes, as part of the said Constitution; viz.

    ARTICLES in addition to, and Amendment of the Constitution of the United States of America, proposed by Congress, and ratified by the Legislatures of the several States, pursuant to the fifth Article of the original Constitution.

Amendment I

Congress shall make no law respecting an establishment of religion, or prohibiting the free exercise thereof; or abridging the freedom of speech, or of the press; or the right of the people peaceably to assemble, and to petition the Government for a redress of grievances.

Amendment II

A well regulated Militia, being necessary to the security of a free State, the right of the people to keep and bear Arms, shall not be infringed.

Amendment III

No Soldier shall, in time of peace be quartered in any house, without the consent of the Owner, nor in time of war, but in a manner to be prescribed by law.

Amendment IV

The right of the people to be secure in their persons, houses, papers, and effects, against unreasonable searches and seizures, shall not be violated, and no Warrants shall issue, but upon probable cause, supported by Oath or affirmation, and particularly describing the place to be searched, and the persons or things to be seized.

Amendment V

No person shall be held to answer for a capital, or otherwise infamous crime, unless on a presentment or indictment of a Grand Jury, except in cases arising in the land or naval forces, or in the Militia, when in actual service in time of War or public danger; nor shall any person be subject for the same offence to be twice put in jeopardy of life or limb; nor shall be compelled in any criminal case to be a witness against himself, nor be deprived of life, liberty, or property, without due process of law; nor shall private property be taken for public use, without just compensation.

Amendment VI

In all criminal prosecutions, the accused shall enjoy the right to a speedy and public trial, by an impartial jury of the State and district wherein the crime shall have been committed, which district shall have been previously ascertained by law, and to be informed of the nature and cause of the accusation; to be confronted with the witnesses against him; to have compulsory process for obtaining witnesses in his favor, and to have the Assistance of Counsel for his defence.

Amendment VII

In suits at common law, where the value in controversy shall exceed twenty dollars, the right of trial by jury shall be preserved, and no fact tried by a jury, shall be otherwise reexamined in any Court of the United States, than according to the rules of the common law.

Amendment VIII

Excessive bail shall not be required, nor excessive fines imposed, nor cruel and unusual punishments inflicted.

Amendment IX

The enumeration in the Constitution, of certain rights, shall not be construed to deny or disparage others retained by the people.

Amendment X

The powers not delegated to the United States by the Constitution, nor prohibited by it to the States, are reserved to the States respectively, or to the people.

AMENDMENTS XI–XXVII TO THE CONSTITUTION

Amendment XI (1798)

The judicial power of the United States shall not be construed to extend to any suit in law or equity, commenced or prosecuted against one of the United States by citizens of another state, or by citizens or subjects of any foreign state.

Amendment XII (1804)

The electors shall meet in their respective states and vote by ballot for President and Vice-President, one of whom, at least, shall not be an inhabitant of the same state with themselves; they shall name in their ballots the person voted for as President, and in distinct ballots the person voted for as Vice-President, and they shall make distinct lists of all persons voted for as President, and of all persons voted for as Vice-President, and of the number of votes for each, which lists they shall sign and certify, and transmit sealed to the seat of the government of the United States, directed to the President of the Senate;—The President of the Senate shall, in the presence of the Senate and House of Representatives, open all the certificates and the votes shall then be counted;—the person having the greatest number of votes for President, shall be the President, if such number be a majority of the whole number of electors appointed; and if no person have such majority, then from the persons having the highest numbers not exceeding three on the list of those voted for as President, the House of Representatives shall choose immediately, by ballot, the President. But in choosing the President, the votes shall be taken by states, the representation from each state having one vote; a quorum for this purpose shall consist of a member or members from two-thirds of the states, and a majority of all the states shall be necessary to a choice. And if the House of Representatives shall not choose a President whenever the right of choice shall devolve upon them, before the fourth day of March next following, then the Vice-President shall act as President, as in the case of the death or other constitutional disability of the President. The person having the greatest number of votes as Vice-President, shall be the Vice-President, if such number be a majority of the whole number of electors appointed, and if no person have a majority, then from the two highest numbers on the list, the Senate shall choose the Vice-President; a quorum for the purpose shall consist of two-thirds of the whole number of Senators, and a majority of the whole number shall be necessary to a choice. But no person constitutionally ineligible to the office of President shall be eligible to that of Vice-President of the United States.

Amendment XIII (1865)

Section 1. Neither slavery nor involuntary servitude, except as a punishment for crime whereof the party shall have been duly convicted, shall exist within the United States, or any place subject to their jurisdiction.

Section 2. Congress shall have power to enforce this article by appropriate legislation.

Amendment XIV (1868)

Section 1. All persons born or naturalized in the United States, and subject to the jurisdiction thereof, are citizens of the United States and of the state wherein they reside. No state shall make or enforce any law which shall abridge the privileges or immunities of citizens of the United States; nor shall any state deprive any person of life, liberty, or property, without due process of law; nor deny to any person within its jurisdiction the equal protection of the laws.

Section 2. Representatives shall be apportioned among the several states according to their respective numbers, counting the whole number of persons in each state, excluding Indians not taxed. But when the right to vote at any election for the choice of electors for President and Vice President of the United States, Representatives in Congress, the executive and judicial officers of a state, or the members of the legislature thereof, is denied to any of the male inhabitants of such state, being twenty-one years of age, and citizens of the United States, or in any way abridged, except for participation in rebellion, or other crime, the basis of representation therein shall be reduced in the proportion which the number of such male citizens shall bear to the whole number of male citizens twenty-one years of age in such state.

Section 3. No person shall be a Senator or Representative in Congress, or elector of President and Vice President, or hold any office, civil or military, under the United States, or under any state, who, having previously taken an oath, as a member of Congress, or as an officer of the United States, or as a member of any state legislature, or as an executive or judicial officer of any state, to support the Constitution of the United States, shall have engaged in insurrection or rebellion against the same, or given aid or comfort to the enemies thereof. But Congress may by a vote of two-thirds of each House, remove such disability.

Section 4. The validity of the public debt of the United States, authorized by law, including debts incurred for payment of pensions and bounties for services in suppressing insurrection or rebellion, shall not be questioned. But neither the United States nor any state shall assume or pay any debt or obligation incurred in aid of insurrection or rebellion against the United States, or any claim for the loss or emancipation of any slave; but all such debts, obligations and claims shall be held illegal and void.

Section 5. The Congress shall have power to enforce, by appropriate legislation, the provisions of this article.

Amendment XV (1870)

Section 1. The right of citizens of the United States to vote shall not be denied or abridged by the United States or by any state on account of race, color, or previous condition of servitude.

Section 2. The Congress shall have power to enforce this article by appropriate legislation.

Amendment XVI (1913)

The Congress shall have power to lay and collect taxes on incomes, from whatever source derived, without apportionment among the several states, and without regard to any census of enumeration.

Amendment XVII (1913)

The Senate of the United States shall be composed of two Senators from each state, elected by the people thereof, for six years; and each Senator shall have one vote. The electors in each state shall have the qualifications requisite for electors of the most numerous branch of the state legislatures.

When vacancies happen in the representation of any state in the Senate, the executive authority of such state shall issue writs of election to fill such vacancies: Provided, that the legislature of any state may empower the executive thereof to make temporary appointments until the people fill the vacancies by election as the legislature may direct.

This amendment shall not be so construed as to affect the election or term of any Senator chosen before it becomes valid as part of the Constitution.

Amendment XVIII (1919)

Section 1. After one year from the ratification of this article the manufacture, sale, or transportation of intoxicating liquors within, the importation thereof into, or the exportation thereof from the United States and all territory subject to the jurisdiction thereof for beverage purposes is hereby prohibited.

Section 2. The Congress and the several states shall have concurrent power to enforce this article by appropriate legislation.

Section 3. This article shall be inoperative unless it shall have been ratified as an amendment to the Constitution by the legislatures of the several states, as provided in the Constitution, within seven years from the date of the submission hereof to the states by the Congress.

Amendment XIX (1920)

The right of citizens of the United States to vote shall not be denied or abridged by the United States or by any state on account of sex.

Congress shall have power to enforce this article by appropriate legislation.

Amendment XX (1933)

Section 1. The terms of the President and Vice President shall end at noon on the 20th day of January, and the terms of Senators and Representatives at noon on the 3d day of January, of the years in which such terms would have ended if this article had not been ratified; and the terms of their successors shall then begin.

Section 2. The Congress shall assemble at least once in every year, and such meeting shall begin at noon on the 3d day of January, unless they shall by law appoint a different day.

Section 3. If, at the time fixed for the beginning of the term of the President, the President elect shall have

died, the Vice President elect shall become President. If a President shall not have been chosen before the time fixed for the beginning of his term, or if the President elect shall have failed to qualify, then the Vice President elect shall act as President until a President shall have qualified; and the Congress may by law provide for the case wherein neither a President elect nor a Vice President elect shall have qualified, declaring who shall then act as President, or the manner in which one who is to act shall be selected, and such person shall act accordingly until a President or Vice President shall have qualified.

Section 4. The Congress may by law provide for the case of the death of any of the persons from whom the House of Representatives may choose a President whenever the right of choice shall have devolved upon them, and for the case of the death of any of the persons from whom the Senate may choose a Vice President whenever the right of choice shall have devolved upon them.

Section 5. Sections 1 and 2 shall take effect on the 15th day of October following the ratification of this article.

Section 6. This article shall be inoperative unless it shall have been ratified as an amendment to the Constitution by the legislatures of three-fourths of the several states within seven years from the date of its submission.

Amendment XXI (1933)

Section 1. The eighteenth article of amendment to the Constitution of the United States is hereby repealed.

Section 2. The transportation or importation into any state, territory, or possession of the United States for delivery or use therein of intoxicating liquors, in violation of the laws thereof, is hereby prohibited.

Section 3. This article shall be inoperative unless it shall have been ratified as an amendment to the Constitution by conventions in the several states, as provided in the Constitution, within seven years from the date of the submission hereof to the states by the Congress.

Amendment XXII (1951)

Section 1. No person shall be elected to the office of the President more than twice, and no person who has held the office of President, or acted as President, for more than two years of a term to which some other person was elected President shall be elected to the office of the President more than once. But this article shall not apply to any person holding the office of President when this article was proposed by the Congress, and shall not prevent any person who may be holding the office of President, or acting as President, during the term within which this article becomes operative from holding the office of President or acting as President during the remainder of such term.

Section 2. This article shall be inoperative unless it shall have been ratified as an amendment to the Constitution by the legislatures of three-fourths of the several states within seven years from the date of its submission to the states by the Congress.

Amendment XXIII (1961)

Section 1. The District constituting the seat of government of the United States shall appoint in such manner as the Congress may direct:

A number of electors of President and Vice President equal to the whole number of Senators and Representatives in Congress to which the District would be entitled if it were a state, but in no event more than the least populous state; they shall be in addition to those appointed by the states, but they shall be considered, for the purposes of the election of President and Vice President, to be electors appointed by a state; and they shall meet in the District and perform such duties as provided by the twelfth article of amendment.

Section 2. The Congress shall have power to enforce this article by appropriate legislation.

Amendment XXIV (1964)

Section 1. The right of citizens of the United States to vote in any primary or other election for President or Vice President, for electors for President or Vice President, or for Senator or Representative in Congress, shall not be denied or abridged by the United States or any state by reason of failure to pay any poll tax or other tax.

Section 2. The Congress shall have power to enforce this article by appropriate legislation.

Amendment XXV (1967)

Section 1. In case of the removal of the President from office or of his death or resignation, the Vice President shall become President.

Section 2. Whenever there is a vacancy in the office of the Vice President, the President shall nominate a Vice President who shall take office upon confirmation by a majority vote of both Houses of Congress.

Section 3. Whenever the President transmits to the President pro tempore of the Senate and the Speaker of the House of Representatives his written declaration that he is unable to discharge the powers and duties of his office, and until he transmits to them a written declaration to the contrary, such powers and duties shall be discharged by the Vice President as Acting President.

Section 4. Whenever the Vice President and a majority of either the principal officers of the executive departments or of such other body as Congress may by law provide, transmit to the President pro tempore of the Senate and the Speaker of the House of Representatives their written declaration that the President is unable to discharge the powers and duties of his office, the Vice President shall immediately assume the powers and duties of the office as Acting President.

Thereafter, when the President transmits to the President pro tempore of the Senate and the Speaker of the House of Representatives his written declaration that no inability exists, he shall resume the powers and duties of his office unless the Vice President and a majority of either the principal officers of the executive department or of such other body as Congress may by law provide, transmit within four days to the President pro tempore of the Senate and the Speaker of the House of Representatives their written declaration that the President is unable to discharge the powers and duties of his office. Thereupon Congress shall decide the issue, assembling within forty-eight hours for that purpose if not in session. If the Congress, within twenty-one days after receipt of the latter written declaration, or, if Congress is not in session, within twenty-one days after Congress is required to assemble, determines by two-thirds vote of both Houses that the President is unable to discharge the powers and duties of his office, the Vice President shall continue to discharge the same as Acting President; otherwise, the President shall resume the powers and duties of his office.

Amendment XXVI (1971)

Section 1. The right of citizens of the United States, who are 18 years of age or older, to vote, shall not be denied or abridged by the United States or any state on account of age.

Section 2. The Congress shall have the power to enforce this article by appropriate legislation.

Amendment XXVII (1992)

No law varying the compensation for the services of the Senators and Representatives shall take effect until an election of Representatives shall have intervened.

FEDERALIST NO. 10

The Same Subject Continued:
The Union as a Safeguard against Domestic Faction and Insurrection

From the New York Packet.
  Friday, November 23, 1787.
  To the People of the State of New York:
  AMONG the numerous advantages promised by a well constructed Union, none deserves to be more accurately developed than its tendency to break and control the violence of faction. The friend of popular governments never finds himself so much alarmed for their character and fate, as when he contemplates their propensity to this dangerous vice. He will not fail, therefore, to set a due value on any plan which, without violating the principles to which he is attached, provides a proper cure for it. The instability, injustice, and confusion introduced into the public councils, have, in truth, been the mortal diseases under which popular governments have everywhere perished; as they continue to be the favorite and fruitful topics from which the adversaries to liberty derive their most specious declamations. The valuable improvements made by the American constitutions on the popular models, both ancient and modern, cannot certainly be too much admired; but it would be an unwarrantable partiality, to contend that they have as effectually obviated the danger on this side, as was wished and expected. Complaints are everywhere heard from our most considerate and virtuous citizens, equally the friends of public and private faith, and of public and personal liberty, that our governments are too unstable, that the public good is disregarded in the conflicts of rival parties, and that measures are too often decided, not according to the rules of justice and the rights of the minor party, but by the superior force of an interested and overbearing majority. However anxiously we may wish that these complaints had no foundation, the evidence, of known facts will not permit us to deny that they are in some degree true. It will be found, indeed, on a candid review of our situation, that some of the distresses under which we labor have been erroneously charged on the operation of our governments; but it will be found, at the same time, that other causes will not alone account for many of our heaviest misfortunes; and, particularly, for that prevailing and increasing distrust of public engagements, and alarm for private rights, which are echoed from one end of the continent to the other. These must be chiefly, if not wholly, effects of the unsteadiness and injustice with which a factious spirit has tainted our public administrations.

By a faction, I understand a number of citizens, whether amounting to a majority or a minority of the whole, who are united and actuated by some common impulse of passion, or of interest, adversed to the rights of other citizens, or to the permanent and aggregate interests of the community.

There are two methods of curing the mischiefs of faction: the one, by removing its causes; the other, by controlling its effects.

There are again two methods of removing the causes of faction: the one, by destroying the liberty which is essential to its existence; the other, by giving to every citizen the same opinions, the same passions, and the same interests.

It could never be more truly said than of the first remedy, that it was worse than the disease. Liberty is to faction what air is to fire, an aliment without which it instantly expires. But it could not be less folly to abolish liberty, which is essential to political life, because it nourishes faction, than it would be to wish the annihilation of air, which is essential to animal life, because it imparts to fire its destructive agency.

The second expedient is as impracticable as the first would be unwise. As long as the reason of man continues fallible, and he is at liberty to exercise it, different opinions will be formed. As long as the connection subsists between his reason and his self-love, his opinions and his passions will have a reciprocal influence on each other; and the former will be objects to which the latter will attach themselves. The diversity in the faculties of men, from which the rights of property originate, is not less an insuperable obstacle to a uniformity of interests. The protection of these faculties is the first object of government. From the protection of different and unequal faculties of acquiring property, the possession of different degrees and kinds of property immediately results; and from the influence of these on the sentiments and views of the respective proprietors, ensues a division of the society into different interests and parties.

The latent causes of faction are thus sown in the nature of man; and we see them everywhere brought into different degrees of activity, according to the different circumstances of civil society. A zeal for different opinions concerning religion, concerning government, and many other points, as well of speculation as of practice; an attachment to different leaders ambitiously contending for pre-eminence and power; or to persons of other descriptions whose fortunes have been interesting to the human passions, have, in turn, divided mankind into parties, inflamed them with mutual animosity, and rendered them much more disposed to vex and oppress each other than to co-operate for their common good. So strong is this propensity of mankind to fall into mutual animosities, that where no substantial occasion presents itself, the most frivolous and fanciful distinctions have been sufficient to kindle their unfriendly passions and excite their most violent conflicts. But the most common and durable source of factions has been the various and unequal distribution of property. Those who hold and those who are without property have ever formed distinct interests in society. Those who are creditors, and those who are debtors, fall under a like discrimination. A landed interest, a manufacturing interest, a mercantile interest, a moneyed interest, with many lesser interests, grow up of necessity in civilized nations, and divide them into different classes, actuated by different sentiments and views. The regulation of these various and interfering interests forms the principal task of modern legislation, and involves the spirit of party and faction in the necessary and ordinary operations of the government.

No man is allowed to be a judge in his own cause, because his interest would certainly bias his judgment, and, not improbably, corrupt his integrity. With equal, nay with greater reason, a body of men are unfit to be both judges and parties at the same time; yet what are many of the most important acts of legislation, but so many judicial determinations, not indeed concerning the rights of single persons, but concerning the rights of large bodies of citizens? And what are the different classes of legislators but advocates and parties to the causes which they determine? Is a law proposed concerning private debts? It is a question to which the creditors are parties on one side and the debtors on the other. Justice ought to hold the balance between them. Yet the parties are, and must be, themselves the judges; and the most numerous party, or, in other words, the most powerful faction must be expected to prevail. Shall domestic manufactures be encouraged, and in what degree, by restrictions on foreign manufactures? are questions which would be differently decided by the landed and the manufacturing classes, and proba-

bly by neither with a sole regard to justice and the public good. The apportionment of taxes on the various descriptions of property is an act which seems to require the most exact impartiality; yet there is, perhaps, no legislative act in which greater opportunity and temptation are given to a predominant party to trample on the rules of justice. Every shilling with which they overburden the inferior number, is a shilling saved to their own pockets.

It is in vain to say that enlightened statesmen will be able to adjust these clashing interests, and render them all subservient to the public good. Enlightened statesmen will not always be at the helm. Nor, in many cases, can such an adjustment be made at all without taking into view indirect and remote considerations, which will rarely prevail over the immediate interest which one party may find in disregarding the rights of another or the good of the whole.

The inference to which we are brought is, that the CAUSES of faction cannot be removed, and that relief is only to be sought in the means of controlling its EFFECTS.

If a faction consists of less than a majority, relief is supplied by the republican principle, which enables the majority to defeat its sinister views by regular vote. It may clog the administration, it may convulse the society; but it will be unable to execute and mask its violence under the forms of the Constitution. When a majority is included in a faction, the form of popular government, on the other hand, enables it to sacrifice to its ruling passion or interest both the public good and the rights of other citizens. To secure the public good and private rights against the danger of such a faction, and at the same time to preserve the spirit and the form of popular government, is then the great object to which our inquiries are directed. Let me add that it is the great desideratum by which this form of government can be rescued from the opprobrium under which it has so long labored, and be recommended to the esteem and adoption of mankind.

By what means is this object attainable? Evidently by one of two only. Either the existence of the same passion or interest in a majority at the same time must be prevented, or the majority, having such coexistent passion or interest, must be rendered, by their number and local situation, unable to concert and carry into effect schemes of oppression. If the impulse and the opportunity be suffered to coincide, we well know that neither moral nor religious motives can be relied on as an adequate control. They are not found to be such on the injustice and violence of individuals, and lose their efficacy in proportion to the number combined together, that is, in proportion as their efficacy becomes needful.

From this view of the subject it may be concluded that a pure democracy, by which I mean a society consisting of a small number of citizens, who assemble and administer the government in person, can admit of no cure for the mischiefs of faction. A common passion or interest will, in almost every case, be felt by a majority of the whole; a communication and concert result from the form of government itself; and there is nothing to check the inducements to sacrifice the weaker party or an obnoxious individual. Hence it is that such democracies have ever been spectacles of turbulence and contention; have ever been found incompatible with personal security or the rights of property; and have in general been as short in their lives as they have been violent in their deaths. Theoretic politicians, who have patronized this species of government, have erroneously supposed that by reducing mankind to a perfect equality in their political rights, they would, at the same time, be perfectly equalized and assimilated in their possessions, their opinions, and their passions.

A republic, by which I mean a government in which the scheme of representation takes place, opens a different prospect, and promises the cure for which we are seeking. Let us examine the points in which it varies from pure democracy, and we shall comprehend both the nature of the cure and the efficacy which it must derive from the Union.

The two great points of difference between a democracy and a republic are: first, the delegation of the government, in the latter, to a small number of citizens elected by the rest; secondly, the greater number of citizens, and greater sphere of country, over which the latter may be extended.

The effect of the first difference is, on the one hand, to refine and enlarge the public views, by passing them through the medium of a chosen body of citizens, whose wisdom may best discern the true interest of their country, and whose patriotism and love of justice will be least likely to sacrifice it to temporary or partial considerations. Under such a regulation, it may well happen that the public voice, pronounced by the representatives of the people, will be more consonant to the public good than if pronounced by the people themselves, convened for the purpose. On the other hand, the effect may be inverted. Men of factious tempers, of local prejudices, or of sinister designs, may, by intrigue, by corruption, or by other means, first obtain the suffrages, and then betray the interests, of the people. The question resulting is, whether small or extensive republics are more favorable to the election of proper guardians of the public weal; and it is clearly decided in favor of the latter by two obvious considerations:

In the first place, it is to be remarked that, however small the republic may be, the representatives must be raised to a certain number, in order to guard against the cabals of a few; and that, however large it may be, they must be limited to a certain number, in order to guard against the confusion of a multitude. Hence, the number of representatives in the two cases not being in proportion to that of the two constituents, and being proportionally greater in the small republic, it follows that, if the proportion of fit characters be not less in the large than in the small republic, the former will present a greater option, and consequently a greater probability of a fit choice.

In the next place, as each representative will be chosen by a greater number of citizens in the large than in the small republic, it will be more difficult for unworthy candidates to practice with success the vicious arts by which elections are too often carried; and the suffrages of the people being more free, will be more likely to centre in men who possess the most attractive merit and the most diffusive and established characters.

It must be confessed that in this, as in most other cases, there is a mean, on both sides of which inconveniences will be found to lie. By enlarging too much the number of electors, you render the representatives too little acquainted with all their local circumstances and lesser interests; as by reducing it too much, you render him unduly attached to these, and too little fit to comprehend and pursue great and national objects. The federal Constitution forms a happy combination in this respect; the great and aggregate interests being referred to the national, the local and particular to the State legislatures.

The other point of difference is, the greater number of citizens and extent of territory which may be brought within the compass of republican than of democratic government; and it is this circumstance principally which renders factious combinations less to be dreaded in the former than in the latter. The smaller the society, the fewer probably will be the distinct parties and interests composing it; the fewer the distinct parties and interests, the more frequently will a majority be found of the same party; and the smaller the number of individuals composing a majority, and the smaller the compass within which they are placed, the more easily will they concert and execute their plans of oppression. Extend the sphere, and you take in a greater variety of parties and interests; you make it less probable that a majority of the whole will have a common motive to invade the rights of other citizens; or if such a common motive exists, it will be more difficult for all who feel it to discover their own strength, and to act in unison with each other. Besides other impediments, it may be remarked that, where there is a consciousness of unjust or dishonorable purposes, communication is always checked by distrust in proportion to the number whose concurrence is necessary.

Hence, it clearly appears, that the same advantage which a republic has over a democracy, in controlling the effects of faction, is enjoyed by a large over a small republic,—is enjoyed by the Union over the States composing it. Does the advantage consist in the substitution of representatives whose enlightened views and virtuous sentiments render them superior to local prejudices and schemes of injustice? It will not be denied that the representation of the Union will be most likely to possess these requisite endowments. Does it consist in the greater security afforded by a greater variety of parties, against the event of any one party being able to outnumber and oppress the rest? In an equal degree does the increased variety of parties comprised within the Union, increase this security. Does it, in fine, consist in the greater obstacles opposed to the concert and accomplishment of the secret wishes of an unjust and interested majority? Here, again, the extent of the Union gives it the most palpable advantage.

The influence of factious leaders may kindle a flame within their particular States, but will be unable to spread a general conflagration through the other States. A religious sect may degenerate into a political faction in a part of the Confederacy; but the variety of sects dispersed over the entire face of it must secure the national councils against any danger from that source. A rage for paper money, for an abolition of debts, for an equal division of property, or for any other improper or wicked project, will be less apt to pervade the whole body of the Union than a particular member of it; in the same proportion as such a malady is more likely to taint a particular county or district, than an entire State.

In the extent and proper structure of the Union, therefore, we behold a republican remedy for the diseases most incident to republican government. And according to the degree of pleasure and pride we feel in being republicans, ought to be our zeal in cherishing the spirit and supporting the character of Federalists.

PUBLIUS.

_____
Source: Federalist No. 10, Library of Congress, http://thomas.loc.gov/home/histdox/fed_10.html.

FEDERALIST NO. 51

The Structure of the Government Must Furnish the Proper Checks and Balances between the Different Departments

From the New York Packet.
Friday, February 8, 1788.
To the People of the State of New York:

TO WHAT expedient, then, shall we finally resort, for maintaining in practice the necessary partition of power among the several departments, as laid down in the Constitution? The only answer that can be given is, that as all these exterior provisions are found to be inadequate, the defect must be supplied, by so contriving the interior structure of the government as that its several constituent parts may, by their mutual relations, be the means of keeping each other in their proper places. Without presuming to undertake a full development of this important idea, I will hazard a few general observations, which may perhaps place it in a clearer light, and enable us to form a more correct judgment of the principles and structure of the government planned by the convention. In order to lay a due foundation for that separate and distinct exercise of the different powers of government, which to a certain extent is admitted on all hands to be essential to the preservation of liberty, it is evident that each department should have a will of its own; and consequently should be so constituted that the members of each should have as little agency as possible in the appointment of the members of the others. Were this principle rigorously adhered to, it would require that all the appointments for the supreme executive, legislative, and judiciary magistracies should be drawn from the same fountain of authority, the people, through channels having no communication whatever with one another. Perhaps such a plan of constructing the several departments would be less difficult in practice than it may in contemplation appear. Some difficulties, however, and some additional expense would attend the execution of it. Some deviations, therefore, from the principle must be admitted. In the constitution of the judiciary department in particular, it might be inexpedient to insist rigorously on the principle: first, because peculiar qualifications being essential in the members, the primary consideration ought to be to select that mode of choice which best secures these qualifications; secondly, because the permanent tenure by which the appointments are held in that department, must soon destroy all sense of dependence on the authority conferring them. It is equally evident, that the members of each department should be as little dependent as possible on those of the others, for the emoluments annexed to their offices. Were the executive magistrate, or the judges, not independent of the legislature in this particular, their independence in every other would be merely nominal. But the great security against a gradual concentration of the several powers in the same department, consists in giving to those who administer each department the necessary constitutional means and personal motives to resist encroachments of the others. The provision for defense must in this, as in all other cases, be made commensurate to the danger of attack. Ambition must be made to counteract ambition. The interest of the man must be connected with the constitutional rights of the place. It may be a reflection on human nature, that such devices should be necessary to control the abuses of government. But what is government itself, but the greatest of all reflections on human nature? If men were angels, no government would be necessary. If angels were to govern men, neither external nor internal controls on government would be necessary. In framing a government which is to be administered by men over men, the great difficulty lies in this: you must first enable the government to control the governed; and in the next place oblige it to control itself. A dependence on the people is, no doubt, the primary control on the government; but experience has taught mankind the necessity of auxiliary precautions. This policy of supplying, by opposite and rival interests, the defect of better motives, might be traced through the whole system of human affairs, private as well as public. We see it particularly displayed in all the subordinate distributions of power, where the constant aim is to divide and arrange the several offices in such a manner as that each may be a check on the other that the private interest of every individual may be a sentinel over the public rights. These inventions of prudence cannot be less requisite in the distribution of the supreme powers of the State. But it is not possible to give to each department an equal power of self-defense. In republican government, the legislative authority necessarily predominates. The remedy for this inconveniency is to divide the legislature into different branches; and to render them, by different modes of election and different principles of action, as little connected with each other as the nature of their common functions and their common dependence on the society will admit. It may even be necessary to guard against dangerous encroachments by still further precautions. As the weight of the legislative authority requires that it should be thus divided, the weakness of the executive may re-

quire, on the other hand, that it should be fortified. An absolute negative on the legislature appears, at first view, to be the natural defense with which the executive magistrate should be armed. But perhaps it would be neither altogether safe nor alone sufficient. On ordinary occasions it might not be exerted with the requisite firmness, and on extraordinary occasions it might be perfidiously abused. May not this defect of an absolute negative be supplied by some qualified connection between this weaker department and the weaker branch of the stronger department, by which the latter may be led to support the constitutional rights of the former, without being too much detached from the rights of its own department? If the principles on which these observations are founded be just, as I persuade myself they are, and they be applied as a criterion to the several State constitutions, and to the federal Constitution it will be found that if the latter does not perfectly correspond with them, the former are infinitely less able to bear such a test. There are, moreover, two considerations particularly applicable to the federal system of America, which place that system in a very interesting point of view. First. In a single republic, all the power surrendered by the people is submitted to the administration of a single government; and the usurpations are guarded against by a division of the government into distinct and separate departments. In the compound republic of America, the power surrendered by the people is first divided between two distinct governments, and then the portion allotted to each subdivided among distinct and separate departments. Hence a double security arises to the rights of the people. The different governments will control each other, at the same time that each will be controlled by itself. Second. It is of great importance in a republic not only to guard the society against the oppression of its rulers, but to guard one part of the society against the injustice of the other part. Different interests necessarily exist in different classes of citizens. If a majority be united by a common interest, the rights of the minority will be insecure. There are but two methods of providing against this evil: the one by creating a will in the community independent of the majority that is, of the society itself; the other, by comprehending in the society so many separate descriptions of citizens as will render an unjust combination of a majority of the whole very improbable, if not impracticable. The first method prevails in all governments possessing an hereditary or self-appointed authority. This, at best, is but a precarious security; because a power independent of the society may as well espouse the unjust views of the major, as the rightful interests of the minor party, and may possibly be turned against both parties. The second method will be exemplified in the federal republic of the United States. Whilst all authority in it will be derived from and dependent on the society, the society itself will be broken into so many parts, interests, and classes of citizens, that the rights of individuals, or of the minority, will be in little danger from interested combinations of the majority. In a free government the security for civil rights must be the same as that for religious rights. It consists in the one case in the multiplicity of interests, and in the other in the multiplicity of sects. The degree of security in both cases will depend on the number of interests and sects; and this may be presumed to depend on the extent of country and number of people comprehended under the same government. This view of the subject must particularly recommend a proper federal system to all the sincere and considerate friends of republican government, since it shows that in exact proportion as the territory of the Union may be formed into more circumscribed Confederacies, or States oppressive combinations of a majority will be facilitated: the best security, under the republican forms, for the rights of every class of citizens, will be diminished: and consequently the stability and independence of some members of the government, the only other security, must be proportionately increased. Justice is the end of government. It is the end of civil society. It ever has been and ever will be pursued until it be obtained, or until liberty be lost in the pursuit. In a society under the forms of which the stronger faction can readily unite and oppress the weaker, anarchy may as truly be said to reign as in a state of nature, where the weaker individual is not secured against the violence of the stronger; and as, in the latter state, even the stronger individuals are prompted, by the uncertainty of their condition, to submit to a government which may pro-

tect the weak as well as themselves; so, in the former state, will the more powerful factions or parties be gradually induced, by a like motive, to wish for a government which will protect all parties, the weaker as well as the more powerful. It can be little doubted that if the State of Rhode Island was separated from the Confederacy and left to itself, the insecurity of rights under the popular form of government within such narrow limits would be displayed by such reiterated oppressions of factious majorities that some power altogether independent of the people would soon be called for by the voice of the very factions whose misrule had proved the necessity of it. In the extended republic of the United States, and among the great variety of interests, parties, and sects which it embraces, a coalition of a majority of the whole society could seldom take place on any other principles than those of justice and the general good; whilst there being thus less danger to a minor from the will of a major party, there must be less pretext, also, to provide for the security of the former, by introducing into the government a will not dependent on the latter, or, in other words, a will independent of the society itself. It is no less certain than it is important, notwithstanding the contrary opinions which have been entertained, that the larger the society, provided it lie within a practical sphere, the more duly capable it will be of self-government. And happily for the REPUBLICAN CAUSE, the practicable sphere may be carried to a very great extent, by a judicious modification and mixture of the FEDERAL PRINCIPLE.

PUBLIUS.

Source: Federalist No. 51, Library of Congress, http://thomas.loc.gov/home/histdox/fed_51.html.

Appendix C:
Charts

Committee Diagram

Committee Name	Date Established	NH	CT	MA	NY	NJ	PA	DE	MD	VA	NC	SC	GA
Rules	28-May					Hamilton				**Wythe**		C. Pinckney	
Compromise on Representation in Congress	2-Jul		Ellsworth	**Gerry**	Yates	Paterson	Franklin	Bedford	Martin	Mason	Davie	Rutledge	Baldwin
Original Apportionment of Congress	6-Jul			Gorham & King			**G. Morris**			Randolph		Rutledge	
Reconsider Proportional Representation	9-Jul		Sherman	**King**	Yates	Brearly	G. Morris	Read	Carroll	Madison	Williamson	Rutledge	Houston
Detail	24-Jul		Ellsworth	Gorham			Wilson			Randolph		**Rutledge**	
State Debts & Militia	18-Aug	Langdon	Sherman	King			Clymer	Dickinson	McHenry	Mason	Williamson	C.C. Pinckney	Baldwin
Slave Trade & Navigation	22-Aug	Langdon	Johnson	King		**Livingston**	Clymer	Dickinson	Martin	Madison	Williamson	C.C. Pinckney	Baldwin
Commercial Discrimination	25-Aug	Langdon	**Sherman**	Gorham		Dayton	FitzSimmons	Read	Carroll	Mason	Williamson	Butler	Few
Interstate Comity & Bankruptcy	29-Aug		Johnson	Gorham			Wilson			Randolph			
Postponed Matters	31-Aug	Gilman	Sherman	King		**Brearly**	G. Morris	Dickinson	Carroll	Madison	Williamson	**Rutledge**	Baldwin
Style	8-Sep		**Johnson**	King	Hamilton		G. Morris	Dickinson		Madison		Butler	
Sumptuary Legislation	13-Sep		Johnson			Livingston	Franklin	Dickinson		Mason			

Bold indicates service as a committee chair.

SIGNERS OF THE U.S. CONSTITUTION

Declaration of Independence

NH
Joshua Barlett
Mathew Thornton
Wm. Whipple

MA
Saml. Adams
John Adams

DE
Tho. M'Kean
Geo. Read
Caesar Rodney

MD
Samuel Chase
Elbridge Gerry
Wm. Paca
Robt. Treat Paine

RI
William Ellery
Step. Hopkins

CT
Samuel Huntington
Roger Sherman
Wm. Willams
Oliver Wolcott

NY
Wm. Floyd
Frans. Lewis
Lewis Morris

NJ
Abra. Clark
John Hart
Fras. Hopkinson
Richd. Stockton
Jno. Witherspoon

PA
Charles Carroll
Geo. Clymer
Benja. Franklin
Robt. Morris
John Morton
Geo. Ross
Benjamin Rush
Jas. Smith
Geo. Taylor
James Wilson

VA
Carter Braxton
Th. Jefferson
Benja. Harrison
Francis Lightfoot Lee
Richard Henry Lee
Thos. Nelson, Jr.
George Wythe

NC
Joseph Hewes
Wm. Hooper
John Penn

SC
Thos. Heywood, Jr.
Thomas Lynch, Jr.
Arthur Middleton
Edward Rutledge

GA
Burton Gwinnett
Lyman Hall
Geo. Walton

Articles of Confederation

NH
Joshua Barlett
John Wentworth, Jr.

MA
Saml. Adams
Francis Dana
Elbridge Gerry
John Hancock
Samuel Holton
James Lovell

DE
John Dickinson
Thos. M'Kean
Nicholas Van Dyke

MD
Daniel Carroll
John Hanson

RI
John Collins
William Ellery
Henry Marchant

CT
Andrew Adams
Titus Hosmer
Samuel Huntington
Roger Sherman
Oliver Wolcott

NY
Jas. Duane
Wm. Duer
Fra. Lewis
Gouv. Morris

NJ
Nathl. Scudder
Jno. Witherspoon

PA
William Clingan
Robt. Morris
Joseph Reed
Daniel Roberdeau
Jno. Bayard Smith

VA
Thomas Adams
John Banister
Jno. Harvie
Francis Lightfoot Lee
Richard Henry Lee

NC
Corns. Harnett
John Penn
Jno. Williams

SC

William Henry Drayton
Thos. Heyward, Jr.
Richd. Hutson
Henry Laurens
Jno. Matthews

GA

Edwd. Langworthy
Edwd. Telfair
Jno. Walton

Mount Vernon Conference

MD

Samuel Chase
Daniel of St. Thomas Jenifer
Thomas Stone

VA

Alexander Henderson
George Mason
George Washington

Annapolis Convention

DE

Richard Bassett
John Dickinson
George Reedy

NY

Egbert Benson
Alexander Hamilton

NJ

Abraham Clarke
William C. Houston
James Schuarman

PA

Tench Cox

VA

James Madison
Edmund Randolph
St. George Tucker

Constitution

NH

Nicholas Gilman
John Langdon

MA

Nathaniel Gorham
Rufus King

DE

Richard Bassett
Gunning Bedford, Jr.
Jaco. Broom
John Dickinson
Geo. Read

MD

Danl. Carroll
James McHenry
Dan. of St. Tho. Jenifer

CT

Wm. Samuel Johnson
Roger Sherman

NY

Alexander Hamilton

NJ

David Brearley
Jona. Dayton
Wm. Livingston
Wm. Peterson

PA

Geo. Clymer
Tho. Fitzsimons
B. Franklin
Jared Ingersoll
Thomas Mifflin
Gouv. Morris
Rob. Morris
James Wilson

VA

John Blair
James Madison
George Washington

NC

Wm Blount
Rich. Dobbs Spaight
Hu. Williamson

SC

Pierce Butler
Charles C. Pinckney
Charles Pinckney
J. Rutledge

GA

William Few
Abr. Baldwin

How Well Do You Know the U.S. Constitution?

1. In what year was the Declaration of Independence signed?

2. Who was the primary author of the Declaration of Independence?

3. What was the name of the first government that the Continental Congress proposed after the writing of the Declaration of Independence?

4. Which delegate to the Continental Congress was most responsible for drawing up a continental government to replace that of Great Britain?

5. How many states were required to amend the Constitution that was adopted before the one now in effect?

6. What Maryland meeting preceded the U.S. Constitutional Convention?

7. In what building and city did the U.S. Constitutional Convention meet?

8. How many delegates attended the Constitutional Convention?

9. How many states were represented at the Constitutional Convention?

10. What rebellion in Massachusetts is credited with stimulating states that might not otherwise have attended to send delegates to the Constitutional Convention?

11. What year did the Constitutional Convention meet?

12. What prominent orator refused to attend the Constitutional Convention reputedly because he "smelt a rat"?

13. Which Virginia delegate served as president of the Constitutional Convention?

14. Which Virginia delegate is most often referred to as the "Father" of the Constitution?

15. Which Pennsylvania delegate was the oldest to attend the Constitutional Convention?

16. Which Massachusetts delegate who refused to sign the Constitution was later elected as vice president?

17. How many future U.S. presidents attended the Constitutional Convention?

18. Which Pennsylvania delegate who attended the Convention had a wooden leg and spoke most frequently?

19. Which Virginia delegate who attended the Constitutional Convention was the second law professor to be appointed in the English-speaking world?

20. Which Connecticut delegate is best known for proposing a compromise between the small states and the large states?

21. What governor of Virginia introduced the Virginia Plan?

22. What New Jersey delegate introduced the New Jersey Plan?

23. What was the most important compromise between the large states and the small states?

24. How did the Convention deal with the issue of slave representation in the U.S. House of Representatives?

25. What is the method for electing the president that the Constitutional Convention adopted?

26. Where would you go today if you wanted to see the original copies of the Declaration of Independence, the U.S. Constitution, and the first ten amendments?

27. What center was opened for the first time on July 4, 2003?

28. On what day was the U.S. Constitution signed?

29. How many of the remaining 42 delegates refused to sign the Constitution?

30. What was the name taken by proponents of the new Constitution?

31. What name was given to the opponents of the new Constitution?

32. According to the Constitution, how many states would have to ratify the document before it went into effect?

33. What was the first state to ratify the Constitution?

34. Which two of the original thirteen states were the last to ratify?

35. Which North Carolina delegate would later serve as the president of Tennessee's first Constitutional Convention and as one of its first two senators?

36. By what name was the current state of Tennessee called at the Constitutional Convention?

37. Other than ratification of the Constitution, what was the most important outcome to emerge from the debates over the ratification of the U.S. Constitution?

38. How many Articles does the U.S. Constitution contain?

39. How many times has the current Constitution been amended?

40. Who was the last president who was an adult at the time that the Constitution was signed?

Answers

1. 1776
2. Thomas Jefferson
3. The Confederation
4. John Dickinson
5. Thirteen
6. The Annapolis Convention
7. The Pennsylvania State House (Independence Hall in Philadelphia)
8. Fifty-five
9. Twelve. Rhode Island did not send delegates.
10. Shays's Rebellion
11. 1787
12. Patrick Henry
13. George Washington
14. James Madison
15. Benjamin Franklin
16. Elbridge Gerry
17. Two—George Washington and James Madison
18. Gouverneur Morris
19. George Wythe
20. Roger Sherman
21. Edmund Randolph
22. William Paterson
23. The Great Compromise or Connecticut Compromise involved state representation in the two houses of Congress.

24. It allowed states to count slaves as three-fifths of a person for purposes of representation in the U.S. House of Representatives.
25. The electoral college
26. The National Archives in Washington, D.C.
27. The National Constitution Center, located in Philadelphia, Pennsylvania
28. September 17, 1787
29. Three—Elbridge Gerry of Massachusetts, and George Mason and Edmund Randolph of Virginia
30. Federalists
31. Anti-federalists
32. Nine
33. Delaware. Its license plates accordingly bear the logo "The First State."
34. Rhode Island and North Carolina
35. William Blount
36. Franklin, or Frankland
37. The adoption of the first ten amendments to the U.S. Constitution, known as the Bill of Rights
38. Seven
39. Twenty-seven
40. James Monroe

Selected Bibliography

Abbott, William W. 1957. "The Structure of Politics in Georgia: 1782–1789." *William and Mary Quarterly,* 3rd ser. 14 (January): 47–65.

Abraham, Henry J. 1999. 1998. *The Judicial Process.* 7th ed. New York: Oxford University Press.

——. *Justices, Presidents, and Senators: A History of the U.S. Supreme Court Appointments from Washington to Clinton.* Rev. ed. Lanham, MD: Rowman and Littlefield Publishers.

Achenbach, Joel. 2004. *The Grand Idea: George Washington's Potomac and the Race to the West.* New York: Simon and Schuster.

Ackerman, Bruce. 1991. *We the People: Foundations.* Cambridge, MA: Belknap Press of Harvard University Press.

——. 1998. *We the People: Transformations.* Cambridge, MA: Belknap Press of Harvard University Press.

Ackerman, Bruce, and Neal Katyal. 1995. "Our Unconventional Founding." *University of Chicago Law Review* 62 (Spring): 475–573.

Adair, Douglass. 1974. "Fame and the Founding Fathers." In Trevor Colburn, ed. *Fame and the Founding Fathers: Essays.* New York: W. W. Norton, 3–26.

——. 1951. "The Tenth Federalist Revisited." *William and Mary Quarterly,* 3rd ser. 8 (January): 48–67.

Adair, Douglass, and Marvin Harvey. 1955. "Was Alexander Hamilton a Christian Statesman?" *William and Mary Quarterly,* 3rd ser. 12 (April): 308–329.

Adams, Willi Paul. 2001. *The First American Constitutions: Republican Ideology and the Making of State Constitutions in the Revolutionary Era.* Lanham, MD: Rowman and Littlefield.

Addison, Joseph. 2004. *Cato: A Tragedy and Selected Essays.* Ed. Henderson, Christine Dunn and Mark E. Yellin. Indianapolis, IN: Liberty Fund.

Adkinson, Danny M., and Christopher Elliott. 1997. "The Electoral College: A Misunderstood Institution." *PS: Political Science and Politics* 30 (March): 77–80.

Ahern, Gregory S. 2004. "Virtue, Wisdom, Experience, Not Abstract Rights, Form the Basis of the American Republic." Center for Constitutional Studies. http://www.nhinet.org/ccs/ccs-res.htm.

——. 1998. "The Spirit of American Constitutionalism: John Dickinson's Fabius Letters." *Humanitas* 11, no. 2. Center for Constitutional Studies. http://www.nhinet.org/ccs/ccs-res.htm.

Alden, George Henry. 1903. "The State of Franklin." *American Historical Review* 8 (January): 271–289.

Aldrich, John H., and Ruth W. Grant. 1993. "The Antifederalists, the First Congress, and the First Parties." *Journal of Politics* 55 (May): 295–326.

Alexander, John K. 1990. *The Selling of the Constitutional Convention: A History of News Coverage.* Madison, WI: Madison House.

Amar, Akhil Reed. 2002. "Architexture +." *Indiana Law Journal* 77 (Fall): 671–700.

——. 1988. "Philadelphia Revisited: Amending the Constitution outside Article V." *University of Chicago Law Review* 55 (Fall): 1043–1104.

American Political Science Association and American Historical Association. 1986. *this Constitution: Our Enduring Legacy.* Washington, DC: Congressional Quarterly.

Ammon, Harry. 1971. *James Monroe: The Quest for National Identity.* New York: McGraw-Hill.

Anastaplo, George. 2000. "Constitutionalism, the Rule

of Rules: Explorations." *Brandeis Law Journal* 39 (Fall): 17–217.

Anderson, Margo, and Stephen E. Fienberg. 1999. "To Sample or Not to Sample? The 2000 Census Controversy." *Journal of Interdisciplinary History* 30, no. 1: 1–36.

Anderson, Thornton. 1993. *Creating the Constitution: The Convention of 1787 and the First Congress.* University Park: Pennsylvania State University Press.

Anderson, William. 1955. "The Intention of the Framers: A Note on Constitutional Interpretation." *American Political Science Review* 49 (June): 340–352.

Appleby, Joyce. 1987. "The American Heritage: The Heirs and the Disinherited." *Journal of American History* 74 (December): 798–813.

——. 1973. "The New Republican Synthesis and the Changing Political Ideas of John Adams." *American Quarterly* 25 (December): 578–595.

——. 1971. "America as a Model for the Radical French Reformers of 1789." *William and Mary Quarterly,* 3rd ser. 28 (April): 267–286.

Arthur, John. 1989. *The Unfinished Constitution: Philosophy and Constitutional Practice.* Belmont, CA: Wadsworth Publishing.

Bailyn, Bernard. 1976. "1776. A Year of Challenge—A World Transformed." *Journal of Law and Economics* 19 (October): 437–466.

——. 1967. *The Ideological Origins of the American Revolution.* Cambridge, MA: Belknap Press of Harvard University Press.

——, ed. 1993. *The Debates on the Constitution: Federalist and Antifederalist Speeches, Articles, and Letters during the Struggle over Ratification.* 2 vols. New York: Library of America.

Baker, Leonard. 1974. *John Marshall: A Life in Law.* New York: Macmillan.

Baker, Paula. 1984. "The Domestication of Politics: Women and American Political Society, 1780–1920." *American Historical Review* 89 (June): 620–647.

Banks, Margaret A. 1966. "Drafting the American Constitution—Attitudes in the Philadelphia Convention towards the British System of Government." *American Journal of Legal History* 10 (January): 15–33.

Banning, Lance. 1985. "From Confederation to Constitution: The Revolutionary Context of the Great Convention." *this Constitution,* no. 6 (Spring): 12–18.

——. 1983. "James Madison and the Nationalists, 1780–1783." *William and Mary Quarterly,* 3rd ser. 40 (April): 227–255.

——. 1974. "Republican Ideology and the Triumph of the Constitution, 1789 to 1793." *William and Mary Quarterly,* 3rd ser. 31 (April): 167–188.

——. 1995. *The Sacred Fire of Liberty: James Madison and the Founding of the American Republic.* Ithaca, NY: Cornell University Press.

Barber, Sotirious A., and Robert P. George. 2001. *Constitutional Politics: Essays on Constitution Making, Maintenance, and Change.* Princeton, NJ: Princeton University Press.

Barnette, Randy E. 2004. *Restoring the Lost Constitution: The Presumption of Liberty.* Princeton, NJ: Princeton University Press.

Baum, Marsha L., and Christian G. Fritz. 2000. "American Constitution-Making: The Neglected State Constitutional Sources." *Hastings Constitutional Law Quarterly* 27 (Winter): 199–242.

Beach, John C., et al. 1997. "State Administration and the Founding Fathers during the Critical Period." *Administration and Society* 28 (February): 511.

Beard, Charles A. 1949. *An Economic Interpretation of the Constitution of the United States.* New York: Macmillan.

——. 1962. *The Supreme Court and the Constitution.* Introduction by Alan F. Westin. Englewood Cliffs, NJ: Prentice-Hall.

Beck, J. Randy. 2002. "The New Jurisprudence of the Necessary and Proper Clause." *University of Illinois Law Review:* 581–649.

Becker, Carl L. 1970. *The Declaration of Independence: A Study in the History of Political Ideas.* New York: Vintage Books.

Beckley, John James. 1995. *Justifying Jefferson: The Political Writings of John James Beckley.* Ed. Gerald W. Gawalt. Washington, DC: U.S. Government Printing Office.

Bedwell, C. E. A. 1920. "American Middle Templars." *American Historical Review* 25 (July): 680–689.

Beer, Samuel H. 1993. *To Make a Nation: The Rediscovery of American Federalism.* Cambridge, MA: Belknap Press of Harvard University Press.

Bellamy, Richard, and Dario Castiglione. 1997. "Constitutionalism and Democracy—Political Theory and the American Constitution." *British Journal of Political Science* 27 (October): 595–618.

Belz, Herman. 1992. "Liberty and Equality for Whom? How to Think Inclusively about the Constitution and the Bill of Rights." *The History Teacher* 25 (May): 263–277.

Belz, Herman, Ronald Hoffman, and Peter J. Albert, eds. 1992. *To Form a More Perfect Union: The Critical Ideas of the Constitution.* Charlottesville: University Press of Virginia.

Benedict, Michael L. 1987. "1787: The Constitution in Perspective: 'We Do Ordain and Establish': The Constitution as Literary Text: Our 'Sacred' Constitution—Another View of the Constitution as Literary Text." *William and Mary Law Review* 29 (Fall): 27–34.

Bennett, William J., ed. 1997. *Our Sacred Honor: Words of Advice from the Founders in Stories, Letters, Poems, and Speeches.* New York: Simon and Schuster.

Benton, Wilbourne E., ed. 1986. *1787: Drafting the U.S. Constitution.* 2 vols. College Station: Texas A and M University Press.

Berkeley, Edmund, and Dorothy Smith Berkeley. 1973. *John Beckley: Zealous Partisan in a Nation Divided.* Philadelphia, PA: American Philosophical Society.

Berkin, Carol. 2002. *A Brilliant Solution: Inventing the American Constitution.* New York: Harcourt.

Berns, Walter. 1968. "The Constitution and the Migration of Slaves." *Yale Law Journal* 78 (December): 198–228.

Bernstein, David. 1987. "The Constitutional Convention: Facts and Figures." *The History Teacher* 21 (November): 11–19.

Bernstein, Richard B. 1987. "Charting the Bicentennial." *Columbia Law Review* 87 (December): 1565–1624.

——. 1991. "The Sleeper Wakes: The History and Legacy of the Twenty-seventh Amendment." *Fordham Law Review* 56 (December): 497–557.

Bernstein, Richard B., with Jerome Agel. 1993. *Amending America: If We Love the Constitution So Much, Why Do We Keep Trying to Change It?* New York: Times Books.

Bernstein, Richard B., with Kym S. Rice. 1987. *Are We to Be a Nation? The Making of the Constitution.* Cambridge, MA: Harvard University Press.

Bicentennial Daybook. 1983–1987. Bicentennial of the Constitution of the United States, Research Project Working Files. Library Archives. Independence National Historical Park, Philadelphia, PA.

"Bicentennial Events." 1987. *U.S. News and World Report* 102 (April 27): 32–33.

"Bicentennial Issue: The Bill of Rights." *Life.* Fall 1999.

Biehl, Katharine L. 1945. "The Indentured Servant in Colonial America." *The Social Studies* 36 (January): 316–319.

Billias, George Athan. 1985. "The Declaration of Independence: A Constitutional Document." *this Constitution,* no. 6 (Spring): 47–52.

——. 1976. *Elbridge Gerry: Founding Father and Republican Statesman.* New York: McGraw Hill.

Bingham, Marjorie Wall. 1990. *Women and the Constitution: Student Textbook.* Atlanta, GA: Communikcorp.

Bishop, Hillman Metcalf. 1950. *Why Rhode Island Opposed the Federal Constitution.* Providence, RI: Roger Williams Press.

Bittker, Boris I. 1999. *Bittker on the Regulation of Interstate and Foreign Commerce.* Gaithersburg, MD: Aspen Law and Business.

Bizzoco, Dennis L., ed. 1994. *The Exhaustive Concordance to the United States Constitution with Topical Index and Rapid Reference Constitution.* Chattanooga, TN: Firm Foundation Press.

Bjerkoe, Ethel Hall. 1978. *The Cabinetmakers of America.* Exton, PA: Schiffer.

Black, Eric. 1988. *Our Constitution: The Myth That Binds Us.* Boulder, CO: Westview Press.

Bloom, Sol. 1937. *The Story of the Constitution.* Washington, DC: United States Constitutional Sesquicentennial Commission.

Boasberg, Leonard W. 1986. "An Opportunity to Hear Music Washington Heard." *Philadelphia Inquirer,* January 16, 1-C, 4-C.

Bogen, David S. 1987. "The Individual Liberties within the Body of the Constitution: A Symposium: The Privileges and Immunities Clause of Article IV." *Case Western Reserve Law Review* 37: 794–861.

——. 2003. *Privileges and Immunities: A Reference Guide to the United States Constitution.* Westport, CT: Praeger.

Boller, Paul F. "George Washington and Religious Liberty." *William and Mary Quarterly,* 3rd ser. 17 (October): 486–506.

Borgeaud, Charles. 1982. "The Origins and Development of Written Constitutions." *Political Science Quarterly* 7 (December): 613–632.

Bork, Robert H. 1990. *The Tempting of America: The Political Seduction of the Law.* New York: The Free Press.

Bowen, Catherine Drinker. 1966. *Miracle at Philadelphia: The Story of the Constitutional Convention, May to September 1787.* Boston: Little, Brown.

Boyd, Steven R. 1979. *The Politics of Opposition: Antifederalists and the Acceptance of the Constitution.* Millwood, NY: kto press.

Boylan, Timothy S. 2001. "The Law: Constitutional Understandings of the War Power." *Presidential Studies Quarterly* 31 (September): 514–528.

Bradford, M. M. 1981. *Founding Fathers: Brief Lives of the Framers of the United States Constitution.* 2nd ed. Lawrence: University Press of Kansas.

——. 1993. *Original Intentions: On the Making and Ratification of the United States Constitution.* Athens: University of Georgia Press.

——. 1982. *A Worthy Company: Brief Lives of the Framers of the United States Constitution.* Marlborough, NH: Plymouth Rock Foundation.

Bradley, Gerald V. 1987. "The Individual Liberties within the Body of the Constitution: A Symposium: The No Religious Test Clause and the Constitution of Religious Liberty: A Machine That Has Gone of Itself." *Case Western Reserve Law Review* 37: 674–747.

Bradley, James E. 1975. "Whigs and Nonconformists: 'Slumbering Radicalism' in English Politics, 1739–1789." *Eighteenth-Century Studies* 9 (Autumn): 1–27.

Brams, Steven J., and Alan D. Taylor. 1995. "Fair Division and Politics." *PS: Political Science and Politics* 28 (December): 697–703.

Brooke, John L. 1989. "To the Quiet of the People: Revolutionary Settlements and Civil Unrest in Western Massachusetts, 1774–1789." *William and Mary Quarterly*, 3rd ser. 46 (July): 425–462.

Brookhiser, Richard. 2003. *Gentleman Revolutionary: Gouverneur Morris–The Rake Who Wrote the Constitution.* New York: The Free Press.

Brooks, Robin. 1967. "Alexander Hamilton, Melancton Smith, and the Ratification of the Constitution in New York." *William and Mary Quarterly*, 3rd ser. 24 (July): 339–358.

Brown, Richard D. 1976. "The Founding Fathers of 1776 and 1787: A Collective View." *William and Mary Quarterly*, 3rd. ser. 33 (July): 465–480.

——. 1983. "Shays' Rebellion and Its Aftermath: A View from Springfield, Massachusetts, 1787." *William and Mary Quarterly*, 3rd ser. 40 (October): 598–615.

Brown, Robert E. 1956. *Charles Beard and the Constitution: A Critical Analysis of "An Economic Interpretation of the Constitution."* Princeton, NJ: Princeton University Press.

Brown, Roger H. 1993. *Redeeming the Republic: Federalists, Taxation, and the Origin of the Constitution.* Baltimore, MD: Johns Hopkins University Press.

Brown, William Garrott. 1905. "A Continental Congressman: Oliver Ellsworth, 1776–1783." *American Historical Review* 10 (July): 751–781.

Browne, Ray B., and Glenn J. Browne, eds. 1986. *Laws of Our Fathers: Popular Culture and the U.S. Constitution.* Bowling Green, OH: Bowling Green State University Press.

Buchanan, James. 2003. *Crowded with Genius: The Scottish Enlightenment: Edinburgh's Moment of the Mind.* New York: HarperCollins.

Buffum, Francis H. 1942. *New Hampshire and the Federal Constitution: A Memorial of the Sesquicentennial Celebration of New Hampshire's Part in the Framing and Ratification of the Constitution of the United States.* 2nd ed. Concord, NH: Granite State Press.

Bullock, Alexander H. 1881. *The Centennial of the Massachusetts Constitution.* Worcester, MA: Press of Charles Hamlin.

Bullock, Charles J. 1900. "The Origin, Purpose and Effect of the Direct-Tax Clause of the Federal Constitution. I." *Political Science Quarterly* 15 (June): 217–239.

——. 1900. "The Origin, Purpose and Effect of the Direct-Tax Clause of the Federal Constitution. II." *Political Science Quarterly* 15 (September): 452–481.

Bullock, Steven C. 2002. "Talk of the Past: American Midrash." *Common-Place* 2, no. 4 (July). www.common-place.org.

Burger, Warren. 1996. "The Judiciary: The Origins of Judicial Review." *National Forum* 76 (Fall): 37–38.

Burnett, Edmund C. 1925. "The Name 'United States of America.'" *American Historical Review* 31 (October): 79–81.

Burns, James MacGregor. 1982. *The Vineyard of Liberty.* New York: Alfred A. Knopf.

Butzner, Jane, compiler. 1941. *Constitutional Chaff–Rejected Suggestions of the Constitutional Convention of 1787 with Explanatory Argument.* New York: Columbia University Press.

Calabresi, Steven G. 1994. "The Vesting Clauses as Power Grants." *Northwestern University Law Review* 33 (Summer): 1377–1405.

Caldwell, Robert G. 1920. "The Settlement of Inter-State Disputes." *American Journal of International Law* 14 (Jan.-Apr.): 38–69.

Carey, George W. 2003/2004. "America's Founding and Limited Government." *Intercollegiate Review* 39 (Fall/Spring): 14–22.

——. 1980. "Comment: Constitutionalists and the Constitutional Tradition–So What?" *Journal of Politics* 42 (February): 36–46.

——. 1989. *The Federalist: Design for a Constitutional Republic.* Urbana: University of Illinois Press.

Carey, George W., and James McClellan. 2001. "Introduction." *The Federalist.* Alexander Hamilton, James Madison, and John Jay. Indianapolis, IN: Liberty Fund.

Carpenter, William Seal. 1928. "The Separation of Powers in the Eighteenth Century." *American Political Science Review* 22 (February): 32–44.

Carr, William G. 1990. *The Oldest Delegate: Franklin in the Constitutional Convention.* Newark: University of Delaware Press.

Carson, Hampton L., ed. 1889. *History of the Celebration of the One Hundredth Anniversary of the Promulgation of the Constitution of the United States.* 2 vols. Philadelphia, PA: J. B. Lippincott.

Casper, Gerhard. 1997. *Separating Power: Essays on the*

Founding Period. Cambridge, MA: Harvard University Press.

Cayton, Mary K., and Peter W. Williams, eds. 2001. *Encyclopedia of American Cultural and Intellectual History.* 2 vols. New York: Charles Scribner's Sons.

Chemerinsky, Erwin. 1987. "The Individual Liberties within the Body of the Constitution: A Symposium: Thinking about Habeas Corpus." *Case Western Reserve Law Review* 37: 748–793.

Chernow, Ron. 2004. *Alexander Hamilton.* New York: Penguin Press.

Chidsey, Donald B. 1964. *The Birth of the Constitution: An Informal History.* New York: Crown Publishers.

Chinard, Gilbert. 1940. "Polybius and the American Constitution." *Journal of the History of Ideas* 1 (January): 38–58.

Claiborne, Louis F. 1987–1988. "Black Men, Red Men, and the Constitution of 1787: A Bicentennial Apology from a Middle Templar." *Hastings Constitutional Law Quarterly* 15: 269–293.

Clark, Bradford R. 2003. "The Supremacy Clause as a Constraint on Federal Power." *George Washington Law Review* 71 (February): 91–130.

Clarke, M. St. Clair, and D. D. Hall. 1832. *Legislative and Documentary History of the Bank of the United States: Including the Original Bank of America.* Washington, DC: Gales and Seaton. Reprinted in New York by August M. Kelley, 1967.

Clarkson, Paul S., and R. Samuel Jett. 1970. *Luther Martin of Maryland.* Baltimore, MD: Johns Hopkins Press.

Clinton, Robert L. 1997. *God and Man in the Law: The Foundations of Anglo-American Constitutionalism.* Lawrence: University Press of Kansas.

Clinton, Robert N. 1990. "A Brief History of the Adoption of the United States Constitution." *Iowa Law Review* 75 (May): 891–913.

Cogan, Neil H. 1998. *Contexts of the Constitution.* New York: Foundation Press.

——, ed. 1997. *The Complete Bill of Rights: The Drafts, Debates, Sources, and Origins.* New York: Oxford University Press.

Cohen, I. Bernard. 1995. *Science and the Founding Fathers: Science in the Political Thought of Jefferson, Franklin, Adams, and Madison.* New York: W. W. Norton.

Cohen, Lester H. 1983. "Mercy Otis Warren: The Politics of Language and the Aesthetics of Self." *American Quarterly* 35 (Winter): 481–498.

Cohn, Mary W., ed. 1991. *Guide to Congress.* 4th ed. Washington, DC: Congressional Quarterly.

Collier, Christopher. 2003. *All Politics Is Local: Family, Friends, and Provincial Interests in the Creation of the Constitution.* Hanover, NH: University Press of New England.

——. 1971. *Roger Sherman's Connecticut: Yankee Politics and the American Revolution.* Middleton, CT: Wesleyan University Press.

Collier, Christopher, and James Lincoln Collier. 1986. *Decision in Philadelphia: The Constitutional Convention of 1787.* New York: Random House.

Collins, Sheldon S. 2000. "A Delaware Initiative for Establishing the Federal Capital." *Delaware History* 29, no. 1: 71–76.

Come, Donald R. 1945. "The Influence of Princeton on Higher Education in the South before 1825." *William and Mary Quarterly,* 3rd ser. 2 (October): 359–396.

Commission on the Bicentennial of the United States Constitution. 1992. *We the People: The Commission on the Bicentennial of the United States Constitution, 1985–1992. Final Report.*

Cone, Carl B. 1948. "Richard Price and the Constitution of the United States." *American Historical Review* 53 (July): 726–747.

——. 1952. *Torchbearer of Freedom: The Influence of Richard Price on Eighteenth Century Thought.* Lexington: University of Kentucky Press.

Conkin, Paul K. 1968. *Puritans and Pragmatists: Eight Eminent American Thinkers.* New York: Dodd, Mead.

Conley, Patrick T., and John P. Kaminski, eds. 1988. *The Constitution and the States: The Role of the Original Thirteen in the Framing and Adoption of the Federal Constitution.* Madison, WI: Madison House.

Conniff, James. 1980. "The Enlightenment and American Political Thought: A Study of the Origins of Madison's *Federalist* Number 10." *Political Theory* 8 (August): 381–402.

——. 1975. "On the Obsolescence of the General Will: Rousseau, Madison, and the Evolution of Republican Political Thought." *Western Political Quarterly* 28 (March): 32–58.

Conrad, Stephen A. 1985. "Polite Foundation: Citizenship and Common Sense in James Wilson's Republican Theory." In Philip B. Kurland, Gerhard Casper, and Dennis J. Hutchinson, eds. *The Supreme Court Review, 1984.* Chicago: University of Chicago Press.

"Constitutional Convention, 1787." 1861. *The Historical Magazine,* 1st ser. 5 (January): 18.

"Constitution of Massachusetts." National Humanities Institute. http://www.nhinet.org/ccs/docs/ma-1780.htm.

"Constitution of the United States: Questions and Answers." http://www.archives.gov/national_archives-experience/constitution_q_and-a.html.

The Constitution of the United States with Tree Planting Instructions by the American Tree Association to Mark the Sesquicentennial: 1787–1937. Washington, DC: American Tree Association.

Constitution Week, September 17–23: An American Legacy. Washington, DC: Commission on the Bicentennial of the United States Constitution.

Cooke, Donald E. 1970. *America's Great Document—The Constitution.* Maplewood, NJ: Hamond.

Cornell, Saul. 1990. "Aristocracy Assailed: The Ideology of Backcountry Anti-Federalism." *Journal of American History* 76 (March): 1148–1172.

———. 1999. *The Other Founders: Anti-Federalism and the Dissenting Tradition in America, 1788–1828.* Chapel Hill: University of North Carolina Press.

———. 1990. "Symposium: Roads Not Taken: Undercurrents of Republican Thinking in Modern Constitutional Theory: The Changing Historical Fortunes of the Anti-Federalists." *Northwestern University Law Review* 85 (Fall): 39–73.

Corwin, Edward S. 1964. "The Progress of Constitutional Theory between the Declaration of Independence and the Meeting of the Philadelphia Convention." *American Constitutional History: Essays by Edward S. Corwin.* Ed. Alpheus T. Mason and Gerald Garvey. New York: Harper and Row, Publishers.

Coulanges, Numa Denis Fustel de. 1956. *The Ancient City: A Study on the Religion, Law, and Institutions of Greece and Rome.* Baltimore, MD: Johns Hopkins University Press.

Cousins, Norman, ed. 1958. *"In God We Trust": The Religious Beliefs and Ideas of the American Founding Fathers.* New York: Harper and Brothers.

Craig, Burton. 1987. *The Federal Convention of 1787: North Carolina in the Great Crisis.* Richmond, VA: Expert Graphics.

Crane, Verner W. 1966. "The Club of Honest Whigs: Friends of Science and Liberty." *William and Mary Quarterly,* 3rd ser. 23 (April): 210–233.

———. 1948. "Franklin's 'The Internal State of America' (1786)." *William and Mary Quarterly,* 3rd ser. 15 (April): 214–227.

Cranston, Maurice. 1973. *What Are Human Rights?* New York: Taplinger Publishing.

Cress, Lawrence Delbert. 1979. "Radical Whiggery on the Role of the Military: Ideological Roots of the American Revolutionary Militia." *Journal of the History of Ideas* 40 (Jan.-Mar.): 42–60.

———. 1981. "Republican Liberty and National Security: American Military Policy as an Ideological Problem, 1783 to 1798." *William and Mary Quarterly,* 3rd ser. 38 (January): 73–96.

———. 1975. "Whither Columbia? Congressional Residence and the Politics of the New Nation, 1776 to 1787." *William and Mary Quarterly,* 3rd ser. 32 (October): 581–600.

Crosskey, William Winslow, and William Jeffrey, Jr. 1980. *The Political Background of the Federal Convention.* Vol. 3 of *Politics and the Constitution in the History of the United States.* Chicago: University of Chicago Press.

Crowe, Charles. 1964. "Bishop James Madison and the Republic of Virtue." *Journal of Southern History* 30 (February): 58–70.

Crowl, Philip A. 1947. "Anti-Federalism in Maryland, 1787–1788." *William and Mary Quarterly,* 3rd ser. 4 (October): 446–469.

———. 1941. "Charles Carroll's Plan of Government." *American Historical Review* 46 (April): 588–595.

Crowley, John E. 2001. *The Invention of Comfort: Sensibilities and Design in Early Modern Britain and Early America.* Baltimore, MD: Johns Hopkins University Press.

———. 1993. *The Privileges of Independence: Neomercantilism and the American Revolution.* Baltimore, MD: Johns Hopkins University Press.

Cummings, Milton C., Jr., and David Wise. 2001. *Democracy under Pressure: An Introduction to the American Political System.* 9th ed. Fort Worth, TX: Harcourt College Publishers.

Cunningham, Noble I., Jr. 1987. *In Pursuit of Reason: The Life of Thomas Jefferson.* Baton Rouge: Louisiana State University Press.

Currie, David P. 1997. *The Constitution in Congress: The Federalist Period, 1789–1801.* Chicago: University of Chicago Press.

Curti, Merle. 1953. "Human Nature in American Thought." *Political Science Quarterly* 68 (September): 354–375.

Curtis, George Ticknor. 1961. *History of the Origin, Formation, and Adoption of the Constitution of the United States with Notices of Its Principal Framers.* 2 vols. New York: Harper and Brothers.

Cushman, Clare, ed. 1995. *The Supreme Court Justices: Illustrated Biographies, 1789–1995.* Washington, DC: Congressional Quarterly.

Dahl, Robert. 2001. *How Democratic Is the American Constitution?* New Haven, CT: Yale University Press.

D'Amato, Anthony. 1988. "The Alien Tort Statute and the Founding of the Constitution." *American Journal of International Law* 82 (January): 62–67.

David, C. W. A. 1924. "The Fugitive Slave Law of 1793 and Its Antecedents." *Journal of Negro History* 9 (January): 18–24.

Davies, Wallace Evan. 1948. "The Society of the Cincinnati in New England 1783–1800." *William and Mary Quarterly,* 3rd ser. 5 (January): 3–25.

Davis, David B. "American Equality and Foreign Revolutions." *Journal of American History* 76 (December): 729–752.

Davis, Joseph L. 1977. *Sectionalism in American Politics, 1774–1787.* Madison: University of Wisconsin Press.

Dellinger, Walter F., III. 1987. "1787: The Constitution and 'The Curse of Heaven.'" *William and Mary Law Review* 29: 145–161.

Delmar, Frances. 2002. "Pastimes: Shouldering Independence." *Common-Place* 2, no. 4 (July). www.common-place.org.

Dewey, Donald O. 1962. "Madison's Views on Electoral Reform." *Western Political Quarterly* 15 (March): 140–145.

Diamond, Martin. 1981. "The Federalist, 1787–1788." In Leo Strauss and Joseph Cropsey, eds. *The History of Political Philosophy.* 2nd ed. Chicago: University of Chicago Press.

——. 1981. *The Founding of the Democratic Republic.* Itasca, IL: F. F. Peacock Publishers.

Dienstag, Joshua Foa. 1996. "Between History and Nature: Social Contract Theory in Locke and the Founders." *Journal of Politics* 58 (November): 985–1009.

——. 1996. "Serving God and Mammon: The Lockean Sympathy in Early American Political Thought." *American Political Science Review* 90 (September): 497–511.

Diggins, John Patrick. 1981. "Power and Authority in American History: The Case of Charles A. Beard and His Critics." *American Historical Review* 86 (October): 601–630.

Dill, Alonzo. 1979. *George Wythe: Teacher of Liberty.* Williamsburg, VA: Independence Bicentennial Commission.

"Documents Relating to Shays' Rebellion, 1787." 1897. *American Historical Review* 2 (July): 693–699.

"Dominion of New England, 1686–1689." u-s-history.com.

Donner, Irah. 1992. "The Copyright Clause of the U.S. Constitution: Why Did the Framers Include It with Unanimous Approval?" *American Journal of Legal History* 36 (July): 361–378.

Donovan, H. H. 1937. "Making the Constitution." *Journal of the National Education Association* 26 (October): 219–234.

Dos Passos, John. 1957. *The Men Who Made the Nation.* Garden City, NY: Doubleday.

Dougherty, Keith L. 2001. *Collective Action under the Articles of Confederation.* Cambridge: Cambridge University Press.

Douglass, Elisa P. 1960. "German Intellectuals and the American Revolution." *William and Mary Quarterly,* 3rd ser. 17 (April): 200–218.

Dreisbach, Daniel L. 1999. "The Constitution's Forgotten Religion Clause: Reflections on the Article VI Religious Test Ban." *Journal of Church and State* 38 (Spring): 261–296.

Dreisbach, Daniel L., Mark D. Hall, and Jeffry Morrison, eds. 2004. *The Founders on God and Government.* Lanham, MD: Rowman and Littlefield.

Dudley, William, ed. 1995. *The Creation of the Constitution: Opposing Viewpoints.* San Diego, CA: Greenhaven Press.

Dunn, Charles W. 1984. *American Political Theology: Historical Perspective and Theoretical Analysis.* New York: Praeger.

Dunn, Susan. 1996. "Revolutionary Men of Letters and the Pursuit of Radical Change: The Views of Burke, Tocqueville, Adams, Madison, and Jefferson." *William and Mary Quarterly,* 3rd ser. 53 (October): 729–754.

Edwards, George C., III. 2004. *Why the Electoral College Is Bad for America.* New Haven, CT: Yale University Press.

Eidelberg, Paul. 1968. *The Philosophy of the American Constitution: A Reinterpretation of the Intentions of the Founding Fathers.* New York: The Free Press.

Einhorn, Robin L. 2002. "Patrick Henry's Case against the Constitution: The Structural Problem with Slavery." *Journal of the Early Republic* 22 (Winter): 549–573.

Eisinger, Chester E. 1947. "The Freehold Concept in Eighteenth-Century American Letters." *William and Mary Quarterly,* 3rd ser. 4 (1947): 42–59.

Elasar, Daniel J. 1980. "The Political Theory of Covenant: Biblical Origins and Modern Developments." *Publius* 10 (Fall): 3–30.

Elkins, Stanley, and Eric McKitrick. 1961. "The Founding Fathers: Young Men of the Revolution." *Political Science Quarterly* 76 (June): 181–216.

Elliott, Jonathan, ed. 1888. *The Debates in the Several State Constitutions on the Adoption of the Federal Constitution.* 5 vols. New York: Burt Franklin.

Ellis, Joseph J. 2000. *Founding Brothers: The Revolutionary Generation.* New York: Vintage Books.

——. 1976. "Habits of Mind and an American Enlightenment." *American Quarterly* 28 (Summer): 150–164.

——. 2004. *His Excellency: George Washington.* New York: Alfred A. Knopf.

——. 1993. *Passionate Sage: The Character and Legacy of John Adams.* New York: W. W. Norton.

Ellis, Richard J., ed. 1999. *Founding the American Presidency.* Lanham, MD: Rowman and Littlefield.

Ely, James W., Jr. 1992. *The Guardian of Every Other Right: A Constitutional History of Property Rights.* New York: Oxford University Press.

Engeman, Thomas S., and Michael P. Zuchert, eds. 2004. *Protestantism and the American Founding.* Notre Dame, IN: University of Notre Dame Press.

Epstein, David F. 1984. *The Political Theory of* The Federalist. Chicago: University of Chicago Press.

Ernst, Robert. 1968. *Rufus King: American Federalist.* Chapel Hill: University of North Carolina Press.

Fairlie, John A. 1013. "The President's Cabinet." *American Political Science Review* 7 (February): 28–44.

Farber, Daniel A. 1995. "The Constitution's Forgotten Cover Letter: An Essay on the New Federalism and the Original Understanding." *Michigan Law Review* 94 (December): 615–650.

Farber, Daniel A., and Suzanna Sherry. 1990. *A History of the American Constitution.* Saint Paul, MN: West Publishing.

Farr, James. 1988. "Political Science and the Enlightenment of Enthusiasm." *American Political Science Review* 82 (March): 51–69.

Farrand, Max. 1921 (1903). "Compromises of the Constitution." *Annual Report of the American Historical Association* 1 (April): 71–84.

——. *The Fathers of the Constitution: A Chronicle of the Establishment of the Union.* New Haven, CT: Yale University Press.

——. 1913. *The Framing of the Constitution of the United States.* New Haven, CT: Yale University Press.

——. 1907. "The Records of the Federal Convention." *American Historical Review* 13 (October): 44–65.

Farrand, Max. ed. 1937. Paperback ed. 1966. *The Records of the Federal Convention.* 4 vols. New Haven, CT: Yale University Press.

The Federal Constitutional Celebration in Pennsylvania, 1937–1938. 1938. Philadelphia, PA: Dunlap Publishing.

Feer, Robert A. 1969. "Shays' Rebellion and the Constitution: A Study in Causation." *New England Quarterly* 42 (September): 388–410.

Fehrenbacher, Don E. 1984. "Race and Slavery in the American Constitutional System: 1787–1865." *this Constitution,* no. 4 (Fall): 31–37.

Ferguson, E. James. 1983. "Political Economy, Public Liberty, and the Formation of the Constitution." *William and Mary Quarterly,* 3rd ser. 40 (July): 389–412.

——. 1951. "State Assumption of the Federal Debt during the Confederation." *Mississippi Valley Historical Review* 38 (December): 403–424.

Ferguson, Robert A. 2000. "The Commonalities of Common Sense." *William and Mary Quarterly,* 3rd ser. 57 (July): 465–504.

——. 1987. "The Constitution in Perspective: 'We Do Ordain and Establish': The Constitution as Literary Text." *William and Mary Law Review* 29 (Fall): 3–25.

Ferris, Robert G., ed. 1976. *Signers of the Constitution.* Washington, DC: United States Department of the Interior, National Park Service.

Fields, William S., and David T. Hardy. 1992. "The Militia and the Constitution: A Legal History." *Military Law Review* 136 (Spring): 1–42.

Finkelman, Paul. 1996. *Slavery and the Founders: Race and Liberty in the Age of Jefferson.* Armonk, NY: M. E. Sharpe.

Fisher, Louis. 1983. "Congress and the Removal Power." *Congress and the Presidency* 10: 63.

Fiske, John. 1888. *The Critical Period of American History, 1783–1789.* Boston: Houghton Mifflin.

Fitzpatrick, John C. 1941. "The Man Who Engrossed the Constitution." In Sol Bloom, director-general. *The History of the Formation of the Union under the Constitution.* Washington, DC: U.S. Government Printing Office.

Fleischacker, Samuel. 2002. "Adam Smith's Reception among the American Founders, 1776–1790." *William and Mary Quarterly,* 3rd ser. 59 (October): 896–924.

Fleming, Thomas. 1997. *Liberty! The American Revolution.* New York: Viking Press.

Flower, Milton E. 1983. *John Dickinson: Conservative Revolutionary.* Charlottesville: University Press of Virginia.

Fogelman, Aaron S. 1998. "From Slaves, Convicts, and Servants to Free Passengers: The Transformation of Immigration in the Era of the American Revolution." *Journal of American History* 85 (June): 43–76.

Foner, Eric, and John A. Garraty, eds. 1991. *The Reader's Companion to American History.* Boston: Houghton Mifflin.

Ford, Lacy K., Jr. 1994. "Inventing the Concurrent Majority: Madison, Calhoun, and the Problem of Majoritarianism in American Political Thought." *Journal of Southern History* 60 (February): 19–58.

Ford, Paul Leicester, ed. 1970. *Essays on the Constitution of the United States Published during Its Discussion by the People, 1787–1788.* New York: Burt Franklin.

Fortenbaugh, Robert. 1948. *The Nine Capitals of the United States.* York, PA: Maple.

"The Founding Fathers: A Brilliant Gathering of Reason and Creativity." 1987. Special issue of *Life* magazine, *The Constitution* (Fall): 51–58.

Fox, Frank W. 2003. *The American Founding.* Boston: Pearson Custom Publishing.

Freehling, William W. 1972. "The Founding Fathers and Slavery." *American Historical Review* 77 (February): 81–93.

Friedman, Dan. 2002. "Tracing the Lineage: Textual and Conceptual Similarities in the Revolutionary-Era State Declarations of Rights of Virginia, Maryland, and Delaware." *Rutgers Law Journal* 33 (Summer): 929–1028.

Fritz, Christian G. 2004. "Fallacies of American Constitutionalism." *Rutgers Law Journal* 35 (Summer): 1327–1369.

Frohnen, Bruce, ed. 2002. *The American Republic: Primary Sources.* Indianapolis, IN: Liberty Fund.

Galloway, George B. 1958. "Precedents Established in the First Congress." *Western Political Quarterly* 22 (September): 454–468.

Galvin, Robert W. 2002. *America's Founding Secret: What the Scottish Enlightenment Taught Our Founding Fathers.* Lanham, MD: Rowman and Littlefield Publishers.

Ganter, Herbert Lawrence. 1937. "The Machiavellianism of George Mason." *William and Mary College Quarterly Historical Magazine,* 2nd ser. 17 (April): 239–264.

Garraty, John A., and Mark C. Carnes, eds. 1999. *American National Biography.* 24 vols. New York: Oxford University Press.

Garver, Frank H. 1936–1937. "Leadership in the Constitutional Convention of 1787." *Sociology and Social Research:* 544–553.

George, Alice L. 2003. *Old City Philadelphia: Cradle of American Democracy.* Charleston, SC: Arcadia Publishing.

Gerber, Scott D. 1995. *To Secure These Rights: The Declaration of Independence and Constitutional Interpretation.* New York: New York University Press.

Gerhardt, Michael J. 1996. *The Federal Impeachment Process: A Constitutional and Historical Analysis.* Princeton, NJ: Princeton University Press.

Gillespie, Michael Allen, and Michael Lienesch, eds. 1989. *Ratifying the Constitution.* Lawrence: University Press of Kansas.

Gilmore, Michael T. 1987. "1787: The Constitution in Perspective: 'We Do Ordain and Establish': The Constitution as Literary Text: The Constitution and the Canon." *William and Mary Law Review* 29 (Fall): 35–40.

Goldwin, Robert A. 1997. *From Parchment to Power: How James Madison Used the Bill of Rights to Save the Constitution.* Washington, DC: AEI Press.

———. 1990. *Why Blacks, Women, and Jews Are Not Mentioned in the Constitution, and Other Unorthodox Views.* Washington, DC: AEI Press.

Goldwin, Robert A., and Art Kaufman, eds. 1986. *Separation of Powers—Does It Still Work?* Washington, DC: American Enterprise Institute for Public Policy Research.

Goodrich, Peter. 1998. "Signs Taken for Wonders: Community, Identity, and a History of Sumptuary Law." *Law and Social Inquiry* 23 (Summer): 707–725.

Gould, Philip. 1993. "Virtue, Ideology, and the American Revolution: The Legacy of the Republican Synthesis." *American Literary History* 5 (Autumn): 564–577.

De Grazia, Sebastian. 1997. *A Country with No Name: Tales from the Constitution.* New York: Pantheon Books.

"Great Essentials: An Exhibition of Democracy at Independence National Historical Part." Pamphlet obtained at Independence Hall, August 30, 2003.

Greene, Evarts B. 1917. "American Opinion on the Imperial Review of Provincial Legislation, 1776–1787." *American Historical Review* 23 (October): 104–107.

Greene, Evarts B., and Virginia D. Harrington. 1966. *American Population before the Federal Census of 1790.* Gloucester, MA: Peter Smith.

Greene, Jack P. 1994. *Negotiated Authorities: Essays in Colonial Political and Constitutional History.* Charlottesville: University Press of Virginia.

———. 1986. *Peripheries and Center: Constitutional Development in the Extended Politics of the British Empire and the United States, 1607–1788.* Athens: University of Georgia Press.

———. 1969. "Political Mimesis: A Consideration of the Historical and Cultural Roots of Legislative Behavior in the British Colonies in the Eighteenth Century." *American Historical Review* 75 (December): 337–360.

Greene, Jack P., and J. J. Pole. 1994. *The Blackwell Encyclopedia of the American Revolution.* Cambridge, MA: Blackwell Publishers.

Greene, Thurston. 1991. *The Language of the Constitution: A Sourcebook and Guide to the Ideas, Terms, and Vocabulary Used by the Framers of the United States Constitution.* Westport, CT: Greenwood Press.

Gregg, Gary L., II. 1999. *Vital Remnants: America's Founding and the Western Tradition.* Wilmington, DE: ISI Books.

Griffin, J. David. 1977. *Georgia and the United States*

Constitution, 1787–1789. Georgia Commission for the National Bicentennial Celebration and Georgia Department of Education.

Griffin, Stephen M. 1996. *American Constitutionalism: From Theory to Politics.* Princeton, NJ: Princeton University Press.

Grimes, Alan P. 1978. *Democracy and the Amendments to the Constitution.* Lexington, MA: Lexington Books.

Grinde, Donald A., Jr., and Bruce E. Johansen. 1977. *The Iroquois and the Founding of the American Nation.* San Francisco: Indian Historian Press.

——. 1996. "Sauce for the Goose: Demand and Definitions for 'Proof' Regarding the Iroquois and Democracy." *William and Mary Quarterly,* 3rd ser. 43 (July): 521–536.

Grundfest, Jerry. 1982. *George Clymer: Philadelphia Revolutionary, 1739–1813.* New York: Arno Press.

Guide to Congress. 1991. 4th ed. Washington, DC: Congressional Quarterly.

Gummere, Richard M. 1962. "The Classical Ancestry of the United States Constitution." *American Quarterly* 14 (Spring): 3–18.

Hall, David W. 2003. *The Geneva Reformation and the American Founding.* Lanham, MD: Lexington Books.

Hall, Kermit L., ed. 1984. *A Comprehensive Bibliography of American Constitutional and Legal History, 1896–1979.* 5 vols. Millwood, NY: Kraus International Publications.

——. 1991. *A Comprehensive Bibliography of American Constitutional and Legal History, Supplement, 1980–1987.* 2 vols. Millwood, NY: Kraus International Publications.

——. 2002. *The Oxford Companion to American Law.* New York: Oxford University Press.

Hall, Kermit L., and James W. Ely, Jr. 1989. *An Uncertain Tradition: Constitutionalism and the History of the South.* Athens: University of Georgia Press.

Hamburger, Philip A. 1993. "Natural Rights, Natural Law, and American Constitutions." *Yale Law Journal* 102 (January): 907–960.

Hamilton, Alexander, James Madison, and John Jay. 1961. *The Federalist Papers.* Ed. Clinton Rossiter. New York: New American Library.

Hammond, Thomas H., and Gary J. Miller. 1987. "The Core of the Constitution." *American Political Science Review* 81 (December): 1155–1174.

Hammons, Christopher W. 1999. "Was James Madison Wrong? Rethinking the American Preference for Short, Framework-Oriented Constitutions." *American Political Science Review* 93 (December): 837–849.

Harding, Samuel B. 1896. *The Contest over the Ratification of the Federal Constitution in the State of Massachusetts.* New York: Longmans, Green, and Co.

Harris, William F., II. 1993. *The Interpretable Constitution.* Baltimore, MD: Johns Hopkins University Press.

Hartz, Louis. 1955. *The Liberal Tradition in America: An Interpretation of American Political Thought since the Revolution.* New York: Harcourt, Brace and World.

Haskett, Richard D. 1950. "William Paterson, Attorney General of New Jersey: Public Office and Private Profit in the American Revolution." *William and Mary Quarterly,* 3rd ser. 7 (January): 26–38.

Hauptly, Denis J. 1987. *"A Convention of Delegates": The Creation of the Constitution.* New York: Atheneum.

Heckathorn, Douglas D., and Steven M. Maser. 1987. "Bargaining and Constitutional Contracts." *American Journal of Political Science* 31 (February): 142–168.

Hemberger, Suzette. 2001. "What Did They Think They Were Doing When They Wrote the U.S. Constitution, and Why Should We Care?" In Sotirios Barber and Robert P. George, eds. *Constitutional Politics: Essays on Constitution Making, Maintenance and Change.* Princeton, NJ: Princeton University Press, 128–161.

Hendrick, Burton J. 1937. *Bulwark of the Republic: A Biography of the Constitution.* Boston: Little, Brown.

Hendrickson, David D. 2003. *Peace Pact: The Lost World of the American Founding.* Lawrence: University Press of Kansas.

Henretta, James A. 1987. "Society and Republicanism: America in 1787." *this Constitution,* no. 15 (Summer): 20–26.

Hieronimus, Robert. 1989. *America's Secret Destiny: Spiritual Vision and the Founding of a Nation.* Rochester, VT: Destiny Books.

Higginbotham, Don. 1998. "The Federalized Militia Debate: A Neglected Aspect of Second Amendment Scholarship." *William and Mary Quarterly,* 3rd ser. 55 (1998): 39–58.

Higonnet, Patrice. 1988. *Sister Republics: The Origins of French and American Republicanism.* Cambridge, MA: Harvard University Press.

Hinds, Asher C. 1909. "The Speaker of the House of Representatives." *American Political Science Review* 3 (May): 155–166.

Hobson, Charles F. 1979. "The Negative on State Laws: James Madison, the Constitution, and the Crisis of Republican Government." *William and Mary Quarterly,* 3rd ser. 36 (April): 214–235.

Hoebeke, C. C. 1995. *The Road to Mass Democracy: Original Intent and the Seventeenth Amendment.* New Brunswick, NJ: Transaction.

Hoffer, Peter C. 2002. "Vox Pop: Consensus and Celebration." *Common-Place* 2, no. 4 (July). www.common-place.org.

Hoffer, Peter C., and H. E. H. Hull. 1979. "Power and Precedent in the Creation of an American Impeachment Tradition: The Eighteenth-Century Colonial Record." *William and Mary Quarterly,* 3rd ser. 36 (January): 51–77.

Hoffert, Robert W. 1992. *A Politics of Tensions: The Articles of Confederation and American Political Ideals.* Niwot: University Press of Colorado.

Hoff-Wilson, Joan. 1989. "Women in American Constitutional History at the Bicentennial." *The History Teacher* 22 (February): 145–176.

Hofstadter, Richard. 1972. *The Idea of a Party System: The Rise of Legitimate Opposition in the United States, 1780–1840.* Berkeley: University of California Press.

Holmes, David L. 2003. *The Religion of the Founding Fathers.* Charlottesville, VA: Ann Arbor, MI: Ash Lawn-Highland: Clements Library.

Holt, Michael F. 1999. *The Rise and Fall of the American Whig Party: Jacksonian Politics and the Outset of the Civil War.* New York: Oxford University Press.

Holton, Woody. 2004. "'From the Labours of Others': The War Bonds Controversy and the Origins of the Constitution in New England." *William and Mary Quarterly,* 3rd ser. 61 (April): 277–307.

Horsnell, Margaret. 1987. "Who Was Who in the Constitutional Convention: A Pictorial Essay of Its Leading Figures." *this Constitution,* no. 15 (Summer): 38–41.

Howard, A. E. Dick. 1993. *The Constitution in the Making: Perspectives of the Original Thirteen States.* Williamsburg, VA: National Center for State Courts.

Howard, John Tasker, and Eleanor S. Bowen, eds. n.d. *Music Associated with the Period of the Formation of the Constitution and the Inauguration of George Washington.* Washington, DC: United States Sesquicentennial Commission.

Howe, Daniel W. 1989. "Why the Scottish Enlightenment Was Useful to the Framers of the American Constitution." *Comparative Studies in Society and History* 31 (July): 572–587.

Hueston, John C. 1990. "Note: Altering the Course of the Constitutional Convention: The Role of the Committee of Detail in Establishing the Balance of State and Federal Powers." *Yale Law Journal* 200 (December): 765–783.

Hume, David. 1948. *Hume's Moral and Political Philosophy.* Ed. Henry D. Aiken. New York: Hafner Publishing Co.

Hunt, John Gabriel, ed. 1997. *The Inaugural Addresses of the Presidents.* New York: Gramercy Books.

Huntington, Samuel P. 1956. "Civilian Control and the Constitution." *American Political Science Review* 50 (September): 676–699.

Hutchison, David. 1975. *The Foundations of the Constitution.* Introduction by Ferdinand Lundberg. Secaucus, NJ: University Books.

Hutson, James H. 1981. "Country, Court, and Constitution: Antifederalism and the Historians." *William and Mary Quarterly,* 3rd ser. 38 (July): 337–368.

——. 1986. "The Creation of the Constitution: The Integrity of the Documentary Record." *Texas Law Review* 65 (November): 1–39.

——. 1984. "The Creation of the Constitution: Scholarship at a Standstill." *Reviews in American History* 12 (December): 463–477.

——. 2003. *Forgotten Features of the Founding: The Recovery of Religious Themes in the Early American Republic.* Lanham, MD: Lexington Books.

——. 1968. "John Adams' Title Campaign." *New England Quarterly* 41 (March): 30–39.

——. 1982. "John Dickinson at the Federal Constitutional Convention." *William and Mary Quarterly,* 3rd ser. 40 (April): 256–281.

——. 1998. *Religion and the Founding of the American Republic.* Washington, DC: Library of Congress.

——. 1987. "Riddles of the Federal Constitutional Convention." *William and Mary Quarterly,* 3rd ser. 44 (July): 411–423.

Hutson, James H., ed. 1987. *Supplement to Max Farrand's* The Records of the Federal Convention of 1787. New Haven, CT: Yale University Press.

Hutson, James L. 1993. "The American Revolutionaries, the Political Economy of Aristocracy, and the American Concept of the Distribution of Wealth, 1765–1900." *American Historical Review* 98 (October): 1079–1105.

Huyler, Jerome. 1995. *Locke in America: The Moral Philosophy of the Founding Era.* Lawrence: University Press of Kansas.

Ingrao, Charles. 1982. "'Barbarous Strangers': Hessian State and Society during the American Revolution." *American Historical Review* 87 (October): 954–976.

Ireland, Owen S. 1995. *Religion, Ethnicity, and Politics: Ratifying the Constitution in Pennsylvania.* University Park: Pennsylvania State University Press.

Isaacson, Walter. 2003. *Benjamin Franklin: An American Life.* New York: Simon and Schuster.

Jacob, James B. 2004. "Corruption and Democracy." *Phi Kappa Phi Forum* 84 (Winter): 21–25.

Jameson, John A. 1887. *A Treatise on Constitutional Con-*

ventions: Their History, Powers, and Modes of Proceeding. 4th ed. Chicago: Callaghan. Reprinted in New York: Da Capo, 1974.

Jamison, King Wells. 2004. *The Letters from Short Mountain.* Murfreesboro, TN: Rubednacoff Press.

Janosik, Robert J. 1991. *The American Constitution: An Annotated Bibliography.* Pasadena, CA: Salem Press.

Jefferson, Thomas. 1964. *Notes on the State of Virginia.* New York: Harper and Row, Publishers.

Jensen, Merrill. 1966. *The Articles of Confederation.* Madison: University of Wisconsin Press.

———. 1958. (1979 reprint). *The Making of the American Constitution.* Malabar, FL: Robert E. Kreiger Publishing.

Jensen, Merrill, ed. 1976. *Constitutional Documents and Records, 1776–1787.* Vol. 1 of *The Documentary History of the Ratification of the Constitution.* Madison: State Historical Society of Wisconsin.

———. 1976. *Ratification of the Constitution by the States Pennsylvania.* Vol. 2 of *The Documentary History of the Ratification of the Constitution.* Madison: State Historical Society of Wisconsin.

———. 1978. *Ratification of the Constitution by the States Delaware New Jersey Georgia Connecticut.* Vol. 3 of *The Documentary History of the Ratification of the Constitution.* Madison: State Historical Society of Wisconsin.

Jillson, Calvin C. 1981. "Constitution-Making: Alignment and Realignment in the Federal Convention of 1787." *American Political Science Review* 75 (September): 598–612.

Jillson, Calvin C., and Thornton Anderson. 1977. "Realignments in the Convention of 1787: The Slave Trade Compromise." *Journal of Politics* 38 (August): 712–729.

———. 1978. "Voting Bloc Analysis in the Constitutional Convention: Implications for an Interpretation of the Connecticut Compromise." *Western Political Quarterly* 31 (December): 535–547.

Jillson, Calvin C., and Cecil L. Eubanks. 1984. "The Political Structure of Constitution Making: The Federal Convention of 1787." *American Journal of Political Science* 28 (August): 435–458.

Johansen, Bruce E. 1990. "Native American Societies and the Evolution of Democracy in America, 1600–1800." *Ethnohistory* 37 (Summer): 279–290.

Johnson, Calvin H. 1998. "Apportionment of Direct Taxes: The Foul-Up at the Core of the Constitution." *William and Mary Bill of Rights Journal* 7 (December): 1–103.

———. 2003–2004. "Homage to Clio: The Historical Continuity from the Articles of Confederation into the Constitution." *Constitutional Commentary* 20 (Winter): 463–513.

Johnson, Eldon L. 1987. "The 'Other Jeffersons' and the State University Idea." *Journal of Higher Education* 58 (March-April): 127–150.

Jordan, Cynthia S. 1988. "'Old Words' in 'New Circumstances': Language and Leadership in Post-Revolutionary America." *American Quarterly* 40 (December): 491–513.

Kaminski, John P. 1995. *A Necessary Evil? Slavery and the Debates over the Constitution.* Madison, WI: Madison House.

———. 1985. "New York: The Reluctant Pillar." In Stephen L. Schechter, ed. *The Reluctant Pillar: New York and the Adoption of the Federal Constitution.* Troy, NY: Russell Sage College.

Kaminski, John P., and Gaspare J. Saladino, eds. 1997. *Ratification of the Constitution by the States Massachusetts.* Vol. 4 of *The Documentary History of the Ratification of the Constitution.* Madison: State Historical Society of Wisconsin.

Kammen, Michael. 1987. *A Machine That Would Go of Itself: The Constitution in American Culture.* New York: Alfred A. Knopf.

———. 1985. *The Problem of Constitutionalism in American Culture.* Irving, TX: University of Dallas.

Kann, Mark E. 1999. *A Republic of Men: The American Founders, Gendered Language, and Patriarchal Politics.* New York: New York University Press.

Kaplan, Sidney. "Veteran Officers and Politics in Massachusetts, 1783–1787." *William and Mary Quarterly,* 3rd ser. 9 (January): 29–57.

Kasson, John A. 1904. *The Evolution of the Constitution of the United States of America and the History of the Monroe Doctrine.* Boston: Riverside Press.

Katz, Stanley N. 1988. "The Strange Birth and Unlikely History of Constitutional Equality." *Journal of American History* 75 (December): 747–762.

Kay, Richard S. 1987. "The Illegality of the Constitution." *Constitutional Commentary* 4 (Winter): 57–80.

Keillor, Steven J. 1996. *This Rebellious House: American History and the Truth of Christianity.* Downers Grove, IL: InterVarsity Press.

Kelley, Joseph, Jr. 1973. *Life and Times in Colonial Philadelphia.* Harrisburg, PA: Stackpole Books.

Kelly, Alfred H., Winfred A. Harbison, and Herman Belz. 1983. *The American Constitution: Its Origins and Development.* 6th ed. New York: W. W. Norton.

Kendall, Willmoore, and George W. Carey. 1970. *The Basic Symbols of the American Political Tradition.* Baton Rouge: Louisiana State University Press.

Kenyon, Cecilia, ed. 1984. *The Antifederalists.* Boston: Northeastern University Press.

Kerber, Linda K. 1998. *No Constitutional Right to Be Ladies: Women and the Obligation of Citizenship.* New York: Hill and Wang.

——. 1985. "'Ourselves and Our Daughters Forever': Women and the Constitution, 1787–1876." *this Constitution,* no. 6 (Spring): 25–34.

——. 1985. "The Republican Ideology of the Revolutionary Generation." *American Quarterly* 37 (Autumn): 474–495.

Kernell, Samuel, ed. 2003. *James Madison: The Theory and Practice of Republican Government.* Stanford, CA: Stanford University Press.

Kesavan, Vasan. 2002. "When Did the Articles of Confederation Cease to Be Law?" *Notre Dame Law Review* 78 (December): 35–82.

Kesavan, Vasan, and Michael Stokes Paulsen. 2003. "The Interpretive Force of the Constitution's Secret Drafting History." *Georgetown Law Review* 92 (August): 1113–1214.

Kessler, Sanford. 1992. "Tocqueville's Puritans: Christianity and the American Founding." *Journal of Politics* 54 (August): 776–792.

Ketcham, Ralph. 1993. *Framed for Posterity: The Enduring Philosophy of the Constitution.* Lawrence: University Press of Kansas.

——. 1963. "France and American Politics, 1763–1793." *Political Science Quarterly* 78 (June): 198–223.

——. 1971. *James Madison: A Biography.* New York: Macmillan.

——. 1958. "James Madison and the Nature of Man." *Journal of the History of Ideas* 19 (January): 62–76.

——. 1987. "Publius: Sustaining the Republican Principle." *William and Mary Quarterly,* 3rd ser. 44 (July): 576–582.

Keyssar, Alexander. 2000. *The Right to Vote: The Contested History of Democracy in the United States.* New York: Basic Books.

Kilbourne, John Dwight (director, Library and Museum of The Society of the Cincinnati). 1986. Memorandum Re: "The Society of the Cincinnati and the Forming of the United States Constitution." April 15. Library Archives of the Independence National Historical Park, Philadelphia, Pennsylvania.

Kincaid, John. 1980. "Influential Models of Political Association in the Western Tradition." *Publius* 10 (Fall): 31–58.

King, Brett W. 1998. "The Use of Supermajority Provisions in the Constitution: The Framers, *The Federalist Papers* and the Reinforcement of a Fundamental Principle." *Seton Hall Constitutional Law Quarterly* 8 (Spring): 363–414.

Kirkham, David M. 1992. "European Sources of American Constitutional Thought before 1787." *United States Air Force Academy Journal of Legal Studies* 3: 1–28.

Klien, Milton M. 1993. *The American Whig: William Livingston of New York.* Rev. ed. New York: Garland Publishing.

——. 1958. "The Rise of the New York Bar: The Legal Career of William Livingston." *William and Mary Quarterly,* 3rd ser. 15 (July): 334–358.

Klinghoffer, Judith Apter, and Lois Elkis. 1992. "'The Petticoat Electors': Women's Suffrage in New Jersey, 1776–1807." *Journal of the Early Republic* 12 (Summer): 159–193.

Kloppenberg, James T. 1987. "The Virtues of Liberalism: Christianity, Republicanism, and Ethics in Early American Political Discourse." *Journal of American History* 74 (June): 9–33.

Kmiec, Douglas M., and Stephen B. Presser. 1998. *The History, Philosophy and Structure of the American Constitution.* Cincinnati, OH: Anderson Publishing Co.

Knupfer, Peter B. 1991. "The Rhetoric of Conciliation: American Civic Culture and the Federalist Defense of Compromise." *Journal of the Early Republic* 11 (Fall): 315–337.

Koch, Adrienne. 1950. *Jefferson and Madison: The Great Collaboration.* New York: Oxford University Press.

——. 1961. "Pragmatic Wisdom and the American Enlightenment." *William and Mary Quarterly,* 3rd ser. 18 (July): 313–329.

Koch, Adrienne, and Harry Ammon. 1948. "The Virginia and Kentucky Resolutions: An Episode in Jefferson's and Madison's Defense of Civil Liberties." *William and Mary Quarterly,* 3rd ser. 5 (April): 145–176.

Kramer, Larry D. 1999. "Madison's Audience." *Harvard Law Review* 112 (January): 511–679.

——. 2004. *The People Themselves: Popular Constitutionalism and Judicial Review.* New York: Oxford University Press.

Kramnick, Isaac. 1986. "Eighteenth-Century Science and Radical Social Theory: The Case of Joseph Priestley's Scientific Liberalism." *Journal of British Studies* 25 (January): 1–30.

——. 1988. "The 'Great National Discussion': The Discourse of Politics in 1787." *William and Mary Quarterly,* 3rd ser. 45 (January): 3–32.

Krauel, Richard. 1911. "Prince Henry of Prussia and

the Regency of the United States, 1786." *American Historical Review* 17 (October): 44–51.

Kraus, Michael. 1934. "George Bancroft 1834–1934." *New England Quarterly* 7 (December): 662–686.

Kreml, William P. 1997. *The Constitutional Divide: The Private and Public Sectors in American Law.* Columbia: University of South Carolina Press.

Kromkowski, Charles A. 2002. *Recreating the American Republic: Rules of Apportionment, Constitutional Change, and American Political Development, 1700–1870.* Cambridge: Cambridge University Press.

Kruman, Marc W. 1997. *Between Authority and Liberty: State Constitution Making in Revolutionary America.* Chapel Hill: University of North Carolina Press.

Kurland, Philip B., and Ralph Lerner. 1987. *The Founders' Constitution.* 5 vols. Chicago: University of Chicago Press.

Kyvig, David E. 1997. *Explicit and Authentic Acts: Amending the U.S. Constitution, 1776–1995.* Lawrence: University Press of Kansas.

Lansky, Dana. 2000. "Proceeding to a Constitution: A Multi-Party Negotiation Analysis of the Constitutional Convention of 1787." *Harvard Negotiation Law Review* 5 (Spring): 279–338.

Larkin, Jack. 1988. *The Reshaping of Everyday Life, 1790–1840.* New York: Harper and Row.

Larson, J. A. O. 1968. *Greek Federal States: Their Institutions and History.* Oxford, UK: Clarendon Press.

Lawrence, Vera Bradsky. 1975. *Music for Patriots, Politicians, and Presidents: Harmonies and Discords of the First Hundred Years.* New York: Macmillan Publishing Co.

Lawson, Gary, and Guy Seidman. 2002. "The First 'Establishment' Clause: Article VII and the Post-Constitutional Confederation." *Notre Dame Law Review* 78 (December): 83–100.

——. 2001. "When Did the Constitution Become Law?" *Notre Dame Law Review* 77 (November): 1–37.

Lawson, Murray G. 1952. "Canada and the Articles of Confederation." *American Historical Review* 58 (October): 39–54.

Lea, James F. 1982. *Political Consciousness and American Democracy.* Jackson: University Press of Mississippi.

Lee, Emery G., III. 1997. "Representation, Virtue, and Political Jealousy in the Brutus-Publius Dialogue." *Journal of Politics* 59 (November): 1073–1095.

Leek, J. J. 1951. "Treason and the Constitution." *Journal of Politics* 13 (November): 604–622.

Lefler, Hugh T. 1947. *A Plea for Federal Union, North Carolina, 1788: A Reprint of Two Pamphlets.* Charlottesville, VA: Tracy W. McGregor Library.

Leibiger, Stuart. 1993. "James Madison and Amend-ments to the Constitution, 1787–1789: 'Parchment Barriers.'" *Journal of Southern History* 59 (August): 441–468.

Leitao, Kevin D. 1996. "Rhode Island's Forgotten Bill of Rights." *Roger Williams University Law Review* 1 (Spring): 31–61.

Leitch, Alexander. "Constitutional Convention of 1787, The." http://etc.princeton.edu/Campus WWW/Companion/constitutional_convention. html. From 1978. *A Princeton Companion.* Princeton, NJ: Princeton University Press.

Lerche, Charles O., Jr. 1949. "The Guarantee of a Republican Form of Government and the Admission of New States." *Journal of Politics* 11 (August): 578–604.

Levinson, Sanford. 1994. "Authorizing Constitutional Text: On the Purported Twenty-seventh Amendment." *Constitutional Commentary* 11 (Winter): 101–113.

——. 1988. *A Constitutional Faith.* Princeton, NJ: Princeton University Press.

——. 2003. "Why I Did Not Sign the Constitution: With a Chance to Endorse It, I Had to Decline." http://www.constitutioncenter.org/explore/View points/WhyIDidNotSigntheConstitution.html.

Levy, Leonard W. 1997. "Foreign Policy and War Powers: The Presidency and the Framers." *American Scholar* 66 (Spring): 271–275.

——. 1988. *Original Intent and the Framers' Constitution.* New York: Macmillan.

——. 1995. *Seasoned Judgments: The American Constitution, Rights, and History.* New Brunswick, NJ: Transaction Publishers.

Levy, Leonard W., and Dennis J. Mahoney. 1987. *The Framing and Ratification of the Constitution.* New York: Macmillan.

Levy, Philip A. 1996. "Exemplars of Taking Liberties: The Iroquois Influence Thesis and the Problem of Evidence." *William and Mary Quarterly*, 3rd ser. 53 (July): 588–604.

Lewis, Jan. 1999. "'Of Every Age Sex & Condition': The Representation of Women in the Constitution." In Edward Countryman, ed. *What Did the Constitution Mean to Early Americans?* Boston: Bedford/St. Martin's.

——. 1987. "The Republican Wife: Virtue and Seduction in the Early Republic." *William and Mary Quarterly*, 3rd ser. 44 (October): 689–721.

"Liberty Bell Facts." http://www.ushistory.org/liberty bell/facts. html.

"Liberty Bell Timeline." http://www.ushistory.org/ libertybell/timeline.html.

Lieberman, Jethro K. 1987. *The Enduring Constitution: A Bicentennial Perspective.* Saint Paul, MN: West Publishing.

Liebiger, Stuart. 1999. *Founding Friendship: George Washington, James Madison, and the Creation of the American Republic.* Charlottesville: University Press of Virginia.

——. 1993. "James Madison and Amendments to the Constitution, 1787–1789: 'Parchment Barriers.'" *Journal of Southern History* 59 (August): 441–468.

Lienesch, Michael. 1980. "The Constitutional Tradition: History, Political Action, and Progress in American Political Thought, 1787–1793." *Journal of Politics* 42 (February): 2–30.

Linder, Douglas O. 1985. "The Two Hundredth Reunion of Delegates to the Constitutional Convention (Or, 'All Things Considered, We'd Really Rather Be in Philadelphia')." *Arizona State Law Journal:* 823–863.

Lindop, Edmund. 1987. *Birth of the Constitution.* Hillsdale, NJ: Enslow Publishers.

Linklater, Andro. 2002. *Measuring America: How the United States Was Shaped by the Greatest Land Sale in History.* New York: Plume.

Lint, Gregg L., and Richard Alan Ryerson. 1986. "The Separation of Powers: John Adams' Influence on the Constitution." *this Constitution,* no. 22 (Summer): 25–31.

Linton, Calvin D. 1975. *The Bicentennial Almanac.* Nashville, TN: Thomas Nelson Inc., Publishers.

Lipset, Seymour Martin. 1988. "George Washington and the Founding of Democracy." *Journal of Democracy* 9, no. 4: 24–38.

Little, David B. 1974. *America's First Centennial Celebration: The Nineteenth of April 1875 at Lexington and Concord, Massachusetts.* Boston: Houghton Mifflin.

Lively, Donald E. 1992. *The Constitution and Race.* New York: Praeger.

Lloyd, Gordon, and Colleen Garot. "Map of Historic Philadelphia in the Late 18th Century." http://teachingamericanhistory.org/convention/map/.

Lloyd, Gordon, and Jeff Sammon. "The Age of Framers in 1787." http://teachingamericanhistory.org.

——. "The Educational Background of the Framers." http://teachingamericanhistory.org.

Locke, John. 1955. *Of Civil Government: Second Treatise.* Chicago: Henry Regnery.

Lofgren, Charles A. 1976. "Compulsory Military Service under the Constitution: The Original Understanding." *William and Mary Quarterly,* 3rd ser. 33 (January): 61–88.

Lohman, Christina S. 2000/2001. "Presidential Eligibility: the Meaning of the Natural-Born Citizen Clause." *Gonzaga Law Review* 36: 349–374.

Lokken, Roy N. 1974. "The Political Theory of the American Revolution: Changing Interpretations." *The History Teacher* 8 (November): 81–95.

Long, Breckinridge. 1926. *Genesis of the Constitution of the United States of America.* New York: Macmillan.

Ludwikowski, Rett R., and William F. Fox, Jr. 1993. *The Beginning of the Constitutional Era: A Bicentennial Comparative Analysis of the First Modern Constitutions.* Washington, DC: Catholic University of America Press.

Lukacs, John. 1987. "Unexpected Philadelphia." *American Heritage* (May/June): 72–81.

Lundberg, David, and Henry F. May. 1976. "The Enlightened Reader in America." *American Quarterly* 28 (Summer): 262–293.

Lutz, Donald S. 1998. *Colonial Origins of the American Constitution: A Documentary History.* Indianapolis, IN: Liberty Fund.

——. 1980. "From Covenant to Constitution in American Political Thought." *Publius* 10 (Fall): 101–134.

——. 1988. *The Origins of American Constitutionalism.* Baton Rouge: Louisiana State University Press.

——. 1984. "The Relative Influence of European Writers on Late Eighteenth-Century American Political Thought." *American Political Science Review* 78 (March) 189–197.

Lynch, Jack. 2004. "Mirroring the Mind of Mason." *Colonial Williamsburg* 26 (Spring): 52–55.

Lynd, Staughton. 1966. "The Compromise of 1787." *Political Science Quarterly* 81 (June): 225–250.

Lyons. 1979. *Rights.* Belmont, CA: Wadsworth Publishing.

Madison, James. 1987. *Notes of Debates in the Federal Convention of 1787 as Reported by James Madison.* Introduction by Adrienne Koch. New York: W. W. Norton.

——. 1977. *The Papers of James Madison.* Vol. 10, *27 May 1787–3 March 1788.* Ed. Robert A. Rutland, Charles F. Hobson, William M. M. Rachal, and Fredericka J. Teute. Chicago: University of Chicago Press.

——. 1973. "Vices of the Political System of the United States, April 1787." *The Mind of the Founder: Sources of the Political Thought of James Madison.* Ed. Marvin Meyers. Indianapolis, IN: Bobbs-Merrill.

Maier, Pauline. 1997. *American Scripture: Making the Declaration of Independence.* New York: Alfred A. Knopf.

——. 1970. "Popular Uprisings and Civil Authority in Eighteenth-Century America." *William and Mary Quarterly,* 3rd ser. 27 (January): 3–35.

Main, Jackson T. 1961. *The Antifederalists: Critics of the Constitution, 1781–1788.* Chicago: Quadrangle Books.

——. 1973. *Political Parties before the Constitution.* New York: W. W. Norton.

Malbin, Michael J. 1984. "Framing a Congress to Channel Ambition." *this Constitution,* no. 5 (Winter): 4–12.

Malone, Dumas. 1948–1977. *Jefferson and His Time.* 6 vols. Boston: Little, Brown.

Mann, Bruce H. 1994. "Tales from the Crypt: Prison, Legal Authority, and the Debtors' Constitution in the Early Republic." *William and Mary Quarterly,* 3rd ser. 51 (April): 183–202.

Manzer, Robert A. 2001. "A Science of Politics: Hume, *The Federalist,* and the Politics of Constitutional Attachment." *American Journal of Political Science* 45 (July): 508–518.

Mapp, Alf J., Jr. 2003. *The Faith of Our Fathers: What America's Founders Really Believed.* Lanham, MD: Rowman and Littlefield.

Markey, Howard T., Donald W. Banner, Beverly Pattishall, and Ralph Oman. 1988. *Celebrating the Bicentennial of the United States Constitution.* American Bar Association Section of Patent, Trademark and Copyright Law.

Marks, Frederick W., III. 1972. "American Pride, European Prejudice, and the Constitution." *The Historian: A Journal of History* 34 (August): 579–597.

——. 1971. "Foreign Affairs: A Winning Issue in the Campaign for Ratification of the United States Constitution." *Political Science Quarterly* 86 (September): 444–469.

Marling, Karal Ann. 1987. "A 'New Historical Whopper': Creating the Art of the Constitutional Sesquicentennial." *this Constitution,* no. 14 (Spring): 11–17.

Martinez, Fernando Rey. 2003. "The Religious Character of the American Constitution: Puritanism and Constitutionalism in the United States." *Kansas Journal of Law and Public Policy* 12 (Spring): 459–482.

Martis, Kenneth C. 2001. "The Geographical Dimensions of a New Nation, 1780s–1820s." In Thomas F. McIlwraith and Edward K. Muller, eds. *North America: The Historical Geography of a Changing Continent.* Lanham, MD: Rowman and Littlefield, 143–164.

Mason, Alpheus T. 1976. "America's Political Heritage: Revolution and Free Government—A Bicentennial Tribute." *Political Science Quarterly* 91 (Summer): 193–217.

——. 1972. *The States' Rights Debate: Antifederalism and the Constitution.* 2nd ed. New York: Oxford University Press.

Mason, Alpheus T., and Gordon E. Baker. 1985. *Free Government in the Making: Readings in American Political Thought.* 4th ed. New York: Oxford University Press.

Mason, Alpheus T., and Donald Grier Stephenson, Jr. 2002. *American Constitutional Law: Introductory Essays and Selected Cases.* 13th ed. Upper Saddle River, NJ: Prentice Hall.

Mason, Ed. 1975. *Signers of the Constitution.* Book 2 of *Builders of a Nation.* Columbus, OH: Dispatch Printing.

Massengill, Stephen E. 1988. *North Carolina Votes on the Constitution: Roster of Delegates to the State Ratifying Conventions of 1788 and 1789.* Division of Archives and History, North Carolina Department of Cultural Resources.

Matson, Cathy, and Peter Onuf. 1985. "Toward a Republican Empire: Interest and Ideology in Revolutionary America." *American Quarterly* 37 (Autumn): 496–531.

Matthews, L. L. 1914. "Benjamin Franklin's Plans for Colonial Union, 1750–1775." *American Political Science Review* 8 (August): 393–412.

Matthews, Marty D. 2004. *Forgotten Founder: The Life and Times of Charles Pinckney.* Columbia: University of South Carolina Press.

Matthews, Richard K. 1995. *If Men Were Angels: James Madison and the Heartless Empire of Reason.* Lawrence: University Press of Kansas.

Mayer, David M. 1994. *The Constitutional Thought of Thomas Jefferson.* Charlottesville: University Press of Virginia.

Mayo, Lawrence Shaw. 1970. *John Langdon of New Hampshire.* Port Washington, NY: Kennikat Press.

McCaughey, Elizabeth P. 1980. *From Loyalist to Founding Father: The Political Odyssey of William Samuel Johnson.* New York: Columbia University Press.

——. 1987. *Government by Choice: Inventing the United States Constitution.* New York: Basic Books.

McClellan, James. 2000. *Liberty, Order, and Justice: An Introduction to the Constitutional Principles of American Government.* Indianapolis, IN: Liberty Fund.

McClendon, R. Earl. 1931. "Origin of the Two-thirds Rule in Senate Action upon Treaties." *American Historical Review* 36 (July): 678–772.

McCormick, Richard P. 1987. "The Miracle at Philadelphia." *Utah Law Review:* 829–846.

McDonald, Forrest. 2000. *States' Rights and the Union: Imperium in Imperio, 1776–1876.* Lawrence: University Press of Kansas.

——. 1958. *We the People: The Economic Origins of the Constitution.* Chicago: University of Chicago Press.

McDonald, Forrest, and Ellen Shapiro McDonald. 1968. *Confederation and Constitution, 1781–1789.* New York: Harper and Row Publishers.

McDowell, Gary L. 1998. "The Language of Law and the Foundations of American Constitutionalism." *William and Mary Quarterly,* 3rd ser. 55 (July): 375–398.

McGee, Dorothy H. 1968. *Framers of the Constitution.* New York: Dodd, Mead.

McGinnis, John O., and Michael B. Rappaport. 2002. "Our Supermajoritarian Constitution." *Texas Law Review* 80 (March): 703–806.

McGuire, Robert A. 1988. "Constitution Making: A Rational Choice Model of the Federal Convention of 1787." *American Journal of Political Science* 32 (May): 483–522.

——. 2003. *To Form a More Perfect Union: A New Economic Interpretation of the United States Constitution.* New York: Oxford University Press.

McLaughlin, Andrew C. 1918. "The Background of American Federalism." *American Political Science Review* 12 (May): 215–240.

——. 1905. *The Confederation and the Constitution, 1783–1789.* New York: Harper and Brothers.

——. 1961. *The Foundations of American Constitutionalism.* Greenwich, CT: Fawcett Publications.

——. 1897. "James Wilson in the Philadelphia Convention." *Political Science Quarterly* 12 (March): 1–20.

McMaster, John Bach. 1887. "The Framers and the Framing of the Constitution." *Century Magazine* 34 (September): 746–59.

McNamara, Peter. 1999. *The Noblest Minds: Fame, Honor, and the American Founding.* Lanham, MD: Rowman and Littlefield Publishers.

McWilliams, Wilson Carey. 1990. "Symposium: Roads Not Taken: Undercurrents of Republican Thinking in Modern Constitutional Theory: The Anti-Federalists, Representation, and Party." *Northwestern University Law Review* 85 (Fall): 12–38.

Mearns, David C., and Verner W. Clapp, comps. 1952. *The Constitution of the United States Together with an Account of Its Travels since September 17, 1787.* Washington, DC: Library of Congress.

"The Medical Men of Virginia." 1911. *William and Mary College Quarterly Historical Magazine* 19 (January): 145–162.

Mee, Charles L., Jr. 1987. *The Genius of the People.* New York: Harper and Row, Publishers.

Mehlinger, Howard D., ed. 1981. *Teaching about the Constitution in American Secondary Schools.* Washington, DC: American Historical Association and American Political Science Association.

Meigs, William M. 1900. *The Growth of the Constitution in the Federal Convention of 1787.* Philadelphia, PA: J. B. Lippincott. Reprinted in Littleton, CO: Fred B. Rothman, 1987.

Melton, Buckner F., Jr. 1998. *The First Impeachment: The Constitution's Framers and the Case of Senator Blount.* Macon, GA: Mercer University Press.

Merritt, Eli. 1991. "Sectional Conflict and Secret Compromise: The Mississippi River Question and the United States Constitution." *American Journal of Legal History* 35 (April): 117–171.

Messerli, Jonathan. 1967. "The Columbian Complex: The Impulse to National Consolidation." *History of Education Quarterly* 7 (Winter): 417–431.

Meyer, D. D. 1976. "The Uniqueness of the American Enlightenment." *American Quarterly* 28 (Summer): 165–186.

Meyers, Marvin, ed. 1973. *The Mind of the Founder: Sources of the Political Thought of James Madison.* Indianapolis, IN: Bobbs-Merrill.

Middlekauff, Robert. 1982. *The Glorious Cause: The American Revolution, 1763–1789.* New York: Oxford University Press.

Miles, Edwin A. 1974. "The Young American Nation and the Classical World." *Journal of the History of Ideas* 35 (April-June): 259–274.

Miller, Joshua. 1988. "The Ghostly Body Politic: *The Federalist Papers* and Popular Sovereignty." *Political Theory* 16 (February): 99–119.

Miller, Perry. 1953. *The New England Mind: From Colony to Province.* Cambridge, MA: Harvard University Press.

——. 1939. *The New England Mind: The Seventeenth Century.* New York: Macmillan.

Miller, William L. 1992. *The Business of May Next: James Madison and the Founding.* Charlottesville: University Press of Virginia.

Millett, Stephen M. 1975. *A Selected Bibliography of American Constitutional History.* Santa Barbara, CA: Clio Books.

Minot, George R. 1910 (reprint 1970). *The History of the Insurrections in Massachusetts in the Year Seventeen Hundred and Eighty Six and the Rebellion Consequent Thereon.* Freeport, NY: Books for Libraries Press.

Mires, Charlene. 2002. *Independence Hall in American Memory.* Philadelphia: University of Pennsylvania Press.

Miroff, Bruce. 1986. "John Adams: Merit, Fame, and Political Leadership." *Journal of Politics* 48 (February): 116–132.

Mitchell, Broadus, and Louise Pearson Mitchell. 1964. *A Biography of the Constitution of the United States: Its*

Origin, Formation, Adoption, Interpretation. New York: Oxford University Press.

Mitchell, Patricia. 1991. *Revolutionary Recipes: Colonial Food, Lore, and More.* Chatham, VA: P. P. Mitchell.

Montesquieu, Baron de. 1949. *The Spirit of the Laws.* Trans. Thomas Nugent. New York: Hafner Press.

Moore, John Allphin, Jr. "Empire, Republicanism, and Reason: Foreign Affairs as Viewed by the Founders of the Constitution." *The History Teacher* 26 (March): 297–315.

Morgan, Edmund S. 1977. *The Birth of the Republic, 1763–89.* Rev. ed. Chicago: University of Chicago Press.

——. 1988. *Inventing the People: The Rise of Popular Sovereignty in England and America.* New York: W. W. Norton.

——. 1961. "John Adams and the Puritan Tradition." *New England Quarterly* 34 (December): 518–529.

——. 1983. "The Witch, and We, the People." *American Heritage* 34 (August/September): 6–11.

Morgan, Kenneth. 2001. "Slavery and the Debate over Ratification of the United States Constitution." *Slavery and Abolition* 22 (December): 40–65.

Morison, S. S. 1929. "Elbridge Gerry, Gentleman-Democrat." *The New England Quarterly* 2 (January): 6–33.

Morris, Richard B. 1956. "The Confederation Period and the American Historian." *William and Mary Quarterly,* 3rd ser. 13 (April): 139–156.

——. 1985. "The Constitutional Thought of John Jay." *this Constitution,* no. 9 (Winter): 25–33.

——. 1987. "A Few Parchment Pages: Two Hundred Years Later." *American Heritage* 38 (May-June): 46–51.

——. 1986. *The Framing of the Federal Constitution.* Washington, DC: U.S. Department of the Interior.

——. 1988. "The Genesis of Project '87." *this Constitution,* no. 18 (Spring/Summer): 76–77.

——. 1985. "The Mount Vernon Conference: First Step toward Philadelphia." *this Constitution,* no. 6 (Spring): 38–40.

——. 1985. *Witnesses at the Creation: Hamilton, Madison, Jay, and the Constitution.* New York: New American Library.

Morris, Thomas D. 1996. *Southern Slavery and the Law, 1619–1860.* Chapel Hill: University of North Carolina Press.

Mullin, John M. 1992. "Fundamental Values, the Founding Fathers, and the Constitution." In Herman Belz, Ronald Hoffman, and Peter J. Albert, eds. *To Form a More Perfect Union: The Critical Ideas of*

the Constitution. Charlottesville: University Press of Virginia.

Munroe, John A. 1952. "Nonresident Representation in the Continental Congress: The Delaware Delegation of 1782." *William and Mary Quarterly,* 3rd ser. 9 (April): 166–190.

Murphy, Walter F., James E. Fleming, Sotirious A. Barber, and Stephen Macedo. *American Constitutional Interpretation.* 3rd ed. New York: Foundation Press.

Murphy, Walter F., C. Herman Pritchett, and Lee Epstein. 2002. *Courts, Judges, and Politics: An Introduction to the Judicial Process.* 5th ed. Boston: McGraw Hill.

Murrin, John M., David E. Narrett, Ronald Hatzenbuehler, and Michael Kammen. 1974. *Essays on Liberty and Federalism: The Shaping of the U.S. Constitution.* College Station: Texas A and M University Press.

Nadelmann, Kurk H. 1957. "On the Origin of the Bankruptcy Clause." *American Journal of Legal History* 1 (July): 215–228.

Narroll, Raoul Soskin. 1953. *Clio and the Constitution: The Influence of the Study of History on the Federal Constitutional Convention of 1787.* Ph.D. diss. University of California, Los Angeles.

Natelson, Robert G. 2003. "The Constitutional Contributions of John Dickinson." *Pennsylvania State Law Review* 108 (Fall): 415–477.

——. 2002/2003. "A Reminder: The Constitutional Values of Sympathy and Independence." *Kentucky Law Journal* 91: 353–423.

——. 2003. "Statutory Retroactivity: The Founders' View." *Idaho Law Review* 39: 489–528.

National Constitution Center. 2003. Visitor's Guide and Map.

Nelson, Caleb. 2003. "Originalism and Interpretive Conventions." *University of Chicago Law Review* 70 (Spring): 519–598.

Nelson, Michael, ed. 2002. *Guide to the Presidency.* 3rd ed. Washington, DC: Congressional Quarterly.

——. 1996. *The Presidency.* London: Salamander Books.

Nelson, William E. 1987. "Reason and Compromise in the Establishment of the Federal Constitution, 1787–1801." *William and Mary Quarterly,* 3rd ser. 44 (July): 458–484.

Nettels, Curtis P. 1946. "A Link in the Chain of Events Leading to American Independence." *William and Mary Quarterly,* 3rd ser. 3 (January): 36–47.

Neustadt, Katherine D. 1982. *Carpenters' Hall: Meeting Place of History.* Philadelphia, PA: Winchell.

Nevins, Jane. 1987. *Turning 200: The Bicentennial of the*

U.S. Constitution. New York: Richardson and Steirman.

Newmark, Mark S. 1997. "Navigating the Internet for Sources in American History." *The History Teacher* 30 (May): 283–292.

Nicholson, Catherine, and Mary Lynn Ritzenthaler. 2002. "Tales from the Vault: Exposed to Air after Fifty Years!" *Common-place* 2, no. 4 (July). www.common-place.org.

"The 1954 Albany Plan of Union." University of Oklahoma Law Center. http://www.law.ou.edu/hist/albplan.html.

Nobles, Gregory H. 1989. "Breaking into the Backcountry: New Approaches to the Early American Frontier, 1750–1800." *William and Mary Quarterly,* 3rd ser. 46 (October): 641–670.

Noelle-Neumann, Elisabeth. 1979. "Public Opinion and the Classical Tradition: A Re-evaluation." *Public Opinion Quarterly* 43 (Summer): 143–156.

Noll, Mark A. 1993. "The American Revolution and Protestant Evangelicalism." *Journal of Interdisciplinary History* 23 (Winter): 615–638.

Nord, David P. 1988. "A Republican Literature: A Study of Magazine Reading and Readers in Late Eighteenth-Century New York." *American Quarterly* 40 (March): 42–64.

Nordham, George Washington. 1987. *George Washington: President of the Constitutional Convention.* Chicago: Adams Press.

"Notes of Major William Pierce on the Federal Convention of 1787." *American Historical Review* 8 (January): 310–334.

O'Brien, David M. 2003. *Storm Center: The Supreme Court in American Politics.* 6th ed. New York: W. W. Norton.

——. 2003. *Struggles for Power and Governmental Accountability.* Vol. 1 of *Constitutional Law and Politics.* 5th ed. New York: W. W. Norton.

O'Brien, Steven G. 1991. *American Political Leaders: From Colonial Times to the Present.* Santa Barbara, CA: ABC-CLIO.

O'Connor, J. J. 1979. *William Paterson: Lawyer and Statesman, 1745–1806.* New Brunswick, NJ: Rutgers University Press.

O'Connor, John F. "The Emoluments Clause: An Anti-Federalist Intruder in a Federalist Constitution." *Hofstra Law Review* 24 (Fall): 89–178.

Ohline, Howard A. 1971. "Republicanism and Slavery: Origins of the Three-fifths Clause in the United States Constitution." *William and Mary Quarterly,* 3rd ser. 28 (October): 563–584.

Olson, Alison Gilbert. 1960. "The British Government and Colonial Union, 1754." *William and Mary Quarterly* 3rd ser. 17 (January): 22–34.

O'Malley, Michael, and Roy Rosenzweig. 1997. *Journal of American History* 84 (June): 132–155.

Onuf, Peter S. 1982. "From Colony to Territory: Changing Concepts of Statehood in Revolutionary America." *Political Science Quarterly* 97 (Fall): 447–459.

——. 1986. "Liberty, Development, and Union: Visions of the West in the 1780s." *William and Mary Quarterly,* 3rd ser. 43 (April): 179–213.

——. 1989. "Reflections on the Founding: Constitutional Historiography in Bicentennial Perspective." *William and Mary Quarterly,* 3rd ser. 46 (April): 341–375.

——. 1987. *Statehood and Union: A History of the Northwest Ordinance.* Bloomington: Indiana University Press.

——. 1981. "State-Making in Revolutionary America: Independent Vermont as a Case Study." *Journal of American History* 67 (March): 797–815.

——. 1985. "Virginia, Vermont, and the Origins of the Federal Republic." *this Constitution,* no. 7 (Summer): 4–10.

Padover, Saul K. 1962. *To Secure These Blessings: The Great Debates of the Constitutional Convention of 1787, Arranged According to Topics.* New York: Washington Square Press/Ridge Press Book.

Paine, Thomas. 1986 (1776). *Common Sense.* New York: Penguin Books.

——. 1780. *Public Good: Being an Examination into the Claim of Virginia to the Vacant Western Territory, and of the Right of the United States to the Same, to Which Is Added, Proposing for Laying off a New State, to Be Applied as a Fund for Carrying on the War, or Redeeming the National Debt.* Albany, NY: Charles R. and George Webster. Reprinted in Berea, KY: Kentucky Imprints, 1976.

Palmer, R. R. 1959. *The Age of the Democratic Revolution: A Political History of Europe and America, 1760–1800.* Princeton, NJ: Princeton University Press.

——. 1953. "Notes on the Word 'Democracy' 1789–1799." *Political Science Quarterly* 68 (June): 203–226.

Pangle, Thomas L. 1988. *The Spirit of Modern Republicanism: The Moral Vision of the American Founders and the Philosophy of Locke.* Chicago: University of Chicago Press.

Patterson, C. Perry. 1949. "The President as Chief Administrator." *Journal of Politics* 11 (February): 218–235.

Patterson, Charles F. 2002. *The True Meaning of the Constitution: Ratifier Understanding.* Xenia, OH: Bentham Press.

Patterson, Thomas E. 2004. *We the People: A Concise Introduction to American Politics.* 5th ed. New York: McGraw-Hill.

Paulsen, Michael S. 1993. "A General Theory of Article V: The Constitutional Issues of the Twenty-seventh Amendment." *Yale Law Journal* 103: 677–789.

Payne, Samuel B., Jr. 1996. "The Iroquois League, the Articles of Confederation, and the Constitution." *William and Mary Quarterly,* 3rd ser. 53 (July): 605–620.

Pease, William H., and Jane H. Pease. 1965. *The Antislavery Argument.* Indianapolis, IN: Bobbs-Merrill.

Peck, Robert S., and Ralph S. Pollock, eds. 1985. *The Blessings of Liberty: Bicentennial Lectures at the National Archives.* Chicago: American Bar Association.

Pelikan, Jaroslav. 2004. *Interpreting the Bible and the Constitution.* New Haven, CT: Yale University Press.

Pencak, William. 1986. "Teaching Eighteenth Century American Politics." *The History Teacher* 19 (February): 169–180.

Pennock, J. Roland, and John W. Chapman, eds. *Constitutionalism.* New York: New York University Press, 1979.

Perrin, John William. 1914. "Presidential Tenure and Reeligibility." *Political Science Quarterly* 29 (September): 423–437.

Persons, Stow. 1954. "The Cyclical Theory of History in Eighteenth Century America." *American Quarterly* 6 (Summer): 147–163.

Pestritto, Ronald J., and Thomas G. West, eds. 2003. *The American Founding and the Social Contract.* Lanham, MD: Lexington Books.

Peters, Ronald M., Jr. 1978. *The Massachusetts Constitution of 1780: A Social Compact.* Amherst: University of Massachusetts Press.

Peters, William. 1987. *A More Perfect Union.* New York: Crown Publishers.

Peterson, Merrill D. 1976. *Adams and Jefferson: A Revolutionary Dialogue.* New York: Oxford University Press.

——, ed. 1966. *Democracy, Liberty, and Property: The State Constitutional Conventions of the 1820's.* Indianapolis, IN: Bobbs-Merrill.

Phelps, Glenn A. 1993. *George Washington and American Constitutionalism.* Lawrence: University Press of Kansas.

Phipps, Frances. 1972. *Colonial Kitchens, Their Furnishings, and Their Gardens.* New York: Hawthorn Books.

Plano, Jack C., and Milton Greenberg. 1989. *The American Political Dictionary.* 8th ed. New York: Holt, Rinehart and Winston.

Plotnik, Arthur. 1987. "The Search for Jacob Shallus." *Pennsylvania Heritage* 13: 24–31.

Pocock, J. G. A. 1975. *The Machiavellian Moment: Florentine Political Thought and the Atlantic Republican Tradition.* Princeton, NJ: Princeton University Press.

——, ed. 1980. *Three British Revolutions: 1641, 1688, 1776.* Princeton, NJ: Princeton University Press.

Pole, J. J. 1962. "Historians and the Problem of Early American Democracy." *American Historical Review* 67 (April): 626–646.

Polishook, Irwin H. 1969. *Rhode Island and the Union, 1774–1795.* Evanston, IL: Northwestern University Press.

Politics and the Constitution: The Nature and Extent of Interpretation. 1990. Washington, DC: National Legal Center for the Public Interest.

Potts, Louis W. 1986. "'A Lucky Moment': The Relationship of the Ordinance of 1787 and the Constitution of 1787." *Mid-America* 68 (October): 141–151.

Powell, H. Jefferson. 1985. "The Original Understanding of Original Intent." *Harvard Law Review* 98 (March): 885–948.

Powell, Thomas Reed. 1938. "From Philadelphia to Philadelphia." *American Political Science Review* 32 (February): 1–27.

Prescott, Arthur Taylor. 1968. *Drafting the Federal Constitution: A Rearrangement of Madison's Notes Giving Consecutive Developments of Provisions in the Constitution of the United States, Supplemented by Documents Pertaining to the Philadelphia Convention and to Ratification Processes, and Including Insertions by the Compiler.* Westport, CT: Greenwood Press.

Prude, Jonathan. 1991. "To Look upon the 'Lower Sort': Runaways Ads and the Appearance of Unfree Laborers in America, 1750–1800." *Journal of American History* 78 (June): 124–159.

Rakove, Jack N. 1979. *The Beginning of National Politics: An Interpretive History of the Continental Congress.* New York: Alfred A. Knopf.

——. 1998. *Declaring Rights: A Brief History with Documents.* Boston: Bedford Books.

——. 1987. "The Great Compromise: Ideas, Interests, and the Politics of Constitution Making." *William and Mary Quarterly,* 3rd ser. 44 (July): 424–457.

——. 1990. *Interpreting the Constitution: The Debate over Original Intent.* Boston: Northeastern University Press.

——. 1990. *James Madison and the Creation of the American Republic.* Glenview, IL: Scott, Foresman.

——. 2002. "James Madison in Intellectual Context." *William and Mary Quarterly* 3rd ser. 59 (October): 866–868.

——. 1996. *Original Meanings: Politics and Ideas in the Making of the Constitution.* New York: Alfred A. Knopf.

——. 1999. "The Super-Legality of the Constitution, or, a Federalist Critique of Bruce Ackerman's Neo-Federalism." *Yale Law Journal* 108 (June): 1931–1958.

——. 2004. "Thinking Like a Constitution." *Journal of the Early Republic* 24 (Spring): 1–20.

Ranney, Austin. 1976. "'The Divine Science': Political Engineering in American Culture." *American Political Science Review* 70 (March): 140–148.

Ranney, John C. 1946. "The Bases of American Federalism." *William and Mary Quarterly,* 3rd ser. 3 (January): 1–35.

Read, Conyers, ed. 1968. *The Constitution Reconsidered.* New York: Harper and Row Publishers.

Read, James H. 1995. "'Our Complicated System': James Madison on Power and Liberty." *Political Theory* 23 (August): 452–475.

Reardon, John J. 1974. *Edmund Randolph: A Biography.* New York: Macmillan.

Reeves, Jesse S. 1917. "The Prussian-American Treaties." *American Journal of International Law* 11 (July): 475–510.

Reichley, James A. 1988. "Religion and the Constitution." *this Constitution,* no. 18 (Spring/Summer): 46–52.

Reid, John Phillip. 1991. *The Authority to Legislate.* Part of *Constitutional History of the American Revolution.* Madison: University of Wisconsin Press.

Report to the Attorney General. 1989. *The Question of Statehood for the District of Columbia.* April 3. Washington, DC: U.S. Government Printing Office.

Return of the Whole Number of Persons within the Several Districts of the United States. 1802. Washington City: William Duane. Reprinted by New York: Arno Press, 1976.

Reveley, W. Taylor, III. 1974. "Constitutional Allocation of the War Powers between the President and the Congress: 1787–1788." *Virginia Journal of International Law* 15 (Fall): 73–147.

Rhodehamel, John H. 1998. *The Great Experiment: George Washington and the American Republic.* New Haven, CT: Yale University Press.

——. 1987. *Letters of Liberty: A Documentary History of the U.S. Constitution.* Los Angeles: Constitutional Rights Foundation.

Richard, Carl J. 1994. *The Founders and the Classics: Greece, Rome, and the American Enlightenment.* Cambridge, MA: Harvard University Press.

Richards, Leonard L. 2002. *Shays' Rebellion: The American Revolution's Final Battle.* Philadelphia: University of Pennsylvania Press.

Riemer, Neal. 1980. "Covenant and the Federal Constitution." *Publius* 10 (Fall): 135–148.

Rigal, Laura. 1998. *The American Manufactury: Art, Labor, and the World of Things in the Early Republic.* Princeton, NJ: Princeton University Press.

——. 1996. "'Raising the Roof': Authors, Spectators and Artisans in the Grand Federal Procession of 1788." *Theatre Journal* 48, no. 3: 253–277.

Riker, William. 1957. "Dutch and American Federalism." *Journal of the History of Ideas* 18 (October): 495–521.

——. 1984. "The Heresthetics of Constitution-Making: The Presidency in 1787, with Comments on Determinism and Rational Choice." *American Political Science Review* 78 (March): 1–16.

Risjord, Norman K. 1992. "Partisanship and Power: House Committees and the Powers of the Speaker, 1789–1801." *William and Mary Quarterly,* 3rd ser. 49 (October): 628–651.

——. 1974. "Virginians and the Constitution: A Multivariant Analysis." *William and Mary Quarterly,* 3rd ser. 31 (October): 613–632.

Ritcheson, Charles R. 1963. "The London Press and the First Decade of American Independence, 1783–1793." *Journal of British Studies* 2 (May): 88–109.

Robbins, Caroline. 1959. *The Eighteenth-Century Commonwealthman: Studies in the Transmission, Development and Circumstances of English Liberal Thought from the Restoration of Charles II until the War with the Thirteen Colonies.* Cambridge, MA: Harvard University Press.

Robert, Joseph C. 1952. *The Story of Tobacco in America.* New York: Alfred A. Knopf.

Roberts, Cokie. 2004. *Founding Mothers: The Women Who Raised Our Nation.* New York: William Morrow.

Robertson, Andrew W. 2001. "'Look on This Picture . . . And on This!' Nationalism, Localism, and Partisan Images of Otherness in the United States, 1787–1820." *American Historical Review* 106 (October): 1263–1280.

Robinson, Blackwell P. 1957. *William R. Davie.* Chapel Hill: University of North Carolina Press.

Robinson, James A. 1957. "Newtonianism and the Constitution." *Midwest Journal of Political Science* 1 (November): 252–266.

Robinson, Paul. 2003. "A Dodgy Constitution: Paul

Robinson on Why Europe's Constitutional Convention Is a Bureaucrat's Dream—Unlike the Philadelphia Convention of 1787." *Spectator* 291 (February 8): 14–15.

Robson, David W. 1983. "College Founding in the New Republic, 1776–1800." *History of Education Quarterly* 23 (Autumn): 323–341.

Roche, John P. 1961. "The Founding Fathers: A Reform Caucus in Action." *American Political Science Review* 55 (December): 799–816.

Rodgers, Daniel T. 1992. "Republicanism: The Career of a Concept." *Journal of American History* 79 (June): 11–38.

Rodick, Burleigh Cushing. 1953. *American Constitutional Custom: A Forgotten Factor in the Founding*. New York: Philosophical Library.

Rohr, John A. 1995. *Founding Republics in France and America: A Study in Constitutional Governance*. Lawrence: University Press of Kansas.

———. 1986. *To Run a Constitution: The Legitimacy of the Administrative State*. Lawrence: University Press of Kansas.

Roll, Charles W., Jr. "We, Some of the People: Apportionment in the Thirteen State Conventions Ratifying the Constitution." *Journal of American History* 56 (June): 21–40.

Rossiter, Clinton. 1964. *Alexander Hamilton and the Constitution*. New York: Harcourt, Brace and World.

———. 1961. "Introduction." *The Federalist Papers*. Alexander Hamilton, James Madison, and John Jay. New York: New American Library.

———. 1966. *1787: The Grand Convention*. New York: W. W. Norton.

Rossum, Ralph A. 2001. *Federalism, the Supreme Court, and the Seventeenth Amendment*. Lanham, MD: Lexington Books.

Rothman, Rozann. 1980. "The Impact of Covenant and Contract Theories on Conceptions of the U.S. Constitutions." *Publius* 10 (Fall): 149–164.

Rozbicki, Michael J. 1997. "The Curse of Provincialism: Negative Perceptions of Colonial American Plantation Gentry." *Journal of Southern History* 63 (November): 737–752.

Ruane, Michael E., and Michael D. Schaffer. 1987. *1787: Inventing America: A Day-by-Day Account of the Constitutional Convention*. Philadelphia, PA: Philadelphia Inquirer.

Rutland, Robert A. 1962. *The Birth of the Bill of Rights, 1776–1791*. New York: Collier Books.

———. 1987. *James Madison: The Founding Father*. New York: Macmillan.

———. 1966. *The Ordeal of the Constitution: The Antifederalists and the Ratification Struggle of 1787–1788*. Norman: University of Oklahoma Press.

———. 1984. "The Virginia Plan of 1787: James Madison's Outline of a Model Constitution." *this Constitution*, no. 4 (Fall): 23–30.

———, ed. 1970. *The Papers of George Mason, 1725–1792*. Vol. 2: *1779–1786*. Chapel Hill: University of North Carolina Press.

Ryn, Claes G. 1992. "Political Philosophy and the Unwritten Constitution." *Modern Age* 34 (Summer). Center for Constitutional Studies. http://www.nhinet.org/ccs/ccs-res.htm.

Samples, John, ed. 2002. *James Madison and the Future of Limited Government*. Washington, DC: Cato Institute.

Sanders, J. J. 1930. "John Fiske." *Mississippi Valley Historical Review* 17 (September): 264–277.

Sandoz, Ellis, ed. 1997. *Index to Political Sermons of the American Founding Era, 1730–1805*. Indianapolis, IN: Liberty Fund.

———. 1991. *Political Sermons of the American Founding Era, 1730–1805*. Indianapolis, IN: Liberty Fund.

Sargent, Mark L. 1988. "The Conservative Covenant: The Rise of the Mayflower Compact in American Myth." *New England Quarterly* 61 (June): 233–251.

Savage, I. Richard. 1982. "Who Counts?" *The American Statistician* 36 (August): 195–200.

Savage, James D. 1988. *Balanced Budgets and American Politics*. Ithaca, NY: Cornell University Press.

———. 1994. "Corruption and Virtue at the Constitutional Convention." *Journal of Politics* 56 (February): 174–186.

Schaedler, Louis C. 1946. "James Madison, Literary Craftsman." *William and Mary Quarterly*, 3rd ser. 3 (October): 515–533.

Schauer, Frederick. 1987. "1787: The Constitution in Perspective: 'We Do Ordain and Establish': The Constitution as Literary Text: The Constitution as Text and Rule." *William and Mary Law Review* (Fall): 41–50.

Schecter, Frank I. 1915. "The Early History and Tradition of the Constitution." *American Political Science Review* 9 (November): 707–734.

Scheef, Robert W. 2001. "'Public Citizens' and the Constitution: Bridging the Gap between Popular Sovereignty and Original Intent." *Fordham Law Review* 69 (April): 2201–2251.

Schofield, Robert E. 1997. *The Enlightenment of Joseph Priestley: A Study of His Life and Work from 1733 to 1773*. University Park, PA: Penn State Press.

———. 2005. *The Enlightened Joseph Priestley: A Study of His Life and Work from 1773 to 1804*. University Park, PA: Penn State Press.

Schudson, Michael. 1998. *The Good Citizen: A History of American Civic Life.* New York: The Free Press.

Schultz, David, and John R. Vile, eds. 2005. *The Encyclopedia of Civil Liberties in America.* 3 vols. Armonk, NY: M. E. Sharpe.

Schulyer, R. L. 1916. "Agreement in the Federal Convention." *Political Science Quarterly* 31 (June): 289–299.

Schulyer, Robert Livingston. 1942. "Galloway's Plans for Anglo-American Union." *Political Science Quarterly* 57 (June): 281–285.

Schwartz, Barry. 1987. *George Washington: The Making of an American Symbol.* New York: The Free Press.

——. 1983. "George Washington and the Whig Conception of Heroic Leadership." *American Sociological Review* 48 (February): 18–33.

Schwarzenbach, Sibyl A., and Patricia Smith, eds. 2003. *Women and the United States Constitution: History, Interpretation, and Practice.* New York: Columbia University Press.

Schweitzer, Mary M. 1993. "The Spatial Organization of Federalist Philadelphia, 1790." *Journal of Interdisciplinary History* 24 (Summer): 31–57.

——. 1989. "State-Issued Currency and the Ratification of the U.S. Constitution." *Journal of Economic History* 49 (June): 311–322.

Scruggs, William L. 1886. "Ambiguous Citizenship." *Political Science Quarterly* 1 (June): 199–205.

Secret Proceedings and Debates of the Convention Assembled at Philadelphia, in the Year 1787, for the Purpose of Forming the Constitution of the United States of America. 1838. Cincinnati: Alston Mygatt.

Seed, Geoffrey. 1978. *James Wilson.* Millwood, NY: kto press.

Senese, Donald J., ed. 1989. *George Mason and the Legacy of Constitutional Liberty: An Examination of the Influence of George Mason on the American Bill of Rights.* Fairfax County, VA: Fairfax County Historical Society.

The Sesquicentennial of the Constitution of the United States of America and Inauguration of George Washington First President 1787–1939. n.d.: n.p.

1787: The Day-to-Day Story of the Constitutional Convention. 1987. Compiled by historians of the Independence National Historical Park, National Park Service. New York: Exeter Books.

Shain, Barry A. 1994. *The Myth of American Individualism: The Protestant Origins of American Political Thought.* Princeton, NJ: Princeton University Press.

Shalhope, Robert E. 1982. "Republicanism and Early American Historiography." *William and Mary Quarterly,* 3rd ser. 39 (April): 334–356.

——. 1972. "Toward a Republican Synthesis: The Emergence of an Understanding of Republicanism in American Historiography." *William and Mary Quarterly,* 3rd ser. 29 (January): 49–80.

Sheehan, Colleen. 2002. "Madison and the French Enlightenment: The Authority of Public Opinion." *William and Mary Quarterly,* 3rd ser. 59 (October): 925–956.

——. 2004. "Madison v. Hamilton: The Battle over Republicanism and the Role of Public Opinion." *American Political Science Review* 98 (August): 405–424.

——. 1991. "The Politics of Public Opinion: James Madison's 'Notes on Government.'" *William and Mary Quarterly,* 3rd ser. 49 (October): 609–627.

Sheehan, Colleen A., and Gary L. McDowell. 1998. *Friends of the Constitution: Writings of the "Other" Federalists, 1787–1788.* Indianapolis, IN: Liberty Fund.

Sheldon, Garrett Ward. 2001. *The Political Philosophy of James Madison.* Baltimore, MD: Johns Hopkins University Press.

Sherry, Suzanna. 1987. "The Founders' Unwritten Constitution." *University of Chicago Law Review* 54 (Fall): 1127–1177.

Shoemaker, Robert W. 1966. "'Democracy' and 'Republic' as Understood in Late Eighteenth-Century America." *American Speech* 41 (May): 83–95.

Siegan, Bernard H. 2003. "Protecting Economic Liberties." *Chapman Law Review* 6 (Spring): 43–121.

Siemers, David J. 2003. *The Antifederalists: Men of Great Faith and Forbearance.* Lanham, MD: Rowman and Littlefield.

——. 2002. *Ratifying the Republic: Antifederalists and Federalists in Constitutional Time.* Palo Alto, CA: Stanford University Press.

Sikes, Lewright B. 1979. *The Public Life of Pierce Butler, South Carolina Statesman.* Washington, DC: University Press of America.

Simmons, R. C., ed. 1989. *The United States Constitution: The First 200 Years.* Manchester, UK: Manchester University Press.

Simpson, Albert F. 1941. "The Political Significance of Slave Representation, 1787–1872." *Journal of Southern History* 7 (August): 315–342.

Simpson, Brooks D. 1992. "Three Who Made the Constitution." *Constitution* 4 (Spring-Summer): 66–73.

Slaughter, Thomas P. 1984. "The Tax Man Cometh: Ideological Opposition to Internal Taxes, 1760–1790." *William and Mary Quarterly,* 3rd ser. 41 (October): 566–591.

Slonin, Shlomo. 1986. "The Electoral College at Philadelphia: The Evolution of an Ad Hoc Congress for the Selection of a President." *Journal of American History* 73 (June): 35–58.

——. 2003. "The Federalist Papers and the Bill of Rights." *Constitutional Commentary* 20 (Spring): 151–161.

Smith, Charles Page. 1956. *James Wilson: Founding Father, 1742–1798.* Chapel Hill: University of North Carolina Press.

Smith, Craig R. 1993. *To Form a More Perfect Union: The Ratification of the Constitution and the Bill of Rights, 1787–1791.* Lanham, MD: University Press of America.

Smith, Daniel Scott. 1999. "Population and Political Ethics: Thomas Jefferson's Demography of Generations." *William and Mary Quarterly,* 3rd ser. 56 (July): 591–612.

Smith, David G. 1965. *The Convention and the Constitution: The Political Ideas of the Founding Fathers.* New York: St. Martin's Press.

Smith, J. Allen. 1965. *The Spirit of American Government.* Cambridge, MA: Belknap Press of Harvard University Press.

Smith, Jean Edward. 1996. *John Marshall: Definer of a Nation.* New York: Henry Holt.

Smith-Rosenberg, Carroll. 1992. "Dis-Covering the Subject of the 'Great Constitutional Discussion,' 1786–1789." *Journal of American History* 79 (December): 841–873.

Smolla, Rodney A. 1992. *Free Speech in an Open Society.* New York: Alfred A. Knopf.

Snyder, K. Alan. 1983. "Foundations of Liberty: The Christian Republicanism of Timothy Dwight and Jedidiah Mores." *New England Quarterly* 56 (September): 382–397.

Solberg, Winton, ed. 1958. *The Federal Convention and the Formation of the Union of the American States.* Indianapolis, IN: Bobbs-Merrill.

Spaeth, Harold J., and Edward Conrad Smith. 1991. *The Constitution of the United States.* 13th ed. New York: HarperCollins.

Spencer, Mark G. 2002. "Hume and Madison on Faction." *William and Mary Quarterly,* 3rd ser. 59 (October): 869–896.

Spicer, Michael W. 1995. *The Founders, the Constitution, and Public Administration: A Conflict in World Views.* Washington, DC: Georgetown University Press.

Spillman, Lyn. 1996. "'Neither the Same nor Different Nations': Constitutional Conventions in the United States and Australia." *Comparative Studies in Society and History* 38 (January): 149–181.

Spitzer, Robert J. 1988. *The Presidential Veto: Touchstone*

of the American Presidency. Albany: State University Press of New York.

Spurlin, Paul M. 1976. "The Founding Fathers and the French Language." *Modern Language Journal* 60 (March): 85–96.

Staff, Independence National Historical Park. 1970. "Furnishing Plan for the Assembly Room, Independence Hall." February. Provided courtesy of James W. Mueller, chief historian and compliance coordinator, Independence National Historical Park.

Staib, Walter. 1999. *City Tavern Cookbook: 200 Years of Classic Recipes from America's First Gourmet Restaurant.* Philadelphia, PA: Running Press.

Stampp, Kenneth M. 1978. "The Concept of a Perpetual Union." *Journal of American History* 65 (June): 5–33.

Staveley, Keith, and Kathleen Fitzgerald. 2004. *America's Founding Food: The Story of New England Cooking.* Chapel Hill: University of North Carolina Press.

Steamer, Robert J. 1962. "The Legal and Political Genesis of the Supreme Court." *Political Science Quarterly* 77 (December): 546–569.

Steiner, Bernard C. 1915. *Connecticut's Ratification of the Federal Constitution.* Worcester, MA: American Antiquarian Society.

——. 1899. "Maryland's Adoption of the Federal Constitution I." *American Historical Review* 5 (October): 22–44.

St. John, Jeffrey. 1987. *Constitutional Journal: A Correspondent's Report from the Convention of 1787.* Ottawa, IL: Jameson Books.

Stoiber, Julie. 2003. "Discovery of Stone Uncovers Syng Plot." May 18. Philly.com. http://www.philly.com/mld/inquirer/2003/05/18/news/local/5884858.thm?lc

Stoner, James R., Jr. 1992. *Common Law and Liberal Theory: Coke, Hobbes, and the Origins of American Constitutionalism.* Lawrence: University Press of Kansas.

——. 2003. *Common-Law Liberty: Rethinking American Constitutionalism.* Lawrence: University Press of Kansas.

Storing, Herbert J. 1981. *What the Anti-Federalists Were For.* Chicago: University of Chicago Press.

——, ed. 1981. *The Complete Anti-Federalist.* 7 vols. Chicago: University of Chicago Press.

Striner, Richard. 1995. "Political Newtonianism: The Cosmic Model of Politics in Europe and America." *William and Mary Quarterly,* 3rd ser. 52 (October): 583–608.

Swift, Elaine K. 1993. "The Making of an American House of Lords: The U.S. Senate in the Constitutional Convention of 1787." *Studies in American Political Development* 7 (Fall): 177–224.

Tansill, Charles C. 1924. "The Treaty-Making Powers of the Senate." *American Journal of International Law* 18 (July): 459–482.

Tansill, Charles C., arranger. 1927. *Documents Illustrative of the Formation of the Union of the American States.* Washington, DC: U.S. Government Printing Office.

Tarr, G. Alan. 1998. *Understanding State Constitutions.* Princeton, NJ: Princeton University Press.

Tatalovich, Raymond, and Thomas S. Engeman. 2003. *The Presidency and Political Science: Two Hundred Years of Constitutional Debate.* Baltimore, MD: Johns Hopkins University Press.

Tate, Thad W. 1965. "The Social Contract in America, 1774–1787: Revolutionary Theory as a Conservative Instrument." *William and Mary Quarterly,* 3rd ser. 22 (July): 375–391.

Taylor, George R., ed. 1993. *The Great Tariff Debate, 1820–1830.* Boston: D. D. Heath.

Taylor, Robert J. 1980. "Construction of the Massachusetts Constitution." *Proceedings of the American Antiquarian Society* 90 (October): 317–340.

——. 1969. "Trial at Trenton." *William and Mary Quarterly,* 3rd ser. 26 (October): 521–547.

Thach, Charles C. 1922. *The Creation of the Presidency 1775–1789: A Study in Constitutional History.* Baltimore, MD: Johns Hopkins University Press.

Thomas, George. 2000. "As Far as Republican Principles Will Admit: Presidential Prerogative and Constitutional Government." *Presidential Studies Quarterly* 30 (September): 534–552.

Thorpe, Francis N., ed. 1907. *The Federal and State Constitutions, Colonial Charters, and Other Organic Laws of the United States.* 7 vols. Washington, DC: U.S. Government Printing Office.

Tillman, Seth B. 2005. "A Textualist Defense of Article I, Section 7, Clause 3: Why *Hollingsworth v. Virginia* Was Rightly Decided and Why *INS v. Chadha* Was Wrongly Reasoned." *Texas Law Review* 85 (Spring).

Treanor, William Michael. 1997. "Fame, the Founding, and the Power to Declare War." *Cornell Law Review* 82: 695–772.

Trees, Andrew S. 2004. *The Founding Fathers and the Politics of Character.* Princeton, NJ: Princeton University Press.

Trenchard, John, and Thomas Gordon. 1995 (first published in four volumes in 1755). *Cato's Letters or Essays on Liberty, Civil and Religious, and Other Important Subjects.* Ed. Ronald Hamowy. 2 vols. Indianapolis, IN: Liberty Fund.

Trenholme, Louise Irby. 1967. *The Ratification of the Federal Constitution in North Carolina.* New York: AMS Press.

Trent, William P. 1889. "The Period of Constitution-Making in the American Churches." In J. Franklin Jameson, ed. *Essays in the Constitutional History of the United States in the Formative Period, 1776–1789.* Boston: Houghton Mifflin.

Turner, Frederick Jackson. 1895. "Western State-Making in the Revolutionary Era I." *American Historical Review* 1 (October): 70–86.

——. 1896. "Western State-Making in the Revolutionary Era II." *American Historical Review* 2 (January): 251–269.

Twiss-Garrity, Beth A. 2002. "Object Lessons: Relics, Reverence, and Relevance." *Common-Place* 2, no. 4 (July). www.common-place.org.

Ulmer, S. Sidney. 1966. "Sub-group Formation in the Constitutional Convention." *Midwest Journal of Political Science* 10 (August): 288–303.

Umbach, Maiken. 1998. "The Politics of Sentimentality and the German Furstenbund, 1779–1785." *The Historical Journal* 41, no. 3: 679–704.

Utley, Robert L., Jr., ed. 1989. *Principles of the Constitutional Order: The Ratification Debates.* Lanham, MD: University Press of America.

Van Doren, Charles. 1948. *The Great Rehearsal: The Story of the Making and Ratifying of the Constitution of the United States.* New York: Viking Press.

Van Doren, Charles, and Robert McHenry, eds. 1975. *Webster's American Biographies.* Springfield, MA: G. and C. Merriam.

Van West, Carroll, ed. 1998. *The Tennessee Encyclopedia of History and Culture.* Nashville: Tennessee Historical Society/Rutledge Hill Press.

Vile, John R. 2001. *A Companion to the United States Constitution and Its Amendments.* 3rd ed. Westport, CT: Praeger.

——. 1992. *The Constitutional Amending Process in American Political Thought.* New York: Praeger.

——. 2003. "Contemporary Constitutional Scholars Missing from Signer's Hall." Posted on National Constitutional Website. October 30. http://www.constitutioncenter.org/explore/Viewpoints?ContemporaryConstitutionalScholarM . . .

——. 1993. *Contemporary Questions Surrounding the Constitutional Amending Process.* Westport, CT: Praeger.

——. 2003. *Encyclopedia of Constitutional Amendments, Proposed Amendments, and Amending Issues, 1789–2002.* 2nd ed. Santa Barbara, CA: ABC-CLIO.

——. 2003. "A Republic Established on Arguments and

Interests: Why I Think the Constitution Is Still Worthy of Signing." findlaw.com. October 23. http://writ.news.findlaw.com/scripts/printer_friendly.pl?page=commentary/20031028_vile.

———. 1994. "The Selection and Tenure of Chief Justices." *Judicature* 78 (October): 96–100.

———. 1992. "Three Kinds of Constitutional Founding and Change: The Convention Method and Its Alternatives." *Political Research Quarterly* 46 (December): 881–895.

———. 1987. "The U.S. Constitution and the Teaching of Economics." *The Social Studies* 78 (November/December): 244–248.

———, ed. 2003. *Great American Judges: An Encyclopedia.* 2 vols. Santa Barbara, CA: ABC-CLIO.

———. 2001. *Great American Lawyers: An Encyclopedia.* 2 vols. Santa Barbara: ABC-CLIO.

Vile, John R., and Mario Perez-Reilly. 1991. "The U.S. Constitution and Judicial Qualifications: A Curious Omission." *Judicature* 74 (December-January): 198–202.

Vile, M. J. C. 1998. *Constitutionalism and the Separation of Powers.* 2nd ed. Indianapolis, IN: Liberty Fund.

———. 1961. *The Structure of American Federalism.* London: Oxford University Press.

Vine, Phyllis. 1976. "The Social Function of Eighteenth-Century Higher Education." *History of Education Quarterly* 16 (Winter): 409–424.

Volcansek, Mary L. 1993. *Judicial Impeachment: None Called for Justice.* Urbana: University of Illinois Press.

Wakelyn, John L. 2004. *Birth of the Bill of Rights: Encyclopedia of the Antifederalists.* 2 vols. Westport, CT: Greenwood Press.

Walker, David M. 1980. *The Oxford Companion to Law.* Oxford, UK: Clarendon Press.

Walker, Joseph B. 1888. *Birth of the Federal Constitution: A History of the New Hampshire Convention for the Federal Constitution and of the Old North Meeting-House of Concord, in Which It Was Ratified by the Ninth State, and Thus Rendered Operative . . . on . . . the 21st of June, 1788.* Boston: Cupples and Hurd, Publishers.

Walker, Juliet E. E. 1989. "Whither Liberty, Equality or Legality? Slavery, Race, Property and the 1787 American Constitution." *New York Law School Journal of Human Rights* 6: 299–352.

Walker, Wendell K. 1976. "Foreword." The Masonic Book Club Edition of *The Signers of the Constitution of the United States.* Bloomington, IL: Masonic Book Club.

Walling, Karl-Friedrich. 2003. "Alexander Hamilton on the Strategy of American Free Government." In Bryan-Paul Frost and Jeffrey Sikkenga, eds. *History of American Political Thought.* Lanham, MD: Lexington Books, 167–191.

Walsh, James J. 1935. (1970 reprint). *Education of the Founding Fathers of the Republic: Scholasticism in the Colonial Colleges, A Neglected Chapter in the History of American Education.* Freeport, NY: Books for Libraries Press.

Ward, Harry M. 1961. *The United Colonies of New England—1643–90.* New York: Vantage Press.

Warren, Charles. 1945. "Fourth of July Myths." *William and Mary Quarterly,* 3rd ser. (July): 237–272.

Warren, Joseph Parker. 1905. "The Confederation and Shays' Rebellion." *American Historical Review* 11 (October): 42–67.

Watson, Henry B. 1983. *George Washington: Architect of the Constitution.* Daytona Beach, FL: Patriotic Education.

Weaver, Glenn. 1957. "Benjamin Franklin and the Pennsylvania Germans." *William and Mary Quarterly,* 3rd ser. 14 (October): 536–559.

Weber, Max. 1992 (1904–1905). *The Protestant Ethic and the Spirit of Capitalism.* New York: Routledge.

Weber, Paul J., and Barbara A. Perry. 1989. *Unfounded Fears: Myths and Realities of a Constitutional Convention.* New York: Praeger.

Webking, Robert H. 1988. *The American Revolution and the Politics of Liberty.* Baton Rouge: Louisiana State University Press.

———. 1987. "Melancton Smith and the Letters from the Federal Farmer." *William and Mary Quarterly,* 3rd ser. 44 (July): 510–528.

Weir, Robert W. 1988. "South Carolinians and the Adoption of the United States Constitution." *South Carolina Historical Magazine* 89 (April): 73–89.

Weisberger, Bernard A. 2000. *America Afire: Jefferson, Adams, and the Revolutionary Election of 1800.* New York: William Morrow.

Werner, John M. 1972. "David Hume and America." *Journal of the History of Ideas* 33 (September): 439–456.

West, John G., Jr. 1996. *The Politics of Revelation and Reason: Religion and Civil Life in the New Nation.* Lawrence: University Press of Kansas.

West, Thomas G. 1997. *Vindicating the Founders: Race, Sex, Class, and Justice in the Origins of America.* Lanham, MD: Rowman and Littlefield Publishers.

"We the People." 1987. Special issue of *Time.* July 6.

Whitaker, A. A. 1926. "The Muscle Shoals Speculation, 1783–1789." *Mississippi Valley Historical Review* 13 (December): 365–386.

White, Leonard D. 1948. *The Federalists: A Study in Administrative History, 1789–1801.* New York: The Free Press.

White, Morton. 1978. *The Philosophy of the American Revolution.* New York: Oxford University Press.

Whitney, David C. 1974. *Founders of Freedom in America: Lives of the Men Who Signed the Constitution of the United States and So Helped to Establish the United States of America.* Chicago: J. J. Ferguson Publishing.

Whitten, Dolphus, Jr. 1961. *The State Delegations in the Philadelphia Convention of 1787.* 4 vols. Ph.D. diss.: University of Texas.

Williams, Frances Leigh. 1978. *A Founding Family: The Pinckneys of South Carolina.* New York: Harcourt Brace Jovanovich.

Wills, Garry. 1987. "Interview with a Founding Father." *American Heritage* 38 (May/June): 83–88.

——. 1978. *Inventing America: Jefferson's Declaration of Independence.* Garden City, NY: Doubleday.

——. 2003. *"Negro President": Jefferson and the Slave Power.* Boston: Houghton Mifflin.

Wilmarth, Arthur E., Jr. 2003. "Symposium: Judicial Review before John Marshall: Elusive Foundation: John Marshall, James Wilson, and the Problem of Reconciling Popular Sovereignty and Natural Law Jurisprudence in the New Federal Republic." *George Washington Law Review* 72 (December): 113–193.

Wilson, Bradford P., and Peter W. Schramm. 1994. *Separation of Powers and Good Government.* Lanham, MD: Rowman and Littlefield Publishers.

Wilson, Rick K., and Calvin Jillson. 1989. "Leadership Patterns in the Continental Congress: 1774–1789." *Legislative Studies Quarterly* 14 (February): 5–37.

Wiltse, Charles M. 1961. *The New Nation, 1800–1845.* New York: Hill and Wang.

Wirls, Daniel, and Stephen Wirls. 2004. *The Invention of the United States Senate.* Baltimore, MD: Johns Hopkins University Press.

Wolf, Edwin, II. 1975. *Philadelphia: Portrait of an American City.* Philadelphia, PA: Wenchell.

Wolfe, Christopher. 1977. "On Understanding the Constitutional Convention of 1787." *Journal of Politics* 19 (February): 97–118.

Wolin, Sheldon S. 1989. *The Presence of the Past: Essays on the State and the Constitution.* Baltimore, MD: Johns Hopkins University Press.

Wood, Gordon S. 2004. *The Americanization of Benjamin Franklin.* New York: Penguin Books.

——. 1982. "Conspiracy and the Paranoid Style: Causality and Deceit in the Eighteenth Century." *William and Mary Quarterly,* 3rd ser. 39 (July): 401–441.

——. 1969. *The Creation of the American Republic, 1776–1787.* Chapel Hill: University of North Carolina Press.

——. 1987. *The Making of the Constitution.* Waco, TX: Markham Press Fund.

——. 1991. *The Radicalism of the American Revolution.* New York: Alfred A. Knopf.

Wooton, David, ed. 2003. *The Essential Federalist and Anti-Federalist Papers.* Indianapolis, IN: Hackett Publishing.

Wormuth, Francis D. 1950. "On Bills of Attainder: A Non-Communist Manifesto." *Western Political Quarterly* 3 (March): 52–65.

Wright, Benjamin Fletcher. 1962. *American Interpretations of Natural Law: A Study in the History of Political Thought.* New York: Russell and Russell.

——. 1958. "Consensus and Continuity–1776–1787." *Boston University Law Review* 53 (Winter): 1–52.

Wright, Esmond. 1961. *Fabric of Freedom, 1763–1800.* New York: Hill and Wang.

Wright, Robert K., Jr., and Morris J. MacGregor, Jr. 1987. *Soldier Statesmen of the Constitution.* Washington, DC: Center for Military History, United States Army.

Wunder, John R. 2000/2001. "'Merciless Indian Savages' and the Declaration of Independence: Native Americans Translate the Ecunnaunuxulgee Document." *American Indian Law Review* 25: 65–92.

——. 1994. *"Retained by the People": A History of American Indians and the Bill of Rights.* New York: Oxford University Press.

York, Neil L., ed. 1988. *Toward a More Perfect Union: Six Essays on the Constitution.* Provo, UT: Brigham Young University.

Zagarri, Rosemarie. 1987. *The Politics of Size: Representation in the United States, 1776–1850.* Ithaca, NY: Cornell University Press.

——. 1998. "The Rights of Man and Woman in Post-Revolutionary America." *William and Mary Quarterly,* 3rd ser. 55 (April): 203–230.

Zahniser, Marvin R. 1967. *Charles Cotesworth Pinckney: Founding Father.* Chapel Hill: University of North Carolina Press.

Zebrowski, Martha K. 1994. "Richard Price: British Platonist of the Eighteenth Century." *Journal of the History of Ideas* 55 (January): 17–35.

Zornow, William Frank. 1954. "The Sandy Hook Lighthouse Incident of 1787." *Journal of Economic History* 14 (Summer): 261–266.

Zvesper, John. 1984. "The Madisonian Systems." *Western Political Quarterly* 37 (June): 236–256.

Selected List of Cases

Barron v. Baltimore, 7 Pet. (32 U.S.) 243 (1833).

Calder v. Bull, 3 Dall. (3 U.S.) 386 (1798).

Cherokee Nation v. Georgia, 30 U.S. (5 Pet.) 1 (1831).

Chisholm v. Georgia, 2 Dall. (2 U.S.) 419 (1793).

Cohens v. Virginia, 6 Wheat. (19 U.S.) 264 (1821).

Dartmouth College v. Woodward, 4 Wheat. (17 U.S.) 518 (1819).

Fletcher v. Peck, 6 Cranch (10 U.S.) 87 (1810).

Gibbons v. Ogden, 9 Wheat. (22 U.S.) 1 (1824).

Home Building and Loan Association v. Blaisdell, 290 U.S. 398 (1934).

Luther v. Borden, 48 U.S. (7 How.) 1 (1849).

Marbury v. Madison, 1 Cranch (5 U.S.) 137 (1803).

McCulloch v. Maryland, 17 U.S. 316 (1819).

Ogden v. Saunders, 12 Wheat. (25 U.S.) 213 (1827).

Owings v. Speed, 18 U.S. (5 Wheat.) 420 (1820).

Pennsylvania v. Nelson, 350 U.S. 497 (1956).

Pollock v. Farmers' Loan & Trust Co., 158 U.S. 601 (1895).

Powell v. McCormack, 395 U.S. 486 (1969).

Reynolds v. Sims, 377 U.S. 533 (1964).

Scott v. Sandford, 19 How. (60 U.S.) 393 (1857).

Texas v. White, 1 Wall. (74 U.S.) 700 (1868).

United States v. Butler, 197 U.S. 65 (1936).

United States v. Lopez, 514 U.S. 549 (1995).

United States v. Morrison, 529 U.S. 598 (2000).

U.S. Term Limits v. Thornton, 514 U.S. 779 (1995).

Selected Bibliography for Schoolteachers and Students

Elementary School

Bradbury, Pamela. 1987. *Men of the Constitution.* New York: Simon and Schuster.

Levy, Elizabeth. 1992. . . . *If You Were There When They Signed the Constitution.* New York: Scholastic.

Maestro, Betsy, and Giulio Maestro. 1990. *A More Perfect Union: The Story of Our Constitution.* New York: Mulberry.

Morris, Richard B. *The Constitution.* 1985. Minneapolis: Lerner Publications.

Prolman, Marilyn. 1969. *The Story of the Constitution.* Chicago: Children's Press.

Spier, Peter. 1987. *We the People: The Constitution of the United States.* Garden City, NY: Doubleday.

We the People: The Citizen & the Constitution. Calabasas, CA: Center for Civic Education.

Junior High and High School

Anderson, Joan. 1987. *1787.* San Diego: Harcourt Brace Jovanovich. (This is a novel.)

Commanger, Henry Steele. 1961. *The Great Constitution: A Book for Young Americans.* Indianapolis, IN: Bobbs-Merrill.

Fisher, Dorothy Canfield. 1950. *Our Independence and the Constitution.* New York: Random House.

Fritz, Jean. 1989. *The Great Little Madison.* New York: Scholastic Inc.

——. 1987. *Shh! We're Writing the Constitution.* New York: Scholastic.

Hagedorn, Hermann. 1927. *The Ten Dreams of Zach Peters and How They Led Him through the Constitution of the United States.* Chicago: The John C. Winston Company.

Hakim, Joy. 2003. *From Colonies to Country.* Book 3 of *A History of US.* New York: Oxford University Press.

Hauptly, Denis J. 1987. *"A Convention of Delegates": The Creation of the Constitution.* New York: Atheneum.

Hayman, LeRoy. 1966. *What You Should Know about the U.S. Constitution and the Men Who Wrote It.* New York: Four Winds Press.

Hudson, David L., Jr. 2002. *The Bill of Rights: The First Ten Amendments of the Constitution.* Berkeley Heights, NJ: Enslow Publishers.

Lomask, Milton. 1980. *The Spirit of 1787: The Making of Our Constitution.* New York: Farrar, Straus and Giroux.

McDonald, Forrest. 1970. *Enough Wise Men: The Story of Our Constitution.* New York: G. P. Putnam.

McPhillips, Martin. 1985. *The Constitution Convention.* Part of *Turning Points in American History.* Morristown, NJ: Silver Burdett Company.

Novick, Minna S. 1986. *Helping Children Understand the United States Constitution.* Chicago: American Bar Association.

Peterson, Helen Stone. 1974. *The Making of the United States Constitution.* Champaign, IL: Garrand Publishing.

Quigley, Charles N., and Charles F. Bahmueller, eds. 1991. *Civitas: A Framework for Civic Education.* National Council for the Social Studies Bulletin no. 86. Calabasas, CA: Center for Civil Education.

Rothschild, Eric, and Werner Feig. 1970. *1787: A Simulation Game.* Pleasantville, NJ: Olcott Forund Division of Educational Audio Visual.

Vaughn, Harold C. 1976. *The Constitutional Convention,*

1787: The Beginning of Federal Government in America. New York: Franklin Watts.

Vile, John R. 1998. *The United States Constitution: Questions and Answers.* Westport, CT: Greenwood Press.

Weidner, Daniel. 2002. *Creating the Constitution: The People and Events That Formed the Nation.* Berkeley Heights, NJ: Enslow Publishers.

We the People: Student Text. 1988. Calabasas, CA: Center for Civil Education. (Junior high)

We the People: The Citizen and the Constitution. 1995. Calabasus, CA: Center for Civic Education. (High school)

"We the People: The Citizen and the Constitution." http://www.civiced.org/wethepeople.php. (Site contains information about a variety of programs sponsored by the Center for Civic Education.)

Wilkie, Katharine E., and Elizabeth R. Moseley. 1963. *Father of the Constitution: James Madison.* New York: Julian Messner.

Williams, Selma R. 1970. *Fifty-five Fathers: The Story of the Constitutional Convention.* New York: Dodd, Mead.

Websites on the Constitutional Convention

Information is increasingly available online for research on the U.S. Constitutional Convention and the U.S. Constitution and for use in classrooms. One of the most helpful is the website of the National Constitution Center in Philadelphia listed under http://www.constitutioncenter.com. In addition to information about the center, this site posts articles on contemporary constitutional issues.

The Avalon Project at Yale Law School is a good source for documents from the Founding era. See "The American Constitution: A Documentary Record" at http://www.yale.edu/lawweb/avalon/constpap.htm.

The National Archives contains a number of documents related to the Founding Fathers as well as biographies of each of the Convention delegates. This site is at http://www.archives.gov/national_archives_experience/constitution/founding_fathers.htm.

The National Archives and Records Administration has also compiled "100 Milestone Documents" from throughout U.S. history. They may be accessed at http://www.ourdocuments.gov/content.php?flash=true&page=milestone. Accessed July 3, 2004.

The Ashbrook Center for Public Affairs at Ashland University has a great website at http://www.teachingamericanhistory.org. It includes a map of eighteenth-century Philadelphia with information about principal places in the city as well as a chart on the age of the Founders in 1787.

On a somewhat lighter note, law professor Doug Linder has prepared a website, "Who Wants to Marry a Founding Father?" in which readers can pair themselves with a Founding Father as a mate. This is found at http://www.law.umkc.edu/faculty/projects/ftrials/conlaw/marry.htm.

The Center for Civil Education, which sponsors mock congressional hearings during which high school students can demonstrate their knowledge of the Constitution, has a very helpful website with links to many other sites with information about U.S. government and the U.S. Constitution. This site is found at: http://www.civiced.org.

FOR FURTHER READING

Newmark, Mark S. 1997. "Navigating the Internet for Sources in American History." *History Teacher* 30 (May): 283–292.

O'Malley, Michael, and Roy Rosenzweig. 1997. "Brave New World or Blind Alley? American History on the World Wide Web." *Journal of American History* 84 (June): 132–155.

Schick, James B. M. 2002. "Designing Interactive Courseware: Creating an Electronic Edition of the Notes of Debates in the Philadelphia Convention of 1787." *History Computer Review* 18 (Fall): 49.

Index

Abolitionism, 5, 10

Achaean League, **1**

Ackerman, Bruce, 96, 183–184, 413, 508

Adair, Douglas, 261, 357, 507

Adams, Abigail, 217 (sidebar), 850 (sidebar)

Adams, John, **1–4**
 Achaean League, 1
 Bassett, Richard, 48
 correspondence with Abigail, 217 (sidebar)
 death of, 98
 Declaration of Independence, 208
 failure to attend, 223
 Gerry's role in the XYZ Affair, 322
 Hamilton and, 347
 impact of three-fifths clause on election, 788
 Jefferson and, 376
 lodging of the delegates, 424–425
 Marshall nomination, 443
 Pilgrim roots, 287 (sidebar)
 presidential title, 615
 progress, 627
 reason and experience, 662–663
 Society of the Cincinnati, 730
 Treaty of Paris, 550
 virtue, 821
 on Washington, 811 (sidebar)

Washington and, 831
 women's rights, 850 (sidebar)

Adams, John Quincy
 Adams, John, 3
 Committee of Style and Arrangement, 109
 50-year anniversary of the Constitution, 98
 Jackson's notes on the Convention, 372
 journal of the proceedings, 665–666
 letter of transmittal, 414
 Monroe Doctrine, 494
 three-fifths clause, 788

Adams, Samuel, 21, 465, 657

Adams, Willi Paul, 807

Addison, Joseph, 90–91

Adoption of the Constitution (portrait), 99

"Advice to my Country" (Madison), 437–438

African Americans, **4–11**
 census provision, 83
 citizenship, 86
 indentured servants, 362–363
 naturalization and citizenship, 520
 See also Slave importation; Slavery; Three-fifths clause

Age as qualification
 Mason's views on elected officials's qualifications, 454

opponents to single executive, 604
 qualifications for members of Congress, 135, 162
 suffrage, 769

Agenda setting, 820 (sidebar)

Ages of delegates, **11**, 204, 216–217, 566–567

Agriculture versus mercantilism, 306

Albany Plan of Union, **11–12**, 290, 301, 790, 800, 856–857

Alexander, John, 621

Alien and Sedition Acts, 3, 376, 436, 444

Amar, Akhil Reed, 413, 508

Ambassadorial appointments, 506

Ambulatory capital, 235 (sidebar)

Amending process, **12–18**
 abolition of slavery, 10
 Articles of Confederation, 36, 251
 authorship of the Constitution, 41
 Brearly's vote on, 67
 bypassing for ratification, 649, 654
 confederal government, 125
 constitutional moments, 183–184
 Gerry's support of, 320–321
 Hamilton's views on, 346
 Madison's proposal, 435

Amending process (*continued*)
    Mason's support of, 459–460
    mechanism for, 182
    modern use of convention,
        684–685
    Morris's preference for
        congressional call, 504
    Pinckney, Charles, 573
    promoting stability, 743
    Randolph's stance on, 647
    ratification and, 654
    supermajorities, 771
    titles of nobility, 789
    U.S. Constitution, 804
    See also Bill of Rights
Amendments XI–XXVII to the
    Constitution, 908–912. *See
    also specific amendments*
American Civil War, 10, 39, 727,
    758, 805, 806
American Historical Review, 565
American Revolution. *See*
    Revolutionary War
Amphictyonic League, 1, **18–19,**
    91
Andros, Edmund, 237
Anecdotes
    Gerry's metaphor of standing
        armies, 320
    rising sun, 681
    Washington, George, 830
    See also Humor
Annapolis Convention, **19–21**
    Bassett, Richard, 48
    Broom's appointment, 67
    calendar, 77
    call for Constitutional
        Convention, 13
    Clark, Abraham, 529 (sidebar)
    congressional consent for the
        Constitutional Convention,
        16
    Delaware's representation, 212
    Madison, James, 428
    motives for holding, xli–xlii
    Mount Vernon Conference
        leading to, 511
    New Jersey Plan, 530
    Resolution from Annapolis
        Convention: September 14,
        1786, 878–880
    signing chart, 922

state appointment of delegates
    to the Convention, 743
Virginia Plan and, 816
Washington, George, 827
Antifederalists, **21–23**
    allocation of power, 590
    Bill of Rights debates, 60, 61
    concerns over injustice, 395
    Congress, terms, 174
    court and country parties, 198
    critical period, 199–200
    forms of government, 281
    House, size of, 144
    implied powers, 591–592
    Jefferson, Thomas, 376
    motives of the Founding
        Fathers, 506
    natural rights, 519
    newspaper coverage of, 622
    North Carolina's ratifying
        convention, 535–536
    ratification debates, 656,
        813–814
    South Carolina's ratification,
        734–735
    sovereignty issues, 736
    trial by jury, 394
    unitary government and,
        799–800
    uses of liberty, 418–419
    Yates, Robert, 854
Anti-Mason Party, 463
Appointments and confirmations,
    23–26, 69
    Committee on Postponed
        Matters, 114
    Dickinson's support of
        congressional appointments,
        228
    executive appointment of the
        judiciary under New Jersey
        Plan, 555
    Gorham's support of
        presidential selection of the
        judiciary with senate consent,
        327–328
    judicial appointments, 646–647,
        689
    Martin's favoring senatorial
        power, 448
    McClurg, James, 471
    militia officers, 483

Morris's views on presidential
    appointment, 502–503
Pinckney's support of legislative
    appointments to the judiciary,
    572–573
Privy Council versus
    presidential appointment and
    senatorial confirmation, 600
senatorial vacancies, 644
Sherman's supporting limits on
    presidential appointments,
    716
state governors, 330, 331
Williamson on congressional
    vacancies, 838
Apportionment of representation
    King's views on states'
        contributions, 399
    Pinckney, Charles Cotesworth,
        578
    Pinckney Plan, 569
    Rutledge on, 686
    See also Congress, House of
        Representatives,
        representation in; Congress,
        representation in; Congress,
        Senate, representation in
Appropriations, 159–160
Architecture of the Pennsylvania
    State House, 560
Aristocracy, **27–29**
    appointment of public officials,
        95
    Congress, terms, 174
    delegates' debates over,
        283–284
    Mason's concerns over the
        Electoral College, 457–458
    Mercer's fear of, 476–477
    Morris's desire for an
        aristocratic Senate, 497
    Pinckney's concerns over wealth
        of legislators, 570
    presidential selection, 611–613
    Senate as, 687
Aristotle, 93, 517
Armies, standing, **29–30**
    Antifederalists' concerns over,
        22
    Bedford's stance on, 52
    congressional governance of the
        military, 479–480

Dayton's opposition to limiting, 205

Gerry's objection to, 320

Langdon's support of, 409

Mason's fear of, 456

Pinckney's opposition to limiting, 571

Randolph's opposition to, 645

Whig ideology, 833–834

Armies and navies, raising and supporting, **30–33**

Article IV. *See* Guarantee clause

Articles of Confederation, **33–37**

Achaean League, 1

admission and creation of new states, 750

Albany Plan of Union, 11–12

ambulatory capital, 235 (sidebar)

amending process, 13–14

Antifederalist view of, 21–22

armies and navies, raising and supporting, 30–31

artistic depictions of the Convention, 38

borrowing power, 64

bureaucracy, 69–70

Canada provisions, 78

collective powers of Congress, 126–128

commerce power, 101, 102, 103

Committee of Detail, 106

confederal government, 124–125

Congress, selection of, 142

Constitutional Convention mechanism, 182–183

critical period, 199–200

debts, 207

Declaration of Independence leading to, 208–210

defects of, 809–810

Delaware's status, 212

delegates' criticism of democracy, 223–224

Dickinson Plan, 230–231, 233

Dickinson's draft of, 226

failure to recognize Vermont, 807

foreign affairs, 279–280

formation of Society of Cincinnatti, 178

general welfare provision, 302

influence of geography on ratification, 303–304

interstate taxation, 779

judicial organization and protections, 386

Kentucky's statehood, 397

land disputes, 407

legality of the Constitution, 413

Madison's dissatisfaction with, 427–428

Maryland, 450–451

Massachusetts, 464–465

Mississippi River navigation, 484–485

New England colonies, 524, 800

New Jersey, 527–528

New Jersey Plan, 530, 554

Northwest Ordinance, 536–538

outline and goals of, xl–xli

plans of government introduced at the Convention, 582

posterity and perpetuity, 587–588

power, 589

presidents, number of, 603

residency requirements for congressional members, 138 (sidebar)

Rhode Island's refusal to accept import duties, 676

Senate representation, 164–167

Sherman, Roger, 717

signing chart, 921–922

similarities to Holland's government, 352

social contract, 728

speech introducing the Virginia Plan, 642–643

state constitutions, 186

state legislatures, 756

state representation issues, 180–181

text of, 874–878

three-fifths clause, 784–785

U.S. Constitution and, 802

Virginia Plan remedies, 819–820

Virginia under, 812

voting at the Convention, 823

war powers of Congress, 825

Artifacts

Liberty Bell, 419–420

rising sun chair, 296–297, 463, 561, 681–682

Syng inkstand, 778

U.S.S. *Constitution,* 479 (sidebar)

Artistic depictions of the U.S. Constitutional Convention, **37–38**

Athens, ancient, 74

Attainder, bills of, **39**, 255, 473, 688

Attendance, **39–41**

collective profile of delegates, 218

delegates who did not attend, 223

Dickinson, John, 226

Ellsworth, Oliver, 243

Fitzsimons, Thomas, 278

Franklin, Benjamin, 291

Gilman, Nicholas, 322

Hamilton, Alexander, 340

Houston, William, 353

Ingersoll, Jared, 366

Jenifer, Daniel, of St. Thomas, 378

King, Rufus, 398

Langdon, John, 408

Lansing's brief stay, 410

Livingston, William, 422

Martin, Alexander, 444

Martin, Luther, 445

McClurg, James, 469

McHenry, James, 471

Mercer, John, 475

Mifflin, Thomas, 478

New York delegates, 532–533

Randolph, Edmund, 645

Yates, Robert, 853

See also Delegates who did not attend the Constitutional Convention

Attorneys general

Martin, Luther, 445

Randolph, Edmund, 649

Attucks, Crispus, 5 (figure)

Authorship of the Constitution, **41**, 107 (sidebar), 108–109, 704

Authorship of the Declaration of Independence, 208–209

Bailyn, Bernard, 507, 762
Balance of power, 700
Baldwin, Abraham, **43–45**
    attendance, 40
    bankruptcy, 47
    committees served on, 113, 115,
        119
    Congress, qualifications for,
        137
    congressional representation,
        104
    education of, 240
    emoluments clause, 151
    new states provision, 755
    number of speeches, 740
    Pierce's character sketch, 542
    on Rhode Island, 679
    on slavery, 10
Baltimore, Lord, 450
Bancroft, Charles, 762
Bancroft, George, 507
Banking, **45–46**
    corporations provision, 192
    Hamilton as Treasury secretary,
        346
    Morris, Robert, 505–506
    Wilson on, 842
Bankruptcies, **47**
    Committee on Interstate
        Comity and Bankruptcy, 112
    Gorham, Nathaniel, 329
    Morris, Robert, 506
    Pinckney, Charles, 571
    Wilson, James, 848
Bankruptcy Act of 1800, 185
    (sidebar)
Banks, Margaret, 334
Banning, Lance, 507
Barron v. Baltimore, 61, 760
Bassett, Richard, **47–48**
    attendance, 40
    lodging of the delegates, 424
    number of speeches, 741
    Pierce's character sketch, 542
    religious affiliation, 668
    religious references during the
        Constitutional Convention,
        56
Baum, Marsha, 747
Bayard, James, 48
Beard, Charles, **48–50**, 86, 167,
    199, 389, 507, 762

Beckley, John, **50–51**
Bedford, Gunning Jr., **50–54**
    appointments and
        confirmations, 25
    armies and navies, raising and
        supporting, 32
    attendance, 40
    classical allusions and
        influences, 91
    congressional origination of
        money bills, 155
    congressional representation,
        104
    Georgia's potential, 309
    Great Compromise, xlix
    impeachment clause, 359
    judicial review, 389–390
    King's concern over foreign
        powers speech, 403
    Masons, 463
    negative on state laws,
        521–522
    number of speeches, 740
    oratory style, 544
    Pierce's character sketch, 542
    presidential term length and
        re-eligibility, 359, 614
    presidential veto, 618
    public opinion, 635
    response to Virginia Plan,
        643–644
    Senate representation, 167
Belgium Confederacy. *See* Holland
Beltway syndrome, 577
Benson, Egbert, 532
Berkin, Carol, 222
Biblical and religious references at
    the Constitutional
    Convention, **54–58**
    Declaration of Independence,
        210
    emoluments clause, 149
    Franklin's proposal of daily
        prayer, 294–295
Biblical references on documents
    and objects
    on liberty, 417
    Liberty Bell, 419–420
    Massachusetts Body of Libertie,
        466–467
Bicameralism. *See* Congress,
    bicameralism

Bicentennial celebration
    assessment of the delegates,
        221–222
    bicentennial of the Declaration
        of Independence and, 100
    Magna Carta, 440
    Philadelphia, 564
    visitors signing the
        Constitution, 722
Bicentennial Covers, 99
Bill of Rights, **58–62**
    Antifederalists' concerns over,
        22
    Baldwin, Abraham, 45
    Butler, Pierce, 76
    citizenship of blacks, 86
    Committee of Detail, 108
    ex post facto laws
        foreshadowing, 255
    Federalists, 275
    freedom of the press, 58, 122
    habeas corpus, 339
    Jefferson's advocacy of, 376
    justice, 395
    limits of written documents,
        186–187
    Madison's support for, 436
    Martin, Luther, 449
    Mason's support for, 460–461
    Massachusetts Body of Liberties,
        466–467
    North Carolina's ratification,
        536
    portrayal in *The Federalist,* 273
    property rights, 628–629
    ratification, 182
    text, 907–908
    U.S. Constitution and, 805
    Washington's support of, 831
Billias, George Athan, 210
Bills of attainder. *See* Attainder,
    bills of
Bills of credit, 73
Bills of rights. *See* Bill of Rights;
    State constitutions
Blacks. *See* African Americans
Blackstone, William, 121, 190,
    230, 255
Blair, John, Jr., **62–63**
    attendance, 40
    education of, 240
    Masons, 463

number of speeches, 741
Pierce's character sketch, 542
Bloom, Sol, 38, 99, 220
Blount, William, **63–64**
  attendance, 40
  impeachment of, 362
  negative on state laws, 522
  number of speeches, 740
  Pierce's character sketch, 542
  posterity and perpetuity, 587
  signing of the Constitution, 720
  Tennessee statehood, 783
Bork, Robert, 26
Borrowing power, **64–65**
Boston Massacre, 2, 5 (figure)
Boston Tea Party, 834
Bowdoin, James, 464, 706
Bowen, Catherine Drinker, 56
Bradford, M.E., 668
Bradford, William, 468
Brearly, David, **65–67**
  amending process, 15
  appointments and
    confirmations, 25
  armies and navies, raising and
    supporting, 32
  attendance, 39
  committees served on, 113, 117,
    118
  House, representation in, 140
  Masons, 463
  Pierce's character sketch, 542
  Senate representation, 165
British influences on Constitution.
    See Great Britain
Broom, Jacob, **67–68**
  artistic depictions of, 37
  attendance, 40
  Congress, compensation of
    members, 132
  Congress, terms, 174
  Masons, 463
  number of speeches, 740
  Pierce's character sketch, 542
  presidential selection, 608
  religious affiliation, 668
  on Rhode Island, 679
  treason provision, 791
Brown, Brockden, 655 (sidebar)
Brown, Robert, 49–50
Brown, William Hill, 655 (sidebar)
Brutus, 271 (sidebar), 854

Bryce, James, 507
Bullock, Steven C., 210
Bureaucracy, **69–70**
Burger, Warren, 100, 748
Burke, Edmund, 624, 664
Burke, Thomas, 33–34, 34
Burns, James MacGregor, 418
Burr, Aaron, 206, 347, 448, 450,
    551, 746 (sidebar), 808
Bush, George W., 26
Butler, Pierce, **70–76**
  admiration for British system of
    government, 332
  age of, 11
  attendance, 40
  borrowing power, 65
  citizenship for senators, 163
  classical allusions and
    influences, 91
  committees served on, 111, 113
  Congress, compensation of
    members, 130, 132
  Congress, qualifications for,
    137
  congressional commerce power,
    102
  congressional origination of
    money bills, 154, 155
  congressional power to organize
    and govern militia, 482
  debts, 207
  emendation of the rules, 684
  emoluments clause, 149, 150
  extradition provision, 259
  fugitive slave clause, 299
  Holland and, 351
  judicial organization, 386–387
  location of nation's capital, 235
  new states provision, 754
  number of speeches, 740
  Pierce's character sketch, 542
  plural executive as alternative to
    sectionalism, 697
  posterity and perpetuity, 587
  president as Commander in
    Chief, 596–597
  presidential veto, 618
  property rights, 627
  qualifications of voters for
    Congress, 139
  ratification provision, 652
  references to Montesquieu, 495

three-fifths clause, 786
treaty-making and ratification,
    795
Virginia Plan, 817
war powers of Congress, 826
Butler, Weedon, 75–76

Cabinet. *See* President, council
Caesar, Julius, 91
Calder v. Bull, 255
Calendar, **77**
Calhoun, John C., 437, 699
Calvert, Cecilius, 450
Calvert, Sir George, Lord
    Baltimore, 450
Calvin, John, 630–631. *See also*
    Protestantism
Canada, **77–79**, 303, 753
Canals, 192–193, 293, 711–712
Capital, location of
  ambulatory capital, 235
    (sidebar)
  Carroll's role in, 81, 82
  criteria for location, 305
  District of Columbia, 234–235
  Gorham's views, 327
  Langdon's views on, 408
  Madison's views on, 432
  Mason, George, 456
  Morris's concerns over siting in
    state capital, 503–504
  Philadelphia, 95, 564
  Pinckney's opinion on, 571
  transfer of U.S. Constitution
    document, 514
  Washington's role in, 831
  Williamson on, 840
Capital punishment, 467
Capitalism, 631
Carroll, Daniel, **79–82**
  attendance, 40
  commerce power, 102
  committees served on, 111, 113,
    117, 119
  Congress, compensation of
    members, 132
  Congress, qualifications for,
    135–136, 137
  education of, 242
  ex post facto laws, 254
  expulsion of congressional
    members, 134

Carroll, Daniel (*continued*)
  guarantee clause, 336
  House, size of, 144
  judicial review, 392
  letter of transmittal, 415
  location and permanence of
    nation's capital, 236
  Masons, 463
  new states provision, 754–755
  number of speeches, 740
  presidential selection, 611
  quorums, 161
  ratification provision, 652
  religious affiliation, 630, 668
Carson, Hampton, 98
Catholic Church, 57, 79, 277
Cato: A Tragedy (Addison), 90–91
Cato's Letters (Trenchard and
  Gordon), 672
Celebrations of the Constitutional
  Convention. *See*
  Commemorations of the
  Constitutional Convention
Census, **82–83**
  House, size of, 144–145
  new states provision, 751
  population of the United States,
    586
  protecting new states'
    independence, 306
Centralization of power in a
  confederal government,
  124–125
Charlemagne, 311
Charter of Privileges, 419
Charters, 178, 184–186, 186
Chase, Salmon, 588
Chase, Samuel, 450, 452, 510
Checks and balances, 69, **83–84,**
  700
Chief justice of the United States,
  84–85, 776
  Ellsworth, Oliver, 250
  Jay, John, 374
  Marshall, John, 269, 443
Children of delegates, 216–217,
  217 (sidebar)
Chisholm v. Georgia, 374, 383
  (sidebar), 649, 848
Christianity. *See* Protestantism
Christy, Howard Chandler, 38
Cicero, 93, 517

Cincinnati. *See* Society of the
  Cincinnati
Cincinnatus, 828 (sidebar)
"Circular Letter addressed to the
  Governors" (Washington),
  662
Citizen virtue, 672–673, 820–822
Citizenship, **85–86**
  Congress, qualifications for,
    136–137, 163–164, 836–837
  Congress, selection of, 374
  Morris's views on qualifications
    of electors and voters, 500
  naturalization, 520
  potential for European
    president, 490 (sidebar)
  Price, Richard, 623
  Randolph's stance on Senate
    qualifications, 644
  three-fifths clause, 786
  Whig ideology, 833–834
City Tavern, 424–425
Civil liberties, 3
Civil rights movement, 518
Civil War. *See* American Civil War
Clark, Abraham, 529 (sidebar)
Classes, **86–90**
Classical allusions and influences,
  90–93
  fame, 262
  founding, 287
  Hamilton Plan principles, 348
  judicial organization, 386–387
  natural rights, 517
  pen names, 271 (sidebar)
  Polybius, 585
Classical liberalism, 197–198, 630,
  670
Clay, Henry, 834
Claypoole, David C., 238
Clerks, 50, 704
Cleveland, Grover, 98
Clinton, Bill, 362
Clinton, DeWitt, 368
Clinton, George, 532, 534
Clymer, George, **93–95**
  attendance, 39
  committees served on, 115
  congressional commerce power,
    101
  number of speeches, 740
  presidential selection, 612

ratification process, 653
signing Declaration of
  Independence and the
  Constitution, 209
taxes on imports and exports,
  258, 781
Coalitions, **95–96**
Cohens v. Virginia, 443
Coke, Edward, 121
Cold War, 39
College of New Jersey, 239
Colleges and universities. *See*
  Education of convention
  delegates
Collins, John, 680
Colonial precedents, **97**
Columbia University, 240–241
Commemorations of the
  Constitutional Convention,
  38, **98–100**, 511–512
Commentaries on the Law of England
  (Blackstone), 255
Commerce power, **100–104**
  Committee on Commercial
    Discrimination, 111–112
  favoring ports, 447
  Pinckney's opinion on, 571
  Pinckney's opposition to federal
    control, 579
  Rhode Island's willingness to
    follow, 678
  taxes on imports and exports,
    779–782
  two-thirds majority requirement,
    94
  Williamson on, 837
Committee of Compromise on
  Representation in Congress
  (July 2), **104–105**, 118
  Baldwin's appointment, 44
  Bedford, Gunning Jr., 53
  committee diagram, 920
  congressional origination of
    money bills, 155
  Davie, William Richardson,
    202–203
  Franklin's contribution to, 292
  Gerry's role in founding and
    chairing, 313–314
  House, size of, 144
  Martin, Luther, 447
  Mason, George, 455

other committees and, 118
slave importation, 724–725
vice presidency, 808
Committee of Detail, **105–108**
armies and navies, raising and
supporting, 31–32
Bill of Rights discussion, 58
borrowing power, 64
chief justice provision, 85
commerce power, 101
committee diagram, 920
Congress, collective powers, 128
Congress, compensation of
members, 131–132
Congress, qualifications for,
136, 687
congressional coining of money,
492
congressional power to call
militia, 481
corporations provision, 192
Council of Revision, 599–600
creation and location of
nation's capital, 235
expulsion of congressional
members, 134
extradition provision, 259
full faith and credit clause, 300
guarantee clause, 336–337
impeachment clause, 361
implied powers, 591
judicial jurisdiction, 384–385
land dispute with Connecticut,
407
leaders of Congress, 147
letter of transmittal, 414
naturalization, 520
new states provision, 753
oaths, 605
other committees and, 118, 119
police powers, 761
post offices and post roads,
586–587
posterity and perpetuity, 588
power, 589
power of the purse, 158
presidential correspondence
with state governors, 330
presidential qualifications, 606
presidential selection, 610–611
presidential title, 615
ratification provision, 652–653

Rutledge's selection as chair, 686
secrecy, 693
Senate qualifications, 162–163
slave importation, 723
state coining of money, 492
suffrage, 767–769
supermajority requirement, 771
supremacy clause, 774
Supreme Court, 776
taxation of imports and exports,
780
time and frequency of
congressional meetings,
175–176
times, places, and manners of
congressional election, 176
treason provision, 790
Treasury secretary, 793
treaty-making and ratification,
795
trial by jury, 393
United States name, 801
vacancies in the House,
146–147
vice presidency, 808
Virginia Plan alterations, 802
war powers of Congress,
825–826
Wilson, James, 847
Committee of Eleven. *See*
Committee of Compromise
on Representation in
Congress
Committee of Style and
Arrangement (September 8),
41, **108–109**, 920
contracts clause, 190
fugitive slave clause, 299
Johnson, William Samuel,
381–382
letter of transmittal, 414
liberty, 417
Preamble to the Constitution,
595
privileges and immunities
clause, 625
Supreme Court, 776
treason provision, 792
United States name, 801
Virginia Plan alterations, 802
"We the People," 832
women's rights, 849

Committee of the Whole (May
30–June 19), **109–111**
age of members of Congress,
162
Congress, compensation of
members, 130
continuance of Congress
provision, 133
Gorham as chair, 324
guarantee clause, 335
other committees and, 118
Paterson, William, 556
ratification provision, 649–650
recall of congressional members,
161
Rutledge's nomination to the
chair, 686
Supreme Court, 775–776
Virginia Plan, 818–819
Washington and, 830
women's rights, 849
Committee on Commercial
Discrimination (August 25),
111–112
committee diagram, 920
Dayton, Jonathan, 205
other committees and, 118
Committee on interstate comity
and bankrupty (August 29),
112, 847, 920
Committee on original
apportionment of Congress
(July 6), **112–113,** 118, 920
Committee on Postponed Matters
(August 31), **113–114**
Brearly, David, 66–67
Butler, Pierce, 74
chief justice provision, 85
committee diagram, 920
congressional power over
location of nation's capital,
236
copyrights and patents, 191
impeachment clause, 361
leaders of Congress, 148
other committees and, 118
power of the purse, 158
presidential qualifications, 606
presidential selection, 502,
611–612
presidential term length and
re-eligibility, 615

Committee on Postponed Matters
(*continued*)
state coalitions, 96
treaty-making and ratification,
795
Committee on rules (May 25),
114
committee diagram, 920
creation of, 683
other committees and, 117
Pinckney, Charles, 567
Wythe, George, 852
Committee on slave trade and
navigation (August 22), **115,**
118, 422, 920
Committee on State Debts and
Militia (August 18), **115–116,**
118, 920
Clymer, George, 94
Committee on Slave Trade and
Navigation, 115–116
congressional militia powers,
153, 483
general welfare clause, 302
Livingston, William, 422
Mason, George, 456
Committee on sumptuary
legislation (September 13),
116, 118–119, 292, 381, 920
Committee on Unfinished Parts.
See Committee on Postponed
Matters
Committee to Reconsider
Representation in the House
(July 9), 67, 104–106,
116–117, 118, 353, 920
Committees at the Constitutional
Convention, **117–119**
daily schedule, 201
diagram of committees, 920
Dickinson, John, 232
Madison's service, 436
*See also individual committee
names*
Common good, 637
Common law, **120–123**
Magna Carta, 440
Massachusetts Body of Liberties,
466–467
women's rights, 850
Common man, Franklin's defense
of, 295

Common Sense (Paine), 208, 549
Commonwealth of Oceana
(Harrington), 2
*The Commonwealth of Virginia v.
Caton et al.,* 62
Commonwealthmen, 197–198
Compacts
Articles of Confederation as,
566
constitutionalism, 184–186
Mayflower Compact, 185,
468–469, 630, 637, 855–866
Compromise, **123–124,** 166–167
Confederal government, 21,
124–125, 281
Germany, 311
Iroquois, 368
New York's proposal, 532
small states' concerns over, 554
See also Articles of
Confederation
Confederate States, 806
Congregationalists, 668
Congress
appointments and
confirmations, 69
Articles of Confederation,
33–34, 35, 36
Articles of the Constitution,
803–804
Bedford's opposition to
boundaries on, 51–52
borrowing power, 64–65
bureaucracy, 69–70
Butler's views on structure and
power, 71–74
collective powers, 126–130
Committee on State Debts and
Militia, 115–116
determination by the
Committee of the Whole,
110
Dickinson Plan, 231, 233
Great Compromise, 43–44
Hamilton Plan principles, 349
implied powers, 591–592
oversight of congressional
elections, 501
Pinckney Plan, 567–568
presidential veto, 617–620
Randolph's stance on, 644–645
ratification process, 653

report of proceedings, February
21, 1787, 880–881
representation by wealth, 71–72
rights under the Articles of
Confederation, 34
separation of powers, 700–704
setting salaries, 67–68, 72
Spaight on, 737
state legislatures, 755–758
Virginia Plan provisions,
817–819
war powers, 825–826
Congress, apportionment of
Committee on Original
Apportionment of Congress,
112–113
Morris, Gouverneur, 497
role of wealth, 628
Congress, bicameralism, 2–3,
125–126
Adams's advocating for
bicameralism, 2–3
Articles of Confederation, 35
determination by the
Committee of the Whole,
110
judicial review balancing,
388–393
Pierce's support of, 566
as protection against injustice,
395
providing stability, 741–742
Sherman on, 714
Virginia Plan, 817–819
Yates, Robert, 853
Congress, collective powers,
126–130
Articles of the Constitution,
803–804
banking provision, 46
bicameralism, 125
Carroll's views, 80
collective powers, 126–130
congressional coining of money,
491–492
Dickinson Plan, 233–234
elections, 400–401
Ellsworth's views, 247
general welfare clause, 302–303
Gorham's vies on, 326–327
Ingersoll's economic powers,
366

Jay's support of increased
powers, 373
limits on, 148
location and permanence of
nation's capital, 236
militia powers, 151–154
Morris's views on, 501
negative on state laws, 521
New Jersey Plan, 531
Pinckney, Charles, 571
piracy, 581–582
piracy punishment, 581–582
post offices and post roads,
586–587
Randolph's stance on, 645
Rutledge, John, 688
Sherman, Roger, 710–712
treason, 790–792
treaty-making and ratification,
794–796
Virginia Plan, 818–819
Williamson on, 839
See also Congress, power of the
purse
Congress, compensation of
members, **130–133**
amendment affecting, 805–806
Carroll, Daniel, 81
Dickinson's opposition to states'
paying, 230
Ellsworth on states' payment,
245
Franklin's concerns over,
292–293
Franklin's proposal of state
expenditure for, 292
Gerry's concerns over, 316
Gorham's opposition to states'
setting, 324
Hamilton's opposition to states'
paying, 341, 345
Langdon's objections to states'
paying, 408
Madison's views on, 431–432
Mason's support of national
treasury paying, 459
Pierce, William, 566
Pinckney's opposition to
senatorial pay, 577–578
Randolph's objections to states'
paying congressional salaries,
645

Sherman, Roger, 714
state legislature providing
congressional salaries, 757
Williamson on congressional
salaries, 836
Congress, Continental. *See*
Continental Congress;
Second Continental Congress
Congress, continuation of under
Articles, **133–134**
Congress, expulsion of members,
80, **134**, 771
Congress, House of
Representatives, 44
attempt to expel Powell, 134
Committee of Detail, 106
Fitzsimons's service in, 278
mixed government, 488
money bills, 661
portrayal in *The Federalist*,
272–273
president, disability of, 601
presidential selection, 611–612
See also Representation
Congress, House of
Representatives, qualifications
of members, **134–139**, 246,
687
citizenship, 85–86
Mason, George, 455
Mercer's criticism of residency
requirements, 475
Pinckney, Charles, 570
residency requirements, 72–73
Sherman, Roger, 713
Wilson on, 842–843
See also Residency
Congress, House of
Representatives, qualifications
of voters for, **139–140**
Congress, House of
Representatives,
representation in, 118,
140–142, 166–167
Carroll, Daniel, 80
census provision, 82–83
Committee to Reconsider
Representation in the House,
116–117
Connecticut Compromise,
180–181
Dickinson, John, 226–227

Georgia's allotment, 309
Johnson's support of
proportional representation,
380–381
Northwest Ordinance provision
of representation, 537
Pinckney Plan, 569–570
representation by wealth, 71–72
Sherman, Roger, 712–713
See also New Jersey Plan
Congress, House of
Representatives, selection of,
142–143
Dickinson Plan, 230–231
Martin, Luther, 447
Mason's support of the popular
vote, 454
Mercer's criticism of direct
election, 475
Pinckney, Charles Cotesworth,
577
popular election, 635–636
selection process, 72
Sherman, Roger, 713
Sherman on, 711
Wilson on, 842–843
Congress, House of
Representatives, size, **143–145**
corruption concerns, 194
Ellsworth's views, 245
Gerry's views on, 316
Hamilton's preference of larger
House, 341
Madison, James, 431
Mason, George, 454
Rutledge's stance, 686–687
Congress, House of
Representatives, terms,
145–146
determination by the
Committee of the Whole, 110
Ellsworth, Oliver, 244
Gerry's support of annual
elections, 314
Hamilton's three-year proposal,
341
Jenifer's preference for three-
year terms, 379
longer terms providing stability,
741–742
Pierce, William, 566
Randolph's stance on, 644

Congress, House of
    Representatives, terms
    (*continued*)
  Rutledge, John, 687
  Sherman, Roger, 713
Congress, House of
    Representatives, vacancies,
    146–147, 330
Congress, leaders designated by
    Constitution, **147–148**
Congress, limits on, **148,** 254–255,
    661, 841–842
Congress, members' ineligibility
    for other offices, **148–151**
  Committee on Postponed
    Matters, 113
  corruption concerns, 194
  Ellsworth's lack of objection to,
    248
  Gerry's objection to, 316
  Gorham's objection to, 324
  Jenifer's views on, 379
  King's arguments, 400
  Pinckney, Charles, 570
  Pinckney, Charles Cotesworth,
    577
  Randolph's stance on, 645–646
  Rutledge, John, 687
  Sherman, Roger, 714
  Spaight on, 737
  Williamson on, 837
Congress, militia power, **151–154,**
    479–480, 480–481, 482–484.
    See also Militia, congressional
    power to call; Militia,
    congressional power to
    organize and govern
Congress, origination of money
    bills, **154–157**
  Butler's views on, 71
  Carroll on, 80
  Committee of Compromise on
    Representation in Congress,
    118
  congressional origination of,
    154–157
  Dickinson's "reason and
    experience" approach, 664
  Dickinson's view on House
    origination, 228
  Gerry's opposition to Senate
    origination, 313

Gorham's views on, 325
King's opposition to House
    origin, 400
Madison's support of
    congressional origination, 432
Mason's support of
    congressional control over,
    456
McHenry's stance on House
    origin, 472
Mercer's concerns over House
    originating, 475
Morris's views on, 498
Pinckney, Charles Cotesworth,
    577
Pinckney Plan, 569
Read's support of limiting to
    House, 661
Rutledge, John, 687
Sherman, Roger, 713–714
Virginia, 812
Williamson, Hugh, 836
Wilson on, 844–845
Congress, power of the purse,
    157–159
  commerce power, 100–103
  Committee on Postponed
    Matters, 113–114
  Mason's views on, 455
  taxes on imports and exports,
    256–259, 779–782
  Treasury secretary, 793–794
Congress, presidential selection
    by, 606–613
Congress, privileges of members,
    159
Congress, publication of
    appropriations, **159–160**
Congress, quorums, **160–161**
Congress, recall, **161–162**
Congress, representation in
  committees addressing, 118
  Franklin's views on, 291–293
  Morris, Gouverneur, 497–498
  Sherman, Roger, 712–713
  Williamson, Hugh, 835–836
  See also Congress, House of
    Representatives,
    representation in; Congress,
    Senate, representation in
Congress, Senate
  Antifederalists' view of, 22

appointments and
    confirmations, 23–26
Committee of Detail, 106
congressional militia powers,
    480–481, 482–484
Gilman's service to, 323
governance of the military,
    479–480
Hamilton Plan, 349
impeachments, 194
longer terms providing stability,
    742
mixed government, 488
Morris on, 497
portrayal in *The Federalist,*
    272–273
president, disability of, 601
presidential selection, 607,
    611–612
publishing proceedings, 688
representation by wealth, 71–72
small states' rights, 43–44
Strong's election to, 764
Congress, Senate, compensation,
    131
  Dickinson's support of higher
    pay for the Senate than the
    House, 230
  Ellsworth, Oliver, 245
  Franklin's objection to salaries,
    293
  Morris's desire for an
    aristocratic Senate, 497
  Rutledge, John, 687
  Sherman, Roger, 714
Congress, Senate, popular
    election, 569
Congress, Senate, qualifications,
    162–164
  citizenship, 85–86
  Dickinson, John, 227–228
  Ellsworth's views on self-
    regulation, 246
  Mason, Goerge, 455
  Pinckney, Charles, 570
  Pinckney Plan, 569
  Randolph's stance on, 644
  Read's opposition to residency
    requirements, 660
  Rutledge, John, 687
  Sherman, Roger, 713
  See also Residency

Congress, Senate, representation in, **164–170**
  Connecticut Compromise, 180–181
  Dickinson, John, 226–227
  Gerry's concerns over powers and representation, 314
  King's opposition to equal state representation, 400
  New Jersey Plan, 531
  Williamson on, 836
  Wilson on, 844
Congress, Senate, selection, **170–172**
  Davie on, 202–203
  Dickinson Plan, 230–231
  Ellsworth's support of legislative selection, 245
  Gerry's insistence on selection by the Senate, 313
  Madison, James, 431
  Pinckney, Charles Cotesworth, 577
  Pinckney Plan, 568–569
  selection by state legislatures, 686
  Sherman, Roger, 713
  Sherman on, 711
  Wilson on, 844
Congress, Senate, size, **172–173,** 326
Congress, Senate, terms, 67, **173–175,** 713, 835
  classes, 88
  determination by the Committee of the Whole, 110
  Gerry's views on, 316
  Gorham's proposal, 326
  Hamilton's push for life terms, 348
  Jenifer's views on, 379
  Pinckney's opposition to long terms, 577
  Randolph's stance on, 644
  Read's good behavior proposal, 661
  Williamson, Hugh, 835, 837
  Wilson on, 844
Congress, Senate, vacancies, 330, 644
Congress, Senate, voting, 246

Congress, time and frequency of meetings, **175–176**
Congress, times, places, and manners of election, **176**
Congress, war powers. *See* War powers of Congress
Congressional call for Constitutional Convention, xliii, **176–178,** 179,
Connecticut, **178–180**
  allocation of House seats, 117
  Committee on Original Apportionment of Congress, 113
  Davie's stance, 202–203
  Ellsworth, Oliver, 242–250
  Johnson, William Samuel, 379–382
  land dispute with Pennsylvania, 407
  ratification of the Constitution, 657
  Sherman, Roger, 709–717
  state appointment of delegates to the Convention, 744
  state constitution, 747
Connecticut Compromise, **180–181**
  Bedford's role in, 53
  bicameralism, 126
  Carroll, Daniel, 79, 80
  coalitions, 96
  Ellsworth, Oliver, 243–244
  Franklin's proposal, 292
  importance of compromise at Convention, 123
  Maryland delegates' support of, 452
  New Jersey's support of, 528
  Senate representation, 164–169, 165
  Senate size, 173
  three-fifths clause, 787
  U.S. Constitution, 804
Connecticut Wits, 678 (sidebar)
U.S.S *Constitution,* 38, 479 (sidebar)
Constitution, document, physical location of. *See* National Archives
Constitution, United States. *See* U.S. Constitution
Constitution Week, 100, 704

Constitutional Convention mechanism, **181–183,** 184
  amending process, 806
  appointments and confirmations, 23–26
  Articles of the Constitution, 803–805
  Committee of the Whole, 109–111
  committees, 117–119
  Constitutional Convention, 181–183
  dispute resolution, 328, 381
  legality of the Convention, 413–414
Constitutional durability, 16–17 (sidebar)
A Constitutional Faith (Levinson), 722
Constitutional moments, 96, **183–184,** 200, 413
Constitutionalism, **184–188,** 210, 468, 557
Constitutions, state. *See* State constitutions
Continental Congress, **188–189**
Contracts
  constitutionalism, 184–186
  King's introduction of the provision, 403
  Morris's opposition to states' interference in, 501
  state interference, 255
  See also Constitutionalism
Contracts clause, **189–191**
Conway Cabal, 478
Copyrights and patents, **191–192,** 627
Corporations, **192–194,** 628, 645
Corruption, **193–194**
  bureaucracy, 70
  concerns over allocation of power, 589–590
  criticism of British system of government, 332–333
  emoluments clause, 149
  Franklin's views on presidential salaries, 293
  presidential selection, 81, 345, 607
  presidential term length and re-eligibility, 614

Corruption (*continued*)
  prohibition from accepting
    other offices as foil for, 72
  Sherman on, 716
  trial by jury as preventive
    measure, 393–394
  Whig ideology, 833–834
Cost of Constitution. *See* Expenses
    of delegates
Council of Advice, 293–294, 792
Council of Revision, **195–197**, 249
  Dickinson's opposition to, 228
  Gorham's objection to, 328
  judicial review, 389, 392
  King's opposition to, 401–402,
    402
  Madison's support of, 434
  Martin's opposition to, 448
  Mason's support of, 457
  Mercer's fear of aristocracy and
    support of executive
    authority, 476–477
  Pinckney's opposition to,
    572–573
  presidential veto, 617
  reason and experience, 663
  Rutledge's opposition to, 689
  separation of powers, 701–702
  stabilizing purpose, 742
  Strong's views, 764
  Virginia Plan provisions, 84–85,
    818
  Williamson's favoring a
    tripartite executive, 838
  Wilson's defense of, 846
Council of State, 108, 196–197,
    294
Counterfeiting, 501
Country party. *See* Court and
    country parties
Court and country parties,
    197–199
  Antifederalists as country party,
    22
  Rhode Island as country party,
    678
  Whig ideology, 833–834
Covenant. *See* Constitutionalism
Criminal laws. *See* Ex post facto
    laws
Critical period, **199–200**

Crosskey, William Winslow, 666
Currency printing. *See* Money,
    congressional coining
Cutler, Manasseh, 424, 538

Daily schedule of the
    Constitutional Convention,
    201
Dane, Nathan, 537–538
Dartmouth College v. Woodward,
    191, 443
Daughters of the American
    Revolution, 100, 704, 722
Davie, William Richardson,
    202–204
  attendance, 40
  Committee on Original
    Apportionment of Congress,
    113
  congressional representation,
    104
  impeachment clause, 360
  number of speeches, 740
  Pierce's character sketch, 542
  presidential term length and
    re-eligibility, 615
  Senate representation, 166
  three-fifths clause, 786
Dayton, Jonathan, **204–206**
  age of, 11
  armies and navies, raising and
    supporting, 32
  attendance, 40
  Committee on Commercial
    Discrimination, 111
  Congress, compensation of
    members, 131
  congressional militia powers,
    153, 483
  House, representation in, 141
  land disputes, 407
  Masons, 463
  number of speeches, 740
  Pierce's character sketch, 542
  prayer at the Convention, 593
  presidential selection, 611
  on Rhode Island, 679
  Senate representation, 167, 168
  slavery stance, 205
  treaty-making and ratification,
    796

Debates
  Madison's preface, 883–889
  mentions of New York, 533
  original intent, 545–547
Debtors' prison
  Morris, Robert, 506
  Shallus, Jacob, 704
Debts, **206–208**
  Committee on State Debts and
    Militia, 115–116
  Congress, qualifications for,
    135–136, 447
  a constitution for prisoners,
    185 (sidebar)
  continuance of Congress
    provision, 133–134
  contracts clause, 190
  Ellsworth's views on state debts,
    247
  Fitzsimon's ruin, 279
  general welfare clause affecting,
    302
  Georgia's refusal to pay war
    debts, 310, 383 (sidebar)
  Gerry's excluding debtors from
    election to office, 315
  Gerry's views on state
    responsibility for, 315
  Gorham's views on
    qualifications for election to
    office, 327
  Langdon's views on holding
    office, 408
  Massachusetts, 464
  Morris's requirements for
    accepting office, 500
  New Jersey, 527–528
  Revolutionary War debts to
    France, 289
  Treaty of Paris, 550
Declaration of Independence,
    208–211
  Articles of Confederation, 33
  bureaucracy, 69
  Constitution and, 405
  equality, 251–252
  Franklin, Benjamin, 290
  independence from monarchy,
    489
  Jefferson, Thomas, 375
  justice, 394

liberty, 417
natural rights, 518
physical dimensions, 514
  (sidebar)
role in film, 462
signing chart, 921
slavery and slave importation, 7,
  10, 726
text of, 859--860
Wilson, James, 841
women's rights, 849
Wythe, George, 851–852
*Defence of the Constitution of
  Government of the United States*
  (Adams), 1, 2–3
Defense and security
  Albany Plan of Union, 12
  Antifederalists' concerns over,
    22
  armies and navies, raising and
    supporting, 30–32
Deists, 629–630
Delaware, **212–213**
  Bassett, Richard, 47–48
  Bedford, Gunning Jr., 51–53
  Broom, Jacob, 67–68
  Committee of Detail, 105–106
  Committee on Original
    Apportionment of Congress,
    113
  congressional origination of
    money bills, 157
  congressional representation,
    104
  Dickinson, John, 225–232
  expenses of delegates, 256
  new states provision, 754
  ratification of the Constitution,
    656
  Read, George, 659–662
  residency requirements of
    representatives, 138 (sidebar)
  state appointment of delegates
    to the Convention, 744
  state constitution, 747
  voting at the Convention, 823
Delegates
  ages of, 11
  attendance, 39–40
  authorship of the Constitution,
    41

Baldwin, Abraham, 43–45
Bassett, Richard, 47–48
Bedford, Gunning Jr., 51–53
Blair, John Jr., 62–63
Blount, William, 63–64
Brearly, David, 65–67
Butler, Pierce, 70–76
Carroll, Daniel, 79–82
classes of citizens and delegates,
  86–90
Clymer, George, 93–95
Davie, William Richardson,
  202–203
Dayton, Jonathan, 204–206
Delaware, 212
Dickinson, John, 225–232
Ellsworth, Oliver, 242–250
Few, William, 276–277
Fitzsimons, Thomas, 277–279
Franklin, Benjamin, 290–297
Gerry. Elbridge, 312–322
Gilman, Nicholas, 322–323
Gorham, Nathaniel, 323–329
Hamilton, Alexander, 340–347
Houston, William, 352–353
Houston, William Churchill,
  353–354
Ingersoll, Jared, 365–368
Jackson, William, 371–372
Jenifer, Daniel, of St. Thomas,
  378–379
Johnson, William Samuel,
  379–382
King, Rufus, 398–405
Langdon, John, 408–410
Lansing, John, 410–412
Livingston, William, 421–422
Martin, Alexander, 443–444
Martin, Luther, 445–450
Maryland, 451
Mason, George, 452–453
Massachusetts, 465
McClurg, James, 469–471
McHenry, James, 471–474
Mercer, John, 474–477
Mifflin, Thomas, 478–479
Morris, Gouverneur, 496–505
Morris, Robert, 505–506
occupations of, 541
Paterson, William, 553–557
Pennsylvania, 557–558

Pierce's character sketches of,
  542–544, 565
Pinckney, Charles, 566–574
Pinckney, Charles Cotesworth,
  575–579
Randolph, Edmund, 641–649
Read, George, 659–662
response to the congressional
  call to the Convention, xliii
Rutledge, John, 685–690
Sherman, Roger, 709–717
size of the Convention, 722–723
slavery, 726–727
Society of the Cincinnati, 732
South Carolina, 734
Spaight, Richard Dobbs, 737–738
stability, 741–743
state appointment to the
  Convention, 743–745
state constitutions, 747–748
Strong, Caleb, 763–764
Washington, George, 827–832
Williamson, Hugh, 834–840
Wilson, James, 840–848
Wythe, George, 851–852
Yates, Robert, 853–854
Delegates, collective assessments,
  213–215
Delegates, collective profile,
  215–219
Delegates, individual rankings,
  219–222
Delegates who did not attend the
  Constitutional Convention,
  xliii, **223**
  Henry, Patrick, 350–351
  Jay, John, 373–374
  Jefferson, Thomas, 375–377
Democracy, 27, **223–225**
  delegates' debates over, 284
  Framer's use of the term,
    281–282
  mixed government, 488
  versus republican government,
    671–672
Democratic Party. *See* Democratic-
  Republican Party; Federalist
  Party
Democratic-Republican Party
  Antifederalists and, 23
  banking controversy, 46

Democratic-Republican Party
  (*continued*)
  court and country parties, 198
  Jefferson's role in establishing,
    376
  Langdon's movement towards,
    410
  Martin's alignment, 444
  republicanism, 673
Deuteronomy, Book of, 54
Diamond, Martin, 507
Dickinson, John, **225–232**
  admiration for British system of
    government, 332
  age of, 11
  aristocracy, 28, 283
  Articles of Confederation, 33,
    34
  assessment of the delegates, 214
  attendance, 40
  Biblical and religious references
    during the Convention, 55
  checks and balances, 84
  classical allusions and
    influences, 91
  committees served on, 113, 115,
    116, 119
  Congress, compensation of
    members, 132
  Congress, qualifications for,
    135, 138 (sidebar)
  Congress, selection of, 143
  congressional militia powers,
    152, 482
  congressional origination of
    money bills, 156
  contracts clause, 190
  Dickinson Plan, 583
  education of, 240
  ex post facto laws, 121, 255
  executive council proposal, 196
  general welfare clause, 302
  guarantee clause, 337
  House terms, 146
  Hume, David, 356
  impeachment clause, 359
  inspection duties for taxes, 75
  judicial independence, 387–388
  judicial organization, 386
  judicial review, 392
  lodging during the Convention,
    424

  monarchy views, 282
  negative on state laws, 521
  new states provision, 754
  number of speeches, 740
  Pierce's character sketch, 542
  piracy punishment, 581
  president, disability of, 601
  presidential selection, 610
  presidential veto, 618, 620
  Privy Council, 600
  qualifications of voters for
    Congress, 139
  ratification provision, 652
  Read's signing the Constitution
    for, 662
  reason and experience, 664
  Senate selection, 170
  Senate size, 172–173
  separation of powers, 701
  slave importation, 724
  suffrage, 767
  taxes on imports and exports,
    258, 781
  three-fifths clause, 787
  treason provision, 791
  treaty-making and ratification,
    795
Dickinson, Philemon, 138
  (sidebar)
Dickinson Plan, 230–232,
  232–234, 489, 583
Diet, German, 311–312
Diet, Polish, 583–585
Direct taxation, 158
  Langdon's objection to, 409
  McHenry's support of state
    collection, 472–473
  Morris's support of, 501
  See also Three-fifths clause
Disability. *See* President, disability
Dispute resolution mechanism,
  328, 381
Distributing articles of the
  Constitution, 803–804
District of Columbia, **234–237**
Documents
  Albany Plan of Union, 856–857
  Amendments XI–XXVII,
    908–912
  Articles of Confederation,
    874–878
  Bill of Rights, 907–908

  Constitution of Massachusetts,
    860–874
  The Debates in the Federal
    Convention of 1787, reported
    by James Madison: The
    Virginia Plan, 889–891
  Declaration of Independence,
    208–211, 859–860
  Dickinson's accomplishments,
    226
  Dominion of New England,
    237–238
  Dunlap and Claypoole's
    printing of, 238
  Federalist No. 10, 912–915
  Federalist No. 51, 915–917
  James Madison's Preface to
    Debates in the Convention,
    883–889
  letter of transmittal, 414–415,
    900
  Madison's notes of the
    Convention, 438–439
  Magna Carta, 440–441
  Massachusetts Body of Liberties,
    466–467
  Mayflower Compact, 468,
    855–856
  The New Jersey Plan: June 15,
    1787, 891–894
  *Pennsylvania Packet and Daily
    Advertiser,* 559
  physical dimensions of the U.S.
    Constitution, 514 (sidebar)
  Preamble, 594–595
  records of the Constitutional
    Convention, 665–667
  Report of Proccedings in
    Congress; February 21, 1787,
    880–881
  Resolution from Annapolis
    Convention; September 14,
    1786, 878–880
  Resolution of Federal
    Convention to Continental
    Congress, 899–900
  Speech and Proposal of
    Alexander Hamilton at
    Federal Convention: June
    18,1787, 894–898
  Speech of Benjamin Franklin
    delivered to Constitutional

Convention: September 17, 1787, 898–899
U.S. Constitution, 801–806, 900–907
Virginia Declaration of Rights, 857–858
See also State constitutions; *The Federalist*
Domestic violence, protection against. *See* Guarantee clause
Dominion of New England, **237–238**
Door-keeper of the Convention. *See* Fry, Joseph
Double jeopardy, 466
Dred Scott decision, 520, 727, 805
Dualist democracy, 183, 413
Dudley, Joseph, 237
Due process, 39, 417, 441, 466
Dueling, 579, 738, 746 (sidebar)
Duer, William, 185 (sidebar), 270
Dunlap, John, 238
Dunlap and Claypoole, **238**
Dutch Reformed Church, 668
Duties. *See* Taxes on imports and exports
Duties versus imposts, 780
Duvall, William, 363

E Pluribus Unum, 267 (sidebar)
East-West divisions, 308–309
Eastern states, 305–306
Eating, 201, 474
Economic issues
banking, 45–46
bankruptcy, 47
borrowing power, 64–65
class divisions, 86–90
commerce power, 100–103
Committee on Interstate Comity and Bankruptcy, 112
copyrights and patents, 191–192
critical period, 199
expenses of delegates, 255–256
motives of the Founding Fathers, 507
plantation slavery, 6, 9, 10
presidential compensation, 597–598
presidential selection by Congress, 619

property rights, 627–629
Protestantism and capitalism, 631
Education
Baldwin's contribution to, 45
College of New Jersey, 528
Davie's involvement in, 203
Ellsworth, Oliver, 242
establishment of national university, 571
national university, 516
Northwest Ordinance provisions, 537
Witherspoon, John, 241 (sidebar)
Education of Convention delegates, xliv, **239–242**
classical allusions and influences, 90–93
Dayton, Jonathan, 204
delegates' educational histories, 217
Few, William, 276
Edwards, Jonathan, 630
Eighth Amendment, 61, 805, 815
Elections. *See* President, selection
Electoral College
allowance for presidential re-eligibility, 615
amendments affecting, 805
Baldwin on, 45
Butler's support of, 74
Committee on Postponed Matters, 114
compromise, 123
geographical differences affecting, 307–308
introduction of, 607, 611–612, 613
Mason's views on, 457–458
Pinckney's opposition to, 572
Polish election of the monarch, 585
Randolph's concerns over, 646
as safeguard against corruption, 194
separation of powers, 702
Sherman's role in, 715–716
states legislatures, 757
Strong's views, 764
supermajority requirement, 771
vice presidency, 808

Washington selection, 830–831
Williamson on, 838–839
See also President, selection
Electoral system, Connecticut's, 178
Eleventh Amendment, 310, 383 (sidebar), 805, 848
Elkins, Stanley, 675
Ellis, Richard, 604
Ellsworth, Oliver, **242–250**
age of, 11
amending process, 14
appointments and confirmations, 25
aristocracy, 27, 283
assessment of the delegates, 215
attendance, 40
borrowing power, 65
chief justice provision, 84–85
citizenship for senators, 163
Committee of Detail, 106
concerns over government of a large area, 397
Congress, compensation of members, 131, 132
congressional militia powers, 152, 482
congressional origination of money bills, 155
congressional representation, 104
Connecticut Compromise, 180–181
correspondence with his wife, 217 (sidebar)
Council of Revision, 195, 599
education of, 239, 242
ex post facto laws, 80, 120, 254
guarantee clause, 336
House, size of, 144
House terms, 145
judicial review, 391
lodging of the delegates, 424
number of speeches, 740
Pierce's character sketch, 542
piracy punishment, 582
posterity and perpetuity, 588
presidential qualifications, 606
presidential selection, 619–620
presidential veto, 619
qualifications of voters for Congress, 139

Ellsworth, Oliver (*continued*)
  quorums, 161
  ratification, 182, 650, 651
  Revolutionary War, 675
  on Rhode Island, 680
  Senate representation, 165, 169
  slavery and slave importation, 7,
    8–9, 724
  small states' rights, 43–44
  social contract, 729
  state governors filling senatorial
    vacancies, 330
  state legislature providing
    congressional salaries, 757
  suffrage, 767–768
  sumptuary legislation, 769
  taxes on imports and exports,
    257, 780–781
  three-fifths clause, 786
  time and frequency of
    congressional meetings, 175
  treason provision, 790–791
Emancipation Proclamation, 727
Embargoes, 323, 377, 501
Embossing of Constitution. *See*
  Shallus, Jacob
Emoluments clause, 148–151, 571,
  598, 689
Engagements clause. *See* Debts
English bill of rights, 58
Enlightenment. *See* Reason and
  experience; Scottish
  Enlightenment
Entrepreneurs, constitutional, **251**
Enumeration, 82–83
Episcopalian Church, 668
Equal representation
  Brearly's support for, 66
  Dayton's support of, 204–205
  Dickinson, John, 226
  Hamilton's objection to, 341
  Jenifer, Daniel, of St. Thomas,
    378
  Lansing's defense of, 412
  Martin's insistence on,
    445–446
  Monroe's criticism of, 494
  Morris's approval of, 497
  New Jersey Plan's intention,
    530
  Senate, 164–169
  Senate depriving states of, 501

See also Congress, House of
    Representatives,
    representation in; Congress,
    representation in; Congress,
    Senate, representation in;
    Connecticut Compromise;
    Representation; Small states
Equality, **251–253**
Ernst, Robert, 221
"The Essex Result," 631
Eubanks, Cecil, 534
European influences on delegates
    to the Convention, **253–254**,
    311–312
  France, 289–290
  Germany, 311–312
  Holland, 351–352
  Spain, 739–740
  See also Great Britain
Ex post facto laws, **254–255**
  Carroll and Ellsworth on, 80
  common law, 120–121
  contracts clause and, 190
  Dickinson on, 230
  Ellsworth's views, 248
  importance of experience, 663
  Johnson's views on, 381
  McHenry's opposition to, 473
  Rutledge's support for, 688
  Wilson on, 842
Executive Branch of government.
    *See entries beginning with
    President*
Expenses of delegates, **255–256**
  Committee on Postponed
    Matters, 114
  Langdon's personal payment of,
    408
Export taxes, **256–259**
  Morris's views on, 501
  Rutledge's call for prohibition
    of, 688
  Williamson on, 837
  Wilson on, 842
  See also Taxes on imports and
    exports
Expulsion of members, 134
Extended republic, Madison's
    concept of, 345
Extradition, **259**, 299
Extralegality of the Constitution,
    413

Fabias, 232
Factions. *See* Parties, factions, and
    interests
Fairlie, John, 600
Fame, **261–262**, 355
Families of delegates, 216–217,
    217 (sidebar), 424
Farber, Daniel, 415
Farrand, Max, **262–263**, 819
  assessment of the delegates, 214,
    220–221
  Madison's notes of the
    Convention, 439
  notes of the proceedings,
    666–667
  sentries, 298
Father of the Constitution,
    263–264
*The Federal Constitutional Celebration
    in Philadelphia* (Bloom), 99
Federal Processions, 98
Federal ratio. *See* Three-fifths
    clause
Federalism, **264–268**
  Bedford's stance on, 52–53
  Butler, Pierce, 74–75
  Carroll, Daniel, 81
  checks and balances, 84
  common law, 120–122
  concerns over governing a large
    territory, 306
  confederal roots of, 125
  court and country parties, 198
  critical period, 199–200
  E Pluribus Unum, 267 (sidebar)
  factions and parties, 553
  Gerry's opposition to, 312
  Gerry's views on, 319–320
  Hamilton on, 342, 344–345
  Ingersoll's views on, 366–367
  King's proposal on
    representation, 402
  Madison, James, 430
  Martin, Luther, 445–448
  Pinckney, Charles Cotesworth,
    575–576
  Read, George, 659–660
  Revolutionary War, 675
  Rhode Island as propaganda
    source, 680
  Senate representation, 169
  separation of powers, 703

Sherman, Roger, 710–712
state constitutions, 186
state power and state
    representation, l
Swiss Cantons, 777–778
unitary government versus, 799
U.S. Constitution, 804
Virginia Plan, 643
Washington and, 831
Wilson on, 846–847
The Federalist (Hamilton, Madison,
    Jay), **269–274**
allocation of power, 590
amending process, 17–18
Antifederalist critiques and, 21
Bill of Rights, 58
bureaucracy, 69
checks and balances, 83–84
classes, 87–88
common law, 122
constitutional revision, 251
democracy and republic, 225
determining original intent of
    the Framers, 546
factions, 552–553
Federalism, 264–265, 266–267,
    276
history of, 346
Hume's influence on, 357
implied powers, 592
inequality in America, 253
Jay's contribution to, 374
Jefferson's praise of, 376
judicial jurisdiction, 383
    (sidebar)
justice, 394–395
on justice, 395
large land area as obstacle to
    republican government, 274
love of fame, 261, 262
Madison's essays, 436
Montesquieu's influence on,
    495
Morris's declining to author,
    505
new government as a
    combination of nationalism
    and federalism, 281
occupations of the delegates,
    541
presidential power, 602
on progress, 626

public opinion as a support for
    a new government, 636
publication of, 533
on reason and experience, 664
religious references contained
    in, 56
republican government, 286
size of the new nation, 306
standing armies, 30
state coining of money, 493
Swiss Cantons, 777
text of *Federalist* No. 10,
    912–915
text of *Federalist* No. 51,
    915–917
Federalist Party
    banking controversy, 46
    Ellsworth, Oliver, 250
    Marshall, John, 443
    Pinckney's (Charles Cotesworth)
        candidacy, 579
    Strong's support of, 764
Federalists, **274–276**, 281
    Antifederalists and, 22
    Bill of Rights debates, 60, 61
    Congress, terms, 174
    factions and parties, 553
    The Federalist, 269–273
    Henry, Patrick, 351
    Marshall, John, 443
    Massachusetts's ratification,
        465–466
    mercantilism versus agriculture,
        306
    motives of the Founding
        Fathers, 506
    natural rights, 519
    New Hampshire's ratification,
        526
    North Carolina's ratifying
        convention, 535–536
    ratification debates, 656,
        813–814
    women's suffrage, 765 (sidebar)
Few, William, **276–277**
    attendance, 40
    Committee on Commercial
        Discrimination, 111
    number of speeches, 741
    Pierce's character sketch, 543
    religious affiliation, 668
Fifteenth Amendment, 140, 805

Fifth Amendment, 60
    justice, 395
    liberty, 417
    property rights, 628–629
    U.S. Constitution and, 805
Filibuster mechanism, 26
Finkelman, Paul, 538
First Amendment, 58–59, 60, 61
    Carroll, Daniel, 82
    religious influence on, 629
    U.S. Constitution and, 805
First Continental Congress, 2, 685
First Volunteer Corps of
    Pennsylvania, 833
Fishing industry, 306
Fiske, John, 199, 507
Fitzpatrick, John C., 704
Fitzsimons, Thomas, **277–279**
    attendance, 39
    Committee on Commercial
        Discrimination, 111
    number of speeches, 740
    Pierce's character sketch, 543
    qualifications of voters for
        Congress, 139
    ratification provision, 653
    religious affiliation, 630, 668
    treaty-making and ratification,
        795
Fletcher v. Peck, 310, 450
Folwell, John, 681
Forefathers, 287 (sidebar)
Foreign Affairs, secretary of, 373
Foreign affairs and the
    Convention, **279–281**
Foreign powers
    Bedford's concern over, 403
    Canada, 77–79
    concerns over size of
        confederation, 304–305
    France, 289–290
    Germany, 311–312
    Great Britain, 331–334
    Indians, 364
    McClurg, James, 470
    new states provision debates,
        753
    Poland as model for
        government, 583–585
    presidential qualifications, 606
    Spain, 739–740
    supremacy clause, 774

Forms of government, **281–286**
  aristocracy, 27–29
  confederalism, 124–125
  democracy, 223–225
  federalism, 264–267
  foundings, 286–288
  Framers' objectives, liv–lv
  mixed government, 488
  monarchy, 488–491
  New Jersey Plan, 529–534
  Northwest Ordinance, 537
  republic, 670–672
  unitary government, 799–800
Fortifications, 316
Founding, **286–288,** 413
Founding Fathers, 211 (sidebar),
  263–264
Fourteenth Amendment
  Declaration of Independence
    and, 210
  equality, 251
  liberty, 417
  naturalization and citizenship,
    520
  overturning *Dred Scott*, 727
  potentially broad scope of, 61
  state legislatures' ratification of,
    758
  U.S. Constitution and, 805
  women's rights, 849–850
Fourth Amendment, 60, 805, 815
Fox, Frank W., 288
Framers, 211 (sidebar), 286–287,
  288–289
France, **289–290**
  Jefferson's ministry, 376
  origins of public opinion, 633
  XYZ Affair, 322
  XYZ mission, 250
Franklin, Benjamin, **290–298**
  age of, 11
  Albany Plan of Union, 11
  appointments and
    confirmations, 24
  aristocracy, 283
  assessment of the delegates, 214,
    215
  attendance, 40
  Biblical and religious references
    during the Convention, 54, 56
  Committee on sumptuary
    legislation, 116

  on compromise, 123–124
  concerns over foreign affairs,
    280
  concerns over monarchy, 489
  Congress, compensation of
    members, 130, 131
  Congress, qualifications for,
    163
  congressional origination of
    money bills, 155
  congressional representation,
    104, 578
  corporations provision, 192
  criticism of British system of
    government, 332
  Declaration of Independence,
    208
  executive council proposal,
    196
  on experience, 663
  German trade treaty, 311
  historical assessment of, 222
  Holland and, 351
  House, representation in, 141
  impeachment clause, 360
  Indians, 364
  judicial salaries, 387
  lack of education, 239
  letter of transmittal, 414
  lodging of the delegates, 425
  Masons, 462
  monarchy views, 282
  naming the state of Tennessee,
    783
  negative on state laws, 331
  number of speeches, 740
  Pierce's character sketch, 543
  Pilgrim roots, 287 (sidebar)
  prayer at the Convention,
    592–593
  preference for republican
    government, 670
  president of the Convention,
    616
  presidential compensation, 597
  presidential qualifications, 606
  presidential salary, 830
  presidential veto, 617–618
  presidents, number of, 603
  Priestley and, 623–624
  Privy Council, 600
  progress, 627

  qualifications of voters for
    Congress, 140
  religious affiliation, 668
  Revolutionary War, 676
  rising sun, 681
  secrecy, 695
  Senate representation, 165–166,
    166–167, 169
  signing of Declaration of
    Independence and the
    Constitution, 209, 718–719,
    720
  on slavery, 5, 9 (sidebar)
  speech delivered to
    Constitutional Convention,
    September 17, 1787, 898–899
  suffrage, 768
  Syng and, 778
  Temple Franklin's nomination
    for secretary of the
    Convention, 371, 372
    (sidebar)
  treason provision, 791
  Treaty of Paris, 550
  two-headed snake, 297 (sidebar)
  virtue, 821
  Washington, George, 827
  Williamson and, 834
  wisdom of, lix
Franklin, William Temple, 50, 291,
  371, 372 (sidebar), 527, 696
Fraternal organizations. *See*
  Masons; Society of the
  Cincinnati
Free-masons. *See* Masons
The Freemen's Journal, 138 (sidebar)
French and Indian War, 289
French Revolution, 290, 550, 789
Frequency of meeting, 715
Fritz, Christian, 747
Fry, Joseph, **298–299,** 833
Fugitive slave clause, 4, 75,
  299–300
  Northwest Ordinance
    provisions, 537–538
  Pinckney's support of, 573
  U.S. Constitution, 804
  Wilson on, 842
Fugitive Slave Law of 1793, 299
Full faith and credit clause, 112,
  300, 381
Full-timers, 39–40

Fundamental Orders of
    Connecticut, 185
Future achievements of the
    delegates, 218

Gallatin, Albert, 109
Galloway, Joseph, 12, 301
Galloway Plan, **301**
Gardoqui, Diego de, 373, 374–375,
    740
Garrison, William Lloyd, 419
Garver, Frank, 220
General welfare clause, **302–303**
Genet, E.C., 695
Geneva, Switzerland, 631
The Genuine Information (Martin),
    450, 451–452
Geography, **303–308**
    distribution of the delegates,
        215
    Georgia, 308–309
    land disputes, 407–408
    New York, 532
    as obstacle to republican
        government, 274
    plural executive, 583
George III, 489, 828 (sidebar)
Georgia, **308–310**
    allocation of House seats, 117
    Baldwin, Abraham, 43–45
    Baldwin's support of slave
        importation, 44
    Committee on Original
        Apportionment of Congress,
        113
    Few, William, 276–277
    Houston, William, 352–353
    Pierce, William, 565–566
    ratification of the Constitution,
        656
    refusal to pay war debts, 310,
        383 (sidebar)
    Senate representation, 167
    small-state coalition, 96
Germanic League, 311
Germany, **311–312**
Gerry, Elbridge, **312–322**
    age of, 11
    amending process, 15
    Antifederalism, 21
    appointments and
        confirmations, 25

aristocracy, 283
armies and navies, raising and
    supporting, 31–32
assessment of the delegates, 215
attainder, bills of, 39
attendance, 39
Biblical and religious references
    during the Convention, 55
Bill of Rights discussion, 59
chief justice provision, 85
classes, 88
commerce power, 103
committees served on, 105,
    107–108, 113, 118
concerns over monarchy, 489,
    491
Congress, qualifications for,
    135–136, 136
Congress, selection of, 142
Congress, terms, 174
congressional militia powers,
    153, 481, 483, 484
congressional origination of
    money bills, 154–155, 156
congressional representation,
    104
contracts clause, 190
Council of Revision, 195–196,
    598
criticism of British system of
    government, 332
debts, 207
democracy, 284
education of, 240
emoluments clause, 149, 150
ex post facto laws, 254
House, size of, 144
House terms, 145
impeachment clause, 360
implied powers, 591
judicial review, 389
Langdon's opposing views, 409
leaders of Congress, 147–148
location and permanence of
    nation's capital, 236
lodging during the Convention,
    424
monarchy views, 283
negative on state laws, 521
new states provision, 752
number of speeches, 740, 741
oaths, 539

Pierce's character sketch, 543
post offices and post roads, 586
posterity and perpetuity, 587
presidential selection, 329,
    607–608, 612, 646
presidential term length and re-
    eligibility, 614–615
presidential veto, 617, 618, 619
presidents, number of, 604
public opinion, 634, 635
publication of appropriations,
    160
quorums, 161
ratification provision, 650, 651,
    652, 653
references to Pennsylvania, 558
Revolutionary War veterans, 676
Senate representation, 167
Senate selection, 171
Shays's Rebellion, 708
signing of the Declaration of
    Independence and the
    Constitution, 209, 719
on slavery, 6, 10
Society of the Cincinnati, 732
standing armies, 29–30
state legislatures, 756
sumptuary legislation, 769
tax apportionment, 73
taxes on imports and exports,
    257, 780
temperatures in the summer of
    1787, 782
three-fifths clause, 785, 786, 787
treaty-making and ratification,
    795, 796
trial by jury, 393
vice presidential bid, 368
Virginia Plan, 13
virtue, 821
war powers of Congress, 826
Gerrymandering, 322
Gibbons v. Ogden, 443
Gillespie, Michael, 466
Gilman, Nicholas, **322–323**
    attendance, 40
    Committee on Postponed
        Matters, 113
    expenses of delegates, 256
    number of speeches, 741
    supporting Langdon's political
        career, 410

Gilmore, Michael, 655 (sidebar)
Gilpin, H.D., 438–439, 666
Gladstone, William, 214, 507
Glanzman, Louis, 37, 68
Glorious Revolution (1688), 197
Goldsmith, Oliver, 564 (sidebar)
Goodrich, Charles A., 38
Gordon, Thomas, 672
Gorham, Nathaniel, **323–329**
  appointments and
    confirmations, 24–25
  armies and navies, raising and
    supporting, 31
  attendance, 39
  Biblical and religious references
    during the Convention,
    56–57
  Bill of Rights discussion, 59
  borrowing power, 65
  commerce power, 102
  committees served on, 106, 110,
    111, 112, 113, 118, 119
  Congress, compensation, 131,
    132
  Congress, qualifications for,
    135–136, 137
  Congress, terms, 174
  emoluments clause, 149
  guarantee clause, 336
  judicial organization, 387
  judicial review, 391
  land disputes, 407
  location of nation's capital, 235
  Maine, 441
  new states provision, 751
  number of speeches, 740
  oaths, 14, 539–540
  Pierce's character sketch, 543
  posterity and perpetuity, 588
  presidential selection, 611
  presidential veto, 619
  presidents, number of, 603
  Prince Henry of Prussia as
    potential president, 490
    (sidebar)
  progress, 626–627
  public opinion, 634
  quorums, 160, 161
  ratification provision, 651
  on Rhode Island, 679, 745
  Senate representation, 165–166
  Senate size, 173

  state coining of money, 492
  state legislature providing
    congressional salaries, 757
  taxes on imports and exports,
    781
  Tennessee statehood, 783
  three-fifths clause, 786
  time and frequency of
    congressional meetings, 175
  times, places, and manners of
    congressional election, 176
  Treasury secretary, 793
  treaty-making and ratification,
    795, 796
  trial by jury, 393, 394
  on Vermont, 807
  Western states admission, 699
Government. *See* Forms of
  government
Governors, state, **329–331**
Governors selecting the president,
  317, 607–608
Grand Committee. *See* Committee
  of Compromise on
  Representation in Congress
Great Awakenings, 625
Great Britain, **331–335**
  Albany Plan of Union, 11–12
  attainder, bills of, 39
  Bedford's stance on equal
    representation in Congress,
    53
  bicameralism, 126
  bureaucracy, 69
  Canada, 78–79
  colonial precedents, 97
  common law, 121
  confederal government and, 125
  corruption, 194
  court and country parties,
    197–198
  Declaration of Independence,
    208–210
  Dominion of New England,
    237–238
  English Bill of Rights, 58
  English Parliament, 125
  foreign affairs influencing the
    Convention, 279
  Galloway Plan, 301
  Gerry's support of independence
    from, 321 (sidebar)

  Hamilton's admiration for, 343
  lack of constitutionalism, 184
  Magna Carta, 440–441
  as model for Committee of the
    Whole, 110
  monarchy, 488–491
  natural rights, 518
  Parliamentary selection, 171
  Price, Richard, 622–623
  Priestley, Joseph, 623–624
  refusal to honor the Treaty of
    Paris, 35
  Revolutionary War, 675–677
  roots of the Constitution,
    xxxix–xxl
  slavery, 8
  sovereignty issues, 736
  state governors, 329
  treason provision, 790–791, 792
  Treaty of Paris, 550
  trial by jury, 393
  tripartite government, 281–282
  unitary government, 799
  unwritten constitution, 802
  Whig ideology, 833–834
Great Compromise
  amending process, 15
  appointments and
    confirmations in light of, 25
  Baldwin's views on
    representation, 43–44
  Franklin's contribution to, 292
  history and goals of, xlviii–li
  Mason's support of, 455
  role of wealth in representation,
    628
  Williamson, Hugh, 836
  Yates, Robert, 853
  See also Connecticut
    Compromise
Greece, ancient
  Achaean League, 1
  Butler's views on the judiciary,
    74
  classical allusions and
    influences, 90–93
  democracy, 223–225
  founding, 287
  See also Classical allusions and
    influences
Grimke, Angelina and Sarah, 685
Grinde, Donald A. Jr., 368

Guarantee clause, 230, **335–337**
  Ellsworth's views, 247
  Gorham's support of, 326
  Morris's objection to, 501
  state governors, 330
Gummere, Richard, 90, 93
Gun-Free School Zones Act
    (1990), 130
Gunpowder Joe, 624

Habeas corpus, **339**
  Pinckney, Charles, 571
  Rutledge's support for, 688
  Wilson on, 842
Half-pay for military, 732
Hall, David, 630–631
Hamilton, Alexander, **340–347**
  Adams and, 3
  admiration for British system of
    government, 332
  advocacy of monarchy, 490
    (sidebar), 491
  age of, 11
  amending process, 14, 15
  Antifederalists, 21
  appointments and
    confirmations, 24, 331
  assessment of the delegates, 214
  attendance, 40
  banking provision, 46
  Bill of Rights, 58
  bureaucracy, 69
  classes, 88
  classical allusions and
    influences, 91
  coalitions, 95
  collective powers of Congress,
    128
  Committee of the Whole, 111
  Committee on Rules, 114
  concerns over allocation of
    power, 590
  concerns over Canada, 78
  Congress, compensation of
    members, 131
  Congress, qualifications for, 137
  Congress, selection of, 143
  Congress, terms, 174
  corporations provision, 192, 628
  corruption concerns, 194
  criticism of Connecticut
    government, 179

criticism of democracy, 224–225
  death of, 746 (sidebar)
  debts, 207
  education of, 241
  emoluments clause, 149
  The Federalist, 269–273
  Franklin's proposal of daily
    prayer, 295
  general welfare clause, 302–303
  Great Compromise, xlviii–l
  House, representation in, 141
  House terms, 146
  human nature, 354–355
  implied powers, 592
  on Indians, 364
  Jefferson's conflict with, 376
  judicial jurisdiction, 383
    (sidebar), 384
  judicial review, 390
  justice, 395
  Livingston and, 422
  lodging of the delegates, 424
  Madison's suspicions of, 436
  natural rights, 518
  New York delegation, 533
  number of speeches, 740
  oratory style, 544
  Pierce's character sketch, 543
  Polish election of the monarch,
    583
  prayer at the Convention, 593
  presidential compensation, 598
  presidential stability, 742
  property rights, 627
  public opinion, 634–635
  ratification, 182–183, 653
  references to German Diet, 311
  references to Montesquieu, 495
  religious affiliation, 668
  religious references during the
    Constitutional Convention,
    56
  republican government, 285, 671
  resolution accompanying the
    Constitution, 674
  secrecy, 695
  Senate representation, 165
  signing of the Constitution, 719
  slave revolts, 5–6
  social contract, 729
  speech and proposal at federal
    Convention, 894–898

standing armies, 29
  suffrage, 766
  supremacy clause, 774
  Swiss Cantons, 777
  taxes on imports and exports,
    256, 779
  Treasury secretary, 793
  vice presidency, 808
  Virginia Plan, 13
  voting at the Convention, 823
  war powers of Congress, 825
  Washington, George, 830
  Yates and, 853
  See also The Federalist (Hamilton,
    Madison, Jay)
Hamilton, Andrew, 560
Hamilton Plan, **347–350,** 661
  impeachment clause, 360
  plans of government introduced
    at the Convention, 583
  president as Commander in
    Chief, 596
  Read's support of, 660
  terms of, 341–344
Hammons, Christopher, 107
    (sidebar), 748
Hancock, John, 464, 465, 657, 682,
    706–707
Harding, Warren G., 211 (sidebar),
    562 (sidebar)
Harrington, James, 2
Harrison, Benjamin, 321 (sidebar)
Hartford Convention (1814), 307,
    505, 764
Hartz, Louis, 507
Harvard University, 240
Hemmings, Sally, 377
Henry, Patrick, **350–351**
  Antifederalism, 21
  Galloway Plan, 301
  Madison and, 436
  Marshall's response to, 442
  oratory style, 544–545
  Preamble to the Constitution,
    595
  ratification, 657, 813
  refusal to attend the
    Convention, 223, 812
Henry of Prussia, 490 (sidebar)
Hertzberg, Hendrik, 211 (sidebar)
Hiltzheimer, Jacob, 782
Hindus, 44

Historians and historical references, 663
    assessment of the delegates, 220–221
    Beard, Charles, 48–50
    Farrand, Max, 262–263
    founding, 288
    Hume, David, 356
Historiography. *See* Motives of the Founding Fathers
History, delegates' use of. *See* Reason and experience
History of England (Hume), 356
Hobbes, Thomas, 416, 728
Holland, 312, **351–352**
Holmes, Oliver Wendell, 479 (sidebar)
Holmes, Oliver Wendell, Jr., lix
Holy Roman Empire. *See* Germany
Home Building and Loan Association v. Blaisdell, 191
Hopkinson, Francis, 235 (sidebar), 511, 562 (sidebar)
Horsnell, Margaret, 221–222
House, representation
    Dickinson Plan, 233
Houston, William, **352–353**
    attendance, 40
    Committee to Reconsider Representation in the House, 117
    criticism of Georgia's constitution, 309
    Great Compromise, 44
    guarantee clause, 336
    Pierce's character sketch, 543
    presidential selection, 619
    presidential term length and re-eligibility, 614
Houston, William Churchill, **353–354**
Hueston, John, 106
Human nature, 344, **354–356**
Hume, David, 194, **356–357**, 633, 672, 691–692
Humor
    Franklin on judicial selection, 294
    Gerry's potential death by hanging, 321 (sidebar)
    standing armies, 320
    See also Anecdotes

Huntington, Samuel, 179
Hutchinson, Thomas, 834
Hutson, James H., 232–233, 439, 782

Ideology. *See* Philosophy and ideology
Illinois, 537
Immigrants
    Congress, qualifications for, 44, 136–137, 163–164, 687, 837, 843
    contribution to the Revolutionary War, 676
    Davie, William Richardson, 202–203
    delegates' profile, 215–216
    Fitzsimons, Thomas, 277–279
    Gerry's objections to immigrants holding office, 315
    Hamilton, Alexander, 340–347
    Houston, William, 352–353
    Jackson, William, 371
    McHenry, James, 471–474
    Morris, Robert, 505–506
    Morris's views on qualifications of electors and voters, 500
    naturalization, 520
    Paterson, William, 553–557
    presidential qualifications, 606
    Williamson, Hugh, 834–840
    Wilson, James, 840–848
Immortality, 262
Immunities clause. *See* Privileges and immunities clause
Impeachment clause, **359–362**
    Blount, John Jr., 64
    chief justice provision, 85
    Committee on Postponed Matters, 114
    corruption concerns, 194
    Davie's support of, 203
    Dickinson Plan, 234
    Franklin's support of, 294
    Gerry's support of, 317–318
    Hamilton Plan, 349
    King's opposition, 402
    Madison's views on, 433–434
    Mason's support for, 457
    Morris's support of popular election as alternative to, 502–503

Pinckney's opposition to, 572
Randolph's views on, 646, 648
separation of powers, 702
supermajority requirement, 771
vice president, 809
Williamson on, 839
Implied powers. *See* Powers, implied
Import taxes. *See* Taxes on imports and exports
Imposts versus duties, 257, 780
Inaugural Address, Washington's, 831
Inauguration, 512, 605
Incompatibility and ineligibility clauses. *See* Congress, members' ineligibility for other offices
Incorporation, 760
Indentured servants, **362–363**
Independence Day, 295, 594, 676, 704
Independence Hall. *See* Pennsylvania State House
Indian Queen Tavern, 424
Indiana, 537
Indians, **363–365**
    Blount's attempts to exploit, 64
    commerce regulation, 114
    equality, 252
    Georgia's concerns over threat from, 309
    Iroquois, 368
    Morris's emotional outburst over, 664
    Pierce's concerns over Indian attacks, 566
    Proclamation Line of 1763, 306
Indigo crop, 576 (sidebar)
Individual rights
    King's emphasis on, 403
    privileges and immunities clause, 624–625
    treason provision, 790–791
Industrializaiton, 10
Influence, Hamilton Plan principles and, 348
Ingersoll, Jared, **365–368**
    attendance, 40
    Committee of Style and Arrangement, 109
    education of, 240

letter of transmittal, 414
number of speeches, 740
Pierce's character sketch, 543
public opinion, 633
relations with France, 290
signing of the Constitution, 720
Inkstand, 778
Inns of Court, 240
Insanity, 690
Insurrections
  Morris's views on controlling, 501
  slave revolts, 5–6
  See also Shays's Rebellion
Interests. See Parties, factions, and interests
Interpretation of the Constitution, 443, 545–547
Interpretivists, 545–546
Interstate commerce and taxation, 304, 779
Iredell, James, 535, 737–738
Irish immigrants, 70–76
Iroquois, **368–369**

Jackson, Andrew, 70, 202, 746 (sidebar)
Jackson, William, **371–372**
  attendance, 40
  Beckley as potential clerk, 50
  Committee of Style and Arrangement, 109
  lack of notes and records, 696
  letter of transmittal, 414
  signing of the Constitution, 721, 734
James II, 237–238
Jay, John, **373–374**
  concerns over presidential qualifications, 606
  The Federalist, 21, 56, 270–273
  Livingston as father-in-law, 422
  religious references in The Federalist, 56
  Treaty of Paris, 550
Jay Treaty of 1794, 374
Jay-Gardoqui negotiations, **374–375**
  geographical divisions, 306
  Georgia's concerns over, 309
  Mississippi River navigation, 484–487

sectionalism and, 698
Southern states' blocking, 740
Virginia's opposition to, 812
Jefferson, Thomas, **374–378**
  Adams and, 2, 3
  amending process, 16–17 (sidebar), 18
  Beckley and, 50
  bicameralism, 126
  Bill of Rights debates, 60
  on constitutions, 182
  corporations provision, 192, 193
  death of, 98
  Declaration of Independence, 208–209
  failure to attend, 223
  impact of three-fifths clause on election, 788
  implied powers, 592
  limits of written documents, 186–187
  Madison and, 436
  Martin's criticism of, 450
  presidential term limits, 615
  Priestley and, 624
  religious affiliation, 630
  Shays's Rebellion, 708–709
  on slavery, 8
  Treaty of Paris, 550
  United States name, 801
  virtue, 822
  Washington, George, 830
Jenifer, Daniel, of St. Thomas, **378–379**
  attendance, 39, 40
  House terms, 145
  Maryland delegates' unity over issues, 472
  Mount Vernon Conference, 509, 510, 511
  number of speeches, 740
  Pierce's character sketch, 543
Jensen, Merrill, 199, 221, 507
Jewish history, 287
Jews
  religious tests, prohibition on, 669
  Washington's Rhode Island visit, 680
Johansen, Bruce E., 368
Johnson, Andrew, 362

Johnson, Herbert, 443
Johnson, Samuel, 418, 535–536
Johnson, William Samuel, **379–382**
  attendance, 39
  committees served on, 108–109, 112, 115, 116, 118, 119
  education of, 240, 241
  full faith and credit clause, 300
  Hamilton Plan, 344
  Hamilton's oratory, 544
  House, representation in, 141
  land disputes, 407
  new states provision, 754
  number of speeches, 740
  Pierce's character sketch, 543
  Preamble to the Constitution, 595
  sumptuary legislation, 770
  Vermont, 807
Jones, Willie, 535
Journal of the Constitutional Convention. See Records of the Constitutional Convention
Journal of the proceedings, 665–666
Judges, selection and removal of, 689
  Dickinson Plan, 234
  Dickinson's views, 229
  Franklin's humorous proposal, 294
  Gerry's views on, 319
  good behavior provision, 387–388
  Virginia Plan provisions, 819
Judicial increase, 473
Judicial independence, 319, 387–388, 689
Judicial jurisdiction, **382–386**
Judicial organization and protections, **386–388**
Judicial review, **388–393, 814**
  Council of Revision, 195–197
  Dickinson's objection to, 229
  Federalist view of, 275
  interpreting the Constitution, 805
  Marshall's support of, 442
Judicial salaries, 386, 387

Judiciary
  Antifederalists' view of federal courts system, 22
  appointments and confirmations, 23–24
  Articles of the Constitution, 804
  authorship of the Constitution, 41
  Bedford's support of judicial selection, 52
  Bill of Rights provisions, 60
  Blair, John Jr., 62
  bureaucracy, 69
  Butler, Pierce, 74
  chief justice, 84–85
  common law, 120–122
  Delaware's state constitution, 212
  Dickinson's support for national judiciary, 229
  dispute resolution between states, 205–206
  Ellsworth's support of judicial-executive connection, 249
  executive appointment under New Jersey Plan, 555
  Franklin's proposal for judicial selection, 294
  Gerry's objection to linking with the executive, 318–319
  Hamilton Plan, 349
  impeachment clause, 359–360
  Johnson, William Samuel, 381
  judicial organization and protections, 386–388
  land disputes, 407–408
  Madison's views, 434–435
  Marshall's support of federal judiciary, 442
  Martin's views on, 448
  Mason's views, 458
  Morris's views on judicial selection and pay, 503
  Pinckney's (Charles Cotesworth) opinions on pay, 579
  Pinckney's support of legislative appointments, 572–573
  portrayal in *The Federalist*, 273
  presidential veto, 618
  Randolph's proposed structure, 646–647
  Read's proposal of separate courts, 662
  Rutledge's stance on, 689
  separation of powers, 700–704
  Sherman, Roger, 716
  Strong's views, 764
  supremacy clause, 774–775
  Supreme Court, 775–776
  trial by jury, 393–394
  Virginia Plan provisions, 818, 819
  Virginia's constitution, 812
  Wilson on, 846
  See also Council of Revision
Judiciary Act of 1789, 76, 250, 764
Jurisdiction, judicial. *See* Judicial jurisdiction
Jury, trial by, **393–394**
Justice, **394–395**

Kaminski, John, 680
Kammen, Michael, 405
Kasson, John A., 98
Katyal, Neal, 413
Kay, Richard, 413
Kemble, Fanny, 76
Kennedy, John F., 307
Kent, Melanie Taylor, 38
Kentucky, 306, **397–398**, 753, 813
Kentucky Resolution of 1798, 376, 436
Kesavan, Vasan, 545, 547
King, Brett, 771
King, Rufus, **398–405**
  age of, 11
  assessment of the delegates, 215
  attendance, 39
  banking provision, 45
  Bedford's Federalist leanings and, 53
  bicameralism, 126
  committees served on, 113, 115, 117, 118
  Congress, compensation of members, 131
  Congress, selection of, 143
  congressional power to organize and govern militia, 483
  contracts clause, 190
  corporations provision, 192–193
  Council of Revision, 195
  education of, 240
  emoluments clause, 149, 150
  executive council proposal, 196
  Federalist stance, 710
  House, size of, 144
  impeachment clause, 360
  journal of the proceedings, 665
  judicial organization, 387
  judicial review, 389
  limits of written documents, 186
  location and permanence of nation's capital, 236
  Masons, 463
  number of speeches, 740
  overdue library books, 421
  Pierce's character sketch, 543
  presidential selection, 608–609
  presidential term length and re-eligibility, 614–615
  presidential veto, 617
  Prince Henry of Prussia as potential president, 490 (sidebar)
  private contracts, 255
  publication of appropriations, 160
  quorums, 160–161
  ratification, 650, 651, 652, 653
  reason and experience, 664
  on reason and experience, 663–664
  rollcall vote, 683
  Senate representation, 167
  Senate selection, 170
  Senate size, 172
  separation of powers, 703
  Shays's Rebellion, 708
  on slave importation, 6, 723–724
  sovereignty issues, 735–736
  three-fifths clause, 786
  time and frequency of congressional meetings, 175
  times, places, and manners of congressional election, 176
  treason, 68, 791
  Treasury secretary, 793
King's College, 240–241, 382
Kingship. *See* Monarchy
Knott's Berry Farm, 561
Knowledge of the Constitutional Convention, **405–406**

Laboratories of democracy, 747
Lame-duck legislators, 176
Land disputes, **407–408,** 839
Langdon, John, **408–410**
　armies and navies, raising and
　　supporting, 32
　attendance, 40
　borrowing power, 65
　commerce power, 102
　committees served on, 111, 115,
　　119
　Congress, compensation of
　　members, 132
　Congress, qualifications for,
　　136
　congressional militia powers,
　　152
　on the Convention rules, 684
　expenses of delegates, 256
　Gilman's political support, 323
　guarantee clause, 336
　location of nation's capital, 235
　Masons, 462
　new states provision, 754
　number of speeches, 740
　president of the Convention,
　　616
　taxes on imports and exports,
　　257, 780
　Washington and, 828
Language, 303
Lansing, John, **410–412**
　Antifederalism, 21
　attendance, 40
　coalitions, 95
　congressional representation,
　　104
　House, representation in, 141
　negative on state laws, 522
　New York delegation, 533
　number of speeches, 740
　Pierce's character sketch, 543
　public opinion, 635
　secrecy, 695
　support of New Jersey Plan, 531
　Yates and, 853
Laurens, Henry, 550, 574
Law, rule of. *See* Constitutionalism
Lee, Richard Henry, 812, 831
　Antifederalists, 21
　Declaration of Independence,
　　208

ratification controversy, 657
refusal to attend, 223
Legal system
　common law, 120–122
Legality of the Convention,
　413–414
Legaux, Peter, 782
Legislation. *See* Judicial review;
　Negative on state laws
Legislative branch of government.
　See Entries beginning with
　Congress
Legitimacy of the Convention. *See*
　Legality of the Convention
L'Enfant, Pierre Charles, 82
Letter of transmittal, 123,
　414–415, 900
*A Letter to the Electors of President
　and Vice-President of the United
　States* (Yates), 695
Levinson, Sanford, 722
Liberalism, 252, **415–417,** 821
The Liberator publication, 419
Liberty, **417–419**
　Ingersoll's views on potential
　　success of new government,
　　367
　Locke's defense of, 423
　Whig ideology, 833–834
Liberty Bell, 54, **419–420,** 560,
　561
Library privileges, **420–421**
Lienesch, Michael, 210
Lighthouse tax, 103, 473, 711
Lincoln, Abraham
　artistic depictions of, 38
　copyrights and patents
　　provision, 192
　oaths, 540
　posterity and perpetuity, 588
　on slavery, 726
　slavery and the Constitution, 4
Lincoln, Benjamin, 371, 706
Livingston, Brockholst, 422
Livingston, Robert, 208, 831
Livingston, William, **421–422**
　attendance, 40
　committees served on, 115, 116,
　　118, 119
　debts, 206–207
　education of, 240
　governor of New Jersey, 527

Hamilton and, 340
Indians and, 364
New York delegation, 533
number of speeches, 741
Pierce's character sketch, 543
Locke, John, **423–424**
　court and country parties, 197
　executive prerogative, 602
　influence on the Declaration of
　　Independence, 208–209
　liberalism, 416
　minimalist state, 624
　natural rights, 517
　origins of public opinion, 633
　property rights, 627
　republicanism and, 672
　social contract, 728
Lodging of the delegates, **424–425**
Louisiana Purchase
　Butler supporting, 76
　code law in Louisiana, 120
　foreign powers as threat to
　　Mississippi navigation, 78
　Jay-Gardoqui negotiations and,
　　487
　Jefferson's role in, 377
　Monroe's negotiation, 494
　new states provision, 753
Lowndes, Rawlins, 734–735
Ludlum, David M., 782
Luther v. Borden, 337
Lutz, Donald, 54, 184–186, 746,
　747

Machiavelli, Niccolo, 672
Madison, Dolley Todd, 436
Madison, James
　Achaean League, 1
　Adams and, 3
　age of, 11
　age of members of Congress,
　　162
　allocation of power, 589–590,
　　590
　amending process, 13, 14, 16–17
　　(sidebar), 17–18
　Antifederalists, 21, 22
　appointments and
　　confirmations, 23–26
　aristocracy, 27, 283
　armies and navies, raising and
　　supporting, 31

Madison, James (*continued*)
  Articles of Confederation, 36
  artistic depictions of, 37
  assessment of the delegates, 215
  attendance, 40
  banking provision, 45–46
  Beard on, 49
  Biblical and religious references during the Convention, 56–57
  Bill of Rights ratification by North Carolina, 536
  checks and balances, 83–84
  citizenship for senators, 163
  classes, 87–88, 90
  classical allusions and influences, 91
  commerce power, 102
  committees served on, 107–108, 108–109, 109, 113, 115, 117, 119
  common law, 120, 121, 122
  Congress, compensation of members, 130, 131, 132
  Congress, qualifications for, 136, 137, 162–163
  Congress, selection of, 142–143
  Congress, terms, 174
  congressional militia powers, 152, 153–154, 480–481, 482–484
  congressional origination of money bills, 155–156
  congressional representation, 104
  as constitutional entrepreneur, 251
  constitutional revision, 636
  continuance of Congress provision, 133
  contracts clause, 190
  corporations provision, 192
  corruption, 194
  Council of Revision, 195–197, 598
  criticism of British system of government, 333
  criticism of Connecticut government, 179
  criticism of Georgia's judiciary, 309

  The Debates in the Federal Convention of 1787: The Virginia Plan, 889–891
  democracy and republic, 225
  education of, 239
  emoluments clause, 149–150
  expulsion of congressional members, 134
  factions, 552–553
  failures of the Articles of Confederation, 809–810
  Father of the Constitution, 263–264
  federalism, 265
  The Federalist, 270–273
  France, 289–290
  fugitive slave clause, 299
  full faith and credit clause, 300
  guarantee clause, 335–336
  Hamilton's criticism of, 345
  House, representation in, 141
  House, size of, 144
  House terms, 145–146
  human nature, 354–355
  impeachment clause, 359, 361
  implied powers, 592
  on Indians, 364
  individual rights, 806
  inequality in America, 252–253
  Jefferson's influence on Madison's support of the Bill of Rights, 376
  Jenifer and, 379
  judicial jurisdiction, 384
  judicial organization, 386
  judicial review, 391–392
  judicial salaries, 387
  letter of transmittal, 414–415
  limiting Congress members from taking office, 72
  limits of written documents, 186–187
  lodging during the Convention, 424
  Mississippi River navigation negotiations, 486
  monarchy views, 282–283
  Monroe and, 494
  Mount Vernon Conference, 509, 511
  natural rights, 518
  naturalization, 520

  negative on state laws, 521–523
  new states provision, 751, 753
  notes of the proceedings, 666
  number of speeches, 740
  oaths, 605
  occupations of the delegates, 541
  opinion of Pinckney, 567
  original intent, 546
  origins of public opinion, 633
  peace treaties, 73
  Pierce's character sketch, 543
  piracy punishment, 581
  Polish election of the monarch, 584–585
  political campaigns, 437 (sidebar)
  posterity and perpetuity, 587
  prayer at the Convention, 594
  Preface to debates in the convention, 883–889
  president of the Convention, 616
  presidential selection, 612, 619
  presidential veto, 618, 619, 620
  presidential victory, 368
  proportional representation, 66
  public opinion, 634
  publication of appropriations, 160
  quorums, 161
  ratification, 649, 651, 652, 657, 813
  references to Germany, 311
  references to Montesquieu, 495
  references to Pennsylvania, 558
  religious affiliation, 668
  religious references during the Constitutional Convention, 56
  republican government, 285, 286, 671–672
  on Rhode Island, 679
  rising sun anecdote, 681
  Scottish Enlightenment influencing, 691–692
  secrecy, 694
  sectionalism, 697–698
  Senate representation, 166, 167, 169
  Senate selection, 170–171
  Senate size, 172

separation of powers, 701–702
Shays's Rebellion, 706
on slavery, 6, 7
social contract, 728–730
stability, 741, 742
standing armies, 30
state coining of money, 493
state governors selecting the president, 329
states legislatures, 758
on statesmanship, 762
suffrage, 766–767, 768
supermajority requirement, 771
supremacy clause, 773–774
Swiss Cantons, 631, 777
taxes on imports and exports, 257, 258, 780, 781
three-fifths clause, 785–786
time and frequency of congressional meetings, 175
times, places, and manners of congressional election, 176
treason provision, 790–791, 792
treaty-making and ratification, 795
Treaty of Paris, 550
Virginia delegates' meeting, xliii
Virginia Plan, 815–820, 820 (sidebar)
virtue, 821
war powers of Congress, 826
Washington and, 828
Madison, James, Jr., **427–438**
Madison Amendment, 133
Madison's notes of the Convention, **438–440**
Madison as Father of the Constitution, 263
Madison's method, xlv
Martin's speeches, 446
nem. con., 524
oaths, 539
Magna Carta, **440–441**
Maine, **441–442**
Majority
under the Pinckney Plan, 568
rules, 683
rules for, 683
supermajorities, 315, 572, 771–772
Mansbridge, Jane, 394
Marbury v. Madison, 3, 443, 814

Marital status of delegates, 216–217, 217 (sidebar)
Marshall, John, 3, 269, **442–443**, 814
banking controversy, 46
Bill of Rights discussion, 61
on brevity of Constitution, 107 (sidebar)
common law, 121
corporations provision, 628
Fletcher v. Peck, 310
implied powers, 592
Jefferson and, 377
judicial jurisdiction, 383 (sidebar)
judicial review, 388
Owings v. Speed, 654–655
ratification, 657, 813
Marshall's Boarding House, 424–425
Martin, Alexander, **443–445**
attendance, 40
emoluments clause, 149
number of speeches, 741
Pierce's character sketch, 543
Prince Henry of Prussia as potential monarch, 490 (sidebar)
secrecy, 692
Martin, Luther, **445–450**
age of, 11
appointments and confirmations, 24
armies and navies, raising and supporting, 31–32
attendance, 40
Biblical and religious references during the Convention, 55
bicameralism, 3, 126
commerce power, 101
committee mechanisms, 118
committees served on, 115
concerns over Kentucky, 397
Congress, compensation of members, 132
Congress, qualifications for, 136
congressional commerce power, 101
congressional militia powers, 153, 483–484
congressional representation, 104–105

contracts clause, 190–191
Council of Revision, 196
Declaration of Independence, 210
forms of government, 281
on Georgia's potential, 309
Great Compromise, 44
guarantee clause, 336
House, representation in, 141
Jenifer, Daniel, of St. Thomas and, 378
judicial review, 391
limits on states' powers, 758
Maine, 441
mention of John Locke, 423
negative on state laws, 522
new states provision, 753, 754, 755
number of speeches, 740, 741
oaths, 539
objection to federalist terminology, 265
oratory style, 544
overdue library books, 421
Pierce's character sketch, 543
port provisions, 80
presidential selection, 608
presidential term length and re-eligibility, 614–615
Price, Richard, 623
ratification controversy, 657
religious tests, prohibition on, 669
Revolutionary War, 675
rights of men and states rights, 519
secrecy, 693
Senate size, 172–173, 173
on slavery and slave importation, 6, 7, 723–724
social contract, 729
Swiss Cantons, 777
treason provision, 791
unitary government, 799
Vermont, 807
Yates's attendance, 853
Marxism, 49
Mary House's Boarding House, 424
Maryland, **450–452**
allocation of House seats, 117
Carroll, Daniel, 79–82

Maryland (*continued*)
    committees served on, 113
    congressional origination of
        money bills, 157
    delegates not in attendance,
        223
    expenses of delegates, 256
    Jenifer, Daniel, of St. Thomas,
        378–379
    McHenry, James, 471–474
    Mount Vernon Conference,
        509–511
    new states provision, 754
    ratification controversy, 657
    state appointment of delegates
        to the Convention, 744
    state constitution, 747
Maryland Ratifying Convention,
    452
Mason, Alpheus, 423
Mason, George, **452–462**
    age of, 11
    age of congressional members,
        135
    amending process, 15, 17
    Antifederalism, 21
    appointments and
        confirmations, 24
    aristocracy, 27–28, 283
    armies and navies, raising and
        supporting, 32
    Articles of Confederation, 36
    assessment of the delegates, 214,
        215
    attendance, 40
    banking provision, 45
    Biblical and religious references
        during the Convention, 55
    bicameralism, 125
    Bill of Rights discussion, 59
    borrowing power, 65
    census provision, 83
    classes of citizens and delegates,
        86
    commerce power, 103
    committees served on, 107–108,
        111, 115, 116, 119
    common law, 121
    concerns over allocation of
        power, 590
    Congress, compensation of
        members, 131

    congressional militia powers,
        151, 482
    congressional origination of
        money bills, 155, 156, 498
    congressional representation,
        104
    contracts clause, 190
    corporations provision, 193
    corruption, 194
    Council of Revision, 195
    criticism of democracy, 224
    debts, 207
    democracy, 284
    education of, 239
    emoluments clause, 150
    ex post facto laws, 255
    experience of the Council of
        Revision, 663
    guarantee clause, 335–336
    House, size of, 144
    human nature, 355
    impeachment clause, 359, 361
    judicial organization, 387
    on liberty and property, 418
    lodging of the delegates, 424
    monarchy views, 282, 489
    Mount Vernon Conference,
        509, 511
    nation's capital, 234–235
    natural rights, 518
    negative on state laws, 847
    new states provision, 751–752,
        753
    number of speeches, 740
    oaths, 605
    opposition to vice presidency,
        600
    Pierce's character sketch, 543
    piracy punishment, 581
    power of the purse, 158
    president, number of, 604
    presidential qualifications, 606
    presidential selection, 607, 608,
        610, 611
    presidential term length and
        re-eligibility, 614, 615
    public opinion, 634
    publication of appropriations,
        160
    qualifications of voters for
        Congress, 139
    quorums, 160

    ratification, 650, 652, 653, 657,
        813
    references to Pennsylvania, 558
    relations with France, 290
    republican government,
        284–285, 670–671
    republicanism and citizen
        virtue, 672–673
    Revolutionary War, 675
    roll-call vote, 683
    secrecy, 692
    Senate qualifications, 162
    Senate selection, 171
    Senate size, 173
    separation of powers, 702
    signing of the Constitution, 719
    on slavery, 6, 8–9, 724, 726–727
    Society of the Cincinnati, 732
    standing armies, 29, 30
    state legislatures, 756
    suffrage, 767
    sumptuary legislation, 769, 770
    Swiss Cantons, 631, 777
    taxes on imports and exports,
        258, 781
    taxing exports, 94
    three-fifths clause, 786
    time and frequency of
        congressional meetings, 175
    treason provision, 790
    treaty-making and ratification,
        795, 796
    trial by jury, 394
    vice presidency, 600, 809
    Virginia Declaration of Rights,
        814
    Virginia Plan, 13–14
    war powers of Congress, 826
    Washington and, 830
    Western states admission, 699
Masons, **462–463**, 649, 681
Massachusetts, **463–466**
    allocation of House seats, 117
    committee members, 119
    Committee on Original
        Apportionment of Congress,
        113
    Gerry, Elbridge, 312–322
    Gorham, Nathaniel, 323–329
    King, Rufus, 398–405
    large-state coalition, 96
    Maine, 441

ratification controversy, 657
Senate representation, 165–166
Shays's Rebellion, 705–709
state appointment of delegates
to the Convention, 744
state constitution, 2–3, 467–468,
747, 748, 806
Strong, Caleb, 763–764
Massachusetts Body of Liberties,
466–467
Massachusetts Constitution of
1780, 2–3, **467–468**, 806
Massachusetts Ratifying
Convention, 329, 404, 512
Mayflower Compact, 185,
468–469, 630, 637, 855–856
McClurg, James, **469–471**
attendance, 40
education of, 240
guarantee clause, 336
lodging during the Convention,
424
number of speeches, 740
Pierce's character sketch, 543
president as Commander in
Chief, 596
presidential terms, 68
McCulloch v. Maryland, 3, 46, 107
(sidebar), 121, 129, 346, 443,
450, 592
McDonald, Forrest, 49, 541
McGillivray, Alexander, 310
McGinnis, John O., 771
McHenry, James, **471–474**
attainder, bills of, 39
attendance, 40
commerce power, 102
Committee on State Debts and
Militia, 115
congressional power to call
militia, 481
ex post facto laws, 254
judicial salaries, 387
Masons, 463
number of speeches, 740
Pierce's character sketch, 543
public opinion, 634
references to Montesquieu, 495
signing of the Constitution, 721
taxes on imports and exports,
781
McKean, Thomas, 138 (sidebar)

McKitrick, Eric, 675
Mead, Walter, 214
Media, 621–622
Meese, Edwin, 545
Meeting times, 248, 327, 401, **474**,
690, 715
Mercantile monopolies, 192–193
Mercantilism versus agriculture,
306
Mercer, John, **474–477**
aristocracy, 28, 283–284
attendance, 40
borrowing power, 65
Congress, qualifications for,
136, 137
congressional origination of
money bills, 155
Council of Revision, 196
education of, 240
emoluments clause, 150
guarantee clause, 336
limits of written documents, 186
location and permanence of
nation's capital, 236
Maryland delegates' unity over
ratification, 472
number of speeches, 740
piracy punishment, 581
post offices and post roads, 586
qualifications of voters for
Congress, 140
quorums, 160
references to France, 290
suffrage, 768
taxes on imports and exports,
257, 780
treaty-making and ratification,
795
Messenger. *See* Weaver, Nicholas
Mexico, 206
Michigan, 537
Middle states, 305–306
Mifflin, Thomas, **478–479**
attendance, 40
education of, 242
emoluments clause, 150
Pierce's character sketch, 543
religious affiliation, 668
secrecy, 694
Military
armies and navies, raising and
supporting, 30–32

Bill of Rights provision, 60
Brearly's service, 65
Canada as threat, 77–79
civilian control of, 828 (sidebar)
Committee on State Debts and
Militia, 115–116
defects of the U.S. political
system, 809–810
military service of the delegates,
216
New Jersey Plan provisions for
power over, 555
president as Commander in
Chief, 596–597
Revolutionary War, 675–677
Shays's Rebellion, 705–709
Society of the Cincinnati,
730–732
standing armies, 29–30
supremacy clause, 773–775
war powers of Congress,
825–826
Washington, George, 827
Military, congressional governance
of, **479–480**
Militia
Davie's command of North
Carolina's, 203
Dickinson's support for state
control, 230
enforcing law, 470–471
states' role in regulating, 230
Whig ideology, 833–834
See also Committee on State
Debts and Militia (August 18)
Militia, congressional power to
call, **480–482**
armies and navies, raising and
supporting, 30–32
congressional militia powers,
151–154
Ellsworth's objection to
congressional power over,
247–248
Gerry's objections to, 319–320
Gorham's support for, 326
King's defense of congressional
control, 401
Langdon's support of, 409
Martin's objection to
congressional control of, 447
Pinckney, Charles, 570–571

Militia, congressional power to call (*continued*)
  Pinckney Plan, 568
  Randolph's stance on training and arming, 645
  Sherman, Roger, 711
  Sherman on, 716
  standing armies, 29–30
Militia, congressional power to organize and govern, 348, **482–484**
Miller, Samuel, 98
Minimalist state, 624
Mississippi River, 373–374, 374–375, 439, **484–487**, 528. *See also* Navigation
Missouri Compromise, 441
Mrs. Dailey's Boarding House, 424, 425
Mrs. Marshall's Boarding House, 424
Mitchell, Broadus, 221
Mitchell, Louise Pearson, 221
Mixed government, **488**, 700
Mob rule, 27
Monarchy, **488–491**
  aristocracy and, 27
  delegates' criticism of, 282–283
  Federalists, 275
  Franklin's concerns over, 293
  mixed government, 488
  motives of the Founding Fathers, 506
Money, congressional coining, 233, **233, 409**, 476, **491–492**, 677–678, 678 (sidebar)
Money, state coining and emissions of, **492–493**
Money bills. *See* Congress, origination of money bills
Monroe, James, **493–495**
  death of, 98
  Madison and, 436
  ratification, 657, 813
  transfer of U.S. Constitution document, 514
Monroe Doctrine, 494
Montesquieu, Charles Louis de Secondat de, **495–496**
  court and country parties, 197
  foundings, 286–287
  Hume and, 357

Locke's philosophy, 423
Madison's argument on republics and democracies, 225
republican government, 274, 285, 671–672
republican governments over large land areas, 22
Montpelier, 427
Moral issues. *See* Slave importation; Slavery
Morgan, Edmund, 144
Morris, Gouverneur, **496–505**
  admiration for British system of government, 332
  age of, 11
  amending process, 14, 15
  appointments and confirmations, 24–26, 67, 330
  aristocracy, 27, 283
  armies and navies, raising and supporting, 32
  assessment of the delegates, 215
  attainder, bills of, 39
  attendance, 40
  authorship of the Constitution, 41
  bankruptcy, 47
  Biblical and religious references during the Convention, 54, 57
  bills of credit, 73
  borrowing power, 65
  census provision, 82
  chief justice provision, 85
  citizenship for senators, 163
  classes, 89
  classical allusions and influences, 91
  commerce power, 101–102, 102
  committees served on, 108, 109, 112–113, 113, 115, 116–117, 118, 119
  common law, 121
  concerns over allocation of power, 589–590
  Congress, compensation of members, 132
  Congress, qualifications for, 135–136, 137, 163
  Congress, terms, 174

congressional origination of money bills, 155, 156
congressional privileges, 159
congressional representation, 104
Congressional suffrage, 72
continuance of Congress provision, 133
contracts clause, 190
corporations provision, 193
corruption, 194
Council of Revision, 599
debtor's prison, 185 (sidebar)
education of, 241
emoluments clause, 150
ex post facto laws, 254
executive council proposal, 196–197
expulsion of congressional members, 134
factions and parties, 553–554
The Federalist, 270
general welfare clause, 302
guarantee clause, 335, 336
habeas corpus, 339
human nature, 355
impeachment clause, 360–361
Indians as savages, 364
judicial independence, 387–388
judicial review, 390, 392
judicial salaries, 387
leaders of Congress, 147
letter of transmittal, 414
on liberty and property, 418
location and permanence of nation's capital, 235, 236
lodging of the delegates, 425
Mississippi River navigation, 486–487
monarchy views, 283
national university, 516
natural rights, 518–519
negative on state laws, 522
new states provision, 751, 752, 753–754
New York delegation, 533
number of speeches, 740
Pierce's character sketch, 543
piracy punishment, 581–582
Polish election of the monarch, 584, 585
posterity and perpetuity, 588

Preamble to the Constitution, 595

president of the Convention, 616

presidential selection, 608, 610, 612, 619

presidential stability, 742

presidential term length and re-eligibility, 294, 614

presidential veto, 619–620

public opinion, 634

publication of appropriations, 160

qualifications of voters for Congress, 139

quorums, 160–161

ratification provision, 651, 652–653

reason and experience, 664

references to France, 290

references to Germany, 311–312

references to Pennsylvania, 558

religious tests, prohibition on, 669

on Rhode Island, 679, 745

role of fame in Convention, 262

secretary of the Convention, 371

sectionalism, 698

Senate representation, 167, 168

Senate selection, 170–171

Senate size, 173

signing of the Constitution, 719

slavery and slave importation, 6, 7–8, 205, 725, 726–727

suffrage, 767–768

sumptuary legislation, 769

taxes on imports and exports, 256, 257, 258, 779, 780–781

territory of the United States, 784

three-fifths clause, 786, 787

time and frequency of congressional meetings, 175

times, places, and manners of congressional election, 176

treason provision, 791, 792

Treasury secretary, 793

treaty-making and ratification, 795, 796

vice presidency, 808–809

Virginia Plan, 817

virtue, 821

Washington, George, 830

"We the People," 832

Western states admission, 364, 698–699

Morris, Richard, 199

Morris, Robert, **505–506**

assessment of the delegates, 214

attendance, 40

lodging during the Convention, 424, 425

Morris (Gouverneur) and, 505–506

number of speeches, 741

Pierce's character sketch, 543

president of the Convention, 683

relations with France, 290

signing Declaration of Independence and the Constitution, 209

Washington and, 828

Wilson and, 841

Morris, Thomas, 782

Motives of the Founding Fathers, xliii–xliv, 261–262, 394–395, **506–509**

Mount Vernon Conference, xli–xlii, 378, 452, **509–511**, 827, 922

Music, **511–512**

National Archives, **513–514**

National Constitution Center, **515–516**, 561, 564, 832

National government. *See* Federalism; Unitary government

National identity, 676

National Treasure (film), 462

National University, **516–517**

Nationalism

Carroll, Daniel, 81

Hamilton, Alexander, 340

Ingersoll's views on, 366–367

Marshall, John, 442

Morris, Gouverneur, 496–505

unitary government, 799–800

"We the People," 832

Wilson on, 847

See also Antifederalists; Hamilton Plan

Native Americans. *See* Indians

Natural rights, 208–209, **517–520**

Naturalization, **520**

Navies, 30–32, 479 (sidebar)

Navigation

duties for erecting lighthouses and clearing harbors, 473

Ellsworth's support of supermajority requirement, 248

Fitzsimon's views on, 278

general welfare clause affecting, 302

Langdon's views on taxation of, 409–410

Maryland delegates' proposal on duties, 379

Mason, George, 456

Mississippi River, 373, 484–487

Morris's views on taxation of, 501

Mount Vernon Conference addressing customs and duties along the rivers, 509–511

piracy, 581–582

requiring two-thirds majority, 472

Sherman on, 711, 714

Spaight on, 738

Virginia's rights, 812

Nebraska legislature, 126

Necessary and proper clause. *See* Powers, implied

Negative on state laws, **521–524**

Dickinson's support for, 230

Ellsworth's opposition to, 248

judicial review debates, 390

Langdon's views on, 409

Morris's objection to, 501

Pinckney's proposal for, 68

Rutledge's views on, 688

state governors and legislatures and, 331

Nelson, Michael, 809

Nelson, Thomas Jr., 812

Nem. Con., **524**

Nemine contradicente, 524

Netherlands. *See* Holland

New Deal era, 70, 183–184

New England, Dominion of, 237–238

New England, United colonies of, 800–810

New England Confederation, **524–525**

New Hampshire, **525–527**
  apportionment of House seats, 117, 686
  Brearly's encouragement to summon delegates from, 66
  coalitions, 96
  committee members, 119
  Committee on Original Apportionment of Congress, 113
  expenses of delegates, 256
  Gilman, Nicholas, 322–323
  Langdon, John, 408–410
  lowering representation, 836
  ratification of the Constitution, 655, 657
  state appointment of delegates to the Convention, 744
  state constitution, 746

New Jersey, **527–529**
  allocation of House seats, 117
  Clark, Abraham, 529 (sidebar)
  College of New Jersey, 239
  Committee on Original Apportionment of Congress, 113
  congressional representation, 104
  Dayton, Jonathan, 204–206
  expenses of delegates, 256
  Houston, William Churchill, 353–354
  interstate taxation, 779
  lighthouse tax, 103
  Livingston, William, 421–422
  Paterson, William, 553–557
  ratification of the Constitution, 656
  state appointment of delegates to the Convention, 744
  state constitution, 747
  women voters in New Jersey, 765 (sidebar)

New Jersey Plan
  admission and creation of new states, 750–751
  amending process, 13–15
  armies and navies, raising and supporting, 31

artistic depictions of the Convention, 38
  bicameralism, 125
  chief justice, 84–85
  coalitions, 95
  collective powers of Congress, 127
  commerce power, 101
  Committee of the Whole, 111, 118
  congressional power of the purse, 157–158
  congressional power to call militia, 481
  Connecticut Compromise, 181
  continuance of Congress, 133
  corporations, 192–194
  Dayton's support of equal representation, 204–205
  debt to France, 289
  Dickinson Plan and, 227, 234
  extradition provision, 259
  Hamilton Plan principles and, 348
  Hamilton's criticism of, 342–343
  history and goals of, xlvii–xlviii
  impeachment clause, 360
  judicial jurisdiction, 384
  judicial review, 390
  Lansing's support of, 410–411
  legislative branch provisions, 803–804
  Mason's support of the Virginia Plan, 454
  negative on state laws, 522
  objectives of, 528
  plans of government introduced at the Convention, 583
  post offices and post roads, 586
  power, 589
  president as Commander in Chief, 596
  presidential compensation, 597
  presidential selection, 608
  purpose of, 802
  ratification provision, 650
  recall of congressional members, 161
  rejection by Committee of the Whole, 110

removal of state governors, 331
  Senate representation, 165
  Senate selection, 171
  separation of powers, 701
  social contract, 728–729
  sovereignty, 380
  state legislatures, 756–757
  supremacy clause, 773–774
  Supreme Court, 775–776
  taxes on imports and exports, 779
  text, 891–894
  three-fifths clause, 785
  treaty-making and ratification, 795
  Virginia Plan and, 643–644
  war powers of Congress, 825
  Wilson's summary of, 843–844

New states. *See* States, admission and creation

New York, **532–535**
  allocation of House seats, 117
  coalitions, 95
  committee members, 119
  Committee on Original Apportionment of Congress, 113
  Connecticut's ratification of the Constitution, 179
  Jay, John, 373–374
  King's political career in, 404–405
  Lansing, John, 410–412
  lighthouse tax, 103
  nation's capital, 235 (sidebar)
  New Jersey and, 527
  ratification controversy, 657
  state appointment of delegates to the Convention, 744
  voting at the Convention, 823
  Yates, Robert, 853–854

New York Journal, 854

Newspapers, 559, 621–622

Newton, Isaac, 84

Nineteenth Amendment, 86, 140, 210, 765 (sidebar), 850 (sidebar)

Ninth Amendment, 61, 805

Nixon, Richard, 362

Nobility, titles of, 789

Noninterpretivists, 545–546

Norman, John, 38
Normandy Liberty Bell, 420
North Carolina, **535–536**
  Blount, William, 63–64
  Committee on Original
    Apportionment of Congress,
    113
  Davie, William Richardson,
    202–203
  Martin, Alexander, 443–444
  ratification of the Constitution,
    657–658
  small-state coalition, 96
  Spaight, Richard Dobbs,
    737–738
  state constitution, 747
  Tennessee, 783
  Williamson, Hugh, 834–840
North-South conflict
  commerce regulations, 837
  Committee on Slave Trade and
    Navigation, 115
  congressional commerce power,
    101–103
  controversy over Spain, 739–740
  divisions within the
    Convention, li–lii
  factions and parties, 553
  fugitive slave clause, 299
  Jay-Gardoqui negotiations,
    374–375
  Morris's objections to slave
    representation, 499–500
  proportional and equal
    representation, 202
  sectionalism, 698
  taxes on imports and exports,
    94, 258, 780–782
  three-fifths clause, 784–788
  See also Slave importation;
    Slavery
Northern states, 6–7
Northwest Ordinance of 1787, 35,
  190, 375, 517, **536–538**, 784
Notes on the State of Virginia
  (Madison), 16 (sidebar), 182,
  251
Novels, 655 (sidebar)

Oaths of Office, 14, 328, 445,
  539–541, 605, 669–670, 847

*Observations on the Importance of the
  American Revolution, and the
  means of making It a Benefit to
  the World* (Price), 625
Occupations of the delegates, 218,
  309, **541–542**
Ogden v. Saunders, 47
Ohio, 537
Ohio Company, 538
Oligarchy, 27
Oratory and rhetoric, **542–545**
  Henry, Patrick, 350–351
  Martin, Luther, 445, 446
  rhetoric of conciliation, 124
Ordinance of 1784, 375
Original intent, **545–547**
Originalists, 545
Otis, Harrison Gray, 574 (sidebar)
Otto, Louis Guillaume, 289
Owings v. Speed, 654–655

Paca, William, 452
Paine, Thomas, 208, 303, **549–550**,
  814
Paintings, 37–38
Palladio, Andrea, 560
The Papers of James Madison
  (Madison), 666
Parades, 98
Pardon power, 646, 703, 792
Paris, Treaty of, 2, 35, 199–200,
  373, **550**, 812
Parsons, Theophilus, 631
Parties, factions, and interests,
  551–553
  classes, 86–90
  coalitions, 95–96
  compromise, 123–124
  justice as a counter of special
    interests, 394–395
Partitioning the states, 686
Pass, John, 420
Patents. *See* Copyrights and patents
Paterson, William, **553–557**
  appointments and
    confirmations, 24
  attendance, 40
  commerce power, 101
  Committee of the Whole, 111
  congressional representation,
    104

Connecticut Compromise,
  180–181
education of, 239
on experience, 663
Galloway Plan and, 301
House, representation in, 66,
  140–141
Masons, 463
naturalization, 520
New Jersey Plan, 14, 816,
  891–894
number of speeches, 740
Pierce's character sketch,
  543–544
Polish election of the monarch,
  585
presidential selection, 619
public opinion, 635
ratification provision, 650
secrecy, 68, 693
Senate representation, 165, 168,
  169
on slavery, 4, 6
three-fifths clause, 785
on Vermont, 807
See also New Jersey Plan
Paterson Plan. *See* New Jersey Plan
Paulsen, Michael Stokes, 545, 547
Peace treaties, 73
Pen names, 271 (sidebar)
Pendleton, Nathaniel, 309
Pendleton Act (1883), 70
Penn, William, 12, 54, 212, 557,
  563
Pennsylvania, **557–559**
  Clymer, George, 93–95
  commemorative exposition, 98
  Committee on Original
    Apportionment of Congress,
    113
  Delaware's ratification of the
    Constitution, 213
  dueling provision, 746 (sidebar)
  expenses of delegates, 256
  Fitzsimons, Thomas, 277–279
  Franklin, Benjamin, 290–297
  Ingersoll, Jared, 365–368
  land dispute with Connecticut,
    407
  large-state coalition, 96
  Mifflin, Thomas, 478–479

Pennsylvania (*continued*)
   Morris, Gouverneur, 496–505
   Morris, Robert, 505–506
   New Jersey and, 527
   presidential selection by popular
      vote, 608
   ratification of the Constitution,
      656
   state constitution, 747, 848
   voting at the Convention, 823
   Wilson, James, 840–848
Pennsylvania Gazette, 298
Pennsylvania Herald, 491, 621,
   622
*Pennsylvania Packet and Daily
   Advertiser*, 210, 238, **559**
Pennsylvania Society for the
   Abolition of Slavery, 5, 9
   (sidebar)
Pennsylvania State House
   (Independence Hall),
   559–562
   artistic depictions of the
      Convention, 37
   Liberty Bell, 54, 419–420
   rising sun chair, 681–682
   Syng inkstand, 778
   Weaver, Nicholas, 833
Pennsylvania v. Nelson, 792
Perot, Ross, 440
Perpetuity. *See* Posterity and
   perpetuity
Person, Thomas, 535
Phantom Amendment, 789
Phelps, Glenn, 829
Philadelphia, **563–565**
   Franklin, Benjamin, 291
   geographical advantage for
      Convention location, 305
   lodging of the delegates, 424
   musical performances, 511
   National Constitution Center,
      515
   nation's capital, 235 (sidebar)
   Pennsylvania State House, 560
Phillips, Jonas, 669
Philosophers
   Hume, David, 356–357
   Locke, John, 423
   Montesquieu, Charles Louis de
      Secondat de, 495–496
   Price, Richard, 622–623

Philosophy and ideology
   coalitions, 95–96
   court and country parties,
      197–198, 198
   liberalism, 415–416
   motives of the Founding
      Fathers, 506–508
   Puritanism, 637
   Scottish Enlightenment,
      691–692
   social contract, 728–730
   virtue, 820–822
   Whigs, 833–834
Pickering, Timothy, 108
Pierce, William, **565–566**
   assessment of the delegates, 214
   attendance, 40
   character sketches of the
      delegates, 542–544, 666
   Congress, selection of, 143
   Congress, terms, 174
   education of, 240
   House, representation in, 141
   lodging of the delegates, 424
   number of speeches, 740
   secrecy, 694–695
   Washington and, 828–829
Pinckney, Charles, **566–575**
   admiration for British system
      of government, 332
   age of, 11
   amending process, 17
   appointments and
      confirmations, 24, 25, 26
   aristocracy, 27, 28
   armies and navies, raising and
      supporting, 32
   assessment of the delegates,
      215
   attendance, 40
   bankruptcy, 47
   Biblical and religious references
      during the Convention, 57
   Bill of Rights discussion, 58, 59
   census provision, 82
   chief justice provision, 85
   classes, 88, 90
   classical allusions and
      influences, 91, 92–93
   collective powers of Congress,
      127
   commerce power, 103

   committees served on, 107–108,
      113, 114, 683
   Congress, qualifications for,
      136, 137
   Congress, selection of, 142
   congressional commerce power,
      101
   congressional origination of
      money bills, 155
   congressional power to organize
      and govern militia, 482
   congressional powers, 688
   congressional privileges, 159
   Connecticut Compromise, 181
   corporations provision, 193
   Council of Revision, 196, 599
   education of, 240
   emoluments clause, 150
   executive council proposal,
      196–197
   extradition provision, 259
   factions and parties, 553
   fugitive slave clause, 299
   full faith and credit clause, 300
   guarantee clause, 336
   habeas corpus, 339
   impeachment clause, 360
   invalidating state legislation, 68
   judicial review, 392
   leaders of Congress, 147
   location of nation's capital, 235
   monarchy views, 282, 489
   money bills, 155, 734
   negative on state laws, 521, 522
   on New Jersey Plan, 528
   Pierce's character sketch, 544
   Polish election of the monarch,
      585
   president as Commander in
      Chief, 596
   presidential qualifications, 606
   presidential selection, 608,
      611–612
   presidential term length and re-
      eligibility, 614, 615
   presidential veto, 618, 619
   publication of appropriations,
      160
   ratification, 650, 652, 653
   references to Germany, 311
   religious tests, prohibition on,
      669

secrecy, 695

sectionalism, 698

Senate, qualifications for, 163

Senate representation, 165, 167, 168

Senate selection, 170–171

Senate size, 172–173

slavery and slave importation, 9, 724

standing armies, 29

three-fifths clause, 785, 787

time and frequency of congressional meetings, 175

times, places, and manners of congressional election, 176

titles of nobility, 789

trial by jury, 394

Virginia Plan, 13

war powers of Congress, 825–826

Pinckney, Charles Cotesworth, **575–580**

age of, 11

attendance, 40

Biblical and religious references during the Convention, 55

committees served on, 105, 115

Congress, compensation of members, 131

Congress, selection of, 143

Congress, terms, 174

congressional commerce power, 101

congressional militia powers, 151–152, 153, 482, 483

congressional representation, 104

education of, 240, 242

emoluments clause, 149, 150

judicial salaries, 387

Madison's defeat of, 436

money bills, 155, 734

number of speeches, 740

Pierce's character sketch, 544

privileges and immunities, 625

Senate qualifications, 162

Senate representation, 167

slavery and slave importation, 9, 723

taxes on imports and exports, 256, 779–780

three-fifths clause, 786

Treasury secretary, 793

trial by jury, 394

wife of, 217 (sidebar)

Pinckney, Elizabeth Lucas, 576 (sidebar)

Pinckney, Thomas, 735

Pinckney Plan, 567–568

armies and navies, raising and supporting, 31

Committee of Detail, 106

congressional coining of money, 492

New York constitution, 533

plans of government introduced at the Convention, 582

privileges and immunities, 624–625

Piracies, punishing, 384, **581–582**

Plans of government introduced at the Convention, **582–583**

Plato, 93

Pledge of Allegiance, 285, 394, 417

Plural executive. *See* President, number of

Pocahontas, 424

Poetry, 512

Poland, 312, **583–585**

Political and Commercial Register, 372

Political experience of the delegates, 216

Poll tax, 769, 805

Polling, 633

Pollock v. Farmers' Loan & Trust Co., 158

Polybius, 93, **585–586**

Population of the United States, **586**

Post offices and post roads, 192, 315, 476, **586–587**

Postage stamps, 37, 99, 129, 586–587. *See also* Post offices and post roads

Posterity and perpetuity, 261, 325, **587–588**

Potomac River, 509–511

Powell, Adam Clayton, 134

Powell v. McCormack, 134, 138

Power, **588–591**

Antifederalist view of, 21–22

Articles of Confederation, 34, 35

Blount's attempts to grab, 63–64

borrowing power, 64–65

Committee of Detail, 107–108

Dickinson Plan, 231

forms of government, 281

Hamilton Plan principles, 348

judicial review, 388–393

presidential power, 602–603

property rights, 628

Puritan influence on limiting, 637

Rutledge on congressional limits, 688

unitary government, 799–800

vice presidency, 808

Whig ideology, 833–834

Williamson on congressional limits, 837

See also Congress, collective powers; President, executive power; Presidential veto

Power, presidential. *See* President, executive power; Presidential veto

The Power of Sympathy (Brown), 655 (sidebar)

Powers, implied, **591–592**

corporations provision, 192

Marshall's interpretation of the Constitution, 107 (sidebar)

McHenry's concerns over, 473

Prayer at the Convention, 141, **592–594**

Franklin's proposal, 294–295

Hamilton's objection to, 346

Randolph's proposed alternative to, 647

Sherman's support of daily prayer, 716

Washington, George, 830

Williamson on, 840

Preamble, **594–595**

Committee of Detail, 106

Committee of Style and Arrangement, 109

general welfare clause, 302

inscription at National Constitution Center, 515

Morris's authorship of, 496

United States name, 801

Virginia Declaration of Rights and, 815

See also "We the People"

Preface to Debates in the Convention, 883–889
Presbyterians, 564 (sidebar), 630–631, 668
Presentment clause. *See* Presidential veto
Presidency
    Articles of the Constitution on powers and structure, 803–804
    executive council proposal, 196–197
    Jefferson's election to, 377
    Madison's views on, 433–434
    Morris's views on, 501–502
    Pinckney, Charles, 572
    presidential power, 602–603
    Randolph's views on powers and structure, 646
    Spaight's views on powers and structure, 738
    stability through curbing power, 742
    Strong's views, 764
    Virginia Plan provisions for powers and structure, 818–819
    See also Presidential veto
President, cabinet. *See* President, council
President, Commander in Chief, **596–597**
President, compensation, 282, 292–293, 293, 345, **597–598**
President, council, 69, 317, **598–601**, 600–601, 793–794
President, disability, 228, 231, 433, **601**, 757
President, executive power, **601–603**
    Articles of the Constitution, 803–804
    bureaucracy and, 69
    Committee of Detail, 107
    The Federalist view of, 273
    judicial review balancing, 388–393
    Mason's suspicion of executive powers, 457
    Mercer's fear of aristocracy, 476–477
    Morris' support of, 502
    pardon power, 792

presidential veto, 617–620
    separation of powers, 700–704
    Sherman's supporting limits, 716
    state coalitions, 96
    treaty-making and ratification, 794–796
    Washington's influence on, 829–830
    Williamson's support of tripartite executive and Council of Revision, 839
    Wilson's role in construction of the presidency, 845–846
President, inauguration. *See* President, oath
President, number of, **603–604**
    Dickinson Plan for tripartite executive, 229, 231, 233, 234, 583
    Gerry's objections to tripartite executive, 317
    Mason's objections to unitary executive, 457
    McClurg, James, 470
    plural executive, 306–307
    plural executive as alternative to sectionalism, 697
    Rutledge's single executive with no power of war and peace, 689
    single executive, 74
    tripartite executive, 457, 838
    unitary presidency, 603–604
President, oath of office, **605**
President, qualifications, 114, 570, **605–607**
President, selection, 607, **607–614**
    Brearly's support of a joint ballot, 66
    Carroll, Daniel, 81
    congressional oversight, 568
    Dickinson Plan, 231
    Ellsworth's views, 248–249
    Gerry's plan for selection by state governors, 317
    Gorham's views on joint ballot proposal, 325–326, 327
    Langon's support of a joint ballot, 410
    Madison's belief in popular election, 430–431

Madison's references to Germany and Poland, 312
Madison's support of, 434
Mason, George, 456–457
Morris's support of popular election, 501–502
Pinckney, Charles, 572
Pinckney, Charles Cotesworth, 576
Polish election of the monarch, 583–585
public opinion, 635–636
Randolph's stance on, 646
Read's tiebreaker proposal, 661–662
reason and experience, 664
Rutledge's proposal of congressional selection, 689
separation of powers, 702
Sherman on, 715–716
Spaight's views, 738
state governors, 329–330
supermajority requirement, 771
Wilson on, 845–846
See also Electoral College
President, term, length, and re-eligibility, **614–615**
    amendments affecting, 805
    Articles of the Constitution, 803–804
    Broom's support of shorter terms and reelection, 68
    Butler's concern over too-frequent elections, 74
    Davie, William Richardson, 203
    Dickinson Plan's rotation system, 234
    Franklin's one-term support, 294
    Gerry's proposal of 15 years, 318
    Jefferson's concerns over, 376
    King's concern over short terms, 402
    life terms, 348, 583, 716
    Martin, Luther, 448
    Mason, George, 456–457
    McClurg on "good behavior," 470
    mixed government, 488
    Morris on, 502
    Pinckney, Charles, 572

Pinckney (General) on "good behavior," 577
presidential council proposal, 599
presidential selection and, 607–613
term limits, 52
Virginia Plan, 818, 819
Washington's decision, 831
Wilson's role in construction of, 845–846
President, title, **615–616**
President of the Convention, 505, **616–617**, 683, 827–831
Presidential veto, **617–621**
  appointments and confirmations, 25
  Carroll, Daniel, 80
  Council of Revision, 195–197
  Franklin's argument against, 293–294
  Gerry's disfavoring a supermajority, 316–317
  Hamilton's support of, 345
  Indians used as argument against, 364
  judicial review and, 389–390
  King's support of absolute veto, 401–402
  Morris's support of, 503
  Pinckney, Charles, 571–572
  Randolph's proposed revision, 646
  Read's support of, 661
  religious influence, 629
  Williamson on, 839
  Wilson on, 845–846
Press, freedom of. *See* Bill of Rights
Press coverage, **621–622**
Price, Richard, 197–198, **622–623**, 625
Priestley, Joseph, 197–198, **623–624**
Primogeniture, 121
Princeton University, 239–240
Printers. *See* Dunlap and Claypoole; *Pennsylvania Packet and Daily Advertiser*
Prisoners. *See* Habeas corpus
Prisoners, a constitution for, 185 (sidebar)

Privileges and immunities clause, **624–625**
Privy Council, 85, 108, 147, 196, 212, 599–600, 809. *See also* President, Council
Probable cause provision, 60
Proclamation Line of 1763, 306
Progress, **625–627**
Progressive Movement, 49, 199
Project '87, 100
Property
  citizen virtue, 822
  classes and, 88
  Congress, qualifications for, 135–136
  contracts clause protecting private property, 191
  copyrights and patents provision, 191–192
  fugitive slave clause, 299
  Gerry's opposition to congressional qualification, 313
  King's objection to congressional qualification, 400
  liberalism, 416
  versus liberty, 418
  Mason's views on, 455
  Morris's desire for a wealthy House, 498
  Morris's desire for an aristocratic Senate, 497
  Pinckney's views on, 570
  qualifications for Senate members, 162–164
  representation by, 71–72, 74–75
  slaves as, 6–8
  suffrage based on property ownership, 608
  See also Wealth, representation by
Property rights, **627–629**
Proportional representation
  Brearly's support for, 66
  Butler's stance, 71
  equal versus proportional representation in the Senate, 166
  Franklin's support of, 291–293
  House, representation in, 140–142

Johnson's support of, 380–381
Madison's belief in, 66, 430–431
North-South conflict, 202
Northwest Ordinance provisions, 537
Senate, 164–169, 170
See also Congress, House of Representatives, representation in; Congress, Senate, representation in; Connecticut Compromise; Equal representation
Protestantism, 416, **629–632**, 637, 668
Public administration. *See* Bureaucracy; President, executive power
Public good, 395
Public opinion, **633–637**
Publius, 21, 270, 271 (sidebar). *See also The Federalist*
Puritanism, 630–631, **637–638**
Purse, power of the. *See* Congress, power of the purse

Quakers, 594, 629, 668, 765 (sidebar)
Qualifications. *See* Congress, House of Representatives, qualifications of members; Congress, Senate, qualifications; President, qualifications
Quartering of troops, 60
Quorums, 160–161, 316, 401, 475, **639**, 683

Rakove, Jack, 413
Randolph, Edmund, **641–649**
  age of, 11
  amending process, 14, 17
  Antifederalism, 21
  appointments and confirmations, 25
  aristocracy, 28, 283
  assessment of the delegates, 215
  attendance, 40
  Biblical and religious references during the Convention, 55
  bicameralism, 125
  borrowing power, 65
  census provision, 82

Randolph, Edmund (*continued*)
  collective powers of Congress, 127
  committees served on, 106, 109, 112, 113, 119
  Congress, compensation of members, 131
  Congress, qualifications of members, 136, 163
  Congress, representation in, 104, 167, 169
  Congress, terms, 146, 174
  congressional origination of money bills, 155–156, 156
  continuance of Congress, 133–134
  criticism of democracy, 223–224
  debts, 207
  democracy, 284
  education of, 240
  expenses of delegates, 256
  federalism and the Virginia Plan, 264–265
  full faith and credit clause, 300
  guarantee clause, 336
  impeachment clause, 360
  judicial organization, 387
  liberty, 417
  lodging during the Convention, 424
  Mount Vernon Conference, 509, 511
  natural rights, 519
  new states provision, 751
  number of speeches, 740
  oaths, 539
  Pierce's character sketch, 544
  prayer at the Convention, 594
  Preamble to the Constitution, 595
  presidential selection, term length and re-eligibility, 329, 607–608, 612, 614
  public opinion, 634, 635
  quorums, 161
  ratification, 652, 653, 657, 813
  reconsideration of representation, 836
  references to Montesquieu, 495
  republican government, 284
  secrecy, 693
  separation of powers, 73, 703
  Shays's Rebellion, 708
  signing of the Constitution, 719, 720
  on slavery, 5
  standing armies, 30
  state coining of money, 492
  state governors filling senatorial vacancies, 330
  territory of the United States, 784
  three-fifths clause, 786–787
  time and frequency of congressional meetings, 175–176
  treason provision, 790, 792
  unitary executive, 603–604
  vice presidency, 809
  Virginia Plan, 13, 802, 816–817
  See also Virginia Plan
Randolph Plan. *See* Virginia Plan
Rappaport, Michael B., 771
Ratification
  Articles of Confederation, 810
  Articles of the Constitution, 804
  convention mechanism, 182
  Franklin, Benjamin, 295–296
  Pierce's commitment to, 566
  resolution accompanying the Constitution, 674
  Rutledge's stance on, 690
  sectionalism, 699
  Spaight's support of, 738
  states legislatures, 758
  supermajority requirement, 771
  Washington, George, 830
Ratification, Convention debates, and constitutional provision, lvii–lviii, **649–655**
  concerns over aristocracy, 28–29
  federalism, 266–267
  forms of government, 285–286
  Gorham's support for state conventions, 328
  Hamilton's concerns over, 346
  Henry, Patrick, 350
  human nature and, 355–356
  Johnson's views on, 381–382
  King's advocacy of state conventions, 404
  Lansing and Yates opposing, 412
  Madison's insistence on ratification, 435–436
  Martin's objections to, 449–450
  Mason's objections to ratification, 461
  Mercer's attempt to block Maryland's ratification, 477
  Morris's objection to ratification, 504
  natural rights, 519
  role of foreign affairs, 280
  Randolph's stance on, 647–648
Ratification in the states, **655–659**
  Butler's support for, 75
  Committee of Detail, 652
  Connecticut, 179–180
  Delaware, 213
  Dickinson Plan, 232
  Ellsworth, Oliver, 249–250
  Federal Processions, 98
  geographical issues affecting, 307
  Georgia, 310
  influence of *The Federalist* on, 273
  majority provision, 94–95
  Marshall, John, 442
  Maryland, 81–82, 451–452
  Massachusetts, 465–466
  McHenry's concerns over, 472
  New Hampshire, 525–526
  New Jersey, 528–529
  New York, 533–534
  North Carolina, 444, 535–536
  original intent, 546
  Pennsylvania, 558
  public opinion, 635–636
  Rhode Island's tardiness in ratifying, 677–678, 678 (sidebar)
  South Carolina, 734–735
  Virginia, 813
  Williamson on, 840
  Wilson on, 848
Rawle, W., 421
Read, George, **659–662**
  abolishing state legislatures, 74–75
  attendance, 40

Biblical and religious references during the Convention, 54–55, 56
borrowing power, 65
committees served on, 111, 117
Congress, qualifications of members, 136
Congress, selection of members, 143, 171
Congress, terms, 174
congressional power to organize and govern militia, 153, 482
House, size of, 144
lodging during the Convention, 424
number of speeches, 740
Pierce's character sketch, 544
signing Declaration of Independence and the Constitution, 209, 232, 721
Reagan, Ronald, 26, 545
Reapportionment of Congress, 645
Reason and experience, 262, 377, **662–665**
Recall, 161
Records of the Constitutional Convention, **665–667**
determining original intent, 545–546
inadequacy of, 372
Pierce's character sketches of delegates, 542–544, 565–566
The Records of the Federal Convention of 1787 (Farrand), 263, 666–667
Reed, Philip, 789
Re-eligibility. *See* President, term, length, and re-eligibility
Regionalism, 305–306, 697–699
Regulator Movement, 444
Rehnquist, William, 748
Reinagle, Alexander, 511, 512
Religion
Biblical and religious references at the Convention, 54–57
contracts, compact, and covenants, 185–186
Franklin's proposal of daily prayer, 294–295
Hamilton, Alexander, 345–346
Jefferson's support of religious freedom, 375

Masons, 462–463
Mason's favoring three executives, 604
Northwest Ordinance provisions, 537
Protestantism, 629–631
Puritanism, 637
religious freedom, 630
Sherman on, 715
See also Prayer at the Convention
Religious affiliations of the delegates, 218, **667–668**
Religious references at the Constitutional Convention. *See* Biblical and religious references at the Constitutional Convention
Religious tests, prohibition on, 539–541, 571, 605, 629, **669–670**
Rendition clause. *See* Fugitive Slave clause
Report of Proceedings in Congress; February 21, 1787, 880–881
Representation, 334
African American slaves, 4–10
Albany Plan of Union, 12
Committee on Original Apportionment of Congress, 112–113
Committee to Reconsider Representation in the House, 116–117
Connecticut's role in convention debates, 180
Gorham's plea for compromise on, 324–325
Indians, 364
replacing the Articles of Confederation, 35–36
role of wealth in, 628
Senate, 164–169
small states' rights in Senate representation, 43–44
taxation linked to, 779
Washington on, 829
Western states, 845
See also Congress, House of Representatives, representation in; Congress,

Senate, representation in; Equal representation; Proportional representation; Three-fifths clause; Virginia Plan
Republic, 284–285, 344, **670–672**
Republicanism, **672–673**
Antifederalists and, 22
armies and navies, raising and supporting, 31
corruption, 194
court and country parties, 197–198
equality, 252
Madison's supporting an extended democratic republic, 435
mercantilism versus agriculture, 306
mixed government, 488
Montesquieu's views on, 495
Pennsylvania's government, 557
standing armies, 29–30
Swiss Cantons, 777–778
virtue, 821
Whig ideology, 833–834
women's suffrage, 765 (sidebar)
Reserved powers of the states. *See* States, police powers
Residency requirements for congressional members
citizenship and residency requirements for Senate members, 163–164
Ellsworth's views on, 247
Hamilton's views on, 341
Madison's views on, 432
residency and inhabitancy requirements for House members, 136, 138 (sidebar)
Rutledge's concerns about immigrants, 687
Williamson on, 836–837
Resolution accompanying the Constitution, **674**
Resolution from Annapolis Convention: September 14, 1786, 878–880
Resolution of Federal Convention to Continental Congress, 899–900
Restraint, attendance under, 659

Revolutionary War, **675–677**
  British supporters, 197–198
  critical period, 199–200
  Davie, William Richardson, 202
  French participation, 289
  Hamilton's activism, 340
  hiding of the Liberty Bell, 420
  Ingersoll's views on potential
    success of new government,
    367
  Jackson's service, 371
  McHenry, James, 471
  Pinckney's service to, 567
  rewriting state constitutions,
    182, 186
  Treaty of Paris, 2, 35, 199–200,
    373, 550, 812
Rhetoric. *See* Oratory and rhetoric
Rhode Island, **677–681**
  committee members, 119
  Committee on Original
    Apportionment of Congress,
    113
  Connecticut's ratification of the
    Constitution, 179
  failure to respond to the call,
    744–745
  ratification of the Constitution,
    658
  state constitution, 747
  Williamson on representaion,
    834
Rights
  British system of government,
    333–334
  individual rights, 403, 624–625,
    790–791
  natural rights, 517–519
  property rights, 627–629
  states bills of rights, 59, 810
  See also Bill of Rights
Riker, William, 351–352
Riots, 707 (sidebar)
Rising sun, 296, 627, **681**
Rising sun chair, 296–297, 463,
    561, **681–682**
Roberts, Owen, 371
Robinson, Paul, 722–723
Roche, John, 507, 613
Rogue Island, 678 (sidebar), 745
Rohr, John, 70
Roll-call vote, 327, 398, 453, 683

Rome. *See* Classical allusions and
    influences
Roosevelt, Franklin D., 99, 615,
    776
Rossiter, Clinton, 221
Rotten boroughs, 138 (sidebar),
    194, 333, 412
Rousseau, Jean-Jacques, 728
Rule of law. *See* Constitutionalism
Rules of the Constitutional
    Convention, **682–685**
  Committee on Rules, 114
  Mason's objection to roll call
    voting, 453
  reason and experience, 663
Rural populations, 306
Rush, Benjamin, 516, 624
Rutledge, John, **685–690**
  amending process, 15
  appointments and
    confirmations, 24
  attendance, 40
  Biblical and religious references
    during the Convention, 55
  chief justice provision, 85
  collective powers of Congress,
    127
  commerce power, 102
  committees served on, 106,
    107–108, 112, 113, 117, 118,
    119
  Congress, compensation, 130
  Congress, qualifications for,
    136, 137, 164
  Congress, selection of, 72, 142,
    143
  Congress, terms, 145
  congressional origination of
    money bills, 156
  congressional representation,
    104
  Council of Revision, 196, 599
  education of, 240
  emoluments clause, 149
  ex post facto laws, 254
  full faith and credit clause, 300
  guarantee clause, 336
  habeas corpus, 339
  House, size of, 144
  impeachment clause, 361
  judicial independence, 388
  judicial organization, 386

  judicial review, 391
  on Kentucky's statehood, 397
  land disputes, 407
  letter of transmittal, 415
  on liberty and property, 418
  lodging of the delegates, 425
  money bills, 734
  negative on state laws, 522
  new states provision, 754, 755
  number of speeches, 740
  presidential qualifications, 606
  presidential selection, 607, 611
  presidential veto, 619–620
  presidents, number of, 603
  property rights, 627
  proportional representation, 71
  qualifications of voters for
    Congress, 140
  ratification process, 653
  Senate representation, 169
  slave importation, 724
  suffrage, 768–769
  supremacy clause, 774
  Tennessee statehood, 783
  times, places, and manners of
    congressional election, 176
  Treasury secretary, 793
  treaty-making and ratification,
    796
  Vermont, 807

Salaries
  Fry, Joseph, 298
  judicial, 386, 387
  Shallus, Jacob, 704
  Weaver, Nicholas, 833
  See also Congress, compensation
    of members; President,
    compensation
Salutary neglect policy, 303
Sanctions, 680, 810
Scott v. Sandford, 10, 86
Scottish Enlightenment, **691–692**
  court and country parties, 197
  Hume, David, 356–357
  liberalism and, 416
  Montesquieu, Charles Louis de
    Secondat de, 495–496
  motives of the Founding
    Fathers, 508
  progress concept, 625–627
Searches and seizures, 60

Secession, threats of, 307, 447–448
Second Amendment, 30, 60, 805
Second Continental Congress
  Adams, John, 32
  Articles of Confederation, 33
  Declaration of Independence, 208
  Dickinson, John, 226
  Jefferson, Thomas, 375
  Rutledge, John, 685
  state constitutions, 746
Secrecy, **692–696**
  Butler's mandatory attendance and secrecy proposal, 71
  creation of secrecy rule, 684
  destruction of the Journals of the Convention, 398–399
  Dunlap and Claypoole's abiding by, 238
  Franklin's anecdote breaching, 297 (sidebar)
  Freemasons, 462–463
  Martin's objections to, 450
  Mercer's objections to, 475
  Mississippi River navigation negotiations, 485
  Paterson's proposal for adjournment, 68
  prayer at the Convention, 593
  Sherman on military secrecy, 715
  Washington and, 828–829, 830
Secret Proceedings and Debates of the Convention (Martin), 450
Secretary of the Convention, 371–372, 372 (sidebar), **696**
Sectionalism, **696–700**
Security, national. *See* Defense and security
Sedition Act (1798), 122
Self-evident truths, 208–209
Senate Judiciary Committee, 250
Senatorial terms, 67
Seneca Falls convention, 210
Sentries, **700**
  Fry, Joseph, 298
  Weaver, Nicholas, 833
Separation of powers, **700–704**
  Adams's advocating for, 2–3
  British government and, 333
  bureaucratic behavior, 69, 70
  Butler on, 73
  Council of Revision, 195–197

Federalist No. 51, 272
Federalists, 275
  influence of Montesquieu on, 495
  Jay's support of, 373
  Jefferson's views, 375–376
  judicial review, 388–393
  Madison's support of, 433
  presidential veto, 617–620
  providing stability, 741–742
  vice presidency, 808
  Virginia's constitution, 811–812
September 17, 1787, 211, 656, 674, **704**
Sesquicentennial celebration, 99, 564, 704
Setting sun remark. *See* Rising sun
Seventeenth Amendment, 171
Seventh Amendment, 60, 121, 394, 805
Shallus, Francis, 704
Shallus, Jacob, **704–705**
Shays's Rebellion, **705–709**
  classes, 88
  delegates addressing through stability provision, 741
  Jefferson's response to, 376
  slavery and, 6
  timing of the Constitutional Convention, 788
She Stoops to Conquer (Goldsmith), 564 (sidebar)
Shepard, William, 706
Sherman, Roger, **709–717**
  age of, 11
  amending process, 15, 18
  appointments and confirmations, 24–25
  armies and navies, raising and supporting, 32
  assessment of the delegates, 215
  attendance, 39
  bankruptcy, 47
  bicameralism, 125
  Bill of Rights discussion, 59
  census provision, 82–83
  classes, 87
  commerce power, 101, 102
  committees served on, 109, 111, 113, 115, 116, 119
  Congress, compensation of members, 131

Congress, qualifications for, 136, 137
Congress, selection of, 142, 143
Congress, terms, 174
congressional militia powers, 151, 153–154, 482
congressional origination of money bills, 154–155
congressional representation, 104
Connecticut Compromise, 180–181
corporations provision, 192
Council of Revision, 599
criticism of democracy, 224
Declaration of Independence, 208
democracy, 224, 284
education of, 240
emoluments clause, 149
fugitive slave clause, 299
general welfare clause, 302
House, representation in, 141
House terms, 145, 146
impeachment clause, 359, 361
judicial independence, 387–388
judicial review, 390, 392
land disputes, 407
on liberty, 417–418
lodging of the delegates, 424
Masons, 462
naturalization, 520
negative on state laws, 521
new states provision, 752, 753–754, 754
number of speeches, 740
oaths, 539
Pierce's character sketch, 544
Pilgrim roots, 287 (sidebar)
posterity and perpetuity, 587
president as Commander in Chief, 597
presidential power, 602
presidential selection, 608, 611, 613
presidential term length and re-eligibility, 614
presidential veto, 618, 620
presidents, number of, 603
publication of appropriations, 160
ratification provision, 649, 652

Sherman, Roger (*continued*)
  religious tests, prohibition on, 669
  Senate representation, 165, 167, 168–169, 169
  Senate selection, 170–171
  separation of powers, 702
  signing Declaration of Independence and the Constitution, 209
  slavery and slave importation, 7, 723, 725
  social contract, 729
  state coining of money, 492
  state legislatures, 756
  states police powers, 760
  taxes on imports and exports, 257–258, 780, 781
  time and frequency of congressional meetings, 175
  times, places, and manners of congressional election, 176
  Treasury secretary, 793
  treaty-making and ratification, 795, 796
  vice presidency, 809
  war powers of Congress, 826
Signing of the Constitution, **717–722**
  artistic depiction of, 37–38
  attendance, 39–40
  authorship of the Constitution, 41
  Baldwin, Abraham, 45
  Bassett, Richard, 47–48
  Bedford, Gunning Jr., 53
  Blair, John Jr., 63
  Blount, John Jr., 64
  Brearly, David, 65–67
  Carroll, Daniel, 82
  chart of signers, 921
  Clymer, George, 93–95
  debates and controversy, lv–lvii
  Gerry's reasons for not signing, 321–322
  Jackson, William, 371
  Livingston, William, 422
  Mason's failure to sign, 453
  McHenry, James, 473
  Randolph's decision not to sign, 647–648
  Read, George, 662

refusal by delegates, 656
  rising sun anecdote, 681
  September 17, 1787, 704
  voting at the Convention, 823
Sixteenth Amendment, 805
Sixth Amendment, 60, 394, 805, 815
Size of the Convention, **722–723**
Sketches of delegates, 542–544, 565, 666
Slave importation, **723–725**
  African Americans, 4–10
  amending process, 15
  Baldwin's defense of, 44
  Committee on Slave Trade and Navigation, 115
  congressional commerce power, 101
  Langdon's support of congressional prohibition, 409
  Madison's objection to, 434
  Mason's efforts to ban, 460
  Mississippi River navigation negotiations influencing recognition of, 486
  Pinckney's (Charles Cotesworth) views on, 578–579
  religious references concerning, 55
  Rutledge's call for prohibition of taxation, 688
  Rutledge's defense of, 690
  South Carolina's defense of, 734
  taxes on, 258, 781–782
  Williamson on, 839–840
  Wilson on, 842
Slavery, **725–728**
  African Americans, 4–10
  Amendments prohibiting, 805
  aristocratic government and, 27–28
  Butler's stance on three-fifths clause, 72, 75
  classical allusions and influences, 92–93
  coalitions, 95
  compromises on, 123
  Dayton's opposition to counting slaves for representation, 205

fugitive slave clause, 299
  Gorham's lack of views, 325
  indentured servants, 362–363
  infringement on natural rights, 518
  Jay's opposition to, 374
  Jefferson's views and actions, 375, 377
  Jenifer's freeing his slaves, 379
  King's pragmatic and moral concerns about, 403–404
  liberty and, 418
  Livingston's freeing his slaves, 422
  Madison's views of, 434, 437
  Martin's proposal of taxation on, 449
  Mason's criticism of, 460
  Morris's objection to, 499–500
  New Hampshire's opposition, 526
  Northwest Ordinance provisions, 537–538
  as obstacle to establishing equality, 252
  Pinckney's (Charles Cotesworth) views on, 578–579
  Pinckney's views on, 573, 574 (sidebar)
  Revolutionary War as argument against, 675
  Rutledge's defense of, 689–690
  South Carolina's defense of, 734
  taxation of imports and exports, 779–780
  Tennessee provision, 783
  three-fifths clause, 784–788
  Washington, George, 831
Small, William, 691
Small states
  coalitions, 96
  Committee of Detail, 106
  Committee on Original Apportionment of Congress, 113
  divisions within the Convention, li–lii
  Federalist No. 37, 272
  geographical influences on Convention issues, 305
  Gorham's plea for compromise on representation, 324–325

Hamilton's views on, 341, 344–345

House, representation in, 140–141

Martin's passionate defense of, 446, 451–452

negative on state laws, 521–522

new states provision, 753

Paterson's concerns over representation, 554

Pennsylvania's stand against, 505

Read's upholding representational rights of, 659–660, 661

supremacy clause, 775

Williamson's views on representation, 835–836

See also Equal representation

Smith, Adam, 416, 691–692

Smith, J. Allen, 199

Smith, Melancton, 214, 412, 533

Smoke-filled room, 562 (sidebar)

Snakes, two-headed, 297 (sidebar)

Snuff, 562 (sidebar)

Social contract, 423, **728–730**

Society for the Manumission of Slaves, 374

Society of the Cincinnati, **730–733**

Dayton, Jonathan, 206

Jackson, William, 372

Masons and, 463

Philadelphia, 564

Pierce, William, 565

Pinckney, Charles Cotesworth, 579

Socioeconomic status, 86–90

Solon, 91, 387

Sons of the American Revolution, 100, 704

South Carolina, **733–735**

Butler, Pierce, 70–76

Committee on Original Apportionment of Congress, 113

Pinckney, Charles, 567–574

Pinckney, Charles Cotesworth, 575–579

ratification controversy, 657

Rutledge, John, 685–690

slave importation, 724

small-state coalition, 96

state appointment of delegates to the Convention, 744

state constitution, 746

Southern states, 6–7

geographical similarities, 305–306

Virginia, 811–814

See also North-South conflict; individual states

Sovereignty, **735–736**

amending process jeopardizing, 15

Georgia's assertion after ratification, 310

Hamilton Plan principles, 348

Johnson's speech on, 380–381

King's objection to sovereignty being applied to states, 402–403

Lansing's views on the New Jersey Plan, 411

Martin's views on, 446–447

riots as expressions of popular sovereignty, 707 (sidebar)

state bills of attainder, 39

state sovereignty under the Articles of Confederation, 34

unitary government, 799–800

Spaight, Richard Dobbs, **736–739**

attendance, 40

Congress, terms, 174

congressional commerce power, 102

education of, 242

emendation of the rules, 684

expenses of delegates, 256

location and permanence of nation's capital, 236

number of speeches, 740

presidential selection, 619

ratification convention, 535–536

Senate selection, 170

Senate size, 172

treaty-making and ratification, 795

Spain, **739–740**

Jay, John and, 373

Jay-Gardoqui negotiations over Mississippi River navigation, 374–375, 484–487

Pinckney's appointment, 574

as threat, 77–78

Speech, freedom of, 122. *See also* First Amendment

Speech and Proposal of Alexander Hamilton at Federal Convention: June 18,1787, 894–898

Speech of Benjamin Franklin delivered to Constitutional Convention: September 17, 1787, 898–899

Speeches

Fitzsimons, Thomas, 278

Franklin, Benjamin, 291, 296, 898–899

Gilman's failure to make, 322

Gorham, Nathaniel, 324

Hamilton Plan, 894–898

honoring our forefathers, 287 (sidebar)

Ingersoll, Jared, 366

Lansing's contributions, 410–411

Livingston's lack of, 422

ranking delegates by number of, 219

rules governing, 683

Virginia Plan, 642–643

Speeches, number of, **740–741**

Spencer, Samuel, 535

Spicer, Michael W., 70

Spillman, Lyn, 633

Spitting boxes, 562 (sidebar)

Spitzer, Robert, 620

Spoils system, 70

Stability, **741–743**

Stampp, Kenneth, 588

Stamps, 37, 99, 129, 586–587. *See also* Post offices and post roads

Stanhope, Philip Dormer, 352

Stanly, John, 738

State, secretary of

Jefferson, Thomas, 376

Madison, James, 377

Marshall, John, 443

president's council, 600–601

Randolph, Edmund, 649

State appointment of delegates to the Constitutional Convention, **743–745**

State constitutions, **746–749**
  Bill of Rights, 59
  Connecticut, 178–180
  Delaware, 212
  failures of the Articles of
    Confederation, 810
  Georgia, 308–309, 309, 310
  Massachusetts, 463, 467–468,
    860–874
  Massachusetts Body of Liberties,
    466–467
  natural rights, 518
  New Jersey, 527
  New York, 532
  Pennsylvania, 557, 558, 841
  religious tests, 669
  rewriting after the
    commencement of the
    Revolution, 182, 186
  South Carolina, 685, 733–734,
    735
  Vermont, 807
  Virginia, 811–812
State delegations to the
  Convention, **749–750**, 823
State governments. *See* State
  constitutions
State house. *See* Pennsylvania State
  House
State laws. *See* Negative on state
  laws
State sovereignty. *See* Sovereignty,
  state
States, admission and creation,
  750–755
  Committee of the Whole, 111
  Dickinson Plan, 233
  Kentucky, 397
  King's concerns over
    representation of new states,
    399
  Langdon's support of fewer
    privileges for, 409–410
  Maine, 441
  Martin, Luther, 447–448
  Morris's proposal, 498
  New Jersey Plan provision, 531
  Northwest Ordinance, 536–538
  Sherman, Roger, 714–715
  Tennessee, 783
  territory of the United States,
    784

  Vermont, 807–808
  See also Western states
States, Hamilton's advocating
  abolishing, 343
States, legislatures, **755–759**
  abolishing, 74–75
  apportionment in state houses,
    334
  bicameralism and
    unicameralism, 125
  congressional control over, 568,
    688
  invalidating, 68
  New Hampshire, 525
  nominating senatorial
    candidates, 660–661
  Spaight on, 737
  See also Negative on state laws
States, police powers, 501,
  760–761, **760–761**
States' rights
  Bedford's concerns over small
    states, 52–53
  Bedford's opposition to
    boundaries on, 51–52
  bicameralism, 125–126
  Blount on, 64
  Broom's stance, 67
  Committee of Detail, 106
  common law, 120
  Congress, compensation of
    members, 131–132
  contracts clause restraining
    states' powers, 189–191
  debts, 206–207
  equal versus proportional
    representation in the Senate,
    166
  limits on congressional powers,
    34, 129
  limits on states, 759–760
  Mason's support of, 458–459
  Northwest Ordinance, 537
  presidential selection by state
    governors, 607–608
  rights of men and, 518–519
  Senate selection, 170
  "We the People," 832
  See also Congress, House of
    Representatives, representation
    in; Congress, Senate,
    representation in; Federalism

Statesmanship, **761–762**
Statute of Anne, 191
Stearns, Junius Brutus, 37, 99
Steele, Richard, 718
Steele, William, 593
Stone, Thomas, 510
Stoner, James R. Jr., 122
Story, Joseph, 158–159, 302–303
The Story of the Constitution
  (Bloom), 99
Stow, John, 420
Strong, Caleb, **763–764**
  attendance, 40
  congressional origination of
    money bills, 156–157
  congressional representation,
    104
  Council of Revision, 195–196
  education of, 240
  House terms, 146
  number of speeches, 740
  Pierce's character sketch, 544
  presidential veto, 619
  Senate representation, 167, 169
Style and arrangement. *See*
  Committee of Style and
  Arrangement
Suffrage, **764–769**
  Ellsworth's opposition to fixing
    voting qualifications, 247
  Madison's views on, 432
  Morris's views on qualifications
    of electors and voters, 500
  qualifications of voters for
    Congress, 139
  Virginia Declaration of Rights,
    815
  voting rights based on wealth,
    628
  women, 805, 849–850
  See also President, selection
Sullivan, John, 525
Sumptuary legislation, **769–771**
  Committee on sumptuary
    legislation, 116
  Ellsworth's views on, 248
  Gerry's opposition to, 320
  Morris's views on, 501
  See also Congress, origination of
    money bills
Super-legality of the Constitution,
  413

Supermajorities, 315, 572, **771–772**
Supremacy clause, 448, 530–531, **772–775**
  Dickinson nad, 231
  Dickinson Plan, 234
  judicial review, 389
Supreme Court, **775–777**
  amendments overturning, 805
  attainder, bills of, 39
  bankruptcy, 47
  congressional powers, 129–130
  constitution for prisoners, 185 (sidebar)
  contracts clause, 191
  direct taxation, 158
  general welfare clause, 302–303
  implied powers, 592
  Indians' rights, 365
  judicial jurisdiction, 382–386
  Marshall, John, 442–443
  naturalization and citizenship, 520
  Rutledge nomination, 690
  selection of, 776
  Shays's Rebellion, 706
  Sherman, Roger, 716
  state constitutions, 748
  territory of the United States, 784
  Wilson, James, 841, 848
  See also individual cases
Swiss Cantons, 631, **777–778**
Syng, Philip Jr., 778
Syng inkstand, **778**

Taney, Roger, 10, 86
Taxes, 73
  apportionment by House apportionment, 73
  congressional power of the purse, 157–159
  death and, 297
  general welfare clause affecting, 302
  Indians, 364
  influence of Jay-Gardoqui negotiations on, 375
  lighthouse tax, 103
  linking representation to, 117
  Madison's views on, 432
  New Jersey's double payments, 527

  property rights, 628
  Protestantism and capitalism, 631
  Read's proposal to limit taxes, 661
  Rhode Island's refusal to accept, 676
Taxes on imports and exports, **779–782**
  Committee on Slave Trade and Navigation, 115
  duties and customs along the Potomac, 509–511
  Ellsworth's opposition to taxing exports, 247
  Fitzsimon's views on, 278
  Gerry's unwilling to trust Congress with, 315
  King's support of, 403
  King's views on slavery and taxation, 403–404
  Langdon's concerns over state power, 409
  Martin's proposal of taxation on slaves, 449
  Martin's proposed mechanism for, 447
  Mercer's objections to congressional power, 476
  New Jersey Plan, 530
  Pinckney's (Charles Cotesworth) views on, 579
  slave importation, 4, 44, 724
  three-fifths clause, 786
  Virginia's proposal, 812
  Williamson on, 837
Temperatures in the summer of 1787, **782–783**
Tennessee, 64, 306, 397, 447, 753, **783**
Tenth Amendment, 61, 82, 376, 592, 761, 805
Terms, congressional. *See* Congress, House of Representatives, terms; Congress, Senate, terms
Terms, presidential. *See* President, term, length, and re-eligibility
Territory of the United States, **783–784**
  geography, 303–308
  land disputes, 407–408

  partitioning, 686
  Read's proposing abolishing states, 659–660
  treaties affecting territorial rights, 738
Texas v. White, 588
Theatrical productions, 564 (sidebar)
Third Amendment, 59, 60
Thirteenth Amendment, 727, 769, 805
Thomas, Clarence, 26
Thoughts on Government (Adams), 2
Three-fifths clause, **784–788**
  African Americans, 4–10
  Butler's views on, 72, 75
  census provision, 83
  Ellsworth's objection to government regulation of slavery, 246
  Gerry's support of, 314
  Gorham's support for, 325
  Johnson's objection to, 381
  King's views on, 399, 723
  Mason's objections to, 460
  Morris, Gouverneur, 499–500
  Northwest Ordinance and, 538
  Pinckney, Charles, 570, 573
  Pinckney, Charles Cotesworth, 578
  sectionalism over, 698
  Senate representation, 168
  South Carolina's ratification controversy, 657
Timing, **788–789**
Titles of nobility, **789**
Tobacco, 562 (sidebar)
Tory Party, 197–198, 212, 213, 356
Touro Synagogue, 680
Trade
  commerce power, 100–103
  Committee on Commercial Discrimination, 111–112
  Committee on Slave Trade and Navigation, 115
  corporations provision, 192–193
  See also Slave importation; Taxes; Taxes on imports and exports
Transcribing the Constitution. *See* Shallus, Jacob

Treason, **790–793**
  Dickinson on, 229
  Ellsworth's views, 248
  extradition, 259
  Franklin's views on, 294
  King's support of national
    punishment for, 401
  Madison's defining, 433
  Martin's views on, 448
  Randolph's stance on pardon
    power, 646
  separation of powers, 703
  Wilson's role, 847
Treasury, secretary of the, **793–794**
  Hamilton, Alexander, 346–347
  Mason, George, 456
  McHenry, James, 473–474
  Sherman's views on
    appointment of, 717
Treaties
  confederal government as, 124
  German trade treaty, 311
  Jay-Gardoqui negotiations,
    374–375
  ratification of, 844
  United Colonies of New
    England, 800
Treaty-making and ratification,
  795–797
  Dayton's stance on, 205
  Fitzsimons's views on, 278
  Gerry's proposal of full
    congressional participation,
    315
  Hamilton Plan principles, 349
  influence of Jay-Gardoqui
    negotiations on, 375
  King's disapproval of
    supermajority requirement,
    401
  Mason, George, 455
  Sherman on, 715
  supermajority requirement, 771
Trenchard, John, 672
Trent, William, 57
Trescot, William Henry, 199
Trumball, John, 37–38
Turner, Frederick Jackson, 307
Twelfth Amendment, 76, 551
Twentieth Amendment, 176
Twenty-fifth Amendment, 601,
  809

Twenty-second Amendment, 376,
  831
Twenty-seventh Amendment, 133
Twenty-sixth Amendment, 140
Two Treatises on Government
  (Locke), 423
Tyler, John, 510
Tyranny, 27

Unconstitutional legislation, 65
Unfinished Parts. *See* Committee
  on Postponed Matters
Unicameral Congress
  Articles of Confederation, 34
  Franklin's preference, 291–292
  Martin's support of, 445–446,
    447
  New Jersey Plan's provision,
    555
  Sherman on, 714
Unitary government, 281,
  799–800
United colonies of New England,
  800–810
United States, name, **801**
United States v. Butler, 302–303
United States v. Lopez, 130
United States v. Morrison, 130
University of North Carolina, 203
University of Pennsylvania, 241
U.S. Constitution
  Adams's models, 2–3
  outline of, liii–liv
  physical dimensions of, 514
    (sidebar), 801–806
  Declaration of Independence
    and, 210
  location of, 514
  number of words, 107 (sidebar)
  signing chart, 922
  text, 900–907
U.S. Term Limits v. Thornton, 138
Utrecht, Union of, 800

Vacancies in the House, 146–147
Van Doren, Calr, 221
Varnum, James M., 40, 678
Vermont, 306, 382, 447, 532, 747,
  807–808
Veterans, 676
Veto. *See* Negative on state laws;
  Presidential veto

Vice presidency, **808–809**
  chief justice provision, 85
  Gerry, Elbridge, 322
  Gorham's objection to the
    second-place vote plan, 327
  Ingersoll's bid for, 368
  Jefferson's election to, 376
  Mason's objections to office,
    458, 600
  Morris's supporting creation of,
    502
  president, disability of, 601
  selection mechanisms, 611, 613
  separate votes for, 551
  separation of powers, 702
  Williamson's objection to, 839
Vices of the political system of the
  United States, **809–811**
  Achaean League, 1
  Articles of Confederation, 35
  failure to address foreign affairs,
    279–280
  lack of guarantee clause, 335
  slavery, 4–5
  Virginia Plan remedies,
    819–820
  weaknesses of government, 1
Violence against Women Act
  (1994), 130
Virginia, **811–814**
  allocation of House seats, 117
  Blair, John Jr., 62–63
  committee members, 119
  Committee on Original
    Apportionment of Congress,
    113
  congressional power to call
    militia, 480–481
  congressional powers, 129
  expenses of delegates, 256
  Henry, Patrick, 350–351
  House, size of, 143–144
  Jefferson, Thomas, 375–377
  Kentucky's statehood, 397
  large-state coalition, 96
  Madison, James, 427–438
  Mason, George, 452–453
  McClurg, James, 469–471
  Mercer, John, 474–477
  Monroe, James, 493–494
  Mount Vernon Conference,
    509–511

Randolph, Edmund, 641–649
ratification of the Constitution,
657
state appointment of delegates
to the Convention, 743–744
state constitution, 746–747
voting at the Convention, 823
Washington, George, 827–832
Wythe, George, 851–852
See also Virginia Plan
Virginia Declaration of Rights,
452, 518, **814–815,** 857–858
Virginia House of Burgesses, 452
Virginia Plan, **815–820**
acceptance by the Committee of
the Whole, 110
admission and creation of new
states, 750
agenda setting, 820 (sidebar)
amending process, 13–15
appointments and
confirmations, 23–24
armies and navies, raising and
supporting, 31
artistic depictions of the
Convention, 38
Bedford's concerns over small
states' rights, 52–53
bicameralism, 125
census provision, 82
chief justice, 84–85
coalitions, 95
collective powers of Congress,
127
commerce power, 101
Committee of the Whole, 110,
118
compacts with foreign powers,
279–280
Congress, qualifications for, 135
Congress, recall of members,
161
Congress, selection of, 142, 143
Congress, terms of, 173–175
congressional power of the
purse, 157–158
congressional recall, 161
Connecticut Compromise,
180–181
Constitutional Convention
mechanism, 183
Constitutional wording, 41

continuance of Congress,
133–134
corporations, 192–194
Council of Revision, 195–197,
598–599
debt to France, 289
Dickinson's views on, 226
distributing articles, 803–804
emoluments clause, 149
federalism, 265
force against states, 728
Galloway Plan and, 301
history and goals of, xlv–xlvii
House, representation in, 140
impeachment clause, 359–360
implied powers, 591
influence of geography on, 305
judicial jurisdiction, 384, 385
judicial organization and
protections, 386
judicial review, 389
King's support of, 403
lack of "foreign invasion"
provision, 550
Lansing's objections to,
411–412
Madison's formation of,
428–430
Martin's strong objections to,
445–448
Mason's probable role in, 454
Morris's approval of, 497
negative on state laws, 521, 522
New Jersey Plan and, 555
plans of government introduced
at the Convention, 582
post offices and post roads, 586
power, 589
president as Commander in
Chief, 596
presidential compensation, 597
presidential qualifications,
605–606
presidential selection, 607
presidential term, length, and re-
eligibility, 614
presidential veto, 617
presidents, number of, 603
proposal and subsequent
alterations of, 802
ratification provision, 649–650,
653–654

reason and experience, 664
role of wealth in representation,
628
Senate qualifications, 162
Senate representation, 164
Senate selection, 170–172
Senate size, 172–173
separation of powers, 701
sovereignty, 380
speech introducing the plan,
642–643
state legislatures, 756–757
states police powers, 760
supremacy clause, 772–773
Supreme Court, 775–776
terms and goals of, 813
three-fifths clause, 784–785
tripartite government, 282
unitary government and,
799–800
war powers of Congress, 825
Washington, George, 829
Wilson's summary of, 843–844
Virginia Ratifying Convention,
442, 493, 649
Virginia Resolution of 1798, 436
Virginia Statute for Religious
Freedom, 375
Virtue, 672, **820–823,** 833–834
von Steuben, Friederich, 490
(sidebar)
Voting. *See* Rollcall vote
Voting at the Convention, **823**
Voting blocs. *See* Coalitions
Voting qualifications. *See* Suffrage

Walton, George, 309
War, secretary of, 600–601
War of 1812, 323
War powers of Congress, **825–827**
foreign affairs, 280
Gerry's objection to presidential
control, 318
Madison's semantic choice, 433
number and power of
presidents, 603
Pinckney, Charles, 570
Pinckney's concerns over
congressional power, 578
president as Commander in
Chief, 596–597
Sherman, Roger, 711

Ward, Nathaniel, 466
Warren, Charles, 220
Warren, Earl, 61, 334
Warren, Mercy Otis, 210
Warren Court, 251, 748
Washington, George, **827–832**
　Adams on, 811 (sidebar)
　Adams's nomination of, 2
　age of, 11
　artistic depictions of, 37
　assessment of the delegates, 214, 215
　attendance, 40
　bicameralism, 126
　Blair and, 63
　classical allusions and influences, 90–91
　Committee of the Whole's adoption of the Virginia Plan, 111
　committees served on, 119
　conspiracy to remove as Commander in Chief, 478
　on the Constitution, 806 (sidebar)
　education of, 239, 240
　historical assessment of, 222
　House, size of, 144
　Jackson and, 372
　letter of transmittal, 415
　lodging of the delegates, 425
　Masons, 462
　Morris's views on, 501
　Mount Vernon Conference, 509–511
　national university, 516
　nation's capital, 235 (sidebar)
　number of speeches, 740
　oaths, 605
　observations on motives and goals, xlv
　Paine's attacks on, 550
　prayer at the Convention, 593
　president of the Convention, 616
　presidential term limits, 615
　presidential title, 615
　presidents, number of, 603, 604
　on progress, 625–626
　Randolph's appointment, 649
　ratification, 813

religious references during the Constitutional Convention, 56
religious tests, prohibition on, 669
resolution accompanying the Constitution, 674
Revolutionary War, 675
　on Rhode Island, 680
　rising sun chair, 681–682
　Rutledge appointment, 690
　Rutledge's support of, 686
　secrecy, 694
　signing of the Constitution, 719, 721
　Society of the Cincinnati, 730, 732
　standing armies, 30
　supporting Gorham's representation proposal, 326
Watson, Gregory, 133
"We the People," **832**
　artistic depictions of of the Convention, 38
　authorship of the Constitution, 41
　commemorative poster, 99
　Committee of Style and Arrangement, 109
　indicating forms of government, 285
　precluding riots as expressions of popular sovereignty, 707 (sidebar)
　sovereignty issues, 736
　Virginia Declaration of Rights, 814
Wealth, representation by
　Butler's advocacy for, 71–72, 74–75
　Dickinson's views, 227–228
　Franklin's defense of the common man, 295
　Morris's desire for an aristocratic Senate, 497
　Pinckney's opposition to senatorial pay, 577–578
　property rights, 627–629
　senators' compensation, 131
　sumptuary legislation, 769–770
　See also Property

Weather during the Convention, 616, 782–783
Weaver, Nicholas, **833**
Weber, Max, 631
Webster, Noah, 191
Welliver, Judson, 211 (sidebar)
Western states
　Clymer's concerns over westward expansion, 94
　debates over admission and creation of new states, 751–755
　Delaware's hope for westward expansion, 656
　geographical divisions with Eastern states, 306
　Gerry's objections to admitting, 314–315
　Gorham's views on, 325, 326
　Indians, 363–365
　Jay-Gardoqui negotiations on Mississippi River navigation, 375, 484–487
　Northwest Ordinance, 536–538
　Read's proposal to limit representation for, 661
　Williamson's concerns over representation, 835
　Wilson's argument for equal representation, 845
　See also States, admission and creation
Wharton, Samuel, 138 (sidebar)
Whig ideology, **833–834**
　court and country parties, 197–198
　Delaware, 212, 213
　Magna Carta, 440
　motives of the Founding Fathers, 507
　republicanism, 672
　standing armies, 31
Whiskey Rebellion, 95
Wiecke, William, 299, 696–697
Wieland, or The Transformation (Brown), 655 (sidebar)
William and Mary, College of, 240
Williamson, Hugh, **834–840**
　age of, 11
　on Alexander's reticence over participation, 444

armies and navies, raising and supporting, 32
assessment of the delegates, 214, 215
attendance, 40
Bill of Rights discussion, 59
census provision, 83
committees served on, 111, 113, 115, 117
Congress, compensation of members, 131
Congress, payment, 757
Congress, qualifications for, 136–137, 163
Congress, terms, 174
congressional commerce power, 102
congressional origination of money bills, 155–156, 157
congressional representation, 104
education of, 242
ex post facto laws, 254, 688
full faith and credit clause, 300
historical assessment of, 222
impeachment clause, 361
judicial review, 392
land disputes, 407
location and permanence of nation's capital, 236
Mississippi River navigation, 487
negative on state laws, 521
new states provision, 753
number of speeches, 740
oaths, 539
Pierce's character sketch, 544
prayer at the Convention, 593–594
presidential selection, 607, 612–613
presidential term length and re-eligibility, 614
presidential veto, 620
qualifications of voters for Congress, 139
ratification, 651, 653
religious references during the Constitutional Convention, 56
Senate representation, 167
Senate size, 172–173

signing of the Constitution, 720
slave importation, 724
state governors filling senatorial vacancies, 330
suffrage, 767
supermajority provision, 771
taxes on imports and exports, 257–258, 780, 781
Tennessee statehood, 783
three-fifths clause, 786
treaty-making and ratification, 795, 796
trial by jury, 393
vice presidency, 808
Wills, Garry, 788
Wilson, James, **840–849**
  Achaean and Amphictyonic leagues, 1
  age of, 11
  amending process, 15
  appointments and confirmations, 24
  aristocracy, 27
  Articles of Confederation, 34
  attainder, bills of, 39
  attendance, 40
  banking provision, 45
  Biblical and religious references during the Convention, 55, 57
  bicameralism, 125
  borrowing power, 65
  census provision, 82
  classical allusions and influences, 91–92
  colonial prcedents, 97
  committees served on, 106, 112–113
  common law, 120
  concerns over monarchy, 489
  Congress, compensation of members, 131
  Congress, qualifications for, 135, 136, 137, 163
  Congress, selection of, 142
  Congress, terms of, 174
  congressional commerce power, 102
  congressional origination of money bills, 155
  congressional representation, 104

Connecticut Compromise, 244
continuance of Congress provision, 133
corporations provision, 192–193
Council of Revision, 195–197, 599
criticism of British system of government, 333
criticism of democracy, 224
Declaration of Independence, 210
education of, 242
emoluments clause, 149, 150
ex post facto laws, 120–121, 254
on experience, 663
extradition provision, 259
fugitive slave clause, 299
full faith and credit clause, 300
guarantee clause, 335, 336
habeas corpus, 339
House, representation in, 141
House terms, 146
impeachment clause, 359, 360
imposts versus duties, 257
journal of the proceedings, 665
judicial independence, 388
judicial organization, 386
judicial review, 390–391, 392
land disputes, 407
on liberty, 417–418
lodging of the delegates, 425
monarchy views, 282
national university, 516
negative on state laws, 521
new states provision, 752
number of speeches, 740
oaths, 14, 539, 605
Pierce's character sketch, 544
Polish election of the monarch, 583
post offices and post roads, 587
posterity and perpetuity, 588
presidential selection, 81, 607, 611, 612
presidential term length and re-eligibility, 614
presidential veto, 617, 618
presidents, number of, 603–604
Privy Council, 600
public opinion, 634
publication of appropriations, 160

Wilson, James (*continued*)
qualifications of voters for Congress, 139
ratification, 650, 652, 656
references to Germany, 311
religious affiliation, 668
republican government, 284, 670
response to Johnson's views on sovereignty, 380
Revolutionary War, 675
rights of men and states rights, 519
Scottish Enlightenment influencing, 692
secretary of the Convention, 371
Senate representation, 164, 165, 166–167, 168, 169
Senate selection, 170–171
Senate size, 172
separation of powers, 701
signing Declaration of Independence and the Constitution, 209
slave importation, 724
social contract, 729, 730
state coining of money, 492
state governors filling senatorial vacancies, 330
state legislatures, 756
suffrage, 767
Supreme Court, 776
Swiss Cantons, 777
taxes on imports and exports, 258, 780, 781
three-fifths clause, 785, 786, 787
time and frequency of congressional meetings, 175
treason provision, 791, 792

treaty-making and ratification, 795–796
virtue, 821
Western states admission, 699
women's rights, 849
Wilson, Sarah, 363
Wilson, Woodrow, 84, 334
Winthrop, John, 800
Wisconsin, 537
Witherspoon, John, 239, 241 (sidebar), 630, 691
Wolcott, Erastus, 179
Women, **849–851**
citizenship, 86
equality, 252
Pinckney, Elizabeth Lucas, 576 (sidebar)
Pinckney's involvement with slave, 574 (sidebar)
Violence against Women Act, 130
wives of the delegates, 217 (sidebar)
women voters in New Jersey, 765 (sidebar)
Wood, Gordon, 507, 762, 828 (sidebar)
Words in the Constitution
brevity of the Constitution, 107 (sidebar)
fugitive slave clause, 299
impeachment provision, 318
Johnson's influence on judicial power wording, 381
Work ethic, 631, 637
Wright, Benjamin, 123
Wright, James, 309
Wrong Island, 678 (sidebar)
Wythe, George, **851–852**
assessment of the delegates, 214

attendance, 40
Committee on Rules, 114, 117, 683
education of, 239, 240
number of speeches, 741
Pierce's character sketch, 544
signing Declaration of Independence and the Constitution, 209–210

XYZ Affair, 250, 322, 443

Yale University, 240
Yates, Robert, **853–854**
Antifederalism, 21
attendance, 40
Brutus, 271 (sidebar)
coalitions, 95
Committee to Reconsider Representation in the House, 117
congressional representation, 104
Lansing and, 410
on liberty, 418
New Jersey Plan, 531
New York delegation, 533
notes of the proceedings, 666
number of speeches, 741
Pierce's character sketch, 544
preference for republican government, 671
secrecy, 695
Secret Proceedings and Debates of the Convention, 450
Senate representation, 167

Zip codes, 99

About the Author

Dr. John R. Vile is a professor in and chair of the Department of Political Science at Middle Tennessee State University. He has written, edited, and coedited more than 15 books and sets of books including *Great American Lawyers: An Encyclopedia,* 2 vols. (2001); *A Companion to the United States Constitution and Its Amendments,* 3rd ed. (2001); *Presidential Winners and Losers: Words of Victory and Concession* (2002); *Proposed Amendments to the U.S. Constitution, 1787–2002,* 3 vols. (2003); *Great American Judges: An Encyclopedia,* 2 vols. (2003); the award-winning *Encyclopedia of Constitutional Amendments, Proposed Amendments, and Amending Issues,* 2nd ed. (2003); and *The Encyclopedia of Civil Liberties in America,* 3 vols. 2005 (coedited with David Schultz).

Vile has written numerous articles, reviews, encyclopedia entries, and book chapters. Vile earned his B.A. degree at the College of William and Mary and his Ph.D. at the University of Virginia, where he served for a time as a guide at the home of President James Monroe. The American Mock Trial Association, in which Vile has long been active, awarded him the Congressman Neal Smith Award in 2000 "in recognition of outstanding and exemplary contributions to law-related education and its mission to promote public understanding of law and the legal process." Vile is also active in the programs of the Center for Civic Education, which fosters knowledge of the U.S. Constitution through high school competitions.